RUSSIA

MONGOLIA

CHINA

N. KOREA
S. KOREA
JAPAN

KAZAKHSTAN

UZBEKISTAN

KYRGYZSTAN

TURKMENISTAN
TAJIKISTAN

GEORGIA
ARM. AZER.
TURKEY

AFGHAN-
ISTAN

IRAN

PAKISTAN

NEPAL BHUTAN
BANGLADESH

TAIWAN

PACIFIC
OCEAN

SWEDEN FINLAND
NORWAY

ESTONIA
LATVIA
LITHUANIA

UNITED
KINGDOM
DENMARK
BELARUS

IRELAND
NETH.
POLAND
GERMANY
BELGUM LUX. CZECH
LIECH.
SLOVAKIA
UKRAINE
FRANCE SW. AUST HUNGARY MOLDOVA
SLO.
CRO. RO.
ITALY HER.
YUGO
ALB. MACE.
BULGARIA
GREECE

SPAIN

PORTUGAL

MALTA

TUNISIA

CYPRUS LEB.
ISRAEL
JORDAN

SYRIA
IRAQ

KUWAIT

BAHRAIN
SAUDI
UNITED ARAB
ARABIA EMIR.

OMAN

YEMEN

INDIA

SRI
LANKA

MYANMAR VIETNAM
LAOS

THAILAND
CAMBODIA

PHILIPPINES

MOROCCO

AHARA
(Mor.)

ALGERIA

LIBYA

EGYPT

MAURITANIA
MALI
NIGER
CHAD

SUDAN

ERITREA

DJIBOUTI

ETHIOPIA

SOMALIA

NEGAL

A
U

BURKINA
FASO
BENIN
GUINBA
NIGERIA
A LEONE IVORY
LIBERIA COAST

CENTRAL
AFRICAN REP.

GHANA TOGO CAMEROON

EQUATORIAL
GUINEA GABON

CONGO REP.

CABINDA
(Ang.)

ANGOLA

RWANDA
DEM. REP.
OF THE
CONGO

BURUNDI

UGANDA
KENYA

TANZANIA

ZAMBIA

NAMIBIA

BOTSWANA

ZIMBABWE

MALAWI

MOZAMBIQUE

MADAGASCAR

SWAZILAND

SOUTH LESOTHO
AFRICA

COMOROS

MAURITIUS (Fr.)

REUNION
(Fr.)

SEYCHELLES

INDIAN

BRUNEI
MALAYSIA

I N D O N E S I A

PAPUA
NEW GUINEA

AUSTRALIA

ANTIC

OCEAN

NTARCTICA

VOLUME II: SINCE 1500

WORLD CIVILIZATIONS

THIRD
EDITION

Philip J. Adler

EAST CAROLINA UNIVERSITY

THOMSON

™

WADSWORTH

Australia • Canada • Mexico • Singapore • Spain
United Kingdom • United States

THOMSON

WADSWORTH

Publisher/Executive Editor: Clark Baxter

Development Editor: Sue Gleason

Assistant Editor: Kasia Zagorski

Editorial Assistant: Jonathan Katz

Technology Project Manager: Steve Wainwright

Marketing Manager: Caroline Croley

Marketing Assistant: Mary Ho

Advertising Project Manager: Brian Chaffee

Print Project Manager, Editorial Production: Ray Crawford

Print/Media Buyer: Karen Hunt

Permissions Editor: Joohee Lee

Production Service: Penmarin Books

Photo Researcher: Connie Hathaway

Copy Editor: Laura Larson

Cover and Text Designer: Diane Beasley Design

Cover Image: Dryburgh Abbey, Scotland © Superstock

Compositor: Carlisle Communications, Ltd.

Cover and Text Printer: Transcontinental-Interglobe

Wadsworth/Thomson Learning
10 Davis Drive
Belmont, CA 94002-3098
USA

Asia
Thomson Learning
5 Shenton Way #01-01
UIC Building
Singapore 068808

Australia
Nelson Thomson Learning
102 Dodds Street
South Melbourne, Victoria 3205
Australia

Canada
Nelson Thomson Learning
1120 Birchmount Road
Toronto, Ontario M1K 5G4
Canada

Europe/Middle East/Africa
Thomson Learning
High Holborn House
50/51 Bedford Row
London WC1R 4LR
United Kingdom

Latin America
Thomson Learning
Seneca, 53
Colonia Polanco
11560 Mexico D.F.
Mexico

Spain
Paraninfo Thomson Learning
Calle/Magallanes, 25
28015 Madrid, Spain

FOR BEN

WITH LOVE

AND HOPE

Contents in Brief

CONTENTS

PART FOUR DISEQUILIBRIUM: THE WESTERN ENCOUNTER WITH THE NON-WESTERN WORLD 1500–1850 C.E.   303

PART FIVE WESTERN REVOLUTIONS, INDUSTRY, AND IDEOLOGY 1700–1920 419

Maps

PREFACE

World Civilizations in its third edition is a brief survey of the history of civilized life since its inceptions in the Middle East some 5,000 years ago. It is meant to be used in conjunction with a lecture course at the introductory level. A majority of the students in such a course will probably be encountering many of the topics for the first time, and this book reflects that fact. The needs and interests of the freshman and sophomore students in two- and four-year colleges and universities have been kept constantly in mind by the author, whose familiarity with those needs has been sharpened by nearly thirty-five years of classroom experience.

While it deals with the history of civilization throughout the globe, this book does not attempt to be comprehensive in detail or evenly balanced among the multiple fields of history. World Civilizations does attempt to walk a middle line between exhaustive detail and frustrating brevity; its narrative embraces every major civilized epoch in every part of the globe, but the treatment of topics is selective and follows definite patterns and hierarchies. It deliberately tilts toward social and cultural topics and toward the long-term processes that affect the lives of the millions, rather than the acts of "the captains and the kings." The evolution of law and the formative powers of religion upon early government, as examples, receive considerably more attention than wars and diplomatic arrangements. The rise of an industrial working class in European cities is accorded more space than the trade policies of the European governments. Such selectivity, of course, is forced on any author of any text, but the firm intent to keep this a *concise* survey necessitated a particularly close *review* of the material. The short chapters are structured so as to leave considerable leeway to the classroom instructor for additional material or expansion of the topics touched upon. That this approach was relatively successful and found favor among many teachers is confirmed by the appearance of this third edition.

Relatively few changes have been necessitated by the tenor of reviews. These deal almost entirely with questions of emphasis. Among others, more focus on the place and role of women in several societies has been attempted; more attention has been given to the impacts of imperialism on the non-European countries; the space devoted to Marxism and its collapse in eastern Europe has been cut. The final chapter has been rewritten, as has the initial one, to bring these better in line with the most recent events and discoveries.

ORGANIZATION

The organization of *World Civilizations* is largely dictated by its nature: as a history, the basic order is *chronological.* There are six parts, dealing with six chronological eras from ancient civilizations (3000–500 B.C.E.) to recent times (post-1920 C.E.). The parts have several binding threads of development in common, but the main point of reference is the relative degree of contact with other civilizations. This ranges from near-perfect isolation, as, for example, in ancient China, to close and continual interaction, as in the late twentieth-century world.

The second organizing principle is the *prioritization of certain topics and processes.* Sociocultural and economic affairs are generally emphasized, and the longer term is kept in perspective, while some short-term phenomena are deliberately minimized. In terms of the space allotted, the more recent epochs of history are emphasized, in line with the recognition of growing global interdependence and cultural contact.

Although this text was, from its inception, meant as a world history and contains proportionately more material on non-Western peoples and cultures than any other currently in print, the Western nations receive sustained attention, consonant with their importance to the history of the globe. (In this respect, *Western* means not only European but also North American since the eighteenth century.) The treatment adopted in this book should allow any student to find an adequate explanation of the rise of the West to temporary dominion in modern times and the reasons for the reestablishment of worldwide cultural equilibrium in the latter half of the twentieth century.

PEDAGOGY

An important feature of *World Civilizations* is its division into a number of short chapters. Each of the fifty-eight chapters is meant to constitute a unit suitable in scope for a single lecture, short enough to allow easy digestion, and with strong logical coherence. Each chapter offers the following features:

- A chapter outline
- A brief chapter chronology
- A chapter summary

- A "Test Your Knowledge" section at the end of the chapter, thoroughly checked and revised
- Terms and individuals for identification in boldface type
- Color illustrations, many of them new, and abundant maps
- Thematic inserts illustrating changing or contrasting attitudes. Chapter inserts are now keyed to five broad themes: Exercise of Authority, Religion and Philosophy, Family and Gender Relations, Science and Technology, and Tradition and Innovation. All chapters have one or more of these inserts, some of which are based on biography, others on events.
- Frequent boxed sidebars illustrating contemporary events. Many new sidebars have been introduced.

Other features include the following:

- An end-of-book glossary gives explanations of unfamiliar terms.
- Each of the six parts begins with a short essay that describes the chapter contents and major trends covered in that part.
- A "Links" feature at the end of each part provides a comparative capsule review of the characteristics and achievements of the epoch as experienced by the different peoples and regions.
- An extensive bibliography organized by chapter appears at the end of each volume. It has been updated to include more 1990s imprints.

Supplements

The following supplements are available for the instructor:

Instructor's Manual and Test Bank
Prepared by Joseph Dorinson, Long Island University. One volume accompanies all three versions of the text. Includes chapter outlines, lecture topics, definitions of terms to know, chapter summaries, InfoTrac and Web site links, and a special guide for instructors making the transition from teaching Western civilization to teaching world history. The test bank includes over 3,000 multiple-choice, true/false, long and short essay, matching, and fill-in-the-blank questions.

ExamView
Professors can create, deliver, and customize tests and study guides (both print and online) in minutes with this easy-to-use assessment and tutorial system. ExamView offers both a Quick Test Wizard and an Online Test Wizard that guides the user step by step through the process of creating tests, while its unique "WYSIWYG" capability allows one to see the test on the screen exactly as it will print or display on-line. Users can build tests of up to 250 questions using up to 12 question types. Using ExamView's complete word processing capabilities, users can enter an unlimited number of new questions or edit existing questions. Available for Windows and Macintosh.

Transparency Acetates
Includes over 100 four-color maps from the text.

World HistoryLink 2001–2002
World HistoryLink is an advanced, PowerPoint presentation tool containing text-specific lecture outlines, figures, and images that allows users to deliver dynamic lectures quickly. In addition, it provides the flexibility to customize each presentation by editing provided content or by adding one's own collection of slides, videos, and animations. All of the map acetates and selected photos have also been incorporated into each of the lectures. In addition, the extensive Map Commentaries for each map slide are available through the "Comments" feature of PowerPoint.

Sights and Sounds of History
Short, focused video clips, photos, artwork, animations, music, and dramatic readings are used to bring life to historical topics and events that are most difficult for students to appreciate from a textbook alone. For example, students will experience the grandeur of Versailles and the defeat felt by a German soldier at Stalingrad. The video segments (averaging four minutes in length) are available on VHS and make excellent lecture launchers.

CNN Video—*World History*
This compelling video features footage from CNN. Twelve two- to five-minute segments are easy to integrate into classroom discussions or as lecture launchers. Topics range from India's caste system to Pearl Harbor.

New History Video Library
A new selection of videos for this edition. Available to qualified adoptions.

The following supplements are available for the student:

Study Guide
Prepared by Eugene Thompson, Brigham Young University of Idaho. Includes chapter outlines, sample test questions, map exercises, and identification terms. Available in two volumes.

Primary Source Document Workbook
Prepared by Robert Welborn, Clayton State College. One volume accompanies all versions of the text. A collection of primary source documents (approximately two per chapter) with accompanying exercises. Students learn to think critically and use primary documents when studying history.

Map Workbook
Prepared by Cynthia Kosso, Northern Arizona University. One version accompanies all versions of the text. Features

approximately thirty map exercises that help students improve their geographic understanding of the world.

Migration in Modern World History, 1500–2000 CD-ROM with User Guide

An interactive media curriculum on CD-ROM developed by Patrick Manning and the World History Center at Northeastern University. Migration goes beyond the mere chronicling of migratory paths. Over 400 primary source documents in *Migration* provide a springboard to explore a wide range of global issues in social, cultural, economic, and political history during the period 1500–2000.

Journey of Civilization CD-ROM

This CD-ROM takes the student on eighteen interactive journeys through history. Enhanced with QuickTime movies, animations, sound clips, maps, and more, the journeys allow students to engage in history as active participants rather than as readers of past events.

Internet Guide for History

Prepared by John Soares. Section One introduces students to the Internet, including tips for searching on the Web. Section Two introduces students to how history research can be done and lists URLs by topic. Available on the Web.

History: Hits on the Web

Recently revised for 2002, Hits on the Web (HOW) is an exciting, class-tested product specially designed to help history students utilize the Internet for studying, conducting research, and completing assignments. HOW is approximately eighty pages of valuable teaching tools that can be bundled with any Wadsworth textbook at a very affordable price. Available through Thomson Custom Publishing.

Magellan Historical Atlas

Available to bundle with text for a nominal price. Contains forty-four four-color historical maps.

Kishlansky, Sources in World History, 3/e, Volumes I and II

This two-volume reader is a collection of primary source documents designed to supplement any world history text.

WebTutor

This on-line ancillary helps students succeed by taking the course beyond classroom boundaries to a virtual environment rich with study and mastery tools, communication tools, and course content. Professors can use WebTutor to provide virtual office hours, post their syllabi, set up threaded discussions, track student progress with the quizzing material, and so on. For students, WebTutor offers real-time access to a full array of study tools, including flashcards (with audio), practice quizzes and tests, on-line tutorials, exercises, discussion questions, web links, and a full glossary. Professors can customize the content in any way they choose, from uploading images and other resources, to adding Web links, to creating their own practice materials.

Exploring the European Past: Text & Images

A new Custom Reader for Western Civilization. Written by leading educators and historians, this fully customizable reader of primary and secondary sources is enhanced with an on-line module of visual sources, including maps, animations, and interactive exercises. Each reading also comes with an introduction and a series of questions. To learn more, visit http://etep.thomsonlearning.com or call Thomson Learning Custom Publishing at (800) 355-9983.

Web Site

Historic Times: Wadsworth History Resource Center
http://history.wadsworth.com
Both instructors and students will enjoy our Historic Times Web Page. From this full-service site, instructors and students can access many selections, such as a career center, lessons on surfing the Web, and links to great history-related Web sites. Students can also take advantage of the online Student Guide to InfoTrac College Edition, featuring lists of article titles with discussion and critical-thinking questions linked to the articles to invite deeper examination of the material. Instructors can visit book-specific sites to learn more about our texts and supplements, and students can access chapter-by-chapter resources for the book, including interactive quizzes.

InfoTrac® College Edition

Create your own collection of secondary readings from more than 900 popular and scholarly periodicals such as *Smithsonian, Historian,* and *Harper's* magazines for four months. Students can browse, choose, and print any articles they want twenty-four hours a day by using the PIN code wrapped with their textbook.

ACKNOWLEDGMENTS

The author is happy to acknowledge the sustained aid given him by many individuals during the long incubation period of this text. Colleagues in the history department at East Carolina University, at the annual meetings of the test planners and graders of the Advanced Placement in European History, and in several professional organizations, notably the American Association for the Advancement of Slavic Studies, are particularly to be thanked.

In addition, the following reviewers' comments were essential to the gradual transformation of a manuscript into a book; I am indebted to all of them and to the students in

HIST 1030–1031, who suffered through the early versions of the work.

William S. Arnett
West Virginia University

Kenneth C. Barnes
University of Central Arkansas

Marsha Beal
Vincennes University

Charmarie J. Blaisdell
Northeastern University

Laura Blunk
Cuyahoga Community College

William Brazill
Wayne State University

Alice Catherine Carls
University of Tennessee–Martin

Orazio A. Ciccarelli
University of Southern Mississippi

Robert Clouse
Indiana State University

Sara Crook
Peru State University

Sonny Davis
Texas A&M University at Kingsville

Joseph Dorinson
Long Island University, Brooklyn Campus

Arthur Durand
Metropolitan Community College

Frank N. Egerton
University of Wisconsin–Parkside

Ken Fenster
DeKalb College

Tom Fiddick
University of Evansville

David Fischer
Midlands Technical College

Jerry Gershenhorn
North Carolina Central University

Erwin Grieshaber
Mankato State University

Eric Haines
Bellevue Community College

Mary Headberg
Saginaw Valley State University

Daniel Heimmermann
University of Northern Arizona

Charles Holt
Morehead State University

Kirk A. Hoppe
University of Illinois–Chicago

Raymond Hylton
Virginia Union University

Fay Jensen
DeKalb College–North Campus

Aman Kabourou
Dutchess Community College

Louis Lucas
West Virginia State College

Ed Massey
Bee County College

Bob McGregor
University of Illinois–Springfield

John Mears
Southern Methodist University

Will Morris
Midland College

Gene Alan Müller
El Paso Community College

David T. Murphy
Anderson University

Tim Myers
Butler County Community College

Elsa A. Nystrom
Kennesaw State University

William Paquette
Tidewater Community College

Nancy Rachels
Hillsborough Community College

Enrique Ramirez
Tyler Junior College

Bolivar Ramos
Mesa Community College

Robin Rudoff
East Texas State University

Anthony R. Santoro
Christopher Newport University

Shapur Shahbazi
Eastern Oregon State University

John Simpson
Pierce College

John S. H. Smith
Northern Nevada Community College

Maureen Sowa
Bristol Community College

Irvin D. Talbott
Glenville State College

Maxine Taylor
Northwestern State University

Eugene T. Thompson
Ricks College

Susan Tindall
Georgia State University

Kate Transchel
California State University, Chico

Bill Warren
Valley City State University

Robert Welborn
Clayton State College

David Wilcox
Houston Community College

Steve Wiley
Anoka-Ramsey Community College

John Yarnevich
Truckee Meadows Community College–Old Towne Mall
Campus

John M. Yaura
University of Redlands

Many thanks, too, to Lee Congdon, James Madison University; Maia Conrad, Christopher Newport University; Theron E. Corse, Fayetteville State University; Dennis Fiems, Oakland Community College, Highland Lakes; Lauren Heymeher, Texarkana College; Maria Iacullo, CUNY Brooklyn College; Rebecca C. Peterson, Graceland College; Donna Rahel, Peru State College; Thomas J. Roland, University of Wisconsin–Oshkosh; James Stewart, Western State College of Colorado; and Brian E. Strayer, Andrews University.

I would also like to acknowledge Clark Baxter's contribution as executive editor.

Note: Throughout the work, the pinyin orthography has been adopted for Chinese names. The older Wade-Giles system has been included in parentheses at the first mention and retained in a few cases where common usage demands it (Chiang Kai-shek, for example).

ABOUT THE AUTHOR

PHILIP J. ADLER has taught college courses in world history to undergraduates for almost thirty years prior to his recent retirement. Dr. Adler took his Ph.D. at the University of Vienna following military service overseas in the 1950s. His dissertation was on the activity of the South Slav emigrés during World War I, and his academic specialty was the modern history of eastern Europe and the Austro-Hungarian empire. His research has been supported by Fulbright and National Endowment for the Humanities grants. Adler has published widely in the historical journals of this country and German-speaking Europe. He is currently professor emeritus at East Carolina University, where he spent most of his teaching career.

INTRODUCTION TO THE STUDENT

WHY IS HISTORY WORTH STUDYING?

A few years ago a book about women in the past appeared with an eye-catching title: *Herstory.* Suddenly, the real meaning of a commonly used word became a lot clearer. History is indeed a *story,* not specifically about women or men, but about all those who have left some imprint on the age in which they lived.

History can be defined most simply as the story of human actions in past times. Those actions tend to fall into broad patterns, regardless of whether they occurred yesterday or 5,000 years ago. Physical needs, such as the need for food, water, and breathable air, dictate some actions. Others stem from emotional and intellectual needs, such as religious belief or the search for immortality. Human action also results from desires rather than absolute needs. Some desires are so common that they recur in every generation; some examples might be literary ambition, or scientific curiosity, or the quest for political power over others.

History is the record of how people tried to meet those needs or fulfill those desires, successfully in some cases, unsuccessfully in others. Many generations of our ancestors have found familiarity with that record to be useful in guiding their own actions. The study of past human acts also encourages us to see our own present possibilities, both individual and collective. Perhaps that is history's greatest value and has been the source of its continuous fascination for men and women who have sought the good life.

Many people are naturally attracted toward the study of history, but others find it difficult or (even worse) "irrelevant." Some students—perhaps yourself!—dread history courses, saying that they can see no point in learning about the past. My life, they say, is here and now; leave the past to the past. What can be said in response to justify the study of history?

Insofar as people are ignorant of their past, they are also ignorant of much of their present, for the one grows directly out of the other. If we ignore or forget the experience of those who have lived before us, we are like an amnesia victim, constantly puzzled by what should be familiar, surprised by what should be predictable. Not only do we not know what we should know, but we cannot perceive our true possibilities, because we have nothing to measure them against. The nonhistorical mind does not know what is missing—and contrary to the old saying, that can definitely hurt you!

A word of caution here: this is not a question of "history repeats itself." This often-quoted cliché is clearly nonsense if taken literally. History does *not* repeat itself exactly, and the difference in details is always important. But history does exhibit general patterns, dictated by common human needs and desires. Some knowledge of and respect for those patterns has been a vital part of the mental equipment of all human societies.

But there is another, more personal reason to learn about the past. Adult persons who know none of their history are really in the position of a young child. They are *objects,* not subjects. Like the child, they are acted upon by forces, limited by restrictions, or compelled by a logic that they not only can do little about, but may not even perceive. They are manipulated by others' ideas, wishes, and ambitions. They never attain control of their lives, or, at least, not until the young child grows up. The sad thing is that the unhistorical adult *has* grown up, physically, but less so mentally.

The historically unconscious are confined within a figurative wooden packing crate, into which they were put by the accident of birth into a given society, at a given time, in a given place. The boards forming the box enclose these people, blocking their view in all directions. One board of the box might be the religion—or lack of it—into which they were born; another, the economic position of their family; another, their physical appearance, race, or ethnic group. Other boards could be whether they were born in a city slum or a small village, or whether they had a chance at formal education in school (about three-fourths of the world's children never go beyond the third year of school). These and many other facts are the boards of the boxes into which we are all born.

If we are to fully realize our potential as human beings, some (at least some!) of the boards must be removed so we can see out, gain other vistas and visions, and have a chance to measure and compare our experiences with others outside. Here "outside" refers to the cross section of the collective experience of other human beings, either now in the present, or what is more manageable for study, in the knowable past.

Thus, the real justification for studying history is that it lets us see out, beyond our individual birth-box, into the rich variety of others' lives and thoughts. History is a factual introduction into humans' past achievements; its breadth and complexity vary, depending on the type. But whatever the type of history we study, by letting us see and giving us perspective that enables us to contrast and compare our lives with those of others, history liberates us from the invisible boards that confine us all within our birth-box.

For many people, the study of history has been a form of liberation. Through history, they have become aware of the ways other people have dealt with the same concerns and questions that puzzle them. They have been able to gain a perspective on their own life, both as an individual and as a member of the greater society in which they work and act. Perhaps, they have successfully adapted some of the solutions that history has revealed to them and experienced the pleasure of applying a historical lesson to their own advantage. For all these reasons, the study of the historical past is indeed worth the effort. *Not* to have some familiarity with the past is to abdicate some part of our human potential.

About This Book

Organization

The textbook you are holding is a beginning survey of world history. It is meant to be studied as part of a lecture course at the freshman/sophomore level, a course in which a majority of the students will probably be encountering world history for the first time in any depth.

Some students may at first be confused by dates followed by "B.C.E.," meaning "before the common era," and "C.E." meaning "common era." These terms are used to reflect a global perspective, and they correspond to the Western equivalent B.C. (before Christ) and A.D. (anno Domini). Also, a caution about the word "century" is in order: the term "seventeenth century" C.E. refers to the years 1601 to 1699 in the common era. "The 1700s" refers to the years 1700–1799. With a little practice these terms become second nature and will increase your fluency in history.

Although this text includes a large number of topics, it is not meant to be comprehensive. Your instructor's lectures will almost certainly bring up many points that are not discussed in the book; that is proper and should be expected. To do well in your tests, you must pay close attention to the material covered in the lectures, which may not be in this book.

Three principles have guided the organization of this book. First, the basic order is dictated by chronology, for this is a history text, and history can be defined as action-in-time. After an introductory chapter on prehistory, we look first at Mesopotamia and Egypt, then at India and China. In these four river valley environments, humans were first successful in adapting nature to their needs on a large scale, a process that we call civilization. Between about 2500 B.C.E. and about 1000 C.E., the river valley civilizations matured and developed a "classic" culture in most phases of life: a fashion of thinking and acting that would be a model for emulation so long as that civilization was vital and capable of defending itself.

By 500 B.C.E., the Near Eastern civilizations centered in Egypt and Mesopotamia were in decline and had been replaced by Mediterranean-based ones, which drew on the older civilizations to some extent but also added some novel and distinct features of their own. First the Greeks, then the Romans succeeded in bringing much of the known world under their influence, culminating in the great Roman Empire reaching from Spain to the Persians. For the West, the greatest single addition to civilized life in this era was the combination of Jewish theology and Greco-Roman philosophy and science. During the same epoch (500 B.C.E.–500 C.E.), the civilizations of East and South Asia were also experiencing growth and change of huge dimensions. India's Hindu religion and philosophy were being challenged by Buddhism, while China recovered from political dismemberment and became the permanent chief factor in East Asian affairs. Japan emerged slowly from a prehistoric stage under Chinese tutelage, while the southeastern part of the Asian continent attained a high civilization created in part by Indian traders and Buddhist missionaries.

From 500 to about 1500 C.E., the various civilized regions (including sub-Saharan Africa and the Americas) were either still isolated from one another or maintained a power equilibrium. After 500, Mediterranean civilization underwent much more radical changes than occurred elsewhere on the globe, and by about 1000, an amalgam of Greco-Roman, Germanic, and Jewish-Christian beliefs called Europe, or Western Christianity, had emerged. By 1500, this civilization began to rise to a position of worldwide domination, marked by the voyages of discovery and ensuing colonization. In the next three centuries, the Europeans and their colonial outposts slowly wove a web of worldwide commercial and technological interests anchored on military force. Our book's treatment of the entire post-1500 age will give much attention to the West, but also to the impacts of Western culture and ideas upon non-Western peoples. In particular, it will look at the Black African civilization encountered by the early European traders and what became of it and at the Native American civilizations of Latin America and their fate under Spanish conquest and rule.

From 1800 through World War I, Europe led the world in practically every field of material human life, including military affairs, science, commerce, and living standards. This was the golden age of Europe's imperial control of the rest of the world. The Americas, much of Asia, Oceania, and coastal Africa all were the tails of the European dog; all became formal or informal colonies at one time, and some remained under direct European control until the mid-twentieth century.

After World War I, the pendulum of power swung steadily away from Europe and toward what had been the periphery: first, North America; then, Russia, Japan, and the non-Western peoples. As we enter a new millenium, the world has not only shrunk, but has again been anchored on multiple power bases, both Western and non-Western. A degree of equilibrium is rapidly being restored, this time built on a foundation of Western technology that has been adopted throughout the globe.

Our periodization scheme, then, will be a sixfold one:

- Ancient Civilizations, 3500 B.C.E.–500 B.C.E.
- Classical Mediterranean Civilizations, 500 B.C.E.–500 C.E.
- Equilibrium among Polycentric Civilizations, 500–1500 C.E.
- Disequilibrium: The Western Expansion, 1500–1800 C.E.
- Industry and Western Hegemony, 1800–1920
- Equilibrium Reestablished: The Twentieth-Century World

Each period will be introduced by a brief summary and followed by an outline comparing the various contemporary civilizations. These six outlines are termed "Links" and will afford a nutshell review of the topics covered in the preceding part of the book.

Text Emphases and Coverage

As a second principle of organization, this book reflects the author's particular concerns, so the material treated is selective.

There is a definite tilt toward social and economic topics in the broadest sense, although these are usually introduced by a treatment of political events. Wars and military matters are treated only as they seem relevant to other topics. Only the most prominent and most recognizably important governmental, military, or diplomatic facts and figures are mentioned in the text. The author believes that students who are interested in such factual details will hear them in lectures or can easily find them in the library or an encyclopedia. Others, who are less interested in such details, will appreciate the relative focus on broad topics and long-term trends.

The third organizing principle of the book is its approach to Western and non-Western history. A prominent place is given throughout to the history of the Western world. Why this emphasis in a world that has grown much smaller and more intricately connected over the last generation?

At least three reasons come to mind: (1) Western culture and ideas have dominated most of the world for the past 500 years, and much of this text deals with that period; (2) the rest of the planet has been westernized in important ways during the twentieth century, either voluntarily or involuntarily; and most importantly, (3) the majority of the people reading this book are themselves members and products of Western civilization. If one agrees with the philosopher Socrates that to "know thyself" is the source of all knowledge, then a beginning has to be made by exploring one's own roots—roots growing from a Western soil.

About one-third of the text chapters deal with the period since the end of the eighteenth century, and about one-fifth with history since World War I. This emphasis on the most recent past fits with the interests of most students; but should you be particularly attracted to any or all of the earlier periods, be assured that an immense amount of interesting writing on almost all of the world's peoples in any epoch is available.

Many instructors will wish to supplement the text by assigning outside readings and/or by material in their lectures. The bibliography is a helpful source for much of the information omitted from the text and for much else besides; your college library will have many of the titles listed. They have been chosen because they are up-to-date, readily available, and highly readable.

As a good student, your best resource, always, is your own sense of curiosity. Keep it active as you go through these pages; remember, this and every textbook is the *beginning,* not the ending of your search for useful knowledge. Good luck!

Introduction to Volume II

This second volume of *World Civilizations* begins with the opening of the previously unknown globe to the avid and adventurous Europeans. Conjoined with the secular attitudes fostered by the Renaissance and the challenges to traditional authority embodied in the Protestant Reformation, this expansion produced fundamental changes in the course of world history. For the West, these partly cultural, partly geographic movements introduce the Modern Age, the subject of this volume. Before then, however, civilized life had taken many forms, in many locales.

The Earliest Civilizations

The Middle East

The earliest civilizations developed in the Middle East and Egypt in the fifth millennium B.C.E., when an agricultural surplus that was sufficient to support sizable populations living in towns first appeared. Here men and women were freed from the daily tasks of producing or gathering food and could devote themselves to specialized labors and techniques that eventually brought all manner of innovation.

Chief among these places were the cities of lower Mesopotamia, along the Tigris and Euphrates Rivers. Here, by 2500 B.C.E. an elaborate division of society into warrior kings and their priests, nobles and commoners, freemen and slaves had been accomplished and would be imitated many times over by other civilizations. Among their many achievements, the early Mesopotamians (Sumerians) developed the wheel, writing, monumental architecture, a sophisticated math, and a calendar, to mention only a few. Egyptian civilization developed in the Nile valley almost as early, but despite Egypt's creativity and prosperity, its examples were generally less important to later ages. The divine kings (pharaohs) and self-contained culture of the upper class could not be replicated without the extraordinary protections afforded by Egypt's unique geography. Instead, it was Mesopotamian urban society and the religion of the Hebrews that became the first building blocks of Western civilization.

The Hebrews

The ancient tribes of Israel, called the Hebrews, left northern Mesopotamia about 1800 B.C.E. as poverty-stricken nomads under their legendary leader Abraham. After the centuries-long march south, they arrived in Egypt, staying under Pharaoh's rule until in the thirteenth century they departed for the Promised Land of Palestine—Israel, or the Land of Canaan. There, they engaged in a long and ultimately successful struggle for possession and set up a kingdom that soon split in two but whose independent parts persisted for several hundred years, until finally overrun by their more potent neighbors.

It was not the conquests or governance of the Jews that make them vital to later history; rather, it was their religion and moral beliefs, conveyed in the gradually accumulating books of the Old Testament. They show us a people obsessed with their relation to an all-powerful, universal, and sole God they called Yahweh. According to the Jewish Scripture, Yahweh had conceived them to be his Chosen. He gave the Jews hopes of eternal life, based on their individual and collective conformity to a code of ethics he had prescribed for them: the Ten Commandments. The Jews were thus the first to make the all-important connection between supernatural gods and an ethical and comprehensible universe in which humans moved as possessors of free will to choose good or evil.

Greeks and Romans

The Jews' theological contributions were matched in importance by the philosophical, artistic, and legal concepts generated by the Greeks and Romans. The Greeks became a force in history after about 600 B.C.E., when the small city-states of their mountainous peninsula produced a previously unparalleled activity in the quest for knowledge of human beings and their natural environment. Among the consequences were the idea of democracy, the outlines of philosophy, and several of the natural sciences. Some of the basic art forms of civilization also were originated or carried to unprecedented perfection in the Greek *poleis* between 500 and 300 B.C.E. Many of the West's later intellectual achievements rested on the Greeks' pioneering efforts during this brief Classical Age.

The Classical Age was brought to an end by the inability of the Greeks to unite politically, even to defend their freedom. In the 300s the Macedonian kingdom to the north brought the quarreling *poleis* under its control. Under Alexander the Great, a Greek-Macedonian army conquered much of the known world, extending to the borderlands of India in the East. This impressive empire remained under central control only briefly, but it served as the channel for the long-term dissemination of Greek culture and thought into the already civilized areas of western Asia. The resultant hybrid is called the Hellenistic civilization, and it formed the basis for continuing advances in science, philosophy, and the arts during the ensuing three centuries.

The Roman republic began as one of the communities on the periphery of the Hellenistic world. Originally a tiny city-state in the middle of the Italian peninsula, the republic gradually expanded through constant wars to become the master of the entire Mediterranean basin. A prolonged crisis followed as the republican political forms were overwhelmed by the demands of imperial government. By the end of the first century B.C.E., the republic had given way to a barely disguised monarchy.

The first and second centuries C.E. saw Rome establish a model of successful imperial rule. More pragmatic than the Greeks and less speculative about the nature of the universe, the Romans developed systems of law and administration that served them well for several centuries and provided the basis of European political and legal theory into modern times. The Romans leaned heavily and unashamedly on their Greek subjects, incorporating the Hellenistic cultural models into their own intellectual and artistic lives without significant change.

In the 200s C.E., however, the smooth functioning of the Roman government broke down at the center. A series of usurping generals seized power. One of these generals, Diocletian, tried to restore and reform the system of shared powers, but this attempt collapsed in renewed upheaval, which was ended only by the establishment of an absolute monarchy in the early 300s. The capital was no longer in Rome but was moved to the eastern metropolis of Constantinople, which was more defensible. In the fourth and fifth centuries, the western half of the empire was overrun again and again by barbarous Germanic tribes, as the emperors focused their efforts on the defense of the richer and more populated East. By 600 the Roman empire was only a memory west of the Balkan peninsula, but the eastern or Byzantine rulers would retain their grip on a small part of the original territories for nearly a millennium.

The decline of the empire's government did not prevent the greatest of Rome's legacies from being passed on to later Europe: the Latin language, government and law, and the Christian religion. Latin was the universal channel of learned or legal discourse for the next thousand years. Roman law and government established the basic concepts of justice and administration in the West. The Christian religion was not a Roman creation, but its adoption as the state religion (by Constantine, Diocletian's successor) dramatically changed its nature and role.

Christianity had begun as a reform movement within Judaism, preached and propagated by Jesus of Nazareth in Judea, a Roman province inhabited mainly by Jews. Soon after Jesus' death by crucifixion, his effort to change a ritualistic Judaic creed into a religion of spirituality and love was transformed into a call to convert all peoples. This transformation was largely the work of a Hellenized Roman citizen, later known as St. Paul.

By the 200s small Christian cells or colonies were scattered throughout Rome's possessions. Though occasionally persecuted by the authorities, they throve on their martyrdom and gradually came to be numerous enough to attract the sympathetic attention of Constantine. Once taken under the government's protection in the mid-300s, what had been a minority religion soon spread into every region and every social group within the empire. As the Roman pagan world shook under the blows of the Germanic invasions, more and more people found their way to the consolations of a religion that promised its faithful a life of bliss without end. In the former western provinces, the Christian religion and its clerical organs were almost the only institutions that carried over intact into the emergent society of medieval Europe.

THE EASTERN CIVILIZATIONS

India

The Hellenistic tide, propelled by the conquests of Alexander, had been halted at the valley of the Indus River. The Indians here were the descendants of an ancient urban civilization that had been conquered about 1500 B.C.E. by the nomad Aryan tribes of central Asia. The Aryans introduced their religious practices, their language, and their social divisions, or castes, to India. A thousand years later, the Aryans had been absorbed into the Indian mass, but the caste system and the religion they had introduced had struck deep roots.

Vedic Hinduism, as the mix of Aryan and prehistoric Indus valley religions is known, was at once a philosophy, a theology, and an intricate code of ethics and manners. Like other world religions, it has spawned an entire civilization. Distinctive to it are its embrace of myriad deities and theologies, its doctrine of reincarnation according to previous conduct, and its insistence on the impermanence and unimportance of the material universe.

Not essential to Hindu theology but intimately bound up with its practice is the caste system. The caste system originated with the Aryan division of society into four groups: priests, warriors, freemen, and serfs. Over time the castes multiplied as they were defined ever more precisely. The caste system has been far more important than government in holding the Indians together as a nation. As the socioeconomic group into which a person is born (and can only rarely leave), caste gives Indians their identity and defines their niche in society.

A strong challenge to Hindu belief was raised in the fifth century B.C.E. by the teachings of Siddartha Gautama, known as the Buddha. Dismayed by the priestly ceremonial that Vedic Hinduism had become, the Buddha sought spiritual enlightenment. Finally, he achieved his goal through prolonged meditation and set out to teach others. More a naturalistic philosophy than a supernatural religion, the Buddha's message aimed at liberating men and women from the bonds of desire, the source of all unhappiness. Through his Eightfold Path, he attempted to lead his faithful to nirvana, or the conquest of suffering.

Within a few generations, his followers had converted his message to a religion, which divided into two major paths: the stricter Theravada and the more liberal Mahayana. Buddhism was from the start a proselytizing faith and was soon exported from India throughout East and Southeast Asia, where it replaced the original Hindu affiliations. Adopting much from its rival's teachings, a reformed Hinduism gradually rewon India's allegiance, whereas Buddhism was extinguished there by about 1200 C.E.

Political unity was a rarity in India's long history. The Mauryan dynasty in the fourth century C.E. was the last native ruler of most of the subcontinent until contemporary times. Alien tribes frequently invaded, and the huge region was the scene of many cultures and ethnic groups clashing for predominance at one time or another. In the long run, Hinduism proved to be the cement of India; its extraordinarily flexible beliefs allowed the various invaders and colonizers to adapt it to their own needs.

China

China possesses the longest continuous civilization in the world. The Chinese begin their history with legendary kingdoms in the third millennium B.C.E.; archaeology reveals that a settled agrarian society existed in the middle reaches of the Yellow River valley by at least 1500 B.C.E. The educated class (mandarins) took their basic tenets and attitudes from the teachings of Confucius (Kung fu-tzu), the fifth-century B.C.E. sage who has probably had more spiritual influence over more people than anyone else save Jesus Christ. Signally disinterested in supernatural religion, Confucius taught his fellow Chinese to concentrate on achieving earthly harmony and well-being. The family served him as the model for the state: the benevolent father properly held supreme authority over wife and children. So long as he fulfilled his duties to them, he could expect their devotion and obedience. The same could be said of the relations between a king and his subjects.

Another cast of mind, however, was directly responsible for the establishment of the Chinese form of imperial government. After 250 years of mutual hostilities among several fragments (the "Era of the Warring States"), a single-minded strongman termed the First Emperor put China back together. An enemy of all talk of mutual obligations between governor and governed, the emperor burned the Confucian books. He adopted instead the philosophy of the Legalists, who held that the end (stability) justifies the means (any, including harsh brutality) in politics and government.

The members of the Han dynasty that followed the First Emperor avoided his brutality but retained his effective measures of governance. The country was greatly expanded from its original territory in the Yellow River basin, allowing China to escape its former isolation. Somewhat later, Buddhism was brought from its Indian birthplace by a stream of traders and missionaries and became the nearest thing to a national religion China has ever seen. The Chinese governing class had little difficulty blending the pragmatic teachings of Confucius with the more ethereal wisdom of the Buddha. Among the other 99 percent of the people, Daoism's nature philosophy held reign, also with an admixture of Buddhist viewpoints.

After a period of disunity, the Tang and Song dynastic periods (from the 600s to the 1200s C.E.) constituted another apex of Chinese civilized life. Major technological advances were impelled by basic knowledge in the natural sciences. Introduction of new grains allowed the expansion of the population and the establishment of huge cities, dwarfing contemporary Europe. The constant challenges on the northern frontiers by barbarian hordes were contained by measures ranging from the building of the Great Wall to the use of pyrotechnics in battle. By the time the savage Mongol tribes were gathering under the leadership of Chingis Khan to assault an astonished world, China had already experienced 2,000 years of civilized life and led the globe in the accomplishments of science and technology.

Japan

Just off the northern coast of China and the Korean peninsula lie the four islands that constitute the Japanese heartland. The beginnings of Japanese civilization are lost in the mists of time. Whereas the Chinese had developed a written language as early as 1200 B.C.E. and Chinese histories from the 800s survive, the Japanese produced little literature until well into the first millennium C.E. What we know of very early Japan is derived mostly from Chinese travelers' remarks and archaeology.

Many of the fundamental models of Japanese culture were taken from Chinese originals, which came to Japan through Korean intermediaries. One such import was Buddhism, which had a powerful impact on Japan as early as the seventh century and has remained the most important of imported religions. It was often alloyed with the native Shinto animism to form peculiarly Japanese hybrids. The Japanese also borrowed the Chinese writing system and employed Chinese ideographs to denote Japanese concepts. Similarly, many Japanese art forms such as landscape painting, calligraphy, ceramics, and poetry came originally from China. In all cases, however, the Japanese altered and adapted these models to fit their own particular visions, desires, and needs. The Japanese are no more indebted to the originals than are modern-day Latin Americans, say, to their Iberian colonial ancestors.

By the tenth century C.E., the Japanese had evolved a peculiar form of government. A quasi-divine ruler, the descendant of the legendary Sun Goddess, performed rituals and exercised religious powers, while the political and military strength lay with a *shogun,* or regent who sat at the apex of a complicated feudal clan hierarchy. Although this system sometimes broke down into feudal warfare fought by the *samurai* for their lords, on the whole it worked well enough to allow steady progress in the civilized arts. Attempts by mainland potentates, such as the thirteenth-century Mongols, to invade the islands were successfully repelled.

THE MIDDLE AGE OF EUROPEAN CIVILIZATION

The Germanic invaders of the Roman Empire had established themselves in several tribal kingdoms by the seventh century. Some of these had adopted Christianity and were therefore admissible to the realm of civilization according to Roman standards and attitudes. With Christianity came a written language (Latin), law codes, some elements of education, and a concept of government based on institutions rather than personal charisma.

The most important of the early medieval Germanic kings was Charlemagne, king of the Franks and the first Holy Roman Emperor. As his second title indicates, he attempted to resurrect the old Roman Empire, this time in collaboration with the pope so as to unite state and church in one irresistible authority. But this attempt failed soon after Charlemagne's death, and his empire dissolved within a few years into three major components: France, Germany, and the lands along the Rhine and down into Italy.

The dissolution of Charlemagne's empire allowed a series of invasions in central and western Europe in the ninth and tenth centuries to succeed. From the east came the wild Magyars, a mounted host who settled in the great plains along the middle Danube and became Christian after the year 1000. From the south came Muslims (see the next section) across the Mediterranean to the coasts of Spain and Italy. And from the north came the Vikings, or Norsemen, who were initially the most destructive of the newcomers and then the most constructive.

Most Europeans had by now become Christian, and the church authorities used their influence to strengthen the kings' powers. Enhancing royal powers not only benefited civil peace but was to the church's advantage as well, for it was already the largest property owner in Europe. But the temptations presented by the administration of this property, among other things, led to corruption, which had already become a major problem for the church despite the periodic efforts of reformers such as St. Francis to combat it.

The most aggressive reformers were the popes of the eleventh and twelfth centuries who contested the traditional rights of the kings to appoint high churchmen in their kingdoms. Thus began the quarrels between church and state that have troubled Western Christianity into modern times.

In contrast, the Eastern, or Orthodox, Christians enjoyed an amicable relationship with the secular authorities. The Eastern Christians split off from the papal church in the eleventh century ostensibly over matters of doctrine. In reality, the division within Christianity had been developing during the centuries of differing traditions since the fall of the western Roman Empire to the barbarians. As early as the sixth century, the Eastern church and its emperor-protector refused to subordinate themselves to the bishop of German-ruled Rome, known as the pope. In the East, clerical leaders reached a mutually advantageous understanding with the emperor and did not sympathize with the papal efforts to subordinate the secular authorities to the clergy that began in the eleventh century.

The High Middle Age (1100–1300) was a period of intensive expansion and development in many fields, aided by beneficial climatic change and a decline in internal warfare. After 1096, much of the destructive energy of the warrior nobility was channeled into the Crusades to the Holy Land. These adventures also added considerably to European knowledge of the rest of the world.

Commerce and manufacturing also revived after the invasions ceased, and it became possible to travel safely again along the land and sea routes laid out by the Romans. The towns, which had been almost deserted for centuries, again attracted a settled population of professionals and merchants. They gradually came to play a leading role in the local governments that replaced the power of the feudal estates of the nobles and became the driving force behind the new capitalist economy. After about 1300, they were numerous enough to insist on recognition by king and church as a fourth element in the traditional division of European society: those who served God (clergy), those who ruled (nobility), and those who supported the first two groups (commoners).

But the stimuli eventually failed, intra-Christian warfare resumed, and the climate became harsher. The later 1300s and 1400s were a long tale of misery and prolonged conflicts that affected most of European society. In 1347 Europe was struck by the worst epidemic in Western history—the Black Death—and within a few years, at least a quarter of the population had died. The resultant shortage of labor brought a century-long economic slump in much of western Europe, and a savage struggle ensued between the landholding nobles and the enserfed peasants who tried to take advantage of the bargaining powers they had as survivors of the plague. Initially crushed, the peasantry eventually won out, and serfdom in western Europe died.

The prestige and authority of the church sharply declined with the scandals of the Babylonian Captivity of the papacy and the Great Schism. Not until the end of the

Hundred Years' War (1337–1453) between England and France and the simultaneous beginning of Portugal's search for a sea route to the East did Europeans experience a renewed sense of opening possibilities.

The World of Islam

A chief impetus for Portugal's interest in finding a sea route to the East was the rise of a new power in the eastern Mediterranean that threatened to cut off the traditional trade routes. This was the Turkish Ottoman dynasty, which had seized the leadership of Islamic civilization in the previous 100 years. Flushed with recent victories over several Muslim and non-Muslim opponents, they crowned their campaigns with the capture of the Christian stronghold of Constantinople in 1453. Islam ("submission to God") had sprung from the teachings of the Arab Muhammad, who claimed to be the last of the line of prophets of God that began with Abraham. Spreading with extraordinary rapidity among the Bedouins of Arabia, the new faith claimed most of the Near and Middle East and all northern Africa within a generation after Muhammad's death. Two centuries later, it ruled from the Spanish Pyrenees to the borders of China and was being carried still further east into the islands of the Pacific.

This fantastic expansion could not be controlled for long from a single center, and the Islamic political world began to fragment into kingdoms and caliphates almost as soon as it appeared. Baghdad in Iraq, Cairo in Egypt, and Córdoba in Spain were the chief early centers. By the eleventh century, each of them presented a magnificent display of the wealth and power of the followers of Muhammad. Originally Arab and Persian, the governing class became Mongol/Turkic after about 1200, when both of the latter peoples entered on campaigns of conquest that brought them into the Islamic orbit.

All Muslims accepted the Qur'an as the word of God, dictated by his angel to Muhammad and containing what was necessary to know in order to attain salvation. In essence, this came down to a public "submission" to God's will and the following of a few simple prescriptions for worship and diet. The ease of comprehending God's message as portrayed in Islam was an important reason for the rapid spread of the religion; another was the belief that those who died in the *jihad*—the holy war—to expand the faith would be rewarded with instant bliss in eternity.

Muslims segregated people solely on the basis of religious belief; the faith was open to all. It subordinated the female to the male (as did most other civilizations of the period) but was otherwise relatively free of social and ethnic prejudices. Under Muslim rule, both Jews and Christians enjoyed a degree of respect as forerunners of Islam and were allowed a significant autonomy.

Muslim scholarship and artistry were highly sophisticated and very cosmopolitan, drawing inspiration and research material from a dozen different sources in Asia, Africa, and the Mediterranean basin. Particularly striking was the Muslims' role in preserving the Greek and Roman classic authors, whose work was almost entirely forgotten or obscured in the Christian European centers. Muslim, Arab, and Persian commentaries on Aristotle and Plato, Muslim medical treatises, Muslim essays on the natural sciences, and Muslim mathematics were the absolutely vital foundations for much of the elevated culture of medieval Europe. In addition to their own achievements, Muslims often served as the conduit through which East Asian (especially Hindu) knowledge and technology reached the West. The Spanish Muslims were especially important in this regard.

THE AFRICAN AND AMERICAN PEOPLES

The early histories of both Africa south of the Sahara and the Americas are lost in obscurity that has been slightly lifted but by no means illuminated in recent years. A major problem has been the complete absence of written language in Africa until the arrival of Arab Muslims and the near-absence of writing in the Americas until the Spanish landings. Archaeology supplies some information in both places—more in the Americas than in Africa—and in Mexico the Spanish conquerors of the early 1500s preserved some fragments of the Aztec civilization in written as well as architectural forms.

Africa

The huge African continent (about three times as large as the United States) is a study in topographical and climatic variety. Much of it has been uninhabitable by humans until very modern times, and much of it is still inhospitable even in the twentieth century. (North of the Sahara the African continent belongs to the Mediterranean basin, and until recently, its cultures and civilizations were quite distinct from those of the peoples south of that barrier.)

The earliest African civilization was that of the Nile valley in the far northeast, which had some contact with the nomads of the surrounding deserts and the upper valley of the river. By perhaps as early as the second century B.C.E., agriculture had spread from Egypt into the grasslands (savanna) south of the Sahara, and the great desert itself was beginning to be crossed regularly by the recent Asian import, the camel.

Armed with iron tools and weapons, the Bantu-speaking peoples of the western "bulge" apparently began to move east and south in the first centuries C.E., bringing a more advanced pastoral and agricultural lifestyle with them to the peoples they encountered, including the Bushmen and Pygmies. Gradually, the Bantu speakers penetrated down to the southern tip of the continent and absorbed most of the peoples they had encountered in their 1,000-year migration.

Urban centers arose in and just south of the Sahara from about the 900s C.E., when the desert became simply an obstacle rather than a barrier to the steadily increasing trade between the Mediterranean and the savanna regions. This trade was largely the result of Muslim demands for gold and slaves, as well as for some tropical luxury items from equatorial Africa. These demands were met by the establishment of kingdoms or even empires, located in the bulge of West Africa and controlling the flow of gold and slaves northward.

Islam had a very strong impact on the savanna kingdoms from the 900s onward. The urban-based kingdoms (Ghana, Mali, Songhai) of West Africa were ruled by a Muslim upper class, which combined native customs with the received cosmopolitan culture of the Arab-Berber traders who settled among them and helped them emulate other Muslim states. The Arabic language offered a majestic channel for communications, but Africans were not accustomed to written record keeping, and our only written histories of these highly sophisticated governments and their customs come from the accounts of Muslim visitors. As these accounts make clear, these kingdoms were in some ways on the same level as their counterparts in the Christian and Muslim worlds.

On the east coast along the Indian Ocean, Islam was also a civilizing factor. From as early as the 700s, Arab traders and slavers had visited these coasts and gradually established colonies among the Bantu-speaking peoples. Here, as in the Sudanese states of the western savanna, intermarriage led to a mixed ruling group composed of Arabs and native peoples, which operated a lively trade over the Indian Ocean routes to Arabia and the Red Sea. Coastal city-states and interior kingdoms were created after about 1100, but their histories must be derived almost exclusively from fragmentary accounts of travelers and some architectural remains. The same is true of the only non-Negro civilization of sub-Saharan Africa, the Ethiopian kingdom of Axum, which flourished from about the first to the sixth century C.E. This state was Christian after its ruling house converted in the fourth century, making it the oldest continuous Christian state in the world and the only one in Africa after the Muslim conquest of the north.

Americas

Nowhere else in the world is there such disparity between the levels of material culture and immaterial culture as in the pre-Columbian Americas. On the one side was a level of political and administrative development that enabled the Inca to govern effectively over some 3,000 miles of mountainous territory and eight million people; on the other was a tool-making and metalworking ability that scarcely approached that of the Egyptians of 2,500 years earlier. The Mayan Indians of 1000 C.E. developed perhaps the most complex system of timekeeping ever seen, but their society proved incapable of solving its most urgent economic problems.

The oldest known civilized society in the Americas was located in central Mexico, on the Gulf coast. Here, the Olmecs developed an agrarian-based civilization that lasted about 700 years (1200–500 B.C.E.) and displayed most of the elements of advanced technology. What we know of the civilization comes from excavated urban sites and some magnificently carved stonework. There is no written history.

After the decline of the Olmec, the Indians of central interior Mexico and those of the Yucatán peninsula developed, separately, the Teotihuacán and the Mayan civilizations, roughly from 100 to 900 C.E. Both of these were centered on cities that fulfilled a combination of religious and mercantile functions. Teotihuacán itself seems to have been a huge place, perhaps with a population of upward of 100,000 at its height in the fifth and sixth centuries.

The Mayan ruins, which were rediscovered in the mid-nineteenth and early twentieth centuries in Yucatán (Peten), Guatemala, and Belize, are the most fascinating of all the Mesoamerican remnants. The Maya had a written language, which is just now being gradually deciphered; unfortunately, very few texts survived the Spanish conquerors. The Maya were obsessed with the correct fixing of dates, which apparently had a religious significance we can only guess at. Many of the very elaborate carved hieroglyphs on their stone buildings deal with astronomy and calendar making, expressed in "long" and "short" systems of counting.

Around 900, the southern Mayan city-states went into sudden decline; the reasons are unknown, but historians suspect that a decline in the food supply, caused either by exhaustion of the soil or by a peasant rebellion, was a major factor. Earlier, the same fate overtook Teotihuacán and its surrounding villages. Although some of the northern Maya continued into the twelfth century, the classic age of their people had drawn to an end.

The Aztecs were the final Mexico-based Indian civilization to arise. These nomadic warriors came into the Valley of Mexico as a conquering horde as late as the mid-1300s. Here they established themselves as a ruling caste over far more numerous tribes and created the impressive center of Tenochtitlán (now Mexico City) from the tribute of their subjects. When the Spanish *conquistadores* under Cortéz arrived in 1519, Tenochtitlán was the governing center of an empire of perhaps fifteen million and was itself one of the two or three largest cities in the world outside China. The Aztecs were totally dedicated to the arts of war and ruled harshly over their subjects, bringing many to the capital to serve as human sacrifice to the various gods.

Meanwhile, in South America, the Inca flourished about the same time as the Aztecs. Like the Aztecs, they had only very recently succeeded in subordinating many other Andean tribes and petty chieftancies. But unlike the Aztecs, the Inca were apparently not hated by their subjects. Despite the total absence of a written language, some evidence exists that suggests Incan rule was benevolently received. The Inca strongly encouraged the spread of new crops in the highland fields, which was essential to the rise of higher civilization. Their political and social institutions allowed their subject Indians considerable autonomy, and their engineering and architectural prowess is clear from the fantastic fortress city of Machu Picchu high in the Peruvian mountains. Just before the Spanish arrived, the Incan empire extended from present-day southern Colombia through Ecuador and Peru and down into central Chile—a distance of nearly 3,000 miles.

Both the Mesoamerican and the South American civilizations rose and fell in long waves, with each succeeding civilization building on the foundations established by the predecessors. Whether pre-1492 contacts took place between the Americas and other civilized areas, as some assume, is a tantalizing mystery. Most expert opinion believes not, but certain areas of human activity in the New World are structurally or conceptually so similar to Old World forms that the similarities are hard to ignore.

FOUR

DISEQUILIBRIUM: THE WESTERN ENCOUNTER WITH THE NON-WESTERN WORLD

1500–1850 C.E.

Within fifty years on either side of 1500 C.E., a host of events or processes contributed to an atmosphere of rising confidence in the power of European governments and their supportive institutions. In the political and military realm, the Mongol yoke in Russia was lifted; the Turks, victorious at Constantinople, failed in an attempt to seize Vienna and central Europe; the Hundred Years' War had ended and the French recovery commenced. The economy finally recovered from the ravages of the Black Death, and maritime trade had increased significantly, as had the sophistication of commercial and financial instruments. The shameful derogation of the papal dignity brought about by the Babylonian Captivity and the Great Schism had ended. The worst of the peasant Jaqueries had been put down, and a peaceable transition from feudal agrarianism seemed possible, at least in the West.

But aside from these general developments, the epoch centered on 1500 is usually heralded as the beginning of the modern era because of two specific complexes of events: the questioning of traditional authority manifested in the Protestant Reformation, and the voyages of discovery that revealed the possibilities of the globe to Europeans' imagination—and greed. Both of these complexes contributed, in very different ways, to the expansion of Europe's reach and authority that took place in the next 300 years, until Europeans began to claim a prerogative to decide the fates of others as almost a God-given right. This tendency was particularly striking in the American colonies, where the native Amerindians were either obliterated or virtually enslaved by their overlords. But it was also the case, though in a much more limited way, for eastern and southern Asia, the coast of Africa, and the island or Arctic peripheries of a world that was larger and more varied than anyone had formerly supposed.

The difference between 1500 and 1850 in this regard might well be illustrated by comparing the Aztecs' Tenochtitlán, which amazed the envious Cortés, with the sleepy, dusty villages to which Mexico's Indians were confined later. Similarly, one might compare the army of the

Persian Safavid rulers of the early sixteenth century that reduced the mighty Moghuls to supplicants for peace with the raggedy mob that attempted—in vain—to stop a handful of British from installing themselves on the Khyber Pass three centuries later. The West, whether represented by illiterate Spanish freebooters or Oxfordian British bureaucrats, seemed destined to surpass or be invincible against what one unrepentant imperialist called the "lesser breeds."

Part Four examines the massive changes that were slowly evincing themselves during these three centuries of heightening interactions between the West and the rest of the world, interactions that by the end of the period had effected a state of disequilibrium in the oecumene that existed since the early stages of the common era.

The voyages of discovery of the fifteenth and sixteenth centuries, the opening of maritime commerce across the Indian and Atlantic Oceans, and the resultant Columbian Exchange and the slave trade are the subject of Chapter 26. Chapter 27 considers in detail the successful Lutheran and Calvinist challenges to the papal church and their permanent effects on Western sensibilities. Chapters 28 and 29 examine the absolutist idea, constitutionalism, and their expression in religious warfare and the desire for stability; the evolving differences in the social and economic structures of western and eastern Europe are also considered.

Chapter 30 shifts the focus to East Asia, where China's centuries of glory following the ejection of the Mongols through the early Qing dynasty are analyzed. The history of pre–Meiji Restoration Japan and the colonial epoch in Southeast Asia follow in Chapter 31. In Chapter 32, the rise and fall of the great Muslim empires of central Asia and India are discussed, and this is succeeded by an overview in Chapter 33 of the disparate histories of the regions of precolonial Africa. Finally, the Iberian colonies of America and their struggle for independent existence are outlined in Chapter 34.

A LARGER WORLD OPENS

I have come to believe that this is a mighty continent which was hitherto unknown.

CHRISTOPHER COLUMBUS

Mid-1400s	Portuguese begin voyages of exploration
1492	Christopher Columbus reaches Americas
1498	Vasco de Gama arrives in India
EARLY 1500s	Transatlantic slave trade begins
1519–1540	Spanish conquer Aztecs and Incans
1522	First circumnavigation of globe completed
1602	Dutch East India Company founded

THE UNPARALLELED OVERSEAS EXPANSION of Europe in the later fifteenth and early sixteenth centuries opened a new era of intercontinental contacts. What were the motives for the rapid series of adventuresome voyages? They ranged from Christian missionary impulses to the common desire to get rich. Backed to varying degrees by their royal governments, Portuguese, Spanish, Dutch, French, and English seafarers opened the world to European commerce, settlement, and eventual dominion. Through the Columbian Exchange initiated in 1492, the New World entered European consciousness and was itself radically and permanently changed by European settlers. In most of the world, however, the presence of a relative handful of foreigners in coastal "factories" or as occasional traders meant little change in traditional activities and attitudes. Not until the later eighteenth century was the European presence a threat to the continuation of accustomed African, Asian, and Polynesian lifestyles.

MARITIME EXPLORATION IN THE 1400S

The Vikings in their graceful longboats had made voyages across the North Atlantic from Scandinavia to Greenland and on to North America as early as 1000 C.E. But the northern voyages were too risky to serve as the channel for European expansion, and Scandinavia's population base was too small. The Vikings' tiny colonies did not last.

Four hundred years later, major advances in technology had transformed maritime commerce. The development of new sail rigging, the magnetic compass, and the astrolabe (an instrument used to determine the altitude of the sun or other celestial bodies); a new hull design; and systematic navigational charts enabled Western seamen, led by the Portuguese, to conquer the stormy Atlantic. Their claims to dominion over their newly discovered territories were backed up by firearms of all sizes. Most of these inventions were originally the products of the Chinese and Muslims. The Europeans had found them in the traditional interchange ports of the eastern Mediterranean and then improved on them.

By the end of the fifteenth century, the map of the Eastern Hemisphere was gradually becoming familiar to Europeans. Knowledge of the high culture of China was current

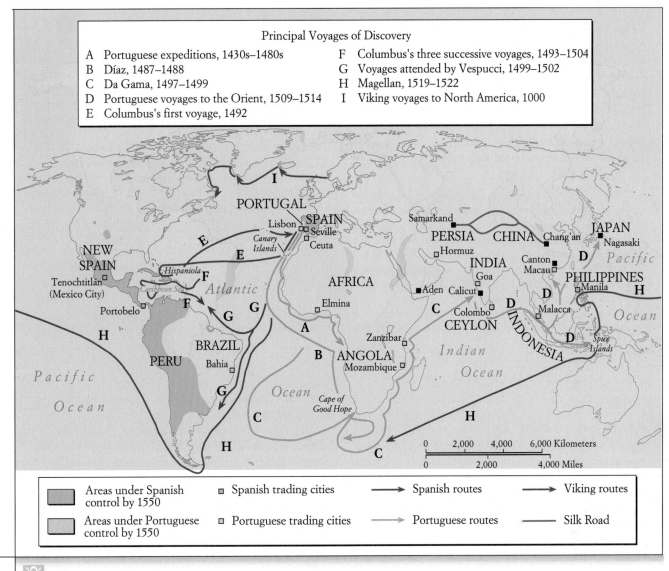

Principal Voyages of Discovery

A   Portuguese expeditions, 1430s–1480s
B   Díaz, 1487–1488
C   Da Gama, 1497–1499
D   Portuguese voyages to the Orient, 1509–1514
E   Columbus's first voyage, 1492

F   Columbus's three successive voyages, 1493–1504
G   Voyages attended by Vespucci, 1499–1502
H   Magellan, 1519–1522
I   Viking voyages to North America, 1000

Areas under Spanish control by 1550
Areas under Portuguese control by 1550
Spanish trading cities
Portuguese trading cities
Spanish routes
Portuguese routes
Viking routes
Silk Road

MAP 26.1   Spanish and Portuguese Voyages in the Fifteenth and Sixteenth Centuries.

by the early 1400s. Overland traders, mostly Muslims, had established an active trade with that country via the famous Silk Road through central Asia and served as intermediaries to Europe. Marco Polo's great adventure was well known even earlier, after the appearance of his book about his many years of service to Kubilai Khan (see Chapter 18).

Most of Europe's luxury imports came from China and India, while the Spice Islands (as they were called by Europeans) of Southeast Asia were the source of the most valuable items in international exchange (see Map 26.1). But in the fourteenth century, this trade was disrupted, first by the Ottoman Turkish conquest of the eastern Mediterranean, and then by the breakup of the Mongol empire, which had formed a single unit reaching from China to western Russia. Security of transit across Asia was threatened, as was the Europeans' long-established and profitable interchange

of goods with the Arabs and Persians. In 1453, the great depot of Eastern wares, Constantinople, fell into the hands of the Turks. Europeans now became much more interested than ever before in finding a direct sea route to the East by circumnavigating Africa. This would allow them to make an "end run" around the hostile Turks and perhaps even cut out the Arab, Persian, and Indian middlemen—a tempting prospect.

OVERSEAS EMPIRES AND THEIR EFFECTS

First the Portuguese and the Spanish and then the Dutch, English, and French created overseas empires that had far-reaching effects both at home and abroad.

First Contacts in East Africa

One of the most daring of all the explorers sailing in the name of Portugal or Spain was Vasco da Gama, the first to round the tip of Africa and sail on to India. Da Gama made landfall on the Indian coast in 1498 before returning safely to Lisbon the following year. He kept a detailed diary of his epoch-making voyage, from which the following comments on the natives of the east African littoral are taken. Note the relaxed African attitude toward these first Europeans, the result of several centuries of experience with Arab and Hindu visitors along this coast.

> These people are black, and the men are of good physique, they go about naked except that they wear small pieces of cotton cloth with which they cover their genitals, and the Senhores [chiefs] of the land wear larger cloths. The young women in this land look good; they have their lips pierced in three places and they wear some pieces of twisted tin. These people were very much at ease with us, and brought out to us in the vessels what they had, in dugout canoes. . . .
>
> After we had been here two or three days there came out two Senhores of this land to see us, they were so haughty that they did not value anything which was given to them. One of them was wearing a cap on his head with piping worked in silk, and the other a furry cap of green satin. There came in their company a youth who, we gathered from gestures, came from another far country, and said that he had already seen great vessels like those that carried us. With these signs we rejoiced greatly, because it seemed to us that we were going to reach where we wanted to go. . . .
>
> This land, it seemed to us, is densely populated. There are in it many villages and towns. The women seemed to be more numerous than men, because when there came 20 men there came 40 women. . . . The arms of these people are very large bows and arrows, and assagais [spears] of iron. In this land there seemed to be much copper, which they wore on their legs and arms and in their kinky hair. Equally used is tin, which they place on the hilts of daggers, the sheaths are of iron. The people greatly prize linen cloth, and they gave us as much of this copper for as many shirts as we cared to give.

Source: The Diary of Vasco da Gama (Travels through African Waters 1497–1499), ed. Harry Stephan (Sydney: Phillips, 1998), pp. 32–33.

Portuguese Pioneers

In the middle of the 1400s, insignificant and impoverished Portugal took advantage of its geographical position to begin the rapid phase of European expansion. Under the guidance of the visionary Prince Henry the Navigator (1394–1460), the Portuguese sponsored a series of exploratory voyages down the west coast of Africa and out into the ocean as far as the Azores (about one-third of the distance to the Caribbean). In 1488, the Portuguese captain **Bartolomeo Diaz** made a crucial advance by successfully rounding the Cape of Good Hope. A few years later, Vasco da Gama sailed across the Indian Ocean to the west coast of India. (For a closer look at Da Gama's exploits, see the box.) Trying to go down the west African coast, the captain Alvarez Cabral got blown all the way across the Atlantic, making landfall in Brazil, which he promptly claimed for Portugal. By 1510, Portuguese flags were flying over Goa in India and **Macao** on the coast of China (see Map 26.1). In 1511, the extraordinary admiral Albuquerque seized the great port-depot of Malacca at the tip of the Malay peninsula. This act established Portugal as the controller of the most profitable sea trade in the world (see Chapter 19).

The Portuguese empire was really only a string of fortified stations called "factories," from which the Portuguese brought back shiploads of the much sought-after spices, gold, porcelain, and silk obtained from their trading partners in East Africa and the Southeast Asian mainland and islands. The Portuguese paid for these imports initially with metalwares, cloth, and trinkets and later with firearms and liquor. The Lisbon government was the initiator and main beneficiary of this trade, because Portugal's small upper and middle classes were unable to pay sufficiently to outfit ships for the expeditions.

The era of Portuguese leadership was brief. The country was too poor and its population too small to maintain this fantastic but very thinly spread network. By the late 1500s, the aggressively expanding Dutch merchants had already forced Portugal out of some of its overseas stations. Previously independent Portugal was incorporated into Catholic Spain in 1580, which gave the Dutch and English Protestants an excuse to attack the Portuguese everywhere. Eventually, by the end of the seventeenth century, Portugal was left with only Macao, Goa, and a few trading posts scattered along the African and Indian coasts.

How did a relative handful of European intruders establish themselves as regionally dominant authorities in these distant corners of the globe? In the Indian Ocean and Southeast Asia, the patterns established by the Portuguese were followed by all their successors. The European outreach was seaborne, and control of the sea was the crucial element. The militant natives quickly learned that it was not profitable to confront the European ships by arms, because the Europeans would generally win. Their naval cannon, more advanced methods of rigging, more maneuverable hulls, better battle discipline, and higher levels of training assured them of success in almost all engagements. The intruders avoided land warfare, unless and until mastery of the surrounding seas was assured. And in that case, land warfare was rarely necessary.

After an initial display of martial strength, the newcomers were usually content to deal with and through the established native leadership in securing the spices, cotton cloth, silk, and other luxuries that they sought. In the normal course of events, the Europeans made a treaty with the paramount regional ruler that assured them a dominant position in the export market. This action meant the elimination of the Muslim or Hindu merchants, who until the sixteenth century controlled the Indian Ocean trade and who were the instigators of whatever initial resistance was made. The local ruler's position was not directly threatened unless he should put up armed resistance—a rare occurrence in view of the Europeans' military superiority.

A kind of partnership thus evolved between the local chieftains and the new arrivals, in which both had sufficient reasons to maintain the status quo against those who might challenge it. The Portuguese frequently made the mistake of alienating the local population by their brutality and their attempts to exclude all competition, but the Dutch and, later, the British were more circumspect. Unlike the Portuguese, they made no attempt until the nineteenth century to bring the Asians into the Christian belief. As a very general rule, after the sixteenth-century Portuguese mis-

sionary efforts had subsided, the Europeans interfered little with existing laws, religion, and customs unless they felt compelled to do so to gain their commercial ends. Such interference was rare in both Asia and Africa. There, the European goal was to attain maximal profit from trade, and they avoided anything that threatened to disrupt the smooth execution of that trade. The Spanish and Portuguese empires in the Americas were a different proposition.

The Spanish Empire in the Americas

The newly unified Spanish kingdom was close behind and in some areas simultaneous with Portugal in the race for world empire. A larger domestic resource base and extraordinary finds of precious metals enabled Spain to achieve more permanent success than its neighbor. The Italian visionary Christopher Columbus was able to persuade King Ferdinand and Queen Isabella of his dream of a shortcut to the "Indies" by heading *west* over the Atlantic, which he

A Portuguese Galleon. In what kind of vessel did the early explorers set sail? Ships like these opened the trade routes to the East and to Brazil and the Caribbean for the Lisbon government in the sixteenth and seventeenth centuries. In their later days, two or three rows of cannons gave them heavy firepower as well as cargo space. (*National Maritime Museum Picture Library*)

thought was only a few hundred miles wide. The first of Columbus's Spanish-financed voyages resulted in his discovery of the American continents. He made three more voyages before his death and was still convinced that China lay just over the horizon of the Caribbean Sea.

By then, the Spanish crown had engaged a series of other voyagers, including **Amerigo Vespucci,** who eventually gave his name to the New World that Columbus and others were exploring. In 1519–1521, the redoubtable **Hernan Cortés** conquered the Aztec empire in Mexico. Soon Spanish explorers had penetrated north into what is now California and Arizona. By the 1540s, Spain controlled most of northern South America as well as all Central America and the Caribbean islands.

Perhaps the greatest of these ventures was the fantastic voyage of **Ferdinand Magellan.** Starting from Spain in 1519, his ships made the first circumnavigation of the globe. A few survivors (not including the unlucky Magellan) limped back into Sevilla in 1522 and reported that, yes, the world was indeed round. Most educated people already thought so, but Magellan's voyage proved that the Earth had no real ends and that it was possible to go around the southern tip of the New World into the more or less familiar waters of East Asia.

Like the Portuguese, the Spaniards' motives for exploration were mixed between a desire to convert the heathen to the papal church and thus gain a strong advantage against the burgeoning Protestants (see Chapter 27) and the desire for wealth and esteem. Gold, God, and glory were the motives most frequently in play. It is often difficult to tell which was uppermost. Sometimes, however—as in the cases of Francisco Pizarro in Peru and Cortés in Mexico—it is easier. By whatever motivation, the middle of the 1500s saw the Spanish adventurers creating an empire that reached nearly around the world. In the terms of the royal charters granted to Columbus and his successors, the Spanish Crown claimed the lion's share of special treasures found by the explorers. Indian gold and silver (*bullion*) thus poured into the royal treasury in Madrid. Those metals, in turn, allowed Spain to become the most powerful European state in the sixteenth and seventeenth centuries.

Unlike the Portuguese, the Spanish frequently came to stay at their overseas posts. Whereas the Portuguese were primarily interested in quick profits from the trade in luxury items from the East, the Spanish noble explorers were accompanied by priests, who set up missions among the Indians, and by a number of lowborn men (later women, also), who were prepared to get rich more slowly. They did so by taking land and workers from among the native population.

Finding that the much dreamed-of cities of gold and silver, or the *El Dorados,* were mirages, the Spanish immigrants gradually created agricultural colonies in much of Central and South America, using first Amerindian and then black labor. Some of these workers were more or less free to come and go, but an increasing number were slaves, imported from Africa. The Spanish colonies thus saw the growth of a multiracial society—blacks, Indians, and whites—in which the whites held the dominant political and social positions from the outset. The dominance of the whites was to assume increasing importance for the societies and economies of these lands both during their 300 years as colonies and later as independent states.

The African Slave Trade Opens

The African slave trade commenced in the fifteenth century. When the Portuguese ventured down the West African coast, they quickly discovered that selling black houseslaves to the European nobility could be a lucrative business. But the slave trade remained very small scale through the 1490s and only began to grow when slaves started to be shipped across the Atlantic. The first known example occurred in 1502. By the mid-1530s, Portugal had shipped moderate numbers of slaves to the Spanish Caribbean and to its own colony of Brazil, and the transatlantic trade remained almost a Portuguese monopoly until into the next century. At that time, Dutch and then English traders moved into the business and dominated it through its great expansion in the eighteenth century until its gradual abolition.

Few European women traveled to the Americas in the early years of colonization, so the Spaniards often married Amerindian or black women or kept them as concubines. As a result, **mestizos** (the offspring of Amerindians and whites) and **mulattos** (the children of Africans and whites) soon outnumbered Caucasians in many colonies. The same happened in Portuguese Brazil, where over time a huge number of African slaves were imported to till the sugarcane fields that were that colony's chief resource. Here, the populace was commonly the offspring of Portuguese and African, rather than the Spanish-Indian mixture found to the north.

Dutch and English Merchant-Adventurers

Holland When Portugal's grip on its Indian Ocean trade began to falter, the Dutch Protestant merchants combined a fine eye for profit with religious prejudice—the Portuguese were after all minions of the pope and the Spanish king—to fill the vacuum. In the sixteenth century, the Netherlands were under Spanish control until the failure of the Spanish *Armada* in 1588 (see Chapter 27). Controlling their own affairs after that, the bourgeois shipowners and merchants of the Dutch and Flemish towns quickly moved into the forefront of the race for trade. By the opening of the seventeenth century, Amsterdam and Antwerp were the major destinations of Far Eastern shippers, and Lisbon had fallen into a secondary position.

Dutch interest in the eastern seas was straightforward and hard-edged. They wanted to accumulate wealth by creating a monopoly of demand, buying shiploads of Southeast Asian luxury goods at low prices and selling the goods

The Slave Ship. This engraving shows the usual arrangements for transport of black slaves in the Atlantic trade. The ship was the *Albanez,* with cargo from the Guinea coast and headed for the Caribbean. It was boarded and taken as a prize by HMS *Albatross* in 1840, as part of the British effort to outlaw slave trading. Food and water were lowered into the hold through the hatch on a once-daily basis. Some slavers permitted short periods on deck for their cargo; most did not.
(The Art Archive)

at very high prices in Europe. Many of the Asian suppliers were Muslims, and their relationship with the Catholic Portuguese had been strained or hostile. They preferred to deal with the Dutch Protestants, who were simply businessmen with no desire to be missionaries. If the suppliers were for one or another reason reluctant to sell, the Dutch persuaded them by various means, usually involving Dutch superiority in naval gunnery.

The Dutch focused on the East Indies spice and luxury trade, but they also established a settler colony in New Amsterdam across the Atlantic, and several island colonies in the Caribbean. These were less attractive to the Dutch and eventually surrendered to other powers, such as England. New Amsterdam became New York at the close of the first of two naval wars in the seventeenth century that made England the premier colonial power along the East Coast of the future United States.

How did such a small nation (Holland did not possess more than 2.5 million people at this juncture) carry out this vast overseas enterprise at the very time it was struggling to free itself from its Spanish overlords? A chief reason for the Dutch success was the East India Company: a private firm chartered by the government in 1602, the company had a monopoly on Dutch trading in the Pacific. The company eventually took over the Portuguese spice and luxury trade from the East and proved an enormous bonanza for its stockholders. The traders were usually temporary partners. A partnership would be set up for one or more voyages with both cost and profits split among the shareholders. The traders hired captains and crews who would be most likely to succeed in filling the ship's hold at minimal cost, whatever the means or consequences. Later in the seventeenth century, the focus of attention shifted from importing spices and luxury goods to the alluring profits to be made in the transatlantic trade in African slaves.

England The English colonial venture was slow in getting started. When the Portuguese and Spaniards were dividing up the newly discovered continent of America and the Far Eastern trade, England was just emerging from a lengthy struggle for dynastic power called the War of the Roses (see Chapter 25). Starting in the 1530s, the country was then preoccupied for a generation with the split from Rome under Henry VIII and its consequences (see Chapter 27). Then came the disappointing failure of Sir Walter Raleigh's "Lost Colony" on the Carolina coast in the 1580s and a war with Spain.

Only in the early 1600s did the English begin to enter the discovery and colonizing business in any systematic way. Like the Dutch, the English efforts were organized by private parties or groups and were not under the direction of the royal government. The London East India Company, founded in 1600, is a good example. Similar to its Dutch counterpart, it was a private enterprise with wide political as well as commercial powers in dealing with foreigners and with its own military resources.

After two victorious wars against the Dutch in the 1650s and 1660s, the English were the world's leading naval power, although the Dutch still maintained their lead in the carrying trade to and from Europe. The East Asian colonial trade was not important to them, however, and they soon gave up their attempts to penetrate the Dutch monopoly on East Indian luxuries, choosing to concentrate on India. (The only important English station in Southeast Asia was the great fortress port of Singapore, which was not acquired until the nineteenth century.)

English colonies in the seventeenth century were concentrated in North America, and an odd mixture they were. The northern colonies were filled with Protestant dissidents who could not abide the Anglican church regime: Puritans, Congregationalists, and Quakers. Maryland was a refuge for persecuted Catholics. Virginia and the Carolinas began as real estate speculations. They were essentially get-rich-quick schemes devised by nobles or wealthy commoners who thought they could sell off their American holdings to individual settlers at a fat profit. Georgia began as a noble experiment by a group of philanthropists who sought to give convicts a second chance.

Elsewhere, the English were less inclined to settle new lands than to make their fortunes pirating Spanish galleons or competing with the Dutch in the slave trade. What the Dutch had stolen from the Portuguese the English stole in part from the Dutch. This was equally true in the New World, where the Dutch challenge to Portuguese and Spanish hegemony in the Caribbean was superseded by the English and French in the eighteenth century.

France   The colonial empire of France parallels that of England. Relatively late in entering the race, the French sought overseas possessions and/or trade factories throughout the world to support their prospering domestic economy. From Canada (as early as 1608, one year after Jamestown in Virginia), to the west coast of Africa (as early as 1639) and India (in the early eighteenth century), the servants of the Bourbon kings contested both their Catholic coreligionists (Portugal, Spain) and their Protestant rivals (Holland, Britain) for mercantile advantage and the extension of royal powers. Thus, the French, too, reflected the seventeenth-century trend to allow state policies to be dictated more by secular interests than by religious adherences, a process we will examine in detail in Chapter 28.

MERCANTILISM

During this epoch, governments attempted to control their economies through a process later termed **mercantilism.**

Under mercantilism, the chief goal of economic policy was a favorable balance of trade, with the value of a country's exports exceeding the cost of its imports. To achieve this goal, the royal government intervened in the market constantly and attempted to secure advantage to itself and the population at large by carefully supervising every aspect of commerce and investment. The practice reached its highest development in seventeenth- and eighteenth-century France, but it was subscribed to almost everywhere.

As for colonial policy, mercantilism held that only goods and services that originated in the home country could be (legally) exported to the colonies and that the colonies' exports must go to the home country for use there or reexport. Thus, the colonies' most essential functions were to serve as captive markets for home country producers and to provide raw materials at low cost for home country importers. Portugal, Spain, and France practiced this theory of economics rigorously in their colonies, whereas Holland and England took a more relaxed approach in theirs.

THE COLUMBIAN EXCHANGE

The coming of the Europeans to the New World resulted in very important changes in the resources, habits, and values of both the Amerindians and the whites. Among the well-known introductions by the Europeans to the Western Hemisphere were horses, cattle, sheep, and goats; iron; firearms; sailing ships; and, less tangibly, the entire system of economics we call capitalism.

But the **Columbian Exchange** had another side: a reverse flow of products and influences from the Americas to Europe and through Europe to the other continents. Educated Europeans after about 1520 became aware of how huge and relatively unknown the Earth was and how varied the peoples inhabiting it were. This knowledge came as a surprise to many Europeans, and they were eager to learn more. The literature of discovery and exploration became extraordinarily popular during the sixteenth and seventeenth centuries.

From this literature, Europeans learned, among other things, that the Christian moral code was but one of several; that the natural sciences were not of overwhelming interest or importance to most of humanity; that an effective education could take myriad forms and have myriad goals; and that viewpoints formed by tradition and habit are not necessarily correct, useful, or the only conceivable ones. Initially just curious about the Earth's other inhabitants, upper-class Europeans gradually began to develop a certain tolerance for their views and habits. This tolerance slowly deepened in the seventeenth and especially the eighteenth century as Europe emerged from its religious wars. The previously favored view of unknown peoples probably being "anthropophagi" (man eaters) began giving way to the

Indian Labor. The Amerindian population was put to hard labor by the Spanish conquistadores either through arrangements between the Spaniards and local chiefs or by force. This sixteenth-century sketch shows the shipment of arms (including a cannon barrel and balls) across a range of mountains in Mexico. The absence of beasts of burden in Mesoamerica meant that humans had to shoulder every load. (© *The Granger Collection, New York*)

concept of the "noble savage," whose unspoiled morality might put the sophisticated European to shame.

Contacts with the Americas also led to economic changes in Europe. Some crops such as sugarcane and rice that were already known in Europe but could not be profitably grown there were found to prosper in the New World. Their cultivation formed the basis for the earliest plantations in the Caribbean basin and the introduction of slavery into the New World.

In addition, a series of new crops were introduced to the European Asian and African diet. Tobacco, several varieties of beans and peas, squashes, rice, maize, bananas, manioc, and others stemmed originally from American or Far Eastern lands. First regarded as novelties—much like the occasional Indian or black visitor—they came to be used as food and fodder. The most important for Europe was the white or Irish potato, an Andean native, which was initially considered fit only for cattle and pigs but was gradually adopted by northern Europeans in the eighteenth century. By the end of that century, it had become the most important part of the peasants' diet in several countries. The potato was the chief reason European farms were able to feed the spectacular increase in population that started in the later 1700s.

So much additional coinage was put into circulation from the Mexican and Peruvian silver mines that it generated massive inflation. In the seventeenth century, the Spanish court used the silver to pay army suppliers, shipyards, and soldiers, and from their hands, it went on into the general economy. Spain itself suffered most in the long run from the inflation its bullion imports caused. Spanish gold and silver went into the pockets of foreign suppliers, carriers, and artisans rather than into domestic investments or business. This would prove fateful in the next century.

In a period of inflation, when money becomes cheap and goods or services become dear, people who can convert their wealth quickly to goods and services are in an enviable position. Those whose wealth is illiquid and cannot be easily converted are at a disadvantage. As a result, the landholders—many of whom were nobles who thought it beneath them to pay attention to money matters—lost economic strength. The middle classes, who could sell their services and expertise at rising rates, did well. Best off were the merchants who could buy cheap and hold before selling at higher prices. But even the unskilled or skilled workers in the towns were in a relatively better position than the landlords: wages rose about as fast as prices in this century.

In many feudal remnant areas, where serfs paid token rents in return for small parcels of arable land, the landlord was dealt a heavy blow. Prices rose for everything the noble landlords needed and wanted, while their rents, sanctioned by centuries of custom, remained about the same. Many of them had been living beyond their means for generations, borrowing money wherever they could with land as security. Unaware of the reasons for the economic changes and unable to anticipate the results, many landlords faced disaster during the later sixteenth century and could not avoid bankruptcy when their long-established mortgages were called. Much land changed hands at this time, from impoverished nobles to peasants or to the newly rich from the towns. Serfdom in the traditional pattern became impractical or unprofitable. Already weakened by long-term changes in European society, it was abolished in most of western Europe.

EUROPEAN IMPACTS AND VICE VERSA

How strong was the European impact on the native cultures of the Western Hemisphere and on the peoples of the Far East, sub-Saharan Africa, and the Pacific Rim? Historians agree that it was enormous in some areas, but much less so in others. The Portuguese and others' trading factories on the African and Asian coasts had minimal impacts on the lives of the peoples of the interior. Only in exceptional circumstances was the presence of the Europeans a prominent factor in native consciousness. Even in the areas most directly affected by slaving such as Senegambia and Angola, the consensus of recent scholarly opinion believes that there were few if any massive changes in the course of ordinary affairs, social or economic, brought by slaving alone. Rather, the foreign slavers' interests were filtered through the existing networks of local authority and custom.

Spain's American settler colonies and Brazil were quite different in these respects. Here the intruders quickly and radically terminated existing Amerindian authority structures, replacing them with Spanish/Portuguese models. In the economy, the collectives of the villages with their free laborers were replaced by *encomienda* estates on which first Amerindians and later Africans were forced to reside and labor. Although the encomiendas were soon abolished, the exploitation of the helpless by their Spanish and Portuguese overseers continued unabated on the rice and sugar plantations, which replaced gold and silver mines.

As with the exchanges in agricultural products, the stream of external influences was not simply one way, from Europe to the rest of the world. In the Americas, there was a noticeable degree of change wrought in the Spanish and Portuguese culture by prolonged exposure to Amerindian habits and attitudes. An example would be the adoption of maize culture by the mestizo Spanish in Mexico. Another would be the incorporation of Amerindian hydraulic farming technique. In another part of the early imperial world created by the voyages of discovery, the architecture of the Dutch colonial town of Batavia (Jakarta), was soon converted from the trim and tight homes and warehouses of blustery Amsterdam to the very different demands of the Javanese climate.

Perhaps it is most accurate to say that in the settler colonies of the Western Hemisphere, the local peoples were extensively and sometimes disastrously affected by the arrival of the whites, but in the rest of the world, including sub-Saharan Africa, the Asian mainland, and the South Pacific islands, the Europeans were less disruptive to the existing state of affairs. Sometimes native governments even succeeded in manipulating the Europeans to their own advantage, as in West Africa and Mughal India. This would remain true until the nineteenth century. Promoted by industrialization at that time, the European impacts multiplied, became more profound, and changed in nature so as to subordinate the natives in every sense.

The Fate of the Amerindians

By far the worst human consequences of the European expansion were the tragic fates imposed on the native Amerindians of the Caribbean and Central America in the first century of Spanish conquest (see the report by **Bartolome de Las Casas** in the Exercise of Authority box). Although the Spanish Crown imposed several regulatory measures to protect the Indians after 1540, little could be done to inhibit the spread of epidemic disease (measles and influenza, as well as the major killer, smallpox) in the Amerindian villages. As a general rule, the immune systems of the Amerindians were unable to cope with the diseases brought by the newcomers, whereas the Spaniards were much less affected by the Amerindian maladies. (Which ethnic group is responsible for the appearance of syphilis is much argued.)

Smallpox was a particular curse. The population of Mexico, which was perhaps 25 million at the coming of Cortez, was reduced to 2 million only sixty years later, largely as a result of smallpox epidemics. On the Caribbean islands, no Amerindians remained after a generation of Spanish occupancy. The same story repeated itself in the viceroyalty of Peru, where as many as 80 percent of the native population died in the sixteenth century. Only in modern times have the Amerindians recovered from this unprecedented disaster.

Racism's Beginnings

Blacks came into European society for the first time in appreciable numbers during the fifteenth century. At the same time appeared the first faint signs of white racism. The black slaves from Africa, who were brought to Europe through Muslim channels, were mostly regarded as novelties by the rich and were kept as tokens of wealth or artistic taste. Some free blacks lived in Mediterranean Europe where they worked as sailors, musicians, and actors, but they were not numerous enough for the average European to have any firsthand contact.

Many whites thought of blacks in terms dictated either by the Bible or by Muslim prejudices imbibed unconsciously over time. The biblical references were generally negative: black was the color of the sinful, the opposite of light in the world. "Blackhearted," "a black scoundrel," and "black intentions" are a few examples of the mental connection between the color black and the evil and contemptible. The Omani Arab slave traders in East Africa who supplied some of the European as well as the Asiatic markets were another source of prejudice. They were contemptuous of the non-Muslim blacks on the Zanzibar coast whom they ruled and with whom they traded in human flesh. These traders' point of view was easily transferred to their Italian and Portuguese partners.

BARTOLOME DE LAS CASAS'S REPORT ON THE INDIES

Violence toward the conquered is a commonplace in history, and nowhere is this more evident than in the history of the state religions. Using inhumane means to propagate Christianity was a cynical cover for some of the Spanish conquistadores in their obsessive search for Indian gold. They were resisted, however, in this bloodthirsty enterprise by one of their own number.

Bartolome de Las Casas (1474–1567), a Dominican priest who had been a conquistador and slaveholder in the Caribbean in his youth, turned his back on his former life and devoted himself to protecting the Amerindians under Spanish rule. In his bold exposé entitled *Brief Relation of the Destruction of the Indies* (1522), he began an uncompromising campaign to show the horrendous treatment meted out by his fellow Spanish to the native populations of the New World. So graphic and terrible were his accounts that foreign powers hostile to Spain (notably, England) were able to use them for centuries to perpetuate the so-called Black Legend of the viciousness of Spanish colonialism.

The Conquistadores Arrive. This Aztec painting shows a skirmish between the Spaniards on horse and their Amerindian allies, and Aztec defenders. The Amerindians are armed with obsidian-edged swords capable of cutting off the head of a horse with a single blow. *(© The Granger Collection, New York)*

Of the Island of Hispaniola

The Christians, with their horses and swords and lances, began to slaughter and practice strange cruelties among them. They penetrated into the country and spared neither children nor the aged, nor pregnant women, nor those in childbirth, all of whom they ran through the body and lacerated, as though they were assaulting so many lambs herded into the sheepfold.

They made bets as to who could slit a man in two, or cut off his head at one blow . . . they tore babes from their mothers' breasts by the feet, and dashed their heads against the rocks. Others, they seized by the shoulders and threw into the rivers, laughing and joking, and when they fell into the water they exclaimed, "boil the body of So-and-so! . . ."

They made a gallows just high enough for the feet to nearly touch the ground, and by thirteens, in honour and reverence of our Redeemer and the 12 Apostles, they put wood underneath and, with fire, they burned the Indians alive.

They wrapped the bodies of others entirely in dry straw, binding them in it and setting fire to it; and so they burned them. They cut off the hands of all they wished to take alive, made them carry them pinned on to their bodies, and said "Go and carry these letters," that is, take the news to those who have fled to the mountains. . . .

I once saw that they had four or five of the chief lords [Indians] stretched on a gridiron to burn them, and I think there were also two or three pairs of gridirons, where they were burning others. And because they cried aloud and annoyed the Captain or prevented him from sleeping, he commanded that they should be strangled; the officer who was burning them was worse than a hangman and did not wish to suffocate them, but with his own hands he gagged them, so that they should not make themselves heard, and he stirred up the fire until they roasted slowly, according to his pleasure. I know this man's name, and knew his relations in Sevilla. I saw all the above things and numberless others.

And because all the [Indian] people who could flee, hid among the mountains and climbed the crags to escape from men so deprived of humanity . . . the Spaniards taught and trained the fiercest boarhounds to tear an Indian to pieces as soon as they saw him. . . . And because sometimes, though rarely, the Indians killed a few Christians for just cause, they made a law among themselves that for one Christian whom the Indians might kill, the Christians should kill a hundred Indians.

FOR REFLECTION

Beside de las Casas, other Spanish priests attempted protection of the Amerindians against cruelty, but usually in vain. What measures could be undertaken by the clergy to diminish such cruelty? Was it logical to expect the priests or bishops to intervene effectively? What does the colonial record show?

SOURCE: *Bartolome de las Casas*, A Very Brief Account of the Destruction of the Indies, *trans. F. A. McNutt (Cleveland: Clark, 1909), pp. 312–319.*

SUMMARY

The explosive widening of Europe's horizons in the sixteenth century, in both the geographic sense and the psychological sense, was one side of the Columbian Exchange. A series of colonial empires were created, first by the Portuguese and Spanish and then by the Dutch, English, and French. The original objective of the government-funded explorers was to find new, more secure trade routes to the East, but soon their motives changed to a mixture of enrichment, missionary activity, and prestige: gold, God, and glory.

The import of great quantities of precious metals created severe inflation and promoted the rise of the business/commercial classes. The discovery of customs and values that were quite different from those of Europeans contributed to the beginning of a new attitude of tolerance. The overseas expansion added important new foods to the European diet.

For the non-Western hosts, this colonial and commercial outreach had mainly negative consequences, although circumstances varied from place to place. The most devastating effects were certainly in Spain's American colonies, where the indigenous peoples were almost wiped out by disease and oppression. In West Africa, East Africa, and the Asian mainland, the European trading presence had overall little effect on ordinary life at this time. Racism's beginnings, however, can be traced to its roots in the African slave trade commencing in this era.

TEST YOUR KNOWLEDGE

1. The fifteenth- and sixteenth-century voyages of exploration were stimulated mainly by
   a. European curiosity about other peoples.
   b. the determination to obtain more farming land for a growing population.
   c. the individual explorers' hopes of enrichment.
   d. the discovery that the Earth was in fact a sphere without "ends."
2. Which of the following was *not* proved by Magellan's epic voyage?
   a. The globe was more compact than had been believed.
   b. The globe was indeed spherical.
   c. A sea passage existed south of the tip of South America.
   d. The islands called "Spice Lands" could be reached from the East.
3. Which of the following reasons was *least* likely to be the motive for a Dutch captain's voyage of discovery?
   a. A desire to deal the Roman church a blow
   b. A search for personal enrichment
   c. A quest to find another lifestyle for himself in a foreign land
   d. The intention of establishing trade relations with a new partner
4. What is the correct sequence of explorer-traders in the Far East?
   a. Spanish, English, French
   b. Spanish, Portuguese, Dutch
   c. Dutch, English, Spanish
   d. Portuguese, Dutch, English
5. The sixteenth-century inflation affected which group most negatively?
   a. Landholding nobles
   b. Urban merchants
   c. Wage laborers
   d. Skilled white-collar workers

6. Which proved to be the most important of the various new foods introduced into European diets by the voyages of discovery?
   a. Tomatoes
   b. Rice
   c. Potatoes
   d. Coffee
7. Which of the following nations was most persistently committed to converting the natives of the newly discovered regions to Christianity?
   a. Spain
   b. Holland
   c. England
   d. Portugal
8. The most devastating effects on the native population brought about by European discovery was in
   a. India.
   b. Latin America.
   c. West Africa.
   d. Southeast Asia.
9. Mercantilism aimed first of all at
   a. securing financial rewards for the entrepreneurs.
   b. allowing the impoverished a chance at rising in society.
   c. bringing maximal income to the royal throne.
   d. securing favorable balance of foreign trade.

IDENTIFICATION TERMS

Columbian Exchange

Cortés, Hernan

de Las Casas, Bartolome

Diaz, Bartolomeo

Macao

Magellan, Ferdinand

mercantilism

mestizo

mulatto

Vespucci, Amerigo

INFOTRAC COLLEGE EDITION

Enter the search term "Vasco da Gama" using Key Words.
Enter the search term "Christopher Columbus" using the Subject Guide.

Enter the search term "mercantilism" using the Subject Guide.

THE PROTESTANT REFORMATION

*I have often been resolved to live uprightly,
and to lead a true godly life,
and to set everything aside that would
hinder this, but it was far from being put
in execution. I am not able to effect that
good which I intend.*

MARTIN LUTHER

THE SPLIT IN CHRISTIAN belief that is termed the Protestant Reformation brought enormous consequences in its wake. Its beginning coincided with the high point of the era of discovery by Europeans. Taken together, these events provide the basis for dividing Western civilization's history into the premodern and modern eras around 1500.

What the opening up of the transatlantic and trans–Indian Ocean worlds did for the consciousness of physical geography in European minds, the Reformation did for the mental geography of all Christians. New continents of belief and identity emerged from the spiritual voyages of the early Protestants. Luther and Calvin worked not only a reformation but also a transformation of the church and its members.

LUTHER AND THE GERMAN NATIONAL CHURCH

The upheaval called the **Reformation** of the early sixteenth century had its roots in political and social developments as much as in religious disputes. The long-standing arguments within the Christian community over various points of doctrine or practices had already led to rebellions against the Rome-led majority on several occasions. In the major affairs in thirteenth-century France, fourteenth-century England, and fifteenth-century Bohemia, religious rebels (the official term is *heretics,* or "wrong thinkers") had battled the papal church. Eventually, all of them had been suppressed or driven underground.

But now, in sixteenth-century Germany, **Martin Luther** (1483–1546) found an enthusiastic reception for his challenges to Rome among the majority of his fellow Germans. Why were they particularly susceptible to the call for reform? The disintegration of the German medieval kingdom had been followed by the birth of dozens of separate, little principalities and city-states, such as Hamburg and Frankfurt, that could not well resist the encroachments of the powerful papacy in their internal affairs. Unlike the nations of centrally governed France, England, and Spain, whose monarchs jealously guarded their sources of revenue, the German populations were systematically milked by Rome and forced to pay taxes and involuntary donations. Many of the German rulers were becoming angry at seeing the tax funds they needed going off to a foreign power and sometimes used for goals they did not support. These rulers were eagerly searching for some excuse to challenge Rome. They found it in the teachings of Luther.

Luther was a monk who had briefly witnessed at first hand the corruption and crass commercialism of the Roman *curia* (court). When he returned to the University of Wittenberg in Saxony, where he had been appointed chaplain, he used his powerful oratory to arouse the community against the abuses he had seen. He especially opposed the church's practice of selling *indulgences*—forgiveness of the spiritual guilt created by sins—rather than insisting that the faithful earn forgiveness by prayer and good works.

In 1517, a major indulgence sales campaign opened in Germany under even more scandalous pretexts than usual. Much of the money raised was destined to be used to pay off a debt incurred by an ambitious noble churchman, rather than for any ecclesiastical purpose. Observing what was happening, the chaplain at Wittenberg decided to take his stand. On October 31, 1517, Luther announced his discontent by posting the famous ***Ninety-five Theses*** on his church door. In these questions, Luther raised objections not only to many of the papacy's practices, such as indulgence campaigns, but also to the whole doctrine of papal supremacy. He contended that if the papacy had ever been intended by God to be the moral mentor of the Christian community, it had lost that claim through its present corruption.

Luther's Beliefs

Luther had more profound doubts about the righteousness of the papal church than merely its claims to universal leadership, however. His youth had been a long struggle against the conviction that he was damned to hell. Intensive study of the Bible eventually convinced him that only through the freely given grace of a merciful God might he, or any person, reach salvation.

The Catholic Church, on the other hand, taught that men and women must manifest their Christian faith by doing good works and leading good lives. If they did so, they might be considered to have earned a heavenly future. Martin Luther rejected this. He believed that faith alone was the factor through which Christians might reach bliss in the afterlife and that faith was given by God and not in any way earned by naturally sinful man. It is this doctrine of **justification by faith** that most clearly marks off Lutheranism from the papal teachings.

As the meaning of Luther's statements penetrated into the clerical hierarchy, he was implored, then commanded, to cease. Instead, his confidence rose, and in a series of brilliantly forceful pamphlets, he explained his views to a rapidly increasing audience of Germans. By 1520, he was becoming a household word among educated people and even among the peasantry. He was excommunicated in 1521 by the pope for refusing to recant, and in the same year, he was declared an outlaw by Emperor Charles V.

The Catholic emperor was an ally of the pope but had his hands full with myriad other problems, notably the assault of the Ottoman Turks. Charles had no desire to add an unnecessary civil war to the long list of tasks he faced. He took action against Luther only belatedly and half-heartedly, hoping that in some way an acceptable compromise might be reached.

Threatened by the imperial and papal officials, Luther sought and quickly found the protection of the ruler of Saxony, as well as much of the German princely class. They saw in his moral objections to Rome the excuse they had been seeking for advancing their political aspirations. They encouraged Luther to organize a national church free from papal overlords.

With this protection and encouragement, Luther's teachings spread rapidly, aided by the newly invented printing press and by the power and conviction of his sermons and writings, which were in German (rather than the traditional Latin). By the mid-1520s, Lutheran congregations, rejecting the papal authority and condemning Rome as the fount of all evil, had sprung up throughout most of Germany and were appearing in Scandinavia as well. The unity of Western Christianity had been shattered.

Martin Luther. This contemporary portrait by Lucas V. Cranach is generally considered to be an accurate rendition of the great German church reformer in midlife. Both the strengths and weaknesses of Luther's peasant character are revealed. (© *The Granger Collection*)

John Calvin. This Flemish portrait of the "pope of Geneva" in his younger days depicts Calvin in a fur neckpiece. This bit of bourgeois indulgence would probably not have been worn by an older Calvin. (© *Erich Lessing/Art Resource*)

CALVIN AND INTERNATIONAL PROTESTANTISM

It was not Luther, the German peasant's son, but **John Calvin** (1509–1564), the French lawyer, who made the Protestant movement an international theological rebellion against Rome. Luther always saw himself as a specifically German patriot, as well as a pious Christian, and his translations of the Scriptures were written in a powerful idiomatic German. (Luther's role in creating the modern German language is roughly the same as the role Shakespeare played in the development of English.) Calvin, on the contrary, detached himself from national feeling and saw himself as the emissary and servant of a God who ruled all nations. Luther wanted the German Christian body to be cleansed of papal corruption; Calvin wanted the entire Christian community to be made over into the image of what he thought God intended. When he was done, a good part of it had been.

Calvin was born into a middle-class family of church officeholders who educated him for a career in the law. When he was twenty-five, he became a Protestant, inspired by some Swiss sympathizers with Luther. For most of the rest of his life, Calvin was "the pope of Geneva," laying down the law to that city's residents and having a major influence on much of the rest of Europe's religious development.

Calvin believed that the papal church was hopelessly distorted. It must be obliterated, and new forms and practices (which were supposedly a return to the practices of early Christianity) must be introduced. In ***The Institutes of the Christian Religion*** (1536), Calvin set out his beliefs and doctrines with the precision and clarity of a lawyer. From this work came much of the intellectual content of Protestantism for the next 200 years.

Calvin's single most dramatic change from both Rome and Luther was his insistence that God predestined souls. That is, a soul was meant either for heaven or hell for all eternity. But at the same time, the individual retained free will to choose good or evil. The soul destined for hell would inevitably choose evil—but did not have to! It was a harsh theology. Calvin believed that humanity had been eternally stained by Adam's sin and that the majority of souls were destined for hellfire.

Despite its doctrinal fierceness, Calvin's message found a response throughout Europe. By the 1540s, Calvinists were appearing in Germany, the Netherlands, Scotland, England, and France, as well as Switzerland. Geneva had become the Protestant Rome, with Calvin serving as its priestly ruler until his death in 1564.

Calvinism and Lutheranism Compared

What were some of the similarities and differences between the beliefs of Luther and Calvin (who never met and had little affection for one another)? First, Luther believed that faith alone, which could not be earned, was the only prerequisite for salvation. Good works were encouraged, of course, but they had little or no influence on the Last Judgment. Calvin demanded works as well as faith to indicate that a person was attempting to follow God's order on Earth.

Later Calvinists saw their performance of good works as a mark that they were among the Elect, the souls predestined for heaven. The emphasis in some places and times shifted subtly from doing good works as a sign of serving God to believing that God would logically favor the members of the Elect. Therefore, those who were "doing well" in the earthly sense were probably among the Elect. From this, some later students of religion saw Calvinist beliefs as the basis for the triumph of the capitalist spirit in certain parts of Europe. In effect, God could rationally be expected to smile on those who did his bidding in this life as well as the next.

Second, Luther saw the clergy as civic as well as spiritual guides for mankind. He believed in a definite hierarchy of authority within the church, and he retained bishops, who maintained their power to appoint priests. In time, the Lutheran pastors and bishops became fully dependent on the state that employed them, rarely defying it on moral grounds. Lutheranism became a state church, not only in Germany but also in Scandinavia where it had become dominant by the mid-1500s. In contrast, Calvin insisted on the moral independence of the church from the state. He maintained that the clergy had a duty to oppose any im-

moral acts of government, no matter what the cost to themselves. In conflicts between the will of God and the will of kings, the Calvinist must enlist on the side of God.

More than Lutherans, the Calvinists thought of the entire community, lay and clerical alike, as equal members of the church on Earth. Calvinists also insisted on the power of the congregation to select and discharge pastors at will, inspired by God's word. They never established a hierarchy of clerics. There were no Calvinist bishops but only presbyters, or elected elders, who spoke for their fellow parishioners. The government of the church included both clerical and lay leaders. The combination gave its pronouncements great moral force.

By around 1570, Calvin's followers had gained control of the Christian community in several places: the Dutch-speaking Netherlands, Scotland, western France, and parts of northern Germany and Poland. In the rest of France, Austria, Hungary, and England, they were still a minority, but a growing one. Whereas Lutheranism was confined to the German-speaking countries and Scandinavia and did not spread much after 1550 or so, Calvinism was an international faith that appealed to all nations and identified with none. Carried on the ships of the Dutch and English explorers and emigrants of the seventeenth and eighteenth centuries, it continued to spread throughout the modern world.

OTHER EARLY PROTESTANT FAITHS

The followers of a radical sect called **Anabaptists** (Rebaptizers) were briefly a threat to both Catholics and Lutherans, but they were put down with extreme cruelty by both. The Anabaptists originated in Switzerland and spread rapidly throughout German Europe. They believed in adult baptism, a priesthood of all believers, and—most disturbingly—a primitive communism and sharing of worldly possessions. Both as radicals in religious affairs and as social revolutionaries, the Anabaptists were oppressed by all their neighbors. After their efforts to establish a republic in the Rhineland city of Münster were bloodily suppressed, the Anabaptists were driven underground. They emerged much later in the New World as Mennonites, Amish, and similar groups.

Yet another Protestant creed emerged very early in Switzerland (which was a hotbed of religious protest). Founded by Ulrich Zwingli (1484–1531), it was generally very similar to Lutheran belief, although Zwingli claimed he had arrived at his doctrine independently. The inability of Zwingli's adherents and the Lutherans to cooperate left Zwingli's stronghold in Zurich open to attack by the Catholic Swiss. The Protestants were defeated in the battle, and Zwingli himself was killed. This use of bloody force to settle religious strife was an ominous note. It was to be increasingly common as Protestant beliefs spread and undermined the traditional religious structures.

The Church of England

As was often the case, England went its own way. The English Reformation differed from the Reformation on the Continent yet followed the general trend of European affairs. The English reformers were originally inspired by Lutheran ideas, but they adopted more Calvinist views as time went on. However, the Church of England, or Anglican Confession, came to be neither Lutheran, nor Calvinist, nor Catholic, but a hybrid of all three.

The reform movement in England had its origins in the widespread popular resentment against Rome and the higher clergy who were viewed as more the tools of the pope than as good English patriots. As we have seen, already in the 1300s a group called the Lollards had rebelled

A Protestant View of the Pope. Clothed in hellish splendor and hung about with the horrible symbols of Satan, the Roman pope is revealed for all to see in this sixteenth-century cartoon. (© *Stock Montage, Inc.*)

Ego fum Papa.

against the clerical claim to sole authority in interpreting the word of God and papal supremacy. The movement had been put down, but its memory persisted in many parts of England.

But it was the peculiar marital problems of King **Henry VIII** (1490–1547) that brought the church in England into conflict with Rome. Henry needed a male successor, but by the late 1520s, his chances of having one with his elderly Spanish wife Catherine were bleak. Therefore, he wanted to have the marriage annulled by the pope (who alone had that power), so that he could marry some young Englishwoman who would presumably be able to produce the desired heir.

After trying to evade the issue for years, the pope refused, for reasons that were partly political and partly moral. Between 1532 and 1534, Henry took the matter into his own hands. Still believing himself to be a good Catholic, he intimidated Parliament into declaring him the "only supreme head of the church in England"—the **Act of Supremacy** of 1534. Now, as head of the church, Henry could dictate to the English bishops. He proceeded to put away his unwanted wife and marry the tragic Anne Boleyn, already pregnant with his child.

Much other legislation followed that asserted that the monarch, and not the Roman pope, was the determiner of what the church could and could not do in England. Those who resisted, such as the king's chancellor Thomas More, paid with their heads or were imprisoned. Henry went on to marry and divorce several more times before his death in 1547, but he did at least secure a son, the future King Edward VI, from one of these unhappy alliances. Two daughters also survived, the half-sisters Mary and Elizabeth.

Henry's Successors Henry's actions changed English religious beliefs very little, although the Calvinist reformation was gaining ground in both England and Scotland. But under the sickly boy-king Edward (ruled 1547–1553), Protestant views became dominant among the English governing group, and the Scots were led by the powerful oratory of John Knox into Calvinism (the Presbyterian church). At Edward's death, it seemed almost certain that some form of Protestant worship would become the official church.

But popular support for Mary (ruled 1553–1558), the Catholic daughter of Henry VIII's first wife, was too strong to be overridden by the Protestant party at court. Just as they had feared, Mary proved to be a single-minded adherent of the papal church, and she restored Catholicism to its official status during her brief reign. Protestant conspirators were put to death without hesitation (hence, she is called "Bloody Mary" in English Protestant mythology).

Finally, the confused state of English official religion was gradually cleared by the political skills of Mary's half-sister and successor, **Elizabeth I** (ruled 1558–1603). She ruled for half a century with great success while defying all royal traditions by remaining the Virgin Queen and dying childless (see the Exercise of Authority box). She was able to arrive

ELIZABETH I OF ENGLAND
(1533–1603)

In the late sixteenth century, England became for the first time a power to be reckoned with in world affairs. What had been an island kingdom with little direct influence on any other country except its immediate neighbors across the Channel gradually reached equality with the other major Western military and naval powers: France and Spain. But England's achievement was not just in military affairs. It also experienced a magnificent flowering of the arts and a solid advance in the economy, which finally lifted the nation out of the long depression that had followed the fourteenth-century plague and the long, losing war with France.

The guiding spirit for this comeback was Elizabeth I, queen of England from 1558 until her death in 1603. The daughter of Henry VIII and his second wife, the ill-fated Anne Boleyn, Elizabeth emerged from a heavily shadowed girlhood to become a symbol of the effective exercise of authority and one of the most beloved of British lawgivers.

Elizabeth was an intelligent, well-educated woman with gifts in several directions. One of her most remarkable achievements was that she managed to retain her powers without a husband, son, or father in the still very male-oriented world in which she moved.

Born in 1533, she was only three years old when her mother was executed. She was declared illegitimate by order of the disappointed Henry, who had wished for a son. But after her father's death, Parliament established her as third in line to the throne, behind her half-brother Edward and her Catholic half-sister Mary. During Mary's reign (1553–1558), Elizabeth was imprisoned for a time, but she was careful to stay clear of the hectic Protestant-Catholic struggles of the day. By so doing, she managed to stay alive until she could become ruler in her own right.

Her rule began amid many internal and external dangers. The Catholic party in England opposed her as a suspected Protestant. The Calvinists opposed her as being too much like her father Henry, who never accepted Protestant theology. The Scots were becoming rabid Calvinists who despised the English halfway measures in religious affairs. On top of this, the government was deeply in debt.

Elizabeth I of England. The Armada Portrait, perhaps the most famous, was painted by an anonymous artist in the late sixteenth century. *(Private Collection/Bridgeman/Art Resource)*

Elizabeth showed great insight in selecting her officials and maintained good relations with Parliament. She conducted diplomatic affairs with farsightedness and found she could use her status as an unmarried queen to definite advantage. Philip of Spain, widower of her half-sister Mary, made several proposals of marriage and political unity that Elizabeth cleverly held off without ever quite saying no. She kept England out of the religious wars raging in various parts of Europe for most of her reign. But it was in one of these wars, against her ex-suitor Philip, that the Virgin Queen led her people most memorably.

In 1588, after long negotiations failed, Philip sent the Spanish Armada to punish England for aiding the rebellious Dutch Calvinists across the Channel. The queen rallied her own sailors in a stirring visit before the battle. The resulting defeat of the Armada not only signaled England's rise to naval equality with Spain but also made Elizabeth the most popular monarch England had ever seen.

A golden age of English literature coincided with Elizabeth's rule, thanks in some part to her active support of all the arts. Her well-known vanity induced her to spend large sums to ensure the splendor of her court despite her equally well-known miserliness. The Elizabethan Age produced Shakespeare, Marlowe, Spenser, and Bacon. By the end of the sixteenth century, English literature for the first time could hold a place of honor in any assembly of national arts.

Elizabeth's version of Protestant belief—the Church of England—proved acceptable to the large majority of her subjects and finally settled the very stormy waves of sixteenth-century English church affairs. By the end of her long reign, "Good Queen Bess" had become a stock phrase that most people believed, from barons to peasants.

FOR REFLECTION

Given that an unmarried queen was considered a political risk, what reasons of state could have impelled Elizabeth to remain "the Virgin Queen"? What political capital did she make out of creating the hybrid Church of England that otherwise would have been denied her?

at a compromise between the Roman and Protestant doctrines, which was accepted by a steadily increasing majority and came to be termed the Church of England. In most respects, it retained the theology and doctrine of the Roman church, including bishops, rituals, and sacraments. But its head was not the pope but the English monarch, who appointed the bishops and their chief, the archbishop of Canterbury. The strict Calvinists were not happy with this arrangement and wished to "purify" the church by removing all remnants of popery. These **Puritans** presented problems for the English rulers throughout the seventeenth century.

The Counter-Reformation

Belatedly realizing what a momentous challenge was being mounted, the papacy finally came to grips with the problem of Protestantism in a positive fashion during the 1540s. Pope Paul III (served 1534–1549) moved to counter some of the excesses that had given the Roman authorities a bad name and set up a high-level commission to see what might be done to "clean up" the clergy. Eventually, the church decided to pursue two major lines of counterattack against the Protestants: a thorough examination of doctrines and practices, such as had not been attempted for more than 1,000 years, combined with an entirely novel emphasis on instruction of the young and education of all Christians in the precepts of their religion. These measures together are known as the **Counter-Reformation.**

The **Council of Trent** (1545–1563) was the first general attempt to examine the church's basic doctrines and goals since the days of the Roman Empire. Meeting for three lengthy sessions divided by years of preparatory work, the bishops and theologians decided that Protestant attacks could best be met by clearly and conclusively defining what Catholics believed. (Protestants were invited to attend, but only as observers; none did.) As a means of strengthening religious practice, this was a positive move, for the legitimacy of many church doctrines had come increasingly into doubt since the 1300s. But the council's work had an unintended negative effect on the desired reunification of Christianity: the doctrinal lines separating Catholic and Protestant were now firmly drawn, and they could not be ignored or blurred by the many individuals in both camps who had been trying to arrange a compromise. Now one side or the other would have to give in on specific issues, a prospect neither side was prepared for.

The founding of the **Jesuit Order** was the most striking example of the second aspect of the Counter-Reformation. In 1540, Pope Paul III accorded to the Spanish nobleman Ignatius of Loyola the right to organize an entirely new religious group, which he termed the Society of Jesus, or Jesuits. Their mission was to win, or win back, the minds and hearts of humanity for the Catholic Church through pa-

tient, careful instruction that would bring the word of God and of his deputy on Earth, the pope, to everyone. While the Jesuits were working to ensure that all Catholics learned correct doctrine, the *Index* of forbidden books was created and the **Inquisition** revived to ensure that no Catholic deviated from that doctrine. These institutions greatly expanded the church's powers to censor the writings and supervise the beliefs of its adherents. Both became steadily more important in Catholic countries during the next century, as what both sides regarded as a contest between ultimate Truth and abhorrent falsity intensified.

Religious Wars and Their Outcomes to 1600

The Counter-Reformation stiffened the Catholics' will to resist the Lutheran and Calvinist attacks, which had, at first, almost overwhelmed the unprepared and inflexible Roman authorities. By 1555, the **Peace of Augsburg** had concluded a ten-year civil war by dividing Germany into Catholic and Lutheran parcels, but it made no allowances for the growing number of Calvinists or other Protestants.

In the rest of Europe, the picture was mixed by the late 1500s (see Map 27.1). England, as we have just seen, went through several changes of religious leadership, but it eventually emerged with a special sort of Protestant belief as its official religion. Scandinavia became Lutheran in its entirety, almost without violence. Austria, Hungary, and Poland remained mostly Catholic, but with large minorities of Calvinists and Lutherans who received a degree of tolerance from the authorities. Spain and Italy had successfully repelled the Protestant challenge, and the counter-reform was in full swing. Russia and southeastern Europe were almost unaffected by Protestantism, being either hostile to both varieties of Western Christianity (Russia) or under the political control of Muslims. In two countries, however, the issue of religious affiliation was in hot dispute and caused much bloodshed in the later 1500s.

France

France remained Catholic at the level of the throne but developed a large, important Calvinist minority, especially among the nobility and the urbanites. For a brief time the Catholic monarchs and the Calvinists attempted to live with one another, but religious wars began in the 1570s that threatened to wreck the country. The box on the St. Bartholomew's Day Massacre gives an eyewitness view of the violence.

After some years, the Calvinists found a politician of genius, Henry of Navarre, who profited from the assassination of his Catholic rival to become King Henry IV of France. In 1593, he agreed to accept Catholicism to win the support of most French ("Paris is worth a mass," he is reported to have said). He became the most popular king in French history. His Protestant upbringing inspired the Calvinist minority to trust him, and he did not disappoint them.

In 1598, Henry made the first significant attempt at religious toleration as state policy by issuing the **Edict of Nantes.** It gave the million or so French Calvinists—the Huguenots—freedom to worship without harassment in certain areas, to hold office, and to fortify their towns. This last provision demonstrates that the edict was more in the nature of a truce than a peace. It held, however, for the bet-ter part of a century. During that time, France rose to be-come the premier power in Europe.

The Spanish Netherlands

The Spanish Netherlands (modern Holland and Belgium) were ruled from Madrid by King Philip II, the most potent monarch of the second half of the sixteenth century. He had inherited an empire that included Spain, much of Italy, and the Low Countries in Europe, plus the enormous Spanish overseas empire begun by the voyages of Columbus.

MAP 27.1 Catholics, Protestants, and Orthodox Christians in Europe by 1550. The radical sects included Unitarians in eastern Europe, Anabaptists in Bohemia and Germany, and Waldensians in France. All of these rejected the idea of a privileged clergy and a priestly hierarchy.

THE ST. BARTHOLOMEW'S DAY MASSACRE

During the sixteenth-century religious wars in Europe, no battlefield was contested more ferociously by both sides than France. Not only did France contain Europe's largest population, but it lay between the Protestant North and the Catholic South. Though the bulk of the peasantry and the royal family remained Catholic, an influential and determined minority of nobles and bourgeoisie became Calvinists, or "Huguenots."

By 1572, because of the political astuteness of their leader, Gaspard de Coligny, the Huguenots were close to a takeover of the French government. However, the queen mother, Catherine de Medici, and the Catholic warlord Henry, duke de Guise, turned the weak-minded King Charles IX against Coligny. The result was a conspiracy that began with Coligny's assassination on August 24, 1572 (St. Bartholomew's Day), and quickly degenerated into a wholesale massacre of the entire Protestant population of Paris: men, women, and children. The death toll is estimated to have approached 10,000, and the streets and alleys reeked of the stench of decaying corpses for weeks afterward.

According to an anonymous Protestant who was among the fortunate few to escape the carnage, vicious cruelties were committed without number, setting the scene for what would become twenty years of intermittent civil war in France:

> In an instant, the whole city was filled with dead bodies of every sex and age, and indeed amid such confusion and disorder that everyone was allowed to kill whoever he pleased, whether or not that person belonged to the [Protestant] religion, provided that he had something to be taken, or was an enemy. So it came about that many Papists themselves were slain, even several priests. . . .
>
> No one can count the many cruelties that accompanied these murders. . . . Most of them were run through with daggers or poniards; their bodies were stabbed, their members mutilated, they were mocked and insulted with gibes sharper than pointed swords . . . they knocked several old people senseless, banging their heads against the stones of the quay and then throwing them half dead into the water [the Seine River]. A little child in swaddling clothes was dragged through the streets with a belt round his neck by boys nine or ten years old. Another small child, carried by one of the butchers, played with the man's beard and smiled up at him, but instead of being moved to compassion, the barbarous fiend ran him through with his dagger, then threw him into the water so red with blood that it did not return to its original color for a long time.

Source: Excerpted from Julian Coudy, The Huguenot Wars, trans. Julie Kernon (Radnor, PA: Chilton, 1969).

But Philip was a man with a mission, or rather two missions: the reestablishment of Catholicism among the Protestant "heretics" and the defeat of the Muslim Turks in the Mediterranean and the Near East. These missions imposed heavy demands on Spanish resources, which even the flow of gold and silver out of the American colonies could not fully cover. Generally successful in his wars against the Turks, Philip could not handle a combined political-religious revolt against Spain's recently acquired province of the Netherlands that broke out in the 1560s. The Netherlands were a hotbed of both Lutheran and Calvinist doctrines, and the self-confident members of the large middle class were much disturbed at the Spanish aliens' attempt to enforce on them the Counter-Reformation and papal supremacy.

Thanks to Spanish overextension, the revolt of the Netherlanders succeeded in holding Philip's feared professional army at bay. The wars were fought with ferocity on both sides. While Philip saw himself as the agent of legitimacy and the Counter-Reformation, the Dutch rebels were aided militarily and financially by the English Protestants across the Channel. The English support was due in part to religious affinity, but even more to the traditional English dislike of a great power's control of England's closest trading partners.

In the mid-1580s, the friction came to a head. Philip (who had earlier tried to convince Elizabeth I to become his wife) became incensed at the execution of the Catholic queen of Scots by order of Elizabeth, who had imprisoned this possible competitor for England's throne. With the reluctant support of the pope, Philip prepared the vast Armada of 1588 to invade England and reconquer that country for the "True Church."

The devastating defeat of the Armada—as much by a storm as by English ships—gave a great boost to the Protestant cause everywhere. It relieved the pressure on the Huguenots to accept Catholic overlordship in France. It saved the Dutch Calvinists until they could gain full independence some decades later. And the defeat of the Armada marks the emergence of England as a major power, both in Europe and overseas.

Spain remained the premier military power long after the Armada disaster, but the country in a sense never recovered from this event. Other fleets were built, bullion from Mexican and Peruvian mines continued to pour into Madrid's treasury, and the Spanish infantry were still the best trained and equipped of all the European armies, but the other powers were able to keep Spain in check from now on, until its inherent economic weaknesses reduced it to a second-line nation in the seventeenth century.

The Legacy of the Reformation

The Protestant movement made a very deep impression on the general course of history in Europe for centuries. It is one of the reasons European history is conventionally divided into "modern" versus "medieval" around 1500. The religious unity of all western Europe was irrevocably shattered, and with the end of such unity inevitably came political and cultural conflicts. For a century and a half after Luther's defiance of the papal command to be silent, much of Europe was engaged in internal acrimony that wracked the continent from the Netherlands to Hungary. In some countries such as Italy, Spain, and Sweden, one or the other faith was dominant and proceeded to harass and exile those who thought differently. Separation of church and state was not even dreamed of, nor was freedom of conscience. These are strictly modern ideas and were not seriously taken up by educated persons until the eighteenth century.

In the Protestant societies, the abolition of the monasteries and convents and the emphasis on vernacular preaching helped integrate the clergy and the laity and thus blurred one of the chief class divisions that had been accepted in Europe since the opening of the Middle Age. Combined with the important roles of the middle-class Protestants in spreading and securing reform, this development provided new opportunities for the ambitious and hardworking to rise up the social ladder.

Some of the other long-term cultural changes that resulted from the Reformation included the following:

1. *Higher literacy and start of mass education.* In much of Protestant Europe in particular, the exhortation to learn and obey Scripture provided an incentive to read that the common folk had never had before. The rapid spread of printing after 1520 was largely due to Protestant tracts and the impact they were seen to have on their large audiences.

2. *Emphasis on individual moral responsibility.* Rejecting the Catholic assurance that the clergy knew best what was necessary and proper in the conduct of life, the Protestants underlined the responsibility of individual believers to determine through divine guidance and reading Scripture what they must do to attain salvation.

3. *Closer identification of the clergy with the people they served.* Both the Catholic and Protestant Churches came to recognize that the church existed as much for the masses of faithful as it did for the clergy—a realization that was often absent previously—and that the belief of the faithful was the essence of the church on Earth.

4. *Increase in conflicts and intolerance.* Much of Europe fell into civil wars that were initially set off by religious disputes. These wars were often bloody and produced much needless destruction by both sides in the name of theological truth. Religious affiliation greatly exacerbated dynastic and the emergent national conflicts.

The Catholic-Protestant clashes led to intellectual arrogance and self-righteousness not only in religion but in general among those who wielded power. Open debate and discussion of contested matters became almost impossible between the two parts of Western Christianity for a century or more.

Summary

As much as the discovery of the New World, the Protestant movement gave birth to the modern era in the West. The protests of Luther, Calvin, and many others against what they saw as the unrighteous and distorted teachings of the Roman papacy had immense long-term reverberations in Western culture. The reformers combined a new emphasis on individual morality with assertions of the ability and duty of Christians to read the Gospels and take into their own hands the search for salvation.

Among Calvinists, the material welfare of the Elect on Earth was linked to their quality of being saved, a link that would gradually produce what later generations called the "Protestant ethic." The Catholic response was the Counter-Reformation, which, spearheaded by the Jesuits, eventually reclaimed much of the Protestant territories for the Roman church at the cost of an alarming rise in religiously inspired conflict. Warfare of an unprecedentedly bloody nature broke out in the Netherlands and in France and Germany between groups asserting their possession of the only correct theology. Europe entered the Modern Age in a flurry of fierce antagonisms among Christians, some of which were to continue for generations and permanently split apart previous communities.

TEST YOUR KNOWLEDGE

1. The posting of the *Ninety-five Theses* was immediately caused by
   a. Luther's outrage over the ignorance of the clergy.
   b. Luther's conviction that he must challenge papal domination.
   c. Luther's anger over the sale of indulgences.
   d. the tyranny of the local Roman Catholic bishop.
2. Which of the following practices/beliefs is associated with Calvinism?
   a. The basic goodness of humans
   b. Predestination of souls
   c. Religious freedom for all
   d. Indulgences
3. Henry VIII's reform of English religious organization occurred
   a. after study in the Holy Land.
   b. for primarily religious-doctrinal reasons.
   c. for primarily political-dynastic reasons.
   d. at the urging of the pope.
4. The Jesuit Order was founded specifically
   a. to train Catholic soldiers for battle.
   b. to recover through education fallen-away Catholics.
   c. to act as the pope's first-line troop in religious wars.
   d. to open a new type of monastery.
5. Which of the following countries remained most strongly attached to Rome in the wake of the Reformation?
   a. Scotland
   b. France
   c. The Netherlands
   d. Spain
6. The term *Counter-Reformation* applies to
   a. a movement in Germany aimed at extinguishing the Lutherans.
   b. the strong resistance of the Roman clergy to real reforms.
   c. a Europe-wide campaign to win back the Protestants to Rome.
   d. the political and military efforts of the German emperor to crush the Protestants.
7. The St. Bartholomew's Day bloodshed was
   a. the result of the Catholic fanatics' hatred of Protestants in France.
   b. the revenge of the English Calvinists on the English Catholics.
   c. the upshot of a failed attempt to overturn the Catholic dynasty in Spain.
   d. the slaughter of rebel peasantry in Flanders.
8. The *Edict of Nantes*
   a. expelled all Protestants from Catholic France.
   b. gave Protestants in France a degree of official toleration.
   c. brought civic and legal equality to Protestants in France.
   d. ended the war between Catholic France and Protestant England.
9. One of the chief negative effects of the Reformation on Europe was
   a. the lessening of educational opportunity.
   b. the loss of national identities.
   c. the diminished tolerance for variations from official doctrine.
   d. the decreased opportunities for social climbing.

IDENTIFICATION TERMS

Act of Supremacy of 1534
Anabaptists
Calvin, John
Council of Trent
Counter-Reformation
Edict of Nantes

Elizabeth I
Henry VIII
Inquisition
Institutes of the Christian Religion

Jesuit Order
justification by faith
Luther, Martin
Ninety-five Theses

Peace of Augsburg
Puritans
Reformation

INFOTRAC COLLEGE EDITION

Enter the search term "Reformation" using the Subject Guide.
Enter the search term "Counter-Reformation" using the Subject Guide.

Enter the search terms "Martin and Luther not King" using Key Words.

28

FOUNDATIONS OF THE EUROPEAN STATES

The great and chief end of men's uniting into commonwealths, and putting themselves under governments, is the preservation of their property.

JOHN LOCKE

IN EUROPE, THE SEVENTEENTH CENTURY saw the birth of the modern state. During this century, the powers of government began to be separated from the person or family of the occupant of the office, creating a group of professional servants of the state, or bureaucrats. Religious conflict continued but gave way to political-economic issues in state-to-state relations. The maritime countries of northwestern Europe became steadily more important thanks to overseas commerce, while the central and eastern European states suffered heavy reverses from wars, the Turkish menace, and commercial and technological stagnation.

Royal courts constantly sought ways to enhance their growing powers over all their subjects. These varied from west to east in both type and effectiveness. But by the early eighteenth century, some form of monarchic absolutism was in force in every major country except Britain. In this chapter, we will focus on the Germanies, France, and England.

THE THIRTY YEARS' WAR

The Thirty Years' War, which wrecked the German states and was the most destructive conflict Europe had seen for centuries, arose from religious intolerance, but it quickly became a struggle for territory and worldly power on the part of the multiple contestants. The war began in 1618, when the Habsburg Holy Roman Emperor attempted to check the spread of Protestant sentiments in part of his empire, the present-day Czech Republic or Bohemia, as it was then called. This led to a rebellion, which the Habsburg forces put down decisively at the Battle of White Mountain near Prague in 1621. A forced re-Catholicization began.

The defeated Protestants did not submit but found allies among their coreligionists in southern and eastern Germany. From this point, the war became an all-German civil war between Lutherans and Calvinists, on the one side, and the imperial armies under the Catholic emperor, on the other. By 1635, the war had become an international struggle beyond consideration of religion. The Protestant kings of Scandinavia and the Catholic French monarchy supported the Protestants, whereas the Spanish cousins of the Habsburgs assaulted the French.

The Thirty Years' War. In this panorama by Jan Breughel, the horror of war in the seventeenth century is brought home. Turned loose on the hapless peasants and townspeople, the mercenaries who made up the professional armies of the day killed and stole as they pleased.
(© Erich Lessing/Art Resource, NY)

The Treaty of Westphalia, 1648

For thirteen more years, France, Holland, Sweden, and the German Protestant states fought on against the Holy Roman Emperor and Spain. Most of the fighting was in Germany. The country was thoroughly ravaged by both sides, which sent forces into the field with instructions to "forage"—that is, to rob the natives of food and fodder, while killing any who resisted.

Finally, a peace, the **Treaty of Westphalia,** was worked out in 1648 after five years of haggling. The big winners were France and Sweden, with the latter suddenly emerging as a major power in northern Europe (see Map 28.1). The losers were Spain and, to a lesser degree, the Austrian-based Habsburgs, who saw any chance of reuniting Germany under Catholic control fade. From 1648 on, Germany

✿ **Henry IV and His Queen.** The great Flemish painter Peter Paul Rubens created this imaginary scene of the French king taking leave of his wife, Marie de Médici, to take command of the army fighting the Habsburg emperor. Between the royal figures is the little son who would grow to be King Louis XIII and father of Louis XIV.
(Louvre, Paris, France/Lauros-Giraudon/Bridgeman Art Library)

MAP 28.1 The Thirty Years' War. This destructive war had three distinct phases: first, it was an internal challenge to Habsburg Catholic rule by the Bohemian Protestants; second, from 1622 it was an all-German civil war between Lutherans and Calvinists and the imperial Catholic forces; third, from about 1635 it was an international conflict in which religious affiliation only played a minor role.

ceased to exist as a political concept and broke up into dozens, then hundreds of small kingdoms and principalities, some Catholic and some Protestant (see Map 28.2).

The Peace of Westphalia was the first modern state treaty. From start to finish, its clauses underlined the decisive importance of the sovereign state, rather than the dynasty that ruled it or the religion its population professed. Theological uniformity was replaced by secular control of territory and population as the supreme goal of the rival powers.

What did the treaty bring? In religious affiliations, despite all the bloodshed, things were left much as they had been in 1618. The principle that had first been enunciated in the Peace of Augsburg 100 years earlier—*cuius regio, eius*

religio (the ruler determines religious affiliation)—was now extended to the Calvinists, as well as Lutherans and Catholics. Northern and eastern Germany were heavily Protestant, while the south and most of the Rhine valley remained Catholic. This division negated any chance of German political unity for the next two centuries.

The Thirty Years' War was an economic disaster for the Germans. Plague, smallpox, famine, and the casualties of war may have carried off as many as one-third of the population. The division of Germany into small states made it all the harder to recover as a nation. For a long while to come, there would be a political power vacuum in the center of Europe, and the Germans would be thought of as a nation of poets and musicians.

MAP 28.2 Europe in the Seventeenth Century. After the Thirty Years' War, the Holy Roman Empire was an empty phrase, with an emperor whose powers were nonexistent in the Protestant lands. The Habsburg emperors, always Catholics, were consistently opposed by the equally Catholic French Bourbons, whose country lay between those of the Habsburgs and their Spanish cousins.

Spain's Decline

For Spain, the results were almost as painful, though the war was not fought on Spanish territory. The Dutch gained full independence from Madrid, and Portugal, which had been under Spanish rule for sixty years, rebelled successfully in 1640. The war with France was foolishly resumed until Spain was forced to make peace in 1659. By that date, the tremendous military and naval advantages that Spain's government had once possessed had all been used up. Spain was bankrupt, and its incoming shipments of overseas bullion were now much reduced. Worse, its domestic economy had seen little or no development for a century and a half.

How did this happen? The influx of Mexican and Peruvian silver had made much of Europe rich in one way or another (see Chapter 26). But ordinary Spaniards—still overwhelmingly rural and agrarian—were as poor as ever and perhaps even poorer, because the Spanish Crown, the nobility, and the church were notoriously unproductive users of the vast wealth that went through their hands in the sixteenth and seventeenth centuries. A capitalist middle class failed to develop, and traces of feudalism were everywhere apparent in the economy as well as the social structures. Despite much effort in the eighteenth century to regain its former status, Spain was condemned to a second rank in European and world affairs.

ROYAL ABSOLUTISM

The theory of royal absolutism existed in the Middle Age, but the upheavals caused by the Hundred Years' War in France and England, the Black Death in the fourteenth century (see Chapter 24), and the wars of religion following Luther's revolt had distracted the rulers' attention and weakened their powers. Now, in the seventeenth century, they got back to the business of asserting their sacred rights (see the Religion and Philosophy box).

The outstanding theorist of absolutism was a French lawyer, **Jean Bodin,** who stated in a widely read book that "sovereignty consists in giving laws to the people without their consent." Sovereignty cannot be divided; it must remain in the hands of a single individual or one institution. For France, Bodin insisted that this person should be the French monarch, who had "absolute power" to give his people law. Another Frenchman, Bishop Bossuet, gave a theological gloss to Bodin's ideas by claiming that kings received their august powers from God and that to defy them as a rebel was to commit a mortal sin.

Does this mean that the monarch had to answer to no one or could safely ignore what his people said and felt? No, the king had to answer to his Christian conscience and eventually to his Creator, as did everyone. And any king who attempted to rule against public opinion or the well-meant advice of his councilors was a fool. But the *king was and should be the final source of legitimate authority* in politics and law. Bodin arrived at this theory in part because of the times he lived in. His book was published at the height of the French religious struggles in the 1570s, when it appeared that without a strong, respected monarch, France might collapse as a state.

Bodin found his most potent and effective adherent in **Cardinal Richelieu** (1585–1642), the prime minister for the young Louis XIII in the 1620s and 1630s. Richelieu was the real founder of absolute monarchy in France—and most of Europe soon imitated Paris.

Following the murder of the peacemaking Henry IV in 1610, Protestant-Catholic antipathy in France had increased. Henry's Italian widow Marie de Médici was the regent for her young son, but much of the Huguenot nobility held her in contempt, despising her frivolity and her partisan Catholicism in equal measure. Unable to control the constant intrigues around her, she turned to the strong-minded and talented Richelieu. Despite being a prince of the church, Richelieu believed wholeheartedly in the primacy of the state over any other earthly institution. *Raison d'état* (reason of state) was sufficient to justify almost any action by government, he thought. The state represented order, the rule of law, and security for the citizenry. If it weakened or collapsed, general suffering would result. The government had a moral obligation to avoid that eventuality at all costs.

The cardinal set up a cadre of officials (***intendants***) who kept a sharp eye on what was happening in the provinces and reported to the king's ministers. Thus, the faint outlines of a centralized and centralizing bureaucracy began to appear: these men were picked for their posts at least partially on merit, were dependent on the central authority for pay and prestige, and subordinated local loyalties and personal preferences to the demands and policies of the center. The cardinal-minister used them to check the independence of the provincial nobles, particularly the Huguenots. He used armed force on several occasions and summarily executed rebels.

Richelieu was the real ruler of France until he died in 1642, followed a bit later by his king. The cardinal had handpicked as his successor as chief minister another Catholic churchman, Cardinal Mazarin, who had the same values as his master. The new king, **Louis XIV** (ruled 1643–1715), was but five years old, so the government remained in Mazarin's hands for many years. The young

Louis XIV. This masterful portrait by the court painter Rigaud shows Louis as he would have liked to appear to his subjects. The "well-turned leg" was considered to be an absolute essential for royal figures. Louis's wig and ermine cape were also necessities for a king. (© *The Granger Collection, NY*)

QUEEN CHRISTINA OF SWEDEN
(1626–1689)

"Far from beautiful, short in stature, pockmarked in face and with a slight humpback": such was the less than prepossessing description of a woman who would make her mark on her nation and her contemporaries in ways still not forgotten—or forgiven. Her political foibles might be overlooked, but it was impossible for her fellow Lutherans to accept her conversion to Rome in an era when religious affiliation was frequently the trigger for civil war.

Christina of Sweden was the sole surviving child of King Gustavus Adolphus, the warrior-king who died at the head of his Lutheran troops in the Thirty Years' War in Germany. When he died, Christina was only six years old, and a regency was established for the next twelve years. Prodigal and imperious by nature, the young girl did not take kindly to advice in matters public or private. She was brilliant in intellect and passionate in temperament and found it irritating to listen to those she regarded as her social or intellectual inferiors.

In 1644, she was crowned queen of Sweden, which at that time included most of Scandinavia and had the best army in Europe. Wanting to rid herself of the chief regent Oxenstierna and knowing that she could not do so as long as the war in Germany raged, she pressured her advisers to end the war as soon as possible. Still Sweden emerged from the conflict as a major power, and its twenty-two-year-old queen now became a major player in the intricate game of high diplomacy. But like the English with Elizabeth a generation earlier, many Swedes thought it unnatural—perhaps foolhardy—to allow the nation's fate to hang on the actions of a mere unmarried woman.

The Swedish estates (clerics, nobles, and commoners) put great pressure on the queen to marry as soon as possible, but she resisted just as strongly. Raised to believe herself the linchpin of her country's fate, she found it difficult to think of herself as only the channel by which a male could steer the ship of state. Disgusted with her countrymen, she was only barely persuaded to withdraw her abdication in 1651. In the same year, Christina also rejected the Lutheranism of almost all her compatriots and began to neglect the business of state in favor of her personal affairs, including her various lovers.

Queen Christina of Sweden. *(© Giraudon/Art Resource, NY)*

Her relations with the nobility worsened when she created more than 400 new nobles in an attempt to gain popularity and thus angered the proud old Swedish families. Friction mounted steadily, and in June 1654 her second offer to abdicate was gladly accepted. Dressed in the male attire she often wore that gave rise to many speculations regarding her sexuality, Christina left Stockholm at once and proceeded to Rome. En route, she insulted her fellow Swedes and her upbringing by accepting the Catholic faith and proclaiming herself the ally of the pope. To her surprise and dismay, practically none of her former subjects chose to follow. Instead, she became a "nonperson" in Stockholm's seats of power. She spent most of the rest of her sixty-three years in Rome, where she involved herself with papal politics and with lovers from both clergy and laity. Christina's authentic fame rests on her extraordinary artistic taste and her lavish generosity in acting on it. The queen-in-exile, as she liked to think of herself, was the Roman patroness of the great musicians Alessandro Scarlatti and Arcangelo Corelli, who wrote some of their finest work in her honor; the protector of the gifted architect and sculptor Giovanni Bernini, who crowned his lifework with the plans for St. Peter's Square; and the sponsor of the first opera company in Rome. Her house was a treasure trove of seventeenth-century Italian and Flemish artworks, and at her death her library became an important addition to the Vatican's library, the greatest in all Europe.

Left alone and living off the charity of the pope, Christina, the heiress of the great Gustavus Adolphus, had her last wish fulfilled by being buried in the cathedral of St. Peter's. Her Swedish Lutheran subjects erected no monuments to her memory.

FOR REFLECTION

Why was it particularly difficult for Sweden's nobility to accept a woman as ruler in the seventeenth century? How significant do you believe it to be that a woman chooses to dress like a man, as Christina often did, when she occupies high public positions?

Versailles. The view is from the garden side, with the grand fountain in the foreground. The palace lies a few miles outside Paris and is now one of the most visited tourist centers in Europe. Built by increments from the seventeenth through the eighteenth century, Versailles set the architectural and landscaping pace for the rest of the Western world's royalty. *(Robert Harding Picture Library)*

Louis was brought up to believe that kingship was the highest calling on Earth and that its powers were complete and unlimited except by God—and perhaps not by him, either!

French Government under Louis XIV

Louis XIV had the longest reign of any monarch in European history. In the last fifty-four of those years, he was his own chief minister, totally dominating French government. He was the incarnation of absolute monarchy, believing in *divine right,* which said that the monarchy's powers flowed from God and that the king's subjects should regard him as God's representative in civil affairs.

The later seventeenth and eighteenth centuries were the Age of France or, more precisely, the Age of Louis XIV. Not only in government, but also in the arts, the lifestyle of the wealthy and the highborn, military affairs, and language and literature, France set the pace. What Florence had been to the Renaissance, Paris was to the European cultural and political world of the eighteenth century. Once King Louis allegedly said, "I am the state," a statement he truly believed. He saw himself as not just a human being with immense powers and prestige but as the very flesh and blood of France. It is to his credit that he took kingship very seriously, working twelve hours a day at the tedious, complex task of trying to govern a country that was still subdivided

in many ways and notoriously difficult to govern. In this task he was greatly aided by a series of first-rate ministerial helpers—the marquis of Louvois, Jean-Baptiste Colbert, Sebastien de Vauban, and others—each of whom made major contributions to the theory and practice of his chosen field.

Below these top levels, the intendants continued to serve the monarch as his eyes and ears in the provinces. Louis's bureaucrats were the best-trained and most reliable servants their king could obtain. He selected their middle and lower ranks from the middle classes as much as from the nobility. Many latter-day French nobles were the heirs of commoners who were rewarded for outstanding service to King Louis XIV or were given the much sought opportunity of purchasing an office that carried noble status with it.

Louis was steeped in Richelieu's concepts from childhood and was determined to establish the royal throne as the sole seat of sovereignty. To do so, he had to nullify the independent powers of the aristocrats in the provinces. He did this by forcing them to come to *Versailles,* his magnificent palace outside Paris, where they vied for his favor and he could keep them under a watchful eye. He was generally successful. By his death, the previously potent nobles had been reduced to a decorative, parasitic fringe group, with few real powers and few responsibilities save those granted by the king.

Louis's revocation of the Edict of Nantes in 1685 was a mistake, which led to the loss of a valuable asset: the Huguenots, who emigrated en masse in the following decade. By allowing them to do so, the king hoped to emphasize the unity of Catholic France. He mistakenly thought that most of the Calvinists had been reconverted anyway and that the edict was no longer needed. Welcomed to Protestant Europe, some 200,000 Huguenots served as bastions of anti-French activity and propaganda against the monarch in the series of wars on which he now embarked.

Wars of Louis XIV   Although Louis kept the peace for the first thirty-five years of his reign, his overpowering thirst for glory led him to provoke four conflicts with England, Holland, and most of the German states, led by the Austrian Habsburgs in the last twenty years. The most important was the final one, the War of the Spanish Succession (1700–1713), in which France tried to seize control of much weakened Spain and its empire and was checked by a coalition led by England. The war bankrupted France and was extremely unpopular among the French people by its end. France succeeded only in placing a member of the Bourbon family (the French dynasty) on the Spanish throne, but under the condition that Spain and France would never be joined together. England, the chief winner, gained control of part of French Canada, the Spanish Caribbean islands, and the key to the Mediterranean, Gibraltar. The war began the worldwide struggle between England and France for mastery of a colonial empire.

Strengths and Weaknesses of French Absolutism Louis XIV gave all of Europe a model of what could be accomplished by a strong king and a wealthy country. His officials were the most disciplined and most effective that any Western country had seen. Through them, the king kept a constant watch on the country as a whole. Anything that happened in the provinces was soon known at Versailles and received a royal response whenever necessary. The palace itself was awe-inspiring, serving to reinforce Louis's prestige and power in visible fashion. Versailles, originally a mere hunting lodge for Louis XIII, was made into the largest and most impressive secular structure in Europe. It was surrounded by hundreds of acres of manicured gardens and parks and was large enough to house the immense court and its servants. Its halls were the museums of the Bourbon dynasty and remained so until the Revolution.

But problems also persisted. Finance was always the sore point for aspiring kings, and Louis spent huge amounts of cash in his quest for military and civil glory. A helter-skelter system of tax "farms," concessions for tax collection in the provinces, did not work well. Begun in the early seventeenth century, the system suffered from a growing disparity between what was collected and what was eventually forwarded to the court. Pushed by his ministers, the king considered the possibility of introducing taxes on the lands of the church and the nobles but was dissuaded from this

radical step. Instead, taxes on the peasant majority were increased, especially after the wars began.

The financial problem of the monarchy was in fact never solved. Of all European countries, France was the most favored by nature, and its agricultural economy was the most diverse. But the French peasants were slowly becoming aware of the contrasts between the taxes they had to bear and the exemptions of various sorts enjoyed by the privileged orders of the clergy and nobility. When that discontent would be later joined by the resentment of the much enlarged group of middle-class townspeople during the course of the eighteenth century, the potential for revolution would exist.

Revolt against Royal Absolutism: England under the Stuarts

At the death of Queen Elizabeth in 1603, the English Crown passed by prearrangement to her nearest male Protestant relative, the Stuart king James VI of Scotland, who became James I (ruled 1603–1625) of England. James was a great believer in absolutism and the divine right of kings and quickly alienated the English Parliament with his insistence that the Crown should have sole control over taxes and the budget. James's lack of respect for English customs, his blatant homosexuality, and his arrogance combined to make him highly unpopular by the end of his reign. His greatest achievement was his selection of a committee of distinguished churchmen who produced in short order the most influential English book ever written: the King James Version of the Bible.

The England that James ruled was fast developing into a society in which the commercial and professional classes had a great deal of political "savvy" and were becoming used to the exercise of local and regional power. Although the highest level of the government in London was still, as everywhere, dominated by the nobility, the well-off merchants and municipal officials who were represented by Parliament's House of Commons were by now insistent on their rights to have final input on taxation and much else in national policy. They were armed with a tradition of parliamentary government that was already four centuries old. They could not be intimidated easily.

Another topic of acrid debate between the king and his subjects was the proper course in religious affairs. James had been brought up a Scot Calvinist but had agreed to adopt Anglicanism (the Church of England) as king of England. In truth, he seemed to many to sympathize with Rome, which made the Anglicans nervous and appalled the growing number of Puritans.

It is impossible to say how numerous the Puritans were because Puritanism was more a state of mind than a formal affiliation. Puritans were inclined to accept the Calvinist social values: hard work, thrift, and a sober lifestyle that aimed at finding its true rewards in eternity. The Puritans liked to think of poverty as the deserved accompaniment of sin and of wealth and social status as the just rewards of a good Christian, a member of the Elect. The "capitalist ethic" was well rooted in them, and they, in turn, had extensive representation in the business classes of England. In the House of Commons, they were now a majority.

Absolutist king and Puritan Parliament clashed again and again in the 1620s over taxation and religion. By the time James died in 1625, Parliament was on the point of revolt. James was succeeded by his son Charles I (ruled 1625–1649), who soon turned out to be as difficult as his father. When the Commons attempted to impose limits on his taxing powers, he refused to honor the ancient custom of calling a Parliament at least every third year. He attempted to bring England into the Thirty Years' War against strong opinion that held that England had no interest in that conflict. He appointed an archbishop of Canterbury, who seemed to many to be a sympathizer with popery, and he was at least as provocatively stubborn as his father had been. Finding that Parliament would not cooperate with him, he sent it home in 1629 and ruled without its advice and consent.

Charles's marriage to a French Catholic princess had stirred up much resentment, and his high-handed attitude toward the Calvinist clergy finally offended his Scot subjects so badly that in 1640 they rose in revolt. Charles needed money—lots of it—to raise an army against them. That meant he had to impose new taxes, which in turn meant he had to summon Parliament.

Parliament had not met for eleven years, and when the representatives came together, they were in no mood to support an arrogant and unpopular king's demands. Instead, Parliament passed a series of restrictive laws on the royal powers, but the king maneuvered to bypass them in clear violation of English traditions. When the increasingly radical Puritans in Parliament took direct control of military affairs, Charles raised an army of royalist supporters, and this action led directly to the beginning of civil war in 1642.

Civil War: Cromwell's Commonwealth

Britain divided about evenly between supporters of the king (the Anglican clergy, most of the nobility, and most peasants) and supporters of Parliament (the majority of the townspeople, the merchant and commercial classes, the Puritans, and the Scots). Regional and local economic interests often dictated political allegiance. After several years of intermittent struggle, the war ended with Charles's defeat. Parliament then tried the king for treason. After a rump trial, he was found guilty and executed in 1649. (See the box for more on Charles's death.)

This was the first and only time that the British had executed their king and the first time since the beginnings of the modern state system that *any* European people had turned so decisively on their legitimate sovereign. The experience was agonizing even for the king's sworn enemies

THE DEATH OF CHARLES I

Most shocking to tradition and the pieties of medieval beliefs about royalty, the English Revolution actually put to death a legitimate king, Charles I. After losing the civil war to the troops of the Roundheads' leader, Cromwell, the king was captured and brought to trial on the count of treason. The Roundhead Parliament convicted him, and by one vote they condemned him to death. An eyewitness who was a royalist sympathizer describes the king's last moments:

> To the executioner, he said: "I shall say but very short prayers, and when I thrust out my hands—".
>
> Then he called to the bishop for his cap, and having put it on, asked the executioner:
>
> "Does my hair trouble you?"
>
> [The executioner] desired him to put it all under his cap; which, as he was doing by the help of the bishop and executioner, he turned to the bishop and said:
>
> "I have a good cause and a gracious God on my side . . . ."
>
> After a very short pause, his Majesty stretching forth his hands the executioner at one blow [of his axe] severed his head from his body; which, being held up and shown to the people, was with his body put into a coffin covered with black velvet and carried into his lodging [in the Tower of London].
>
> His blood was taken up by diverse persons for different ends: by some as trophies of their villainy; by others as relics of a martyr; and in some hath had the same effect, by blessing of God which was often found in his sacred touch when living.

Source: Louis L. Snyder and Richard B. Morris, eds., They Saw It Happen (Harrisburg, PA: Stackpole, 1951).

among the Puritans, and it led to a great deal of debate over where sovereignty resided and how legal process in government should be defined and protected. Over time, the modern Anglo-American ideals of constitutional government evolved from this debate.

After the king's execution, Parliament declared that England was a *commonwealth*—that is, a republic with no monarch. Its executive was the chief organizer of the triumphant Puritan army, **Oliver Cromwell,** who had gained a deserved reputation as a man of iron will and fierce rectitude. During his turbulent tenure as Lord Protector (1653–1658), there was a comprehensive attempt to eliminate such vices as dancing, drinking, making merry on the Sabbath, and theatrical performances. Such efforts to limit human enjoyment had the predictable result: when Cromwell died, few people wanted to hear more about Puritan government.

Cromwell's rule had also become unpopular because of the high taxes he levied (with the cooperation of an intimidated Parliament) to pay for frequent military expeditions. He put down rebellions against English rule in Catholic

Ireland and Calvinist Scotland with bloody force, thereby laying the groundwork for a Great Britain that would include these formerly quite separate countries as well as England and Wales. A maritime war with Holland in the 1650s brought England far along the road to control of the seven seas and in North America the rich prize of the former Dutch colony of New Amsterdam.

Three years before his death, the Lord Protector tired of parliamentary quibbling and instituted a forthright military dictatorship. When Cromwell's weak son attempted in vain to fill his father's shoes, parliamentary negotiations with the exiled son of Charles I were begun. After eighteen months, the **Restoration** was completed with the return of King Charles II (ruled 1660–1685) to his native land.

Restoration and Glorious Revolution of 1688

King Charles had learned the lessons that had cost his father his head. Charles also wished to exercise absolute powers but knew when he had to compromise. As he once said, he had "no wish to go on my travels again."

The pendulum of power in British government had swung decisively toward the House of Commons during the revolutionary era, and Charles made his peace with the Commons by establishing the beginnings of the ministerial system. The king appointed several of his trusted friends to carry out policy, but these men had to answer to parliamentary questioning. Gradually, this informal arrangement became a fundamental part of government and was formalized when the party system got under way in the eighteenth century. From it came the modern British cabinet, with its collective responsibility for policy and its reliance on parliamentary votes of confidence to continue its authority as a government.

Charles cared little about religion (his private life was a continual sexual scandal, and real or alleged royal bastards abounded), but many members of Parliament did. They proceeded to make it legally impossible for anyone but an Anglican to hold office, vote, or attend the universities. The measure was a reaction against the Puritans, Quakers, and Catholics who had caused such turmoil for England over the past quarter century. But this law—the **Test Act**—was too restrictive to be supported by the majority in the long run. It was gradually eased, first for other Protestants, then for Catholics and Jews until it was finally abandoned in the nineteenth century.

One aspect of Charles's religious policy helped create problems for his successor, however. Under a secret arrangement with King Louis XIV of France, Charles was to receive a large annual money payment in exchange for returning England to Catholicism. Although nothing ever came of the rather absurd pact, the news inevitably leaked out in Britain and created a wave of anti-Catholicism that led to a virtual panic. Thus, when it became clear that the aging and (legitimately) childless Charles would be succeeded by his younger brother, James, who had indeed become a practicing Catholic while in exile in France, the English viewed their new king with a great deal of suspicion from the outset.

James II (ruled 1685–1688) made things worse by flinging insult after insult at the Protestants in and out of Parliament and by deliberately ignoring the provisions of the Test Act in his official appointments. So long as the king had no Catholic children to succeed him, the English could grit their teeth and wait for the elderly man's death. But in 1688 his young second wife produced a healthy baby son who would be raised a Catholic and would presumably rule Britain for many years. To many, this prospect was too much to bear.

Practically all England rebelled against King James in the **Glorious Revolution of 1688** that ended the Stuart male line on the English throne. James again went into French exile accompanied by his family, while parliamentary committees stepped into the vacuum in London. After brief negotiations, William of Orange, the Dutch Calvinist husband of James's daughter Mary, was invited to rule England jointly with his wife. So began the reign of William and Mary (1689–1702).

Significance of the Glorious Revolution

The revolution against James Stuart had been almost bloodless; its significance was political and constitutional, not military or economic. Sovereignty shifted from the monarch to his or her subjects, as represented by their elected Parliament. From now on England was a constitutional state. The king or queen was the partner of Parliament in matters of high policy, both domestic and foreign. William and Mary had accepted the offer of the throne from a parliamentary delegation. What parliamentary committees had given, they could also legitimately take away. Though relations were generally cordial, the royal pair was never allowed to forget that.

The most concrete result of the Glorious Revolution was the **Bill of Rights,** which was adopted by Parliament in 1689. Its most important provisions spelled out the rights and powers of Parliament versus the Crown:

- Law was to be made only by Parliament and could not be suspended by the king.
- Members of Parliament were immune from prosecution when acting in their official capacities.
- The king could not impose taxes or raise an army without prior approval by Parliament.

In addition, the Bill of Rights assured the independence of the judiciary from royal pressures, prohibited standing armies in peacetime, extended freedom of worship to non-Anglican Protestants, and stipulated that the throne should always be held by a Protestant.

The Glorious Revolution was the world's first significant move toward full parliamentary government, but it was definitely *not* a democratic revolution. The great majority of the English and other Britons did not have the vote at any

The change in females' economic status from the Middle Age to the early modern epoch was clearly downward. The near-equality that working women had enjoyed with males in the fifteenth century had deteriorated sharply by the late seventeenth, when this statement was made by a young German tradesman:

> Women are shut out from our guild and cannot be trained by a master. The reason is, they are given the leadership of the family, under the supervision of their husbands. Because it is impossible to know who will be their husband when girls are still children, it is better and more suitable to their sex to teach them the domestic arts, which any husband will appreciate. It is also better for everyone that each sex does what is proper for it, and doesn't attempt to butt into the other's affairs while ignoring or neglecting their own.

I might add, that a woman who moves in male circles [namely, journeymen, who were almost always bachelors] puts herself in danger to her good reputation. . . . It is certainly better that men, and not women, learn a trade, as not everything can be learned at home or during the apprenticeship, but must be picked up through experience and "wandering." From this comes the old saying of the journeymen: "what I haven't learned, I got from my wandering." But wandering doesn't suit women's place in the world, as they would return from their Wanderjahre with their reputation in tatters, and therefore there is another axiom: "journeymen who haven't done their Wanderjahre, and maidens who have, are equally dubious." To lead, protect and command is the duty of a master, and is rightly given over to the male sex.

Source: Dora Schuster, Die Stellung der Frau in der Zunftverfassung (Berlin: 1927).

---

level beyond the village council. That would have to wait until near the end of the nineteenth century. And women of any class would not have political equality in Britain until the twentieth century (see the box for a view of their status in guilds).

In accord with the 1701 Act of Succession worked out by Parliament and the king, Mary's younger sister Anne succeeded William and Mary on the English throne. Like them, she died without surviving children. Now Parliament exercised its new powers under the act to invite the duke of Hanover, a distant German relative of King James I and the nearest male Protestant relation to the deceased queen, to become King George I (ruled 1714–1727). George thus introduced the **Hanoverian dynasty** to Great Britain.

The first two Georges lived mostly in Hanover, could barely speak English, and showed little interest in the intricacies of English political life. Both were content to leave policymaking to trusted confidants among the aristocrats and landed gentry who still dominated both houses of Parliament. Robert Walpole, the prime minister for more than twenty years (1721–1742), was the central figure in British government and the key developer of the ministerial government that had begun under King Charles II. Under Walpole, the monarchs were manipulated by the parliamentary leadership more and more so that Parliament became the more important force in most aspects of internal policy. While foreign affairs and the military still belonged primarily in the Crown's domain, Parliament was supreme in legislation and finance.

POLITICAL THEORY: HOBBES AND LOCKE

Two British political philosophers formed the basis of public debate on the nature of government during the tumultuous seventeenth century. **Thomas Hobbes** (1588–1679) thought that the pregovernmental "state of nature" had

been a riotous anarchy, a "war of all against all." A strong government was essential to restrain humans' natural impulses to improve their own lot by harming their neighbors. Recognizing this need to restrain the violence, early societies soon gave birth to the idea of the state and to the state's living embodiment, the monarch. The state, which Hobbes termed *Leviathan* in his famous book of 1651, was both the creature and the master of man. The state commanded absolute obedience from all. Those who rebelled should be crushed without mercy for the protection of the rest (see the Exercise of Authority box).

Hobbes's uncompromising pessimism about human nature was countered at the end of the seventeenth century by the writings of **John Locke** (1632–1704). In his most famous work, the *Two Treatises of Civil Government,* Locke said that all men possess certain natural rights, derived from the fact that they were reasonable creatures. Some of those rights were voluntarily given up to form a government that would protect and enhance the remaining ones: the rights to life, liberty, and property. No prince might interfere with such rights or claim to have one-sided powers to define the citizenry's welfare. Insofar as the government fulfilled its duties, it should enjoy the citizens' support and loyal service. When it did not, it had no claim to their support, and they could righteously push it aside and form a new government.

Whereas Hobbes's words were harsh and shocking to most English people of his time, Locke's message fell on much more welcoming ground. His readers, like the author, were members of the middle and upper classes, who possessed properties and freedoms they were determined to protect from the claims of absolutist monarchs. The English Revolution of the 1640s and the events of the 1680s had given them confidence that their views were both correct and workable. Locke's arguments made good sense to them, and he was also to become the most important political philosopher for the English colonials in North America.

HOBBES'S *LEVIATHAN*

Thomas Hobbes published *Leviathan* in 1651 to provide a philosophical basis for absolutist monarchy that went beyond the conventional idea of "divine right." Much influenced by the events of the day in England—the civil war was raging—Hobbes wished to demonstrate that strong control of the body politic by a monarch was a political necessity. Note how he bases all effective lawmaking on people's fear of punishment by a superior force, and not at all by the action of reason or compassion. He is interested in establishment of an effective governing authority, and not in the moral and/or reasonable basis for it. He had no illusions about the benign nature of mankind. The following excerpts come from the opening section of the second part of *Leviathan*, where the author summarizes his case:

> The final cause, end, or design of men (who naturally love liberty, and dominion over others) in the introduction of that restraint upon themselves . . . is the foresight of their own preservation, and of a more contented life thereby; that is to say, of getting themselves out of that miserable condition of war, when there is no visible power to keep them in awe, and tie them by fear of punishment to the performance of their covenants.

> For the laws of nature . . . without the terror of some power to cause them to be observed, are contrary to our natural passions. . . . And covenants without the sword are but words, and of no strength to secure a man at all. . . . And in all places where men have lived in small families, to rob and spoil one another has been a trade, and so far from being reputed against the law of nature, the greater spoils they gained, the greater was their honor. . . . And as small families did then; so now do cities and kingdoms, which are but greater families. . . .

> It is true that certain living creatures, as bees and ants, live sociably with one another . . . and therefore some man may perhaps desire to know, why mankind cannot do the same. To which I answer

> First, that men are continually in competition for honor and dignity, which these creatures are not. . . .

> Secondly, that amongst these creatures, the common good differs not from the private; and being by nature inclined to their private, they procure thereby the common benefit.

> Thirdly, that these creatures, having not [as man] the use of reason, do not see, nor think they see any fault, in the administration of their private business: whereas among men, there are very many that think themselves wiser, and abler to govern the public, better than the rest; and these strive to reform and innovate, one this way, another that way; and thereby bring it into distraction and civil war.

> Lastly, the agreement of these creatures is natural; that of men, is by covenant only, which is artificial; and therefore it is no wonder if there be somewhat else required to make their agreement constant and lasting; which is a common power, to keep them in awe, and to direct their action to the common benefit.

> The only way to erect such a common power . . . [is] to confer all their power and strength upon one man, or upon one assembly of men, that may reduce all their wills, by plurality of voices, unto one will . . . as if every man should say to every man, *I authorize and give up my right of governing myself to this man, or to this assembly of men, on this condition, that thou give up thy right to him, and authorize all his actions in like manner.*

> And he that carries this power is called *sovereign,* and said to have *sovereign power,* and everyone besides him is his *subject.*

> The attaining of this sovereign power is by two ways. One, by natural force . . . the other, is when men agree amongst themselves to submit to some man or assembly of men, voluntarily, in confidence to be protected by him against all others. This latter may be called a political Commonwealth.

FOR REFLECTION

Do you believe Hobbes wrong in his assumption that only fear of superior force keeps people in a more or less peaceable community? What might a devout Calvinist have to say about that assumption? How do *Leviathan* and *The Prince* by Machiavelli resemble or contradict one another?

SOURCE: *From* The English Works of Thomas Hobbes, *ed. Thomas Molesworth, vol. 3, chap. 17.*

SUMMARY

The Thirty Years' War wrecked Germany while providing a forcible resolution to the question of religious conflict in post-Reformation Europe. The Treaty of Westphalia, which ended the war, was founded on state interests, rather than religious doctrine or dynastic claims. From the early seventeenth century on, doctrines of faith took an ever-decreasing role in forming state policy. The Catholic but anti-Habsburg French emerged as the chief beneficiaries of the conflict in Germany. France replaced Habsburg Spain as the prime force in military and political affairs and, under the guidance of Richelieu and the long-lived Louis XIV, became the role model for the rest of the aspiring absolutist monarchies on the Continent.

The English Revolution, sparked by the attempts of the Stuart kings to emulate Louis XIV, ended in clear victory for the antiabsolutist side. Led by the Puritan rebels against Charles I, the wealthier, educated segment of the English people successfully asserted their claims to be equal to the

Crown in defining national policies and the rights of citizens. The Glorious Revolution of 1688 cemented these gains. The seeds thus planted would sprout continuously in the Western world for the next two centuries, especially in the British colonies in North America. Given a theoretical underpinning by philosophers such as John Locke and practical form by the 1689 Bill of Rights, the idea of a society that was contractual rather than authoritarian in its political basis began to emerge. Along with this came the ideal of a state that guaranteed liberty and legal equality for all its subjects.

TEST YOUR KNOWLEDGE

1. The Thirty Years' War began
   a. as a struggle for religious freedom for reformers in Bohemia.
   b. as a contest between Calvinists and Lutherans in Germany.
   c. as a political contest between Germans and French in the Rhineland.
   d. as none of these.
2. In its final stage, the Thirty Years' War became
   a. the first religious war in Europe.
   b. a political struggle for additional extra-European colonies.
   c. a struggle between the Roman pope and various Protestant groups.
   d. a struggle between the Habsburgs and Bourbons.
3. *Raison d'état* is most accurately translated as
   a. the power of a duly constituted government to do what it wishes within its own borders.
   b. a false reason given by a spokesperson to justify what the government desires.
   c. a pretext used by a government to justify illegal acts.
   d. the state's legal power to make war.
4. Which of the following characteristics was *not* true of the government of Louis XIV?
   a. It was based on parliamentary policymaking.
   b. It was Catholic in religion.
   c. It was staffed by many members of the middle classes.
   d. It was highly concentrated in the person of the king.
5. Which of the following seventeenth-century English monarchs was most successful in retaining the support of Parliament?
   a. James II
   b. Charles I
   c. James I
   d. Charles II
6. William and Mary came to rule England
   a. at the invitation of Parliament.
   b. as the successors to Cromwell after his death.
   c. as the conquerors of Cromwell's Commonwealth.
   d. as the brother and sister of the last Stuart king.
7. The message conveyed by Hobbes's *Leviathan* was in brief that
   a. man would find his way to a better future.
   b. man could make more progress once religion was abolished.
   c. man was irredeemably stained by original sin.
   d. man needed a powerful government to avoid anarchy.

IDENTIFICATION TERMS

Bill of Rights	**Glorious Revolution of**	***intendants***	**Richelieu, Cardinal**
Bodin, Jean	**1688**	**Louis XIV**	**Test Act**
Christina of Sweden	**Hanoverian dynasty**	**Locke, John**	**Treaty of Westphalia**
Cromwell, Oliver	**Hobbes, Thomas**	**Restoration (English)**	**Versailles**

 INFOTRAC COLLEGE EDITION

Enter the search term "Thirty Years' War" using Key Words.
Enter the search term "Louis XIV" using Key Words.

Enter the search term "Oliver Cromwell" using Key Words.

EASTERN EUROPEAN EMPIRES

After I had seen [Peter I] often and had conversed with him, I could not but adore the depth of the providence of God that raised up so furious a man to so absolute an authority over so great a part of the world.

BISHOP BURNET

1533–1584	Ivan IV, the Terrible (Russia)
EARLY 1600s–1613	Time of Troubles (Russia) ended by first Romanov czar
1640–1688	Frederick William, the Great Elector (Prussia)
1682–1724	Peter I, the Great (Russia)
LATE 1600s–1700s	Ottoman decline
1713–1740	Frederick William I (Prussia)
1740–1786	Frederick II, the Great (Prussia)
1740–1748	War of the Austrian Succession
1740–1780	Maria Theresa (Austria)
1762–1796	Catherine II, the Great (Russia)
1772–1795	Polish Partitions

ABSOLUTISM BEGAN TO DEVELOP in eastern Europe at about the same time as in western Europe—that is, in the sixteenth century—but it proceeded further and was not disturbed or checked until much later. The gap between East and West in this regard is one of the outstanding determinants of modern European history. Eastern Europe, lagging in the evolution toward personal freedoms and the abolition of class privilege, became a different society from western Europe. In the seventeenth and eighteenth centuries, three states—Russia, Austria, and Prussia—came to dominate this "other Europe" in which feudal society still prevailed.

The borders of the eastern European states were extremely unstable partly because of war, political backwardness, and centuries of forced and voluntary migrations. This instability both contributed to the rise of absolutist monarchic government and acted against its effectiveness. By the end of the eighteenth century, eastern Europe had westernized its ruling classes, but deep differences remained between Europe east of the Elbe River and west of that traditional dividing line.

ABSOLUTISM EAST OF THE ELBE

The reasons for these differences varied, some being economic, others social and political in character. What were the most important of these factors? Absolute monarchy was able to develop more forcefully in eastern Europe largely because of the nature of *its agrarian economy.* Feudal estates lasted much longer in Russia, Poland, and Hungary than in France, England, and Sweden. The social cleavage between noble lord and peasant serf was enabled and perpetuated by the rising profits that the landlords were able to wring from their large estates. The grain necessary for the expanding populations of the cities of western and central Europe was produced on these feudal holdings—a business that became increasingly profitable for landlords who could produce the crop cheaply with nonfree labor.

The struggle between autonomous noble landowners and the royal government was resolved in eastern Europe by *a silent compromise:* the monarchies surrendered full control over the peasants to the landlords in return for the landlords' loyalty and service to the Crown. As time passed, the once-weak monarchs steadily gained power, and the nobles became their servants, just as the peasants were servants to the nobles. No effective middle-class voice was ever heard. Why? The towns were too few, and the small urban populations never gained self-government and economic freedom as in the West. In Russia, Prussia, and Austria, the royal dynasts were gradually able to subordinate all classes and interests to themselves, and *the continuity of royal power* had become the pivot on which all society revolved by the eighteenth century.

The three states' political constitutions were not identical, however. Russia became the most autocratic by far. The Romanov czar was not beholden to any earthly power in Russian legal theory; his will was law. On the contrary, the power of the Austrian emperor—always a member of the Habsburg dynasty—was sharply limited by the high nobility until the later eighteenth century. The Prussian king—a Hohenzollern—originally had fewer supreme powers than the Romanovs but more than the Habsburgs. Eventually, the Prussian king was to become in fact the most powerful and successful of the three, and from Prussia came modern Germany. We will look at Prussia first and then at the other two states.

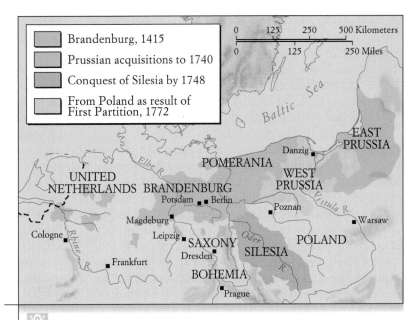

MAP 29.1   The Expansion of Prussia, 1640–1795.

PRUSSIA'S RISE

As we have seen, after the Thirty Years' War (1618–1648), much of Germany was in a state of economic decay and political confusion. The 300-odd German states and statelets were divided along religious lines: about half were Catholic and half Protestant. Neither accepted the other, and distrust and animosities were always present. The famines and epidemics that accompanied the war had led one-third of the population to an early death, and whole regions almost reverted to wasteland. From this very unpromising situation, however, arose one of the major powers of modern Europe, Prussia-Germany (see Map 29.1).

The rise of the small and commercially insignificant Prussia during the later seventeenth and eighteenth centuries was largely due to the Hohenzollern princes who occupied the Prussian throne from 1640 to 1786. **Frederick William, the Great Elector** (ruled 1640–1688), was a man of iron will and great talent. He united his previously quite separate family holdings of Prussia, Brandenburg, and some small areas in western Germany into a single government that was known thereafter simply as Prussia. During his reign, Berlin began its rise from a simple market town to a capital city. A sign of his strength was his victory over the powerful feudal lords in a struggle over who would have the final word regarding taxes.

Through such measures, the Great Elector tripled the government's revenues and then spent much of the increase on his prize: a new professional army. Every fourteenth male citizen was a member of the army on active service. No other European country even came close to this ratio. Frederick William only once had to use this force directly against a foreign enemy. Its existence was enough to intimidate his many opponents both inside and outside Prussia's borders.

Frederick William also began the understanding between king and nobles that gradually came to characterize Prussian politics until the twentieth century. The Crown handed over the peasants to the noble landlords, who acted as their judge and jury and reduced most of them to a condition of misery as serfs. In return, the Crown was allowed almost total control over national policy, while the noble landlords' sons were expected to serve in the growing military and civil bureaucracy that Frederick William was creating.

During the reign of the Great Elector and for a long time thereafter, many of the Prussian *Junkers* (landowning nobles) were not yet resigned to their inferior position as adjuncts to the monarch. But they could not bring themselves to look for help from the most likely quarter. In the struggle over constitutional rights, the nobles ignored the third party that might have been able to tip the balance against the king: the townspeople. As in the rest of eastern Europe, the Prussian urban middle classes did not play the crucial role that they had in western Europe. They could not strike a "deal" with either king or nobles to guarantee their own rights. They had to pay the taxes from which the nobles' lands were exempt, and their social and political status remained much lower than that of the estate-owning Junkers.

After Frederick William's death, his son Frederick I and grandson Frederick William I ruled Prussia until 1740. By clever diplomacy in the War of the Spanish Succession, Frederick I was able to raise his rank from prince to king of Prussia, while Frederick William I was even more intent than his grandfather on building the finest army in Europe. He was the real founder of Prussia-Germany's military tradition and its deserved reputation as the most efficiently governed state on the Continent.

During the reign of Frederick William I (ruled 1713–1740), Prussia was aptly called "an army with a country." Military priorities and military discipline were enforced everywhere in government, and the most talented young men by now automatically entered state service, rather than going into business or the arts and sciences. The aristocratic bureaucrats were known far and wide as dedicated, hardworking servants of their king, whether in uniform (which they generally preferred) or in civilian clothing. The officer corps became the highest social group in the nation, enjoying its own legal code quite separate from the civil society.

The series of notable Hohenzollern monarchs culminated in the eighteenth century with Frederick II, the Great (ruled 1740–1786), who is generally seen as one of the most talented kings in modern history. A shrewd judge of people and situations, Frederick was cultivated and cynical, daring, and calculating. A fine musician, his artistic inclinations as a youth were so strong as to have him defy his overbearing father and toy with the idea of abdicating his

rights to become a private citizen. But a sense of duty combined with unlimited ambition to abort this romantic notion.

As king, Frederick proved to be one of the most effective in an age of outstanding monarchs. His victories in Silesia (and later in the Seven Years' War) enabled Prussia to rise into the first rank of European powers. Under Frederick's rule, the Prussian economy prospered. The universal adoption of the potato as a staple enabled the rising population to subsist on the product of the marginal agricultural land of northeast Germany. The Prussian territorial gains in western Germany were brought together under the efficient bureaucracy that Frederick continued to develop. Frederick II cleverly associated the Prussian monarchy with a reviving sense of national unity. With him began the "German dualism," the century-long contest between Austria and Prussia for leadership of the German-speaking people, the most numerous in Europe.

THE HABSBURG DOMAINS

Prussia's rival for eventual political supremacy over the fragmented Germans was **Habsburg** Austria. Based in Vienna, the dynasty ruled over three quite different areas: Austria proper, Bohemia (the present-day Czech republic), and Hungary (see Map 29.2). In addition, the Habsburgs

MAP 29.2   The Growth of the Austrian Empire, 1536–1795.

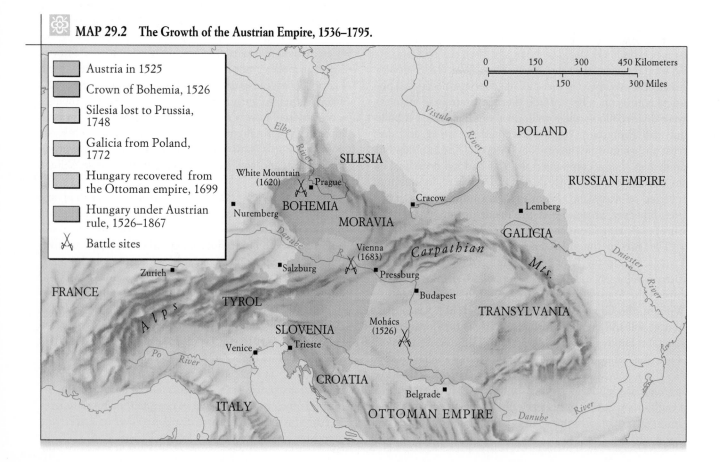

 **The Belvedere in Vienna.** This palace was built by and for Prince Eugen of Savoy, greatest of the Habsburg generals in the wars of the late seventeenth and early eighteenth centuries. It is a perfect example of Austrian baroque architecture. (© *The Granger Collection, NY*)

found allies among the south German Catholics, who sympathized with their Austrian cousins and had strong antipathies toward the Prussian Protestants.

The dynasty had acquired Hungary and Bohemia through lucky marriages in the sixteenth century. At that time, much of Hungary was still occupied by the Ottoman Turks (see the next section). It was liberated by Habsburg armies at the end of the seventeenth century. Though a potentially rich agricultural country, Hungary had been laid to waste by the Turks during their long occupation. By the end of the eighteenth century, it had been revivified and repopulated by Catholic Germans and others under the close control of the Vienna government.

Bohemia was even more valuable. It had been severely hurt by the Thirty Years' War but had scored a quick comeback. Commerce and manufacturing were more developed here than in any other Habsburg dominion. As a center of the arts and commerce, Prague at this juncture was almost as important as Vienna. It was inhabited almost entirely by Germans and Jews, however. The Czechs were still peasants, ruled over by foreign nobles imported by the Catholic emperor as a result of the native nobles' support of the Protestants in the Thirty Years' War.

The Struggle against Turkey

Toward the end of the seventeenth century, Austria was being threatened on several sides. Against its southern and eastern flanks, the Ottoman Turks were still a menacing foe, and mounted an invasion which reached the outskirts of Vienna in 1683. In the west, the French monarch Louis XIV was readying the War of the Spanish Succession (1700–1715).

Louis's object was to make Spain, including its overseas possessions, an integral part of France and thereby make France the decisive power in continental affairs. The Ottomans' attack was beaten off, and the counterattack against Turkey went well at first. But then preparations for the imminent war with France allowed the Turks to recoup their strength. The Treaty of Karlowitz in 1699 regained Hungary for the Habsburgs but did not definitively end the Ottoman menace to Austria. In this conflict, the chief architect of Austrian greatness in the eighteenth century, **Prince Eugen of Savoy,** first won renown. He then successfully led the imperial forces against the army of Louis XIV along the Rhine before returning to the Ottoman front where he won a decisive victory at Belgrade in 1716. From this point on, the Ottomans were almost always on the defensive against the Christian powers opposing them. The threat of a Turkish invasion of central Europe was eliminated, and Austria became a leading power for the first time.

This new power, however, had a flaw that became apparent with time. Ethnically, the empire of Austria was the least integrated of all European countries. It included no fewer than ten different nationalities: Germans, Hungarians, Italians, Croats, Serbs, Slovenes, Poles, Czechs, Slovaks, and Ukrainians. At this historical epoch few if any Europeans were conscious of their national affiliations in the modern, political sense and were thus not disturbed at being ruled by nonnatives or being unable to use their native tongues in court proceedings or schools. Nevertheless, as late as the mid–eighteenth century, the Habsburg lands resembled a "salad" of nations and regions that had little in common except rule by the dynasty in Vienna.

MOTHER AND SON IN THE HABSBURG FAMILY

We get an extraordinary insight into royal family relations among the Austrian Habsburg dynasty of the eighteenth century via a letter composed by Leopold, younger son of Maria Theresa and younger brother of her coruler, Kaiser Joseph. Although the two brothers supported each other in many ways, Leopold had an unsparing eye for Joseph's weak points. It should be noted that Leopold succeeded his brother on the Habsburg throne after Joseph's early death, and in the opinion of many contemporaries, he was the most talented ruler in that family's lengthy history. However, his reign lasted only two years (1790–1792) before he, too, died of sudden illness.

> When they [that is, the empress and her coruler Joseph] are together there is uninterrupted strife and contradictions, and if the Kaiser takes a step or gave an order without telling her, she is always put out of sorts. . . . She sees how many want to curry the Kaiser's favor by complaining about her and telling him how much better things will go when he is in command. She claims she will abdicate, as people can't seem to wait for the passing of the crown to Joseph. . . . She has the greatest jealousy of all who speak or even write to the Kaiser, suspecting them of making common cause against her. With Joseph she is always arguing, even over trifles, and they are never of one voice and mind.

Maria Theresa. This somewhat idealized portrait shows the young queen as she settled into the rigorous routine of government in the 1740s. (© Giraudon/Art Resource, NY)

The worst is, all these arguments and conflicts of opinion are publicly known, because both of them speak openly about such things, and that means that among the officials and in fact among all the public there are people who claim that they are either of the Kaiser's faction or that of the empress, and are therefor being persecuted. This makes a very bad impression upon the diplomats at court, as well as harming the affairs of government and discouraging everybody. . . .

The Kaiser has many talents and capabilities; he quickly comprehends, and has the gift of both good memory and articulate speech. He understands well how to get his ideas across, verbally and on paper. In recent days he has been of a bad temper, it seems because of frustration that he is not yet able to exercise sole power, but must still depend on the empress' acquiescence. He complains a lot about that. He is a hard, powerful man, full of ambition, who will do most anything to be talked about and be praised. . . . He can stand for no contradiction, and is a believer in wilful, even brutal principles of action, and is an adherent of the most uncompromising, strongest despotism. He loves no one, makes a friendly face towards only those whom he thinks he needs because of their special talents, but makes mockery even of them when it pleases him. He contemns everything that did not originate with himself.

SOURCE: Adapted from Karl Guthas, Kaiser Joseph II (Munich: Zsolnay, 1989).

Maria Theresa, the only surviving child of the previous emperor, became the first and only female to rule Austria (1740–1780). Accepted only reluctantly by the still-semifeudal nobility, she became one of the most successful of the Habsburg rulers. She and her son Joseph II (ruled 1780–1790) did much to modernize the Austrian armed forces and civil bureaucracy. (See the Family and Gender Relations box for more on the prickly relationship of these two.) She was also the first to introduce some coherence and uniformity to the Habsburg government. Despite losing Silesia to the Prussians in the **War of the Austrian Succession** (1740–1748) at the outset of her reign, she slowly welded the various provinces and kingdoms into a single entity under a centralized government headquartered in the impressive royal city. Thanks to Russian initiatives (see the next section), Austria even gained some territory from neighboring Poland.

Much later, in the mid–nineteenth century, when it gradually became clear that Austria was losing the battle over the future allegiance of the German-speaking people, the Austrians turned east and south to realize their version of colonial expansion. By so doing, they encountered the Turks, who had sunk into second-level status and would not have been a serious obstacle had they been forced to stand alone. But in the nineteenth century, Europe's diplomats agreed to let the Turks continue to control southeastern Europe (the Balkans), so as to avoid the inevitable conflicts that would ensue if the Turks were pushed aside and replaced by others. Foremost among those contenders were the newly powerful Russians.

Russia under the Czars

Russia's government rose from centuries of retardation and near-disintegration to attain great power status in the eighteenth century (see Map 29.3). Until the 1200s, Russia had been an independent Christian principality based on the impressive city of Kiev, with extensive trading and cultural contacts with both western and Mediterranean Europe through the Baltic and Black Seas. The Russians had been converted to Orthodox Christianity by Greek missionaries in the late 900s and had remained closely attached to Constantinople in secular, culture, and religious doctrine for the next three centuries.

But in 1241, the fierce, pagan Mongols under the successors of Genghis Khan had conquered the principality of Kiev and settled down to rule the Russians for the next 240 years (see Chapter 32). During that period, Russia's formerly numerous contacts with both eastern and western Europe were almost completely severed or neglected, and the Russians retrogressed in many differing fashions, ranging from literacy rates to peasant superstitions. Even their crafts and skills declined. For example, in the sixteenth century, after the Mongols were overthrown, the seat of Russian government, the Kremlin in Moscow, was rebuilt in stone rather than wood, but Italian masons had to be brought in because the Russians could no longer handle large-scale projects as they had in the eleventh and twelfth centuries when they built their great churches in Kiev.

Their governmental institutions also deteriorated. The Russian princes connived and maneuvered to serve as agents and intermediaries of the Mongol khan, who played them off against each other for almost two centuries. Moscow, one of the dozen or so principalities into which Russia was divided after the conquest, came through cunning, perseverance, and good luck to overshadow its rivals even during the Mongol era.

Shifting alliances between Russians, Mongols, and the briefly potent Lithuanian state on the western borders marked the entire fourteenth century. Taking advantage of a temporary split in the upper rank of the occupying *orda* (horde), one Muscovite prince actually defeated the Mongol cavalry in 1380, but he could not follow up his victory. But in the fifteenth century the princes of Moscow gained steadily on their several rivals. Using every available means, from marriages to bribery, the Muscovites brought neighboring Slavic principalities under their control as the Mongol grip slowly loosened.

The **Mongol Yoke,** as the Russians call it, was finally thrown off in a bloodless rebellion led by Moscow in 1480. The once-fearsome Golden Horde's remnant retired eastward into the Siberian steppe, and the Russians slowly reemerged into European view. The English traders, the German diplomats, and the Greek clerics who now arrived looked on the Russians as residents of a "rude and barbarous kingdom."

MAP 29.3   From Muscovy to Russia, 1584–1796.

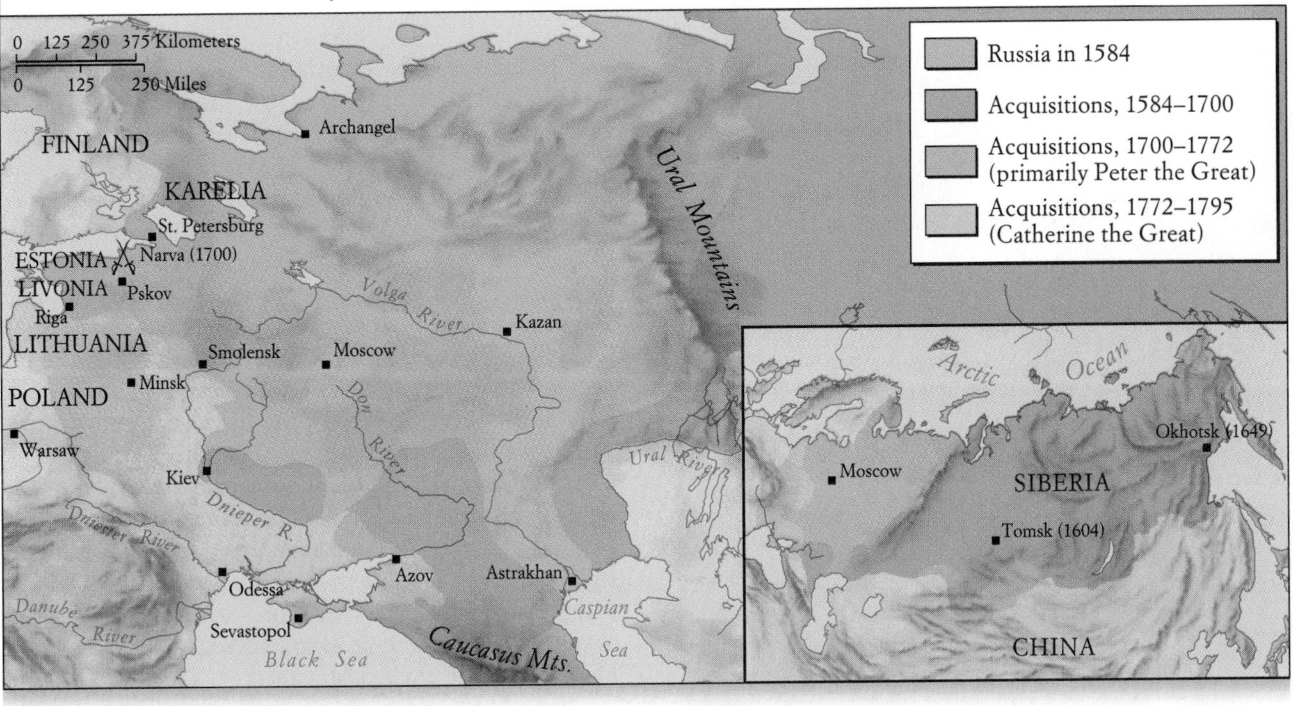

In fact, as late as the 1600s, few western Europeans gave any thought to Russia or the Russians. Trade relations were eventually established with Britain through the Arctic seas and later with the Scandinavians and Germans through the Baltic. But beyond some raw materials available elsewhere and some exotic items such as ermine skins, there seemed little reason to confront the extraordinary challenges involved in trading with this alien society. Militarily and politically it had nothing to offer the West, and whatever technical and cultural progress was made in Russia during these centuries usually stemmed from Western—particularly German and Swedish—sources.

Russia's Antipathies to the West

The Russians were in any case not inclined to welcome Western ideas and visitors except on a highly selective basis. The Orthodox church had been crucially important in keeping alive national identity during the Yoke, and most Russians responded with an uncompromising attachment to its doctrines and clergy. Their distrust of Western Christians was strong. The sporadic attempts of both papal and

Peter the Great. The great reformer/modernizer of backward Russia, painted in the middle years of his reign, 1682–1724. In the background are the Russian navy that the czar created and St. Petersburg, his new capital on the Baltic Sea. (© *The Granger Collection, NY*)

Protestant missionaries to convert the Russian "heretics" contributed, of course, to this distrust and dislike on the Russians' side. The ill-concealed disdain of the Europeans for their backward hosts in Moscow, Novgorod, and other trade markets sharpened native xenophobia (antipathy to foreigners).

Culturally, Russia experienced almost nothing of the consequences of the Protestant revolt against Rome or the Renaissance, a situation that greatly heightened the differences between it and the rest of Europe. The Renaissance glorification of individuality, of examination of the human potential, of daring to oppose was to make no impact east of Poland. And in religious affairs, the Russians either were ignorant of or rejected the changes Western Christianity had undergone such as the enhanced role of the laity in the church, the emphasis on individual piety and Bible reading, and the restrictions on the clergy's power. Protestant doctrines were regarded either as negligible tamperings with a basically erroneous Roman faith or—worse—Western surrender to the lures of a false rationalism that could only lead to eternal perdition.

Above all, from their Byzantine-inspired beginnings, the Russian clergy had accepted the role of partner of the civil government in maintaining good order on Earth. Unlike the papal or Protestant West, the Russian Christian establishment accorded the government full authority over the earthly concerns of the faithful. This tradition had been much strengthened by the church's close support of the Muscovite princes' struggle to free Russia from the Mongols. The high Orthodox clerics saw their role as helper and moral partner of the government in the mutual and interdependent tasks of saving souls and preserving Russia.

Absolutism in Russia: Peter I

The expansion of the Muscovite principality into a major state picked up its pace during the sixteenth century. The brutally effective czar **Ivan IV**, the Terrible (ruled 1533–1584), encouraged exploration and settlement of the vast and almost unpopulated Siberia. He brushed aside the Mongol remnants in a program of conquest that reached the Pacific shores as early as 1639—6,000 miles from Muscovy proper. Soon after, Russia was brought into formal contacts with China for the first time—a fateful meeting and the onset of a difficult relationship along the longest land border in the world.

Like the countries of western Europe, Russia adopted a form of divine right monarchy in the seventeenth century. Already in the previous century, Ivan the Terrible had established a model by persecuting all who dared question his rights. So fearful had been his harassment of his nobles—*boyars*—that many of them abandoned their lands and positions and fled. Those who chose to remain often paid with their lives for nonexistent "treason" or "betrayal." Whether or not Ivan became clinically paranoid is open to question. Mad or not, he bullied and terrified the Russian upper

A Prospect of St. Petersburg. The beautiful neoclassical facades of the government buildings in St. Petersburg were ordained by the eighteenth-century Russian rulers, notably by Catherine the Great, whose winter palace later became the Hermitage art museum. *(© Giraudon/Art Resource, NY)*

classes in a fashion that would have certainly led to revolt in other countries of the age. But in Russia, no such rebellion occurred.

A *Time of Troubles* in the early seventeenth century threatened the state's existence. The ancient dynasty of Kiev died out, and various nobles vied with armed force for the vacant throne. A serf rebellion added to the turmoil, and the Poles and Swedes took advantage of the confusion to annex huge slices of Russian territory. Nevertheless, recovery under the new **Romanov dynasty** (1613–1917) was fairly rapid. By the middle 1600s, Moscow was pressing the Poles and Swedes back to the Baltic shores and reclaiming some of the huge territories lost to these invaders and to the Ottoman Turks in the far south during the previous fifty years.

Peter I, the Great (ruled 1682–1724), is the outstanding example of Russian royal absolutism. There is no question of Peter's sanity. In fact, his foreign policy was one of the shrewdest of his age. But, like Ivan IV, he was in no way inclined to share power with any group or institution and believed the fate of the country was solely his to decide. There *were* indeed attempts to rebel against Peter, but they were put down with great cruelty. Nobles and peasants suffered equally if they resisted.

The impact of the human whirlwind called Peter on stolid and conservative Russia is impossible to categorize. He was the first Russian ruler to set foot outside the country and to recognize how primitive Russia was in comparison with the leading countries of Europe. He brought thousands of foreign specialists, craftsmen, artists, and engineers to Russia on contract to practice their specialties while teaching the Russians. These individuals—many of whom eventually settled in Russia—acted as yeast in the Russian dough and had inordinate influence on the country's progress in the next century.

Peter was the driving force for an enormously ambitious, partly successful attempt to make Russia into a fully European-style society. He did westernize many Russian public institutions and even the private lives of the upper 2 to 3 percent of the society. This tiny minority of gentry or noble landowners/officials assisted the czar in governing his vast country; they were swept up into lifelong service to the state, much against their will. In Peter's scheme, the peasants (five-sixths of the population) were to serve the nobility on their estates and feed the townspeople; the nobles were to serve the government as both military and civil bureaucrats at the beck and call of the czar; and the czar, in turn, styled himself the chief servant of the state.

Defeating the Swedes and Poles, Peter established a new capital at St. Petersburg to be Russia's long-sought "window on the West," through which all sorts of Western ideas and values might flow. He began the slow, state-guided modernization of what had been a very backward economy; he built a navy and made Russia a maritime power for the first time; he also encouraged such cultural breakthroughs as the first newspaper, the first learned journal, the Academy of Sciences, and the first technical schools.

But Peter also made Russian serfdom even more rigid and more comprehensive. He used his modernized, professional army not only against foreign enemies in his constant wars but also against his own peasant rebels. He discouraged any independent political activity and made the

Раскольникъ говоритъ: слушаи цырюльникъ я бороды стрицъ не хочю вотъ гляди я на тебя скоро ударю заплачю

цырюлъникъ хочетъ раскольнику бороду стрицъ ∙ ∙

✿ **A Royal Barber.** Peter's many domestic opponents saw him as an atheistic upstart and vandalizer of all that the conservative Russians held sacred. Here Peter personally clips the beard of a dignified noble who refused to pay the tax on beards that the czar imposed in his modernization drive. *(© The Granger Collection, NY)*

Orthodox clergy into mere agents of the civil government under a secular head. His cruelty bordered on sadism, and his personal life was filled with excess. Perhaps, as he himself said, it was impossible to avoid every evil in a country as difficult to govern as Russia. In any event, he remains the watershed figure of Russia's long history.

Two Eastern Powers in Eclipse

In the East, two former powers—Poland and Turkey—were gradually eclipsed by the rising stars of their competitors.

Poland

The Polish kingdom had come into existence in the 900s under native Slavic princes who converted to Western Christianity. Under pressure from the Germans pushing eastward, the Poles expanded into Lithuanian and Russian/Ukrainian territory between the twelfth and sixteenth

centuries. In the 1500s, Poland reached from the Baltic to the Black Sea, making it easily the largest European state west of Russia. It shared in the western European Christian culture in every way, while rejecting and condemning the Orthodox culture of the Russians. The Polish nobles were numerous and powerful, and they had instituted a system of serfdom over their Polish and non-Polish subjects that was as oppressive as any in the world.

The native dynasty died out in the 1500s, and the Polish nobles successfully pressed for an elective monarchy that would give them decisive powers. From then on, the succession to the Polish throne was a type of international auction: whoever promised the most to the noble voters was the winner and next king. As a result, centralized and effective government ceased to exist. Poland became a series of petty feudal fiefdoms headed by the great magnate—that is, large landholding families.

Under the famous *liberum* veto—perhaps the most absurd technique for governance ever devised—a single individual could veto any proposed legislation of the *sejm* (national parliament of nobles). Poland was truly what its proud motto asserted: a "republic of aristocrats." No one else counted. The small urban middle classes lost all influence on national policy, and the peasantry had never had any. The king, often a foreigner who had no roots whatever among the Poles, had to be content with being a figurehead, or he could not attain the post in the first place. The clergy was a noble domain. In the 1700s, Poland resembled a feudal monarchy of western Europe five centuries earlier. Even the royal army ceased to exist, and the nation's defense was put into the very unstable hands of the "confederations"— that is, the magnates and their clients.

The Polish Partitions   This situation was too tempting to Poland's neighbors to be allowed to continue. In the seventeenth century, the kingdom was seriously weakened by rebellions among the Ukrainian peasants and invasions by the Swedes. A long war against the Muscovites for control of the lower stretches of the important Dnieper waterway to the Black Sea had resulted in a decisive defeat. And the Turks had seized and kept the area along the Black Sea coast that had formerly been under Polish sovereignty.

In 1772, the Russian empress Catherine II decided that a favorable moment had arrived to "solve" the problem of a weakening Poland on Russia's western borders. Coordinating her plans with Frederick II of Prussia and Maria Theresa of Austria, she found a transparent pretext to demand Polish subordination. When the nobles attempted resistance, the upshot was the First Partition, whereby about a third of Poland was annexed to the three conspirators' lands (see Map 29.3).

The tremendous shock at last awakened a reform party among the aristocrats in Warsaw. Further impetus to reform was provided by the example of the American Revolution and its constitutional aftermath in the 1780s. In 1791, the noble Diet produced a remarkably liberal, forward-looking document for future Polish government. Serfdom was abolished, and many other significant reforms were enacted.

Catherine used this "unauthorized" constitution as a pretext for renewed armed intervention in the form of the Second Partition, which took another very large slice for Russia and Prussia in 1793. The Poles in desperation then rebelled in an uprising led by the same Thaddeus Kosciusko who had assisted General George Washington in America a few years earlier. After a brave fight, the rebels were crushed, and Poland disappeared from the map in the ensuing Third Partition of 1795 (Russia, Prussia, and Austria).

Throughout the nineteenth century, Polish patriots in and outside the country constantly reminded the world that a previously unthinkable event had happened: an established nation had been swallowed up by its greedy neighbors. They attempted two major uprisings (1831 and 1863–1864) against foreign rule. Much later, in the waning days of World War I, the revolution in Russia and the defeat of the Germans and Austrians allowed the Polish state to be re-created by the peace treaty.

Turkey

The other unsuccessful empire in eastern Europe was Ottoman Turkey. The Turks had invaded the Balkans in the later 1300s and gradually expanded their territory north, west, and east through the later 1500s. After a period of equilibrium of power, they then began to lose ground. The decisive turning point came in 1683, at the second siege of Vienna when the Ottoman attackers were beaten off with heavy loss.

At this point, Russia joined with Austria to counter the Turks throughout the eighteenth century, and the fortunes of the Ottomans came to depend on how well the two Christian empires were able to coordinate their policies and armies. When they were in harmony, the Turks were consistently pushed back. But when, as often, the two powers were pursuing different aims, the Turks were able to hold their own.

From 1790 on, the Austrians came to fear Russian territorial ambitions more than Turkish assault and ceased to make war on the Ottomans. But in the nineteenth century, the Turks had weakened sufficiently that they were repeatedly defeated by the Russians acting alone. Finally, all the other great powers stepped in to restrain Russia and support the sultan's government in its feeble attempts to modernize and survive.

Why was the Ottoman government unable to adapt effectively to the demands of a modern state and civil society? Certainly, a basic problem was the inability to devise an effective substitute for military conquest as the reason for government to exist. Thus, when military conquest was no longer easily possible against the Europeans (roughly about

Stanislas Lesczinski, King of Poland. One of several Polish monarchs in the seventeenth and eighteenth centuries who were installed in power through foreign intervention or bribery of the noble electors. Lesczinski was supposed to be a Russian puppet but discovered Polish patriotism once on the throne. Note the artist's balancing of military armor with a decidedly unmilitary face. (*Chateau de Versailles, France/Bridgeman Art Library*)

1600), the government no longer commanded the respect and moral authority it had enjoyed earlier.

Furthermore, the entire tradition of the Ottoman state emphasized the crucial importance of religion as the foundation stone of public life and institutions. Islam was never intended to be merely a matter of conscience. This attitude—which grew stronger rather than weaker as time passed—meant that a large part of the population was always excluded from consideration as a creative or constructive force. In southeastern Europe, 80 to 90 percent of the native populace remained Christian everywhere except Bosnia. These were the *raja*, the barely human who were destined to serve and enrich the Islamic ruling minority. A modern civic society could not be created on such a basis.

In addition, the bureaucracy and military, which had originally served the sultan faithfully and effectively in the conquered lands, became corrupt and self-seeking as time passed. Foremost in this were the **Janissaries,** the professional soldiers who gradually became a kind of parallel officialdom in eastern Europe, rivaling and often ignoring the Istanbul appointees. The Janissaries also blocked every effort to modernize the armed forces of the sultan after 1700 because the changes would have threatened their privileges. For example, they resisted the introduction of modern field artillery drawn by horses because their tradition was to employ heavy siege guns, which could only be moved very slowly and were meant to be used only against immobile targets. The Turks were therefore consistently outgunned in battles in the open field after about 1700 and suffered heavy casualties before they could engage the enemy.

The Janissaries' corruption and greed in dealing with their Christian subjects and serfs triggered several rebellions in the Balkans in the eighteenth and nineteenth centuries. Too entrenched to be disciplined by the central government, the Janissaries were ultimately eliminated by government-inspired massacre in Istanbul in the 1830s.

Finally, the Ottomans as an economic entity were weakened by corrupt local governors who withheld taxes from the central government and so oppressed their non-Muslim subjects that they rebelled and/or failed to produce. The local officials could then justify their failure to forward tax money to Istanbul by claiming that it was needed to combat rebellion or to supervise an increasingly restive subject population. In many parts of the Balkans, the Christian peasants habitually went "into the hills" to evade the Muslim landlords, which, of course, further reduced the tax funds collected. Banditry was widespread. In some of the more backward areas such as Montenegro and Albania, it became a profession. So long as most of the victims were Muslims, no social stigma attached to it.

For all these reasons, the Ottomans were destined to fall behind their European enemies and were unable to catch up despite sporadic reform attempts by the sultans and grand viziers. The government's problem was not that it was ignorant of what was happening in its domains but that it was physically and morally unable to correct the situation. In the end, this inability condemned the government in Istanbul to a slow death.

SUMMARY

The eastern European dynasties were able to grow and foil the occasional efforts to restrict their royal powers because neither of the two potential counterforces, the peasant majority and the nobility, could substitute themselves for the throne. The clergy in all three eastern Christian empires were mainly a part of the machinery of government rather than an autonomous moral force. These factors, while true everywhere to some extent, were particularly noteworthy in the Orthodox lands.

The rise of the Prussian Hohenzollern kingdom began in earnest in the mid-1600s when the Great Elector cleverly made his petty state into a factor in the Thirty Years' War, while subordinating the nobility to a centralized government. Continued by his successors, the Elector's policies culminated in the reign of his great-grandson Frederick II, one of the most effective monarchs of European history.

The Habsburgs of Austria took a different path. Through fortunate marriage alliances, they gradually created a large empire based on Bohemia and Hungary as well as Austria proper. The weaknesses of this state were partially addressed by the efforts of Empress Maria Theresa, who brought a degree of centralization and uniformity to the government. But Austria's great problem—its competing nationalities—remained.

After an obstacle-filled climb from obscurity under the Mongols, the Muscovite principality "gathered the Russian lands" in the 1500s and began to expand eastward. Its Polish, Turkish, and Swedish rivals in the west were gradually overcome by lengthy wars. The Russian nobility, once all-powerful, were reduced by the various devices of the czars to mere servants of the imperial throne. As in Prussia, this collaboration of throne and noble had been secured by giving the estate-owning nobility full powers over the unfortunate serfs and the sparse and insignificant townspeople.

Two other would-be great powers in the East had been either swallowed up by their neighbors or reduced to impotence by the late eighteenth century. Poland was made to disappear as a sovereign state by the partitions, and the Ottomans were checked and weakened by both internal and external factors so as to become a negligible factor in European affairs.

TEST YOUR KNOWLEDGE

1. East of the Elbe, the feudal landlords of the fifteenth through seventeenth centuries
   a. maintained or increased their local powers and prestige.
   b. regularly overthrew the royal governments.
   c. suffered a general decline economically.
   d. practically became extinct with the rise of urban life.

2. Which of the following did the Great Elector of Prussia *not* do?
   a. He made a tacit alliance with the landlord-nobles.
   b. He ensured the political and social prestige of the peasants.
   c. He greatly increased the financial resources of the government.
   d. He began the tradition of noble military and civil service to the government.

3. The foundation of Frederick William's success in establishing strong royal government in Prussia was his
   a. ability to intimidate the rebellious nobles into submission.
   b. success at waging war against the rebel peasants.
   c. ability to bribe his enemies.
   d. tacit bargain with his nobles.

4. Maria Theresa's major achievement for Austria was
   a. to conquer more territories from the Turks.
   b. to bring order into the workings of government.
   c. to defeat the claims of the Prussians to Austrian lands.
   d. to clean up the corruption in society.

5. A great difference between Ivan IV, the Terrible, and Peter I, the Great, is
   a. the savagery of the first and the subtlety of the second.
   b. the minimal successes of Ivan and the tremendous ones of Peter.
   c. the tender consideration shown to the nobles by Peter.
   d. the degree of foreign influences apparent in each czar's policymaking.

6. The most striking difference between the absolutist governments in East and West was
   a. the degree of local powers retained by the townspeople.
   b. the ability of the peasants to express their political opinions to the central government.
   c. the coordination of the policies of the official church and the government.
   d. the degree to which constitutions restrained them in their policies.

7. The two nations that had least success in the competition for power in East Europe were
   a. Austria and Russia.
   b. Turkey and Poland.
   c. Poland and Russia.
   d. Turkey and Prussia.

8. The liberum veto was a device by which
   a. one individual could prohibit the passage of a proposed law.
   b. a family member had the right to secure liberty for a political prisoner.
   c. the king could veto any measure passed by the Polish parliament.
   d. only a noble had the right to full liberty.

9. All but one of the following factors contributed to the decline of Turkish prestige after 1600:
   a. The rise of army garrisons in the provinces who had local connections and loyalties
   b. The squeezing of the flow of taxes to the capital because of corruption
   c. The questioning on religious grounds of the right of the sultan in Constantinople to govern
   d. The decline of the effectiveness of Turkish weaponry and tactics in war

IDENTIFICATION TERMS

Great Elector (Frederick William)

Habsburg dynasty

Ivan IV

Janissaries

Junker

liberum veto

Maria Theresa

Mongol Yoke

Peter I, the Great

Prince Eugen of Savoy

Romanov dynasty

War of the Austrian Succession

INFOTRAC COLLEGE EDITION

Enter the search terms "Habsburg" or "Hapsburg" using Key Words.

Enter the search term "Ottoman Empire" using Key Words.
Enter the search term "Peter the Great" using Key Words.

CHINA FROM THE MING
TO THE EARLY QING DYNASTY

Great wealth is from heaven; modest wealth is from diligence.

CHINESE FOLK SAYING

1368–1644	Ming dynasty
1400s	Maritime expeditions
1500s	First contacts with Europeans
1644–1911	Qing (Manzhou) dynasty
1700s	Economic growth; population rises, trade increases

THE AGES OF CHINA do not coincide with those of Europe. China had no Middle Age or Renaissance of the fourteenth century. The outstanding facts in China's development between 1000 C.E. and 1500 C.E. were the humiliating conquest by the Mongols and their overthrow by the rebellion that began the Ming dynasty. For over 200 years, the Ming remained vigorous, providing the Chinese with a degree of stability and prosperity that contemporary Europeans would have envied. But the sustained creative advance in the sciences and basic technologies that had allowed China to overshadow all rivals during the thousand years between the beginning of the Song and the end of the Ming dynasties (600–1600) was slowly drawing to a close. Indeed, China was being overtaken in these fashions by the West, but as late as the eighteenth century, this was hardly evident to anyone. Possessed of an ancient and marvelous high culture, China was still convinced of its own superiority and was as yet far from being forced to admit its weaknesses.

MING CHINA, 1368–1644

The Ming was the last pure Chinese dynasty. It began with the overthrow of the hated Mongols who had ruled China for 100 years. Founded by the peasant Zhu who had displayed masterful military talents in leading a motley band of rebel armies, the Ming would last 300 years. Zhu, who took the imperial title **Hongwu** (meaning The Generous Warrior), was an individual of great talents and great cruelty. In many ways his fierce ruthlessness was reminiscent of the First Emperor. He built the city of Nanjing (Nanking) as his capital near the coast on the Yangtze River. His son and successor Yongle was even more talented as a general and an administrator. During his twenty-two-year reign (1402–1424), China gained more or less its present heartlands, reaching from Korea to Vietnam and inward to Mongolia (see Map 30.1). The eastern half of the Great Wall was rebuilt, and the armies of China were everywhere triumphant against their Mongol and Turkic nomad opponents.

In the Ming era, China generally had an effective government. One sign of this was the sharp rise in population throughout the dynastic period. When the Ming took power, bubonic plague (the same epidemic that was simultaneously raging in Europe; see Chapter 24) and Mongol

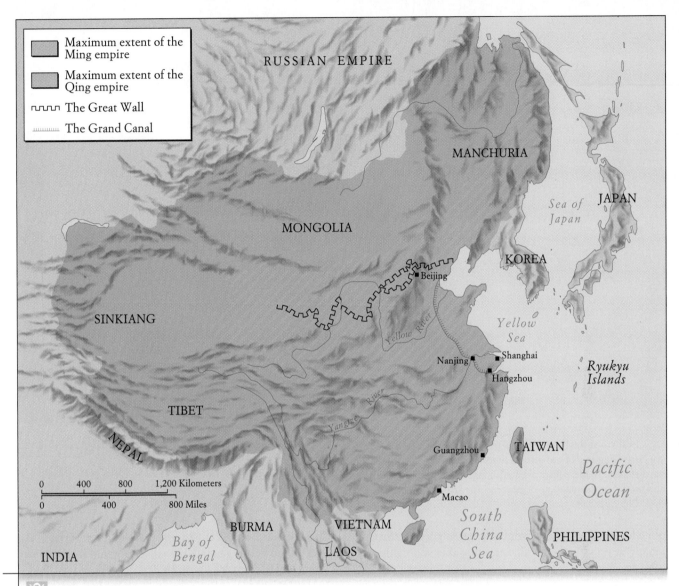

MAP 30.1 The Empire under the Ming and Qing Dynasties. By the time of the Ming dynasty, China had reached its modern territorial extent, with the exception only of Tibet and the far western deserts. Beijing and Nanjing alternated as the capital cities. At the height of the empire under the Qing dynasty in the middle of the eighteenth century, both Tibet and the huge desert province of Sinkiang came under its control.

savagery had reduced the population to about 60 million, the same size it had been in the Tang period, 500 years earlier. The population rose to perhaps 150 million by 1600—the most dramatic rise yet experienced by any society.

This new population necessitated an equally dramatic rise in food supply. The old center of Chinese food production, the Yangtze basin in south-central China, was not able to meet the demand. A new area for rice cultivation in the extreme south near Vietnam was developed during the Ming, while some new crops from the Americas such as corn, squash, peanuts, and beans made their way into Chinese fields via the trans-Pacific trade with the Portuguese and Spanish. Interestingly, the Irish potato, which would become the staple food crop of northern European peas-

ants in the eighteenth century, was introduced into China but did not catch on. Since rice has a greater nutritional value than the potato, this turned out to be a boon for China.

Economic Progress

Commercial activity steadily increased until it was probably more commonplace in China than in any other country of the world by the 1600s. A larger percentage of the labor force was directly engaged in buying, selling, and transporting goods than in any other land. The merchants remained

🏵 **Festival at the River.** This is part of a thirty-three-foot-long scroll painted in the Ming dynasty era portraying one of the several civic festivals that marked the Chinese calendar. The emperor's participation in these festivals was an important part of his functions as head of government and holder of the mandate of heaven. *(The Metropolitan Museum of Art, Fletcher Fund, 1947, The A. W. Bahr Collection)*

quite low on the social ladder but were acquiring sufficient money to provide them with a comfortable and cultivated lifestyle.

Commercial contact with the Europeans started in the early 1500s with the coming of the Portuguese. Originally welcomed, the Portuguese behaved so badly that the Chinese quickly limited them to a single port, Macao. Here, in return for silver from the Americas, the Portuguese obtained luxurious and exotic goods that brought exorbitant prices from European nobles who coveted them for the prestige they lent. A merchant who could take a single crate of first-class Chinese porcelain tableware back to Europe could make enough profit to start his own firm.

Urbanization and Technology

The Ming period also saw an enormous increase in the number of urban dwellers. Some Chinese cities, serving as marketplaces for the rural majority and as administrative and cultural centers, grew to have several hundreds of thousand inhabitants; one or two had more than a million at a time when no European town had a population of even 100,000. In these Chinese metropolises, almost anything was available for money, and all available evidence indicates

that the kind of abject poverty that would arise later was still unknown. In general, the villagers and city dwellers of Ming China seem to have been decently housed and fed.

Historians have often asked why China with its large, financially sophisticated commercial class and a leadership role in so many ideas and techniques did not make the breakthrough into a mechanical mode of industry. Why, in other words, did the Chinese fail to make the leap from the "commercial revolution" of the later Ming period to an "industrial revolution" of the kind that began in the West a century later? Various answers have been proposed, and no single one is satisfactory. The Chinese esteem for artists and scholars and the tendency of such people to place little emphasis on accumulation of material goods must be part of the explanation. Engineers and inventors were never prominent in China's culture, even though Chinese science and technology led the world until the 1200s at least. Also, the Confucian ethos did not admire the entrepreneur or his activities. It was the retention of the old, not the invention of the new, that inspired a properly educated Chinese. In the end, we can only attest that China did not experience an industrial-technical breakthrough. If it had, China and not western Europe would have been the dominant power of the world in the past three centuries.

The Ming Political System

As always since Han times, the Chinese government culminated in the person of an all-powerful but not divine emperor who ruled by the mandate of Heaven through a highly trained bureaucracy derived in substantial part from talented men of all classes and backgrounds. Hongwu, the peasant rebel commander, brought militaristic and authoritarian ways to the government he headed. The first Ming ruler divided China into fifteen provinces, subdivided into numerous counties, an arrangement that has survived almost intact into the present day. He made occupations hereditary and classified the population into three groups: peasants, soldiers, and workers. Supposedly, the class people were born into would determine the course of their lives, but this was much truer on paper than in reality. China was far too vast and the bureaucracy far too small to allow the theory to be put successfully into practice.

But the emperor's powers during the early Ming were probably greater than ever before. Hongwu created a corps of palace eunuchs, men who had been raised since boyhood to be totally dedicated servants of the ruler. They served as his eyes and ears, and during periods of weak leadership, the eunuchs often exercised almost dictatorial powers over the regular officials, because they alone had direct access to the emperor. This practice, of course, led to much abuse, and the eunuchs were hated and feared by most Chinese. Curiously, the eunuchs never seem to have attempted to overthrow a legitimate ruler, although some Ming emperors practically turned the government over to them. The imperial corps of eunuchs lasted into the twentieth century, though their powers were much diminished by then.

After a brief sojourn in Nanjing during the rule of the first Ming emperor, the government was returned to the northern city of Beijing (Peking) originally built by the Mongols. In its center was the **Forbidden City,** a quarter-mile-square area of great palaces, offices, and living quarters for the higher officials. No ordinary person was ever permitted within its massive walls. The Forbidden City was expanded several times during the Ming, until it came to house more than 20,000 men and women who served the emperor or his enormous official family. Its upkeep and the lavish entertainments and feasts that were regularly put on for thousands were a heavy burden on the whole country.

The Bureaucracy

The basis for entry and success in the bureaucracy remained the same as it had been for the last 1,500 years: mastery of the Confucian philosophy and ethics. Confucianism grew stronger than ever. Many schools were founded solely

Examinations for Government Posts. This seventeenth-century painting shows the examinations for government posts in progress. Despite years of preparation, very few candidates were successful at the higher levels. *(© Giraudon/Art Resource, NY)*

Women Bathing Their Children. This domestic scene is taken from a twelfth-century Song dynasty painting of life in the palace. *(Courtesy of the Freer Gallery of Art, Smithsonian Institution, Washington, DC, F1935.8)*

to prepare boys for the government service exams. These exams, which had been suspended by the Mongols, were immediately reinstated by the first Ming emperor. Their essentials would not change until the twentieth century. The exams were administered every other year at the lowest (county) level and every third year at the provincial capitals. Each candidate was assigned a tiny cubicle where he slept and ate under constant surveillance when not writing his essays during the three to five days of the examination. Only a tiny minority was successful in obtaining an official post even at the province level. The most distinguished of these would then compete for the central government posts every third year, and the successful ones were considered the most prestigious of all of the "men of Han."

Unchanged for centuries, the exams influenced all Chinese education and kept what we now call the curriculum to a very narrow range. After basic reading, writing, and arithmetic, most Chinese schooling was aimed only at preparing the student for the civil service examinations. It consisted of a good deal of rote memorization and required very extensive knowledge of the various interpretations of Confucian thought. Imagination, creativity, and individuality were definitely not desired. Over the long term, this limited education put China's officials at a distinct disadvantage when confronted with situations that required flexibility and vision. On the other hand, the uniform preparation of all Chinese officials gave the country an especially cohesive governing class, the mandarins (see Chapter 18), and conflicts generated by differing philosophies of government were rare or nonexistent. Until very recent times, civil upheaval and antagonism never occurred *within* the governing class, only *between* it and some outer group (usually foreigners, eunuchs, or provincial usurpers). This unity of view and the loyalty it engendered was very valuable in preserving China from threatened disintegration on repeated occasions.

In the early Ming period, both the government and the great majority of the educated population agreed on the vital principles of a good civic life and how to construct it. All officials, from the emperor down to the minor collector of customs in some obscure port, were accepted by the masses as their proper authorities. Unfortunately, this harmony declined in later years, as weak emperors ignored the examples set by the dynasty's founder.

DEALING WITH FOREIGNERS

The Mongols on the northern and northwestern frontiers were still a constant menace after they had been expelled from China proper. Much of the large military budget of Ming China was spent on maintaining the 2,000 miles of the Great Wall, large sections of which had to be rebuilt to defend against them. To do this job, a huge army—well over a million strong—was kept in constant readiness. The main reason for moving the capital back to Beijing from Nanjing was to better direct the defense effort.

The rulers at Beijing followed the ancient stratagem of "use the barbarian against the barbarian," whenever they could. But twice they miscalculated, and the Mongol tribes were able to put aside their squabbles and unite in campaigns against the Chinese. The first time the Mongols actually defeated and captured the emperor, holding him for a tremendous ransom. The second time, they smashed a major army and overran Beijing itself in 1550. Eventually, both incursions were forced back, and the dynasty was reestablished.

With the Japanese, relations proceeded on two planes: that of hostility toward pirates and smugglers and that of legitimate and beneficial exchange. From the fourteenth century, pirate-traders (there was little distinction) from Japan had appeared in Korean and north Chinese waters. Gradually, they became bolder and often joined Chinese pirates to raid coastal ports well into the south. Because the Japanese could always flee out of reach in their islands, the Chinese could only try to improve their defenses, rather than exterminate the enemy fleets. During the sixteenth century, the Beijing government actually abandoned many coastal areas to the pirates, hoping this tactic would enable them to protect the rest.

Otherwise, the Ming period was a high point in cultural and commercial interchange between China and Japan. Direct Chinese-Japanese relations concentrated on trading between a few Japanese *daimyo* and Chinese merchants, a private business supervised by the respective governments. Several of the shoguns of Japan (see the next chapter) were great admirers of Chinese culture and saw to it that Japan's doors were thrown widely open to Chinese ideas as well as artifacts.

The trading activity with the Japanese was exceptional, however. Generally speaking, China's rulers believed that the Empire of the Middle needed little from the outside world. A brief excursion onto the Indian Ocean trade routes seemed to underline this conviction. The **Maritime Expeditions** of the early 1400s are a notable departure from the general course of Chinese expansionist policy, in that they were naval rather than land ventures. Between 1405 and 1433, huge fleets carrying as many as 30,000 sailors and soldiers traveled south to the East Indies, and as far west as the east coast of Africa. The expeditions were sponsored by the government, and at the emperor's order, they stopped as suddenly as they had begun. Their purpose remains unclear, but it does not seem to have been commercial. The fleets made no attempt to plant colonies or to set up a network of trading posts. Nor did the expeditions leave a long-term mark on Chinese consciousness or awareness of the achievements and interests of the world outside.

The Maritime Expeditions were a striking demonstration of how advanced Chinese seamanship, ship design, and equipment were and how confident the Chinese were in their dealings with foreigners of all types. Although China possessed the necessary technology (shipbuilding, compass, rudder, sails) to make a success of overseas exploration and commerce, the government decided not to use it. The government's refusal was the end of the matter. The mercantile class had no alternative but to accept it because the merchants had neither the influence at court nor the high status in society that could have enabled the voyages to continue. In this sense, the failure to pursue the avenues opened by the expeditions reflects the differences between the Chinese and European governments and the relative importance of merchants land entrepreneurial vision in the two cultures.

Contacts with Westerners during the Ming era were limited to a few trading enterprises, mainly Portuguese or Dutch, and occasional missionaries, mainly Jesuits from Spain or Rome. The Portuguese, who arrived first of all Europeans in 1514, made themselves so offensive to Chinese standards of behavior that they were expelled, then confined to the tiny Macao port, near Guangzhou. The missionaries got off to a considerably more favorable start. They made enormous efforts to empathize with the Confucian mentalities of the upper-class Chinese officials and adapt Christian doctrines to Chinese psyches.

Outstanding in this regard was **Matteo Ricci** (1551–1610), a Jesuit who obtained access to the emperor thanks to his scientific expertise, adoption of Chinese ways of thought, and mastery of the difficult language. Ricci and his successors established a Christian bridgehead in the intellectual focal point of China that for a century or more looked as though it might be able to broaden its appeal and convert the masses. But this was not to be. (See the Science and Technology box for some of Ricci's insights into Chinese culture.)

THE MANZHOU INVADERS: QING DYNASTY

The end of the Ming dynasty came after a slow, painful decline in the mid–seventeenth century. A series of ineffective emperors had allowed government power to slip into the hands of corrupt and hated eunuchs, who made decisions on the basis of bribes, without responsibility for their consequences. Court cliques contended for supreme power. The costs of the multitude of imperial court officials and hangers-on were enormous and could be met only by squeezing taxes out of an already hard-pressed peasantry. Peasant rebellions began to multiply as the government's ability to restrain rapacious landlords declined (see the Family and Gender Relations box). The administrative apparatus, undermined by the eunuch cliques at court, ceased to function. Adding to the troubles was the popularity among the mandarins of an extreme version of scholarly Confucianism that paralyzed innovation.

The Manzhou tribesmen living north of the Great Wall in **Manchuria** had paid tribute to the Beijing emperor but had never accepted his overlordship. When the rebellions led to anarchy in several northern provinces, the Manzhou saw their chance. The Manzhou governing group admired Chinese culture and made it clear that if and when they were victorious, conservative Chinese would have nothing to fear from them. Presenting themselves as the alternative to banditry and even revolution, the Manzhou invaders gradually won the support of much of the mandarin class. One province after another went over to them rather than face continuous rebellion. The last Ming ruler, faced with certain defeat, committed suicide. Thus was founded the

CHINESE INVENTIONS

In the sixteenth century, an Italian priest named Matteo Ricci was invited by the emperor to reside at the court in Beijing in the capacity of court astronomer. Ricci had learned Chinese and drew on his learned background in the sciences to both instruct and entertain his hosts. His journals were published shortly after his death in 1610, and gave Europeans their first eyewitness glimpse of the Ming dynasty civilization and the first knowledgeable insight into Chinese affairs since Marco Polo's report three centuries earlier.

All of the known metals without exception are to be found in China. . . . From molten iron they fashion many more things than we do, for example, cauldrons, pots, bells, gongs, mortars . . . martial weapons, instruments of torture, and a great number of other things equal in workmanship to our own metalcraft. . . . The ordinary tableware of the Chinese is clay pottery. There is nothing like it in European pottery either from the standpoint of the material itself or its thin and fragile construction. The finest specimens of porcelain are made from clay found in the province of Kiam and these are shipped not only to every part of China but even to the remotest corners of Europe where they are highly prized. . . . This porcelain too will bear the heat of hot foods without cracking, and if it is broken and sewed with a brass wire it will hold liquids without any leakage. . . .

Finally we should say something about the saltpeter, which is quite plentiful but which is not used extensively in the preparation of gunpowder, because the Chinese are not expert in the use of guns and artillery and make but little use of these in warfare. Saltpeter, however, is used in lavish quantities in making fireworks for display at public games and on festival days. The Chinese take great pleasure in such exhibitions and make them the chief attraction of all their festivities. Their skill in the manufacture of fireworks is really extraordinary and there is scarcely anything which they cannot cleverly imitate with them. They are especially adept at reproduc-

ing battles and in making rotating spheres of fire, fiery trees, fruit, and the like, and they seem to have no regard for expense where fireworks are concerned. . . .

The art of printing was practiced in China at a date somewhat earlier than that assigned to the beginning of printing in Europe. . . . It is quite certain that the Chinese knew the art of printing at least five centuries ago, and some of them assert that printing was known to their people before the beginning of the Christian era. . . .

Their method of making printed books is quite ingenious. The text is written in ink, with a brush made of very fine hair, on a sheet of paper which is inverted and pasted on a wooden tablet. When the paper has become thoroughly dry, its surface is scraped off quickly and with great skill, until nothing but a fine tissue bearing the characters remains on the wooden tablet. Then with a steel graver, the workman cuts away the surface following the outlines of the characters, until these alone stand out in low relief. From such a block a skilled printer can make copies with incredible speed, turning out as many as fifteen hundred copies in a single day. Chinese printers are so skilled at turning out these blocks that no more time is consumed in making one of them than would be required by one of our printers in setting up a form of type and making the necessary corrections. . . .

The simplicity of Chinese printing is what accounts for the exceedingly large number of books in circulation here and the ridiculously low prices at which they are sold. Such facts as these would scarcely be believed by one who had not witnessed them.

FOR REFLECTION

Why do you think the Chinese did not use gunpowder technology in war as in entertainments? In light of what Ricci reports, is contemporary European preference for metallic type justified?

SOURCE: Documents in World History: Vol. 2. The Modern Centuries, ed. P. Stearns et al. (New York: Harper & Row, 1988).

---

last dynasty of imperial China, the Manzhou or **Qing** (1664–1911). In its opening generations it was to be one of the most successful as well.

Manzhou Government

When the Qing dynasty was at the apex of its power and wealth, China had by far the largest population under one government and the largest territory of any country in the world (see Map 30.1). China reached its biggest territorial extent at this time. The Manzhou had been close to Chinese civilization for many years and had become partially sinicized (adopted Chinese culture), so the transition from Ming to Qing rule was nothing like the upheaval that had followed the Mongol conquest in the 1200s. Many Ming officials and generals joined with the conquerors voluntarily

from the start. Many others joined under pressure or as it became apparent that the Manzhou were not savages and were adopting Chinese traditions in government. High positions in the central government were in fact occupied by two individuals: one Manzhou, one Chinese. Chinese provincial governors were overseen by Manzhou, and the army was sharply divided between the two ethnic groups, with the Manzhou having superior status.

Like most new dynasties, the Manzhou were strong reformers in their early years, bringing order and respect for authority, snapping the whip over insubordinate officials in the provinces, and attempting to ensure justice in the village. The two greatest Manzhou leaders were the emperors **Kangxi** (Kang-hsi; ruled 1662–1722) and his grandson **Qienlong** (Chien Lung; ruled 1736–1795). Their unusually long reigns allowed them to put their stamps on the bu-

A PEASANT'S REVENGE

A story written in the 1670s tells of the rough behavior of the conquering Qing soldiery toward Chinese women and the way one woman got her revenge:

In the year 1674 ... the expeditionary troops being sent south were bivouacked with their horses in the area of Yen; not a dog or a chicken was left, the hearths were empty, women and girls suffered their outrages.

At this season there had been heavy rains, and the fields were covered in water, like lakes; the people had nowhere to hide. . . . Only the wife of a certain Chang did not lie low but stayed quite openly in her home. At night, with her husband, she dug a deep pit in her kitchen and filled it with dried reeds; she screened over the top and laid matting upon it so that it looked like a bed. And then she went on with her cooking by the stove.

When the troops came she went out of doors, as if offering herself. Two Mongol soldiers seized her and prepared to rape her, but she said to them, "How can I do such a thing in the presence of others?" One of them chuckled, jabbered to the other, and went away. The woman went into the house with the other and pointed to the bed, to get him to climb up first. The screening broke, and the sol-

dier tumbled in. The woman took the matting again and placed it over the hole; then she stood by it, to lure the other when he came back. He returned after a short while and heard the shouting from the pit, though he couldn't tell where it was; the woman beckoned to him with her hand and her smile, saying, "Over here." The soldier climbed onto the matting and also fell in. The woman threw more brushwood on top of them and set the whole pile on fire. The flames blazed up and the house itself caught fire. The woman called out for help. When the fire was extinguished, there was a strong smell of roasted meat; people asked her what it was, and the woman replied, "I had two pigs, and feared they would be taken from me by the troops. So I hid them in that pit."

FOR REFLECTION

This story indicates that by no means were all Chinese peasant women passive accepters of their fate. Note that the woman's husband is enlisted by her into this daring—and dangerous—scheme.

SOURCE: J. Spence, *The Death of Woman Wang* (New York: Viking, 1979). © by J. Spence.

---

reaucracy and develop long-range policies. Both were strong, well-educated men who approached their duties with the greatest seriousness. Both attempted to keep Manzhou and Chinese separate to some degree, though the Manzhou were always a tiny minority (perhaps 2 percent) of the population and were steadily sinicized after the early 1700s by intermarriage and free choice. (See the Exercise of Authority box for more on Kangxi.)

Kangxi was the almost exact contemporary of Louis XIV of France and, like him, was the longest-lived ruler of his country's history. From all accounts, Kangxi was a remarkable man with a quick intellect and a fine gift for administration. He did much to improve the waterways, which were always of great importance for transportation in China. Rivers were dredged, and canals and dams built. He was particularly active in economic policymaking, both domestically and toward the Western merchants whose vessels were now starting to appear regularly in Chinese ports. After decades of negotiations, Kangxi opened four ports to European traders and allowed them to set up small permanent enclaves there. This decision was to have fateful consequences in the mid–nineteenth century when the Beijing government was in much weaker hands.

Kangxi's grandson Qienlong was a great warrior and intelligent administrator. He eradicated the persistent Mongol raiders on the western borders and brought Tibet under Chinese control for the first time (see Map 30.1). The peculiar fashion of dealing with neighboring independent

kingdoms as though they were voluntary satellites of China (tributaries) was extended to much of Southeast Asia at this time. Qienlong ruled through the last two-thirds of the eighteenth century, and we know a good deal about both him and his grandfather because Jesuit missionaries still resided in Beijing during this era. Their perceptive reports to Rome contributed to the interest in everything Chinese that was so manifest in late eighteenth-century Europe.

The early Manzhou emperors were unusually vigorous leaders, and the Chinese economy and society responded positively to their rule until the middle of the nineteenth century, when their prestige suffered under a combination of Western military intrusions and a growing population crisis. (This period is covered in Chapter 43.)

QING CULTURE AND ECONOMY

No break in fundamental cultural styles occurred between the Ming and Qing dynasties. As in earlier China, the most respected cultural activities were philosophy, history, calligraphy, poetry, and painting. In literature, a new form reached maturity in the 1500s: the novel. Perhaps inspired by the Japanese example, a series of written stories about both gentry life and ordinary people appeared during the late Ming and Qing eras. Best known are the *Book of the Golden Lotus* and ***The Dream of the Red Chamber,*** the latter a product of the eighteenth century. Most of

KANGXI REFLECTS ON A LONG LIFE

Emperor Kangxi, the seventeenth-century Qing dynast, was perhaps the greatest of all the Chinese rulers, in part because of the extraordinary duration of his hold on the throne. Here, in his sixties, he muses on the trials of being the "son of Heaven" and not being fully appreciated by his countrymen:

When I had been twenty years on the throne I didn't dare conjecture that I might reign thirty. After thirty years I didn't dare conjecture that I might reign forty. Now I have reigned sixty-one years. The "Great Plan" section of the *Book of History* says of the five joys:

The first is long life

The second is riches

The third is soundness of body and serenity of mind

The fourth is the love of virtue

The fifth is an end crowning the life.

The "end crowning the life" is put last because it is so hard to attain. I am now approaching seventy, and have the world as my possession, and my sons, grandsons, and great-grandsons number over one hundred and fifty. The country is at peace and happy. You can say that my good fortune has been extensive. Even if I should suddenly die my mind would be truly content. I have thought that ever since I came to the throne . . . we have improved all manners and customs, and made all the people prosperous and contented. . . . I have worked with unceasing diligence and intense watchfulness, never resting, never idle. So for decades I have exhausted my strength day after day. How can all this be summed up in a two word phrase like "hard work"?

Those among the rulers of earlier dynasties who did not live long have all been discussed in the Histories as having caused this by drink and sex. Such remarks are just the sneers of pedants who have to find some blemishes in even the purest and most perfect of rulers. I now exonerate these earlier rulers, saying that because the affairs of the country are so troublesome one can't help getting exhausted. . . . If an official wants to serve, then he serves; if he wants to stop, then he stops. When he grows old he resigns and returns home, to look after his sons and play with his grandsons, he still has the chance to relax and enjoy him self. Whereas the ruler in all his hardworking life finds no place to rest.

FOR REFLECTION

Kangxi's reflections on the tribulations of the man who rules seem clearly aimed at making him more human in the eyes of those who counted in China: the mandarin class. Why might such an impression be important to such a powerful man? Do you think his humble attitude is authentic or a pretense?

SOURCE: Jonathan Spence, Emperor of China (New York: Vintage, 1975), pp. 361–362.

---

the authors are unknown, and the books that have survived are probably a small portion of those actually produced. Some of the stories are pornographic, a variety of literature that the Chinese evidently enjoyed despite official disapproval.

Porcelain reached such artistry in the eighteenth century that it became a major form of Chinese aesthetic creation. Throughout the Western world, the wealthy sought fine "china" as tableware and objects of art and were willing to pay nearly any price for the beautiful blue-and-white Ming wares brought back by the Dutch and English ships from the south China ports. Chinese painting on scrolls and screens was also imported in large amounts, as were silks and other luxury items for the households of the nobility and wealthy urbanites. The very popular decorative style termed *chinoiserie* reflected Europe's admiration for Chinese artifacts and good taste. The "Clipper ships" of New England made the long voyage around Cape Horn and across the Pacific in the first half of the nineteenth century to reap enormous profits carrying luxury goods in both directions: sea otter furs from Alaska and the Pacific Northwest and porcelain, tea, and jade from China.

During the Ming and Qing periods, far more people were participating in the creation and enjoyment of formal culture than ever before. By the 1700s, China had a large number of educated people who were able to purchase the tangible goods produced by a host of skilled artists. Schools and academies of higher learning educated the children of anyone who could afford the fees, generally members of the scholar-official class who had been governing China since the Han dynasty.

In this era (from the 1500s on), however, China definitely lost its lead in science and technology to the West, a lead that had been maintained for the previous thousand years. Developing a sensitivity to beauty, such as the art of calligraphy, was considered as essential to proper education in China as mastering literacy and basic math. Painting, poetry, and meditation were considered far more important than physics or accounting or chemistry. This ongoing downgrading of the quantitative sciences and the technical advances they spawned in the West was to be a massively negative turning point in international power relations for China. Aesthetic sensitivities and artistic excellence proved to be little aid when confronted by cannons and steam engines.

Progress and Problems

Among the outstanding achievements of the early Qing emperors were improvements in agriculture and engineering that benefited uncounted numbers of ordinary Chinese. Kangxi, for example, did much to ensure that the south

China "rice bowl" was made even more productive and that the Grand Canal linking the Yellow River with the central coast ports was kept in good order. New hybrid rice allowed rice culture to be extended and increased yields, which in turn led to an expansion in population.

Internal trade in the large cities and many market towns continued the upsurge that had begun during the Ming dynasty and became ever more important in this era. Although most Chinese remained villagers working the land, there were now large numbers of shopkeepers, market porters, carters, artisans, moneylenders, and all the other occupations of commercial life. Money circulated freely as both coin and paper, the coins being minted of

Ming Vase. This superb example of Chinese porcelain was made in the seventeenth century, possibly for the developing export trade with Europe. (© *Giraudon/Art Resource, NY*)

Spanish silver brought from the South American colonies to Manila and Guangzhou to trade for silk and porcelain.

All in all, the Chinese in the early Qing period were probably living as well as any other people in the world and better than most Europeans. But this high standard of living was to change for the worse in later days, when for the first time the population's growth exceeded the ability of the economy to find suitable productive work for it. By the nineteenth century, almost all the land that had adequate precipitation for crops had already been brought under the plow. The major improvements possible in rice farming had already been made, and yields did not continue to rise as they had previously. Machine industry had not yet arrived in China (and would not for many years), and trade with the outside world was on a relatively small scale that government policy refused to expand. (China wanted very few material things from the non-Chinese, in any case.) In the nineteenth century, rural China began to experience massive famines that were the result of too rapid growth in population in a technically backward society without the desire or means to shift to new production modes.

SUMMARY

The overthrow of the Mongols introduced another of the great Chinese dynasties: the Ming. Blessed by exceptionally able emperors in the early decades, the Ming imitated their Tang dynasty model and made notable improvements in agriculture and commerce. Urban life expanded and the urban bourgeoisie of merchants became economically (but not politically) important. The borders were extended well to the west and north, and the barbarian nomads thrust once again behind the Great Wall for a couple of centuries.

In the classic pattern, however, the Ming's grip on government and people weakened, and the costs of a huge court and army pressed heavily on the overtaxed population. When rebellions began in the northern provinces, they were encouraged by the promises of change offered by the invading Manzhou in the northeast. Triumphant, the

Manzhou leader began the final dynastic period in China's 3,000-year history, that of the Qing.

The Qing emperors of the first half of the dynasty were able men, who in the eighteenth century led China to one of the summits of its national existence. The economy and the fine arts prospered, and overpopulation was not yet a problem. But in science and technology, China now lagged far behind the West, and the coming century was going to be filled with political and cultural humiliations. China entered the modern age unprepared to handle the type of problems that it now faced: impoverishment, military backwardness, and technical retardation. First the Europeans and then the Japanese would find ways to take advantage of these handicaps.

TEST YOUR KNOWLEDGE

1. The most serious menace to China's stability during the 1300s and 1400s was
   a. the Japanese coastal pirates.
   b. the Mongol tribes in the north.
   c. the conspiracies of the palace eunuchs.
   d. the invasions of the Vietnamese in the south.
2. The last dynasty to be of pure Chinese origin was the
   a. Manzhou.
   b. Song.
   c. Tang.
   d. Ming.
3. During the Ming period, Chinese-Japanese contacts were
   a. restricted to occasional commerce and raids by Japanese pirates.
   b. thriving on a number of fronts, both commercial and cultural.
   c. hostile and infrequent.
   d. marked by the Japanese willingness to accept China's dominance.
4. The Maritime Expeditions of the fifteenth century were
   a. the product of contacts with Arab traders.
   b. the result of Mongol invaders who had occupied China.
   c. the government-sponsored explorations of the Indian Ocean.
   d. begun at the initiative of private traders.
5. The replacement of the Ming by the Manzhou Qing dynasty was
   a. caused by a Japanese invasion of China and collapse of the Ming.
   b. a gradual armed takeover from a demoralized government.
   c. carried out by Westerners, anxious to install a "tame" government in Beijing.
   d. caused by Western Christian missionaries hostile to the Ming.
6. Which of the following did *not* figure prominently in Manzhou cultural achievement?
   a. Poetry
   b. Landscape painting
   c. Theology
   d. Fictional narratives
7. During the Ming/Manzhou era, China was ruled by a bureaucracy that was
   a. selected on the basis of aristocratic birth.
   b. controlled by a professional military establishment.
   c. dominated by the Buddhist priesthood.
   d. selected on the basis of written examinations.
8. The outstanding Qing emperors of the eighteenth century
   a. learned much of political value to them from the West.
   b. were cruel tyrants in their treatment of the common Chinese.
   c. split governmental responsibility between Manzhou and Chinese.
   d. tried hard to expand commerce between China and Europe.

IDENTIFICATION TERMS

The Dream of the Red Chamber

Forbidden City

Hongwu

Kangxi

Manchuria

Maritime Expeditions

Qienlong

Qing dynasty

Ricci, Matteo

INFOTRAC COLLEGE EDITION

Enter the search term "Ming China" using Key Words.

Enter the search term "China history" using Key Words.

31

JAPAN AND COLONIAL SOUTHEAST ASIA TO THE MID–NINETEENTH CENTURY

The white chrysanthemum
Even when lifted to the eye
Remains immaculate.

BASHO

1543	First European contacts with Japan
c. 1600	Tokugawa shogunate established
c. 1630s	Christianity suppressed; foreigners expelled/ *sakoku* begins
1600s–1700s	Money economy and commercial society develop
1853–1854	Perry opens Japan to trade; *sakoku* ends

PRIOR TO THE 1500s, the Japanese islands' contacts with the outer world were with Korea and China, only. The arrival of Portuguese trader-explorers brought change to a substantial segment of society, which adopted Christian belief. But this trend was later reversed by government action, and in a remarkable turnabout, the Japanese entered a long period of self-imposed seclusion.

Southeast Asia also experienced the European outreach, but in highly localized and restricted fashion, linked to the exclusive interest of the newcomers in the spice trade. Only much later, in the nineteenth century, did Europeans begin to develop Southeast Asian colonies.

JAPAN

Though akin to China in some ways, Japan was very different in many others. The political power of the emperor in Kyoto was quite weak throughout early modern times, and Japan became a collection of feudal provinces controlled by clans. In the century between the 1460s and the 1570s, the warrior-nobles—*daimyo*—had engaged in a frenzy of the "strong eating the weak." Finally, a series of military strongmen managed to restore order, culminating in the establishment of a type of centralized feudalism, the **shogunate.**

The first European contacts occurred in the mid-1500s, when traders and missionaries were allowed to establish themselves on Japanese soil. One of the most important trade items brought by the Portuguese was firearms. Another was the Christian Bible. Contacts with Europe were complicated by Japanese distrust of the Christian faith and its hints of submission to an alien culture. The shogun eventually decided that this danger was intolerable. Within a generation's time, Japan withdrew behind a wall of enforced isolation from the world, from which it would not emerge until the nineteenth century.

FIRST EUROPEAN CONTACTS: CHRISTIANITY

The Portuguese arrived in Japanese ports for the first time in 1543, looking for additional opportunities to make money from their active trading with all the Eastern countries.

They took Chinese silk to Japan and Japanese silver to China and used the profits from both to buy spices in the South Pacific islands to bring back to Portugal.

One of the first influences from the West to reach the thus-far isolated Japanese was Christianity, which arrived via the numerous Catholic missionaries sponsored by the Society of Jesus. The Jesuit order had been founded to fight Protestantism only a few years earlier, and its missionaries were well educated and highly motivated. For various reasons, a fair number of the daimyo were sympathetic to the Jesuit efforts and converted to Christianity during the 1550s and 1560s. By the year 1600, it is estimated that 300,000 Japanese had converted. That number would have

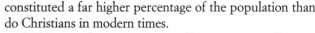 **Arrival of the Portuguese.** Note the black slave unloading the goods, showing that the Portuguese were already using black labor in their trans–Indian Ocean trade in the first half of the seventeenth century. The Japanese observer is possibly the merchant for whom the goods were consigned, and the monkey is the ship's mascot. (*© Giraudon/Art Resource, NY*)

constituted a far higher percentage of the population than do Christians in modern times.

At this time, the great majority of Japanese were adherents of either Shinto or one of the many varieties of Buddhism. Why did the ruling group allow the missionaries free access to the people? And why did the Japanese initially prove more receptive to Christianity than, for example, the Chinese or the Indians? It is impossible to say with certainty. One reason, certainly, was the personal example of the Jesuits, led by St. Francis Xavier, who greatly impressed their hosts with their piety and learning.

Other changes were under way. In the later 1500s, a movement for Japanese national unity led by **Oda Nobunaga** (1523–1582), a feudal lord who had fought his way to regional power, was getting under way. In the 1570s, the brutal Nobunaga succeeded in capturing Kyoto and most of the central island of Honshu, but he was killed by one of his cohorts. Following Nobunaga's death, his lieutenant **Toyotomi Hideyoshi** took over. Aided by the first large-scale use of firearms in Japan, Hideyoshi had visions of Asian, if not worldwide, supremacy. He invaded Korea with a well-equipped army of 150,000 as a first step toward the conquest of Ming China. Repulsed in 1592, he was in the midst of a second attempt when he died in 1598. After a couple of years of struggle among Hideyoshi's would-be successors, the baton was seized by the formidable warrior and statesman, **Tokugawa Ieyasu** (ruled 1603–1616). (See the Exercise of Authority box.)

Tokugawa ceased the abortive invasion of the mainland and by 1600 had beaten down his several internal rivals. Thus began the two and a half centuries of the Tokugawa shogunate, a military regency exercised in the name of a figurehead emperor. Tokugawa "ate the pie that Nobunaga made and Hideyoshi baked" goes the schoolchildren's axiom in modern Japan. He was the decisive figure in premodern Japanese history, using a selective violence against the daimyo to permit a special form of centralized governance.

THE TOKUGAWA SHOGUNATE

Once in power, Tokugawa continued and expanded the changes that Hideyoshi had begun. By disarming the peasants, Tokugawa removed much of the source of the rebellions that had haunted Japan during the preceding century. From this time on, only the professional warrior class, the **samurai,** and their daimyo employers had the right to own weapons. The daimyo, who were roughly equivalent to the barons of Europe some centuries earlier, were expected to spend half their time at the court of the shogun

TOKUGAWA IEYASU
(1542–1616)

On March 8, 1616, the shogun Tokugawa Ieyasu died. According to his wish, he was buried in Nikko, a beautiful wood ninety miles north of Tokyo. His tomb stands at the end of a long avenue of great gardens. Posthumously, Tokugawa was given the title "Noble of the First Rank, Great Light of the East, Great Incarnation of the Buddha." He was already acknowledged as the individual who brought law to a lawless society.

Tokugawa Ieyasu (that is, Ieyasu of the Tokugawa clan) was born in 1542. During the last decades of the sixteenth century, he became an ally of Toyotomi Hideyoshi, the most powerful of all the feudal aristocrats who divided the country among themselves. When Hideyoshi died unexpectedly in 1598, Ieyasu and another man were the prime candidates to succeed him. Tokugawa assembled a force of 80,000 feudal warriors, while his opponent led a coalition of 130,000. In the decisive battle of Sekigahara in 1600, the outnumbered Tokugawa forces claimed the field. In the next few years, Ieyasu destroyed the coalition's resistance and secured the shogun's office for himself and his second son. Ieyasu's victory was a turning point of great importance. For the next two and a half centuries, the Japanese were forced to live in peace with one another. This "Era of Great Peace" was marked by the Tokugawa clan's uninterrupted control of the shogunate in Edo (Tokyo), while the semidivine emperor resided in Kyoto and remained the symbolic center of Japanese patriotism.

Ieyasu was an extraordinarily gifted man. Coming out of the samurai tradition of military training, he was nevertheless able to appreciate the blessings of a permanent peace. He carefully redivided the feudal lords' domains throughout the islands so as to assure his control over all of them. He established the daimyo as the officials of his kingdom. They were given considerable freedom to do as they pleased in their own backyards, so long as their loyalty to the shogun was not in doubt.

Ieyasu and his successors in the 1600s did much to improve and nationalize Japan's economy, particularly among the peasant majority. The *heimin* or plain folk were divided into three basic groups: farmers, artisans, and traders, in that rank order. Farmers were generally regarded as honorable people, while traders were originally looked down upon, as in China. At the bottom of the social scale were the despised *hinin*, who were equivalent to the Indian untouchables. Unlike the untouchables, however, the hinin were able to rise in status.

In many ways, Tokugawa Ieyasu was the father of traditional Japan. The political institutions of the country did not change in any significant way after him until the late nineteenth century. He lives on in the pantheon of Japan's heroes as a model of military virtue, who reluctantly employed harsh and even brutal measures in order to bring about the rule of law in a lawless society.

FOR REFLECTION

Would there have been many alternatives to Tokugawa's method of imposing order in sixteenth-century Japan? What problems may arise from having absolute powers assertedly in one man's (the emperor's) hands, while another actually exercises them?

Tokugawa Ieyasu. This portrait was done after the powerful warrior had assured his position as shogun in 1603. *(Portrait of Tokugawa Ieyasu. The Tokugawa Art Museum, Nagoya, Japan)*

🔆 **Hideyoshi as Samurai.** This later illustration of General Hideyoshi allows close inspection of the traditional samurai costume and weapons. *(The Art Archive)*

country for half a century and put heavy pressure on the Christian Japanese to reconvert to Buddhism. After Christian peasants supported a revolt in 1637, pressure turned into outright persecution. Death became the standard penalty for Christian affiliation. In a few places, the Christians maintained their faith through "underground" churches and priests, but the majority gradually gave up their religion in the face of heavy state penalties and their neighbors' antagonism.

At the same time, Japan's extensive mercantile contacts with the Europeans and Chinese were almost entirely severed. Only a handful of Dutch and Portuguese traders/residents were allowed to remain in two ports (notably, Nagasaki, where two Dutch ships coming from the East Indies were allowed to land each year). The building of oceangoing ships by Japanese was forbidden. No foreigners could come to Japan, and no Japanese were allowed to reside abroad (with a few exceptions). Japanese who were living abroad were forbidden to return. The previously lively trade with China was sharply curtailed.

This isolation—called *sakoku* in Japanese history—lasted until the middle of the nineteenth century. It was a remarkable experiment with highly successful results so far as the ruling group was concerned. Japan went its own way and was ignored by the rest of the world.

Shogun, Emperor, and Daimyo

The Tokygawa shoguns continued the dual nature of Japanese government, whereby the shogunate was established at **Edo** (later Tokyo) while the emperor resided in the imperial palace at **Kyoto** and occupied himself with ritual and ceremony as the current holder of the lineage of the Sun Goddess who had created Japan eons earlier (see Chapter 19). True power in both a military and a political sense remained, of course, with the shogun, who now headed a council of state composed of daimyo aristocrats. An individual who was always a member of the Tokugawa clan acted in the name of the emperor while closely overseeing some twenty large and perhaps two hundred small land-holding daimyo who acted both as his agents and as autonomous regents in their own domains. The shogun himself controlled about one fourth of Japan as his own fiefdom. This system continued without important change until 1867.

The daimyo were the key players in governance and posed a constant potential threat to Tokugawa's arrangements. As the source of military power on the local level, they could tear down any shogun if they united against him. Therefore, to secure the center, the shogun had to play the daimyo against each other in the countryside. He did this

where they would be under the watchful eyes of the shogun and his network of informers.

In the early 1600s, the Tokugawa shoguns began to withdraw Japan into seclusion from outside influences. Earlier, Hideyoshi had had misgivings about the activities of the Jesuits within his domains, and in 1587 he had issued an order, later revoked, that they should leave. After newly arrived members of the Franciscan order attempted to meddle in the shogunate's internal affairs, Tokugawa acted. He evicted the Christian missionaries who had been in the

by constant intervention and manipulation, setting one clan against another in the competition for imperial favor. The shogun controlled the domains near Edo himself or put them in the hands of dependable allies. Domains on the outlying islands went to rival daimyo clans who would counterbalance one another. Meanwhile, the wives and children of the more important daimyo families were required to live permanently at Edo, where they served as hostages for loyal behavior. The whole system of supervision and surveillance much resembled Louis XIV's arrangements at Versailles in seventeenth-century France.

Economic Advances

Japan's society and economy changed markedly during the centuries of isolation. One of the most remarkable results of sakoku was the great growth of population and domestic trade. The population doubled in the seventeenth century and continued to increase gradually throughout the remainder of the Tokugawa period. The closing off of trade with foreigners apparently stimulated internal production, rather than discouraged it, and domestic trade rose accordingly. The internal peace imposed by the powerful and respected government of the shogunate certainly helped. The daimyo aristocracy had an ever-increasing appetite for fine wares such as silk and ceramics. Their fortress-palaces in Edo and on their domains reflected both their more refined taste and their increasing ability to satisfy it.

The merchants, who previously had occupied a rather low niche in Japanese society (as in China) and had never been important in government, now gradually gained a much more prominent place. Formerly, the mercantile and craft guilds had restricted access to the market, but the early shoguns forced them to dissolve, thereby allowing many new and creative actors to come onto the entrepreneurial stage. Even so, the merchants as a class were still not as respected as were government officials, scholars, and especially the daimyo and their samurai. Nevertheless, the merchants' growing wealth, which they often lent—at high interest—to impoverished samurai, began to enhance their prestige. A money economy gradually replaced the universal reliance on barter in the villages.

Commercialization and distribution networks for artisans invaded the previously self-sufficient lifestyle of the country folk. Banks and the use of credit became more common during the later Tokugawa period. Some historians see the growth of a specifically Japanese form of capitalism long before Japan's entry into the world economic system in the later nineteenth century.

Peasants and Urbanites

The condition of the peasants, who, of course, still made up the vast majority of the population, improved somewhat under the early Tokugawa regime. Since the beginnings of the shogunate under the Fujiwara clan, the peasantry had

"Sunrise." This woodcut by the famed engraver Hiroshige (1797–1858) shows a typical procession of laborers going to work in a seaside town, while the fishermen raise sail and the rice sellers ready their booths for the morning trade along the quay. The long net is presumably for capturing birds that will be put into the cages and sold. (*Musée des Beaux-Arts, Angers, France. © Giraudon/Art Resource, NY*)

been sacrificed to keep the daimyo and their samurai retainers satisfied. In most of the Japanese lands, the peasant was no better than a serf and lived in misery. In the early Tokugawa era, the peasants received some protection from exploitation, and the shogun's government claimed that agriculture was the most honorable of ordinary occupations. But the government's taxes were heavy, taking up to 60 percent of the rice crop, which was by far the most important harvest. In later years, the increasing misery of some of the peasants led to many provincial rebellions, not against the shogun but against the local daimyo who were their landlords. These revolts, though numerous, were on a much smaller scale than those that would trouble Manzhou China in the same nineteenth-century epoch.

Cities grew rapidly during the first half of the Tokugawa period, more slowly later. Both Osaka and Kyoto were estimated to have more than 400,000 inhabitants in the eighteenth century, and Edo perhaps as many as 1 million. All three cities were bigger than any town in Europe at that date. The urban population ranged from very rich daimyo and merchants at the top, through tens of thousands of less fortunate traders, shopkeepers, and officials of all types in the middle, and many hundreds of thousands of skilled and unskilled workers, casual laborers, beggars, prostitutes, artists, and the unlucky samurai at the bottom. Most Japanese, however, still lived as before in small towns and villages. They depended on local farming, timbering, or fishing for their livelihood and were in only occasional and superficial contact with the urban culture. Until the twentieth century, the rhythms of country life and rice culture were the dominant influence on the self-image and the lifestyle of the Japanese people.

TAMING THE SAMURAI

In the seventeenth and eighteenth centuries, the samurai caste, which had been the military servants of the wealthy daimyo and their "enforcers" with the peasants, lost most of its prestige in Japanese society. Estimated to make up as much as 7 percent of the population at the establishment of the Tokugawa regime, the samurai had now become superfluous. With the establishment of the lasting domestic peace, there was literally nothing for them to do in their traditional profession. They were not allowed to become merchants or to adopt another lifestyle, nor could they easily bring themselves to do so after centuries of proud segregation from the common herd. The Edo government encouraged the samurai to do what they naturally wished to do: enjoy themselves beyond their means. Borrowing from the merchants, the samurai tried to outdo one another in every sort of showy display. After a generation or two, the result was mass bankruptcies and social disgrace.

The fallen samurai were replaced in social status by newcomers who were finding they could advance through commerce or through the civil bureaucracy. As in the West,

this bureaucracy was slowly assuming the place of the feudal barons and becoming the day-to-day authority in governance. The samurai lost out to a new class of people—men who did not know how to wield a sword but were good with a pen. Trained only to make war and raised in the bushido code of the warrior, most of the samurai were ill equipped to make the transition from warrior to desk-sitting official of the shogun or a daimyo lord. The majority seem to have gradually sunk into poverty and loss of status as they reverted to the peasant life of their long-ago ancestors.

TOKUGAWA ARTS AND LEARNING

The almost 250 years of peace of the Tokugawa period produced a rich tapestry of new cultural ideas and practices in Japan. Some of the older ideas, imported originally from China, were now adapted so as to become almost entirely Japanese in form and content. The upper classes continued to prefer Buddhism in one form or another, with a strong admixture of Confucian secular ethics. Among the people, Shinto and the less intellectual forms of Buddhism formed the matrix of belief about this world and the next. Japanese religious style tended to accept human nature as it is without the overtones of penitence and reform so prominent in Western thought. As before, there was a very strong current of eclecticism, blending Buddhism with other systems of belief and practice.

Literature and Its Audiences

Literacy rates were quite high in Japan and became still higher in the later years of the Tokugawa period, when perhaps as many as 50 percent of the males could read and write the cheap product of woodblock printing presses. This percentage was at least equal to the literacy rate in central Europe of the day and was facilitated by the relative ease of learning the phonetic written language (in distinct contrast to Chinese, the original source of Japanese writing).

Literature aimed at popular entertainment began to appear in new forms that were a far cry from the elegant and restrained traditions of the past. Poetry, novels, social satires, and Kabuki plays were the foremost types of literature. By this era, all had liberated themselves from imitation of classical Chinese models. Several were entirely original with the Japanese.

Haiku poems, especially in the hands of the revered seventeenth-century poet Basho, were extraordinarily compact revelations of profound thought. In three lines and seventeen syllables (always), the poet reflected the Zen Buddhist conviction that the greatest of mysteries can only be stated—never analyzed. Basho's contributions in poetry were matched by those of Saikaku in fiction, also during the late seventeenth century. His novels and stories about ordinary people are noteworthy for their passion and the underlying sense of comedy with which the characters are observed. Saikaku's stories, like Basho's verse, are read today in Japan with the same admiration they have enjoyed for centuries.

Kabuki is a peculiarly Japanese form of drama. It is highly realistic, often humorous and satirical, and sometimes violent in both action and emotions. For its settings, it often made use of the "floating world," the unstable but attractive world of brothels, shady teahouses, and gambling dens. Kabuki was wildly popular among the upper classes in seventeenth- and eighteenth-century Japan. It was not unusual for a particularly successful actor (males played all parts) to become a pampered "star." Actors were often also male prostitutes, just as actresses in the West often were female prostitutes at this time. Homosexuality was strongly frowned upon by the shogunate authorities, but it had already had a long tradition among the samurai and some branches of Buddhism.

Himeji Castle. This relatively late construction, known as the White Egret to the Japanese, stands today as a major tourist attraction. The massive stone walls successfully resisted all attackers. *(Steve Vidler/eStock Photo)*

Adaptation and Originality

In the fine arts, Japan may have drawn its initial inspiration from Chinese models, but it always turned those models into something different, something specifically Japanese. This pattern can be found in landscape painting, poetry, adventure and romance stories, gardens, and ceramics—indeed, in any art medium that both peoples have pursued. The Japanese versions were often filled with a playful humor missing in the Chinese original and were almost always consciously close to nature, the soil, and the peasantry. The refined intellectualism common to Chinese arts appeared less frequently in Japan. As a random example, the rough-and-tumble of Kabuki and the pornographic jokes that the actors constantly employed were specifically Japanese and had no close equivalent in China.

The merchants who had prospered during the Tokugawa era were especially important as patrons of the arts. Again, there is a parallel with the European experience, but with differences. The European bourgeoisie became important commissioners of art two centuries earlier than the Japanese merchants and did so in self-confident rivalry with the nobles and church. Japan had no established church, and the bourgeoisie never dared challenge the daimyo nobility for taste-setting primacy. Nevertheless, high-quality painting and wood-block prints displaying a tremendous variety of subjects and techniques came to adorn the homes and collections of the rich merchants. In fact, much of what the modern world knows of seventeenth- and eighteenth-century Japanese society is attributable to the knowing eye and talented hands of the artists rather than to historians. Unlike the Chinese, the Japanese never revered compilers of records. There are no Japanese equivalents of the great Chinese histories.

Response to the Western Challenge

In the later Tokugawa, the main emphasis of Japanese thought shifted from Buddhist to Confucian ideals, which is another way of saying that it shifted from an otherworldly emphasis to an empirical concern with this world. The Japanese version of Confucianism was, as always, different from the Chinese. The secular, politically pragmatic nature of Confucius's doctrines comes through more emphatically in Japan. The Chinese mandarins of the nineteenth century had little tolerance for deviation from the prescribed version of the Master. But in Japan, several schools contended, unimpeded by an official prescription of right and wrong. Another difference was that whereas China had no room for a shogun, Japan had no room for the mandate of Heaven. Chinese tradition held that *only* China could be the Confucian "Empire of the Middle." The Japanese, on the other hand, while confident they were in that desirable position of centrality and balance, believed they need not ignore the achievements of other, less fortunate but not entirely misguided folk.

What was the significance of this pragmatic secularism for Japan? It helped prepare the ruling daimyo group for the invasion of Western ideas that came in the mid–nineteenth century. The Japanese elite were able to abandon their seclusion and investigate whatever Western technology could offer them with an open mind. In sharp contrast to China, when the Western avalanche could no longer be evaded, the Japanese governing class accepted it with little inherent resistance or cultural confusion.

At the outset of the Tokugawa shogunate, the Japanese educated classes were perhaps as familiar with science and technology as were the Westerners. Sakoku necessarily inhibited further progress. The Scientific Revolution and its accompanying technological advances were quite unknown in Japan, and the Enlightenment of the eighteenth century was equally foreign to the cultural landscape of even the most refined citizens (see Chapter 35). From the early 1800s, a few Japanese scholars and officials were aware that the West (including nearby Russia) was well ahead of them in certain areas, especially the natural sciences and medicine, and that much could be learned from the Westerners. These Japanese were in contact with the handful of Dutch merchants who had been allowed to stay in Japan and occasionally read Western science texts. "Dutch medicine," as Western anatomy, pharmacy, and surgery were called, was fairly well-known in upper-class Japan in the early nineteenth century, although it did not yet have much prestige.

When the American naval commander **Matthew Perry** arrived with his "black ships" to open the country forcibly to foreign traders in 1853 and 1854, the Japanese were not as ill prepared as one might assume after two centuries of isolation. Aided by the practical and secular Confucianist philosophy they had imbibed, the sparse but important Western scientific books they had studied, and the carefully balanced government they had evolved by trial and error, the Edo government, the daimyo, and their subofficials were able to absorb Western ideas and techniques by choice rather than force. Rather than looking down their cultured noses at what the "hairy barbarians" might be bringing, the Japanese were able to say, "If it works to our benefit (or can be made to), use it." Unlike China, the Japanese were decidedly not overwhelmed by the West. On the contrary, they were true to their nation's tradition by showing themselves to be confident and pragmatic adapters of what they thought useful to themselves, rejecting the rest.

Southeast Asia

The territories in Southeast Asia that had succeeded in achieving political organization prior to the appearance of European traders and missionaries had little reason to fear or even take much notice of them until a much later era. Contacts were limited to coastal towns and were mainly commercial in nature. In the 1600s, the Dutch had driven the Portuguese entirely out of the islands' spice trade, and they had established a loose partnership with the local Muslim sultans in Java and Sumatra in assuring the continuance of that trade with Europe. After a brief contest with the Dutch, the British, in the form of the East India Company,

Asian Wildlife

The sights and sounds of Southeast Asia were a series of novel, sometimes frightening impressions on the first European explorers on those lands and waters. One of the early Portuguese pathbreakers, Fernando Mendes Pinto, was exceptional in leaving a journal of his experiences from which the following glimpse of the exotic wildlife of the island of Sumatra is taken:

> Journeying upriver from the Sumatran coast: we could see between the thick jungle growth a large number of snakes and other creatures of such extraordinary sizes and shapes that one would very much fear to mention it, at any rate, to people who have not seen much of the world, for inasmuch as they have seen little, they are also apt to give little credence to what others have seen a great deal of.
>
> All along the river, which was not very wide, there were a great many lizards* though serpents would be a more appropriate name for them because some of them were as big as a good sized almadia [dugout canoe] with scales on their backs and mouths more than two spans wide; and from what the natives told us, they were extremely bold and quick to attack, and very often they would lunge at an almadia that had only three or four blacks on board, upsetting it with a swish of their tail and devouring the occupants one by one as they floundered in the water, without tearing them to pieces, just swallowing them whole.

*These are the Komodo dragons, the world's largest lizards, found only in the Indonesian archipelago. Their fierceness is well attested to by modern researchers.

Source: Rebecca Catz, ed. and trans., The Travels of Mendes Pinto (Chicago: University of Chicago Press, 1989), pp. 23–24.

had withdrawn from the Spice Islands to concentrate on Indian cotton goods. Only in the Spanish Philippines was a European presence pervasive and politically dominant over a sizable area.

Most of the insular Asians were by now converted to Islam, a process begun in the 1400s through contact with Arab and Indian Muslim traders. Except for the island of Bali, the original syncretic blend of Hindu with animist beliefs that had been India's legacy had faded away. Only in the Philippines was there a Christian element.

If the islands were relatively untouched by the early European traders, the mainland populations were even less so. In the 1700s, the three states of Thailand, Burma, and Vietnam dominated the area. The first two were by then part of the *Hinayana* Buddhist world, while Vietnam under Chinese influence had remained with the *Mahayana* version of the faith. The once-potent Khmer state of Cambodia had been divided between the Thais and the Viets by stages during the fifteenth through seventeenth centuries. Nowhere was there a visible European influence so late as the end of the eighteenth century, but this was to change radically in the next.

The Colonial Experience

In the early nineteenth century, a generation of European administrator-scholars entered on colonial careers following the Napoleonic wars (see Chapter 37). These men were products of the Enlightenment and often sincerely dedicated to a humane treatment of their Southeast Asian charges while still convinced adherents of Western cultural superiority. Foremost among them was Sir Thomas Raffles, the founder of Singapore and the first European to take serious interest in the history and archaeology of the precolonial societies. Although Raffles was entrusted with oversight of affairs only for a few brief years in Java, his reforming policies aimed at promoting peasant prosperity and local government autonomy persisted as a model, unfortunately not often followed in the century to come.

Indonesia was returned to Dutch rule in 1824 by a treaty that finally settled the ancient Anglo-Dutch rivalry. In the century that followed, Dutch administrators gradually expanded their controls, both political and economic, over the hundreds of inhabited islands that make up the "East Indies" (see Map 31.1). The bloody five-year Java War (1825–1830) was the decisive step, establishing Dutch sovereignty once and for all over this most important of the Indonesian lands. Others had to be fought in Sumatra and in the Celebes at the end of the nineteenth century. Only then was a true Dutch colony, rather than a trade partnership, created.

In the economic sphere the Dutch directed a change from a limited, spice export trade with the homeland to an expansive, commodity-oriented trade during the middle of the nineteenth century. This change was accomplished via the "**culture system,**" a refined form of peonage through which the peasants were obliged to deliver a major part of their crops to Dutch buyers at minimal prices. It brought poverty to the Indonesians and great profits for the Dutch and Chinese middlemen, especially from the export of coffee, which replaced spices as the most important crop in the colony. The blatant abuses of the peasant laborers finally led to humanitarian reforms in the latter part of the century. But by this time, Java and Bali had been thrust into a cycle of declining availability of land and a rising population of rural tenants working absentee landlord estates. The resentments thus bred would inspire a tide of nationalist sentiment in the early twentieth century.

In mainland Asia, the assertion of Western colonial power extended first to the Burmese kingdom. As the British East India Company gradually transformed itself from a private commercial venture to a colonial government in India (see Chapter 32), its agents came into conflict with the claims of the Burmese rulers to certain frontier districts. A brief war ensued, with the customary results in favor of the Europeans. The process was renewed twice more in the middle of the nineteenth century, and the Burmese eventually submitted to imperial oversight as a province of British India.

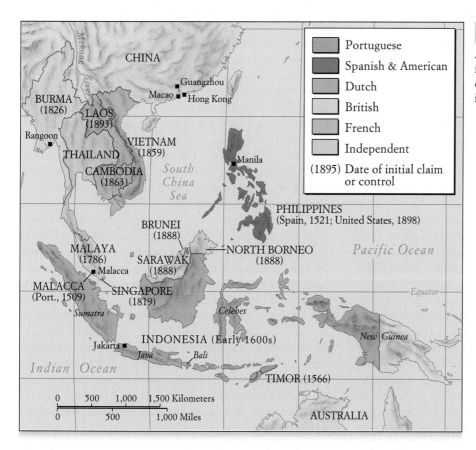

MAP 31.1 Colonial Southeast Asia, c. 1850. At this point, European imperialism was just getting under way on the mainland but had a long history in the islands of Java and the Philippines.

Singapore's Inner Harbor. The hundreds of sampans crowding the waterways of modern Singapore have not changed in design or use for several hundred years, since the Europeans first arrived in the Straits area. (*© Charles Rotkin/Corbis*)

The sultans of Malaya (in the lower reach of the long Malay peninsula) followed a somewhat different route into the imperial camp. Here, the British at Singapore were joined by an influx of Chinese who quickly came to dominate the increasing trade going through the Straits of Malacca. By the 1870s (following the opening of the Suez Canal linking the Mediterranean and the Red Sea), this was the world's busiest waterway. Steamships and sailing vessels of many nations carried trade between Asian countries and took part in the long-distance transport between Asia and Europe. The remarkable growth of world markets for tin and rubber, both of which were found in abundance in the peninsula, also spurred alien business interests there. One after the other, the undeveloped sultanates were peaceably melded into the British "Straits Settlements," with a large population of immigrant Chinese in the mines and plantations. By the opening of the twentieth century, this jerry-built aggregation had become the colony of Malaya.

Vietnam fell under French dominion in this same epoch, largely because of the imperial ambitions of a handful of French leaders who felt that Paris was falling behind London in the race for colonial riches. A secondary reason was the determination of the Catholic leadership in France to use Vietnam as the portal to the conversion of China to the Roman faith. French missionaries had been engaged among the Viets since the seventeenth century and had made considerable progress by the early years of the nineteenth. At that time, they and their converts were subjected to an intense anti-Catholic campaign by a successful contestant in the recurrent civil wars that marked Vietnamese nineteenth-century history. This was the justification for French military intervention beginning in the 1850s and continuing at intervals until all of the **Union of Indochina**—the official name for the colony—was under Parisian oversight by the end of the century. It included the present-day states of Vietnam, Laos, and Cambodia.

As in Malaya, economic development picked up rapidly after the coming of the Europeans. Capital and steam power brought the great rice-growing area of the lower Mekong River valley into production for the first time, and Vietnam became the premier exporter of rice to the world markets. Rubber plantations followed. Unfortunately, the rice fields and plantations were owned either by aliens or by a small clique of francophile aristocrats. The economic lot of the Vietnamese villagers deteriorated as a result of the new developments. Just as in Dutch-ruled Indonesia, the visible and growing cleft between the mass of the inhabitants and the European/bourgeois governmental class inspired the rise of a strong nationalism among some of the newly educated.

Among the Southeast Asian nations, only Thailand (still known as Siam) escaped the colonial net and remained independent. How did this happen? It was due in part to the 1893 agreement between the British in India and the French in Indochina that it would be convenient to maintain a buffer between their respective colonies and that could only be Thailand. It was also partly due to the quite remarkable vision and diplomatic skills of two of the nineteenth-century Thai kings, **Mongkut** (ruled 1851–1868), and his son and successor, Chulalongkorn (ruled 1868–1910). The two kings together brought their country into the modern age, introducing a wide variety of Western-style governmental and technical ideas into the still very traditional Thai culture. These reforms ranged from overhauls of the judicial system to setting up a telegraph line, from abolition of the traditional prostration in the royal presence to the first printing press.

Although the premier foreign influence remained Britain, the Thai kings made it a point to invite advisers from many nations to assist them in their campaign of modernization. Not only were foreigners made to feel secure and well rewarded for their efforts, but the numerous members of the ruling clan were encouraged to undergo Western education in several different countries before returning to take up their governmental duties. As a result of these policies of openness and technical progress, Thailand entered the twentieth century not only independent but also poised to meet Western cultural imperialism with an awakening sense of Thai national pride and a conviction of equality with the aliens.

SUMMARY

After a century of unchecked feudal warfare in Japan, three strongmen arose in the late sixteenth century to re-create effective centralized government. Last and most important was Tokugawa Ieyasu, who crushed or neutralized all opposition, including that of the Christian converts who were the product of the first European contacts with Japan in the mid-1500s.

By the 1630s, Japan was rapidly isolating itself from the world under the Tokugawa shogunate. The chief goal of the Tokugawa shoguns was a class-based political stability, which they successfully pursued for centuries. The shogun controlled all contacts with foreigners and gradually ended them so as to isolate the island empire for over 200 years. The daimyo nobility were carefully controlled by the shogun in Edo who ruled from behind the imperial throne. Social changes took place on a massive scale at the same time the feudal political structure remained immobile. While urban merchants rose in the socioeconomic balance and peasants became wage laborers, the samurai slowly declined into obsolescence.

Population surged and the general economy prospered. The arts, particularly literature and painting, flourished. When Japan's solitude was finally broken, the governing elite were ready to deal with the challenge of Western science and technology in a constructive manner.

In Southeast Asia, the colonial period commenced with Dutch and Spanish presence in the Indonesian and Philippine Islands, respectively. But as late as the end of the eighteenth century, the Western traders and missionaries had had relatively very little impact on the mass of the native inhabitants of the islands and even less on the mainland. This situation changed gradually but with increasing rapidity. The nineteenth century saw both a transformation of the former subsistence economy of the peasantry and the introduction of direct European control of government both in the islands and on the mainland. By 1900, the entire region had become a European colony, except for Thailand.

TEST YOUR KNOWLEDGE

1. The early Christian missionaries to Japan
   a. found a very hostile reception.
   b. were mainly Protestants.
   c. made the mistake of trying to conquer the Buddhist natives.
   d. were made welcome and given a hearing.
2. The Shinto faith is best described as
   a. the native Japanese religion.
   b. the Japanese Holy Scripture.
   c. a mixture of Christianity and Japanese pagan belief.
   d. a variety of Buddhism imported from Korea.
3. The Tokugawa shogun is best described as a
   a. military dictator.
   b. military adviser to the emperor.
   c. chief of government under the supposed supervision of the emperor.
   d. symbolic and religious leader under the emperor's supervision.

4. The government system created by the shoguns in the 1600s
   a. allowed the local chieftains called *daimyo* to rule unchecked.
   b. was an imitation of the Chinese system of mandarin officials.
   c. made the daimyo dependent on the shogun's favor.
   d. used the emperor as military chief while the shoguns ruled all else.

5. Which of the following did *not* occur during the Tokugawa period?
   a. Japanese elite thought shifted from Buddhist to Confucian patterns.
   b. Japanese formal culture stagnated in its continued isolation from the world.
   c. Trade and economic activity generally increased.
   d. Internal peace and order were effectively maintained.

6. The reduction of the samurai's influence in public affairs was
   a. carried out through government-ordered purges.
   b. attempted but not achieved during the shogunate period.
   c. achieved by eliminating internal warfare through a strong government.
   d. achieved by encouraging them to become merchants and landlords.

7. The Kabuki drama
   a. specialized in dreamy romantic comedies.
   b. was limited in appeal to the samurai and daimyo.
   c. depicted drama in daily life in a realistic, humorous way.
   d. was an import from China.

8. Which of the following art forms was an original Japanese invention?
   a. Wood-block printing
   b. Haiku
   c. Nature poetry
   d. Weaving of silk tapestry

9. The culture system was introduced in
   a. French Vietnam to assure supply of rice to the peasantry.
   b. Dutch Indonesia to assure export profits.
   c. British Malaya to get the rubber plantations started.
   d. Spanish Philippines to support the Catholic Church clergy.

10. Thailand's continuing independence is largely attributable to
    a. the conflict between Vietnam and Burma.
    b. the determination of the Thai people.
    c. the protection afforded by the Manchu emperors in China.
    d. the desire for a buffer between India and Indochina.

IDENTIFICATION TERMS

culture system	**Hideyoshi, Toyotomi**	**Kyoto**	***sakoku***
daimyo	**Ieyasu, Tokugawa**	**Nobunaga, Oda**	**shogunate**
Edo	**Kabuki**	**Perry, Matthew**	**Union of Indochina**
haiku	**King Mongkut**	***samurai***	

INFOTRAC COLLEGE EDITION

Enter the search term "Japan history" using Key Words.

Enter the search term "Tokugawa" using Key Words.

THE RISE AND FALL OF MUSLIM EMPIRES

*H*e who cannot love another human
being is ignorant of life's joy.

SA'ADI

1200s–MID-1300s	Mongol empire in Eurasia
1300s–1500s	Ottoman empire expands and flourishes
1500s–1722	Safavid empire in Persia
1500s–MID-1800s	Mughal empire in India
LATER 1600s	Ottoman decline begins

WHILE EUROPE WAS SLOWLY finding its way from feudal disintegration to early statehood, and East Asian governments were experiencing challenges from both external and internal rivals, the world of Islam in Asia and Africa was undergoing seemingly endless and enormous upheavals. The Islamic world did not have a Middle Age of governmental evolution and consolidation. Instead, a series of destructive intrafaith wars wracked the West Asian centers of Islamic civilization and contributed much to its slow decline after 1700.

In Chapter 15, we looked at the rapid rise of Islam in the tropical zone between Spain and India. Within a remarkably few decades, the Arab Bedouin armies carried the message of Muhammed the Prophet from Mecca in all directions on the blades of their conquering swords. The civilization created by this message and conquest was soon a mixture of Arab, Greek, Persian, Egyptian, Spanish, and others—the most cosmopolitan civilization in world history.

In the thirteenth century, the capital city of Islam was still Baghdad in Iraq, although various segments of the faithful had long since broken off in both a governmental and doctrinal sense. In that century, the yet-pagan Mongols swept into the Islamic heartland in Southwest Asia, devastating all in their path and establishing brief sway over half the world. After their disappearance, the Ottoman Turks gave the faith of the Prophet a new forward thrust. By the later 1400s, the Ottomans had captured Constantinople and were reigning over enormous territories reaching from Gibraltar to Persia. Farther east and somewhat later, the Safavids in Persia and the Mughals in India established Muslim dynasties that endured into the modern age.

THE MONGOL WORLD EMPIRE

Ethnically speaking, Islam's origins were Arabic and Persian. The Bedouins who had conquered Persia in the 640s were quickly absorbed by the much more sophisticated and numerous Persians. Unlike the Arabs, the Persians had long been accustomed to serving as rulers and models for others, and they reasserted those talents after mass conversion to Islam. For two centuries, the message of the Qur'an came through an Arab-Persian filter. In the 900s a new ethnic group, the Turkic peoples, began to dominate the religion and culture. In the next centuries, the Seljuks who initially took over the Baghdad caliphate and their Mongol successors gave Islam a Turco-Mongol cast that it retained for centuries.

The Conquering Khans

The Mongol invasion of what the West calls the Middle East began in the early thirteenth century under the leadership of the fierce Temujin, better known to history as **Chinghis Khan** (1167–1227) (see the Exercise of Authority box in this chapter). As Chapter 16 described, by the mid–thirteenth century, the Mongols had amassed the largest land empire ever created, extending from Korea to the Danube in eastern Europe (see Map 32.1).

Everywhere, the invaders distinguished themselves by their exceptional bloodthirstiness toward those who resisted (see the box on the Mongol Army), and everywhere they were despised as cultural inferiors. This was particularly true in China, but also in the Christian and Muslim lands they overran. Many of the conquered territories had been under Persian Muslim rule for centuries and had developed a highly civilized lifestyle. Cities such as Samarkand,

Bokhara, Herat, and Baghdad itself suffered terrible devastation, and some never recovered their former wealth and importance.

The Mongols believed that their great spirit-god, Tengri, had commanded them to conquer the world, and they came very close to doing so. Neither Christians nor Hindus nor Buddhists were able to stop them, and only their defeat at **Ain Jalut,** near Nazareth in Palestine, by an Egyptian commander saved the remaining Muslim lands. Coming two years after the Mongol conquest of Baghdad in 1258, this victory revived Muslim resistance and is one of the handful of truly decisive battles of world history.

Along with the destruction they brought, the Mongol hordes also opened some notable possibilities for the traders and merchants among the peoples they had conquered. For about a century, the ***pax Mongolica*** (peace of the Mongols) extended for many thousands of miles, all under the supervision of the Great Khan and the relatives and clan leaders he appointed as his subordinates from his headquarters in Karakorum. Goods could be safely transported from the coast of China to the towns of the eastern Mediterranean, so long as a tribute or tax was paid to the khan's agents. It was the first and only time that all of main-

MAP 32.1 The Mongol Empire in 1255. In the early 1200s, Chinghis Khan created the vastest empire ever seen. His sons and grandsons expanded and divided the empire after his death in 1227. Except for India and the far southeast, almost all of Asia and eastern Europe was under Mongol sway. The Yuan dynasty in China was the host of Marco Polo.

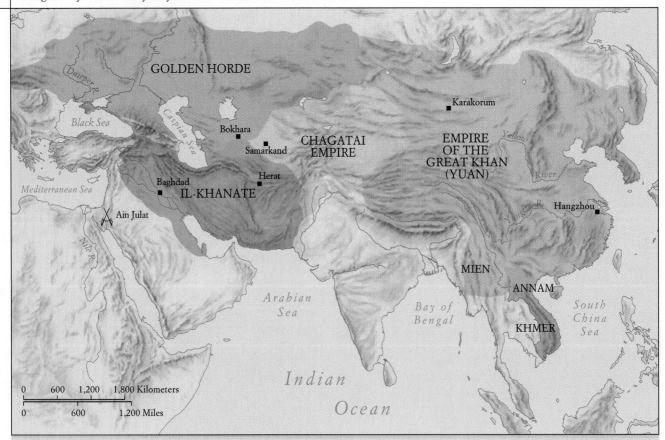

CHINGHIS KHAN
(1167–1227)

If one measures greatness by area, there can be no doubt at all as to who is the greatest ruler in world history. It is the illiterate son of a twelfth-century Mongol who was named Temujin but adopted the title of Chinghis Khan in later life. Before his death in 1227, he had come to rule a vast territory from the south Russian steppes to the China Sea. His sons and successors expanded the Mongol empire even farther, until it was easily the largest the world has ever seen.

Temujin was born about 1167 into a violent landscape and had to struggle almost from birth against harsh competitors. Mongolia at this time was the home of primitive nomads who warred against one another continuously when they were not assaulting the richer lands of the Chinese and Koreans. By 1200, Temujin had established his claim by right of conquest to be the leader of a confederation of several tribes. A few years later in his capital at Karakorum, he accepted the title of Great King (Chinghis Khan) of the Mongols and imposed a tight military order on his several hundreds of thousands of followers.

The prime advantage of the Mongols in war was their ability to cover long distances more rapidly than any of their enemies. Virtually living on their small, hardy ponies, the Mongol warriors combined the tactic of surprise with an uncanny accuracy with the bow and arrow and the ability to use massed cavalry against their mainly infantry opponents. The Mongols would bypass walled strongholds where the cavalry charge would be ineffective and starve them into submission by controlling the surrounding countryside.

Using these tactics, Chinghis Khan conquered much of north China in only two years (1213–1215) and then turned west

Chinghis Khan. (*Bibliothèque Nationale, Paris, France/ Bridgeman Art Library*)

against the Turks and Persians. By his death, all of what is now Central Asia and western Siberia was under Mongol rule. Proud cities such as Bokhara, Samarkand, and Herat, all centers of a high Muslim civilization, were overwhelmed after desperate resistance and their populations massacred or led into slavery. Mosques were turned into stables, and libraries burned. Never had such destruction been seen, and word of an approaching Mongol army was sometimes enough to cause wholesale flight. Russia was spared for a few more years only by Chinghis Khan's death, which necessitated a great conclave of the other Mongol chieftains to determine succession.

Chinghis Khan had ruled by installing members of his family in positions of command as he fought his way into western Asia. His sons and grandsons succeeded him and divided the huge empire among themselves. The richest part, China, went to Kubilai Khan, the host of Marco Polo. Gradually, the wild Mongols came to see that the arts of civilized life brought greater rewards than the practice of terror on defenseless subjects. By the later 1200s, many of them had adopted either the Chinese lifestyle as the rulers of that nation or had joined with their Turkic allies to adopt the Muslim religion and Islamic civilization. The vast empire founded by Chinghis Khan broke into pieces by the later 1300s, but not before it had given the world a name that would always strike terror into the hearts of the civilized.

FOR REFLECTION

Why was the question of succession to Chinghis Khan's position so difficult for the Mongols? Why was the early twelfth century a time of attack from two sides for the Islamic faithful?

land Asia (except southern India) was under the rule of a single power, and a few areas and cities prospered to an unprecedented degree as a result.

Fragmenting Empire

The Mongols had five Great Khans in the 1200s, beginning with Chinghis and ending with the death of Kubilai Khan

in 1294. After that, the ethnic segments of the huge empire went their own ways. The primitive nomadic culture and the Mongols' approach to government (exploitation through conquest) would have made it difficult to maintain their vast domain under a single center, even if much better communications and a much larger pool of loyal officials had been available. Since they were not, the original unified conquest broke up in a century. First China, then Russia

The Mongol Army

Shortly after the devastating Mongol attack, a high-ranking Persian Muslim, Ala-ad-Din-Juvaini, wrote *The History of the World Conqueror.* Clearly impressed by the new overlords, he spoke of the discipline of the Mongol army:

> What army can equal the Mongol army? In time of action when attacking and assaulting, they are like trained wild beasts out after game, and in the days of peace and security they are like sheep, yielding milk, and wool and many other useful things. In misfortune and adversity they are free of dissension and opposition. It is an army after the fashion of a peasantry, being liable to all manner of contributions, and rendering without complaint what is enjoined upon it. . . . It is also a peasantry in the guise of an army, all of them, great and small, noble and base, in time of battle becoming swordsmen, archers and lancers in whatever manner the occasion requires. . . .
>
> Their obedience and submissiveness is such that if there be a commander of a hundred thousand [men] between whom and the Khan there is a distance of sunrise and sunset, and if he but commit some fault, the Khan dispatches a single horseman to punish him after the manner prescribed; if his head has been demanded, he cuts it off, and if gold be required, he takes it from him.

Source: Ala-ad-Din Ata-Malik Juvaini, The History of the World Conqueror, *trans. J. A. Boyle (Manchester: 1958), vol. I, p. 23; cited in* The Islamic World, *ed. W. H. McNeill and M. R. Waldman (Oxford: Oxford University Press, 1973).*

---

and the Middle Eastern lands separated from one another under subkhanates with their own conflicting interests. Successive intra-Mongol fights for regional supremacy after 1280 further weakened the power of the dynasty.

The second and third generations of Mongol rulers were more sensitive to their subjects' needs and expectations and included some exceptionally able men. Their adoption of one or another of the competing religions of Asia also enhanced their prestige for a time at least. Kubilai Khan (ruled 1260–1294), the host of Marco Polo and the introducer of many new ideas into the closed Chinese universe, favored Buddhism. One of the Middle Eastern khans adopted the Muslim faith in the 1290s and simultaneously began the revival of Persian power and prestige. The Russian-based Mongols (the "Golden Horde") also adopted Islam in the late 1200s, but their conversion had no influence on the Russian people, who remained steadfast in their Eastern Orthodox Christianity.

Gradually, the Mongols' far more numerous Christian (Russia, Near East), Muslim (Middle East, India), and Buddhist (China, Tibet) subjects began to make their presence felt, as they civilized and to some degree absorbed their conquerors. By the mid-1300s, the empire was disintegrating into its preconquest component parts, and rebellions against Mongol rulers were multiplying. In China and Persia first (late 1300s), then the Near East and Russia (1400s),

Mongol rule became a bad memory. The former rulers were either absorbed into the subject populations or retired back into their desolate Central Asian homelands.

THE OTTOMAN TURKS

The Mongols had smashed the Persian center of Islam in the 1250s, leaving the caliph himself as one of the corpses in Baghdad. At this time, the all-conquering intruders intended to wipe out the rest of the Islamic states reaching westward to Spain. One of these was the Ottoman principality in what is now Turkey, which took full advantage of the Mongols' defeat at Ain Jalut to maintain its independence.

The Ottomans (the name comes from Osman, their first chieftain) originated as a frontier force, guarding central Turkey from the Greek Christians across the straits in Constantinople. Having converted to Islam in the 1200s, they were famed as fanatical warriors for the jihad. By the 1300s, they had established a beachhead in Europe against the weakening Greeks, while simultaneously taking advantage of the destruction of Baghdad and its caliphate to assert themselves as a new dynasty of *sultans* (protectors).

After several failed attempts to capture Constantinople, the great fortress city of the Christians on the western side of the narrow waterway separating Europe from Asia, Sultan Mehmed the Conqueror succeeded in taking his prize. A long siege weakened the defenders' resistance, and the sultan's new bronze cannon destroyed the walls. In 1453, the city finally surrendered. Present-day Serbia, Bulgaria, and Greece had also fallen by then to the Ottoman forces. By the mid-1500s, Hungary, Romania, southern Poland, and southern Russia had been added to the sultan's domain, while in North Africa and the Middle East all the Islamic states from Morocco to Persia had accepted his overlordship (see Map 32.2). At this stage, Ottoman military power was unmatched in the world.

Ottoman Government

Ottoman glory reached its apex in the reign of **Suleiman the Magnificent,** a sixteenth-century sultan whose resources and abilities certainly matched any of his fellow rulers in an age of formidable women and men (Elizabeth of England, Akbar the Great in India, and Ivan the Terrible in Russia). The government he presided over was composed of the "ruling institution" and the "religious institution." At the head of both stood the sultan. The ruling institution was what we would call the civil government, composed of various levels of officials from the **grand vizier** (prime minister) down. Most members of the ruling institution were originally non-Muslims who had converted to the True Faith.

The religious institution was parallel to the ruling institution. Its members were collectively the ***ulema,*** or learned men of the law, the *sharija,* which was derived from the holy book of Islam, the Qur'an. The religious institution lent its

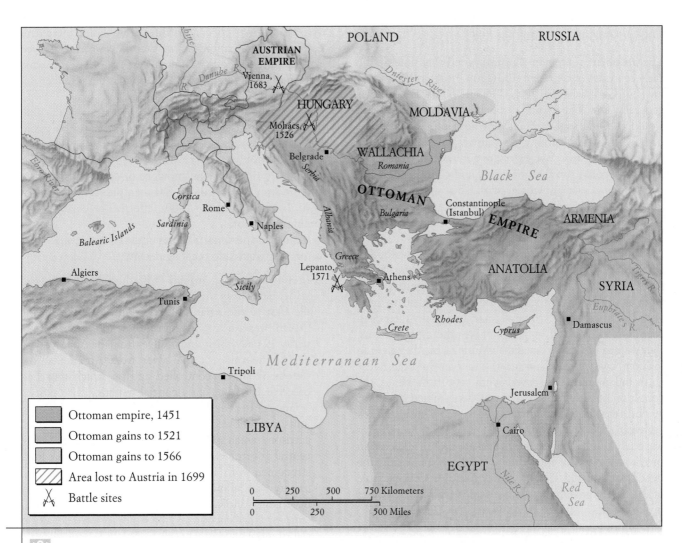

![MAP 32.2] **MAP 32.2   The Ottoman Empire's Growth and Decline.**   At its peak in the late 1500s, the domain of the sultan in Istanbul reached from the Persian Gulf to the Atlantic Ocean. For a short time, the losses in eastern Europe were counterbalanced by advances in the Middle East.

great moral authority to the ruling institution. It was in effect a junior partner of the government. In the ordinary course of events, conflict between the two was unthinkable.

The army was part of the ruling institution. The Ottoman army was far in advance of the Europeans by virtue of its professionalization and discipline. At its heart were the well-trained and well-armed **Janissaries,** an elite infantry created by conscripting Balkan Christian boys at a tender age, converting them to Islam, and giving them unlimited chances to rise high in both army and government. Some of the most brilliant leaders of the Ottoman state in the sixteenth through eighteenth centuries were these willing slaves of the sultan (as they proudly termed themselves), recruited from the infidel.

The Ottoman state for many years successfully avoided the weakening of the central authority that was inevitable with feudalism by refusing to reward military service with land grants. Instead, the bulk of the standing army was a mobile, permanent corps that could be shifted about throughout the huge empire controlled by Istanbul. The soldiers received salaries paid by the central government and supplemented their pay by pillaging defeated enemies. Without local connections and rarely remaining very long in one place, the soldiers were loyal to the central government alone.

As long as the Janissaries, in particular, conformed to this ideal, the Ottoman governmental system operated smoothly and effectively. The provincial authorities obeyed the center or were soon replaced and punished. But after about 1650, when the professional army was able to obtain land and develop the connections to purely local affairs that landholding entailed, a lengthy period of decline commenced.

Non-Muslims under Ottoman Rule

The treatment of the non-Muslims varied over time. In the early centuries of Ottoman rule (1300–1600), official treatment of Christians and Jews ("People of the Book") was generally fair. They were distinctly limited in what we would call civil rights, could not hold office, could not proselytize for converts or bear arms, and suffered many other disadvantages. But they were not forced to convert to Islam and could run their own civil and cultural affairs on the local and even provincial level. They were taxed, but not excessively. Their public life was certainly far more secure than that of most Jews or Muslims living under Christian rule.

The majority of the Balkan population was Orthodox Christian. Under Turkish rule, those peasants were almost always decently treated until the seventeenth century. They were allowed to elect their own headmen in their villages; go to Christian services; baptize, marry, and bury their dead according to tradition; and so on. Like other non-Muslims, they were more heavily taxed than Muslims, but they were allowed to own land and businesses and to move about freely.

In the course of the seventeenth century, however, the condition of the Balkan Christians deteriorated badly for several reasons. These included the central government's increasing need for tax funds, the increasing hostility toward all "infidels" at Istanbul, and a moral breakdown in provincial and local government. "The fish stinks from the head," says the old Turkish proverb, and the bad example of the harem government in the capital was having effects in the villages.

By the middle of the eighteenth century, the condition of the Balkan Christians had become sufficiently oppressive that they were looking for liberation by their independent neighbors, Austria and Russia. From now on, the Ottomans had to treat their Christian subjects as potential or actual traitors, which, of course, made the tensions between ruler and ruled still worse.

This is the background of the widespread Western conception of the Turks as perhaps the most inept of all the peoples who have ruled in Europe, a conception that is partially true at best. It applies only to the last century and a half of Ottoman dominion. In that period, imperial rule had effectively broken down into a kind of free-for-all among crudely ambitious provincial authorities and their rebellious Christian subjects.

The Decline of the Ottoman Empire

Suleiman's reign (1520–1566) was the high point of the sultan's authority and also of the efficiency and prestige of the central government. Beginning with Suleiman's son and successor Selim the Sot (!), many of the sultans became captives of their own viziers and of the intrigues constantly spun within the harem. After 1603, the sultans began to allow their sons to be raised within the harem, where they were subject to every conceivable manipulation by scheming eunuchs and ambitious women. This practice proved highly injurious to official morale and was one of the worst influences on government (see the Family and Gender Relations box).

Nevertheless, the empire did not run straight downhill after 1600. Once every few decades, a dedicated grand vizier or a strong-willed sultan would attempt to reverse the decay. He would enforce reforms, sweep out the corrupt or rebellious officials in one province or another, and make sure the army was obedient. But then the rot would set in again. By the end of the 1700s, effective reversal was becoming impossible.

Besides the personal qualities of the sultan, several other factors contributed to the long decline:

1. *Economic.* Starting around 1550, the shift of European trade routes from the Muslim-controlled Near and Middle East to the Atlantic Ocean (and later the Pacific Ocean) was a heavy, long-term blow to Ottoman prosperity. Equally, the influx of silver from the Americas undercut the value of the silver from Africa that the Ottomans largely controlled and on which they had based their trading and financial systems.
2. *Military.* After the 1570s, the Janissaries and other elite units were allowed to marry and settle down in a given garrison, which gradually eroded their loyalties to the central government and allowed them to become local strongmen with local sympathies. Also, the Turkish cavalry were allowed to meet their heavy expenses by becoming landlords over peasant-worked domains (*ciftlik*), which encouraged the same erosion of loyalty to the Istanbul government.
3. *Technological.* From the 1600s, the Ottomans failed to comprehend how Western technology and science were changing. Increasingly, they found themselves unready when confronted in tests of power. They almost always responded by attempting to ignore the unpleasant realities. They failed to acknowledge or give up old ways when the situation demanded change. This characteristic was spectacularly apparent in military sciences, where the once-pioneering Turks fell far behind the West in weapons and tactics.

Strengths and Weaknesses of Ottoman Civilization

The strengths of the Ottomans are most evident during the earlier centuries of their rule, as one would expect, and the weaknesses later. But some of each are clear throughout. Aside from their military merits, their strengths included their extraordinary artistic sensitivity in literature, architecture, and symbolic imagery; a commitment to justice for all, no matter how weak; a tolerance for nonbelievers that was unusual for its time; and a literary language (Arabic-Persian in origin) that was truly an international bond as well as the channel of a rich literature. In economic and administrative

OTTOMAN HAREMS

In the Turkish sultan's palace, concubines vied for preeminence in his favor. Perhaps the greatest of the sultans was Suleiman, who broke precedent by taking one of the harem as his legal wife rather than merely his concubine because of his affection for her. A Venetian ambassador tells the story:

> This sultan has two highly cherished women: one a Circassian, the mother of Mustafa the firstborn, the other, whom in violation of the custom of his ancestors he has married and considers as his wife, a Russian, so loved by his majesty that there has never been in the Ottoman house a woman who enjoyed greater authority. It is said that she is agreeable and modest, and that she knows the nature of the sultan very well. The way in which she entered into the favor of the sultan I understand to have been the following. The Circassian, naturally proud and beautiful . . . understood that [the Russian] had pleased the sultan, wherefore she insulted her, and as she was doing so she scratched her all over her face and mussed her clothing, saying, "Traitor, sold meat, you want to compete with me?"
>
> It happened that a few days later the sultan had the Russian summoned for his pleasure. She did not let the opportunity pass, and angrily told the eunuch who had come to fetch her that she was not worthy to come into the presence of the sultan because, being sold meat and with her face so spoiled and some of her hair pulled out, she recognized that she would offend the majesty of such a sultan by coming before him. These words were related to the sultan and induced in him an even greater desire, and he commanded that she should come. He wanted to understand why she would not come and why she sent him such a message. The woman related to him what had happened, accompanying her words with tears and showing the sultan her face which still bore the scratches and how her hair had been pulled out. The angry sultan sent for the Circassian and asked her if what the other had said was true. She responded that it was, that she had done less to her than she deserved. She believed that all women should yield to her and recognize her as mistress since she had been in the service of his majesty first. These words inflamed the sultan even more, for the reason that he no longer wanted her, and all his love was given to this other.

SOURCE: Leslie Pierce, The Imperial Harem: Women and Sovereignty in the Ottoman Empire (Oxford: Oxford University Press, 1993), © L. Pierce.

affairs, the Ottomans had a far more efficient tax system and better control of their provincial authorities than any European government of the fourteenth through sixteenth centuries. Unfortunately, these institutions were to weaken very much later on.

Among the Ottomans' weaknesses were a government that depended too much on the qualities and energy of one or two individuals, the sultan and the grand vizier; a theory of government that was essentially military in nature and needed constant new conquests to justify and maintain itself; an inability to convert the Qur'an-based sharija code of law to changing necessities in legal administration; a blind eye to the importance of secular education and to all types of technology; and an overreverence for tradition, which led to stagnation.

From the late 1600s on, the weaknesses of the Ottoman state in Europe rendered it prey to an increasingly aggressive West. First, the Habsburg dynasty in Vienna, then, the Russian Romanovs went on the counterattack against Turkey in Europe, driving back its frontiers step by step. In the early 1800s, the native peoples began to rebel and were assisted by the European powers until the Turks' domain was reduced to Bulgaria, Albania, and northern Greece. At that point, about 1830, the external attacks ceased only because the aggressors became wary of one another. The "Sick Man of Europe" was allowed to linger on his deathbed until 1918 only because his heirs could not agree on the division of the estate.

THE MUSLIM EMPIRES IN PERSIA AND INDIA

In the sixteenth and seventeenth centuries, the **Sufi** and **Shi'ite** currents, which had existed within the theology of Islam for many centuries, became noticeably stronger. The Sufi mystics sought a different path to God than orthodox Muslims (see Chapter 16). Some of the Sufi of Central Asia adopted the historical views of the Shi'ites, who reject all the successors to Muhammed who were not related by blood or marriage to him. In the eighth century, as we saw in Chapter 15, this belief resulted in a major split between the Shi'ite minority and the **Sunni** majority, who believe that the caliph, or successor to the Prophet, can be anyone qualified by nobility of purpose and abilities. From that original dispute over succession gradually emerged a series of doctrinal differences. Much Islamic history can be best conceived of within the framework of the rivalry between Shi'ite and Sunni.

The Safavid Realm

The Shi'ites early on took over much of the Persian Muslim state and from that base made frequent wars on their Sunni competitors. In the early 1500s, a leader named Ismail succeeded in capturing Baghdad and made himself *shah* (king). Thus was founded the **Safavid empire,** which lasted

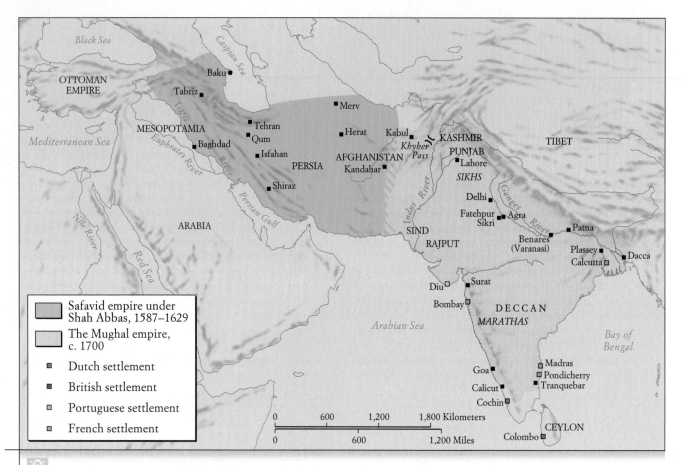

MAP 32.3   Safavid and Mughal Empires.   The Safavid empire, shown at its maximal extent, about 1625 under Shah Abbas I, was crushed by Ottoman and Afghani attacks in the 1720s after two centuries of independent Shi'ite rule. The Mughal empire, shown at its maximal extent, about 1700, included most of north and central India until the late eighteenth century, when losses to the Hindu Marathas and the English multiplied.

for two centuries and was a strong competitor to the Ottomans, who were Sunni Muslims (see Map 32.3). This doctrinal and political rivalry was most vividly apparent in the early seventeenth century, and it reached its height in the reign of **Shah Abbas I** (ruled 1587–1629), the greatest of the Safavid rulers.

Shah Abbas was aided in his conflicts with Istanbul by the European opponents of the Turks, who were then still established deep in central Europe. A number of foreigners occupied high positions in his government, as Abbas strove to avoid favoring any one group within his multiethnic realm. His beautifully planned new capital at Isfahan was a center of exquisite art and artisanry, notably in textiles, rugs, ceramics, and painting. The Safavid period is considered the cultural high point of the long history of Persia and the Iranian people. After Abbas, the empire slowly lost vigor and collapsed altogether in the 1720s under Turkish and Afghani attack.

It is worth noting that, like the European Christians, the various subdivisions within Islam fought as much against each other as against the infidel. A common religion is rarely able to counter the claims of territorial, economic, or military advantage in the choice between war and peace.

The Mughal Empire

We last looked at the Indian subcontinent in Chapter 17, commenting on the gradual revival of Hindu culture under the Gupta dynasty in the fourth and fifth centuries C.E. and the Golden Age that ensued. Very early in Islam's history, during the late 600s, Arabs and Persians had moved into the Indus valley and seized the province of Sind at its lower extremity. This was the beginning of a long ongoing struggle between Hindu and Muslim in the northwest borderlands. From it, 800 years later came one of the most impressive Muslim empires: the one founded in northern India by a branch of the Turks known as **Mughals** or Moghuls.

The word is a corruption of *Mongols,* to whom the Turks were distantly related. Muslims from Central Asia had been raiding and attempting to invade north India since the 900s but had been sooner or later repulsed by the dominant Hindus. Finally, in the early 1200s, the **sultanate of Delhi** was established by a band of Turks operating from their base over the Khyber Pass in Afghanistan. Within a century, they controlled much of the Indian subcontinent, reaching down into the Deccan. Divorced from their Hindu subjects by every aspect of culture, language, and religion, the sultans and their courts attempted at first to convert and then, failing that, to humiliate and exploit them.

The original dynasty was soon overthrown, but it was succeeded by other Central Asian Muslims who fought among themselves for mastery even as they extended their rule southward. For two centuries (1335–1550), the tides of battle surged now in favor of this, now in favor of that claimant. Aided by continuing disunity among their Hindu opponents, Mongol, Turk, Persian, and Afghan contested the entire width of the subcontinent from the Indus to the Ganges. At last, a leader, Babur, arose again from the Afghan base who was able to impose his will or persuade his fellow princes to follow him. Brilliantly successful battle tactics allowed him to conquer much of the territory once ruled by the Delhi sultans. By his death in 1530, he had established a Muslim Indian dynasty, called Mughal. This man's grandson and successor was **Akbar the Great** (ruled 1556–1605). Akbar was the most distinguished Indian ruler since Ashoka in the third century B.C. Indeed, he was perhaps the greatest statesman that Asia has ever produced.

Akbar has several claims to his title. He splendidly fulfilled the usual demands made on a warrior-king to crush his enemies and enlarge his kingdom. Under his guidance and generalship, the Mughal empire came to control most of the subcontinent—the first time a central government had accomplished this since the day of the Mauryan kings. Second, despite his own youthful illiteracy, he completely reorganized the central government, developed an efficient multinational bureaucracy to run it, and introduced many innovative reforms in society. Third and most strikingly, Akbar practiced a policy of religious and social toleration that was most unusual in any part of the sixteenth-century world. He himself was at least formally a Muslim, ruling a Muslim-dominated empire. But he allowed all faiths including Christianity to flourish and to compete for converts in his lands.

Because Hindus made up the large majority of his subjects, Akbar thought it particularly important to heal the breach between them and the Muslim minority. His initiatives toward an ethnically equal society were remarkable. He married a Hindu princess, and one of his sons by a Hindu eventually succeeded him. Hindus were given an equal chance at obtaining all but the highest government posts, and the Hindu warrior caste called Rajputs became his willing allies in governance. By repealing the odious poll tax (*jizya*) on non-Muslims, Akbar earned the lasting gratitude of most of his subjects. The sorrow that existed among both Muslim and non-Muslim at Akbar's death was the most sincere tribute to his character.

Palace at Fatehpur. The palace-city erected by Akbar the Great outside Agra is now mostly ruins. It was abandoned soon after Akbar's death by his successor as Great Mughal. The lovely design and exquisite stonework are still visible in buildings like this, now cared for by the Indian government as national treasures. (© *Wolfgang Kaehler*)

Midway in his long reign, Akbar decided to build an entirely new capital at Fatehpur, some distance from the traditional royal cities of Delhi and Agra. This palace-city was soon abandoned and is now a ruin, but its beauty and magnificence were famous throughout the Muslim world. The court library reputedly possessed over 24,000 volumes, making it easily the largest collection of books in the world at this time. Akbar's love of learning encouraged sages of all religions and all parts of the Asian world to come to his court at his expense as teachers and students. (See the Science and Technology box for his interest in science.) His cultivation of the official Persian language brought new dimensions to Indian literature. The ties with Persian culture enabled by the language contributed substantially to the revival of a sense of national unity among Hindus, lacking since the Gupta era.

None of the rulers who followed Akbar matched his statesmanship. Aurangzeb (ruled 1656–1707), though a triumphant warrior, was responsible for reversing the climate of toleration that Akbar had introduced and that had been generally maintained for the ensuing half century. Aurangzeb was a convinced Muslim, and he reintroduced a distinctly Islamic character to public life. This change heightened the latent frictions between the ruling class and their Hindu, Zoroastrian, Jain, and (a few) Christian

PRACTICAL SCIENCE IN AKBAR'S INDIA

Akbar the Great lived a century earlier than Russia's Peter the Great, but both rulers have certain similar traits that are striking. They shared a strong interest in practical application of scientific knowledge and the desire to learn by doing. We know of Akbar's interests both from the reporting of the several Jesuit priests who resided at the Delhi court while attempting to convert the emperor to Christianity and from the memoirs of the Muslim courtier-scientist, Abul Fazl, one of Akbar's favorites.

In 1580, Jesuit father Henriques noted that "Akbar knows a little of all trades, and sometimes loves to practise them before his people, either as a carpenter, or as a blacksmith, or as an armorer." Another said that he "is so devoted to building that he sometimes quarries stone himself along with the other workmen." These inclinations, so reminiscent of Peter during his grand tour of western Europe, were also employed in learning the goldsmith's and lacemaker's trades and the manufacture of guns. Like the Russian, Akbar believed that to truly value a product by another's hand, you must first learn how to make it yourself.

Akbar prided himself also in his inventions—or what he claimed were his inventions. Abul Fazl tells us that the prince originated the use of a *khas*-frame, a method of using hollow bamboo stalks stuffed with a fragrant root called *khas*, then pouring water over the bamboo, with the effect of cooling the area within the frame, "so that winter seems to arrive in the midst of summer."

Not only that, but His Majesty was a pioneer of refrigeration technique. He apparently was familiar with basic chemical reactions, so that he could enjoy a cooling drink. Akbar "made saltpeter, which creates such tumult in the form of gunpowder, the means of cooling water, so that both the poor and the rich were made happy. . . . A *ser* of water is poured into a bottle made of pewter or silver and its mouth is closed. In a pan two and one half *sers* of saltpeter are mixed with five *sers* of water, and the closed bottle is moved round and round within that mixture for the space of half a *ghari* [about twelve minutes]. The water within the bottle gets very cold."

FOR REFLECTION

If Akbar and Peter were alike in their fascination for technology, can you point out some ways in which their personalities were quite different? Refer to Chapter 29.

SOURCE: Irfan Habib, *Akbar and His India* (Calcutta: Oxford University Press, 1997), p. 128 ff.

---

subjects. Though his large, efficient, and tax-eating army was too big to challenge directly, Aurangzeb's rule set the stage for eventual rebellion by the dispossessed Hindu majority against his weaker successors. The entire eighteenth century witnessed a slow decline of the emperor's powers and prestige, and a gradual whittling off of the territory he controlled. The latter condition was the result of both internal and external (European) challengers.

Relations with Europe to 1800

In the expanding empires of the Safavids in Persia and the Mughals in India, the appearance of European explorers and traders during the 1500s did not create much of a stir. At that time, the European presence in India was limited to a relative handful of traders in a few ports such as Goa and Calicut. Barricaded behind their fortified walls, they had no appreciable influence on Indian life.

The Portuguese were the first Europeans to arrive in India, followed by the Dutch, English, and French. By the end of the 1600s, the Portuguese "factories" except Goa had been absorbed first by the Dutch, then by the English. After some tentative skirmishing on the seas (demonstrating that no non-Western force could hold its own against the European navies), the Mughals had settled into a mutually comfortable relationship with the British centered on luxury trade goods in both directions. The privately owned British East India Company, founded in 1603, was given monopolistic concessions to trade Indian goods, notably tea and cotton cloth, to the West and bring in a few European items in return.

For a long time, the arrangement worked out quite harmoniously. The East India Company made large profits, and the members of the Mughal upper class were pleased with their access to European firearms, metal, and fabrics. Within the company's handful of port enclaves, all power over both Englishmen and Indians was vested in the English superintendent, who had strict reminders not to involve himself in local politics.

The arrival of the French in the 1670s put some strain on English-Mughal relations, as Paris was already in competition with London for a colonial empire. Under the brilliant administrator Dupleix, the French made an effort to enlist the Indians as allies, not just trading partners. The British then responded similarly. By the 1740s, the frequent European wars between Britain and France involved their Indian outposts as well. On the French side, Dupleix commanded tens of thousands of Indian troops. On the British side, Robert Clive was just as active. They fought one another even while the home countries were at peace.

In India as in North America, the Seven Years' War (1756–1763) was the decisive round in the contest. British control of the sea proved more important than French victories on land. By the Treaty of Paris in 1763, control of much of India fell into British hands through the intermediation of the East India Company. But Parliament was by now unwilling to trust such a costly asset entirely to private hands, and a statute in 1773 divided political oversight between London and the company. In the 1780s, Lord Cornwallis (lately commander in chief of the British forces in Virginia) was put in charge of the Indian possessions, and he was followed by others who crushed the occasional Muslim and/or Hindu attempts to defy British power. Increasingly, those rajahs who did not obey London's wishes found themselves forcibly replaced by British civil governors. One after another the many subdivisions of the subcontinent were incorporated into the British-ruled empire.

Society and Culture

India under the Mughals remained a hodgepodge of different peoples, as well as different religions and languages. Besides the civilized Indians, there were still many tribal groups, especially in the jungled areas of the eastern coast, whom neither Hindu nor Muslims considered fully human and often enslaved.

The caste system continued to refine itself in constant subdivisions among Hindus. While the Muslims never acknowledged, of course, the caste system for themselves, it did serve as a useful wall to minimize frictions between subject and ruler. Despite extensive business and administrative dealings between the two religious communities, social intercourse was unusual at any level. Even among the majority Hindus, culturally based barriers existed that had nothing to do with caste.

A new religion, derived from the doctrines of both Hindu and Muslim, arose in the far north during the seventeenth century. At first dedicated to finding a middle ground between the two dominant faiths, it eventually became a separate creed, called the religion of the **Sikhs.** Generally closer to Hindu belief (but rejecting caste), the Sikhs fought the last Mughal rulers and came to dominate the northwestern Panjab province. (They currently represent perhaps 5 percent of the total population of India and strive still for full autonomy on either side of the India–Pakistan border.)

After Emperor Aurangzeb, the governing class was almost entirely Muslim again, and their habits of dress and manners were sometimes imitated by aspiring Hindus. A notable example was ***purdah,*** the seclusion of women, which was adopted by the upper

castes of Hindus. Many foreigners, especially from the Middle East, came into the country to make their fortunes and often did so at the very luxurious and free-spending courts of not only the emperor but subsidiary officials. Prevented by imperial decrees from accumulating heritable land and office, the Muslim upper class took much pride in funding institutions of learning and supporting artists of all types.

In the fine arts, the Mughal rulers made a conscious and successful effort to introduce the great traditions of Persian culture into India, where they blended with the native forms in literature, drama, and architecture. The quatrains

Elephant Hunt. An Indian prince sets out to capture additional elephants in this seventeenth-century Mughal painting. Two assistants ride with him, while he brandishes the short spear that was the usual weapon prior to the coming of firearms. Note the hobbles, which helped control the prince's elephant, and the baby elephant that accompanied its mother at all times. *(Victoria & Albert Museum, London, UK/Bridgeman Art Library)*

🏵 **The Taj Mahal.** This seventeenth-century tomb was designed in Indo-Persian style as the resting place of the beloved wife of Mughal emperor Jahan. Building commenced in 1632 and was completed eleven years later. Four identical facades surround a central dome 240 feet high. The whole complex is supplemented by gardens and the river that flows beside. *(The Bridgeman Art Library, London)*

of **Omar Khayyam's *Rubaiyat,*** which have long been famous throughout the world, held a special appeal for Mughal poets, who attempted to imitate them (see the Religion and Philosophy box for an excerpt from the *Rubaiyat*).

The **Taj Mahal,** tomb of the much-loved wife of the seventeenth-century emperor Jahan, is the most famous example of a Persian-Indian architectural style, but it is only one of many, as exemplified by the ruins of Fateh-Sikri, the equally imposing Red Fort at Agra, as well as a whole series of mosques. Much painting of every type and format from book miniatures to frescos also survives from this era and shows traces of Arab and Chinese, as well as Persian, influence. By this time, Muslim artists ignored the ancient religious prohibition against reproducing the human form. The wonderful variety of portraits, court scenes, gardens, and townscapes is exceeded only by the precision and color sense of the artists.

The Muslims had an extensive system of religious schools (*madresh*), while the local brahmins took care of the minimal needs for literacy in the Hindu villages by acting as open-air schoolmasters. Increasingly, the Muslims used the newly created Urdu language (now the official language in Pakistan) rather than the Sanskrit of the Hindus.

Like the Safavid Persians to their west, the Mughals were an exceptionally cosmopolitan dynasty, well aware of cultural affairs in and outside their own country and anxious to appear well in foreign eyes. They welcomed European travelers. Like Marco Polo's reports about Kubilai Khan's China, the sixteenth- and seventeenth-century tales of visitors to the Great Mughal were only belatedly and grudgingly believed. Such cultivation and display of luxury were still beyond Europeans' experience.

The Mughal Economy

The existing agrarian system was but slightly disturbed by the substitution of Muslim for Hindu authority. Beginning with the Delhi sultans, courtiers and officials were awarded a parcel of land (jagir) consonant with their dignity and sufficient taxes to allow them to maintain a specified number of fighting men and their equipment. This was the *mansabdari* system, a version of rewarding individuals who rendered either civil or military duties to the state. Some mansabdars maintained small armies of 5,000 or even 10,000 men. When the sultanate

THE *RUBAIYAT* OF OMAR KHAYYAM

Perhaps the most quoted poem in the English language is a nineteenth-century translation of a twelfth-century Persian philosopher, who may or may not have written the original. The *Rubaiyat* of Omar Khayyam is a collection of four-line verses that became associated with his name long after his death in 1122. Edward Fitzgerald, who had taught himself Persian while passing his days as a Victorian country gentleman, published them in 1859 in a very free translation. Instantly finding a public, the *Rubaiyat* was reprinted several times during Fitzgerald's life and many more since.

The poem speaks in unforgettably lovely words of our common fate. Morality is all too often a negation of joy. Death comes all too soon: in wine is the only solace. The verse story, of which only a fragment is given here, opens with the poet watching the break of dawn after a night of revelry:

1
Awake! for Morning in the Bowl of Night
Has flung the Stone that puts the Stars to Flight
And lo! the Hunter of the East has caught
The Sultan's Turret in a Noose of Light.

2
Dreaming when Dawn's Left Hand was in the Sky
I heard a Voice within the Tavern cry,
"Awake, my Little ones, and fill the Cup
"Before Life's Liquor in its Cup be dry."

7
Come, fill the Cup, and in the Fire of Spring
The winter Garment of Repentance fling
The Bird of Time has but a little way
To fly—and Lo! the Bird is on the Wing.

14
The Worldly Hope men set their Hearts upon
Turns Ashes—or it prospers; and anon,
Like Snow upon the Desert's dusty Face
Lighting a little Hour or two—is gone.

15
And those who husbanded the Golden Grain
And those who flung it to the Winds like Rain
Alike to no such aureate Earth are turn'd*
As, buried once, Men want dug up again.

16
I think that never blows† so red
The Rose as where some buried Caesar bled;
That every Hyacinth the Garden wears
Dropt in its Lap from some once lovely Head.

19
Ah, my Beloved, fill the Cup that clears
Today of past Regrets and future Fears—
Tomorrow?—Why, Tomorrow I may be
Myself with Yesterday's Sev'n Thousand Years.

20
Lo! some we loved, the loveliest and best
That Time and Fate of all their Vintage prest
Have drunk their Cup a Round or two before,
And one by one crept silently to Rest.

21
And we, that now make merry in the Room
They left, and Summer dresses in new Bloom,
Ourselves must we beneath the Couch of Earth
Descend, ourselves to make a Couch—for whom?

22
Ah, make the most of what we yet may spend,
Before we too into the Dust descend;
Dust into Dust, and under Dust, to lie,
Sans Wine, sans Song, sans Singer, and—sans End!

23
Alike for those who for TODAY prepare,
And those that after a TOMORROW stare,
A Muezzin from the Tower of Darkness cries
"Fools! your Reward is neither here nor there!"

24
Why, all the Saints and Sages who discuss'd
Of the Two Worlds so learnedly, are thrust
Like foolish Prophets forth; their Words to Scorn
Are scatter'd, and their Mouths are stop'd with Dust.

25
Oh, come with old Khayyam, and leave the Wise
To talk; one thing is certain, that Life flies;
One thing is certain, and the Rest is Lies;
The Flower that once has blown for ever dies.

*"Aureate earth . . ." means once buried, the body is no golden treasure.
†The verb "to blow" here means "to bloom."

FOR REFLECTION

Do you sympathize with the poetic point of view? Why or why not?

SOURCE: The Rubaiyat of Omar Khayyam, *trans. and ed. Edward Fitzgerald (New York: Dover, 1991). Used by permission of Dover Publications.*

weakened, they established themselves as petty kings, joining the universal fray in north India for territory and prestige. This system was carried over into the Mughal period. Perhaps half of the mansabdars under Akbar were Hindu, creating a loyalty to the imperial government that continued even under Aurangzeb's determined Islamic regime.

The peasants on the mansabdar's domain were possibly better off than their contemporary counterparts in Europe or China. Most of them were tenants rather than outright proprietors, but they were not yet haunted by the shortage of agrarian land that would arrive, as it did in China, during the later eighteenth century. Their lives were bounded by the village, caste, and tax collectors. The latter were generally no worse than in other places, and their demand for a third to half of the crop was bearable if the harvest was normal.

SUMMARY

The various Muslim empires and subempires that occupied parts of the Asian continent between 1200 and 1800 were able to hold their own with their Chinese, Hindu, and Christian competitors. Often warring among themselves, they were still able to maintain their borders and prestige for 200 to 400 years. After the terrible destruction rendered by the still-pagan Mongols, the Muslims of the Middle East converted their invaders and rebuilt. Chief and most enduring among their states were those of the Ottoman Turks and the Indian Mughals. The Ottomans profited from the destruction of Baghdad by the Mongols to erect their own powerful emirate and then claim the caliph's role by taking Constantinople (Istanbul) for their capital. Under a series of warrior-sultans, they extended their power to the gates of Vienna before weakening internally and being driven back in the 1700s. By the nineteenth century, the Ottomans had become so weak that they were held upright only by the rivalry of their enemies.

For two centuries, the Shi'ite dynasty of the Safavids reclaimed grandeur for Persia and Iraq, where they ruled until they were brought down by the superior power of their Sunni rivals in Istanbul. The Mughals descended upon Hindu India in the early sixteenth century and set up one of the few regimes in Indian history that managed to rule most of this intensely varied subcontinent successfully. Under the extraordinary Akbar the Great, this regime reached its apex, only to enter into slow decline during the following century. The wealth of India's exotic trade items lured European interest from the early sixteenth century and stimulated first Portuguese and then Dutch, British, and French colonial experiments in commercial capitalism. By the end of the eighteenth century, Britain's victories over France and the commercial success of its East India Company had turned much of India into its indirectly ruled colony.

TEST YOUR KNOWLEDGE

1. Taken together at their height, the Ottoman, Mughal, and Safavid empires
   a. extended from the Atlantic Ocean to Australia.
   b. included all of Asia except the Japanese islands.
   c. could be termed a united political territory.
   d. extended from the Atlantic to the Ganges River valley.
2. A major source of internal trouble for the Ottoman rulers of the eighteenth and nineteenth centuries was
   a. the spreading atheism of most of the Turkish upper class.
   b. the professional military units called Janissaries.
   c. the missionaries from Europe in the Ottoman cities.
   d. the attacks from the Mughal empire of India.
3. Which of the following was *not* accepted by Ottoman statecraft?
   a. The precepts and prescriptions of the Qur'an
   b. The function of the sultan as leader of the faithful
   c. The favored situation of the Muslims over the non-Muslim subjects
   d. The necessity to have at least one major Christian ally

4. The treatment of non-Muslims in the Balkans under Ottoman rule
   a. deteriorated sharply in the seventeenth and eighteenth centuries.
   b. improved as the powers of the sultan diminished.
   c. tended to become better the farther away they were from the capital.
   d. depended entirely on the whims of the ruling sultan.
5. Shi'ite Muslims
   a. believe the leader of Islam must be descended from the prophet Muhammed.
   b. make up the largest single group of Islamic people.
   c. reject the prophetic vocation of Muhammed.
   d. believe the Qur'an is only partly correct.
6. The Muslim rulers of the Safavid dynasty were
   a. the conquerors of Constantinople.
   b. the allies of the Mughals in India.
   c. a Persian Shia family.
   d. the first conquerors of Persia for Islam.

7. The most universally revered of the Indian Mughal rulers was
   a. Aurangzeb.
   b. Akbar.
   c. Ashoka.
   d. Abbas.

8. The original objective of the British East India Company in India was to
   a. study native customs.
   b. control the spice and cotton trade with Europe.
   c. conquer and convert the Hindus to Christianity.
   d. colonize southern India for the British Crown.

IDENTIFICATION TERMS

Ain Jalut	Mughals	Safavid empire	Suleiman the Magnificent
Akbar the Great	*pax Mongolica*	Shah Abbas	sultanate of Delhi
Chinghis Khan	*purdah*	Shi'ite	Sunni
grand vizier	*Rubaiyat* of Omar	Sikhs	Taj Mahal
Janissaries	Khayyam	Sufi	*ulema*

 # INFOTRAC COLLEGE EDITION

Enter the search term "Mongol" using Key Words.
Enter the search term "Ottoman Empire" using Key Words.

Enter the search terms "Sufi" or "Sufism" or "Rumi" using Key Words.

33

AFRICA IN THE COLONIAL ERA

We are people because of other people.
SOTHO PROVERB

1650–1870	Height of Atlantic slave trade
c. 1800–1850	North Africa and many coastal areas brought under European control
1840s	Christian missionaries and explorers begin to move into interior
1880s–1914	Almost all Africa brought under European control
1880–1898	Mahdi rebellion in Sudan
1899–1902	Boer War in South Africa

THOUGH DIFFERENT IN PRACTICALLY every other aspect, Africa and Japan share one important similarity: their long-sustained isolation from the European West, even after their respective "discoveries." For centuries interior Africa remained in an isolation that was less self-willed than the result of circumstance. Long after the Europeans had arrived on the coasts in the late fifteenth century, they had penetrated very little into the enormous depths of the continent or into the interior life of the people. Aside from the Cape of Good Hope and one or two Portuguese locations, the Europeans in the three centuries after 1480 established practically no settlements. Their presence was limited to trading posts at wide intervals along the coasts. Staffed by a literal handful, these "factories" had little direct impact on the coastal populations and still less on the interior.

Transatlantic slaving had a strong impact on African life in some places, but more often, it seems, it did not. The African leaders dealt with the white traders on an equal status, as the whites depended entirely on them to gather not only slaves but also the exotic goods that the interior produced for export.

Until about 1850, the Arabs and Moors (Berbers) remained the major external influence on sub-Saharan Africa, as had been true for centuries. After that date, the Europeans moved into Africa in an entirely new fashion, as missionaries and governors and, in a few places, even as settlers. They rapidly explored the previously unmapped interior. By the end of the century, all of Africa had been divided up into new European colonies, governed by greater or lesser numbers of aliens in the spirit of a **New Imperialism,** desiring strategic or economic advantage rather than territorial conquest.

Africa is usually divided into northern, western, southern, and eastern sections. We will review the continent accordingly.

THE ERA OF MINIMAL EUROPEAN PRESENCE

In contrast to the Americas and Asia, the interior of sub-Saharan Africa long remained free from outside interventions.

The chief reason seems to have been the ability of the early trader/explorers to gain what they wanted without establishing extensive settlements or permanent relationships. What they wanted originally was gold and a small list of exotic products peculiar to Africa. In this sense, the early African experience with the Europeans was very similar to that of the Southeast Asian peoples: minimal and highly selective contact. Very soon, however, slaves took the place of gold as the most profitable and most pursued item of trade. Both slaves and goods were delivered to them by the local chiefs on the coast in mutually profitable fashion. The Europeans saw no persuasive reason to risk the dangers of a long journey into unknown territory to get what African middlemen would deliver—for a price. There was certainly profit enough for all.

The coastal chiefs possessed sufficient authority and knowledge of trading practices to deal with the newcomers as equals.

The model established in the 1400s by the exploring Portuguese was followed closely by their several successors along the western African coast. The European traders could not and did not simply overwhelm the Africans and seize what they wanted. Such an attempt would have resulted at the very least in stopping all future trade. And for the entire four centuries of European precolonial contact with West Africa, the Portuguese, Dutch, British, and French were engaged in commercial competition, which the native leaders at times could manipulate to their own advantage.

Also discouraging permanent settlement were the devastating diseases that were endemic. Fevers and infections that were unknown elsewhere were commonplace, and the western coast was long known as "the white man's graveyard." A recent authority on the question thinks that the mortality rate among white traders and seamen on the West African coast was higher than that of the black slaves shipped across the Atlantic: 25 to 50 percent *per year*! Adding to the difficulties were the oppressively hot climate, the difficult terrain, and the dangerous animals that ranged through much of the interior.

As we noted in Chapter 20, Africa's geography and climate make traveling inward from the coast especially difficult. Thanks to the tsetse fly, spreader of "sleeping sickness," no beasts of burden are native to the central and southern two-thirds of the continent, and the wheel was unknown in equatorial Africa when the Europeans arrived. All goods of whatever nature depended on human muscle for transport. The interior plateaus drop off sharply to the coastal plains, creating rapids and waterfalls that make long distance river transport impossible in much of the continent. Only the Nile, the Niger in the west, and the Congo in the center are sporadically navigable far into the interior. All three of these rivers were controlled by substantial states when the Europeans arrived, and the Nile valley was, of course, in Muslim hands.

The Slave Trade and Its Results

No topic in African history is as controversial as the extent and results of the transatlantic slave trade (see Map 33.1). The latest figures, summarized in *A History of Africa* (second edition, 1988) by the English expert J. D. Fage, indicate that a total of about 10 million human beings were exported from Africa to the New World in the 220 years between 1650 and 1870, which were the high point of the trade. Another 3.5 million were involuntarily transported from Africa to the Near East and the Mediterranean in the same period. Fage states (on the basis of recent demographic research) that because the total population of sub-Saharan Africa in 1650 was about 75 to 80 million and the population was growing at a rate of about 1 percent per year (80,000), the estimated annual loss through slaving in the peak years of the eighteenth century was about the same as the annual gain. This means that the population of Africa thus essentially stood still for the 150 years between 1650 and 1800 before beginning to rise again, as it has continued to do until the present.

These statistics do not mean that slaving had little impact on African populations or that the impact was uniform in all areas. Slaves for the Atlantic trade were gathered primarily in two areas: first, Guinea (the southern coast of the great bulge), and somewhat later, Angola. In East Africa, where the trade ran northward by sea to the Muslim countries, the impact was still more narrowly focused on the areas that are now Tanzania and Uganda (inland from Mombasa on Map 33.1). In large regions of Central and East Africa, slaving was of little or no importance, either because the inhabitants successfully resisted it or because the populations were too small and scattered to offer an easy target for capture.

Besides checking the population growth in parts of Africa, the slave trade had other social and economic effects, but their precise nature is the subject of much debate, even among Africans. It is indisputable that some West African leaders (chieftains, kings, even emperors) were able to reap a solid advantage for themselves and for at least some of their people from the trade. They accomplished this by becoming active partners with the whites in securing new human supplies and by using the proceeds of the trade in ways that increased their material prestige and powers. In some West African states, such as Dahomey and the Ashanti kingdoms (present-day Ghana and Nigeria), for example, the leaders traded slaves for firearms, which they then used to enhance their power to gather more slaves.

On the other side, it is equally indisputable that slaving and the raids or local wars that it generated were a major cause of the chaotic bloodshed observed and condemned by nineteenth-century Europeans. Particularly in East Africa, where Arab traders had a free and brutal hand in obtaining human cargoes for shipment north, the

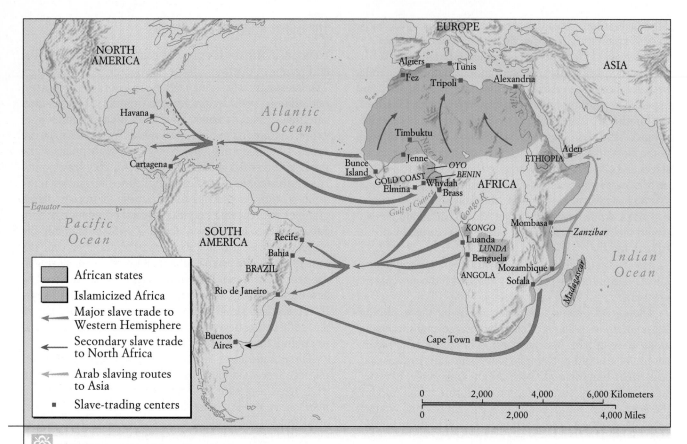

MAP 33.1 The African Slave Trade, c. 1700. During the two centuries of intense slaving (1600–1800), most Africans were captured and shipped from West African ports across the Atlantic. But millions also went north and east into the Islamic areas.

slaving business as it developed in the years after 1840 resulted in not only massive misery for the captured victims but also the degeneration of a previously stable village society.

There seems to have been a clear distinction between traditional African slaving practice, which was based on either raiding or warfare against neighboring communities and primarily aimed at enhancing the social status of the slave taker, and the commercially driven exploitation practiced by both Europeans and Arabs in the modern era. Although the eyewitness **David Livingstone** may have exaggerated when he estimated in the 1860s that ten lives were lost for every slave successfully delivered by Arab captors to the East African coast, he was probably not too far off. The mortality rates of the transatlantic trade were never quite so high because of both its more efficient organization and the emphasis on males to be used for plantation labor. The Arab-controlled trade, on the other hand, emphasized females for concubines and house slaves. Fage estimates 15 percent of those taken perished before landing in the New World. Over time, this rate means that more than a million lives were lost.

INTENSIFICATION OF EUROPEAN CONTACTS

Not until the later nineteenth century did the bulk of sub-Saharan Africans experience the hand of the European in any substantive fashion. The coastal trading factories had dealt only with the African political-social leadership for their desired goods. (There had been limited intermarriage, particularly in the Portuguese colonies, but the upshot was normally the Africanization of the male rather than the Westernization of the African female.) In North Africa and the Muslim northeast, the conquests of the Arabs and the Ottoman Turks (see Chapter 32) had sufficed to restrict European influence until the Napoleonic wars. The interior of the continent was thus still an almost total mystery to Westerners as late as the 1840s.

The coming of the Europeans as political overseers rather than simply as traders proceeded in different ways and at different tempos in various parts of Africa. The process can best be summarized by region and by governing colonial administration (see Map 33.2).

North Africa

In the 1830s, Morocco and Algeria fell under varying degrees of French influence. Morocco remained theoretically independent under its Muslim Berber sultan, who was supervised by a "resident-general" appointed by the French government in Paris. Less populous and less stable, Algeria was militarily seized from a corrupt Turkish clique and made into a formal French colony as early as 1847. More than a million French gradually settled there. Algeria was the sole African region where this type of intensive, agriculturally oriented European settlement occurred until diamonds and gold were discovered in late nineteenth-century South Africa. The native Arabs and Berbers in Algeria were made into second-class citizens, subordinate to the French settlers in every way. Nearly the same process occurred later in neighboring Tunisia. Thus, by the later nineteenth century, the whole western half of Africa north of the Sahara (in Arabic, the *Maghrib*) was within the French orbit.

The eastern Mediterranean coast of Africa was still part of the dying Ottoman Empire, but the Turks had had very little real control over these lands for centuries and could not defend them from European ambitions. The Italians and the British eventually divided the rest of the coast, with the Italians taking over the (then) wastelands of Libya in 1911 and the British adding Egypt and the Sudan to their worldwide empire after 1880.

In all these lands, Islam was the religion of the great majority. As both the local leadership and the Turks in Istanbul proved themselves unable to act effectively in the face of the aggressive Christian "infidels," Islam underwent a fundamentalist revival. Sometimes this revival took the form of armed rejection of the Europeans, most notably in the great **Mahdi rebellion** in the 1880s in the Sudan. The Mahdists were briefly able to set up an independent state,

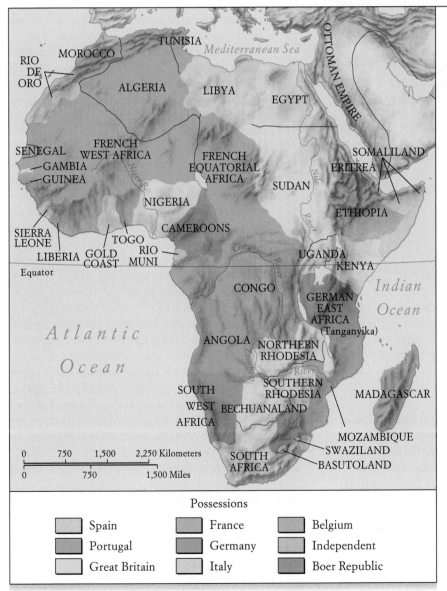

MAP 33.2 Africa before World War I. Following the scramble of the 1880s and 1890s, all of Africa except tiny Liberia in the west and mountainous Ethiopia in the east was brought under European rule. The German possessions were given to either Britain or France following the war.

Possessions

- Spain
- Portugal
- Great Britain
- France
- Germany
- Italy
- Belgium
- Independent
- Boer Republic

ernment was overwhelmed by the foreigners and their hated ways, frustrated men desperately lashed out against them. The upshot was crushing defeat and the sullen recognition that the aliens would have to be accommodated, perhaps even joined.

West Africa

From the early nineteenth century, the French were the leading European influence in West Africa (the great bulge), with strong British competition in the **Niger River** basin (Nigeria) and the Gold Coast (Ghana, Sierra Leone, Gambia). In these areas, the slave trade had been the major occupation of Europeans and their African collaborators for centuries. After slaves were banned by acts of Parliament from British ships in 1807 and from British imperial territory in 1833, the slaving centers moved southward into the Portuguese colony of Angola. Here the trade throve for a time until the American Civil War removed a major destination and the abolition of slavery in Brazil in 1888 the most important one. (The U.S. Congress prohibited the importation of slaves in 1808, but they continued to be smuggled into the southern United States even during the Civil War.)

In West Africa the French and British, as well as the Portuguese, had gradually installed genuine colonial systems during the nineteenth century as the slave trade was replaced by a new economy based on agricultural exports from Africa and imports of European metal, cloth, and manufactured goods. The three European governments had somewhat different goals for their colonies and administered them in different ways, which were arrived at by necessity and experiment rather than by plan.

French possessions were administered from a central office in Dakar and were linked directly with the Paris government. The Africans were given little margin to govern themselves. The French exerted strong pressure on the upper-caste natives to assimilate—that is, to learn French and acquire French manners and values. If they did so, they were officially considered "black Frenchmen and women." They could then enter the colonial bureaucracy and even become French citizens.

Considerable effort was made to convert the Africans to Catholic Christianity, but it met with little success until the twentieth century. Very little economic development occurred in these colonies, which were for the most part desertified regions almost devoid of resources or blanketed by impenetrable rain forest. Only in the twentieth century have modern irrigation works made it possible to develop some agriculture in former French colonies such as Mali,

Drying Sorghum Grain. The Rwanda villagers dry large quantities of sorghum, a coarse grain, for beer brewing. The beer is a standard refreshment for festivity days and, like all food preparation, is considered a woman's task. (© Betty Press/Woodfin Camp and Associates)

and in 1885 they even beat off a British expeditionary force sent to punish them. Not until 1898 were they finally crushed by another British force armed with the forerunner of the machine gun. In the crucial encounter outside Omdurman (in Sudan), something like 11,000 Mahdists died but only 28 British! As the doggerel poem went, "whatever else under the sun, remember who has the Gatling gun."

The Mahdi revolt and several other Islamic fundamentalist plots to throw out the alien whites are strongly reminiscent of the simultaneous Boxer Rebellion in China (see Chapter 48). In each case, as the native gov-

Chad, and Mauretania, which are still among the poorest countries in the world.

The British possessions to the south were more favored by nature and experienced more private entrepreneurial activity. A few colonies (Gold Coast and Nigeria) began as the private possessions of a monopoly firm, similar to the British East India Company in India. Sierra Leone began as a refuge for free blacks from the British colonies and from intercepted slave ships after the maritime slave trade was banned. The British rulers, whether private or governmental, relied heavily on native chiefs to exercise actual day-to-day government under loose British supervision. This system of indirect rule, which was similar to what the British did in India with the Hindu and Muslim *rajahs* and *nabobs,* was inexpensive for the home country and also gave ambitious natives at least some semblance of authority and socioeconomic mobility.

Thanks to the introduction of commercial peanut and oil palm plantations in the late nineteenth century, Britain's West African dominions were integrated into the world market and were the most sophisticated and prosperous of all the African colonies. Protestant missions were scattered about in the back country but had no great effect on the prevalent animism and Muslim beliefs until the twentieth century, when like the French Catholic efforts they became substantially more important. The authorities and missionaries made considerable effort to educate the population in basic terms, and a few blacks—again like their French-ruled counterparts—went on to European university training.

The Portuguese possessions (Guinea in the west, Angola in the southwest, and Mozambique in the southeast) were the descendants of much earlier trading posts and were governed entirely from the home country. Natives were excluded from any meaningful participation in government and were treated mainly as potential labor. There was considerable intermarriage, and Catholic missions attempted to convert the people to Christianity and to educate the most promising. (Portuguese efforts to Catholicize the blacks of the Congo region had a long history. See the Religion and Philosophy box on Doña Beatriz.)

Enormous numbers of slaves were sent out to Brazil and the Caribbean for many years, and the attitude of the Portuguese administrators toward their subjects was highly influenced by this **Angola-to-Brazil trade.** The rubber and coffee plantations that were the mainstay of the economy were run like the cotton plantations of the antebellum U.S. South, but without the occasional benevolent paternalism encountered there.

South Africa

The Cape Colony in extreme southern Africa was the other large area, along with Algeria, where whites settled in some numbers prior to the late nineteenth century. As far back as the mid–seventeenth century, Dutch emigrants had come to the Cape, attracted by the pleasant climate and good agricultural conditions. By the time the British took over in 1815 through the Treaty of Vienna, perhaps 25,000 **Boers** (farmers), as the Dutch called themselves, were living there.

Having enjoyed substantial self-government, the Boers resented the imposed British rule. In particular, they resented the British effort to extend the same legal rights to the Africans as the white Boers enjoyed. In 1836, the Boers marched northward away from the Cape in the Great Trek. Once in the interior, they set up an independent region where they could continue the old ways undisturbed: the **Orange Free State** and its neighboring **Transvaal.**

For a time, all went well, as the Free State and the British Cape Colony were far apart. British and Boers collaborated in eliminating the ancient Bushman (San) and Hottentot (Khoikhoi) hunter-gatherers, pushing them into the Kalahari Desert of the southwest (see Map 20.1). In another joint effort, they crushed the Zulu kingdom (discussed later in this chapter). But when rich diamond and gold deposits were discovered in the Johannesburg area in the 1880s, the old conflicts rose up again. Led by the redoubtable **Cecil Rhodes,** the British capitalists and developers pushed into Boer territory to open mines and build railroads to serve them.

The result was the **Boer War** (1899–1902), won by the British after a bitter struggle. But the Boers still constituted the backbone of white settlements and commerce in South Africa, and the British had to make concessions to them to maintain a manageable colony. The chief concession, which would become increasingly ominous in the future, was to leave the Boers in control of the economic and social *apartheid* (segregation) that they had always maintained against the black tribal groups who far outnumbered them. The blacks were left with the choice of becoming ill-paid and contemptible laborers in the white-owned industries, mines, and farms or remaining in a seminomadic tribalism on barren reservations. Politically, the British maintained oversight of the colony from London and Cape Town, but the Boers dominated in the *veldt* (rural) villages and towns and elected a majority of the colony's legislature.

Central and East Africa

In the center of the continent, the drainage of the great Congo River was a royal plantation, held by a private firm in which the Belgian king held a majority share. Originally explored by Henry Stanley (of Stanley and Livingstone fame), the Belgian Congo was a vast area along Africa's second largest and longest river. It was an important source of several industrial raw materials, especially copper and rubber.

The Congo saw relatively few Europeans ever settled there permanently. The main reason for claiming and keeping this jungled kingdom was to exploit its abundant material resources. A great scandal ensued in the early twentieth century when it was gradually revealed how cruel the royal enterprise had been toward its workers and how little had been done to educate or convert the native peoples to

DOÑA BEATRIZ
(C. 1675–1706)

The kingdom of Kongo was the best-organized and most extensive of all the African states encountered by the Europeans in their early explorations. Extending many hundreds of miles on either side of the great river, Kongo encompassed most of today's Angola and much of the territory of the Congo Republic. The Portuguese, who sent missionaries to the court of Kongo's powerful and wealthy king at the same time as Columbus's voyages to the Caribbean, were delighted at being able to report the conversion of the ruler they dubbed Afonso I (ruled 1506–1543) to Catholic Christianity. Afonso collaborated closely with his Portuguese protectors and business partners in a rapidly expanding slave and luxury goods trade. He also was the founder of the only black African dynasty of Christian rulers, which lasted until the collapse of the Kongo kingdom in the later seventeenth century.

After Kongo's collapse, a variety of visionaries came forward, claiming they could explain why the once mighty kingdom had come to grief and how it could be restored. The most fascinating was a young woman known to the Portuguese as Doña Beatriz, who for two years (1704–1706) was a veritable Joan of Arc for her people. She founded a sect called the Antonians (for St. Anthony), which still has much influence in religious affairs in present-day Congo.

As described by one of the Portuguese priests resident in Kongo, Doña Beatriz was "about twenty-two years old. She was rather slender and fine-featured. Externally she appeared devout. She spoke with gravity . . . foretold the future, and predicted among other things, that the day of Judgement was near." Beatriz believed herself to be the living embodiment of a blend of the ancient animistic beliefs and the Christian religion in which she had been tutored. At the point of death from illness, she had felt St. Anthony (a popular saint among the Portuguese) enter her soul and revive her. He had instructed her to preach to her people, restore the kingdom of Kongo, and punish those who opposed her.

In the next two years, Beatriz succeeded in establishing a doctrine that combined elements of the Christian message with Kongo traditions. She taught that Kongo was the Holy Land, that the founders of Christianity were black, that Christ was born in the Kongo capital city of São Salvador, and that the Virgin Mary was the daughter of a Kongo notable. She gave up all earthly goods and lived among the poor, taking St. Francis of Assisi as her model.

Antonian belief spread quickly, and the Portuguese authorities and priests took measures to squelch it. They attacked Beatriz as a false prophetess, a heretic who sought to mislead and defraud her people for her own ambitions. Although the priests had to admit that Beatriz was the "enemy of vices, superstitions, fetishism," she rejected the forms of the Catholic Church in fundamental ways. Europeans were threatened, and priests driven out of the country. Under her inspiration, "little Anthonys" ran rampant in Kongo, persecuting both blacks and whites who adhered to orthodox Christianity.

Beatriz's downfall came suddenly. After long hesitation, the Portuguese-supported king of Kongo, Pedro IV, came to believe she was more a rival than an ally in his struggles to restore his kingdom. Beatriz's claims to be a holy prophet were severely undermined when she gave birth to a child whose father she would not divulge. Mother and infant were arrested and subjected to an interrogation much akin to what happened to Joan of Arc three centuries earlier in France. Beatriz, too, was found guilty of heresy and condemned to death by burning at the stake. Her baby was at her side when the sentence was carried out on July 2, 1706. According to a witness, she died "with the name of Jesus on her lips."

FOR REFLECTION

What similarities and dissimilarities occur to you when comparing Beatriz with Joan of Arc?

Christianity. Despite many solemn proclamations that European rule was justified by its potential to benefit the natives, the final judgment is spoken by a simple figure: the population declined by half in twenty years (1885–1905) of Belgian royal oversight.

East Africa felt the most direct impact of the Arab traders who had long preceded the Europeans in slaving and other commerce in African goods. Coastal towns such as Zanzibar and Mombasa were busy entrepots in the Indian Ocean trade for centuries. They remained so until the abolition of slavery (1873) and the technology of the Europeans made it impossible for their Muslim Arab rulers to compete.

In these coastal regions, the Bantu populations had developed a highly civilized lifestyle with an extensive trading network into the interior. The ruling urban-based class was a mixture of Arab and African Muslims, while the great majority of the villagers remained animists. These city-states were commercial in nature, trading across the Indian Ocean as partners of their fellow Muslims in India and southeastern Asia's islands.

The slave trade, oriented toward the Red Sea and Persian Gulf destinations, was active here into the late nineteenth and even the twentieth century. (It should be remembered that Muslim law and practice saw nothing wrong with slavery and the slave trade. The idea that enslavement of a fellow being was evil was a viewpoint that the Europeans had only gradually accepted in early modern times. They were now imposing it with their guns and officials on Muslim and animist Africans alike.)

THE SCRAMBLE FOR AFRICA, 1880–1914

Except for the French in North Africa, the Europeans did not attempt to disturb the network of tribal kingdoms that existed until the mid–nineteenth century in most of the continent. The Europeans knew no more about the interior in 1840 than their ancestors had known in the fifth century. Not even the basic geography of the river systems was understood, and the quest for the sources of the Nile, which lasted until the 1860s, is one of the great adventure stories of the Victorian era.

From the 1840s onward, this indifference and ignorance changed radically. The most noted of the nineteenth-century explorers of the interior of the Dark Continent were either missionaries such as David Livingstone or explorer-adventurers such as Richard Burton and Henry Stanley. The sharply competitive search for the source of the Nile River was in large part responsible for opening the vast interior of East Africa in the 1860s and 1870s, while the exploration of the Niger and Congo basins did the same for West and Central Africa. Livingstone was the first European to be acknowledged as having crossed the entire African continent east to west, though there is evidence that he was preceded by a half century by a Portuguese explorer. The British journalist Stanley, made famous by his well-publicized search for an allegedly lost Livingstone, went on to become a major African explorer in the 1870s and "opened up" the Congo to colonial status as an agent of the Belgian throne.

By the 1880s, sufficient geographic information was known about the interior to allow the European nations to begin to stake definite claims. Belgium and Germany vied with the British in Central and East Africa. The Portuguese took Angola and Mozambique under firm control at this time. The French cemented their hold on West Africa and parts of the center. Italy took the area around the Horn of Africa and was repulsed when it attempted to add independent Ethiopia to the list. In 1885, all the major European states met at a conference in Berlin to delineate claims and avoid overlapping jurisdictions.

From the Western point of view, the Berlin conference was one of the more successful diplomatic enterprises of re-

Walled Village, Niger. The distinctive shape of the huts and the camel identify this village as a Hausa settlement, on the southern edge of the Sahara in the former French colony of Niger. (© M&E Bernheim/Woodfin Camp and Associates)

cent history. By 1900, all of Africa had been allocated to European rule with the exception of mountainous Ethiopia and Liberia, the small West African country founded by liberated American slaves. No attention whatever was given to native custom or economic relations when the borders of the various colonies were drawn. Tribes were split, and ecological and economic units were shattered by the survey teams sent out from Paris, London, or Berlin. That this disregard for native geographic and ecological traditions was a burdensome mistake first became clear when the colonial system was dismantled after World War II.

At the completion of the "scramble for Africa" at the turn of the century, perhaps 175 million Africans were newly placed under European rule. In sub-Saharan regions, with the exception of some river valleys and coastal ports, this rule at the outset was of the most tenuous sort; huge areas remained unmapped and their populations—if any—were neither cognizant of nor disturbed by the new white chieftains.

What made possible the extension of European sovereignty over interior Africa? Several factors contributed. First, in the nineteenth century, weapons had been developed (mobile artillery, the Gatling and the Maxim machine guns, the rapid-firing rifle) that tipped the balance sharply in favor of those who possessed them versus those who did not (no Africans did). Second, the diseases that had made much of Africa "the white man's graveyard" were finally understood and countered by tropical medicines (quinine and mosquito control for malaria, above all). Mortality per year for whites dropped to about 5 percent in 1900. This rate was still twice what it would have been for the same persons resident in Europe but was now an acceptable figure. Finally, a misunderstood or contorted Darwinian biology (see Chapter 43) provided a framework for a hierarchical division of human societies, in which the Europeans naturally reserved the highest slot for themselves and the lower ones for darker-skinned peoples such as the blacks in Africa.

One of the first tasks of the new overlords was to train a native constabulary under white officers to break up tribal wars and slaving raids. Another was the establishment of district offices, staffed often by young civil servants fresh from the mother country who were given extraordinary responsibilities in maintaining the peace and establishing justice. In the British colonies, it was not unusual to see a twenty-seven-year-old, three years out of Cambridge and only backed by his constables, given life-and-death authority over a district population of perhaps 30,000 individuals. Direct challenges to the new dispensation were rare. Officers could move about freely without fear in the villages, though the nearest European might be a couple of hundred miles away. Attacks on the Europeans, when they occurred, were almost always motivated either by the whites' breaking of religious taboos or repeated cruelties.

REACTIONS TO EUROPEAN DOMINATION

Although terribly outgunned (literally as well as figuratively), Africans did not passively submit to European overlords. Many African leaders sought to check or defeat the Europeans' encroachments throughout the second half of the nineteenth century. Among the notable struggles were the **Zulu War** in South Africa, the fight against the Germans in Tanganyika, and the Ashanti resistance against the British in the Gold Coast. But like the resistance of the Berber rebels against the French in Algeria and Morocco

and the Mahdists in Sudan, these attempts were hopeless. With the single exception of the Italians' failed campaign in Ethiopia, the Europeans' superiority in weaponry and tactics generally won out rapidly and always did so in the long run. One reason was the Africans' fatal willingness to engage in battles in the open field instead of conducting guerrilla-style campaigns. Against the Gatling and Maxim guns, bravery alone was not enough.

Once conquered, the African elites had a range of choices, which boiled down to essentially two: to submit and attempt to imitate the manners and values of their new masters, or to withdraw as far as possible from contact with an alien overlord. In the French and British colonies, the native leaders generally chose the first way, encouraged by colonial administrators who sometimes had the real interests of the natives at heart. In the Belgian, Italian, Portuguese, and German colonies, the Africans often chose the second way, as they were given very little opportunity to do anything else until the interwar period of the twentieth century. In some cases, those who withdrew and remained committed to African tradition retained more prestige in the eyes of their people than those who associated with the conquerors and mimicked their manners. The majority, however, believed that the whites' ways were superior and sought to associate themselves with those who provided access to them.

What was the attitude of the new rulers toward their African charges? With the exception of the Congo and the Portuguese colonies, the natives were not as a matter of policy treated brutally. Many young white males, stationed in the bush far from social contacts with their own race, took local mistresses and sometimes became much more understanding and sympathetic toward African ways than their superiors in the capital. But anyone who allowed this sympathy to become noticeable ran a strong risk of being reprimanded or dismissed as an eccentric by his white associates.

Of the three types of Europeans with whom Africans now were in contact—merchants, administrators, and missionaries—the latter were most important for the evolution of African culture. Missionary efforts at basic education in the native languages were responsible for the twentieth-century creation of a small group of educated blacks who came to look on their own backgrounds as inferior, even primitive, and were determined to rise to the level of their white mentors. These Africans became the founders of national or regional literatures. A few were eventually sent to Europe for university training.

These men (there was no education beyond the ABCs—and rarely that—for African females) became conscious of the gap between what the European liberals and intellectuals preached and what the governments practiced in their treatment of the colonial peoples. From their ranks in the early twentieth century were to come the nationalist leaders of Africa. They saw that the most telling critique of Western colonial practice was to be found in the classic ideals of the West itself. Like their Asian counterparts, they used the weapons that their Western education delivered to them to free themselves from a sense of their own inferiority and to lead their peoples to independence.

CHANGES IN AFRICAN SOCIETY

By the early twentieth century, the Europeans had completely demolished the traditional division of lands and severely affected the commercial and cultural relations among the Africans. The old boundaries based on topography and tribal and ethnic associations had given way to boundaries based on European diplomatic agreements and horse trading. In the same fashion, traditional African power relations had been either destroyed or severely altered by the imposition of European-style officials, police forces, and courts, manned either by whites or by their satellite blacks.

Personal relations between masters and underlings varied, sometimes even within the same empire. French officials and black subordinates generally got along well in West Africa but badly in Central Africa, because of local variations in the French administration. In some instances, the whites and the black Muslim upper class got on well, but both were resented by the black non-Muslim majority who saw them both as alien exploiters. In colonies with large numbers of settlers, as in British Kenya and South Africa, the whites generally exploited their black labor and established an impenetrable social "color line," regardless of liberal central government policies.

Undermining of the Old Ways

At the beginning of the twentieth century, though Christianity had already made a slight dent in African animism, the Islamic faith had far more prestige throughout the northern half of the continent. Urban life was still rare. The great majority of natives lived in villages or in pastoral nomadic societies. Their standards of living were simple, but they generally were not impoverished in any sense, and certainly not in the sense of having fewer material goods than was necessary to maintain a decent status in their neighbors' eyes. Illiteracy was nearly universal outside the Europeans' towns and the villages with mission schools. (Traditional education is illustrated in the Family and Gender Relations box.)

Everywhere in the villages, "the old ways" of the natives' culture and institutions lingered on, apparently almost untouched except for the handful of educated, Europeanized blacks. But subtle changes were under way beneath the surface. The tribal chiefs left in place by the Euro-

peans no longer were backed by the universal assent of their villagers, who knew all too well that an unknown European official could overrule them at will. The tribal gods were no longer respected in the same fashion now that some of the tribe's most promising youth were the product of Christian missionary schools. The white man's medicine could save lives that the tribal shaman's magic could not help. In these and other fashions, mostly unintended, the Europeans' coming as permanent overlords had a cumulatively erosive effect on the old ways. Many blacks found themselves adrift between the colonialists' preferred models of belief and conduct and the age-old traditions of African life.

Chief and Attendants, West Africa. This nineteenth-century photo was taken in present-day Central African Republic by French administrators. The guards were unusual and show that the photo was posed for European purposes. *(Hulton-Deutsch Collection/Corbis)*

RAISING CHILDREN IN WEST AFRICAN SOCIETY

In the sixteenth and seventeenth centuries, Dutch (and British) traders steadily gained the upper hand over the original Portuguese explorers/commercial men along the Guinea coast of Africa. One of them, Pieter de Marees, left an extensive accounting of his years in this trade. De Marees was an observant man, interested in many things. In the following remarks he outlines his impressions of child raising. Like many other Europeans then and later, de Marees seems somewhat disturbed by the relative freedom that the Africans normally granted small children and even youths to do as they best saw fit.

> They feed the small child with all their coarse food at a tender age, as soon as there is no more food left in the breasts of its Mother, or the Mother has weaned the child, which they do very early, not allowing the child to suck for long . . . and when it begins to accept this [coarse food] and also to drink water, they care little about it and just put it down in their huts as if it were a Dog, grubbing in the earth like a Pig. In addition, the little children learn to walk early, for they allow the young children to do as they like from infancy. Each woman maintains her children, and each child knows its Mother, staying close to her. . . .
>
> Once the children know to walk by themselves, they soon go to the water, in order to learn how to swim and to walk in the water . . . they grow up as savages, running about together, Boys and Girls, beating and fighting one another and stealing one another's food, beginning right from youth to be very jealous of one another. Thus, they grow up in rough circumstances, the Parents not teaching their children any virtues or allowing them to be taught any, leaving them to walk around naked as they were brought into the world, Girls as well as Boys, walking with their private parts exposed and without any sense of shame. . . .

> When the children have thus spent their youth in roughness and reach the age of 8,10, or 12, the Parents begin to admonish them to do something and set their hands to some kind of work. Fathers teach their sons to spin yarn from the bark of trees and to make nets, and once they can make nets, to go with their Fathers to the sea to Fish. . . . But when they are about 18 or 20 years of age, the Sons begin to do their own trade and, taking leave of their Father, go to live with two or three other Boys together in a house.
>
> Regarding the Girls, they begin to do some handiwork, according to their age, earlier than the Boys; they learn how to make Baskets, Hampers, Mats and straw Hats made of green Rushes, which they make with their hands. They begin to make Caps, Purses, and cloth from the bark of Trees, dyed in all sorts of colors and very artfully made, as if made with a Loom, to the wonder of many people: and one can see often enough in our lands [Netherlands] what artful work they make. . . .
>
> What a girl earns she gives to her mother, who provides for her at the time she comes to marry. Thus the girl begins at a very early age to be busy and learns housework; and they are very good at their kind of housekeeping, outdoing the Men in all deftness of manual work, as we shall explain later.

FOR REFLECTION

Consider how much effort it would have taken on de Marees's part to overcome his Calvinist commitment to a proper sense of shame about the naked human body and about the necessity of parents teaching virtues to their children.

SOURCE: Excerpted from A. van Dantzig and A. Jones, eds., Pieter de Marees: Description and Historical Account of the Gold Kingdom of Guinea (Oxford: Oxford University Press, 1987), pp. 26–27.

Economic Changes

What benefits to the home countries came from the establishment of African colonies?

In 1880, the European colonial governments had few if any long-range plans to develop their new territories. The chief concern shared among them was to avoid expense or to find ways in which the Africans could be brought to pay for the military and civil expenditures incurred. A fine line had to be walked between excessive expense to the home country taxpayer and excessive coercion or taxation in the colony. A rebellion would be not only distasteful but expensive to the home government. Ideally, development of African natural resources—especially minerals—would allow a cost-free colony. For most colonial governments, however, this goal proved to be a mirage.

On balance, the home governments put at least as much into the African colonies as they were able to take out. Only a few of the West African colonies (Gold Coast, Nigeria, Senegal) with their agricultural specialty crops such as palm oil and peanuts were better than a break-even proposition for the home nations. The hoped-for large markets for excess European industrial capacity never developed—the natives' cash incomes were far too small to absorb consumer goods, and it proved impossible to attract private investments into Africa on any scale comparable to what was going into the Americas or even Asia. Only in one or two special situations, notably the copper mines and rubber of the Congo and the precious stones and minerals of the Cape Colony, did the African bonanza materialize for the home governments and private investors. Cecil Rhodes, the British capitalist and greatest of the private empire builders

Diamond Mining. The richest diamond mining district in the world was found in the 1860s by British prospectors in South Africa. Massive amounts of hard labor were required to bring the mines into production, leading diretly to much harsher working and living conditions for the natives who supplied it. *(The Granger Collection, New York)*

of the nineteenth century, had envisioned a thorough Europeanization of Africa, driven by railroads and mineral wealth. By 1914, it was already clear that this would not happen, and a degree of disillusion had set in.

In a few colonies, the economic impacts on Africans themselves were visible and direct. In British South and East Africa and in Algeria, whole districts were taken from the natives to be used exclusively by the whites. The blacks and Berbers were coerced into providing agricultural labor by the necessity of having to pay new taxes in money. The same system was used to force men to work in the mines. The "Kaffirs" of South Africa's diamond and gold mines were pressured into their dangerous and exhausting work by colonial governments dominated by local businessmen.

Like it or not, the Africans were being steadily more involved in the Western-created, Western-dominated economy of trade and cash payments. These economic changes also undermined traditional lifestyles and beliefs, shifting prestige in the villages from those who came from respected lineages or who had shamanistic powers to those who accumulated wealth. The way was being prepared for Africa's belated entry into the world marketplaces.

The White Man's Burden. This engraving from 1895 shows the European concept of civilized administration being brought to the Africans. A district official listens judiciously to the complaint before issuing his decision, backed up if necessary by the native soldiery in the background. *(Woodfin Camp and Associates, Inc.)*

SUMMARY

After a long period of isolation, the various regions of interior Africa experienced more or less the same fate in the later nineteenth century: they became satellites of the Europeans' markets and culture. Whether coming as explorers, administrators, or missionaries, the whites were armed not only with guns and steam engines but also with a conviction of cultural superiority that made them irresistible to the politically fragmented and technically primitive blacks. In the three decades between 1880 and 1914, practically the entire continent was divided among the imperialist powers. The British and French took the lion's shares, while Belgium, Italy, Portugal, and Germany picked up smaller portions of varying size. Resistance was common but almost always quickly defeated.

Various motivating forces for this sudden takeover were in play, largely but not always economic in nature. But in general, the imperialist dreams of individual and national wealth from the new colonies were disappointed. Few of the colonies more than repaid the costs of administration.

At first glance, the Africans held on to much of their basic culture at the village level, even when they had lost all political control of their fate and were forced to provide unskilled labor for the whites. But this appearance was deceptive. Over the longer run, the Europeans' demonstrable capacity to work their will on the traditional leadership eroded the latter's authority and the validity of what it represented. Western religion, education, and economic demands collaborated with military and political power to overwhelm the "old ways" and force the Africans into confrontation with the modern world.

TEST YOUR KNOWLEDGE

1. The most widespread, externally introduced religion in Africa is
   a. Buddhism.
   b. Protestantism.
   c. Hinduism.
   d. Islam.
2. In the nineteenth century, most of the northwestern part of Africa fell under the control of
   a. Spain.
   b. France.
   c. Italy.
   d. England.
3. Doña Beatriz believed herself to be
   a. the bringer of a new form of Christianity to her people.
   b. the mother of Jesus.
   c. the war leader of Kongo against the Portuguese colonists.
   d. the bringer of Islam to Kongo.
4. Which of the following best summarizes the African reaction to being placed under European colonial rule in the nineteenth century?
   a. The Africans were consistently rebellious and unwilling to do the whites' bidding.
   b. The reaction varied, ranging from free cooperation to rebellion.
   c. The people's reaction varied, but the leaders were usually rebellious.
   d. The reaction varied from rebellion in the North to collaboration in the South.
5. The coastal cities of East Africa in the nineteenth century
   a. already had centuries of trading history when put under European rule.
   b. were already part of Christian culture.
   c. had never before experienced foreign contacts.
   d. were enclaves of Arab colonists.
6. By 1900, all of the African continent had been colonized by Europeans except
   a. Liberia and Zanzibar.
   b. South Africa and Ethiopia.
   c. Ethiopia and Liberia.
   d. Ethiopia and Egypt.
7. The most important cultural contacts between Europeans and Africans in the nineteenth and twentieth centuries were those initiated by
   a. the traveling merchants.
   b. the Christian missions.
   c. the European sportsmen/hunters.
   d. the medical practitioners on both sides.
8. By 1914, the economic results of the New Imperialism in Africa were
   a. disappointing to the home countries, which now regretted their colonies.
   b. disappointing, but generally not admitted as such by the governments or public.
   c. fairly close to the hopes of the imperialist groups.
   d. good for the European public, but negative for the Africans.

IDENTIFICATION TERMS

Angola-to-Brazil trade	**Livingstone, David**	**Niger River**	**Transvaal**
Boer War	**Mahdi rebellion**	**Orange Free State**	**Zulu War**
Boers	**New Imperialism**	**Rhodes, Cecil**	

INFOTRAC COLLEGE EDITION

Enter the search term "Africa" using the Subject Guide.

Enter the search term "slave trade" using Key Words.

34

LATIN AMERICA FROM COLONY TO DEPENDENT STATEHOOD

America is ungovernable.
SIMÓN BOLÍVAR

1520s–1810s	Latin America under Spanish/Portuguese rule
1650s–1750	Stagnation under a weakened Spain
1760–1790	Revival of economy under Carlos III
1793–1804	Haitian slave rebellion and independence
1810s–1820s	Wars of independence throughout Latin America

THE ARRIVAL OF the Europeans in the New World started an enormous exchange of crops and commodities, modalities, and techniques. The beginning and most important phase of this exchange was conducted under the auspices of the Spanish and Portuguese conquistadores, who so rapidly conquered the Indian populations in the sixteenth century. For the next 300 years, most of the newly discovered lands were administered by a colonial system that superimposed Iberian Christian economic institutions, habits, and values on existing indigenous ones. The form of colonial lifestyle that gradually evolved in Latin America was the product of the native Indians and the imported black slaves, as much as of the whites.

THE COLONIAL EXPERIENCE

We have seen (Chapter 26) that the initial phase of Spanish exploration in the Caribbean was dominated by the search for treasure. The "Indies" of Columbus were reputed to be lands of gold and spices, waiting to be exploited by the first individual who might happen upon them. Within a very few years, however, this image was obliterated by the realities of the Caribbean islands, where gold was nonexistent. The search then shifted to the mainland, and the immediate result was the conquest of the Aztecs in Mexico (1520s) and the Inca in Peru (1530s). Here there was treasure in gratifying abundance, both in gold and, in even greater amounts, silver. Indian resistance was broken, and the small groups of Spaniards made themselves into regional chieftains, each with his Spanish entourage. One-fifth (*quinto*) of what was discovered or stolen belonged to the royal government; the remainder could be divided up as the conquistadores saw fit.

In this earliest period, until about 1560, the Spanish Crown, which in theory was the ultimate proprietor of all the new lands, allowed the conquerors of the Indians the **encomienda,** or the right to demand uncompensated labor from the natives as a reward for the risks and hardships of exploration. This soon led to such abuses that the priests who were charged with converting the Indians to Christianity (especially the determined and brave Dominican Bartolomé de Las Casas) protested vigorously to Madrid, and the encomienda was abolished midway through the sixteenth century on paper, though somewhat later in fact.

It should be noted that the Spanish in America have long had an unjustified reputation for cruelty and indifference to Indian welfare (the "Black Legend"). It is true that most of the motley group of fortune seekers who constituted the conquistadores had no consideration whatever for the Indians; the Carib Taino tribe, for example, literally disappeared within a generation at their tender mercies. But again and again during the sixteenth century, both the Spanish home government and its agents, the viceroyal councils in the Americas, intervened as best they could to ameliorate and protect the welfare of the natives. The colonial histories of other nations have no equivalent to the flat prohibition of Indian slavery or the precise outline of the rights of the Indians and the duties of the Spanish overlords that were features of the Spanish American administration as early as the 1560s. That these prohibitions were sometimes observed in the breach is also, unfortunately, true. But the general thrust of law, legislation, and instructions to the bureaucracy in New Spain (Mexico) and Peru was definitely more solicitous of humane treatment of the natives than the colonial administrations of Holland or Britain in a later and supposedly more enlightened epoch.

This solicitousness, however, could not prevent a demographic disaster without parallel in history. Owing in part to a kind of soul sickness induced by their enslavement and subservience but much more to epidemic diseases brought by the whites and unfamiliar to the Indians, the populations of these civilized, agricultural folk went into a horrific crash (see Chapter 26). By the mid–seventeenth century, the Indian populations had begun to recover but never did so fully. Latin American populations only reached their pre-Columbian levels in the nineteenth century, when the influx of blacks and whites had created a wholly different ethnic mix.

The Spanish administration in most of the Americas and the Portuguese system in Brazil were essentially similar. Under the auspices of the home government, an explorer/conqueror was originally allowed nearly unlimited proprietary powers in the new land. Soon, however, he was displaced by a royal council set up with exclusive powers over commerce, crafts, mining, and every type of foreign trade. Stringent controls were imposed through a viceroy or governor appointed by the Spanish government in Madrid and responsible solely to it. Judicial and military matters were also handled through the councils or the colonial *audiencia* (court) in each province. There was no hint of elective government beyond the very lowest rung, the traditional communes of the Indian villages.

The colonial administration was dominated by Iberian-born nobles (*peninsulares*). It was highly bureaucratized and mirrored the home government in its composition and aims. A great deal of paper dealing with legal cases, regulations, appointment procedures, tax rolls, and censuses flowed back and forth across the Atlantic. From the mid–sixteenth century, the government's basic aim was to maximize fiscal and commercial revenues for the home country. Secondarily, the government wished to provide an avenue of upward mobility for ambitious young men in the administration of the colonies. Viceroys of New Spain and of Peru were established in the mid–sixteenth century, and the holders of these posts were always peninsulares. A few of them were able administrators; most were court favorites being rewarded with a sinecure with opportunities for wealth. Despite all attempts to assure Madrid's controls over colonial policies, the sheer distance involved and the insecurity of ocean travel meant that the local officials—normally *criollos* (native-born people of Iberian race in Latin America)—had considerable autonomy. Their care of their Indian and mestizo charges varied from blatant exploitation to an admirable solicitude.

Another Iberian institution was as strong as the civil government in the colonies: the Catholic Church. Filled with the combative spirit and sense of high mission that were a legacy of the long *reconquista* struggle against the Moors, the missionaries were anxious to add the Central and South American Indians to the church's ranks. In this endeavor they were supported by the Madrid authorities. A church stood at the center of every town in the new lands; all other buildings were oriented around it. The bishops, nominated by the Crown, were as important in the administration of a given area as the civil governors; cultural matters pertaining to both Europeans and Indians were in their hands. In its baroque buildings and artworks, the church left a long-lasting physical imprint throughout the Spanish and Portuguese colonies. The spiritual imprint was even more profound, continuing to the present day.

THE EARLY ECONOMIC STRUCTURE

The major element in the economy of the early Spanish colonies was the mining of precious metals. Everything else served that end. (Brazil, the Portuguese colony, was originally a sugarcane plantation, but later it also emphasized mining.) The agricultural estates, which were first encomiendas and then **haciendas**—rural plantation-villages with at least technically free wage labor—existed primarily to supply food for the mining communities. Handicraft industries made gloves and textiles, prepared foods, and provided blacksmithing services for the same market. There were few exports beyond the produce of the mines and a handful of cash crops such as sugar and indigo.

Rights to export goods to the Spanish colonies were limited to Spaniards; the goods could be carried only in Spanish ships, which left from one port, Seville (later also Cadiz), twice a year. From Latin America, another flotilla laden with the bullion mined the previous year left annually from the Mexican port of Vera Cruz. The restrictions on these flotillas were intended to protect the returning treasure

This church in Guanajuato, Mexico, is a good example of the Spanish baroque style that the colonial governors and artists of the seventeenth century brought to Latin America. The work was performed by native craftsmen who frequently used Indian motifs in combination with the Spanish designs. (© *Robert Frerck/Woodfin Camp and Associates*)

heights in the later eighteenth century before declining again, this time for good.

The input of bullion did not produce lasting constructive results in Spain. Some of it flowed on through royal or private hands to enrich the western European shippers, financiers, merchants, and manufacturers who supplied Iberia with every type of good and service in the sixteenth and seventeenth centuries. Perhaps a third wound up in Chinese hands to pay for the Spanish version of the triangular trade across the Pacific: Spanish galleons left Acapulco, Mexico, loaded with silver and bound for Manila, where they met Chinese ships loaded with silk and porcelain, which, after transshipment across Mexico or Panama, wound up in Seville and might be reshipped back to the Caribbean. Less than half of the Spanish silver remained in Spanish hands. But this was enough to start an inflationary spiral there that seized all of Europe by the end of the sixteenth century and brought ruin to many of the land-holding nobles (see Chapter 26).

STAGNATION AND REVIVAL IN THE EIGHTEENTH CENTURY

The later seventeenth century and the first decades of the eighteenth were a period of stagnation and decline in New Spain. The last Spanish Habsburg kings were so weak that local strongmen in Latin America were able to overshadow the audiencia and *corregidores* (municipal authorities) of the viceroyal governments.

The once-annual treasure fleets were sailing only sporadically, and the total supply of American bullion was down sharply from its high point. Several of the larger Caribbean islands were captured by the British, French, or Dutch or were taken over by buccaneers. The import/export controls imposed by the Madrid government were falling apart, as non-Spaniards were able to ignore the prohibitions against trading with the colonies, were granted exemptions, or collaborated with the criollos in smuggling in systematic fashion. By now the colonies could produce the bulk of their necessities and no longer had to import them.

At this juncture, the Spanish government experienced a revival as a new dynasty, an offshoot of the French Bourbons, took over in Madrid in 1701 as a result of the war of Spanish Succession (see Chapter 28). Especially under King **Carlos III** (ruled 1759–1788), who figured among the most enlightened monarchs of the eighteenth century, thoroughgoing reform was applied to the Indies. A form of free trade was introduced, the navy and military were strengthened, and a new system of *intendants,* responsible to the

from the Americas from pirates and to keep tight control over what was sent to and taken from the colonies.

The great bonanza of the early years was the "mountain of silver" at Potosí in what is now Bolivia. Next to it came the Mexican mines north of Mexico City. The silver that flowed from the New World to Seville (and from Acapulco to Manila) from the 1540s to the 1640s far overshadowed the gold taken from Moctezuma and the Inca in the conquest period. When the volume declined drastically in the 1640s, the Madrid government experienced a crisis. Production stayed relatively low for a century, but thanks to new technology and increased incentives, it reached great

🏵 **A Haciendero and his Family.** This 1830s scene shows a Mexican *haciendero,* owner of a large plantation, with his wife and one of his overseers. The elaborate costumes were impractical but necessary in maintaining social distance from the peons. *(The Granger Collection, New York)*

center on the French Bourbon model, was able to make Spanish colonial government much more effective. Taxes were collected as they had not been for years, and smuggling and corruption were reduced. The two Latin American viceroyalties were subdivided into four: New Spain, Peru, New Granada (northern South America), and Rio de la Plata (Argentina and central South America). The officials for these new divisions continued to be drawn almost exclusively from the Peninsula, an affront that the people in the colonies did not easily swallow.

The reforms did not benefit the mass of Indian and mestizo inhabitants at all. Indian population increased (perhaps doubling) in the eighteenth century, creating an irresistible temptation to hacienda owners to press this defenseless and unskilled group into forced labor in the expanding plantation agriculture. The market for these products was not only the seemingly insatiable demand for sugar in Europe and North America but also the rapidly growing population in the colonies themselves. The foreseeable result was an expansion of brutal serfdom, generating a series of Indian uprisings. The most notable was led by **Tupac Amaru,** a descendant of the Inca, in the 1780s. The viceroyal government of Peru was very nearly toppled before the revolt was put down. A few years later in the Caribbean island of Haiti (then Saint Domingue), a black ex-slave named **Toussaint L'Ouverture** led an uprising of slaves that ended French dominion on that island. The Toussaint rebellion eventually succeeded in attaining complete independence for Haiti, and it made an indelible impression on both the friends and enemies of the daring idea of a general abolition of slavery.

The oppressed Indians and enslaved blacks were by no means the only Latin Americans who were discontented in the last years of the eighteenth century. Economic policy reforms, however needed, were also sometimes painful to the native-born criollos. With free trade, imports from Europe became considerably cheaper, hurting domestic producers. And the remarkable increase in silver production due to new mining techniques and new discoveries did not flow to the benefit of the locals but rather to what was steadily more viewed as an alien government in Madrid. The untying of the former restrictions on trade and manufactures had a distinctly stimulative effect on the intellectual atmosphere of the criollo urbanites. After decades of somnolence came within a small but crucially important minority a spirit of criticism and inquiry, which itself reflected the stirring of European liberalism we shall look at in the next chapter.

In the 1770s, the criollo elite witnessed the successful (North) American revolt against Britain, and a few years later the radical French revolution doctrines seized their attention. In both of these foreign upheavals, they believed they saw many similarities with their own grievances against their government, similarities that were to be ultimately persuasive for their own rebellion.

INDEPENDENCE AND EARLY NATIVE GOVERNMENTS

In the decade between 1810 and 1822, one after another of the Iberian colonies in the Americas declared their independence and fought loose from the grip of the mother countries. The revolts against Spain, Portugal, and France were *not* uprisings of the common people against their masters and landlords. On the contrary, with the single exception of the black slaves in French Haiti, all of the revolutions were led by the native-born whites who formed the elite class. These criollos had become dissatisfied with rule by Madrid and Lisbon for reasons both commercial and political. But most immediately, they were worried that Napoleon's victory over the Spanish and Portuguese monarchies (see Chapter 37) would result in some type of radical, antielite reforms in the colonies. To *prevent* such reforms, when Napoleon occupied Spain, various criollo groups proclaimed that they were severing their colonial ties and taking over political leadership.

Three of the Latin American warriors for independence were particularly important:

1. **Miguel Hidalgo,** the Mexican priest who started the revolt against Spain in 1810;
2. **José de San Martín,** who liberated Argentina and Chile with his volunteer army;
3. **Simón Bolívar,** who liberated northern South America and is the best known and most revered of the three.

In each colony, other men also contributed to the success of the rebellions: Agustin Morelos in Mexico, Bernardo O'Higgins in Chile and Peru, and the Portuguese prince Pedro in Brazil, among many more. But it should be repeated that, outside Haiti, the revolts were led and carried through by conservative and/or wealthy men, who had no interest at all in social reforms or political equality.

The restored monarchs of Spain and Portugal were far too weak and too preoccupied with their internal affairs after Napoleon's eventual defeat to interfere. The faint hope of the Madrid government that it could find European support for an overseas expedition to "restore order" was put to rest in 1823 when the U.S. president James Monroe issued the **Monroe Doctrine,** backed by the British navy. Latin America was thus acknowledged to be independent, at least in terms of international law. Within a few years, no less than nine sovereign states had appeared from the wreckage of the former Spanish dominions, and a generation later this number had reached eighteen. All hope of a large, integrated entity reaching from Texas to Cape Horn had to be soon abandoned, as regional and personal quarrels came to the fore.

The most farsighted and most tragic of the heroes of the early independence era was Simón Bolívar (1793–1847), who struggled through the 1820s to bring the various regions together under a federal constitution modeled on the U.S. Constitution. He failed, and at the end of his life he declared, "America's ungovernable . . . elections are battles, freedom anarchy, and life a torment." This black depression was the result of seeing one reasonable plan for Latin American union and progress after another fail because of the indifference of the people or sabotage by selfish personal interests.

The great question in the early years of the revolutions in Latin America was whether the new governments should be monarchies or republics. The example of the newly independent United States was well known in Latin America, and many criollos thought that a republic was the only form of government suitable for the new nations (see Map 34.1). But many were fearful of the power of the mob, and especially of the mestizos and blacks. They rejected the sharp break with tradition that a republican form of government necessarily represented; instead, they wanted a monarchy. The struggle between the two schools of thought went on throughout the revolutionary decades of the 1810s and 1820s. Except in Brazil, it was eventually won by the republicans, who protected the rights of property and the existing social structure by placing supreme powers in a legislature elected through a narrowly drawn franchise. The efforts of some to introduce democratic forms were generally repulsed until the twentieth century. Only in Mexico was some progress attained. (See the box on Exercise of Authority.)

EARLY POLITICAL GROUPINGS

In most countries, political affairs quickly degenerated into a maneuvering for supreme power among a group of **caudillos** (strongmen). The frequent "revolutions" and "manifestos" were shadow plays, disguising the raw greed that impelled almost all of the actors. Only the names of the people in charge changed after a revolution of this nature. When internal affairs seemed to become too dangerous for their continued survival, many caudillos would find one excuse or another to divert attention by starting a war with their neighbors. For this reason, much of Latin America was at war over pointless territorial disputes through most of the century.

The main outlines of politics were delineated by the struggle between liberals and conservatives. On the liberal side were those inspired by the French Revolution's original goals: the liberty and fraternity of humankind and the abolition of artificial class distinctions. They regarded Bolívar as their leader and thought the proper form of political organization was a federation, exemplified by the United States. Most of the liberals came from a commercial or professional background and were strong promoters of economic development.

The conservatives generally either were landed gentry or had connections with the very powerful Catholic clergy. Like all conservatives, they emphasized stability and protection of property rights first and foremost. They looked on the Indians and mestizos as wards, who could be gradually trained toward full citizenship but in the meantime had to be excluded from political and social rights. The conservatives would support a republic only if their traditional preferences were guaranteed; if not, they could be counted on to finance and direct the next "revolution."

Everywhere in Latin America, the civil government operated in the shadow of the military, and the frequent dictators

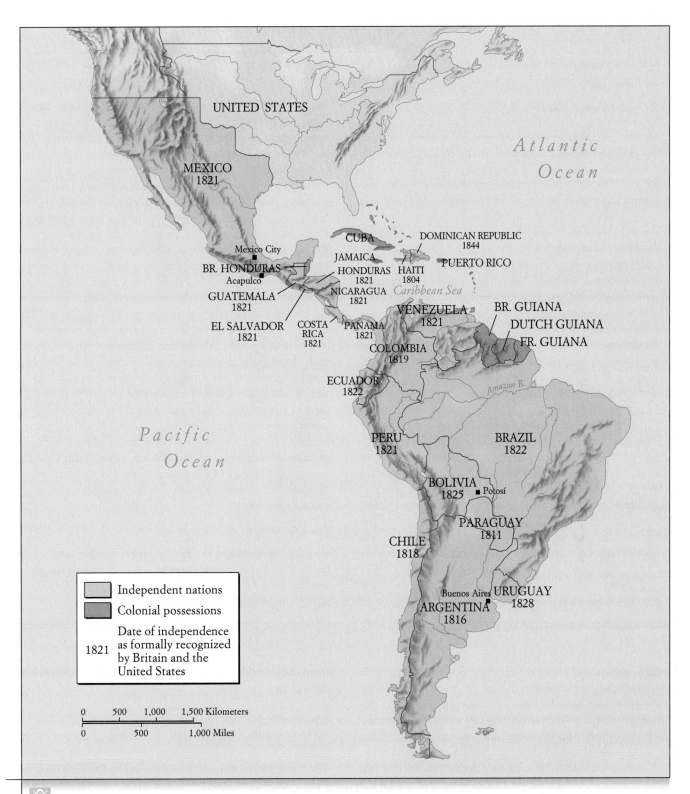

UNITED STATES

Atlantic Ocean

MEXICO
1821

Mexico City

BR. HONDURAS
Acapulco

GUATEMALA
1821

EL SALVADOR
1821

COSTA RICA
1821

PANAMA
1821

CUBA

JAMAICA

HONDURAS
1821

NICARAGUA
1821

HAITI
1804

DOMINICAN REPUBLIC
1844

PUERTO RICO

Caribbean Sea

VENEZUELA
1821

BR. GUIANA

DUTCH GUIANA

FR. GUIANA

COLOMBIA
1819

ECUADOR
1822

Amazon R.

Pacific Ocean

PERU
1821

BRAZIL
1822

BOLIVIA
1825

Potosí

PARAGUAY
1811

CHILE
1818

Buenos Aires

URUGUAY
1828

ARGENTINA
1816

Independent nations

Colonial possessions

1821 Date of independence
as formally recognized
by Britain and the
United States

0   500   1,000   1,500 Kilometers

0   500   1,000 Miles

MAP 34.1 Latin America in the Early Nineteenth Century. This map shows the changes
in status after 1804, when Haiti was effectively made independent by a slave rebellion.

BENITO JUÁREZ
(1806–1872)

The popular image of **Benito Juárez,** the national hero of Mexico and the protector of its independence, stems only partly from his deeds as a political and social reformer. Juárez also planted the seed for a whole series of changes in the national consciousness of his country toward the relative importance of criollo and mestizo values. In a society long known for its aristocratic views, he awakened Mexican nationalism and steered his people on the lengthy and rocky path toward political democracy. In Mexico, he is considered the spirit and soul of his country and one of the greatest of all the Latin American leaders.

A contemporary of Abraham Lincoln, Juárez, too, was of humble birth and very poor. The son of Zapotec Indian peasants from the region of Oaxaca, he could not even speak Spanish in his childhood. At the age of three, he lost both father and mother and went to live with an uncle. At twelve, he set out on foot to Oaxaca because he had lost one of his uncle's sheep and feared severe punishment. Living with a sister, he was lucky enough to find a Franciscan brother who gave him the rudiments of education. Years later, he succeeded in entering the local Institute of Arts and Sciences to study law and graduated in 1831. After a few years, Juárez entered local politics and served in the state and, later, national legislatures. In 1841, he was made a judge, and six years later, he was elected governor of Oaxaca state. Political differences with the dictatorial government of Antonio López de Santa Anna in Mexico City landed Juárez briefly in jail and sent him into exile in the United States in the mid-1850s. When Santa Anna was deposed, Juárez became minister of justice in the new liberal government, and from that position, he was primarily responsible for the creation of the strongly liberal and reformist constitution of 1857.

All these activities brought him the solid opposition of the conservative elements, notably the entrenched *haciendados,* or great landowners, and the higher churchmen. This opposition led to the War of Reform (1858–1861), in which the liberals were able to beat back the challenge of the reactionary groups and preserve the constitution under Juárez's leadership as acting president.

No sooner was the war over than Britain, Spain, and France decided to force Mexico to pay outstanding debts by seizing the country's ports. Although Britain and Spain soon withdrew, the French under Archduke Maximilian and a good-sized army fought their way into Mexico. Despite heroic resistance against the invaders in Puebla (May 5, 1862) and elsewhere, much of Mexico was under the control of the French for several years. Juárez's government retired to El Paso (now Ciudad Juárez), while keeping up the struggle. Finally, the withdrawal of the French and the capture and execution of Maximilian in 1867 ended this major threat to Mexico's independent existence.

Juárez was reelected president, but the years of war against both the dictator Santa Anna and the foreign colonialists had taken a severe toll. The struggle between liberals and conservatives was as fierce as ever and showed no signs of abating after the victory over the French. Like other Latin reformers, Juárez ended his life painfully aware of the difficulties in getting his fellow Mexicans to agree on even the most basic elements of political and social progress. His Indian origins, his commitment to the welfare of the poor masses, and his high-minded dedication to justice and equality have ensured his everlasting memory in Mexico.

FOR REFLECTION

In which ways can you predict that Juárez's Indian race would be an asset and a debit in his attempt to lead an independent Mexico? Why didn't the neighboring United States take a stand against Maximilian?

---

almost always came from the army ranks. Government policy was tightly controlled by a small group of wealthy individuals, closely linked with the military officer corps. The prestige of the military man was an unfortunate consequence of the battles for independence—unfortunate, that is, for constitutional process and the rule of law.

Once in a while, a "man of the people" would rise and assert populist dictatorial rule for a time. Examples are Juan Rosas in Argentina and Agustin Iturbide in Mexico. Almost always, these individuals soon made peace with the large landlords and other criollos who had traditionally governed. Social reforms were forgotten for another generation, while the caudillo became corrupt and wealthy.

In the constitutions worked out in the 1820s, all legal distinctions among the citizens of the new states were declared void. Slavery was abolished in most (but not all) of them. But that did not mean that there were no social class distinctions.

SOCIAL DISTINCTIONS

The Latin society of the colonial period had already evolved a clear scale of prestige: the "pure-blooded" criollos were at the top, various levels of Europeanized mestizos were in the middle, and the non-European ***zambos,*** or Indians and black ex-slaves, were at the bottom. Because people were born into their places on the scale, Latin American society is frequently called a society of ***castas*** (castes). Status was largely visible at a glance because skin color was an important factor in determining who was who. Although Latin society was relatively free of the legal and political

Water Supply in an Indian Village. Bringing fresh water is traditionally the work of women and girls, while the men are in the fields. A central well or fountain can be found in every village, such as this one in Guatemala. (© *Joe Cavanaugh/DDB_Stock*)

prejudice against the dark-skinned population that the North Americans only partly overcame in the Civil War, the society had a distinct social gradient by complexion that was (and is) taken for granted.

States with numerous pure-blooded Indians (most of South and all of Central America) refused to allow them to participate as equals in either political or cultural life and made no effort to introduce them into national public affairs for several generations. These restrictions were not necessarily a bad thing: most of the Indians had neither experience nor interest in government beyond the village or tribal levels.

In free Latin America as under Spain, the towns were the center of everything that was important: politics, administration, cultural events, commerce, and industry. The criollos were disproportionately prominent in the towns. The countryside was inhabited by the bulk of the population: mestizo or Indian small farmers, farm and pastoral laborers, and many hundreds of thousands of people who had no visible means of support. The absentee landlords lived in town, looked toward Europe, and left daily control of the rural plantations to agents and managers.

For the mestizo and Indian masses, life was a losing struggle against poverty; there was not enough good land, not enough industrial jobs, and not enough enterprise in the ruling group to induce change for the better. Though slavery was forbidden, **peonage** became commonplace on the haciendas. Peonage was a form of coerced labor to repay real or alleged debt owed to the employer; it was not much different than slavery for the victim and perhaps more lucrative for the master. (See the box for more details about "Labor in the Americas.")

The universal backwardness of the rural majority was a chief reason for the stagnation of national politics through most of the nineteenth century. Illiteracy and desperate poverty were normal; social castes were fixed from colonial days and did not change. The Indians, blacks, and their zambo offspring remained mostly outside public life, though technically they were free and equal citizens when slavery was abolished (Brazil did not abolish slavery until 1888, when it became the last of the Western Hemisphere countries to do so). Blacks and Indians had more opportunity for mobility in Latin America than in North America, however. Latin American society was willing to consider light-skinned mulattos and mestizos as equivalent to Europeans rather than holding that miscegenation (mixed blood) was an insuperable obstacle to social status. Relative wealth, skills, and education counted for more than blood alone.

LAND AND LABOR

Land (the source of livelihood for the great majority of people) was held in huge blocks by a small number of families, who often claimed descent from the conquistadores. Sometimes they had land grants from the king to prove it; more often, their ancestors had simply taken over vast tracts from the helpless Indians. Since land was useless without labor, first the Indians and then (in Brazil and the Caribbean) imported blacks were forced to work it as slaves.

Slave agriculture is normally only profitable where monoculture plantations can produce for a large market. For this reason, Latin American agriculture came to be

LABOR IN THE AMERICAS

In the 1620s, a Spanish monk traveled through the Spanish colonies in the Americas, making careful observation of what he witnessed, among which was the workings of early textile mills and how they got their labor.

Three centuries later, just before the Mexican Revolution, a couple of Englishmen observed the economy of the henequen (sisal, used before synthetics for rope and cord) haciendas in Yucatán, southern Mexico. What they saw outraged them, and after returning to Europe, they published an account that they hoped would change things—in vain.

1. There are in this city [Puebla, in central Mexico] large woolen mills in which they weave quantities of fine cloth. . . . To keep their mills supplied with labor, they maintain individuals who are engaged and hired to snare poor innocents; seeing some Indian who is a stranger to the town, with some trickery or pretense, such as hiring him to carry something, like a porter, and paying him cash, they get him into the mill; once inside, they drop the deception, and the poor fellow never again gets outside that prison until he dies and they carry him out for burial. In this way they have gathered in and duped many married Indians with families, who have passed into oblivion here for 20 years, or longer, or their whole lives, without their wives and children knowing anything about them; for even if they want to get out, they cannot, thanks to the great watchfulness with which the doormen guard the exits. These Indians are occupied in carding, spinning, weaving, and the other operations of making cloth; and thus the owners make their profits by these unjust and unlawful means.

And although the Royal Council of the Indies, with the holy zeal which animates it in the service of God our Lord, of his Majesty, and of the Indians' welfare, has tried to remedy this evil . . . and the Viceroy of New Spain appoints mill inspectors to visit them and remedy such matters, nevertheless, since most of those who set out on such commissions aim rather at their own enrichment, however much it may weigh upon their consciences, than at the relief of the Indians, and since the mill owners pay them well, they leave the wretched Indians in the same slavery; and even if some of them are fired with holy zeal to remedy such abuses when they visit the mills, the mill owners keep places provided in the mills in which they hide the wretched Indians against their will, so that they do not see or find them, and the poor fellows cannot complain against their wrongs. . . .

2. The Yucatecans have a cruel proverb, "Los Indios no oigan sino por las nalgas" ("The Indians hear only through their backs"). The Spanish halfbreeds have taken a race once noble enough, and broken them on the wheel of a tyranny so brutal that the heart of them is dead. The relations of the two peoples is ostensibly that of master and servant; but Yucatan is rotten with a foul slavery—the fouler and blacker because of its hypocrisy and pretence.

The peonage system of Spanish America, as specious and treacherous a plan as was ever devised for race-degradation, is that by which a farm labourer is legally bound to work for the landowner, if in debt to him, until that debt is paid. Nothing could sound fairer; nothing could lend itself better to the blackest abuse. In Yucatan every Indian peon is in debt to his Yucatecan master. . . . The plantation slave must buy the necessaries of his humble life at the plantation store, where care is taken to charge such prices as are beyond his humble earnings. Thus he is always in debt to the farm; and if an Indian is discovered to be scraping together the few dollars he owes, the books of the hacienda are "cooked"—yes, deliberately cooked—and when he presents himself before the magistrate to pay his debt, say, of twenty dollars the haciendado can show scored against him a debt of fifty dollars. The Indian pleads that he does not owe so much. The haciendado-court smiles. The word of an Indian cannot prevail against the Señor's books, it murmurs sweetly, and back to his slave work the miserable peon must go, first to be cruelly flogged to teach him that freedom is not for such as he, and that struggle as he may, he will never escape the cruel master who under law as at presently administered has a complete a disposal of his body as of one of the pigs which root in the hacienda yard.

Sources: A. Vásquez de Espinosa, Compendium and Description of the West Indies, *trans.* C. Clark (Washington, D.C.: Smithsonian, 1942), *and* C. Arnold *and* F. J. Tabor Frost, American Egypt: A Record of Travel in the Yucatan *(London: Hutchinson, 1909).*

based on one or two export crops in each region—an economically precarious system. Originally, the cash crops were sugar and rice destined for the European or North American markets. Later, bananas, coffee, and citrus in the more tropical lands and cattle and wheat in the more temperate climates became the main exports. Almost all the labor of clearing land, raising and harvesting the crop, and transporting it to market was done by hand. Machinery was practically nonexistent into the twentieth century, because with labor so cheap, the landholders had no need for machines.

The size of the *latifundia* (big rural plantations) actually grew after independence. Their owners were practically little kings within the republics. Although these great landowners did not carry formal titles of nobility after independence, they might as well have done so, as they comprised an aristocracy in the truest sense. Mostly of European blood, they intermarried with one another exclusively; their sons went into high government office or the army officers' cadres by right of birth. In the nineteenth century, this aristocracy lived very well, in both the material and the intellectual senses. But they inherited the lack of social responsibility that also marked their ancestors. They either could not see or would not recognize that the miserable conditions of the majority of their fellow citizens eventually posed a danger to themselves.

Getting Logs to the River. Backbreaking labor is still the rule in most of Latin America for jobs that the developed world performs with machines. Here men are preparing logs for floating to a downstream mill on the Amazon River. (© *Elizabeth Harris/Getty Images*)

LATIN AMERICAN AND CARIBBEAN CULTURES

The prevalent culture of Latin America owes as much to the European background of its original colonists as does the culture of North America. The two differ, of course. The ideas and values introduced into Latin America were predominantly Spanish or Portuguese, Roman Catholic, and patriarchal rather than British, Protestant, and (relatively) genderless as in the United States and Canada.

While Iberian culture is supreme on the mainland, the Caribbean islands reflect the African origins of their black populations. The native Amerindian populations of the islands were exterminated or fled early and have been entirely supplanted by African ex-slaves and mulattos. Thus, the Caribbean culture is very different from the Iberian and is not properly considered a part of Latin America.

From these different roots have developed very different societies. As an example, until recently, public life in Latin countries was as much dominated by males as were ancient Greece and the Islamic civilizations. The adoption of the Napoleonic codes of law in these countries contributed to the persistence of the idea that the male is legally and socially responsible for the female. On the contrary, the black ex-slave societies of the Caribbean islands followed the African example of giving females a quasi-equal position in private and—to some degree—public affairs.

The Catholic Church in Latin America was guaranteed a supervisory role in most aspects of public life and private morals. It was from the start and remained an official church, supported by donations and taxes. It had little competition. Catholicism was the religion of the vast majority of the general population and of the entire ruling group. (As in the European homelands, Latin America has simultaneously had a strong tradition of anticlericalism.) The high clergy were automatically men of influence and did not hesitate to intervene in political affairs when they sensed that the church or their own family interests were threatened.

In the nineteenth century, the church was responsible for most educational institutions and practically all social welfare organs. At times, in some places, the church made a sincere effort at lifting the Amerindians and poor mestizos toward justice and dignity, even when doing so meant breaking with the ruling group from which much of the higher clergy came. But these episodes were the exception. Most of the time, class ties seemed stronger than a sense of obligation to the common people, and the clergy were content to conform to the current ideas of their lay peers.

Cultural stratification is particularly strong in Latin America and has long been an obstacle to national unity. Until the early twentieth century, certainly, the landowner–official group who controlled public life regarded themselves as Europeans resident in another continent, rather than as Latin Americans, in the same way the British colonists regarded themselves as British living in Australia or the French settlers regarded themselves as French living in Africa. The elite read European literature, taught their children European languages in European-directed schools, and dressed in current European fashions. When they grew tired of their surroundings, they often spent a year or two in a European capital. Many sent their older children to European schools and universities as a matter of course. When asked about family origins, young men and women would say they came from some Spanish town, which their ancestors had left (often as poverty-stricken emigrants) 300 years earlier! They did not recognize a Latin American culture that was separate and distinct from Iberia. They spent much of their lives attempting to keep up with contemporary European culture and trying to replicate it in their alien environment.

A powerful reason for the great difference between Latin and North American social habits and history in this regard was that the whites in Central and South America perceived Amerindian culture as a much greater threat than did the European settlers of North America. The Amerindians of Latin America were far more numerous and far more civilized than their North American cousins. The Spanish and Portuguese conquerors wanted to maintain a sharp distinction between themselves and the natives. This distinction gradually gave way for a large number of ordinary people who intermarried with the Indians and created the mestizo culture that predominates in many present-day Latin countries. But the ruling class rigorously maintained the distinction, remaining at heart Europeans who lived in Peru, Brazil, or Colombia, *not* Peruvians, Brazilians, or Colombians. For them, intermarriage was unthinkable.

SUMMARY

The colonial experience in Latin America was quite different from that in Asia, North America, or Africa. A large number of Europeans eventually settled there but remained far outnumbered by the native Indians and the imported blacks. The church and government worked together to create a society that imitated that of the mother countries, while remaining different in many essentials. The unique melding of Iberian with Indian and African cultures proceeded in differing tempos in different places.

After the flow of American bullion to the Old World tapered off in the mid–seventeenth century, a long period of stagnation and neglect ensued. A century later, the Spanish Bourbons supervised an economic and political revival in Latin America with mixed results. While the economies of the colonies were indeed stimulated, so was resentment against continued foreign rule. Armed rebellion followed on the North American and French models, and by 1825 the colonials had established independent republics that Spain and Portugal could not recapture.

Independence proved easier to establish than to govern, however. Military men and local caudillos became the ultimate arbiters of politics despite grand-sounding manifestos and constitutions. An urban elite of absentee landlords maintained power despite numerous "revolutions."

The agrarian economy became dependent on the exports western European and North American states. The rural majority lived in agrarian villages or haciendas that differed little from serfdom. Little manufacturing could develop owing to both the widespread poverty of the internal market and the openness of that market to imports from abroad. By the end of the nineteenth century, Latin America was perhaps tied more closely to foreign economic interests than it had ever been in the colonial era.

The disparities between the governing criollo cliques and the mestizo, black, and Amerindian masses were underlined by cultural orientations. The members of the upper class considered themselves Iberians and Europeans displaced in a Latin American atmosphere.

TEST YOUR KNOWLEDGE

1. Which of following Spanish terms does *not* apply to Latin American social or ethnic divisions?
   a. Criollo
   b. Menudo
   c. Mestizo
   d. Zambo

2. Which of the following does *not* describe the conditions under which the Latin Americans gained independence?
   a. In the wake of the Napoleonic invasion of Spain
   b. As a result of the Spanish king's intolerable tyranny
   c. As a counter to a feared movement toward radical democracy
   d. Inspired by the successful North American and French revolutions

3. Which of the following is most correct? Racism in the Latin countries has traditionally been
   a. wholly contingent on the economic position of the affected person.
   b. expressed as prejudice but not persecution against the dark skinned.
   c. less overt but more harmful overall to good relations than in North America.
   d. divorced from skin color but reflective of religious prejudices.
4. Which was the last country in the Americas to outlaw slavery?
   a. Honduras
   b. Brazil
   c. United States
   d. Mexico
5. The Latin criollos of the independence movement were interested mainly in
   a. obtaining more land for themselves.
   b. keeping U.S. influences out of their homelands.
   c. assuring the installation of popular democratic government.
   d. maintaining political control against the Indian or mestizo masses.

6. Which of the following does *not* describe Benito Juárez?
   a. A pure-blooded Indian
   b. A committed defender of Mexican nationalism
   c. The devout ally of the Catholic clergy
   d. The father of Mexico's constitution
7. The only successful rebellion by slaves in the Western Hemisphere occurred in
   a. Haiti.
   b. Cuba.
   c. Colombia.
   d. Brazil.
8. *Monoculture* and *latifundia* are terms usually associated with
   a. pastoral societies.
   b. self-sufficient farmers.
   c. growing of garden produce for local consumption.
   d. large-scale, forced labor production for export.
9. *Caudillo* is the Latin American term for
   a. a retired general who has been honored in civil life.
   b. an appointed governor of a province.
   c. a usurping strongman.
   d. a priest who has entered politics.

IDENTIFICATION TERMS

Bolívar, Simón	*encomienda*	L'Ouverture, Toussaint	San Martín, José de
Carlos III	*hacienda*	Monroe Doctrine	Tupac Amaru
castas	Hidalgo, Miguel	peonage	*zambo*
caudillo	Járez, Benito		

INFOTRAC COLLEGE EDITION

Enter the search term "Latin America history" using Key Words.
Enter the search terms "Mexico revolution" or "Mexican revolution" using Key Words.

Enter the search term "Monroe Doctrine" using Key Words.

1500–1800 C.E.
DISEQUILIBRIUM: THE WESTERN EXPANSION

	Law and Government	Economy
Europeans	Law and government based on class, but the effect of religious wars is to make them increasingly secular. Absolutist monarchy the rule, with few exceptions (England, Holland). Nobles and landlords rule free peasants in West, serfs in East. State and church still intertwined; religious tolerance considered dangerous to public order by most governments.	Economy continues to diversify, with strong capitalist character, especially in Protestant nations. Urban middle class becomes prominent in business and commerce. Growing number of impoverished people, with abject serfdom common east of the Elbe River. Machine industry begins in later eighteenth century in western Europe.
West Asians	Government continues along traditional Qur'anic lines, and law follows the *sharija*. Ottomans bring Muslim international empire to its apex in sixteenth century, but they cannot sustain the momentum after 1700. Safavid dynasty in Persia has two hundred years of glory but exhausts itself between Ottoman and Mughal rivals in Turkey and India.	Further evolution of highly commercialized, complex trade among Muslim countries as well as between them and the non-Muslims. Slavery remains common, mainly from African sources. Wealth is generated from gold mines in West Africa, spices from East Asia, and carrying trade between India/China and the West via the Mediterranean.
South and East Asians	The Western presence is not yet decisive but steadily more apparent. Many South Pacific island territories have been under Western colonial administration since 1500s. Japan originally welcomes Westerners but then shuts itself off in *sakoku*. China continues as imperial dynasty ruling through mandarins after the Manzhou replace the Ming in 1600s. India's north and center unified under the Mughal dynasts, with European colonies beginning to occupy the coasts after 1700.	Japan prospers and advances in *sakoku* isolation; China has last great age under early Qing before humiliation at European hands: north and south brought firmly together by extensive trade. Mughul India is still a well-organized, prosperous country, with much commerce with Southeast Asia and islands. Merchants and craftsmen multiply, but everywhere the agrarian village is the mainstay of the economy.
Africans	The coming of Europeans to coasts as slavers generally has little immediate effect on African law and tribal government. On east coast, Arab-African trading cities (Zanzibar, etc.) prosper, but Great Zimbabwe declines. Tribal warfare increases after introduction of firearms and large-scale slaving in West. Interior tribes barely affected by Europeans throughout period.	Slaving disrupts some established trade patterns in West, making some of the coastal states (Dahomey) more powerful, undermining others (Hausa, Songhay). Agriculture spreads, aided by introduction of new crops from the Americas and South Asia. Bantu areas in east and south develop extensive trade with Arab and Portuguese coastal towns.
Americans	By the mid-1500s, Spain and Portugal had established Iberian law and viceroyalties. Natives subordinated to small minority of whites. Highly centralized colonial governments committed to mercantilist system and discouragement of autonomy. Temporary reversal of these policies in later 1700s.	Mercantilism enforced until the 1700s, with colonial artisans and manufacturers obstructed by Madrid. Mining and plantation agriculture are the dominant large-scale economic activities. A large majority of population lives in agrarian subsistence economy.

PEOPLES: EUROPEANS, WEST ASIANS, SOUTH AND EAST ASIANS, AFRICANS, AMERICANS

Religion and Philosophy	Arts and Culture	Science and Technology
Christian unity broken by Protestant Reform. Papal church severely challenged, but regains some of lost ground in seventeenth century. Churches become nationalistic and theology more narrowly defined. Skepticism and secularism on rise after 1700, leading to increased religious tolerance by end of eighteenth century. Enlightenment dominates intellectual affairs after c. 1750.	Renaissance continues in plastic arts; great age of baroque architecture, sculpture, and painting in Catholic Europe. Neoclassicism of eighteenth century led by France. Vernacular literature flourishes in all countries. Western orchestral music begins. First professional authors. First signs of democratization of the arts.	Physical, math-based sciences flourish in "Scientific Revolution" of seventeenth century. Science replaces scripture and tradition as source of truth for many educated persons. Technology becomes much more important. Weaponry enables West to dominate all opponents. Agriculture enables population explosion of eighteenth century. The beginnings of the Industrial Revolution are manifested in England.
Ulema and Islamic tradition resist the accumulating evidence of Western superiority and attempt to ignore or refute it on doctrinal grounds. Religious orthodoxy is severely challenged in various parts of empire (Sufi, Shi'a, etc.) and becomes increasingly defensive. Last major surge of Islamic expansion into Asian heartland (Mughal India).	High point of Islamic art forms under Ottoman, Safavid, and Mughal aegis. Architecture, ceramics, miniature painting, and calligraphy are some particular strengths.	Sciences are neglected; original mental capital derived from Greek and Persian sources now exhausted and no new impulses discovered. Technology also lags, with almost all new ideas coming from the West rejected as inferior. By end of period, Westerners moving into preferred posts in commerce of Ottoman and Mughal empires (capitulations, East India Company).
Religious beliefs undergo no basic changes from the prevalent Buddhism (China, Japan, Southeast Asia); Hinduism (most of India, parts of Southeast Asia); Islam (north India, Afghanistan, East Indies); and Shinto (Japan). Christianity briefly flourished in Japan until its suppression by Tokugawa shoguns in 1600s, but makes little headway in China and India.	Superb painting, drawing on porcelain, bamboo, and silk in China and Japan. Calligraphy is major art form. *Kabuki* and *No* plays in Japan, novels in China. Poetry of nature. India: Taj Mahal, frescoes, enamel work, and Mughal architecture are high points.	Sciences throughout Asia falling rapidly behind Europe by end of this period. Exceptions in medicine, pharmacy. China adopts defensive seclusion from new ideas under mandarin officials. Technology lags also, as overpopulation begins to make itself felt at end of period, further reducing the need for labor-saving devices or methods.
African native animism continues unchanged by European "factories," which have no interest in missionary work, but Muslims make steady progress in sub-Saharan conversions, reaching into Congo basin by period's end.	The high point is Benin bronze work and masks. People have oral folk beliefs in place of literature. Wood carving and gold work are chief media.	Sciences and technology remain dormant in the absence of writing and systems of formal education. Some adaptation of European technology by western coastal states in weaponry and ironwork.
Catholicism makes a somewhat deeper impression on Indians, but religion remains a mixed cult of pre-Christian and Christian beliefs, supervised by *criollo* priesthood and Spanish hierarchs.	The church remains the major sponsor of arts in formal sense, but folk arts derived from pre-Columbian imagery remain universal. Baroque churches are center of social life. Little domestic literature, but secular Enlightenment makes inroads into a small educated class by the mid-eighteenth century.	Science and technology are totally dependent on stagnant mother country and have no importance to illiterate masses. Enlightened monarchs of later 1700s make some improvements, but these are temporary and partial.

FIVE

WESTERN REVOLUTIONS, INDUSTRY, AND IDEOLOGY

1700–1920

After a rising secularism had gradually dampened the Europe-wide crisis generated by the Protestant challenge to the papal church, the seventeenth century witnessed the first wave of "scientific revolutions" that would mark modern times. For the first time since the Greeks, the West took the forefront in advances in knowledge about this world and its natural phenomena (Chapter 35).

The same curiosity and willingness to challenge ancient authority that impelled the breakthroughs in natural science were a bit later applied to the Science of Man, as the eighteenth-century Enlightenment called it. The Enlightenment itself was the project of an urban upper class determined to bring Reason and its child Wisdom to take their rightful places in the halls of government as well as the school and home. Filled with a sense of sacred mission, the philosophes fought the intolerance and ignorance of the past, most especially the darkness surrounding the established church and absolutist throne (Chapter 36).

What they desired in political/constitutional affairs seemingly came to pass in the first flush of the popular revolution in France. But the original reforms were soon overshadowed by a radical democracy employing terror against all who opposed. The Napoleonic empire's aggressions confirmed the negative impression gained by most observers outside France and also strengthened the eventual victors' resolve to limit and control both political and social change (Chapter 37).

Following the pattern established in late eighteenth-century Britain, the rest of western Europe entered the industrial epoch in the ensuing century by stages. The initial industrial revolution was powered by steam and concentrated in a few basic commodity production processes (Chapter 38). Its immediate social repercussions were bitter for the masses of poor laborers in the new towns but gradually were ameliorated (Chapter 39). In the meantime, the postrevolutionary peace was disturbed by clashes between reactionary monarchies and the rising forces of economic and political liberalism, culminating in the bloody rebellions of 1848–1849 in much of Europe (Chapter 40).

The short-term failure of most of the 1848 rebellions was caused largely by the new ethnically based nationalism that had arisen in many lands as an indirect result of the French Revolution. It was exacerbated by the cleft between the bourgeois political liberals and the socially radical working classes, which came to light during the revolts. By the 1870s, this cleft was being bridged in the western, democratizing states, though still quite wide in the eastern and southern parts of Europe (Chapter 41). Advancing industrial development, now powered by the new energy sources of petroleum and electricity, helped bring about further democratization as well as a rising wave of Marxian socialism as the nineteenth century entered its final quarter (Chapter 42).

The physical sciences and some of the social sciences took imposing strides in the second half of the nineteenth century and had various effects on the European popular consciousness (Chapter 43). The nineteenth century's naïve faith in Progress had a horrid demise in the catastrophic World War I, with fateful impacts on both the West and the non-Western world (Chapter 44).

35

THE SCIENTIFIC REVOLUTION
AND ITS ENLIGHTENED AFTERMATH

*If I have seen farther than others,
it is because I have stood on the shoulders
of giants.*

ISAAC NEWTON

1543	Nicholas Copernicus, *Revolution of the Heavenly Bodies*
c. 1575–c. 1650	Francis Bacon/Galileo Galilei/René Descartes
1687	Isaac Newton, *Principia Mathematica:* law of gravitation
1690	John Locke, *Essay Concerning Human Understanding*
1730s–1789	Enlightenment flourishes
1776	Adam Smith, *Wealth of Nations*
1776	Thomas Jefferson, Declaration of Independence

PERHAPS THE MOST far-reaching of all the "revolutions" since the introduction of agricultural life in the Neolithic Age was the change in educated persons' thinking about nature and its components during the early modern era. This Scientific Revolution became fully evident in the work of the eighteenth-century *philosophes,* but its major outlines were drawn earlier, when the focus of European intellectual work gradually shifted away from theology to the mathematical sciences. By the end of the eighteenth century, it had proceeded so far among the educated classes that the new worldview was taken for granted. While the consolidation of royal absolutism was proceeding in most of Europe during the seventeenth and eighteenth centuries, the sciences successfully challenged theology's claim to be the summit of intellectual activity.

THE SCIENTIFIC REVOLUTION
OF THE SEVENTEENTH CENTURY

So great were the achievements in science during this epoch that one of the outstanding modern philosophers has said that "the two centuries [that followed] have been living upon the accumulated capital of ideas provided for them by the genius of the seventeenth century." The natural sciences—that is, those based primarily on observed phenomena of nature—experienced a huge upswing in importance and accuracy. A new style of examining phenomena, the **scientific method,** came into common usage. It was composed of two elements: careful observation and systematic experimentation based on that observation. Interpretation of the results of the experiments, largely relying on mathematical measurement, was then employed to achieve new knowledge.

The most significant advances in the sciences came from posing new types of questions rather than from collecting new data. Different questions led directly to novel avenues of investigation, and those led to new data being observed and experimented with. For example, **René Descartes** (1596–1650), one of the founders of the mathematical style of investigation, wished to take humanity to a higher plane of perfection than ever yet achieved. To do so, he separated the material from the nonmaterial universe completely, insisting that the material world could be comprehended by mathematical formulas that existed entirely apart from the human mind. If that was so, knowledge of these broad laws of number and quantity could provide explanations—hitherto lacking—of observed phenomena. The proper way to understand the material world, then, was to formulate broad generalizations of a mathematical nature and employ these to explain specific events or processes. This approach, in which one went from a general law to a particular example of that law observed by the human mind, was called **deductive reasoning.**

The other method of accumulating knowledge about the natural world was exemplified in the writings of the Englishman **Francis Bacon** (1561–1626). Bacon insisted that contrary to traditional belief, the great majority of the ideas and principles that explain nature had not yet been discovered or developed but lay buried, like so many gems under the earth, awaiting uncovering. Like Descartes, he looked forward to a better world, but this world was to be created by the persistent and careful observation of phenomena without any preconceived laws or general explanations of them, a process that became known as **inductive reasoning.**

Bacon was not methodical in his science or his reasoning. His close association with the concept of inductive reasoning is not really deserved. But his writings did encourage later scientists to practice the **empirical method** of gathering data and forming generalizations. *Empirical* means the evidence obtained by observation through the five senses, which is then worked up into hypotheses (assumptions) that may be subjected to experiment. This style of assembling knowledge blossomed in the seventeenth century and later became the normal fashion of proceeding in all the sciences.

Background of the Scientific Revolution

Why did the spectacular advances in natural science occur in the seventeenth century rather than earlier or later? There is no single answer to this question. As with most important changes in the status quo, several factors both material and immaterial came together at that time to encourage more rapid progress than before. But this is not to say that no progress had been under way previously. It is now accepted that the old view of medieval science as a laughable collection of superstitions and crackpot experiments is quite wrong. The medieval universities harbored many people who seriously undertook to widen the horizons of knowledge and had some success in doing so. The long search for magical elements to convert base metal into gold, for instance, did much to found the science of chemistry.

The real problem of medieval and Renaissance science seems to have been its exaggerated reliance on authority, rather than empirical evidence. The great Greek philosophers of science—Aristotle, Ptolemy, Galen, Eratosthenes, and Archimedes—were held in excessive reverence as the givers of final truth. The weakening of this reverence or intimidation by the ancients made possible the breakthroughs of the sixteenth and seventeenth centuries.

Stimulated and aided by the reports of the explorers and voyagers in the New World, scholars accumulated a mass of evidence about nature and geography that both amplified and contradicted some of what the traditional authorities had taught. Such evidence could be ignored only at the risk of retarding the power and wealth of the whole society. Still more important, perhaps, was the rapid advance in the mathematical capabilities of Europeans. At the beginning of the sixteenth century, European math was still at the same level as in the seventh century. Only with the recovery of the Greek and Hellenistic mathematical works could it advance into new areas: logarithms, calculus, and decimals. By the middle of the seventeenth century, math had become as much a device for theoretical exploration as for counting.

Another mass of data that partly contradicted what the Greeks had believed was the product of new instruments. The new math made possible analyses of the physical world that had never before been attempted. New instruments of all sorts (sensitive scales, pressure gauges, microscopes, telescopes, thermometers, chronometers) came along one after the other to assist in this analysis. It was now possible to measure, weigh, divide, and synthesize the world in ways that seemed to explain the previously inexplicable.

THE PROGRESS OF SCIENTIFIC KNOWLEDGE: COPERNICUS TO NEWTON

The rediscovery of the Greco-Roman scientific treatises by the Renaissance scholars (often working from Arabic translations of the Greek and Latin originals) stimulated curiosity while simultaneously providing a series of new insights into the makeup of the natural world—insights that contradicted the conventional wisdom of the day. This progress was sharply interrupted by the wars of religion in the sixteenth century, when the focus shifted away from science to clashing theologies. Only with the exhaustion of those religious antipathies after the Thirty Years' War did scientific endeavors once again take an important position in educated men's affairs.

Our emphasis on seventeenth-century events does not mean that modern science commenced then. The first solid theoretical advance in knowledge of the natural world came a century earlier with the *Revolution of the Heavenly Bodies,* the pioneering treatise on astronomy by the Polish scholar **Nicholas Copernicus** (1473–1543). Copernicus cast severe doubt on the generally accepted theory of an Earth-centered (**geocentric**) universe, which he criticized as unnaturally complex and difficult to understand. Copernicus's observations led him to conclude that the Earth revolved around a fixed sun, a belief first advanced by Hellenistic Greek astronomers. A cautious and devout

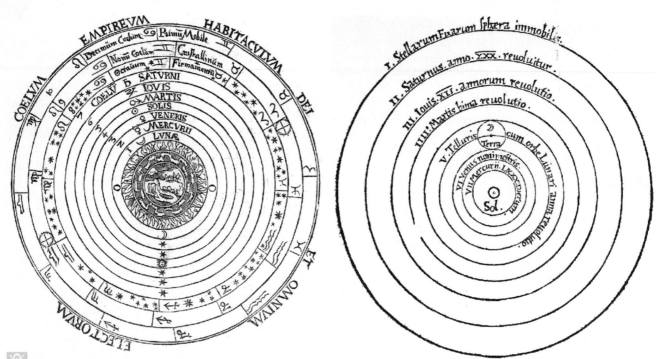

The Two Cosmoses. Contrasted here are the two visions of the cosmos. The first dates from the sixteenth century before Copernicus's death and shows the geocentric universe and the sun (Solis) between Venus and Mars. The second is from the first edition of Copernicus's great work and shows the heliocentric universe. *(Courtesy of the Lilly Library, Indiana University, Bloomington, Indiana)*

man, Copernicus published his conclusions only in the year of his death. The church ignored his theory at first, though it was ridiculed by both Luther and Calvin. But when **heliocentrism** began to win adherents in large numbers, both Rome and the Protestants officially condemned it as contrary to both Scripture and common sense.

Two astronomer-mathematicians who emerged a generation after Copernicus also deserve our attention. The first was an eccentric Dane, Tycho Brahe (1546–1601), who spent much of his life taking endless, precise measurements of the rotation of the visible planets. Using these data, Tycho's student, the German Johannes Kepler (1571–1630), went on to formulate the *three laws of celestial mechanics,* which showed that the heavenly bodies moved in great ellipses (ovals) around the sun, rather than in the perfect circles that had been believed necessary as the handiwork of a perfect Creator. This insight explained what had been previously inexplicable and made Copernicus's proposals still more persuasive.

In the early 1600s, an Italian professor at Pisa named **Galileo Galilei** (1564–1642) used his improvement of the telescope to rewrite the rules of cosmology as handed down from the ancients. His discoveries strongly supported Copernicus's suppositions that the universe was indeed sun centered and that the Earth was a relatively small, insignificant planet in a huge solar system. Not only did Galileo's astronomy force a reconsideration of the condemned theory of Copernicus, but his physics contributed to the final overthrow of Aristotle's long reign as master physicist.

Through his work with falling bodies and the laws of motion, Galileo came close to discovering the fundamental law of all nature: the law of gravity.

When Galileo died in 1642, the whole traditional view of the physical universe as an impenetrable mystery—created by God for his own reasons and not responsive to human inquiries—was beginning to come apart. The horizons that had been in place for many centuries were steadily receding as the seventeenth century progressed. What was still needed was some overarching explanation of the physical world order, which was now being revealed as though through a semitransparent curtain.

The genius of **Isaac Newton** (1642–1727) put the capstone of the new science in place. While still a student at Cambridge University, he theorized that there must be a "master key" to the edifice of the universe. In the century and a quarter since Copernicus, a great deal had been discovered or strongly indicated about the laws of nature. Still lacking, however, was a universally applicable explanation of the most basic property of matter: movement.

In the 1660s, Newton occupied himself with the study of physics. At that time he evolved his deceptively simple-looking theorem, the most famous in the history of the world: $E = M^2/D^2$. This was the formula of the law of gravitation, although it yet lacked mathematical proof. After many more years of research, Newton published his conclusions and their proofs in the *Principia Mathematica* in 1687. The *Principia* was the most influential book on science in the seventeenth century and was soon known from

ISAAC NEWTON
(1642–1727)

The man many consider the most distinguished scientist of all history, Sir Isaac Newton, was born on Christmas Day, 1642, in Lancashire, England. Best recognized as the discoverer of the law of gravity, Newton in his own day was equally famed for his work in optics, higher mathematics, and physics. He was a distinct exception to the rule that pioneers are not appreciated; his career as both a Cambridge professor and government official under William and Mary was brilliant and adequately rewarded.

Although his father was a farmer with little property, Newton received an exceptional education. He completed studies at the local grammar school near his home village, with the aid and encouragement of the Anglican vicar, who was a graduate of Cambridge. With this gentleman's recommendation, Isaac won a scholarship to the university in 1661, graduating in 1665 with what would now be called a major in natural science. He wished to go on for the M.A. degree at once, but an outbreak of plague forced the university to close in both 1666 and 1667, and Newton returned home.

During these years, the great, groundbreaking work on gravity was basically outlined. The notion that all physical being was, so to speak, tied together by a single principle—that of gravity—took shape in the twenty-five-year-old's long studies at his family home in Woolsthorpe. Newton gradually refined and expanded his theory when he returned to Cambridge, first as an M.A. candidate, then as a professor in 1669. He held this post until his honor-filled retirement in 1701.

Although Newton apparently regarded gravitation as a fact as early as the 1660s, he hesitated in publishing his work until 1687. In that year, his *Principia Mathematica,* or *Mathematical Principles of Natural Philosophy,* was finally published in London

Isaac Newton.
(© The Granger Collection)

and soon afterward in most of the capitals of Europe. Rarely has a scientific book been hailed so universally as a work of genius. At the same time, Newton was bringing out fundamentally important work on the spectrum, proving that light was composed of colored particles. Newton is also generally credited with being the codiscoverer of calculus, along with his rival Gottfried Leibniz. The two men were working quite independently, and their quarrel over who was first became one of the Scientific Revolution's less appetizing anecdotes.

In his later years, Newton's dedication to Old Testament studies and theology surpassed his scientific interests. Newton was a master of Greek and Hebrew and spent much energy on his researches into the Old Testament prophecies.

Highly placed friends secured his appointment as warden of the royal mint in 1696, a lucrative post that Newton was very grateful to have. In 1703, he was elected president of the Royal Society, the premier scientific post in England, and was reelected every year thereafter until his death. The queen knighted Sir Isaac in 1705 for services to his country as well as to the realm of science. Newton died at eighty-five years of age, heaped with honors and substantial wealth. On his deathbed he is supposed to have said, "If I have seen farther than others, it is because I have stood on the shoulders of giants." After a state funeral, he was buried in the walls of Westminster Abbey.

The famous story of the falling apple just may be true; no one will ever know.

FOR REFLECTION

Contrast the fashion in which Newton gave his formula on gravitation to the world and the way such as announcement might be made today by modern scientists. Why do you think he chose to use Latin as his vehicle, so late in the 1680s?

---

one end of educated Europe to the other. (See the Science and Technology box for more on Newton.)

Newton created a new universe. The physical cosmos was a sort of gigantic clockwork in which every part played a particular role and every movement and change was explained by the operation of law. It was humans' proud duty and privilege to identify those laws and in so doing to penetrate to the heart of the God-created universe.

RELIGION AND SCIENCE IN THE SEVENTEENTH CENTURY

What was the reaction of the official churches to this challenge to tradition? Both Catholic and Protestant preachers felt that relegating the earth to a secondary, dependent position in the universe was at least an implied rejection of

Holy Scripture (the Old Testament story about the sun standing still at the battle of Jericho, for example). It also downgraded the jewel of God's creation, human beings, who lived on Earth and were presumably limited to it. Galileo was threatened with imprisonment if he did not retract parts of what he had published in one of his books on science. He spent his final years under house arrest by order of the pope.

Were these condemnations justified? Most of the seventeenth-century scientists considered themselves good Christians and made no attempt to rule a divine being out of the universe. Newton himself, a devout Anglican, spent most of his later life in religious speculations and obscure theological inquiries. Descartes, like Copernicus before him, was a Catholic who saw no conflict between what he taught about the nature of the material world and what he believed about the spiritual one. Quite to the contrary, Descartes believed that his speculations only pointed more clearly to the existence of a divine intelligence in the universe.

Most ordinary people were unmoved by the revelations of science. The peasants never heard of them, and even urban dwellers were ignorant of them except for the privileged few whose education went beyond the three Rs. The fourth R, religion, generally retained the strong grip on the daily lives of common folk that it had always had.

But the church's truth, resting as it did on revelation rather than empirical data, was being challenged—at first only tangentially, but later more and more confrontationally—by the truth of science. And science's truth had potent appeal for men and women weary of the strife of theologians and the claims of priests and pastors. Science's truth had no axes to grind for one party or another. It was not linked to politics or to a social group's advantage or disadvantage. It was self-evident and could sometimes be used to benefit the ordinary person, for example, through technology (though the connections between science and technology were as yet almost entirely undeveloped).

Increasingly, educated people were beginning to wonder whether it was indeed more useful to know whether the Holy Eucharist should be given in two forms than to know how digestion takes place in the stomach or some similar aspect of the new physical science. Science came to be seen as an alternative to theology in finding useful knowledge and applying it to society's multiple problems.

In this regard, two of the most important thinkers of the seventeenth century were the agnostic Dutch Jew Baruch Spinoza and the devout Catholic Frenchman Blaise Pascal. Spinoza was a great questioner, who after leaving Judaism finally found some measure of peace by perceiving his God in all creation—*pantheism.* His rejection of a personal deity earned him a great deal of trouble, but his thought influenced generations. Pascal wrote his *Pensées* (*Thoughts*) to calm a troubled mind and produced a work that has ever since been considered one of the greatest of Christian consolations. The fact that Pascal was highly suspect to the French clerical establishment only added to his later fame.

The Science of Man

Until modern times, the natural sciences were regarded as a branch of philosophy rather than a separate intellectual exercise. Already in the Renaissance, math and physics were beginning to establish a place in the university curriculum. Their prestige was still relatively low, and they could not rival medicine, law, or theology in attracting students—but they did begin to form their own rules of evidence and analysis.

As the mathematics-based sciences came to be accepted as the sources of much previously unknown truth, the previous relation between natural science and philosophy underwent a gradual but decisive reversal. Philosophy, which had been the more inclusive term, encompassing science itself, now became for many merely a branch of science. Insomuch as an object of thought could not be measured and weighed, it ceased to be for them worthy of close attention. Such individuals held that *only* what could be determined in its existence by the tools of science was reachable by the intellect and useful to humans. They did not deny that other phenomena that were not reachable by intellectual means existed, but they insisted that these phenomena should have only a secondary place in the hierarchy of values.

Among those phenomena, of course, were religious belief, artistic creativity, wonder, imagination, ethics, and political theory, to mention only a few. None of these could be measured, and none could be brought under uniform and predictable laws. Or could they? A body of thought gradually arose that said these phenomena, too, might be subject to law, analyzable through mathematical computations, and comprehensible in the same way as physics. *The Science of Man,* not as an anatomical construct or an example of biological systems but as a thinker, political actor, and artist, began to form. By the early eighteenth century, this science—which we now call social science—was competing with physical science for the attention of the educated classes.

The Enlightenment

Eighteenth-century intellectual leaders saw no reason why what had been done in the natural sciences could not be attempted in the social and intellectual sciences. They wanted to put history, politics, jurisprudence, and economics under the same logical lenses that had been applied to math and physics. Spurred on by such hopes, the **Enlightenment** was born.

Above all, the eighteenth century in western Europe was distinguished from what had come before by the attitudes that educated persons exhibited in the affairs of everyday life: the atmosphere of their mental life. Two key characteristics marked the Enlightenment: optimism and rationality. Here *optimism* refers to the belief that change is possible and controllable in society at large, while *rationality* refers to the idea that the universe and all creatures within it, especially humans themselves, are comprehensible, predictable, and lawful. The commitment to a rational view of the universe usually embraced a similar commitment to *secularism*—that is, a downgrading or outright rejection of the importance of supernatural religion. The Enlightenment preferred to see humanity as capable of creating its own moral code for its own benefit and in accord with the precepts of a rational mind.

How did this translate to concrete activity? The ways of viewing the physical world that math and physics had introduced were now applied—or an attempt was made to apply them—to the world's social, political, and moral aspects. If physicists could measure the weight of the Earth's atmosphere (as indeed they could), then why couldn't historians isolate the exact causes of cultural retardation and determine how to avoid them in the future? Why couldn't criminologists build a model prison and establish a regime there that would turn out completely rehabilitated prisoners? Why couldn't political scientists calibrate various methods of selecting public officials to ensure that only the best were elected?

Formative Figures and Basic Ideas

The two outstanding fathers of the Enlightenment's ideals were the Englishmen Isaac Newton and John Locke. As we have already seen, Newton was the greatest scientific mind of his age, and Locke was the leading mapper of the political path that England embarked on with the Glorious Revolution of 1688 (see Chapter 28).

Newton's greatest contribution to science—even more important than the law of gravity—was his insistence on rational, lawful principles in physical nature. He rejected supernatural causes as an explanation of the natural world. Because nature is rational, human society as part of nature should be rational in its organization and function.

Locke was as much a psychologist as a political scientist; he set forth his view of the mind in the immensely influential **Essay Concerning Human Understanding** (1690). Here he said that the mind is a blank page until experience writes on it and molds it. Thus, human nature is dynamic and unfixed; it has been in the past and will be in the future formed by external experience, and this experience is capable of being controlled. Thus, humans are *not* condemned to repeat endlessly the mistakes of the past. They can and indeed must take charge of their destiny; they can perfect themselves. (See the box for "Frederick II's Opinions on Human Nature.")

More than anything else, this faith in *perfectibility* is the distinguishing innovation of the Enlightenment. For the previous seventeen centuries, the Christian idea of guilt from the sin of Adam as an insuperable barrier to human perfection had been the foundation stone of Western moral philosophy. Now, the eighteenth century proposed to move

FREDERICK II'S OPINIONS ON HUMAN NATURE

By no means were the philosophes able to sway all throne holders or other important people to their optimism on human capabilities. Here is the opinion of one of their favorites, Frederick II, king of Prussia, on the nature of human beings and the requirements of governing them, as expressed to Voltaire in 1759:

> Superstition, self-interest, vengeance, treason, ingratitude will produce bloody and tragic scenes until the end of time, because we are governed by passions and very rarely by reason. There will always be wars, lawsuits, devastations, plagues, earthquakes, bankruptcies. . . . Since this is so, I presume it must be necessary. . . . But it seems to me that if this universe had been made by a benevolent Being, he should have made us happier than we are. . . . The human mind is weak; more than three fourths of mankind are made for subjection to the most absurd fanaticism. Fear of the Devil and of hell fascinates their eyes, and they detest the wise man who tries to enlighten them. . . . In vain do I seek in them that image of God which the theologians assert they bear. Every man has a wild beast in him; few can restrain it, most men let loose the bridle when not restrained by terror of the law.

Source: W. and A. Durant, *The Story of Civilization* (New York: Simon & Schuster, 1965), vol. 10, p. 496.

the house off this foundation and erect it anew. Progress, both moral and physical, was reachable and real. The study of history showed how far humans had come and how far they still had to go. The past was filled with error and blindness, but it could be—*must* be—learned from, so that it could light the way to a better future.

The reformers believed that religion was generally controlled by those who profited from the continuance of ignorance and was everywhere used as a tool for obscuring the truth. They took an especially harsh view of the Roman Catholic clergy. Where the church had obtained a monopolistic position in the state and was the official church, the reformers believed that inevitable corruption had made it a parasite that should be cast off as soon as possible and replaced with freedom of conscience and worship.

In the reformers' view, education was the salvation of humankind. It should be promoted at every opportunity everywhere. Insofar as people were educated, they were good. The educated would be unerring seekers of the best that life held, defenders of the helpless, teachers of the misguided, and the liberators of the oppressed.

The Philosophes and Their Ideals

The Enlightenment was a view of life, a philosophy, and that meant it must have its philosophers. Generically

⬡ **The Establishment of the French Academy of Sciences and the Observatory.** Louis XIV sits in the center as the scientists who depend on his support for their work scramble around him to display their achievements. (© *Giraudon/Art Resource, NY*)

known by the French term *philosophes,* they included men and women of both thought and action, scientists and philosophers, who were committed to the cause of reform. Despite their often intense personal differences, they were united in their desire for progress, by which they meant controlled changes.

Several of the outstanding philosophes were French. Paris, and secondarily London, was the center of the Enlightenment's activities (the Enlightenment was a decidedly urban phenomenon), but the philosophes kept in frequent touch with one another through a network of clubs and correspondents that covered the map of Europe (see Map 35.1). They included the Frenchmen Voltaire (François-Marie Arouet), Baron Montesquieu, Denis Diderot, and Jean-Jacques Rousseau; the English and Scots David Hume, Adam Smith, and Samuel Johnson; the Germans Josef von Sonnenfels, Gotthold Lessing, and August Ludwig von Schlozer; and the Italians Lodovico Muratori and Cesare Beccaria; but the list could be made as long as one wants. The Americans Thomas Jefferson, Benjamin Franklin, and John Adams belong as well—the Enlightenment had no territorial boundaries, though it was much narrower and shallower in eastern Europe than in the west and had much less impact on the public conduct of government. (See the Science and Technology box for more on Franklin.)

Chronologically, the earliest evidence of enlightened activity in organized fashion dates from the 1730s. The period ended with the French Revolution's political crises. The high point of reform activity was in the 1770s and 1780s, when various governments experimented with or fully adopted one after another of the favored ideas of the philosophes.

Beyond reform, it is difficult to find a common denominator in these ideas because the philosophes themselves are difficult to categorize. Some of them were the first public atheists, while the majority were at least outward Christians, and some were quite pious clergymen. Muratori, for example, was a priest. Most believed constitutional monarchy was the best form of government, whereas others were uncompromising republicans.

In the physical sciences, some believed unreservedly in the Baconian procedure of going to the sense-perceptible data (empirical science), others rejected all knowledge that was not reducible to mathematics, and still others classified quantifiable knowledge as inherently inferior. Some were hopeful of gradual improvement in human affairs (ameliorationism); others were convinced that nothing important could be accomplished without radical, even revolutionary changes in society.

The philosophes did not hesitate to argue with one another as well as with their conservative opponents. Much of the literature of the later eighteenth century consists of pamphlets and newspapers arguing one or another favorite idea. In a society where literacy levels made wide distribution of printed matter a paying proposition for the first time, the philosophes made full use of the available channels to get their various messages out into the public.

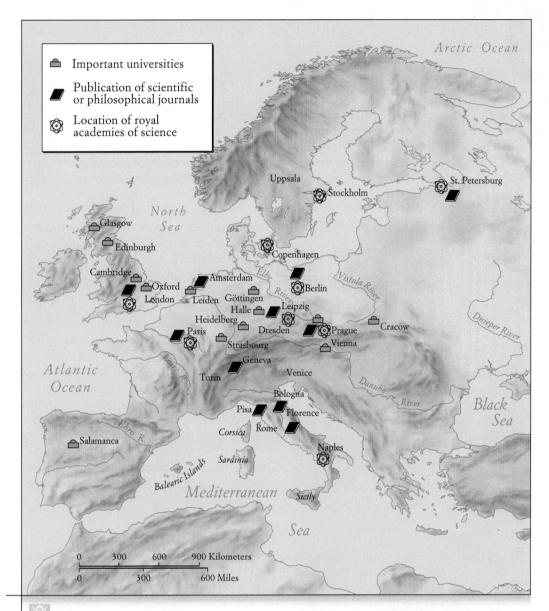

MAP 35.1   Centers of the Enlightenment, circa 1750.   The absence of Enlightenment centers in Turkish-controlled southeast Europe and their paucity east of the Elbe and south of the Pyrenees were decisive influences on the futures of these regions in the ensuing century. Focused on cities and academies, the Enlightened society was the spearhead of later social and political innovation.

Common Goals   Although they differed on specific details, the majority of the philosophes agreed on many general points. For one thing, they universally acclaimed the idea of a *balance of governmental powers* between executive and legislature as presented in Baron Montesquieu's famous ***Spirit of the Laws*** (1748), perhaps the most influential of a century of very influential books on government. In it, the French aristocrat argued for the careful division of powers to prevent any one branch from becoming too strong and dictatorial. He thought that of current governments, the British example came closest to perfection in that line (he did not really understand the British system,

however), and his ideas had great impact on the makers of both the U.S. and the French Revolutions.

The *constitutional limitation of monarchic power* was considered an absolute essential of decent government. The brilliant Voltaire (1694–1778), in particular, led the charge here, as he had a good deal of personal experience with royal persecution in his native France before becoming such a celebrity that kings desired his witty company. He, too, admired the British system of assuring civil rights and condemned the French lack of such safeguards.

The philosophes also agreed that *freedom of conscience* must be assured at least for all varieties of Christians, if not

FRANKLIN AS SCIENTIST

Ben Franklin is better known to Americans as a political activist and philosopher, but he is equally entitled to be in the front rank of those who created the Enlightenment's views of science. His work in isolating and controlling electricity was fundamental, and his interest in the subject was, as almost always with him, closely tied to the practical applications it might contain. But to ascertain those applications, certain experiments were necessary:

Franklin spoke of electricity as fire, but this fire, he thought, was the result of a disturbance between the equilibrium of the

Franklin at his Laboratory. This nineteenth-century French engraving shows the American diplomat-scientist investigating the attraction and repulsion of electrical ions. Franklin was convinced that someday electricity could be rendered useful to mankind. (*The Granger Collection, New York*)

"positive" and the "negative" fiery fluids that he conceived electricity to be. All bodies, in his view, contained such electrical fluid: a "plus" body containing more than its normal amount, is positively electrified, and tends to discharge its surplus into a body containing a normal amount or less; a "minus" body containing less than a normal amount, is negatively electrified and will draw electricity from a body containing a normal amount or more.

His work with lightning rods to protect buildings from such electrical discharges was at first rejected as "visionary" by the Royal Society in London but was soon validated: Two French scientists, de Lor and d'Alibard, put Franklin's theory to trial by erecting a pointed iron rod fifty feet high; they instructed a guard to touch the rod with an insulated brass wire if, in their absence, thunder clouds should pass overhead. The clouds came, the guard touched the rod not only with wire but also with his hands, sparks flew and crackled, and the guard was severely shocked. De Lor and d'Alibard confirmed the guard's report by further tests and informed the Académie des Sciences, "Franklin's idea is no longer a conjecture, but reality."

Franklin himself was not satisfied; he wished to make the identity of lightning and electricity evident by "extracting" lightning with something sent up into the storm cloud itself. In June 1752, as a thunderstorm began, he sent up on strong twine a kite made of silk; a sharply pointed wire projected some twelve inches from the top of the kite; and at the observer's end of the twine a key was fastened with a silk ribbon. In sending to England directions for repeating the experiment, Franklin indicated the results:

> When the rain has wet the kite twine so that it can conduct the electric fire freely, you will find it stream out plentifully from the key at the approach of your knuckle, and with this key a phial [Leiden jar] may be charged, and from electric fire thus obtained spirits may be kindled, and all other electric experiments performed . . . and therefore the sameness of the electrical matter with that of lightning completely demonstrated.

FOR REFLECTION

Why do you think it generally took a century or more to convert knowledge of science into technology useful to man, prior to our own days?

Source: W. and A. Durant, The Story of Civilization *(New York: Simon & Schuster, 1965), vol. 9, p. 520.*

Jews and atheists as well. "Established" or tax-supported churches should be abolished, and no one faith or sect should be identified with governmental powers (as was the case in all European countries at this time).

All persons should enjoy a fundamental *equality before the law.* The philosophes saw this as a basic right that no government could take away or diminish. In line with this principle, punishments were to be blind to class distinctions among criminals; the baron would be whipped just like the peasant. Meanwhile, those who had talent should have increased possibilities for upward mobility. This did not mean that the philosophes were democrats; almost all of them agreed with the majority of educated persons that humans should definitely *not* have equal social and political rights.

The philosophes were convinced that the cause of most misery was ignorance, not evil intentions or sin. They were thus picking up a thread that had been running through the fabric of Western intellectual discussion since the Renaissance: that the main causes of man's inhumanity to man were to be found in ignorance and that in a good society, such ignorance would not be tolerated. This view led the philosophes to call for *state-supervised education* through the elementary grades as perhaps the most important practical reform for the general benefit.

Most philosophes viewed the *abolition of most forms of censorship* as a positive step toward the free society that they wished to see realized. Just where the lines should be drawn was a topic of debate, however; some of them would permit direct attacks on Christianity or any religion, for instance, while others would not.

In addition to censorship, the philosophes were not in agreement on several other broad areas of public affairs. Some would have abolished the barriers to social equality, so that all government posts would be open to commoners; others feared that this would guarantee the rule of the mob. A few, such as the Marquis de Lafayette, became republicans; most thought that monarchy was a natural and necessary arrangement for the good of all.

Economic Thought: Adam Smith

The outstanding figure in eighteenth-century economic thought was undoubtedly the Scotsman **Adam Smith** (1723–1790). In his ***Wealth of Nations,*** which was published in 1776 and soon became a European best-seller in several languages, Smith put forth the gospel of free trade and free markets. Smith is often described as saying that the smaller the government's role in the national economy, the better, and that there is no economic problem that a free market cannot solve to the benefit of all. *Laissez-faire* (Let them do what they will) was supposedly his trademark. But this is a vast oversimplification of Smith's ideas. In reality, he acknowledged that government intervention in one form or another was necessary for society's well-being in many instances.

Smith is, however, rightly credited with being the father of free enterprise as that term is used in the modern West. In *The Wealth of Nations,* he laid out in persuasive detail his conviction that an "unseen hand" operated through a free market in goods and services to bring the ultimate consumers what they needed and wanted at prices they were willing to pay. Smith criticized mercantilism, the ruling economic wisdom of his time, for operating to the disadvan-

tage of most consumers. As in so many other instances, his doctrines followed the Enlightenment's underlying conviction that the sum of abundant individual liberties must be collective well-being. Whether this is true, seen from the perspective of the twenty-first century, is debatable; to the eighteenth-century reformers, it was a matter of faith.

Educational Theory and the Popularization of Knowledge

One of the least orthodox of the philosophes, Jean-Jacques Rousseau (1712–1778), was the most influential of all in the vitally important field of pedagogy and educational philosophy. Rousseau was a maverick in believing that children can and *must* follow their inherent interests in a proper education and that the teacher should use those interests to steer the child in the wished-for directions. Rousseau had little following in his own lifetime, but his ideas had a strong impact on some of the revolutionary leaders a few years later and gained more adherents in the nineteenth century. He is now regarded as the founder of modern pedagogical theory and along with Smith is probably the most important of the philosophes to the present age.

In the mid–eighteenth century, Europeans were able to profit for the first time from the popularization of science and intellectual discourse that had come about through the Scientific Revolution. The upper classes developed a passion for collecting, ordering, and indexing knowledge about the natural world and humans' relations with it and with each other. The century also saw the initial attempts to make science comprehensible and accessible to the masses.

The most noted of these was the immensely successful French ***Encyclopédie,*** which contained thirty-five volumes and thousands of individual articles on literally everything under the sun. Its general editor was Denis Diderot (1713–1784), assisted by Jean d'Alembert, who saw the work through in fifteen years (1751–1765) against enormous odds. Contributors to the *Encyclopedie* (the first of its kind) included the outstanding intellectuals of Europe. The philosophical articles were often very controversial, and their "slant" was always in the direction favored by the more liberal philosophes. (Not the least valuable part of the enterprise were the numerous volumes of illustrations, which are the greatest single source of information on early technology.) The very expensive *Encyclopedie* sold more than 15,000 copies, a huge number for the day, and was found on personal library shelves from one end of Europe to the other, as well as in the Americas and Russia.

Ideals of the Enlightenment: Reason, Liberty, Happiness

Reason was the keyword in every philosophical treatise and every political tract of the Enlightenment. What was reasonable was good; what was good was reasonable. The philosophes took for granted that the reasoning faculty was

The Wheelwrights' Trade. One of the lasting values of the *Encyclopédie* was the exact illustration by copper engravings of the various trades and handicrafts of the eighteenth century. Pictured here are five steps in the making of carriage wheels. (© *The Granger Collection*)

humans' highest gift and that its exercise would, sooner or later, guarantee a decent and just society on Earth.

Liberty was the birthright of all, but it was often stolen away by kings and their agents. Liberty meant the personal freedom to do and say anything that did not harm the rights of another person or institution or threaten the welfare of society.

Happiness was another birthright of all humans. They should not have to defer happiness until a problematic eternity; it should be accessible here and now. In a reasonable, natural world, ordinary men and women would be able to engage in what one of the outstanding philosophes called "the pursuit of happiness" (Thomas Jefferson in the Declaration of Independence).

All of the ideals of the philosophes flowed together in the concept of *progress.* For the first time in European history, the belief that humans were engaged in an ultimately successful search for a new state of being here on Earth crystallized among a large group. The confidence and energy that were once directed to the attainment of heaven

Dual Portraits: Voltaire and Rousseau. Two faces of the Enlightenment are shown here. Voltaire's knowing half-smile suited the man who wrote the savagely satirical *Candide,* while Rousseau's moral seriousness comes across in this portrait of the author as a young man. *(Left, Mary Evans Picture Library; right, National Gallery of Scotland)*

THE ENLIGHTENED FEMALE

The eighteenth century saw the triumph of the idea that women have a specifically female nature. The triumph was essentially the work of physicians and the philosophes. More than ever before they speculated on what makes a woman and what differentiates and separates her from man. . . . All agreed that women are half of humankind, but once that statement was made their positions diverged.

One current of thought . . . introduced the notion of equality into the *querelle*. Asserting that "the mind has no sex" [this current] insisted that reason, which defines membership in the human species was proper to men and women alike. . . .

The opposing and clearly predominant attitude had two illustrious spokesmen, one a physician and the other a philosophe: Jean-Jacques Rousseau and Pierre Roussel. . . . Reducing current opinion to a system, they sparked a dynamic movement that produced a harvest of writings, medical and/or philosophical, on the specificity of the female. For all these authors the woman represented admittedly half of the human species, but a half that was fundamentally different. From difference they passed on rapidly to inequality, and from inequality to inferiority. . . .

The woman could not have the same type of reason as the man. Like the rest of her person, her reason was subject to her genital organs. This explained much of her weakness, hence her inferiority. She was an eternal invalid, regularly subject to ills proper to her—a true handicap that meant she could not possibly lead an active life in society. . . . "Women's status," Rousseau and the physicians asserted, is to be a mother, and they added that her anatomy predestined her to that role. What followed from that maternal function and her physiological weakness was a less active life, a "passive state" (Roussel) dictated by nature. . . . Each sex had its own functions, willed by nature: men's functions were public, women's were private; and it would be subversive to confuse the two.

The century of triumphant reason was thus not free of paradoxes. In a society where the sexes mixed (at least in France) on nearly all occasions, where women were at the heart of social life, both in the street and in the literary circles, a reigning ideology incontrovertibly divided the qualities, the space, and the social roles of the sexes. . . . Whereas the Enlightenment fought prejudice as the enemy of reason, the philosophers had no intention of abandoning their own prejudices where women were concerned.

FOR REFLECTION

What side of this perennial argument over the nature and capacities of women do you take? Do you believe that there is a real difference in the quality of female from male reason, or is this a "male myth"? If true, is it necessarily a mark of inferiority?

SOURCE: Dominique Godineau: :"The Enlightened Woman," in Enlightenment Portraits, ed. M. Vovell (Chicago: University of Chicago Press, 1997), pp. 395–399, 409–411.

---

were now transferred to the improvement of earthly life. Progress was inevitable, and it was the individual's proud task to assist in its coming.

The Audience of the Philosophes

How thoroughly did the Enlightenment penetrate European society? It was not by any means a mass movement. Its advocates, both male and female, were most at home amid the high culture of the urban elite. (See the Family and Gender Relations box on differences between the genders.) There were probably more fans of the acid satire of Voltaire in Paris than in all the rest of France and more readers of Hume in London than in all the remainder of the British Isles. It was an age of brilliant conversationalists, and the hostesses who could bring the celebrated minds of the day together were indispensable to the whole movement. In the "salons" of Madame X or Madame Y were heard the ex-

Cook and Banks in Hawaii. Captain Cook, discoverer of the Hawaiian Islands and much of the southern Pacific, is shown examining some of the exotic birds and wildlife of Hawaii. Beside him is the official naturalist of Cook's carefully planned expeditions, William Banks. (*Mary Evans Picture Library*)

changes of ideas and opinions that were the heartbeat of the Enlightenment.

The movement hardly ever attempted direct communication with the majority of the people. In any case, most were still illiterate and could not absorb this highly language-dependent message. Others, especially among the peasants, rejected it as atheist or antitraditional. Only the upper strata—the educated professional and merchant, the occasional aristocrat and liberal-minded clergyman—made up the audience of the philosophes, bought the *Encyclopedie,* and were converted to the ideals of progress, tolerance, and liberty. The majority of these would un-

doubtedly have been appalled by the prospect of revolution, and they had no sympathy for the occasional voice that considered violence against an evil government acceptable.

The Enlightenment was, then, an intellectual training ground for the coming explosion at the end of the eighteenth century. In its insistence on human perfectibility, the necessity of intellectual and religious freedoms, and the need to demolish the barriers to talent that everywhere kept the privileged apart from the nonprivileged, the Enlightenment spirit served as an unintentional forerunner for something far more radical than itself: the revolution.

SUMMARY

In the sixteenth century, the Renaissance scholars' rediscovery of classical learning and its methods produced an acceptance of empirical observation as a method of deducing truth about the physical world. This new attitude was responsible for the Scientific Revolution, which was at first confined to the physical sciences but inevitably spread to other things. Inductive reasoning based on observation and tested by experiment became commonplace in the educated classes. Mathematics was especially crucial to this process.

A century later, the confidence that the method of science was adequate to unlock previously incomprehensible mysteries had spread to the social sciences: the Science of Man. The same overreaching law that governed the rotation of the planets operated—or should operate—in politics and government. When that law was finally understood, all

would fall into place, and the Earth would cease to be out of joint.

The conviction that progress was inevitable and that humans were good and wanted good for others was the product of a relatively small but very influential group of philosophes in France and other countries. They were the leaders of a significant transformation of Western thought that was gradually embraced by most members of the educated classes during the course of the eighteenth century. This transformation is termed the Enlightenment. The philosophes were obsessed by reason and the reasonable and saw nature as the ultimate referent in these respects. A phenomenon of the urban, educated classes, the Enlightenment made little impact on the masses but prepared the way for middle-class leadership of the coming revolutions.

TEST YOUR KNOWLEDGE

1. The source of the major elements of medieval European thought in the physical sciences was
   a. Augustus Caesar.
   b. Aristotle.
   c. Virgil.
   d. St. Augustine.
2. Developments in which two sciences were at the heart of the advances of the sixteenth and seventeenth centuries?
   a. Physics and astronomy
   b. Math and chemistry
   c. Math and medicine
   d. Biology and chemistry
3. Kepler's great contribution to science was
   a. his theory of the creation of the universe.
   b. the three laws of celestial mechanics.
   c. the discovery of the planet Jupiter.
   d. his theory of the geocentric nature of the universe.

4. Which of the following did *not* make his fame as a natural scientist?
   a. Galileo
   b. Spinoza
   c. Copernicus
   d. Brahe
5. Newton's conception of the universe is often described as
   a. an apparent order that cannot be comprehended by humans.
   b. an incoherent agglomeration of unrelated phenomena.
   c. a mirage of order that exists only in the human mind.
   d. a machine of perfect order and laws.
6. By the end of the seventeenth century, educated Europeans were generally
   a. ready to abandon the search for a more intelligible natural science.
   b. considering applying the scientific method to the study of humans.

c. impelled toward atheism by the conflicts between religion and science.

d. abandoning Bacon's empiricism for Descartes's inductive reasoning.

7. Which of the following was particularly interested in reforming education?

a. Rousseau

b. Diderot

c. Hume

d. Voltaire

8. The Enlightenment is best described as a phenomenon that

a. was generally limited to an urban, educated group.

b. was found more or less equally throughout Christendom.

c. reached quickly into the consciousness of most people.

d. was generally favorable to the idea of an official religion.

IDENTIFICATION TERMS

Bacon, Francis

Copernicus, Nicholas

deductive reasoning

Descartes, René

empirical method

Enlightenment

Encyclopédie

Essay Concerning Human Understanding

Galilei, Galileo

geocentric

heliocentric

inductive reasoning

Newton, Isaac

philosophes

scientific method

Smith, Adam

Spirit of the Laws

Wealth of Nations

 # INFOTRAC COLLEGE EDITION

Enter the search terms "Isaac Newton" or "Copernicus" using Key Words.

Enter the search term "Enlightenment" using the Subject Guide.

Enter the search term "Rousseau" using Key Words.

36

LIBERALISM AND THE CHALLENGE TO ABSOLUTE MONARCHY

The American Revolution broke out, and the doctrine of the sovereignty of the people came out of the townships and took possession of the State.

ALEXIS DE TOCQUEVILLE

THE LIBERAL CREED

THE AMERICAN REVOLUTIONARY WAR

RESULTS OF THE AMERICAN REVOLUTION IN EUROPEAN OPINION

AMONG THE MOST IMPORTANT long-term consequences of the Scientific Revolution and the subsequent Enlightenment was the mental attitude called *liberalism*. It took especially strong root in the Anglo-Saxon countries, where it was also fostered by the events of 1688 and the writings of John Locke (see Chapter 28).

The political revolutions in America and France were quite different in course and outcome, but they were linked by a common origin in the belief in the inherent freedom and moral equality of men. This belief was at the heart of liberal politics and economics and could not be reconciled with the existing state of affairs in either the American colonies or France in the late eighteenth century. In this chapter, we will look at the linkage of liberal thought with the problems of the Americans; in the following one, at the troubles in France.

In America, the more radical colonists' discontent with their status grew to the point of rebellion in the 1770s. The term *rebellion* is usually associated with starving workers or exploited peasants. On the contrary, the American Revolution was led by a prosperous middle class, who had nothing against their government except that final authority was located in London and not directly responsible to them.

THE LIBERAL CREED

Where did the liberal creed begin, and what were its essentials? Liberalism was born in the form identified by the modern world in the late eighteenth century. Its roots go back much further, to the Protestant Reformation and the seventeenth-century political philosophers in England. The basic principles of liberalism are a commitment to (1) the liberty of the individual in religion and person and (2) the equality of individuals in the eyes of God and the laws.

Eighteenth-century liberals were children of the Enlightenment and thus especially noticeable in France and England, much less so in central, southern, and eastern Europe. They believed in the necessity of equality before the law and freedom of movement, conscience, assembly, and the press. They considered censorship both ineffective and repressive, and they despised the inborn privileges accorded to the aristocracy. They thought that a state religion was almost inevitably corrupt and that individuals should have the power to choose in which fashion they would serve their God.

Liberals originally did not believe in equality for all in political or social matters but only in legal and economic concerns. They subscribed to what we would now call "the level playing field" theory—that is, that all people should have the opportunity to prove themselves in the competition for wealth and the prestige that comes with it. Those who were weaker or less talented should be allowed to fail, as this was nature's way of allowing the best to show what they had to offer and keeping the best on top.

The liberals of the eighteenth century reflected the general optimism of the Enlightenment about human nature. Like most of the philosophes, the liberals believed that the good would inevitably triumph and that humans would recognize evil in whatever disguises it might assume for the short term. They believed that rational progress was possible and—in the long run—certain. They believed that education was the best cure for most of society's problems. (The enthusiasm for education carried over to a fascination with new technology that could demonstrate the innate mastery of men over nature. See the Science and Technology box for one of the more exotic examples.)

In matters of government, they sympathized with John Locke and Baron Montesquieu. These men thought that the powers of government must be both spread among various organs and restricted by a checks and balances system in which the legislative, judicial, and executive powers were held by separate hands. Liberals believed that representative government operating through a property-based franchise was the most workable and most just system. They mistrusted total democracy, which they thought would lead to rule by the "mob" of uneducated, propertyless, and easily misled. They rejected aristocracy (even though there were many liberal nobles) as being outmoded, a government by the few for the few. They were willing to have a monarchy, so long as the monarch's powers were checked by a constitution of laws, by a free parliament, and by free judges.

In the liberal view, the legislature should be the most powerful branch of government. It should be elected by and from the "solid citizens"—that is, from among the liberal sympathizers: educated and well-off commoners, professionals, merchants, and the lower ranks of the nobles. They all believed that the government of eighteenth-century England should be the model for the world. They admired its segregation of parliamentary and royal powers, with Parliament holding the whip hand in matters of domestic policies. They thought England after the Glorious Revolution had achieved a happy blend of individual freedoms within proper limits, allowing the responsible and forward-looking elements to retain political and social dominance.

THE AMERICAN REVOLUTIONARY WAR

It was natural that the British American colonies were strongholds of liberal thought and sympathy. Men like George Washington, Thomas Jefferson, James Madison, Benjamin Franklin, and many others were ardent supporters of the liberal view. They had pored over Locke and Montesquieu and digested their ideas (see Chapter 35). They had much less fear of democracy than the home country, because the masses of desperate poor who might threaten the continued leadership of the middle- and upper-class liberals in Europe were not present in America. In fact, the 3 million or so free colonists were probably the materially best-off large group of individuals in the world.

The American Revolutionary War began with a routine dispute between the British government and its subjects over taxation. Winning the **Seven Years' War** (French and Indian War), which lasted from 1754 to 1763 in North America, had cost the British government a considerable sum, while the American colonists had contributed very little to meet those expenses. The necessity of maintaining a much larger standing army to garrison America meant that London would be faced with a budgetary drain for the foreseeable future. Therefore, Parliament imposed a series of new taxes on the colonists, most notably the **Stamp Act of 1765,** which created such a furor that it was quickly repealed. The **Navigation Acts,** demanding the use of British ships in commerce between the colonies and other areas, which had been very loosely enforced until now, were tightened and applied more rigidly.

These British demands fell on colonists who in the Hanoverian dynasty era had become thoroughly accustomed to running their own household. The American colonies had the highest per capita income in the Western world in 1775, and they paid among the lowest taxes. They were the great "success story" of European settlement colonies, and they had achieved this condition without much guidance or interference from the London government. The Americans were used to a high degree of democratic government in local and provincial affairs. Many now felt they were being unduly pushed about by the ministers of King George III, and they resolved to let their feelings be known. The focal point of discontent was in the Massachusetts Bay colony, where commerce was most developed.

The Boston Tea Party of 1773 was a dramatic rejection of the right of the Crown to change the terms of colonial trade in favor of British merchants. When the London government replied to the defiant and illegal acts of the Bostonians by sending troops and closing the crucially important Boston harbor, the clash came much closer. One act led to another as the stakes were raised on both sides. Finally, in April 1775 the "shots heard 'round the world" were fired by the Minutemen in Lexington, and the War for Independence was on.

What did the rebellious colonists want? At the outset, the moderate faction in the Continental Congress, which the rebels summoned to provide political leadership, was in control. They demanded "no taxation without representation" and other, mild slogans upholding the alleged rights of Englishmen after the Glorious Revolution of 1688. But

THE FIRST MANNED FLIGHT IN ENGLAND, 1784

Vicente Lunardi, a Neapolitan diplomat in London, was a pioneer of the new science of aeronautics, born of the Enlightenment. In the 1780s, a rage for balloon flights swept Europe, with the first successful attempts being made in France at the very moment the American Revolution had been completed and the French upheaval was gathering momentum. Lunardi gives us here his recollections of his first flight in London, as an impatient crowd surrounds the anchored balloon and one accident after another delays the ascent:

I now determined on my immediate ascension, being assured by the dread of any accident which might consign me and my Balloon to the fury of the populace, whose impatience had wrought them up to a degree of ferment. An affecting, because unpremeditated testimony of approbation and interest in my fate, was here given. The Prince of Wales, and the whole surrounding assembly almost at one instant, took off their hats, hailed my resolution, and expressed the kindest and most cordial wishes for my safety and success. At five minutes past two, the last gun was fired, the cords [holding the Balloon] were divided, and the Balloon rose, the company returning my signals of adieu with the most unfeigned acclamations and applause. The effect was that of a miracle on the multitudes which surrounded the place; and they passed from incredulity and menace into the most extravagant expressions of approbation and joy.

At the height of twenty yards, the Balloon was a little depressed by the wind, which had a fine effect; it held me over the ground for a few seconds, and seemed to pause majestically before its departure. On discharging a part of the ballast, it ascended to the height of two hundred yards. As a multitude lay before me of a hundred and fifty thousand people who had not seen my ascent from the ground, I had recourse to every stratagem to let them know I was in the gallery [basket] and they literally rent the air with their acclamations and applause. In these stratagems I devoted my flag and worked my oars, one of which was immediately broken and fell from me, a pigeon too escaped, which with a dog and a cat were the only companions of my excursion.

When the thermometer had fallen from 68 to 61 degrees I perceived a great difference in the temperature of the air. I became very cold and found it necessary to take a few glasses of wine. I likewise ate the leg of a chicken, but my bread and other provisions had been rendered useless by being mixed with sand, which I carried as ballast.

When the thermometer was at fifty, the effect of the atmosphere and the combination of circumstances around produced a calm delight, which is inexpressible, and which no situation on earth could give. The stillness, extent, and magnificence of the scene rendered it highly awful. . . . I saw streets as lines, all animated with beings, whom I knew to be men and women, but which I should otherwise have had difficulty in describing. . . . All the moving mass had no object but myself, and the transition from the suspicion, and perhaps contempt of the preceding hour, to the affectionate transport, admiration, and glory of the present moment, was not without its effect on my mind.

Lunardi went on to land safely a few miles outside London in a farmer's yard, and the first balloon flight in England was the topic of every journal and café conversation for a week. Note that the cheerful custom of taking a glass of wine or two while making a balloon flight dates back to the origins, not always because of the cold!

FOR REFLECTION

Only a few days previously, a French balloonist had been threatened and his vehicle destroyed by an angry crowd awaiting the delayed ascent. Why might the common folk be suspicious and/or violent when confronted by new technology?

SOURCE: V. Lunardi, *An Account of the First Aerial Voyage in England* (London, 1784).

The Tea Party in Boston, 1773. This contemporary engraving shows the colonists emptying cases of tea into Boston harbor to express their contempt for the new excise-tax laws imposed by Parliament. Their diguise as Indians neither fooled nor was intended to fool anyone. (© *The Granger Collection*)

THE DECLARATION OF INDEPENDENCE OF 1776 AND THE DECLARATION OF THE RIGHTS OF MAN AND CITIZEN OF 1789

The American 1776 Declaration of Independence and the French 1789 Declaration of the Rights of Man and Citizen were products of individuals who had studied the same authors and were committed to the same visions of government's proper role. The American declaration was intent on dissolving political ties with what the colonists considered an unjust and alien government. The French document was aimed at generic reform of a monarchy that had neglected its duties to its people.

THE DECLARATION OF INDEPENDENCE OF 1776

We hold these truths to be self-evident, that all men are created equal, that they are endowed by their Creator with certain inalienable rights, that among these are life, liberty, and the pursuit of happiness. That to secure these rights, governments are instituted among men, deriving their just powers from the consent of the governed. That whenever any form of government becomes destructive of these ends, it is the right of the people to alter or to abolish it, and to institute new government, laying its foundation on such principles and organizing its powers in such form, as to them shall seem most likely to effect their safety and happiness.

THE DECLARATION OF THE RIGHTS OF MAN AND CITIZEN OF 1789

The representatives of the French people, organized in National Assembly . . . recognize and proclaim, in the presence and under the auspices of the Supreme Being, the following rights of man and citizen:

1. Men are born equal and remain free and equal in rights. . . .
2. The aim of every political association is the preservation of the natural and inalienable rights of man; these rights are liberty, property, security, and resistance to oppression; . . .
4. Liberty consists of the power to do whatever is not injurious to others; thus the enjoyment of the natural rights of every man has for its limits only those that assure other members of society the enjoyment of those same rights;
5. The law has the right to forbid only actions which are injurious to society. Whatever is not forbidden by law may not be prevented, and no one may be constrained to do what it does not prescribe.
6. Law is the expression of the general will. . . . All citizens, being equal before it, are equally admissible to all public offices, positions, and employments.
7. No man may be accused, arrested, or detained except in the cases determined by law, and according to the forms prescribed thereby. . . .
10. No one is to be disquieted because of his opinions, even religious, provided their manifestation does not disturb the public order established by law.
11. Free communication of ideas and opinions is one of the most precious of the rights of man. . . .
17. Since property is a sacred and inviolate right, no one may be deprived thereof unless a legally established public necessity obviously requires it.

July 4, 1776. This well-known painting by the American John Trumbull shows Jefferson as he presented his final draft to the Continental Congress in Philadelphia. (© *The Granger Collection*)

THOMAS PAINE
(1737–1809)

Of all those who might be called the liberal instigators of the American Revolution, Tom Paine must take pride of place. When he came to the colonies in 1774, he was an unknown English acquaintance of Benjamin Franklin. Two years later, he was one of the foremost figures in America. But at that point his extraordinary public career was just beginning.

Paine was born into rural poverty in 1737 and had to leave school at age thirteen to go to work to supplement the family's meager income. For the next quarter century, he failed at everything he tried, from seaman to schoolteacher. His appointment as excise collector (a hated post among the people) in 1762 was revoked because of an improper entry in his records. Although he managed to be reinstated in 1766, he remained under a cloud of suspicion and was dismissed again in 1774 for reasons that are unclear. At this juncture, friends introduced him to Franklin, who had come to London to represent the North American colonies before Parliament.

At his invitation, Paine arrived in Philadelphia in late 1774 and began writing for Franklin's *Pennsylvania Magazine*. A few months later, he became editor of the magazine. His contributions were marked by a gift for rhetoric and a radical turn of mind on public issues.

In early 1776, his pamphlet *Common Sense* appeared. The work immediately became a best-seller in the colonies and was reprinted in several European countries as well. Paine had a way with memorable phrases. *Common Sense* made a powerful argument not only against colonial government but also against the person of George III as a "hardened, sullen Pharaoh." In a mere seventy-nine pages, the pamphlet gave discontented Americans both abstract arguments and very concrete objections against being ruled by a distant, uncaring, and allegedly tyrannical monarch.

General Washington and other leaders at once recognized Paine's merits and his potential to assist in the revolutionary cause. Between 1776 and 1783, in support of the rebels, he produced the papers known collectively as *The Crisis*: "These are the times that try men's souls . . ." with references to "the summer soldier and the sunshine patriot."

In 1787 Paine returned to England for a short visit. Delays kept him until 1789, and while there, he was swept up in the initial liberal euphoria about the French Revolution. He wrote *The Rights of Man* (1791) to defend the Revolution against the increasing number of English critics. Having to flee England, Paine went to France and was elected to the Convention of 1793 despite being a foreigner. But here his independent attitude also made him an uncomfortable ally, and he was imprisoned for almost a year during the Reign of Terror. Released by the intercession of the American minister James Monroe, Paine wrote *The Age of Reason* (1794), a pamphlet denouncing revealed religions, especially Christianity, and challenging people to exercise their capacity to find a morality independent of faith.

When Paine finally returned to America in 1802, he was astonished and depressed to find that the outrage over his attack on religion had overwhelmed all gratitude for his services in the Revolution. Former friends such as John Adams and his family avoided him, and the children in his adopted town of New Rochelle, New York, taunted him. After several years of living as a social pariah on his farm, he died in 1809 and was denied the burial in a Quaker cemetery he had requested. A final bizarre note was added when a project to take his remains back to England failed because of the bankruptcy of one of the principals, and the coffin, which was seized as an "asset," disappeared forever.

FOR REFLECTION

Tom Paine once wrote, "It is absurd that a continent be ruled by an island." Do you agree in the sense that Paine meant? Do you think Paine's treatment after returning to America was justified given that almost all of his fellow citizens were God-fearing Christians?

---

by 1776, after blood had flowed, a more uncompromising group, led by Patrick Henry and Jefferson, assumed the leadership role. This group wanted nothing less than independence from Britain, and in the Declaration of Independence Jefferson wrote their program and battle cry (see the box for excerpts from this work as well as a comparable French declaration). The great popularity of the radical pamphlet **Common Sense** by the newly arrived **Thomas Paine** showed how inflamed some tempers had become (see the Tradition and Innovation box for more on Paine).

Not all the colonists agreed by any means. Besides the very hesitant moderates, many persons in all the colonies remained true to the Crown, and these Loyalists later either were maltreated by their fellow Americans or chose to emigrate at war's end. The conflict was as much a civil war as a rebellion. Even families were split. Washington's troops froze during the savage winter at Valley Forge, while in nearby Philadelphia most of the populace enjoyed their comforts under British protection.

The military outcome was eventually dictated by three factors favoring the rebels: (1) the logistic effort needed to transport and supply a large army overseas; (2) the aid provided to the rebels by the French fleet and French money; and (3) the only halfhearted support given by the Parliament in London to the war.

Under the **Alliance of 1778,** the French supplied the Americans with much material aid, some manpower, and, above all, prevented the British navy from controlling the

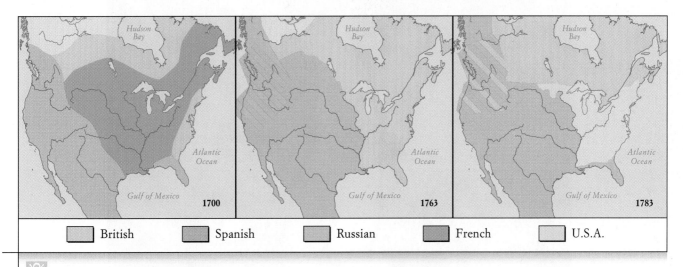

British   Spanish   Russian   French   U.S.A.

MAP 36.1 North America's Possessors, 1700–1783. The changing balance of power in Europe's affairs was closely reflected in North America in the eighteenth century.

coasts. By 1779, it was clear that the second-rate British commanders had no plans worth mentioning and could not put aside their mutual jealousies to join forces against Washington. Even if they had, the many London sympathizers with the Americans, both in and out of Parliament, would negate any full-fledged war effort. The defeat of General Lord Cornwallis at Yorktown in 1781 spelled the end of armed hostilities, and the Peace of Paris officially ended the war in 1783.

RESULTS OF THE AMERICAN REVOLUTION IN EUROPEAN OPINION

What exactly was the American Revolution? We are accustomed to thinking of a revolution as necessarily involving an abrupt change in the economic and social structures. But this was not the case in the new United States. The existing political, economic, and social circumstances of the citizenry, whether white or black, were scarcely changed by independence. The War for Independence had been won, but this was not at all the same as a revolution.

The real American Revolution was slower to manifest itself and did so only by degrees after 1783. At the outset, the thirteen former colonies were recognized as a sovereign nation, equal to any other. All the territory west of the Appalachians to the Mississippi was open to the new nation (see Map 36.1). For the first time, a major state (Switzerland preceded the United States but did not qualify as a major state) would have a republican form of government—that is, one that had no monarch and in which sovereignty rested ultimately in the people at large. Lawmaking power would be exercised by a representative body that was responsible to the citizenry through the electoral process.

Most of the (white male) citizens would be entitled to vote and to hold office. They would enjoy freedom of religion, be fully equal before the law, and have no economic restrictions imposed on them by birth, residence, or circumstance. The establishment of *that* form of government and *those* freedoms was the American Revolution, not the severance of ties with London.

A few years after independence, the ex-colonists acknowledged the severe shortcomings of the 1781 Articles of Confederation, which had been their first try at bonding the states together. They set themselves the task of creating a workable, permanent system of government. The outcome of the effort, the U.S. Constitution of 1789, is now one of the oldest constitutions in the world.

This document was drafted by men raised in the liberal traditions of the eighteenth century. They wished to create a system that would allow free play to individual talent and ambition and protect individual rights, while still asserting the primacy of the state. They believed in freedom of opportunity, while rejecting political and social equality. They believed in equality before the law and in conscience, but like Locke, they believed in the sacred rights of property. The framers of the Constitution under which Americans still live were conservatives in their approach to the life of the society but liberals in their approach to the life of the individual person.

More than the successful war, the U.S. Constitution made a huge impact on educated European opinion. It demonstrated for many that a large number of men could create a moderate system of self-government with elected representatives, and without an aristocracy or a monarch at its head. Many European liberals had informed themselves in detail about the United States. Some of them even came to fight in the rebellion (the French Marquis de Lafayette, the Poles Kazimierz Pulaski and Tadeusz Kościuszko, and the German Baron von Steuben). They were an effective

✦ **Lafayette, Marquis de France.** This engraving shows Lafayette as the adherent of the earliest stage of the revolution in France, when he was commander of the Garde Nationale, 1790. He was soon disillusioned by the increasing terror. *(AKG London)*

propaganda apparatus. And they were seconded by the equally effective work of Americans such as Franklin, Jefferson, and the Adamses, who resided for a time in Europe as officials of the new country.

Naturally, the American innovations received the most attention in France. The rebellion had many friends in enlightened society, including some in the royal government who welcomed this weakening of the British winner of the Seven Years' War. Many French officers had been in America and had contact with the leading American figures. The drawing rooms of the Parisian elite were filled with talk about America. Some of it was negative: the crude Ameri-

cans would soon see that government must be either by the king and his responsible officials or by the mob—no third way was possible, given human nature. But much of the talk was enthusiastically favorable. More and more persons of high social standing were convinced that the present French monarchic system was in terrible need of reform, and they looked to some aspects of the American experiment for models of what they wished to introduce at home.

Like the Enlightenment, the liberal frame of reference in politics was to contribute mightily in a few more years to a movement for reform that would go much further than originally intended.

SUMMARY

Liberal politics was the product of beliefs dating to the Protestant Reformation and the seventeenth-century English revolution against absolutism. Its fundamental principles asserted the equality and liberty of individuals in both

the moral and the legal sense. Liberals believed that all were entitled to the opportunity to prove their merits in economic competition, but they generally rejected social and political equality as impractical for the foreseeable future.

The British colonies in America were strongholds of liberalism, and those convictions led directly to the rebellion against British rule in 1775. Thanks in part to French military and financial aid and the lukewarm support of the war effort by Parliament, the rebellion was successful: the American republic was born, the first large-scale experiment in liberal politics. Although the War for Independence was won, the true American Revolution took longer to develop. Its paramount expression came in the Constitution of 1789, which made a deep impression on educated Europeans, particularly the French adherents of reform.

TEST YOUR KNOWLEDGE

1. Eighteenth-century liberals thought that
   a. all individuals should have equal opportunities to amass wealth.
   b. all individuals should have basic necessities guaranteed to them.
   c. men and women were essentially equal in talents and abilities.
   d. social and cultural position should be about the same for all.
2. In matters of religion, eighteenth-century liberals normally believed that
   a. there should be an officially designated and supported faith.
   b. all individuals should have freedom to believe as they saw best.
   c. the government must have authority over religion because of its connection with politics.
   d. all humans were naturally inclined to evil and sinfulness.
3. The essence of Baron Montesquieu's theses on government is that
   a. power should clearly be concentrated in the executive.
   b. lawmaking powers should be shared between the federal and state levels of government.
   c. elections should be guaranteed to be held within short time periods.
   d. powers should be divided among three branches of government.
4. An important reason for the democratic spirit among the North American colonists in the era before 1776 was
   a. the natural inclinations of colonials toward equality for all.
   b. the total absence of the social divisions commonly found in Europe.

c. the habit of religious tolerance in the American traditions.
   d. the absence of masses of poor people who might have threatened social revolution.
5. Which of the following was *not* a reason for American victory in the Revolutionary War?
   a. The division in Parliament about the conduct of the war
   b. The military mediocrity of the British commanding officers
   c. The better equipment of the American forces
   d. French aid to the rebels
6. The impact in Europe of the American Revolution can best be summarized as
   a. important and influential among the educated classes everywhere.
   b. important in Great Britain but not acknowledged widely elsewhere.
   c. minimal except among a handful of liberals.
   d. important in a military but not a political sense.
7. To liberal-minded Europeans, the success of the American Revolution meant above all that
   a. force is most important in political affairs.
   b. democracy should be introduced to their own governments.
   c. the teachings of the Enlightenment were feasible.
   d. Americans were more aggressive than other Westerners.

IDENTIFICATION TERMS

Alliance of 1778   **Navigation Acts**   **Seven Years' War**   **Stamp Act of 1765**
Common Sense   **Paine, Thomas**

INFOTRAC COLLEGE EDITION

Enter the search term "John Locke" using Key Words.
Enter the search term "American Revolution" using Key Words.

Enter the search terms "Thomas Paine" or "Tom Paine" using Key Words.

THE FRENCH REVOLUTION AND THE EMPIRE OF NAPOLEON

The effect of liberty upon individuals is that they may do as they please; we ought to see what it will please them to do before we risk congratulations.

EDMUND BURKE

THE WATERSHED OF modern political history is the upheaval called the French Revolution that struck France and then all of Europe in the last years of the eighteenth century. Considerably more than what had happened in the American colonies a few years earlier, the unrest in France challenged every tradition and shook every pillar of the establishment. During its unpredictable and violent course evolved the ideas of democracy, equality, and personal liberty, which the Revolution originally stood for but later betrayed. What started as a French aristocratic rebellion against taxes became the milepost from which all modern political and social developments in the Western world are measured.

THE BACKGROUND OF THE CRISIS

The Revolution of 1789 in France was triggered by a dispute over finances and taxation between monarch and subjects, just as the American Revolution was. But the tax question could have been remedied, if the deeper problems of the royal government in Paris had not been so intense and so complex.

Since the death of the "Sun King," Louis XIV, in 1715, the quality and the morale of French officialdom had declined. Louis's immediate successor was his great-grandson (he had outlived both his son and grandsons), Louis XV, a young boy. For many years during his youth, actual power had been exercised by a group of nobles who used the opportunity to loosen the controls put on them by the former regime. Intent mainly on personal luxuries, they abused their powers and their newly regained freedom. Corruption and bribery began to appear in the courts and in administrative offices where it was previously not tolerated. The middle-class professional officials who had been the heart and soul of Louis XIV's bureaucracy were passed over or ignored in favor of the aristocrats who monopolized the highest offices, by right of birth.

How did this deterioration come about? By nature, Louis XV was not suited to the demands of governmental reform. He was intelligent but lazy and preferred play to work. When he did take action, he delegated power to sycophants and careerists and refused to involve himself if he could avoid it.

But the tax revenue problems could not be put off indefinitely. During the mid–eighteenth century, France engaged in a series of costly and losing wars against Britain overseas and against Austria and then Prussia on the Continent (War of the Austrian Succession, 1740–1747; Seven Years' War, 1756–1763). Taxes had to be increased, but from whose pockets? The urban middle classes and the peasantry were already paying a disproportionate amount, while the state church (the greatest single property owner in France) and the nobles were paying next to nothing, claiming ancient "exemptions" granted by medieval kings. By the time of Louis XV's death in 1774, the government was already on the verge of bankruptcy, unable to pay its military forces on time and forced to go to several moneylenders (notably, the Rothschild family) to meet current accounts.

Louis XV was succeeded by his weak-minded and indecisive grandson Louis XVI (ruled 1774–1792). A sympathetic and decent person, Louis was in no way qualified to lead an unstable country that was rapidly approaching a financial crisis. Specifically, he could not be expected to limit the vast expenditures that were wasted on the maintenance and frivolities (such as the amusements of Queen Marie Antoinette) of the royal court. Nor would he take an effective stand against the rising political pretensions of the nobility. These latter, acting through their regional assemblies—the *parlements*—claimed to be the true defenders of French liberties. In practice, this claim translated into an adamant refusal to pay their share in taxes.

This was the situation when the royal government decided to enter the American rebellion on the side of the colonials, to weaken Britain and perhaps to reclaim what it had lost in the Seven Years' War earlier (that is, Canada and the Mississippi valley). The expenses of this effort were very high for France. And by now, much of the entire budget had to be funded by borrowed money at rates of interest that rose higher and higher because of the justified fear that the government would declare bankruptcy and refuse to honor its outstanding debts. (This had happened before in France.) Half of the revenues had to be paid out just to meet the interest due on current accounts. No one knew when or whether the principal could be repaid.

Faced with the refusal—once more—of the nobles and the clergy to pay even a token sum, the king reluctantly agreed to the election of an assemblage that had been forgotten for 175 years: the **Estates General,** or parliament representing all segments of the society of all France. No Estates had been convoked since 1614, for after that time first Richelieu and then Louis XIV had embarked on absolutist royal government.

CONSTITUTIONAL MONARCHY

According to tradition, the members of the delegations to the Estates General would be elected from and by their own colleagues. There were three estates, or orders of society: the First Estate was made up of the clergy, the Second consisted of the nobility, and the Third included everyone else. Rich or poor, rural or urban, educated or illiterate, all people who were neither in the church nor of the nobility, were in the **Third Estate.** Tradition further held that each estate voted as a bloc, so that only three votes would be cast on any issue. Since the two "privileged" estates could always form a majority against the commoners, they were assured of retaining their privileges if they stayed together.

Calling of the Estates

The first two estates made up only about 3 percent of the total population of France. But the nobles and clergy dominated every aspect of public life except commerce and manufacturing. They were the exclusive holders of political power above the local level. They were the king's powerful servants and concession holders, and they had every social privilege imaginable. They lived a life apart from the great majority, with their own customs and their own entertainments. They looked upon the commoners with contempt and, sometimes, fear. They held a very large share of the property in France—about 40 percent of the real estate and an even higher share of income-producing enterprises and offices of all sorts.

Some of the representatives of the First and Second Estates were liberal-minded individuals who sympathized with the demands for reform. Their assistance was crucially important to the success of the Revolution's first phase.

The Third Estate, the commoners, was represented mainly by lawyers and minor officials. A very few delegates were peasants, but there were virtually no representatives from the vast mass of illiterate laborers. The Third Estate's major complaints were the legal and social inequalities in the kingdom and their own lack of political representation. The Estate's guiding principles and its political philosophy were taken straight from the liberal Enlightenment. (See the box for more on the Third Estate.)

In the spring of 1789, the elected Estates General convened at Versailles, the site of the royal palace and government outside Paris. Immediately, a dispute arose over voting. The Third Estate demanded "one man, one vote," which would have given it the majority when joined with known sympathizers from the others. The other two orders refused; and the king was called on to decide. After attempting a vain show of force, Louis XVI caved in to the demands of the commoners. A number of renegades from the privileged then joined with the Third Estate to declare themselves the National Constituent Assembly. On June 20, 1789, they resolved not to disperse until they had given the country a constitution. In effect, this *was* the French Revolution, for if this self-appointed assembly were allowed to stand, the old order of absolutist monarchy would end.

The National Assembly and Its Constitution

What the assembly wanted was a moderate, constitutional monarchy like England's. But the king's hope to reestablish

What Is the Third Estate?

The original ideals of the French Revolution were moderate and primarily concerned with eliminating the special privileges of the church and the nobles. By the 1780s, the large majority of the French populace understood more or less clearly that they were being severely disadvantaged by the various exemptions and concessions that the 3 percent of the population belonging to the privileged classes held.

No one better expressed the sentiments of the middle classes (the bourgeoisie) at this time than the priest Emmanuel Sieyes (1748–1836) in a pamphlet entitled *What Is the Third Estate?*

We must ask ourselves three questions:

1. What is the Third Estate? Everything.
2. What has it been till now in the political order? Nothing.
3. What does it want to be? Something. . . .

Who is bold enough to maintain that the Third Estate does not contain within itself all that is needful to constitute a complete nation? It is like a strong and robust man with one arm still in chains. If the privileged order were removed, the nation would not be something less, but something more!

What then is the Third Estate? All; but an "all" which is fettered and oppressed.

What would it be without the privileged order? It would be all; but free and flourishing. Nothing will go well without the Third Estate; everything would go considerably better without the two others.

Source: Emmanuel Sieyes, What Is the Third Estate? trans. M. Blondel. Reprinted with permission of Greenwood Publishing Group, Inc., Westport, CT.

---

control and the refusal of most of the nobility and clergy to go along with the assembly's project made a confrontation unavoidable. The confrontation came in the summer of 1789, beginning with the storming of the Bastille (the royal prison in Paris). For the next several months, the Parisian mob played a major role in the course of political events, the first time in modern history that the "underclass" asserted such direct influence. The moderates and conservatives who dominated the assembly were forced to listen and heed the demands of the poor, who staged a series of bread riots and wild demonstrations around the assembly's meeting place.

On August 4, 1789, the nobles who had joined the assembly made a voluntary renunciation of their feudal rights, effectively ending serfdom and the nobility's legal privileges in France forever. A little later, the assembly adopted the **Declaration of the Rights of Man and Citizen,** which went much farther than the almost simultaneous first ten amendments—the Bill of Rights—of the American Constitution. (For a sampling from these two historic documents, see the box in Chapter 36.)

This democratic manifesto was followed by the **Civil Constitution of the Clergy,** meaning the Catholic clergy in France. This measure allowed the state to confiscate the church's property and made the priests into (unwilling) agents of the emerging new government—paid by it and therefore controlled by it. This very radical act was a misreading of the country's temper, as the majority of the French were still good Catholics and rallied to the support of the church's continued independence. The pope in Rome condemned the Civil Constitution, and with the resistance against it began the counterrevolution.

By the end of 1791, the new constitution had been completed. It provided for powers to be shared between king and parliament along the English lines, but with even stronger powers for the parliament. A national election for this new Legislative Assembly was ordained and carried through.

Jacobin Terror

The conservative governments of Europe led by Austria and Prussia were closely watching what was happening, and they were determined to restore Louis XVI to his rightful powers with armed force. The counterrevolutionary war began in the summer of 1792. Combined with the misguided attempt of Marie Antoinette and Louis to flee the country, the war changed the internal atmosphere at a blow. Until 1792, the moderates, who wished to retain the monarchy and to avoid any challenge to the rule of property, had been in control. Now the radical element called the **Jacobins** (their original headquarters was in the Parisian convent of the Jacobin order of nuns) took over the Legislative Assembly. The moderates were soon driven into silence or exiled.

What did the new masters of France want? The Jacobins were determined to extend the Revolution, to guarantee the eradication of aristocratic privileges and royal absolutism and to put the "common man" into the driver's seat. They brushed aside the Legislative Assembly and called a National Convention, elected by universal male suffrage, into being. In Paris, a self-appointed Jacobin Commune established itself as the legal authority. By early 1793, the war emergency encouraged the Jacobins to institute a *Reign of Terror* against all enemies within the country. This was history's first mass purge of people on account of their social origins or suspected beliefs. Over the next year or so, between 25,000 and 40,000 victims were guillotined, and many tens of thousands more were imprisoned or exiled by the extraordinary Courts of the People, which were everywhere.

Among the early victims of the Terror was the king. Held as a prisoner since his foiled attempt to escape France, he was given a mock trial for treason and beheaded in January 1793. Marie Antoinette followed him to the guillotine in October. The killing of the king and queen was an enormous shock to the many Europeans who believed in

Female Patriots, 1790. A club of women discusses the latest decrees of the revolutionary government, while a collection plate is set up for the relief of those families who have suffered in the cause. (*© Giraudon/Art Resource, NY*)

liberal ideals and had seen the first stage of the Revolution as their implementation. From 1793 on, the educated classes of Europe were sharply divided between friends and enemies of the Revolution, with more and more tending toward the latter camp as the atrocities of the Terror were recognized. What had started in 1789 as a high-principled campaign for justice, liberty, and progress had degenerated into a bloodbath.

After September 1792, France was no longer a monarchy but a republic. The executive power was exercised by the National Convention's **Committee of Public Safety** with dictatorial authority. **Maximilien Robespierre** was its leading member and the theoretician of the Revolution. (For more about Robespierre, see the Exercise of Authority box.)

The years 1793–1794 were the height of the Revolution. The Jacobins produced many novel ideas and techniques of power that would be imitated in revolutions to come over the next two centuries. They insisted on the following three points:

- That all men were legally, socially, and politically equal—*Egalité*
- That they were free in mind and body—*Liberté*
- That they were, or should be, brothers—*Fraternité*

They elevated reason and patriotism to entirely new heights, making these faculties into virtues that were supposed to supplant the old ones of religion and subservience. They recognized no neutrality, nor would they tolerate neutrals. Those who did not support the People's Revolution were necessarily its enemies and would be treated accordingly. These were novel and shocking thoughts to the conservative forces inside and outside France. It seemed to them that the Jacobins' systematic rejection of traditional authority must lead to chaos rather than freedom.

A French Cartoon from 1792. In this engraving, the enraged peasant finds himself unchained and reaches for his weapons while the shocked priest and noble recoil in horror. (*© The Granger Collection*)

Believing the royal professional military to be a dubious ally, the Jacobins also started the ***levée en masse*** (conscript army) to defend the Revolution. With the aid of many recruits from the former royal forces (such as Napoleon Bonaparte), they developed and used that army so effectively that the French were on the offensive from 1794 onward against the conservative coalition. And they

MAXIMILIEN ROBESPIERRE
(1758–1794)

The most dreaded name in all France during the Reign of Terror of 1793–1794 was that of the leader of the Committee of Public Safety, Maximilien Robespierre. A small figure with a high-pitched voice, he had come to the forefront during the National Assembly in 1790–1791 as an advocate of a republican democracy. His power base was the Society of Jacobins in Paris.

Robespierre was the driving force behind the steady radicalization of the Legislative Assembly in 1792 and its successor, the Convention. He engineered the declaration of the republic in August 1792 and justified the horrific massacre of imprisoned nobles and clerics in September as a necessary step in preparing France to defend its Revolution. Attacked by his enemies in the Convention as a would-be dictator, he defied them to find any stain on his patriotism and his selflessness in the revolutionary cause.

His election to the Committee of Public Safety in July 1793 meant a sharp turn toward even more shocking measures. In the fall, he led the Convention into pronouncing the Republic of Virtue, an attempt to supplant Christianity and indeed all religion in France. Patriotism would henceforth be measured by devotion to reason and the people rather than to God and king. The names of the days and the months were changed to rid them of all overtones of gods and saints, and the counting of the years began anew, with the declaration of the republic in 1792 being Year One. Churches were renamed Temples of Reason, and the Catholic clergy was subjected to both ridicule and bloody persecution. Much of this went far beyond what Robespierre intended, but he was powerless to stop

Robespierre. An anonymous eighteenth-century portrait of the man whom some considered the pure and selfless servant of the little people and others viewed as the personification of evil. (© Giraudon/Art Resource, NY)

the frenzy that he had helped set loose among the *sans-culottes* (urban working class) and the provincial Jacobins.

Robespierre found it necessary to eliminate even his coworkers in the committee and the Convention for being lukewarm supporters of the Revolution. He felt himself destined to cleanse the ranks of all who would falter on the road to perfection. In June 1794, he pushed the notorious Law of 22 Prairial through an intimidated Convention (Prairial was the name of the month in the revolutionary calendar). This allowed kangaroo courts all over France to issue the supreme penalty with or without substantive evidence of hostility to the government. In that summer, thousands of innocents were guillotined, either because they were anonymously denounced or simply because they were members of a "hostile" class such as the nobles. Robespierre justified it in a speech saying that since the Terror was but an inflexible application of justice, it was indeed a virtue and must be applauded.

In July 1794, the increasingly isolated Robespierre rose in the Convention to denounce the backsliders and the hesitant. In the past, such speeches had foretold another series of arrests by the People's Courts. This time, by prearrangement, the Convention shouted him down and arrested him. On the following day, July 28, he was guillotined amid sighs of relief and curses.

FOR REFLECTION

Can you think of the counterpart of Robespierre in a more recent revolution? What case can be made for the application of terror against the internal enemies of a radical political movement? What case against it?

completed the wholesale confiscation and distribution of royal, noble, and clerical land to the peasants, thereby eliminating one of the major causes of complaint in pre-1789 France. The nobility and the church had lost their economic bases. They would never get them back.

REACTION AND CONSOLIDATION

The machinery of terror was quickly dismantled after the execution of Robespierre, as the pervasive fear had become too great for most French, even radicals, to live with. The period 1794–1795 is termed the *Thermidorean Reaction* against the excesses of the Reign of Terror. The name comes from Thermidor, the new name for August, the month after which Robespierre fell. In place of the Jacobin-led poor who had greatly influenced government policy until now, the middle classes and the wealthy came again to the fore. They chose several of their own to form a new executive, called the **Directory,** and created a much more conservative-minded assembly, derived largely from the propertied classes.

The Levée en Masse. In 1792, the National Convention created a new, massive army composed of volunteers from all classes and, later, conscripts. Here, citizens enthusiastically sign up while receiving money payments for their enrollment. (© *Giraudon/Art Resource, NY*)

The five directors were soon maneuvering for power and squabbling among themselves. Meanwhile, the economic condition of the urban poor grew desperate, and the ongoing war created a severe inflation and a new class of wealthy profiteers. The peasantry sought in vain for legal recognition of its newly seized lands, while neither the clergy nor its detractors were satisfied with the relation between state and church. These various discontents could be contained so long as France was winning on the battlefield and the prospect for final victory looked good.

The Bonapartist Era Opens

From 1794 to 1798, French armies seemed irresistible (see Map 37.1). A young and well-connected general named **Napoleon Bonaparte** distinguished himself in the campaigns that forced the Austrians to make a losing peace with France. In 1798, however, Russia joined the anti-French coalition, and Britain remained an enemy that would not give in. Napoleon persuaded the Directors to send him with a large army to Egypt to cut off the British commercial route to the East and thus induce this "nation of shopkeepers" to make peace. The ill-thought-out Egyptian campaign of 1798–1799 was a disaster, but Napoleon saved his reputation by returning home in time and letting his subordinates take the eventual blame. His ambitious wife, Josephine, and his friends had told him that the time was ripe to brush aside the unpopular civilians and take command in France. In November 1799, he acted on their advice.

Finding very little resistance in defense of the by-now vastly unpopular Directors, Bonaparte and his army accomplices pulled off the coup d'état of 18 Brumaire. It made Napoleon **First Consul** of France, holding supreme civil and military power in his ambitious hands. A new era was about to begin, led by a thirty-year-old Corsican who had risen dramatically since entering the revolutionary army six years previously as a young lieutenant.

Confident of his talent and his vast energies, Napoleon as First Consul (1799–1804) pretended to obey a new constitution that was concocted by his agents in the "tame" legislature he allowed to stand. He suppressed all political opposition and solidified his already-high standing with the public by carrying out a series of acts, called collectively the **Napoleonic Settlement.** It embraced the following:

- Establishing the *concordat* with the papacy in 1801. This agreement pacified the French clergy and the peasants by declaring that Catholicism was the semiofficial religion. But it also pleased the strong anticlerical party by making the Catholic Church and clergy a part of the state apparatus and putting them under strict controls.
- Creating administrative and judicial systems that have lasted in France until the present day. Napoleon created a highly centralized network that went far to integrate and make uniform the formerly diverse provinces and connect the regions with the capital.
- Granting legal title to the peasants for the lands they had seized earlier

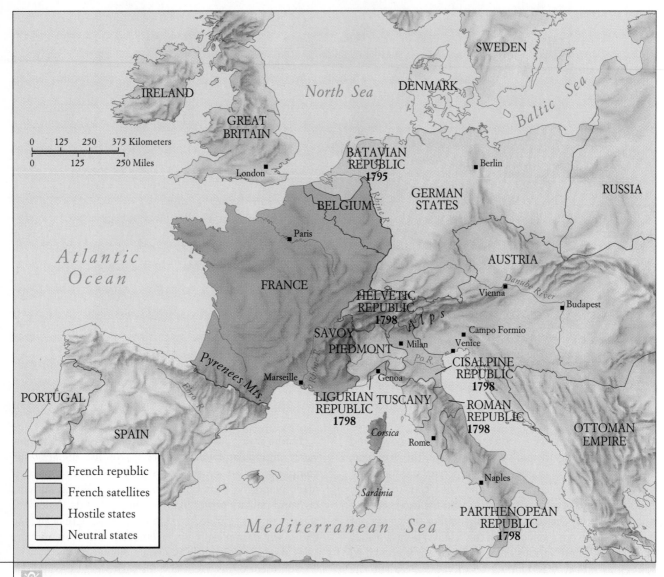

MAP 37.1   The French Republic and Its Satellites, Hostile States, and Neutrals in 1799.

- Giving the country new uniform civil and criminal codes of law (the **Civil Code of 1804;** see the box for more on this code)
- Putting the new single national currency and the government's finances in good order
- Establishing social peace by allowing the exiles to return if they agreed to support the new France
- Crushing royalist plots to return the Bourbons, and also crushing the radical Jacobin remnants

FRENCH DOMINION OVER EUROPE

In 1804, Napoleon felt the time ripe to do what everyone had long expected. He crowned himself monarch of France. His intention was to found a Bonaparte dynasty that would replace the Bourbons. He took the formal title of emperor, for by then France controlled several non-French peoples. As long as his wars went well, he was so popular at home that he could raise vast conscript armies and levy heavy taxes to support their expense, employing a legislature and bureaucracy that were completely his creatures. And the wars went well for France for several years.

Napoleon was perhaps the greatest military strategist of the modern era. He devised and led one victorious campaign after another, often against superior numbers, between 1796 and 1809. His implacable enemy was Britain, which actively supported the various coalitions against him by contributions of troops, ships, and money. War reigned between France and Britain uninterruptedly (save a few

THE CIVIL CODE OF 1804

The systematic reworking of French law called the Civil Code of 1804 proved to be one of the most lasting and most important bequests of the French Revolution. Whereas the radical democratic spirit and the atheism of the Jacobins was soon submerged and the French military dominion over much of the Continent was ended by Waterloo, the Napoleonic code had a supranational influence not only on the continent of Europe but also on Latin America and the European colonies.

One of the code's important aspects was its conservative and patriarchal definition of the rights of females, a definition that would not be substantially altered in France until the twentieth century. Those definitions and distinctions between male and female included the following:

- The legal residence of a married woman was that designated by her husband.
- Women could not serve as witnesses or institute lawsuits in court.
- Female adultery was punishable by imprisonment or fines; male adultery was legally blameless unless the illicit partner was brought into the wife's home.
- Generally, a married or single woman had no control over property.
- Married women's wages were legally the property of their husbands, and a married woman could not engage in business or sign contracts without the permission of her husband.

These restrictions on females remained essentially unchanged until the entry of large numbers of women into the labor force in Europe, and the resultant necessity of allowing them greater management of their independent incomes. The crises generated in society by World Wars I and II also contributed greatly to this movement.

---

months in 1802) for twenty-two years, 1793–1814. French armies conquered Spain, Portugal, the Italian peninsula, Austria (three times), Prussia, and Holland, all of which were incorporated into France directly, made into satellites, or neutralized. He also defeated a Russian army sent against France and was on the verge of invading England when his defeat in a major sea battle at Trafalgar off the Spanish coast in 1805 put that plan to rest forever.

Napoleon's relations with Russia were always edgy, even after its decisive defeat at French hands in 1807. By 1810, Napoleon was convinced that the czar, **Alexander I,** was preparing hostilities again and would form an alliance with the English. He decided on a preemptive strike. In the summer of 1812, the invasion began with a huge army of 600,000, including Frenchmen, their coerced allies, and some volunteers.

Napoleon's campaign in Russia is one of the epic stories of modern war. After initial successes against the retreating Russian army, the French belatedly realized that they had fallen into a lethal trap: exposure and starvation claimed most of those who survived the guerrilla warfare of the long winter retreat from Moscow. Perhaps one-third of the original force found their way to friendly Polish soil.

La Grande Armée, Napoleon's magnificent weapon, was irretrievably broken despite his frantic efforts to rebuild it. The culminating **Battle of the Nations** at Leipzig in 1813 ended in French defeat at the hands of combined Russian, Prussian, and Austrian forces. Occupied Europe was then gradually freed of French troops and governors. In March 1814, Paris was occupied, and Bonaparte was forced to abdicate.

The Plum Pudding in Danger. This satirical cartoon by noted British illustrator James Gillray was done in 1805, when it briefly appeared that Napoleon was more interested in carving off Europe for his empire than in striking a deal with Britain and ending the lengthy war. The Englishman is William Pitt, prime minister throughout the war years. *(The Granger Collection, New York)*

Retreat from Moscow. This rendering of the retreat of Napoleon's Grande Armée through the snowy wastes of Russia in the winter of 1812 captures well the atmosphere of desperation that engulfed the once proud ranks of the French invaders. *(The Granger Collection, New York)*

Napoleon Leading His Troops. This magnificent if imaginary scene of Napoleon crossing the Alps was created by the great French painter J. L. David (1748–1825) to give the French a vision of their emperor they could not forget. *(© Erich Lessing/ Art Resource, NY)*

NAPOLEON PRO OR CON

The debate over Napoleon's greatness as a leader and statesman has occupied the French and others for almost two centuries. Opinions divide nearly as sharply now as during his lifetime. While some see him as a man of genius and the founder of a progressive, stable social order, others see him as a dictator whose visions for society were always subordinate to his concern for his own welfare and glory.

There can be little doubt that he was an able administrator and selector of talent. In those crucial capacities, he came closer to the ideal "enlightened despot" than any other ruler of his day or earlier. In contrast to the recent Bourbon regime, his government was for years efficient, able, popular, and relatively honest. Men of ability could move upward regardless of their social background. Though by no means a revolutionary himself, Napoleon kept the promises that the French Revolution had made to the peasants and to the middle classes. He confirmed, though he may not have originated, many of the liberals' favorite measures, such as the disestablishment of the Catholic Church, equality before the law, and the abolition of privilege by birth. His codes provided a modern, uniform basis for all French law, both civil and criminal (though the subordination of women was kept very much intact). His administrative reforms replaced the huge mishmash that had been the French bureaucracy with a thoroughly rational centralized system. Now power was concentrated in the government in Paris, which appointed and oversaw the provincial and local officials.

But the imperial regime developed more than a few blemishes as well. After about 1808, the French government was a dictatorship in which individual liberties depended on Napoleon's wishes. No political parties were allowed, and the legislature was at all times a sham. The press was so heavily controlled that it became meaningless. Political life was forced underground and degenerated into a series of conspiracies. A spy system had informants everywhere.

In the occupied or satellite territories that made up the Napoleonic empire (see Map 37.2), governmental policies were often harsh even when enlightened, and patriots who opposed French orders were executed without mercy. The non-French populations were steadily exploited. They were expected to pay new and onerous taxes, furnish conscripts for the French armies, and trade on terms advantageous to the French. Napoleon also strongly promoted the nationalist spirit that had been so important to the early years of the Revolution, but only as long as the subject peoples accepted the leadership of Paris. When they did not, they were regarded as traitors and dealt with accordingly. The Prussian liberals, especially, learned this to their dismay when, in true national spirit they attempted to reject French overlords after royal Prussia's defeat in 1806.

There is also no doubt that as time went on, Bonaparte became increasingly cynical and indifferent to the welfare of the masses he once claimed to champion against their aristocratic oppressors. His willingness to create a new class

MAP 37.2 The Napoleonic Empire, 1810–1813. Except for Britain and Russia, Napoleon controlled almost all of Europe by 1810, either directly through incorporation into his empire or by coerced alliances.

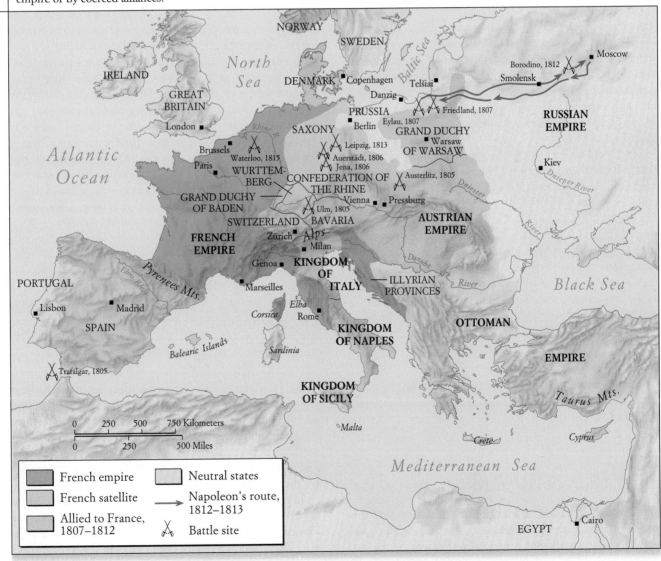

TALLEYRAND
(1754–1836)

Maurice de Talleyrand-Perigord, prince of Benevento, diplomat extraordinaire, and foreign minister of France under five different regimes, was born in 1754 the second son of a high noble family. As was customary for that time and that class, his upbringing was turned over to a nurse and a governess, while his mother and father were in constant attendance at the royal court. When Talleyrand was five, a fall injured his foot and lamed him for life. It also deprived him of the career in the army that would normally have been his lot. When he was thirteen, he was sent to a seminary against his will, and he never forgave the parents who sent him nor the church that he was supposed to serve.

Through family influence consecrated bishop of Autun in 1789, he at once joined with the moderate members of the Third Estate in the deliberations of the Estates General at Versailles. In general, he endorsed the state's confiscation of the church's property, the Civil Constitution of the Clergy, and the subordination of the religious establishment to the government. For these opinions, he was excommunicated by the pope and spent the rest of his long life as a layman.

Talleyrand's demonstrated administrative and diplomatic abilities caused the National Assembly to name him as a special emissary to Great Britain in 1792. But the Revolution's radical turn later in 1792, especially the execution of the king and queen, frightened Talleyrand, who remained all his life an adherent of constitutionalism and tolerance. Expelled from Britain after the war broke out, he went to the United States (whose society he did not care for) for two years and then returned to France under the Directory in 1796. He served as foreign minister both for the Directory and for Napoleon, whose triumphant takeover in 1799 Talleyrand had a hand in preparing. For the next eight years, Talleyrand was the most important man in France except for the emperor himself. He constantly tried to tame Napoleon's ambitions and to work out a permanent peace between France and the rest of Europe. He was convinced that Bonaparte's cynical disregard of the interests of other powers would not succeed in the long run, although it was sustained at the moment by superior force. But he could not get his master to see things in this light, and after the peace of Tilsit in 1807, Talleyrand resigned his ministry.

When Napoleon abdicated and the defeated French began negotiations with the allies, Talleyrand's career resumed with a flourish, as he was able to induce Czar Alexander I of Russia to support the return of the Bourbon family to the throne of France in the name of the sacred principle of "legitimacy." He was also crucial to the decision to allow France to come to the Congress of Vienna as an almost equal member rather than as a defeated enemy. Talleyrand's skill at protecting French national interest at Vienna became legendary. He was rewarded by being appointed France's foreign minister once again in 1815, this time by the restored Bourbon Louis XVIII. Shortly afterward, he resigned the post, however, preferring to retire to a life of ease and social activity at his country mansion.

He was by now immensely rich, having taken full advantage of many opportunities to increase his wealth during the Napoleonic era. His many enemies in Paris claimed that he had acquired his money by illegal means, and the accusations were at least partly true: he had taken part in schemes to manipulate the nation's finances for his own advantage more than once.

In 1830, the old man emerged briefly into the political limelight once again as a supporter of the "Citizen King" Louis Philippe, who took the throne after the July revolution in that year. Louis wished to make him foreign minister once more, but Talleyrand preferred to be ambassador to London, where he negotiated the treaty that made England and France formal allies for the first time in centuries. In 1834, he resigned his post and returned to France to die. In his final weeks, he reconciled himself to the Catholic Church and died with honors showered on him as one of the greatest statesmen of the age. He had terminated a loveless marriage in 1815 and left no heirs.

FOR REFLECTION

Was Talleyrand a flexible diplomat, who attempted in his own way to serve the cause of peace, or a "titled scoundrel" as he was called by many? Does serving many masters well imply moral degradation in an official?

---

of nobles, based on alleged merit but actually too often sycophants of the Bonapartist regime, was not unnoticed by the idealists.

THE VIENNA SETTLEMENT

With Napoleon exiled (in luxurious circumstances) to the island of Elba in the Mediterranean, the allies went to Vienna to try to work out a general settlement of the extremely complex issues that the two decades of war had created. Originally, France was not invited, but the brilliant and slippery **Talleyrand,** foreign minister to the restored Bourbon monarch Louis XVIII (brother to the last king), used his talents to assure that France soon received an equal seat at the bargaining table. (For more about Talleyrand, see the Exercise of Authority box.)

In the midst of the discussions came the news in February 1815 that Napoleon had fled Elba, landed in southern France, and issued a call to all his followers to renew the war. They responded with enthusiasm in the tens of thousands. The "Hundred Days campaign" nearly succeeded but ended in total defeat for the Bonapartists at **Waterloo.** This time, Napoleon was shipped off as a prisoner of war to a rock in the South Atlantic, St. Helena, where he lived out the remaining six years of his life.

In Vienna, the "Big Four" victors—Austria, Prussia, Russia, and England—were busy working out the political and territorial outlines of a new Europe. Actually, the conservative powers, led by Austria's Prince Clemens von **Metternich,** hoped to reconstruct the old Europe but found that was impossible. Too much had happened since 1789: too many hopes had been awakened, borders changed, kings removed, and constitutions issued. In the years since, Europe had passed a great watershed in political and social history. The "Old System" of European government and society (*l'ancien régime*) was like Humpty Dumpty after his fall—it could not be reconstructed.

After nearly coming to blows on the thorny question of what should happen to Poland—a state that had been partially re-created by Napoleon—the four victors hammered out a series of agreements that collectively gave Europe its political borders for the next hundred years. They were guided in their work by some underlying principles:

1. *Legitimacy in government.* Kings were restored to their thrones, and radical constitutions written by pro-French revolutionaries were thrown out or rewritten to reflect more conservative themes. Revolutions would henceforth be suppressed by international collaboration.
2. *International cooperation to maintain peace.* The victors (and soon also France) formed an alliance with regular meetings of foreign ministers. The Quadruple Alliance lasted for only a decade, but its principles of international responsibility for peace guided diplomatic meetings throughout the century from 1815 to 1914.
3. *Discouragement of nationalism and liberalism in politics.* The conservative forces saw both nationalism and liberalism as evils brought by the French radicals to Europe. Neither was recognized as a legitimate demand of the citizenry.
4. *Balance of power.* No single state would be allowed to dominate the Continent as had France under Napoleon.

Within the framework created by these general principles, what now were the agendas of the four chief victors? Each had a separate one which had to be harmonized with others.

Russia, under the visionary Czar Alexander I (ruled 1801–1825), had been the main force in the final military defeat of the French and now for the first time played a leading role in European affairs. Alexander had originally sympathized with liberalism and constitutionalism but came to think better of it after the struggles with Napoleon began. Led by mystical hopes for peace and harmony, the czar became a conservative autocrat in later years. Under Alexander's successor, Nicholas I (ruled 1825–1855), the country became a bastion of reactionary and antiliberal forces.

Austria under the astute diplomat Prince Metternich also took a leading role in the reconstruction. Metternich was convinced that nationalism and popular participation in government would ruin the multinational state of Austria and then all of Europe. He fought these ideas with all his considerable skill and energy. Because he stayed at the helm of Vienna's foreign policy for almost forty years, he became the outstanding example and main voice of European conservatism until 1848. Austria stagnated intellectually and scientifically, however, as conservatism turned into first reaction and then paralysis.

Prussia originally tended toward liberalism and carried out internal reforms under a group of statesmen who admired the constitutional phase of the French Revolution. But, after the defeat of the French, the Prussian king Frederick William III made clear his distaste for constitutional government and succeeded in turning back the political clock for a generation. As a nation, Prussia came out of the wars with France strengthened and expanded, with improved technology and an aggressive entrepreneurial class. By the 1830s, it had the best educational system in Europe and was in a position to contest Austria for the lead in pan-German affairs.

Great Britain was clearly the leading naval power and one of the strongest military forces in Europe by 1815. But the British governing class primarily wanted to concentrate on their business interests to take advantage of the big lead they had established since 1780 in the race to industrialize (see the next chapter). The British liberals always felt uncomfortable on the same side of the table as Czar Alexander and Metternich, and by 1825, they had abandoned the Quadruple Alliance system. Having helped establish the balance of power on the Continent, they retreated into "splendid isolation" for the rest of the nineteenth century. They involved themselves in Europe's affairs only when they deemed their commercial and business interests endangered.

These four powers plus France would mold Europe's destinies for the rest of the nineteenth century. The others had little to say beyond their own borders. Italy was not yet formed into a single power and would in any case remain in the second tier in international affairs. Spain subsided into a third-rank state, especially after losing its empire in the Western Hemisphere early in the nineteenth century (see Chapter 34). Turkey was "the sick man of Europe," increasingly powerless to protect its southeast European possessions. Already during the Napoleonic era, the Scandinavian countries had adopted the neutral course that they would henceforth maintain.

Overall Estimate of the Vienna Settlement

During the later nineteenth century, the treaty making at Vienna was criticized on many grounds. The aristocratic negotiators meeting in their secluded drawing rooms ignored the growing forces of popular democracy, national feeling, liberalism, and social reform. They drew up territorial boundaries in ignorance of and disregard for popular emotions and restored kings to their thrones without citizenry support. The treaty makers were a small handful of upper-class men, contemptuous of the ordinary people and their right to participate in politics and government.

All these criticisms are more or less true. Yet, if success is measured by the practical test of enduring peace, it would be hard to find another great international settlement as successful as the treaty of Vienna of 1815. The borders it established endured without serious challenge for fifty years until the German and Italian petty states were unified into two great powers. With the single exception of the Franco-Prussian conflict of 1870, Europe did not experience an important, costly war until the outbreak of World War I in 1914. The great multilateral conflicts that had marked the late seventeenth and all of the eighteenth centuries were avoided, and Europe had three generations of peaceable economic expansion both at home and overseas.

The Vienna Treaties were followed by a century of cultural and material progress for the middle classes and toward the end, at least, for the common people as well. That this was not the specific intent of the peacemakers is beside the point. Any judgment of the treaties must consider that the massive social and economic changes witnessed by the nineteenth century were successfully accommodated within the international relationships established in 1815.

SUMMARY

The problems of the French monarchy in the late eighteenth century were cumulative and profound. Inspired by the Enlightenment and the example of the U.S. Revolutionary War, many French were convinced that the weak and directionless regime of King Louis XVI must change. In 1789, they were able to overcome the stubborn resistance of both king and nobility to bring about a moderate constitutional monarchy. Within two more years, however, this situation was turned into a radical social upheaval by the Jacobins and their supporters among the nation's poor. The ancien régime of rule by an absolutist monarch and a privileged church and nobility could not survive this challenge despite the attempt by France's conservative neighbors to save it through armed intervention.

The exigencies of war combined to create the Reign of Terror led by the Jacobin Committee of Public Safety. This egalitarian dictatorship was overthrown after two years, and a consolidation begun under the Directory in 1795. Corruption and incompetence weakened the Directory to a point that allowed a military coup by the young general Napoleon Bonaparte in 1799.

Napoleon's authoritarian settlement of the Revolution's conflicts within France was successful, and his wars in the name of defense of the Revolution went well for several years. For a decade most of western and central Europe were under French sway. The 1812 Russia campaign was disastrous, however, and soon led to final defeat in 1814. At the Vienna congress of victors, a framework of compromise between reaction against and grudging acceptance of the Revolution's principles was worked out; despite numerous defects, it allowed Europe a century of relative peace and progress.

TEST YOUR KNOWLEDGE

1. The trigger for the outbreak of revolution in France was
   a. the nobles' refusal to pay their share of taxes.
   b. peasant unrest caused by landlord abuses.
   c. an armed rebellion by outraged middle-class taxpayers.
   d. the assassination of the king.
2. The Third Estate in France consisted of
   a. the peasants.
   b. the urban dwellers of all types.
   c. the nonprivileged.
   d. the children of the nobles who had no right of succession.
3. The opening phase of the French Revolution saw the establishment of a
   a. republic.
   b. military dictatorship.
   c. representative democracy.
   d. constitutional monarchy.
4. Abbé Emmanuel Sieyes wrote a much-read pamphlet in 1789 that
   a. attacked the whole idea of the monarchy in France.
   b. defended the rights of the Third Estate.

c. demanded the separation of church and state.

d. urged the immediate introduction of a proletarian dictatorship.

5. Napoleon came to power in 1799 because of the

a. public reaction against the Terror of the Jacobins.

b. complete anarchy in France after Robespierre's fall.

c. threat of the counterrevolutionaries.

d. unpopularity of the Directory.

6. The battle at Trafalgar

a. assured French domination of most of the Continent.

b. frustrated a potential French invasion of England.

c. knocked the Russians out of the anti-French coalition.

d. made it necessary for France to sell the Louisiana Territory to the United States.

7. Which of the following did Napoleon *not* preside over in France?

a. The signing of a concordat with the Vatican

b. The creation of a new administrative system

c. The enactment of uniform legal codes for the whole country

d. The elimination of the Catholic clergy's influence on French opinion

8. The chief conservative powers at the Vienna peace conference were

a. Prussia, Russia, and Austria.

b. Prussia, Russia, and Britain.

c. Austria, Russia, and France.

d. Russia, Prussia, and France.

9. Which of the following was least considered in the negotiations at Vienna?

a. The right of forcibly deposed monarchs to regain their thrones

b. The right of working people to determine their form of government

c. The right of states to adequate territory and resources for defense

d. The right of nations to be governed by one of their own

10. Which country of post-1815 Europe does the phrase "splendid isolation" apply to most directly?

a. Great Britain

b. France

c. Russia

d. Turkey

IDENTIFICATION TERMS

Alexander I

Battle of the Nations

Bonaparte, Napoleon

Civil Code of 1804

Civil Constitution of the
Clergy

Committee of Public Safety

Declaration of the Rights of
Man and Citizen

Directory

Estates General

First Consul

Jacobins

l'ancien régime

levée en masse

Metternich

Napoleonic Settlement

Robespierre, Maximilien

Talleyrand

Third Estate

Waterloo

INFOTRAC COLLEGE EDITION

Enter the search term "French Revolution" using Key Words.
Enter the search term "Napoleon" using Key Words.

Enter the search term "Napoleonic Wars" using Key Words.

38

EUROPE'S INDUSTRIALIZATION

*S*team is an Englishman.

ANONYMOUS

1700s	Increase in trade, population, and agricultural production
1760s–1820s	First Industrial Revolution in Britain/steam power
c. 1815–c. 1860s	Industrialization of northwestern Europe
1830	First railroad completed in Britain
LATE 1800s	Second Industrial Revolution/petroleum and electricity

THE INDUSTRIAL REVOLUTION that gripped Europe in the nineteenth century was a direct outgrowth of the Scientific Revolution and, like that earlier event, was not really so much a revolution as a gradual accretion of new knowledge and techniques. The Industrial Revolution was made possible by another "revolution": the transformation of agriculture that took place at the same time. Stimulated by several developments, England led in both of these transformations, and the rest of Europe only slowly and unevenly fell into line behind the English.

PREREQUISITES FOR INDUSTRIAL PRODUCTION

Historians have identified several factors that are necessary for an economy to engage in large-scale industrial production. All of these were present in England by the late eighteenth century.

1. *Upsurge in world trade.* The expanding market for European goods and services created by the new colonies was matched by the large volume of exports from those colonies destined for European consumption. From Eastern ports flowed a stream of tea, coffee, and cocoa as well as spices, exotic woods, Chinese jades, porcelain, and, above all, silk and cotton cloth. From the American colonies came not only Spanish bullion but also the sugar, rice, and dried fish that added variety to European tables and tobacco and dyes as well.

   In the eighteenth century, French overseas trading grew more than tenfold, and the English were not far behind. Intra-European trade also grew spectacularly, as the colonial goods were often reexported to third parties. All of this increase reflected much higher demand from consumers and also for the basic needs of overseas commerce: maritime equipment and boats and "trade goods" for the natives.

2. *Rising population.* The increased demand for imports was due in large part to the rapidly rising population of most of the Continent and England. Although the precise reasons for this rise are still in dispute, it is clear that the death rate fell and the birth rate rose in Europe after 1750. The English population, for instance, quadrupled

ADAM SMITH ON SPECIALIZATION

One of the outstanding innovative results of early industrialization was the specialization of labor. Tasks that previously had been performed by two or three individual craftspeople working at their own pace and in their own sequence were broken up by the early factory operators into distinct phases, each with its own machine-supported applications by individual workers.

Adam Smith (1723–1790) anticipated these results in his epoch-making book *The Wealth of Nations*, written in 1776 when the Industrial Revolution's impacts were just barely discernible in Great Britain. Smith provided the economic and philosophical bases of liberalism, as that word was used in the eighteenth and nineteenth centuries. In the following excerpt, he considers the division of labor, which the introduction of factories was greatly stimulating.

Factories. *(Mary Evans Picture Library)*

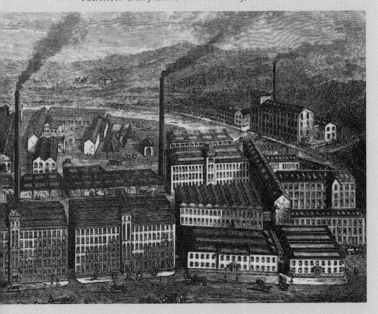

Chapter I: Of the Division of Labor

To take an example, therefore, from a very trifling manufacture; but one in which the division of labor has been very often taken notice of, the trade of the pin-maker; a workman not educated to this business (which the division of labor has rendered a distinct trade), nor acquainted with the use of the machinery employed in it (to the invention of which the same division of labor has probably given occasion), could scarce with his utmost industry, make one pin in a day, and certainly could not make twenty. But in the way in which this business is now carried on, not only the whole work is a peculiar trade, but it is divided into a number of branches, of which the greater part are likewise peculiar trades. One man draws the wire, another straightens it, a third cuts it, a fourth points it, a fifth grinds it at the top to receive the pin-head; to make the head requires two or three distinct operations; to put it on is a peculiar business, to whiten the pins is another; it is even a trade by itself to put them into the paper; and the important business of making a pin is, in this manner, divided into about eighteen distinct operations, which in some manufactures, are performed by distinct hands, though in others the same man will perform perhaps two or three of them.

I have seen a small manufactory of this kind where ten men only were employed . . . they could when they exerted themselves make among them about twelve pounds of pins per day. There are in a pound upwards of four thousand pins of a middling size. Those ten persons, therefore, could make among them upwards of forty-eight thousand pins in a day. Each person, therefore, making a tenth part of forty-eight thousand pins, might be considered as making four thousand, eight hundred pins in a day. But if they had all [worked] separately and independently, and without any of them having been educated to this peculiar business, they certainly could not each of them have made twenty, perhaps not one pin in a day; that is, certainly, not the two hundred and fortieth, perhaps not the four thousand eight hundredth part of what they are at present capable of performing, in consequence of proper division and combination of their different operations.

SOURCE: Adam Smith, *An Inquiry into the Nature and Causes of the Wealth of Nations*, ed. Edwin Canaan (New York: Modern Library, 1994).

most experienced traders and entrepreneurs. The English colonies were spread around the world, and the North American colonies were the biggest markets for goods outside Europe. The English national bank had existed as a credit and finance institution since 1603, rates of interest were lower than anywhere else, and the English stock markets were the world's largest and most flexible for raising capital.

2. *Population increase.* The population was sharply increasing. As mentioned earlier, the English population rose about 15 percent per decade throughout the eighteenth century, generating a huge increase in demand and an equally huge increase in the potential or actual labor supply.

3. *Energy, or "Steam is an Englishman."* The key to industrialization as a mechanical process was a new source of energy: steam. And the English pioneered the inventions that made steam engines the standard form of mechanical energy during the nineteenth century. All over the world, English steam engines opened the path to industrialized production of goods.

4. *Agricultural improvements.* English agriculture underwent its own "revolution." The improvements in agricultural production during the eighteenth century made

Opening of Royal Albert Bridge. Named in honor of Queen Victoria's husband, this span was a design by I. K. Brunel and one of the triumphs of the transport revolution spawned by industrialization. *(Elton Collection/Ironbridge Gorge Museum Trust)*

it possible for the farmers not only to feed the rapidly growing urban sector but to do so with fewer workers in the fields. The excess rural population then migrated from the countryside, contributing to the growth of the urban sector's demand for foodstuffs.

5. *Key raw materials.* England controlled much of the two basic raw materials of early industry: coal and cotton. The English coal fields were large and easy to access. They provided the fuel for the new steam engines and used those engines extensively to produce coal more cheaply than anywhere in Europe. Cotton came from India, by now an English colony, and from the North American colonies. It was carried across the ocean almost entirely in English ships, woven in English factories, and the finished cloth was exported to the rest of Europe without effective competition for a century.

6. *Transportation.* England had the most favorable internal transport system. The geography and topography of England made the country ideal for moving goods to market. Not only were there few natural obstacles to travel and transport, but the river system, connected by canals in the eighteenth century, made transportation cheaper and safer than elsewhere.

As a result of these advantages, it was natural for England to take the lead in industry (see Map 38.1). In the generation between 1740 and 1780, England produced a variety of mechanical inventions, including Richard Arkwright's spinning machine, called the *spinning jenny,* and Samuel Crompton's mule, which made yarn or thread. By 1800, these machines had been joined by others, including the cotton gin, invented by an American, Eli Whitney, and Edmund Cartwright's power loom. Together, these inventions revolutionized the production of cotton cloth. Machines

Isambard Kingdom Brunel. This jaunty figure was the outstanding engineer of ironwork in the mid–nineteenth century. He designed several famous bridges in addition to *The Great Western* steamship, whose anchor chain he is standing in front of here. *(Courtesy George Eastman House)*

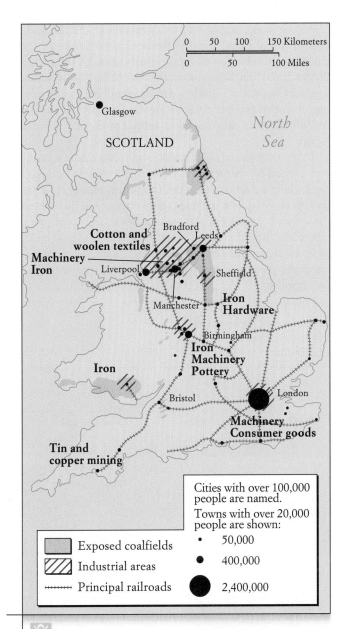

MAP 38.1 Britain's Industrial Revolution. The fastest pace in industrial development was in the north of England, where coal and textile production combined to create strong attraction for laboring immigrants.

SPREAD OF THE INDUSTRIAL REVOLUTION

From England the new processes spread slowly during the eighteenth and early nineteenth centuries. No other country had England's peculiar combination of advantages, but there were other reasons for this slowness. A major factor was England's attempt to treat industrial techniques as state secrets. The English government strictly prohibited the export of any process or machine design that could help another country rival England. For a time, the government went to the extreme of attempting to prohibit the emigration of skilled workers! Needless to say, these restrictions could not be effectively enforced, and the theoretical knowledge of machine design and technology spread into northern Europe and the United States after about 1820.

Another factor retarding industrialization was the long Napoleonic wars, which disrupted the normal communications and commerce between the Continent and England for the quarter-century between 1793 and 1815. After the wars, much of Europe was too impoverished or too unstable to encourage the importation of new processes or machines. It would take another generation before even the more advanced areas of western Europe could rival Britain in industrial techniques.

By about 1830, the areas on the Continent closest to England had begun to industrialize part of their productive capacity. Belgium and northern France began to use steam power first in coal and textile production, the same industries that had initiated the use of steam in England. By the 1860s, industrial techniques had spread to the Rhine valley, especially the Ruhr coal and iron fields, as well as to parts of northern Italy and the northern United States (see Map 38.2).

Nevertheless, even as late as the 1860s, eastern Europe, Russia, and Iberia (Spain and Portugal), as well as most of Italy, were almost untouched by the industrial lifestyle and industrial production. These regions all lacked one or more of the important factors that had to come together for industrialization to proceed. They became the permanent, involuntary clients of the industrialized regions. Some areas, such as eastern Europe and the Balkans, were still untouched well into the middle of the twentieth century. Industrialization was not automatic or inevitable, and large parts of the non-Western world are still only superficially and partially industrialized in their essential production techniques.

EARLY INDUSTRIAL SUCCESSES

The first industries to feel the full weight of industrial processes were cotton textiles and coal mining. Both of these were highly labor-intensive and were uniquely able to use the

that still used water or animal power were now quickly replaced by the perfected steam engines designed by **James Watt** (see the box) and Matthew Boulton. Cheap and reliable steam power became the standard energy source of the Western world's machines for the next hundred years.

Engineers of all sorts, bridge builders, railroad and tramway developers, and mining superintendents—in short, all types of the nineteenth century's burgeoning technical aristocracy—were first and foremost England's contribution to the industrial world.

new steam engines to replace tedious, hand labor. Cotton cloth production in England rose geometrically during the late eighteenth century. Previously, cotton had been a luxury good used only by the rich for fine clothing, tapestries, and upholstery. Now cotton clothing became commonplace. Production of raw cotton in India and the southern United States became a major branch of agriculture.

From cotton the revolution in spinning and weaving spread to wool. Parts of England and Scotland became vast sheep ranges, as former agricultural lands were converted to pastures, which brought in more profit. Meanwhile, the huge increase in coal production provided a great boost for the iron industry, which now used coal in lieu of less efficient and more costly charcoal. British iron production rose from 68,000 tons in 1788 to 260,000 in 1806. It kept on climbing at almost the same pace throughout the nineteenth century.

As the steam engine's capacity increased and the addition of gears, belts, and flywheels expanded the uses to which it could be put, all kinds of products felt the impact of the Industrial Revolution. Instead of having to locate near flowing water as in the past, flour milling, timber sawing, and other industries requiring simple repetitive motion could be located near the labor supply or the raw material source.

In the preindustrial age, most large-scale manufacturing was carried on in rural areas, preferably near a navigable river where a dam could be built to supply energy for a water wheel. Now new mills and foundries could be built on the edge of existing towns, where labor, transport, commerce, and housing were already in place. The urban locale of much new industry was, of course, a major reason for the rapid growth of many towns into cities and cities into metropolises.

MAP 38.2 The Spread of Industry by 1850. The sharp differences between the countries with industrial resources and those without are shown on this map. There is also a notable correlation between industry and the peasantry's freedom from landlords' controls.

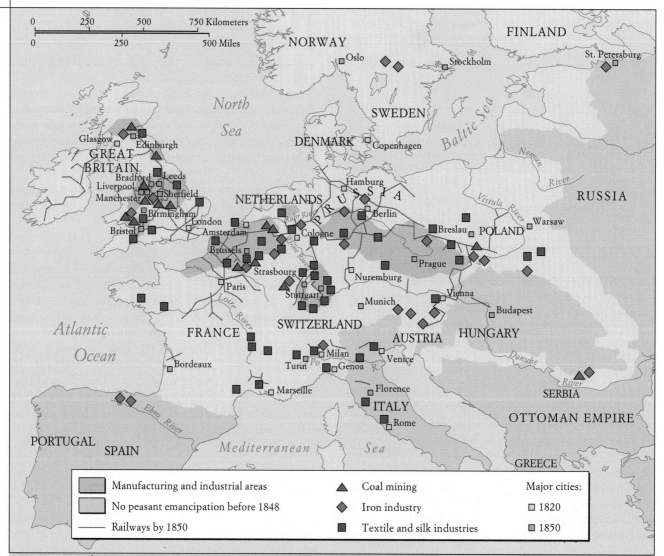

JAMES WATT'S STEAM ENGINES

James Watt was the engineer who made the steam engine into a practical source of industrial power. Although Watt did not invent the engine, his version was the first to use the potential of steam power efficiently. His work was crucial in bringing the Industrial Revolution into being.

Watt was born in Greenock, Scotland, in 1736. He educated himself by studying instruments, working with all types of mechanical devices, and building small machines. In 1757, the University at Glasgow hired him as an instrument maker. There Watt worked with a Newcomen engine, an earlier version of a machine that used steam power, and he was able to make several basic improvements. First, he saw the advantage of a separate condensing chamber and designed a more efficient system of condensing the steam back to water. Then he invented a mechanism that increased the speed of the piston in both directions. A few years later Watt was able to devise a method of gears and wheels that allowed the vertical motion of the piston to be translated into rotary motion, such as in grindstones.

Watt entered into an enormously successful partnership in 1774 with Matthew Boulton, the owner of an English foundry. Within a few years, the Watt–Boulton engine had set an entirely new standard for steam power in Britain; it was cheaper, lighter, more flexible, and far more efficient in its use of fuel and in its applications to industrial tasks.

George Stephenson took the Watt engine, put it on wheels and wooden tracking, and designed the earliest form of locomotive, which was used to pull coal cars in mines. From this gradually evolved the railroad. In 1829, Stephenson's *Rocket* bested several other competitors to become the engine for the first rail line in the world, constructed in 1830 between Manchester and Liverpool. For many years, the locomotive was simply a Watt engine laid on its side and mounted on a wheeled platform with gears and levers connecting the piston in its cylinder to the drive wheels below.

Already by the end of the Napoleonic wars in 1815, Watt engines were to be found everywhere in British factories and mines. Despite the efforts of the government, the patents and designs of Watt and Boulton were soon exported overseas, and by midcentury, steam power spread rapidly on the northern Continent and in the United States. Engineers of all nations continued to improve and refine the engine, and new uses for steam power followed one after another each year. When James Watt died in his eighty-third year, he could look with satisfaction on a world that his engine was transforming in its productive capacities.

Railroads

One of the most spectacular results of steam power was the railroad. Again, Britain led the way, but in this instance, the new invention spread very rapidly. The first commercial use of steam railroading was in 1830, when a line connected Liverpool and Manchester, two of the newly important British industrial towns. By the 1840s, lines were under way in most countries of the old and new worlds, including Russia and the United States.

Most early rail lines were built by private companies. But railroads were costly, and the large debts the owners in-

Rail Station. This magnificent 1862 illustration by the British painter W. Powell Frith captures the bustling activity of a Victorian-era station and the crowds who were glad to board the "iron horse." *(Royal Holloway and Bedford New College, Surrey, UK/Bridgeman Art Library)*

 **The *Rocket*, 1829.** This engraving shows George Stephenson's locomotive as it traveled across the English countryside in 1829. Essentially a steam boiler laid on its side with pistons and wheels, the *Rocket* quickly outdistanced its stagecoach competitors between Liverpool and Manchester. (© *The Granger Collection*)

curred were often more than the lines could sustain during the frequent downturns in the economic cycle. As a result, many railroads went bankrupt and were taken over by the government. By the 1860s, most railroad lines were in government hands everywhere but in the United States.

The steam locomotive was the heart of a railroad. Yet the locomotive's mechanics were so simple that only a few years after the first one was mounted on its track, it had reached a state of perfection that hardly changed over the next century. Bigger and slightly more efficient locomotives were built, but they were essentially the same machine as the famous ***Rocket*** of the 1830 Liverpool–Manchester line.

The railroad dramatically reduced the costs of shipping and personal travel. It also greatly increased the security of moving goods and people long distances. By as early as 1850, trains were steaming along in excess of fifty miles per hour—a speed that seemed almost diabolical to many on-lookers. By that year it was possible to travel from London to Edinburgh overnight in safety and comfort. Twenty years earlier, the same journey had taken four or five jolting, banging days in a stagecoach. And the train cost less as well. The railroad had an impact on the first half of the nineteenth century similar to the impact of the automobile on the first half of the twentieth—another "revolution"!

PHASES OF THE INDUSTRIAL REVOLUTION

Industrial work and lifestyles did not develop rapidly as a onetime occurrence at the end of the eighteenth century. The changes that began then have continued to the present day, but they can be divided into certain discernible stages.

The **First Industrial Revolution,** which lasted in Europe from about 1760 to 1820, was marked by the predominance of Britain, the central importance of a new supply of energy from steam, and the production of textiles and iron in the factory setting.

The **Second Industrial Revolution** began in the later part of the nineteenth century in various parts of western Europe and produced modern applied science or technology. The chemical and petroleum industries especially came to the fore in this phase, and a new source of energy was developed—electricity. National leadership shifted gradually from Great Britain to Germany (after its formation in 1871) and the post–Civil War United States.

In our own time, industrial production has spread very rapidly into many countries that were previously untouched, or almost so, by these revolutions. At the same time, the older industrial countries in the West have moved on to a "postindustrial" society, in which the production of goods in factories and their transport by railroad has given way in importance to the provision of services and information relying on electronic transmissions. We are, in fact, living through a Third Industrial Revolution symbolized and powered by the computer.

SUMMARY

Industrial methods of producing goods via machinery entered European life gradually in the mid–eighteenth century, with England as the leader. The English had several natural advantages and social characteristics that enabled them to expand their lead over the rest of the world until well into the nineteenth century. This First Industrial Revolution was largely dependent on two related changes: the increase in agrarian production and the rapid rise in population and attendant demand for consumer goods. Without these, the fac-

tory system of concentrated labor under single management and discipline would not have been feasible.

The industrial system spread quite slowly at first, owing to the wars and to the difficulty of replicating the English advantages. By the mid–nineteenth century, however, industrialization had spread into much of northern and western Europe and the United States. Coal mining and textiles were two of the initial industries to be affected, and the steam engine became the major energy source for all types of industry. The railroad, introduced in the 1830s, soon effected massive change in the transport of goods and people and contributed to the success of the industrial system in substantial ways. A Second Industrial Revolution commenced in the late nineteenth century, fueled by petroleum and electricity, and a third is currently under way in the provision of services rather than goods.

TEST YOUR KNOWLEDGE

1. Which of the following was *not* a factor in England's leadership in industrialization during the later eighteenth century?
   a. A rapidly growing population
   b. Familiarity with the principles of finance and credit
   c. The government's commitment to stable currency and interest rates
   d. Thorough government supervision of the economy's trends and patterns
2. The basic aim of industrial production technique is to
   a. provide more employment opportunities for the labor force.
   b. allow a greater variety of jobs.
   c. lower the unit cost of production.
   d. discipline and organize the labor force more efficiently.
3. James Watt was the inventor of
   a. an entirely new form of mechanical energy.
   b. the power loom for weaving.
   c. an improved and more flexible form of steam-driven engine.
   d. a device for raising water from flooded mines.
4. The chief driving force for the Industrial Revolution in eighteenth-century England was
   a. the threat of being overshadowed by France in the world economy.
   b. the invention of an improved source of energy.

   c. the creation of the British overseas colonial empire.
   d. the encouragement of the British government.
5. The first major industry to feel the impact of industrial production was
   a. lumbering.
   b. textiles.
   c. grain farming.
   d. paper making.
6. The example used by Adam Smith to demonstrate specialization of labor was
   a. coal mining.
   b. textile spinning.
   c. pin making.
   d. shipbuilding.
7. Development of competitive industry on the Continent was delayed by
   a. the Napoleonic wars and their attendant disruption of trade.
   b. lack of interest.
   c. the upper classes' contempt for profit making.
   d. lack of suitable and basic natural resources.

IDENTIFICATION TERMS

factory system	putting-out system	Second Industrial	Watt, James
First Industrial Revolution	*Rocket*	Revolution	

INFOTRAC COLLEGE EDITION

Enter the search term "industrial revolution" using Key Words.

Enter the search term "industrial development" using the Subject Guide.

THE SOCIAL IMPACTS OF EARLY INDUSTRY

The fall in our wages took place immediately that food got cheaper. The contractors said, since we could live for less, we must do the work for less.

ANONYMOUS LABORER

c. 1750	Europe enters "population explosion"
1750–1850	Change in premarital relationships and family structure
1800–1850	Urbanization of northwestern Europe/First Industrial Revolution completed in Britain, gets under way on the western and central Continent

TO WHAT EXTENT were the lifestyles of ordinary people altered during the transition from a preindustrial to an industrial society? The change was substantial, but it was gradual in most cases and only really remarkable over a generation or more. Taken all in all, the lives of many Europeans changed more in the century between 1750 and 1850 than they had in all preceding centuries together.

In this chapter, we look at four areas of social transformation during this period: family and gender relations, occupations, urbanization, and living conditions. Much of this material is relatively new as an object of formal history writing, and this "new social history" has become one of the major research fields for historians everywhere. Their findings are constantly changing previous ideas and frequently show that innovations formerly presumed to be the result of machine industry actually began earlier.

CHANGES IN SOCIAL RELATIONS

During the later eighteenth century in Britain and France (where the records are best preserved), a change in social habits and relationships became apparent. Why did this happen? The causes of this change are not well understood, but they seem to be linked with the arrival of science as a competing primary source of knowledge with religion and with the philosophy of the Enlightenment as it trickled down into popular concepts (see Chapter 35).

The beginnings of the Industrial Age accelerated changes that had already begun. The mutual stimuli afforded to industry by science, and vice versa, became ever more intense. Eventually, an industrial lifestyle made itself apparent, quite different from what had gone before. It was long believed that one of the changes effected was a new structure of the family. This belief is now being reexamined.

The Structure of the Family and Household

For most people, the family they are born into is the most important social institution in their lives. We tend to think of it as unchanging: a man, a woman, and their children. But is this so? Historians once assumed that for many centuries before industrialization, the European family had a standard structure, which varied little. This family, so it was thought, was characterized by an extended kin group living under one roof, high rates of illegitimate children, and early universal marriage. Now, however, researchers have established that this stereotype of the preindustrial family is false. The characteristics that were assumed to be commonplace were in fact very uncommon during the preindustrial centuries.

Instead, it is now clear that major changes in the family structure took place beginning in the middle of the eighteenth century *before* industry became common. Three changes were particularly noticeable:

- A lowering of the average age of marriage from the previous 27 for both men and women to about 22 for women and 23.5 for men by 1850
- A sharp increase in the bastardy rate, beginning in the towns but soon also becoming common in the rural areas, where the majority of the population lived
- A steady increase in the previously low number of aged persons (over sixty) who lived on to see their grandchildren and share their homes with two younger generations

The Place of Children

Until the eighteenth century, only the very wealthy or the nobility could afford to give much loving attention to infants or very young children. The reason was simple: The mortality rate for infants and children was so high that it discouraged people from putting much financial or emotional investment into them. In many places, three of five children of ordinary people normally would die before age ten, and another would die before age twenty.

Diseases of every type hit children (and the aged) harder than others. In times of famine, young children were often the first victims. Household and farm accidents of a lethal nature were an everyday affair among children (we hear of children drowning in the farm pond or the well, being kicked by a horse, cut by sharp tools, or burned to death). In those days when medical care for rural people was nonexistent, even minor burns or slight infections would become aggravated and often result in death, weeks or months later.

Therefore, the usual attitude toward the infant was a mix of indifference with a good deal of realistic caution about its prospects. Most peasants and agrarian workers viewed children below age seven or so as debit factors: they demanded time-consuming care and feeding without being able to contribute anything to the family resources. Only after they had become strong and rational enough to do adult work were they looked on as assets.

The urban classes and the wealthy could afford to take a more relaxed attitude toward children's work, but their emotional relations with the young child were about as distant as the peasant's. Urban children died as readily and as unpredictably as rural children. It only made "biological sense" to restrict maternal love and paternal pride to those old enough to have a good chance of a long life. And for most people, the point of having children was to provide a primitive form of social security. Children were expected to see to it that their parents did not suffer the ultimate indignity of a beggarly old age or have to throw themselves on the charity of others when ill or disabled.

At some point between 1750 and 1850, a change began, as parents began to show what we now consider normal parental love and tenderness toward newborn and young children. This change occurred first in the better-off segment of society and then seeped downward into the lives of the majority. Why did it happen?

The answer is complex, but several factors can be identified: the declining child mortality rate, which gradually increased the chances that a child would survive; the rising numbers of middle-class people who did not need children's labor but valued them for their own sake; and the influence of educational reformers such as Jean-Jacques Rousseau, Johann Heinrich Pestalozzi, and Friedrich Herbert. These reformers insisted that children should be given more humane education and treated as unformed, responsive individuals rather than as contrary creatures whose naturally mischievous ways must be corrected by strict discipline.

Another influence on the attitudes of adults toward young children was the introduction of general public instruction in state-supervised schools, which began in Prussia and Austria, among other places, in the mid-1700s. Clearly, children worthy of being educated at parental tax expense were valuable for more than just serving as attendants in their parents' old age (for which the children needed no education).

Relations between Men and Women

The premier event of most people's social lives was, of course, marriage. Marriage among the rural folk and most urbanites was still a contract between two families rather than the result of individual erotic attraction. But this, too, changed during the eighteenth century in Europe. Not only did people marry at an earlier age as the century progressed, but also social relations among the young became considerably freer. Premarital sex had always been tolerated among the peasants, as long as it was followed by marriage. In the later eighteenth century, however, premarital sex without marriage plans seems to have occurred with increasing frequency. Both sexes, in countryside and town, were able to "get away" with behavior that previously the full weight of social opinion would have prevented. Why this happened is a subject of some debate among historians. Some say that a psychological sea change occurred after 1750 that allowed new freedoms in the sexual sphere. Others, the majority, say that the young people simply seized the increasing opportunities that a more mobile society gave them to get together outside the watchful oversight of pastors, parents, and elders.

The Flower Girl. "That girl seems to know you, George!" says the suspicious wife as the flower girl recognizes a customer of her other wares. Prostitution was widespread in the early Industrial Age. *(Mary Evans Picture Library)*

For most women, marriage was still the main career option, but demographic changes made it impossible for a number of women to marry. Although the number of males and females is about equal at birth, unmarried females begin to outnumber males after about age twenty-five. This discrepancy was larger in the past than now because males were affected disproportionately by accidents and violence. Consequently, there were fewer eligible males than females in the age cohort most likely to marry. Many women were never able to marry. These "spinsters" were common in all social strata except the very highest. Their married relatives often took shameless advantage of them, forcing them to work as child watchers, laborers, maids, and seamstresses in return for minimal room and board.

Since children were generally considered an absolute necessity for a good marriage, a single female who was beyond childbearing age was a near-hopeless case. Only one thing could improve her chances: if she were well-off, she might attract some ambitious young man as a husband. The well-off widow who was courted by a series of younger men who had their eyes on her money is a stock figure of eighteenth- and nineteenth-century folklore. In return for giving the woman a respected place in society, her husband became the master of her money and expected to find his sexual pleasures, and possibly children, elsewhere.

Occupations and Mobility

The ordinary work of ordinary men and women was changing during the latter part of the eighteenth century. This change steadily picked up momentum as new industrial towns began to emerge in Britain and northern Europe.

Although most people continued to work directly with and on the land (farming, tending orchards, fishing, timbering, shepherding), the number engaged in urban occupations and nonmanual work was gradually increasing by the 1750s. As methods of agriculture improved, large estates could reduce the number of farm laborers they employed. The so-called **enclosure movement** in Britain—by which formerly communal lands were enclosed by private landlords—also forced a good number of independent farmers off the land (see Chapter 38). They could escape poverty only by moving away to a new life as wage earners in the towns.

Some small minority of these ex-farmers had the intelligence, drive, and luck to take up nonmanual work, perhaps as bookkeepers, salesclerks, or schoolteachers (for which the only real qualification was semiliteracy). Any who could make their way into these occupations would move upward in the social scale and find the opportunity to better themselves by imitating the manners and ideas of the socially superior classes.

But ex-peasants could also get ahead in many other ways. They could apprentice themselves to a skilled craftsman for a number of years or take any of the new opportunities for unskilled manual work now opening, such as building canals or railroads. The rapidly increasing overseas commerce of the eighteenth and early nineteenth centuries extended the horizons of ambitious youths, a good many of whom had left their ancestral villages because they saw only too clearly what a miserable future awaited them there. Some of them ended up in one or another of the American colonies, but the majority stayed at home, unable to bring themselves to take the leap into the dark that emigration entailed.

As there were, of course, absolutely no government provisions to aid the needy, the threat of unemployment and of literal starvation was often very real. Many young men spent years teetering on the edge of the abyss, before they had sufficiently mastered a trade, established themselves in business, or inherited some land to farm, so that they could set themselves up as the head of a family household. (See the Tradition and Innovation box for one youth's adventures.)

Female Occupations

For young women, the choices were considerably narrower. There were essentially only two: they could stay at home,

A NAVVY'S LIFE ON THE TRAMP

The anonymous author of this piece was born about 1820 in England. When he left home at about twenty years of age, he was already well acquainted with hard work. Like tens of thousands of other young men, he could find no place in the traditional village economy and went "on the tramp," taking pickup laboring jobs with farmers or railroad gangs. He would do any other unskilled work he could find. Many men (and a few women) who could not find a suitable place for themselves in the home village pursued this life for years, sometimes even into old age.

Family and Earliest Work

My father was a labouring man, earning nine shillings a week in the best of times [about the equivalent of $135 currently]. . . . There was a wonderful large family of us—eleven was born, but we died down to six. I remember one winter, we was very bad off, for we boys could get no employment, and no one in the family was working but father. He only got fourteen pence a day to keep eight of us in firing and everything. It was a hard matter to get enough to eat.

The first work I ever did was to mind two little lads for a farmer, I drawed them about in a little cart, for which I got my breakfast and a penny a day. When I got older, I went to tending sheep. I was about seven years old then.

On the Tramp

After I left home I started on the road "tramping" about the country, looking for work. Sometimes I'd stop a few weeks with one master, then go on again, travelling about; never long at a time in the one place. I soon got into bad company and bad ways. . . . This is the way we'd carry on. Perhaps I'd light on [meet] an old mate somewhere about the country, and we'd go rambling together from one place to another. If we earned any money, we'd go to a public house [tavern], and stop there two or three days, till we'd spent it all, or till the publican turned us out drunk and helpless to the world. Having no money to pay for a lodging, we had to lie under a hedge, and in the morning we'd get up thinking, "What shall we do?" "Where shall we go?" And perhaps it would come over us, "Well, I'll never do the like again."

We'd wander on till we could find a gang of men at work at some railroad or large building; sometimes they would help us and sometimes they would not. Once I travelled about for three days without having anything to eat.

. . . [W]hile I was in Yorkshire I met with a young gentleman who had a fine house of his own, but would spend all his time in the beer-shop. One day he saw me there and called out, "Well, old navvy," he says, "can you drink a quart of ale?"

"Thank you, sir," says I.

"Well, if you will stop along of me, I'll keep you in drink, as long as you like to sing me songs," says he.

"Master," says I, "I'll have you! I do like my beer."

. . . I stopped with him a fortnight drinking Yorkshire ale at 6 pence a quart, while he drank rum and brandy, and soda water between whiles. But at the fortnight's end I had to run away. I could not stand it any longer. He'd have killed me with it if I'd gone on.

It was not long after this that I got sent to prison. I was working at Hastings, when we struck [went out on strike] there. The ganger [foreman], he came up and then he upped with his fist and knocked me down; and as fast as I got up he hit me down again. . . . They come and ta'en us the next day, and had us locked up in Lewes Gaol; two of us got two months, and the other one month. We was all very happy and comfortable there, though we were kept rather short of victuals. There they learnt me to spin mops, and it was there that I got hold of most of my scholarship.

FOR REFLECTION

Does our author think his life exceptional in its hardships? What does the comment on the "eleven . . . who died down to six" tell you of family life and intrafamilial relations at the time?

SOURCE: "Life of a Navvy," in Useful Toil, ed., J. Burnet (New York: Penguin, 1984), p. 55. © 1984, Penguin Classics. Reprinted by permission of Penguin, Ltd.

hoping for a successful marriage to a local youth of their own class, or they could go into service—that is, join the millions of teenaged daughters of peasants and laborers who left home to become servants. The prevalence of servants is hard for twentieth-century Americans to imagine. Practically every household, even relatively poor ones, had one or more. It was not at all unusual for a poor farmer's house to harbor one or two servant girls as well as a male laborer or two. No middle- or upper-class house in the nineteenth century was without its servant staff, mainly females from rural families who came to town to seek work. Sometimes the servants were related by blood or marriage to the household; sometimes not.

Many of these young women left their employers after shorter or longer periods of service, having found a suitable marriage partner with whom to "set up." But many others stayed for life. They remained unmarried, contributing part of their meager wage to support the old folks in the village. Some of these women practically became members of the family and were cared for in their old age, but many were turned out like so many used-up horses when they became too old to work.

By the early nineteenth century, when factory work had become fairly common in Britain, young women also had the option of taking a job tending a machine. The very earliest factories were often staffed by entire families. But increasingly, young women and children replaced the male adults and family units in the unskilled jobs such as cotton spinning and mechanical weaving. The owners of the textile and shoe mills found that young women would work for

Textile Mill Workers. This early photo shows the noisy and dangerous conditions of work in a mid-nineteenth-century mill. The many exposed machinery parts were constantly jamming, often at the expense of a worker's daily wages. *(The Art Archive)*

lower wages than young men commanded and were more reliable. Many country girls preferred factory jobs, where they could be with their peers and have some freedom in their off hours, to going into domestic service with its many restrictions.

THE MIGRATION TO THE CITIES: URBANIZED SOCIETY

Throughout the Western world, a massive flight to the cities began in the eighteenth century and continued almost unchecked through the twentieth century. Most of the migrants from the countryside were young people in the prime of life. The precise reasons for this **urban migration** varied considerably from place to place and era to era, but three motives underlay it everywhere:

- *Human curiosity and the desire for change.* The young in every culture are more open to change and more eager to embrace it than their elders. When it became relatively easy to move about and experience new things, new places, and new people, young people took advantage of the changed conditions.
- *The desire to improve economic and social status.* The variety of occupations that the towns offered, the opportunity to gain at least a minimal education, and the belief that talent and ambition had a freer field in the town than in the ancestral village inspired many persons to move.
- *The desire to find better marital partners.* Young women in particular, whose prospects of finding a desirable husband in their village were tightly restricted by their families' demands and social standing and who could

not easily rebel, took the opportunity to search elsewhere.

Beyond these subjective motivations, we should note the objective economic fact that by the nineteenth century, the shift of an entire society from a rural to an urban majority was, for the first time in history, viable and sustainable. The gradual spread of commerce and long-distance communications and financial credit arrangements allowed towns to grow regardless of the local food-producing capacity. Bristol in England, Lyon in France, Brussels in Belgium, and Oslo in Norway, to cite some examples at random, no longer depended on the ability of the agricultural region close by to supply their daily bread and meat. They could, and did, get their supplies from Canada, Denmark, or wherever it was most convenient.

Urban Growth

In the eighteenth century, this urbanization of society was advancing rapidly: among the metropolises, London's population rose from 700,000 in 1700 to about 1 million in 1800. Berlin tripled in size to about 175,000. Paris rose from about 300,000 to 500,000 in the same period. In every Western country, the number of towns with populations between 10,000 and 25,000 grew considerably. These towns served as important administrative, cultural, and economic centers for the provinces.

It was in these smaller towns that the bulk of the new industry and manufacturing was concentrated as the Industrial Revolution gradually got under way. Land was cheaper there than in the great metropolises, and the smaller towns were usually closer to the raw material sources. **Manchester,** the English textile center, for example, had a population of about 7,000 in the 1740s. By 1790, the population had risen to about 25,000, and it gained at least 50 percent every decade for the next half-century.

The census of 1851 showed that for the first time, a majority of the people in England lived in an urban setting (that is, in places with more than 5,000 inhabitants). About 25 percent of the population of France and Germany lived in urban areas. But the percentage was lower in southern and eastern Europe, where industry was not yet established.

Urban Classes and Lifestyles

In the eighteenth-century towns, social classes were quite distinct. At the top, dominating politics and setting the cultural tone, was the nobility. In some places, particularly in western Europe and Scandinavia, the aristocrats increasingly intermarried with wealthy commoners—bankers, merchants, officials of the self-governing cities—and together they formed the governing group.

Beneath them, but gaining in power and prestige, was an urban upper-middle class, or classes, who included less wealthy merchants, landlords, tradesmen, and professionals. These well-educated, upwardly mobile men and their families constituted what the French called the **bourgeoisie.** Many of them opposed the pretensions of the nobles and their wealthy allies and were on a collision course with the aristocratic governors, a collision that finally exploded in the French Revolution at the end of the century.

Below the bourgeoisie were the lower-middle classes, also primarily urban, composed of clerks, artisans, skilled workers, and independent shopkeepers. They were desperately afraid of falling back into the class from which they had emerged: the workers who labored in semiskilled or unskilled jobs for an employer. The lower-middle classes mimicked their social betters among the bourgeoisie, a class to which they might ascend with luck, time, and good marriages.

This lower-middle class, more than the still relatively small and fragmented working classes, generated most of the social discontents that marked the late eighteenth and early nineteenth centuries. Only in the later nineteenth century, when the industrial working classes had become much larger and more important in the social structure, did they successfully assert themselves.

DIET AND NUTRITION

At the same time that industrialization was beginning, the diet and health of ordinary citizens were gradually transformed. For many centuries, European common people had been accustomed to depending on an uneven mix of grains, cheese, sporadic meats and fowl, and a few seasonal fruits to maintain life. Much depended on local weather and harvests. The season determined what provisions

Manchester, England, at Midcentury. This moody portrait of the outstanding industrial town in Britain conveys the uncompromising ugliness of the environment created by the early factories. (*The Art Archive*)

would be available for human consumption. In late winter and spring, the supplies put away at harvest would begin to run short, and hunger became a constant companion to much of the population.

Local famine was a commonplace through the early eighteenth century everywhere. In such times, it was not unusual for grain to be rotting in barns fifty miles or so from where people were starving for lack of it. Transport networks for bulk goods were primitive or nonexistent in the more backward regions. Only the towns commanded a more or less sophisticated supply system, with stored reserves and emergency powers over the population in times of crisis. In the countryside, every decade or so in one part of Europe or another, people starved in large numbers.

By the end of that same century, famines had become a rarity, and Europeans were in fact eating considerably better than ever. What happened to change the situation? First, water transportation was much improved, as were the roads, which had formerly been in an abysmal condition. Second, new and more productive agricultural methods, seeds, and crop rotations had increased food production in western Europe, while in eastern Europe the spread of serfdom on latifundia estates allowed an increasing amount of grain to be exported to the west. Third, the diet of Europeans had expanded and improved a great deal. The potato had become a dependable staple for the poor, and its nutritional value was exceptional. Milk and dairy products were considerably more common though still viewed with suspicion by many. Meat and fish, always desired but too expensive to be enjoyed by the poor, were coming to be a standard part of the diet of all but the very poor by the end of the century.

Changing diets had a basic impact on health. The diet of the rich was excessively dependent on protein (meat) and carbohydrates (sweets, fats), with a shortage of vitamins.

Slum Life in Late-Nineteenth-Century Britain. This photograph was made in London's East End, where dead-end alleyways like this were the rule and children rarely saw anything green and growing from one month to the next. *(Private Collection/Bridgeman Art Library)*

With the coming of new foods from the colonies such as potatoes, maize, beans, and squash, this protein-loaded diet became more balanced. For the poor, the potato in particular meant the difference between life and death for many hundreds of thousands of northern Europeans who came to depend on it as much as they did on bread. In the latter part of the century, citrus fruits and exotic vegetables began to show up on the tables of the middle and upper classes, adding another dimension to the diet. These were the products of the semitropical colonies, as was sugar from cane, which now replaced honey.

PUBLIC HEALTH

Although the lives of ordinary people were improving in several respects, in many areas conditions were hardly better at all. For example, though diet was generally improving, medical and surgical conditions showed very little change over the century. Being admitted to a hospital was still almost a death warrant, and the poor would absolutely refuse, preferring to die at home. Doctoring was very much a hit-or-miss proposition, with primitive diagnosis backed up by even more primitive treatment. Surgery was a horror, with no pain deadener but whiskey until well into the nineteenth century. Amputations were the last resort in many cases, and the resultant wounds frequently became infected and killed the patient if shock had not already done so.

Doctors and pharmacists still did not receive formal training in schools of medicine. The trainees did a hit-or-miss apprenticeship with a doctor, who may or may not have known more than his apprentice. All sorts of quacks were active, bilking the public with their "Electrical Magnetic Beds" and "Elixirs of Paradise." Both the educated and the uneducated had a very low opinion of doctors.

Medical facts now taken for granted were unknown. The functions of many of the internal organs, germ theory, the dangers of infection, and fever treatment were still guesswork or not known at all. The mentally ill were just beginning to be given some treatment besides the traditional approach, under which violent patients were locked up under awful conditions and others were kept at the family home. All in all, the treatment of the human mind and body when they fell ill was hardly improved over what the Romans had done 2,000 years earlier. Some would say it was worse.

Housing and Sanitation

The most urgent problem facing the industrial towns in the early part of the nineteenth century was sanitation. In the dreary rows of cheap rental housing (hastily built largely by the mill and factory owners as an additional source of income), overcrowding to an incredible degree was commonplace. Even the most basic sanitary facilities were largely missing. Ventilation of interior rooms was nonexistent, and all types of infectious disease ran rampant. Tuberculosis (TB, or consumption) rapidly became the number one cause of death in nineteenth-century Britain. It bred in the damp, unventilated back rooms and spread easily through the workers' slums where several people—often unrelated—crowded into every miserable abode.

Privacy was impossible for the working class to obtain. Illegitimacy and incest were constant menaces to family cohesion and security. In report after report to the British Parliament in the 1830s and 1840s, shocked middle-class investigators noted that sleeping five and six to a bed was common, that boys and girls in their teens were frequently forced to sleep together for lack of space, and that greedy landlords regularly extracted the maximal rent by allowing several poverty-stricken families to share the same tiny apartments.

Similar conditions were soon found on the Continent as industry spread. For many years, civic authorities were either unable or unwilling to tackle the huge tasks of assuring decent living conditions for the poorer classes. (Recall that the poor did not yet have the vote anywhere.) Despite the relative youth of the new urban populations, towns and cities normally had a higher death rate than birthrate. Only the huge influx of new blood from the villages kept the towns expanding.

LIVING STANDARDS

As the Industrial Age began, the gap between the living conditions of the European rich and poor became wider than ever before in history. The aristocracy and the handful of wealthy commoners lived a luxurious and self-indulgent life. The higher nobility and court officials were expected to have squadrons of servants, meals with fourteen courses and ten wines, palaces in the towns and manors in the countryside, and personal jewelry whose value was equal to the yearly cash incomes of a whole province of peasants. Great wealth, though almost always hereditary, was thought to be a reward for merit and should be displayed as an intrinsic duty as well as honor.

The lifestyle of the urban middle classes was much more modest, although some of the richest, such as bankers, might have six times the income of the poorer aristocrats. Secure in their solid townhouses, surrounded by domestic servants, the members of the middle classes entertained modestly if at all and concentrated on their counting-houses, investments, shops, businesses, and legal firms. They devoted much attention to their extensive families. The wife was expected to be a thrifty, farsighted manager of the household, and the husband was the source of authority for the children and the bearer of the most precious possession of all, the family honor.

For most people in urban areas, material life was gradually improving, but the lower fringes of the working classes

Seven Dials. This 1872 engraving by Gustave Doré captures the irrepressible vitality of the worst slum in London. Seven Dials was known far and wide as a thieves' haven and a pickpocket's bazaar. Some of the stolen wares were brazenly put on display immediately for sale, perhaps to the former owners. *(The Granger Collection, New York)*

Cholera Arrives in Manchester, 1832

The most dreaded disease of the nineteenth century was cholera. Borne by polluted water, it was particularly lethal in the crowded industrial slums springing up in the first half of the century throughout western Europe. The worst epidemic occurred in 1832, moving briskly from Russia through central Europe into Britain. In this excerpt, one of the leading medical researchers of the age tells us of the first case in Manchester, where it was going to kill several thousand people in a period of weeks. The unstinting devotion of the doctor and his helplessness in the face of the highly contagious disease are both remarkable. It would take another British cholera outbreak, in the 1850s, to finally prove the disease's spread through germ-laden water and lead to its eventual control. Note also the fear of the effect of the discovery of epidemic among an uneducated and poverty-stricken populace:

I had requested the younger members of the staff, charged with the visitation of outpatients of the infirmary, to give me the earliest information of the occurrence of any cases of cholera. I had a scientific wish to trace the mode of its propagation and to ascertain if possible by what means it would be introduced into the town. My purpose was to ascertain whether there was any, and if so, what, link or connection between the physical and social evils, to which my attention had been so long directed. . . .

[A sick Irish laborer living in the dank, polluted slum called Irishtown is reported to the doctor, who goes to visit him]

I sat by the man's bed for an hour during which the pulse became gradually weaker. In a second hour it became almost extinct, and it was apparent that the patient would die. His wife and three children were in the room . . . as the evening approached I sent the young surgeon to have in readiness the cholera van not far away. We were surrounded by an excitable Irish population, and it was obviously desirable to remove the body as soon as possible, and

then the family, and to lock up the house before any alarm was given. . . .

No case of Asiatic cholera had occurred in Manchester, yet notwithstanding the total absence of characteristic symptoms in this case, I was convinced that the contagion had arrived, and the patient had been its first victim. The Knott Hill Hospital was a cotton factory stripped of its machinery; on my arrival here I found the widow and her three children with a nurse grouped round a fire at one end of a gloomy ward. . . . None of them showed any sign of disease, and I left the ward to take some refreshment. On my return, the infant had been sick in its mother's lap, had made a faint cry, and had died. The mother was naturally full of terror and distress, for the child had had no medicine, had been fed only from its mother's breast, and consequently, she could have no doubt that it perished from the same causes as its father. I sat with her and the nurse by the fire very late into the night. While I was there the children did not wake, nor seem in any way disturbed, and at length I thought I might myself seek some repose. When I returned about six o'clock in the morning, another child had severe cramps and some sickness, and while I stood by the bedside, it died. Then later, the third and eldest child had all the characteristic symptoms and perished in one or two hours. In the course of the day the mother likewise suffered from a severe and rapid succession of the characteristic symptoms and died, so that within twenty-four hours the whole family was extinct.

FOR REFLECTION

What does the doctor mean by "any link or connection between the physical and social evils"? Why was it logical that the early cases of cholera would be found among the inhabitants of a place called "Irishtown" at this time and place?

Source: Frank Smith, The Life and Work of Sir James Kay-Shuttleworth *(London: n.p., 1923).*

---

and the many beggars, casual laborers, and wandering peddlers and craftspeople were hard put to keep bread on the table and their children in clothes. Poverty was perhaps never so grim in European cities as in the early nineteenth century, when it became more visible because of the much increased numbers of abjectly poor, and it had not yet called forth the social welfare measures that would become common by the twentieth century. As industrial work began to become common in the towns, the uprooted ex-peasants who supplied most of the labor often experienced a decline in living standards for a while, until they or their families found ways to cope with the demands of the factory and the town lifestyle. This decline could last for an entire first generation of migrants, and only their children benefited from the often painful transition.

Reforms and Improvements

To the credit of the British aristocrats who still controlled Parliament, as early as the 1820s, after the war emergency had passed, a number of reform proposals to aid the working classes were introduced. By the 1830s, some of the worst abuses in the workplace were attacked. The **Factory Acts** of 1819 and 1833 limited the employment of young children and provided that they should be given at least a little education at their place of work. (Still, it remained entirely legal for a nine-year-old to put in eight-hour workdays and for a thirteen-year-old to work twelve hours a day, six days a week!)

Women and boys under the age of ten were not permitted to work in the mines after 1842. Until then, much of the deep underground work, which was highly dangerous and exhausting to anyone, was done by women and young children. In most textile manufacturing, physical strength was not as important as quickness and endurance. Women and children were paid much less than men demanded, and their smaller size allowed them to move about in the crowded machine halls with more agility than men. Boys as young as seven years of age were regularly employed in twelve- or thirteen-hour shifts until the passage of the 1833 act. The families of young working children often opposed and circumvented the reforms, which diminished the potential family income. No more substantial reform legislation was passed until the early twentieth century.

Little was done to improve basic sanitation in worker housing until the 1860s. In 1842, a pioneering report by **Edwin Chadwick** on the horrible conditions in the slums and how they might be corrected through modern sewage and water purification systems began to draw attention. But not until the great cholera scare of 1858, when London was threatened by a major outbreak of this lethal water-borne disease, was action taken. (Read more about this epidemic in the Science and Technology box.) Then the upper and middle classes realized that although epidemic diseases such as cholera might originate in the slums, they could and would soon spread to other residential areas. At about the same time, the restructuring of its primitive sewer system allowed Paris for the first time to manage its waste disposal problem. Led by the two capitals, the provincial city authorities soon began to plan and install equivalent systems. By the end of the nineteenth century, European city life was again reasonably healthy for all but the poorest slum dwellers.

SUMMARY

The social change introduced by mechanized industry took many forms, impacting family relations, occupational mobility, urbanization, and diet. The family was changed by a decreasing age of marriage and a sharp rise in illegitimacy. Children came to be valued as creatures worthy of love in their own right. A number of new occupations were opened to both men and women in factories and mills as industry spread, while the traditional servant jobs multiplied in the expanding cities and towns.

Living standards varied from an unprecedented opulence among the rich to an actual decline in the conditions of recent urban migrants. Slums appeared in the new industrial quarters, which were horribly lacking in basic sanitation and privacy. Nevertheless, to the working classes, the attractions of the towns were manifold and irresistible, particularly for those who sought a better life than the traditional social and economic restrictions that the villages allowed. A richer and more varied diet even for the poor gradually made itself felt in better health. By the end of the nineteenth century, sanitation and workers' living and labor conditions had visibly improved.

TEST YOUR KNOWLEDGE

1. Around the mid–eighteenth century, the European population
   a. began to rise as a result of declining mortality and rising birthrates.
   b. started to stabilize after a century of steady increase.
   c. tapered off from the sharp decline that had marked the sixteenth and seventeenth centuries.
   d. began to rise as a result of medical breakthroughs against epidemics.
2. Formerly, historians erroneously believed that in preindustrial Europe
   a. the average age at marriage was in the early thirties.
   b. the average life span was no more than twenty-five years.
   c. daughters shared equally with the sons in inheriting land.
   d. there was a great deal of illegitimacy.
3. Marriage in preindustrial European society is best described as
   a. a contractual relation formed mostly by economic and social aspirations.
   b. a contractual relation that conformed closely to biological drives.
   c. an economic relationship between two individuals.
   d. a stratagem to "cover" the sexual activities engaged in by the young anyway.
4. An important function of children in preindustrial society was
   a. to serve as security for their parents in old age.
   b. to elevate themselves socially and thus to honor their parents.
   c. to bring grandchildren into the world for their parents' gratification.
   d. to pray for the departed souls of their deceased parents.

5. In the early industrial period, the most common employment for a female
   a. involved prostitution at least part-time.
   b. was as a domestic household servant.
   c. was in one or another white-collar jobs.
   d. was to substitute for a man temporarily.
6. The governing class in the cities of the eighteenth century was composed of
   a. the hereditary aristocracy.
   b. the aristocracy and the wealthiest commoners, who had intermarried.
   c. the military commanders responsible to the royal government.
   d. the masses of urban commoners who had obtained the vote.

7. As a generalization, living standards in early-nineteenth-century towns
   a. saw a huge differentiation between top and bottom, perhaps the most ever.
   b. were roughly similar to conditions in the countryside for the mass of people.
   c. were better than they would ever be again for the laboring poor.
   d. were much better than ever before in European history.
8. Diet and nutrition in the later eighteenth century were
   a. steadily worsening for the poorer classes.
   b. favorably affected by the trade with the colonies.
   c. about the same for the poor and the rich.
   d. undermined by the frequent famines.

IDENTIFICATION TERMS

bourgeoisie	**enclosure movement**	**Manchester**	**urban migration**
Chadwick, Edwin	**Factory Acts**		

INFOTRAC COLLEGE EDITION

Enter the search terms "family nineteenth century" using Key Words.

Enter the search term "Chartism" using the Subject Guide.

Enter the search term "Romanticism" using the Subject Guide.

40

EUROPE IN IDEOLOGICAL CONFLICT

The folk learn more from a defeat than the kings do from a victory.

ALESSANDRO MANZONI

THE ANCIEN REGIME of pre-1789 Europe could not be brought back despite the efforts of the conservative leaders at the Vienna congress. But in countries other than France, a great many of the political, legal, and social reforms that the French Revolution had brought or attempted to bring were delayed or even temporarily reversed. In France itself, however, the changes since 1789 were too popular to be ignored in the post-1815 settlement. And even outside France, the forces unleashed by the economic changes that had been taking place in England—the First Industrial Revolution, as it has come to be called—were going to remake the society of western Europe by the mid-nineteenth century. The revolts of 1848 were the direct though delayed result of the changes set in motion by industrialization and by the ideas of 1789.

LIBERAL POLITICS AND ECONOMICS

Much of the history of the past two centuries, especially in Europe, has been a reflection of a sustained *dual revolution* in politics and economics. What exactly is meant or implied by that term? The political revolution was highlighted by events in the United States between 1775 and 1789 and in France between 1789 and 1800, which we looked at in earlier chapters. In the first example, a republic of federated states was born, committed to political democracy and the legal equality of all citizens. In the second, the ancient class distinctions and privileges given the highborn were declared extinct, and the way upward was opened to all who had the talent and ambition to tread it.

The economic revolution was slower and less spectacular, but it was at least as important over the long run. It was generated by the changes in industrial production that took place beginning in the second half of the eighteenth century, particularly in Britain; by the conquest of space through the railroads; and by the immense growth of population in Europe and the United States, which provided formerly undreamed of markets for consumer products.

The two revolutions fused together reinforcing one another in all kinds of ways. Two examples will suffice:

1. In the 1790s, during the period of the Directory in France, a tiny group of conspirators tried to popularize the first "socialist" ideas, although they did not use that

🏵 The *Wanderer in the Sea of Clouds.* Caspar Friedrich was the best known and possibly the most technically accomplished of the early generation of Romantic painters. He painted this brooding introspective in 1818. *(Hamburg Kunsthalle, Hamburg, Germany/Bridgeman Art Library)*

term. Their vague hopes of eliminating property-based distinctions and sharing equally the products of human labor got nowhere. The leaders were soon arrested and put to death as pernicious agitators of the poor. A generation later, when the horrible working conditions produced by early industrialization were being recognized simultaneously with the political beliefs of liberal democracy, another group of theorists arose in Britain and France. They were determined to replace the abuses and exploitation of early capitalism by the humane ideals of equality and mutual care. This was the origin of an organized, multinational effort to introduce governmental responsibility for the welfare of the citizenry, which eventually triumphed to a greater or lesser degree in several countries.

2. The eighteenth-century political revolution was guided by the middle classes—the lawyers, teachers, and merchants—on their own behalf. They had little sympathy with democracy as we now understand that term. Later, in the post-1815 period of reaction, the more perceptive among them recognized that without the active assistance of much of the laboring classes, they could not gain and hold power against the aristocracy. The industrial laboring classes were growing rapidly but lacked leadership from within their own ranks. Instead, "renegades" from the middle classes became more or less radical democrats and led the struggle to help the industrial laborers find their rightful voice in the political arena. During the later nineteenth century, a partnership grew up between the middle-class reformers and newly en-

franchised working-class voters, which brought about substantial improvement in the condition of ordinary people.

We have already explored the fundamental principles of liberal thought (see Chapter 36). Inspired by the philosophical concepts of Locke, Montesquieu, and others, middle- and upper-class reformers believed that so long as law and custom prevented most people from enjoying certain fundamental liberties and rights, the human race would fail to fulfill its high destiny.

These liberal sons and daughters of the Enlightenment everywhere formed a *"party of reform,"* dedicated to changing the traditional, class-based system of political representation. By 1815, much had been achieved in those respects in America and France, but the conservative reaction nullified some of those gains everywhere in Europe. Only in France and England was much of the liberal political agenda retained. Here, men of property had the vote, all men were equal in the eyes of the law, and royal powers were sharply curtailed by written laws that could not be easily manipulated. Parliaments in both countries, similar to Congress in the United States, were responsible to the voters, rather than to the king, and freedom of conscience was guaranteed.

The Gospel of Free Enterprise

Another side of the liberal philosophy focused on freedoms in the marketplace and the rebellion against the traditional restrictions imposed by mercantilism. In contrast to political liberalism's gradual evolution, economic liberalism grew directly from the work of Adam Smith, whose ideas were mentioned briefly in Chapter 36. What did Smith's adherents want?

- *Laissez-faire.* If government would only let them alone (laissez-faire), the merchants and manufacturers of every nation would produce goods and services to meet the demands of the market most efficiently and economically.
- *Free trade.* The existing mercantile system of quotas, licenses, and subsidies should be eliminated as quickly as possible, and the most efficient producers should be allowed to trade with any place and anyone who desired their goods at prices that the free market would set.
- *The less government, the better.* As the first two conditions suggest, the economic liberals despised governmental controls of any sort in the economy (even though Smith himself made certain important exceptions to laissez-faire). They believed that the free market alone would provide proper guidance for policy decisions and that it was government's task simply to follow these guidelines as they revealed themselves over time. Any interference in the economy they condemned as an obstruction to the prosperity of the nation. The famous "unseen hand" of the free market should be allowed to do its beneficial work for all.

In early nineteenth-century England, economic liberalism, often called **Manchester liberalism** because of its popularity with the cotton mill owners in Manchester, provided the employers of industrial labor with an excuse for the systematic exploitation of the weak. They drew on theorists such as Thomas Malthus (*An Essay on Population,* published in 1798) and David Ricardo (*The Iron Law of Wages,* published in 1817). Using these sources, the Manchester liberals were able to demonstrate that the poor would always be poor because of their excessive birthrate and other moral faults and that it was the well-off's duty to protect their material advantages by any means they could. Since sympathizers with this line of thought came into control of the British House of Commons after the electoral **Reform Act of 1832,** the government was largely unsympathetic toward the idea of social protection of the lower classes. Only in the 1870s and later did a sufficient number of reformers emerge who rejected this heartless attitude and busied themselves with the improvement of the lot of the poor majority.

CONSERVATISM IN POST-NAPOLEONIC EUROPE

The liberals, though gaining strength, were by no means the sole players in the political field after 1815. Supported by the wave of anti-Napoleonic nationalism, conservative forces in Britain and France were powerful for at least a generation longer. In eastern Europe, the conservative wave became sheer reaction and lasted much longer. Conservatism in the first half of the nineteenth century meant one of two things. One was *moderate conservatism,* an attempt to take the the milder liberal ideas of the day and adapt them to the service of the traditional institutions such as monarchy, established religion, and class-based distinctions. The other was *reaction,* a total rejection of the ideas of the American and French Revolutions and a determination to turn the clock back.

Moderate Conservatism

Conservatives of all stripes believed that an official religion was a necessity for instilling proper respect for law and tradition. They could not imagine a state in which church and government were separated by law. They supported a constitution but rejected political democracy as being the rule of the mob. They believed that only those who had a stake in society, evidenced by property, could and would take on the burdens of self-government with the requisite seriousness and respect for legal procedure. They thought that just as differences in talent would always exist, so also should differences in privilege. Some conservatives rejected the idea of privilege by birth. Others embraced it as the best way to assure a responsible group in continuous command of the ship of state.

Moderate conservatism was supported by a large percentage of ordinary Europeans who had been appalled by Jacobin radicalism and then angered by Napoleon's arrogance and his economic exploitation of non-French subjects. The clergy, both Catholic and Protestant, were the leaders of moderate conservatism in much of the Continent. The more enlightened aristocrats, who could see what would happen if turning the clock back were to be adopted as state policy, also contributed to moderate conservatism. They wished to avoid revolutions in the future by making some necessary concessions now.

In economics, the moderates generally favored the continuation of government controls in trade (especially foreign trade) and industry. They thought that Smith was well meaning but wrong and that without such supervision by the authorities, the national welfare would only be harmed by selfish and greedy entrepreneurs.

Since many of the nonclerical conservatives either were wealthy or had prospects of becoming so, any drastic change in the existing economic system would almost certainly harm their interests. Much of their wealth was tied up in inherited land. They were not happy watching financial speculation, commerce, and manufacturing replace land rent as the primary source of prestige and large income.

Reaction

Reactive conservatism was the rule in Prussia, Austria, and Russia, where few if any political concessions were made to the new social structures being created by the changing modes of production. This led to explosive pressures, which eventually burst forth in the revolts of 1848 and the upheaval of World War I and its revolutionary aftermath. In Prussia and Austria, the reactionary conservatives ruled for a generation after 1815. They denied a constitution; retained the established church, whether Catholic or Protestant; and maintained strict class distinctions in justice, taxation, and voting rights. Both countries also maintained a form of serfdom until 1848.

In Russia (which meant not only the Russian ethnic groups but also much of what is now independent eastern Europe), the reactionaries were also in command. Czar Alexander I had died in 1825 without ever giving his nation the constitutional government that he had toyed with since his accession to the throne twenty-five years earlier. He was followed on the throne by his younger brother, Nicholas I (ruled 1825–1855), a sincere believer in God's designation of autocracy for Russia and a dyed-in-the-wool reactionary. Nicholas's inclinations were reinforced by the botched attempt of a handful of idealistic rebels (the "Decembrists") to organize a revolution and impose a constitution on liberal lines in December 1825. During Nicholas's reign, Russia was called the "**Gendarme of Europe**," eager and ready to put down liberal agitation or revolutionary change wherever it might rear its ugly head. All of Europe was split during the entire post-Napoleonic generation between these reactionary forces and their liberal opponents. Some version of this struggle could be found in every quarter of the European public.

NATIONALISM

Besides the struggle between liberal and conservative, another source of conflict was evidencing itself in post-1815 Europe: nationalist feeling. Modern political nationalism has its origins in France between 1792 and 1795, when the Jacobins insisted on the duties imposed on all citizens by patriotism. Later, when the French occupied half of Europe, their subjects' patriotic reaction against the occupier contributed mightily to nationalism.

Nationalism and liberalism marched well together in several nations, especially Britain and France. Conservatives, on the other hand, were usually split on the question of nationalism. Many conservatives denounced it as a trick exercised by demagogues to fool the common people into supporting ill-advised and revolutionary actions. They could not forget its origins.

Early nationalism was generally a culturally benign phenomenon. It was positive in its goals and tolerant in outlook. Thus, to be aware of being French did not mean to reject the Germans or English as inferiors. One could simultaneously strive for the freedom of the individual and the free nation. Sometime in the 1840s, however, nationalism in much of Europe lost its constructive, tolerant character. This later phase was marked by the rise of negative qualities that we in modern times are thoroughly familiar with: "we" versus "they" and right against wrong; nationalism as a zero-sum game in which one nation's gain is another's loss and vice versa. This nationalism was characterized by a conviction of cultural superiority over other nations and by a sense of mission—the belief that one's nation was bringing the light to other, less fortunate neighbors. It degenerated to its worst in the Balkans and eastern Europe, where many distinct peoples lived in mixed communities and regions without clear territorial lines. Here, nationalism soon became an excuse for one war after another in the later nineteenth and early twentieth centuries. The propaganda campaigns of World War I exemplified this type of negative nationalism.

SOCIALISM IN THE PRE-MARX ERA

Usually, the word *socialism* is associated with the political and economic creed first systematically proposed by **Karl Marx.** But that connection did not always exist. As we have seen, the earliest socialists were a handful of conspirators in France in the 1790s. Once they were eliminated, no others arose to take their place until a generation later. None of these individuals had any link with Marx.

What did the early socialist thinkers wish to achieve? What constituted this phenomenon of socialism? Three chief economic goals were involved:

1. *A planned economy.* The unregulated free market was an entirely wasteful, haphazard way of supplying the needs and wants of most people.
2. *Greater economic equality.* There was too much for the rich, too little for the rest, and too few ways in which that situation could be changed peaceably and fairly.
3. *Ownership of income-producing property by the state rather than private parties.* Only the state was powerful enough to resist the wealthy and ensure that the means of producing wealth were not controlled by a few for their own benefit.

The pre-Marxian nineteenth-century socialists were often later termed "utopian," because what they wanted allegedly could never be secured so long as human nature remained as it was. But that label (originated by Karl Marx) is inherently unfair to them. What they wanted has been, in large part, achieved by modern societies all over the globe.

The most influential of the early socialists worked in France. The reform-minded nobleman **Henri de Saint-Simon** (1760–1825) was perhaps the most important of all. He believed that industrialized society had the potential to be the fairest, as well as the most productive, society that the world had ever seen. He believed further that the state (that is, the government) had the positive duty to look out for those who were unable to look out for themselves—the misfits, the incompetent, and the disabled. Since industrialized production would be so much more lavish than anything previously seen, the economy of scarcity would be abolished soon, and it would be no hardship to care for these "welfare cases." Saint-Simon thought that private industry and government must combine in planning this economy of abundance that was surely coming.

Charles Fourier and **Pierre Proudhon** were active later than Saint-Simon and had differing views. Fourier was an obsessive theorist of technology and organization. His vision of special, self-contained units of precisely 1,620 persons living and working together was one of the oddities of early social thought (see the Science and Technology box). Fourier was particularly important as a forerunner of feminist equality in work and politics and as the upholder of the demands of the emotional, passionate side of human nature in industrialized society.

Proudhon was the first modern anarchist. He believed the power of the state must be destroyed if men and women were ever to be truly free and capable of living humane lives. Unlike most socialists, Proudhon was convinced that government was at best a barely tolerable evil. He thought it was always controlled by the wealthy and was almost always the oppressor of the poor. In 1840, he posed his famous question, *What Is Property?* and gave a resounding answer: Property is nothing but organized theft! It has been stolen from the sole creator of value, the worker, by the owning class. And it should be taken back—by force, if necessary.

In England, utopian socialism's standard-bearer in the early nineteenth century was a businessman, **Robert Owen.** Owen was a remarkable man whose hard work and ambition made him a wealthy mill owner at the age of twenty-seven. He then decided to give much of his wealth and power to his workforce. At his famous cooperative textile mill at New Lanark, Scotland, Owen put his theories into practice and created a profitable enterprise that also provided well for every need of its workers and their families. Although not all of his visions worked out so well (the American experimental community he founded in the 1820s was a quick disaster), Owen remained convinced that industrial production and a decent life for workers were compatible and within reach.

In the 1840s, socialism was still very much an idea or theory of outsiders. It was not taken seriously by most people and condemned as against the laws of God and man by most of those who *did* take notice of it. Economic liberals thundered against it as unnatural. Middle-class political liberals were appalled at the prospect of hordes of uneducated industrial workers being admitted into equality in government. All types of conservatives thought it terribly misunderstood human nature and hence was foredoomed to fail.

POLITICAL EVENTS TO 1848

In the period just after the Vienna settlement of 1815, European international affairs were relatively calm (see Map 40.1). The Quadruple Alliance of the victors formed at Vienna was easily strong enough to suppress any attempts to overthrow the peace, as long as its members agreed. Revolts by liberals in Spain (1820) and Italy (1822) were quickly squelched, but a nationalist guerrilla war by the Greeks against their Turkish overlords (1827–1830) was allowed to commence and eventually succeed because it was a special circumstance of Christian versus Muslim. (The Greek rebellion had a special connection to nineteenth-century English literature; see the Religion and Philosophy box on Lord Byron.)

During this decade, the Spanish-American colonies were also allowed to break away from backward Spain, which was too weak to suppress their revolts by itself. First Mexico, then most of South America rebelled against Madrid and were independent states by 1825. Brazil, Portugal's one colony in the New World, also broke away during this same period (see Chapter 34).

The Liberal States: France and Britain

In an almost bloodless revolution in July 1830, the French middle classes threw out their unpopular Bourbon ruler, who had foolishly attempted to install an absolutist

CHARLES FOURIER
(1772–1837)

The most interesting of all the early socialist theorizers was the Frenchman Charles Fourier. Though perhaps not entirely sane, he nevertheless pinpointed many of the unpleasant truths about modern industrial society seventy-five or a hundred years before those truths were accepted by most.

Fourier was born into a well-off family in a provincial city and received an excellent education, but he lost his property during the French Revolution. He fought for the Napoleonic regime for two years, but ill health forced him to resign his army post. He then began a life of scholarship and propagandizing his ideas.

In 1808, he published, anonymously, his basic work, *The Theory of the Four Movements;* there he explains that human society has been corrupted by the unnatural restraints that we impose on ourselves. Only when those restraints have been lifted will humans achieve their potential. Fourier's focus on the importance of emotions, or passions, and on the necessity of women finding satisfaction in their emotional life make him an important forerunner of the feminist movement. However, Fourier's demand that passions be given free expression quickly stamped him as an eccentric and a dangerous challenger to accepted values.

In the economic aspect of this doctrine, Fourier worked out an answer to the blight of early industrialization: the socioeconomic unit he called the *phalanx* (Greek for a military unit). He insisted that individualism and the competition it fostered were the prime cause of social evils. The new society would consist of voluntary associations, where cooperation would be the rule in every aspect of life.

The phalanx envisioned by Fourier consisted of exactly 1,620 persons, equally divided by sex, with sufficient farmland around the common dwelling and workplace—the *phalanstery*—to supply the members with food. Work would be assigned as much as possible by preference, but the dirty tasks would be rotated, and there would be no "high" or "low" occupations. The work would be suited to the natural temperaments of different age and gender groups. For example, young children with their natural affinity for dirt would be assigned to act as public scavengers and garbage collectors! Those who desired could marry, but all could rightfully engage in free sexual expression, which was considered a basic human need. Needless to add, such reasoning did not convince many in a Europe that was still largely controlled by church and censor.

Though he led a very reclusive life, Fourier continued to publicize his theories to his dying day, but he never had the satisfaction of seeing them translated into fact. Despite the best efforts of his friends and converts, there was but one French experiment with Fourierism, as the theory was termed by the 1830s. It ended quickly in total failure. Instead, Fourier's most important impact was in the New World. Several American experiments in communal living in the first half of the nineteenth century drew their inspiration and some of their structure from Fourier. Brook Farm, the famous New England venture in an intellectual and communal society, was one of these.

In his later life, Fourier devoted his energies to finding a rich backer, who would supply the necessary capital to establish a phalanstery, or a series of them, under his own supervision. Reportedly, having published an appeal for the equivalent of a million dollars or so in his tiny newspaper, Fourier would go to his office at noon on the appointed day to wait for the unknown benefactor to drop the money in his lap. No matter how many times the benefactor failed to appear, the next time the notice ran Fourier would go in all confidence to wait for the gift.

This sort of unworldliness pervaded Fourierism, as well as its founder, and kept the authorities from becoming too concerned about his challenge to the status quo. Fourier was contemptuous of the competing theories of Saint-Simon and Owen, believing that their failure to appreciate the importance of human passions rendered their whole approach to socioeconomic questions invalid. Although it is beyond dispute that much of his own theory would, if applied, do more damage than good to people, it is still impressive to note how well Fourier understood some of the damage that modern individualistic and competitive societies inflict on their members. While the phalanxes and phalansteries may be condemned without hesitation as unworkable daydreams, the emotional repression, social isolation, and alienation from one's fellow beings that they were meant to counter are also indisputably bad for the human body and soul.

FOR REFLECTION

What would happen among your college classmates if a Fourier phalanx were to be erected along his principles? What do you think of Fourier's insistence that human emotions must be considered in providing a work environment?

---

government. In his place came the "Citizen King," Louis Philippe (ruled 1830–1848). Louis gladly accepted from Parliament a moderately liberal constitution, which called him "king of the French," rather than the traditional king of France, and stated that sovereignty lay in the people, not in the throne. This was a novelty in monarchic government that would be widely accepted later.

The **July Monarchy,** as the eighteen years of Louis Philippe's reign are generally called, was a major step forward for both economic and political liberalism. The middle class and especially the new upper class of wealth (not birth) did very well under this government. The rising number of urban poor and industrial workers found very little sympathy from it, however. Troops were repeatedly used to

MAP 40.1 Prussia and Austria after the Peace of Vienna, 1815. The center of the continent was the scene of an increasing rivalry for leadership of the German-speaking peoples. Austria and Prussia both emerged victors in 1815, and both were bulwarks of the reaction against French revolutionary ideas.

break strikes and to control the populace. Citizen rights were granted and usually observed by the government, but those rights were much more extensive for the well-off than for the majority. Social tensions were steadily building and could not be held in check forever. Victor Hugo's great novel *Les Misérables* is the best mirror of this epoch.

In Great Britain, the other country favoring the liberal views, the major fact of political life during the 1820s to 1840s was the rising influence of the mercantile and manufacturing classes. In 1832, the most important reform of voting rights since the Glorious Revolution was finally passed over the protests of the Conservative Party (**Tories**) by their opponents in Parliament, the Liberals (**Whigs**). This Reform Act of 1832 stripped away many of the traditional political advantages of the landholding wealthy aristocrats and strengthened the previously weak urban middle classes. Overnight, the House of Commons seats controlled by *rotten boroughs* (very few voters) and *pocket boroughs*

(controlled by a single family) were eliminated, and the seats thus made free were distributed to urban and industrial districts. Since these latter were controlled by the Liberals, the composition of the Commons changed drastically. The Whigs would remain in charge for the next thirty-five years.

By making Parliament into a more representative national body and giving the vote to a large number of property holders who previously had been denied it, British government diminished the danger of revolution. The British middle classes were assured of a forum—Parliament—in which their voice would be heard and through which they could attain peaceable, orderly change. In the later nineteenth century, these concessions would be extended downward from the propertied classes to the unpropertied, working classes. Revolution and radical socialism never gained much following among the common folk in Britain for that reason.

GEORGE GORDON, LORD BYRON
(1788–1824)

The triumph of the Industrial Age also saw a vigorous reaction against it in the **Romantic movement,** which seized on much of Europe during the middle years of the nineteenth century. Beginning in Britain, this movement first attacked the excessive faith in rationalism that characterized the later eighteenth-century Enlightenment. By the 1820s, it had become a rejection of the narrow moneygrubbing that many believed had come into British urban life with the Industrial Revolution. A recognition of the power of the emotions and of the impenetrable mystery of life came to be seen as essential elements of all the arts, but particularly the art most given to expression of feeling—poetry. Among the British Romantic poets, George Gordon, Lord Byron, took the first place through not only the magnificence of his verse but also the enormous publicity his unconventional life generated. Several of the finest Romantic poems are from his pen, but Lord Byron's place in history has also benefited from what would now be called successful media exposure.

Born to a dissipated and irresponsible father and a loving but unbalanced mother, Byron's early years were very unstable. He was lamed by a clubfoot that grew worse under the attentions of a quack doctor who tried to heal the boy with painful braces. His erratic schooling was successful at least in arousing a love of literature and encouraging his inclination to write. At age sixteen, he fell in love with Mary Chatworth, a slightly older girl whose tantalizing cold-blooded attitude toward her teenage admirer, Byron later said, was the turning point of his emotional life. From this time on, this handsome and passionate man became involved in a steady procession of short- and long-term affairs with women of all descriptions. There is much evidence of sexual ambivalence as well in his relations with men both in Britain and abroad.

Byron's poetic efforts begin to see the light of day in 1807, when he was a student at Cambridge. His gifts were equally apparent in his lyrics and in his satires of his detractors, which could be savage. In 1809, he entered the House of Lords (his father had been a minor noble) and soon took off for a two-year visit to the Continent, despite the Napoleonic wars then raging. Most of his time was spent in Greece, a place and a people for whom he developed a lasting affection.

The major literary product of his trip was the magnificent *Childe Harold's Pilgrimage,* which became the rage of all London and made Byron's reputation overnight. The long poem beautifully caught the moods of the growing reaction against conventional manners and values, personified in the autobiographical Childe Harold. The magnetic Byron now took advantage of his notoriety to enter into one sexual affair after another—an "abyss of sensuality," as he himself put it, enhanced by both wine and drugs.

Seeking perhaps some stable influence, in early 1815, he suddenly married a rich young woman, but the marriage went awry almost as soon as it commenced. Only a scant year later, his wife was hurrying back to her parents and requesting legal separation despite her just-born daughter. After some unpretty squeezing of his in-laws for money, Byron agreed to sign the separation papers; in those days, this was tantamount to an admission of guilt. His social reputation was now destroyed, not only by the scandalous separation but also by dark hints, never denied and much later confirmed, that he had committed incest with his half-sister, Augusta Leigh. In 1816, he left to visit his friend, the poet Percy Bysshe Shelley, in Switzerland. He never set foot in Britain again.

For the final seven years of his life, Byron was mainly in Italy, where he wrote much of his finest work, including the *Don Juan* epic as well as several of his poetic dramas. The Italian years were made happy by his permanent attachment to the young Teresa Guiccioli, the love of his life, who finally released him from the aimless philandering he had engaged in for fifteen years.

In 1823, the Greeks' rebellion against their Turkish overlords attracted Byron's attention, and he hastened to Greece to put his money and energies into the cause. He contracted a lethal fever and died in his adoptive country in 1824. Throughout the rest of the century, his reputation grew, not only as a poet but as the literary symbol of the brave but doomed individual who challenges the destiny of ordinary souls and must eventually pay for his temerity by defeat and death. Denied the honor of burial in Westminster Abbey because of his shocking escapades, Byron finally received a memorial stone in the abbey floor in 1969. His beloved Greeks had acted much earlier to memorialize him in their own country.

Byron as the Giaour. This portrait was painted in 1813, shortly after Lord Byron returned from his tour of the Near East. (© *The Granger Collection*)

FOR REFLECTION

Should the character or private life of a great artist influence one's judgment of him or her as an artist? Do you think Byron's political banning from England was a legitimate expression of society's condemnation of his private life?

The Reactionary States: Austria, Russia, and Prussia

In the reactionary countries, the story was different. In Austria, Russia, and the Germanies, the rulers spent the generation after Napoleon attempting to hold back all thought of political liberalism. Through censorship, police and military force, diplomacy, and eventually war, they threw a dam across the tide of reform, which held more or less tightly until 1848. The Austrian emperor, the Russian czar, and the Prussian king rejected the kind of concessions the French and British governments had made to their citizens. As a result, revolt seemed to many thinking people the only hope of bringing these countries into modern political and economic life.

Austria had a special problem in that it was a multinational society in a time of increasing national conflict. It was for this reason that Prince Metternich was so determined to wall off Austrian politics from liberal ideas. He saw that whereas liberalism fostered nationalism, the conservative point of view generally disregarded national divisions as irrelevant and looked at people solely in terms of social class. Until 1848, in Austria, one's social background was far more important than one's ethnic group. The governing class was composed of a multiethnic aristocracy, where it mattered not at all whether a person was a Pole, a Hungarian, a Croat, or a German by blood. What counted was birth in the aristocracy.

THE REVOLTS OF 1848

The revolt that broke out in the streets of working-class Paris in late February 1848 was destined to sweep through Europe from one end to the other during the next year. These revolts of the lower classes against their stepchild position in society combined with an explosion of nationalist

Liberty Leading the People. This often-reproduced painting by Eugène Delacroix shows the female Liberty (the national symbol of Marianne) leading the way in the revolution of 1830. Delacroix, the foremost Romantic painter of his day, was probably the illegitimate son of Talleyrand. *(© Giraudon/Art Resource, NY)*

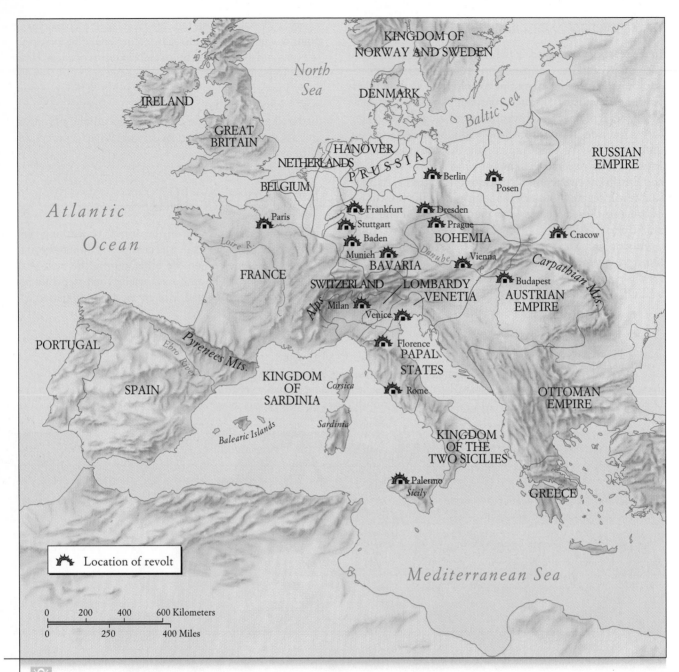

MAP 40.2 Centers of Revolt in 1848–1849.   The revolts in France and German-speaking
Europe were primarily political in nature: liberal versus conservative. In southern and eastern
Europe the revolts were above all nationalistic in nature: native versus alien overlord.

conflicts and assertions of popular sovereignty against
kings and emperors to set all Europe aflame (see Map 40.2).
Of the major countries, only Britain and Russia were
spared, the first because there was no intense dissatisfaction
with the government, and the second because the government seemed too strong to be challenged.

The revolts did not have a single cause, and it is impossible to bring them down to a lowest common denominator. Nor did they have the same outcome. In some cases, the
revolutionaries were partly successful (Italian states, Scan-

dinavia). In others (German states, Austria, France), they
were defeated in the short term.

Nevertheless, at least three underlying similarities can be
established. First, the revolts were led initially by middle-
class liberals, not by the workers and/or the peasants. Second, the workers soon grew disappointed with the liberals'
hesitancy and created their own more violent revolutions
against both aristocrats and the middle classes. Third, national divisions significantly contributed to the failure of
the revolts throughout central and eastern Europe.

Barricades in Vienna. Edouard Ritter painted this canvas shortly after the events it depicts in revolutionary Vienna. Bourgeois revolutionaries atop the hill make common cause for a brief interval with the laborers gathered below. *(Historisches Museum der Stadt, Vienna, Austria/Bridgeman Art Library)*

Two Phases

In the initial stages, the revolts appeared to be on the verge of success. In France, the exhausted and impotent July Monarchy fell within days, and France was turned into a republic for a few years. In the German states, several kings and princes were brushed aside by popular assemblies that claimed supreme powers and enacted liberal constitutions. In the Austrian Empire, the Hungarians and the Italians declared themselves independent, while the German-Austrians attempted to set up a liberal and constitutional monarchy. In the "Springtime of Nations," it looked for a while as though the reactionaries had been routed.

But appearances were deceptive. The military generally remained loyal to the monarchies, and the churches rallied round the throne. The peasants, who were still a majority of the population outside Britain, remained on the sidelines everywhere, as they could see no common ground with the urban liberals or workers after the abolition of serfdom was accomplished.

The second phase of the revolts opened them to defeat. When the workers in Paris, Vienna, and Berlin went into the streets to demand not only constitutional government but also decent working conditions and better pay and housing, the liberals got "cold feet." If they had to choose between the continued rule of the aristocracy and Crown and radical social change in favor of the masses, the middle classes would take the first alternative. They figured, more or less correctly, that time was on their side in their efforts to obtain political power peaceably. If they encouraged thoroughgoing reform of the socioeconomic system, on the other hand, they had no way of knowing what would happen in the long run. The liberals, composed overwhelmingly of urban middle-class property holders, were more afraid of some form of socialism than they were of continued aristocratic privilege and royal absolutism.

THE REVOLTS' CONSEQUENCES

In instance after instance, during 1848 and 1849, this open or barely concealed split between the middle class and the lower class enabled the conservative forces to defeat the goals of both in the short term. The liberals got only a very conditioned increase in political representation. The workers got nothing but bayonets.

1. *France.* The Second Republic established by the revolt lasted but three years before **Louis Napoleon** (Napoleon III), nephew of the great Bonaparte, used the power of the republican presidency to which he had been elected in 1848 to declare himself emperor. So began the Second Empire in France, which was to last twenty years. It saw the realization of most of the liberals' economic and political goals, but little for the workers.

2. *Prussia.* After a year of wrangling about the exact form and provisions of a liberal constitution for a united Germany, the middle-class **Frankfurt Assembly** dissolved in complete failure. Led by Prussia, the bulk of the German states reverted to the conservative regimes that had been briefly pushed aside by the revolts. German liberals had suffered a permanent defeat—one they would not recover for a century.

3. *Austria.* The Austrian emperor, eighteen-year-old **Franz Joseph** (ruled 1848–1916), relied on his aristocratic advisers to gradually regain control of the revolutionary situation, which had forced Metternich out and briefly turned Austria into a constitutional and liberal regime. Playing off one nationality against the other, the Vienna government crushed the independence movements of the Czechs, Hungarians, and Italians within the empire and then intimidated the German liberals in Austria proper. By the summer of 1849, reaction was unchecked, and Austria was embarked on a decade of old-fashioned royal absolutism.

4. *Italy.* It is important to remember that as yet there was no unified Italy. It was rather a collection of small kingdoms and the Papal States. The north was controlled by Austria, the middle was divided between the kingdom of **Sardinia-Piedmont** and the papacy, and the south and Sicily were controlled by the kingdom of Naples. Liberal Italians had long wanted to unite Italy under a constitutional monarchy. They favored the Sardinian kingdom as the basis of this monarchy because it was the only state that had a native Italian, secular ruler. Many middle-class Italians, especially those in the northern cities, were anticlerical and antipapal. They viewed the popes as political reactionaries and upholders of class privilege. For several of the nineteenth-century popes, this was a fair judgment.

In 1848, anti-Austrian and antipapal riots broke out in various parts of Italy. Sardinia declared war on Austria, believing that Vienna was too occupied with other crises to defend its Italian possessions. This proved to be a mistake. The Austrians were decisive victors. Pope **Pius IX** (in power 1846–1875) was so frightened by the Roman mobs that he opposed any type of liberalism from then on. In 1849, it appeared that a united Italy was as far away as it had ever been.

Thus, the revolts and attempted revolutions had accomplished very little by 1850. Both middle-class liberals and working-class radicals had been defeated by military force or its threat. Yet, within a generation's time, almost all that the middle classes had fought for and even some of the demands of the radicals had come into being in many European capitals. Reaction proved unable to meet the needs of the day, and the necessity to introduce a more or less industrialized economy overrode the objections of the Old Guard. Many of the thousands imprisoned for treason or violating public order from 1849 to 1850 would live to see the day when their governments freely gave the rights they had fought for and been punished for seeking.

SUMMARY

The dual revolutions in politics and economics started in the later eighteenth century but matured in the nineteenth. In the era after the Napoleonic wars, Europe divided politically into liberal and reactionary segments, both of which were attempting to meet the new challenges thrown up by the Americans' successful revolt against their colonial overlord and the French Revolution.

In politics, the conservatives reluctantly discovered that the French upheaval and its spread by Napoleon's armies had changed traditional relationships so that they could not be successfully reconstructed. Despite the defeat of the French radicals by their own countrymen and the defeat of Napoleon by the rest of Europe, some of the seeds planted by each would sprout in a generation's time.

The liberal spirit that was forcing its way into prominence in France and Britain took a less benign form in economics than in politics. The ideas of Adam Smith and others were selectively adopted by the Manchester liberals and used to justify harsh exploitation of the workers. They triggered experiments with socialism that attracted little attention because of their utopian nature and, in most cases, quick failure. In the reactionary empires of eastern Europe, the liberals failed to gain ground throughout the generation after the Vienna settlement.

The Europe-wide revolts of 1848 mostly failed in the short run, but the forces in society that had touched them off proved too strong to resist. One reason for the initial failure was the rising sense of conflicting nationalism in multiethnic states. Another was the divergence between the mainly political goals of the liberal middle classes and the mainly economic and social goals of the workers.

TEST YOUR KNOWLEDGE

1. Which of following would a moderate conservative be most likely to support?
   a. An officially established church with preeminent rights in education
   b. An absolutist monarch ruling with no constitutional restraints
   c. A proposal to sever any connections between church and schools
   d. A proposal to give poor and rich alike an equal vote
2. Which of the following did *not* have its modern birth in the 1789–1814 era?
   a. Socialism
   b. Nationalism
   c. Egalitarian democracy
   d. Meritocracy
3. The "Gendarme of Europe" was
   a. France.
   b. Great Britain.
   c. Russia.
   d. Germany.
4. The most uncompromisingly radical of Europe's early socialists was
   a. Henri Saint-Simon.
   b. Pierre Proudhon.
   c. Robert Owen.
   d. Charles Fourier.
5. Charles Fourier propagandized for a society structured
   a. in large states with dictatorial leadership by the working classes.
   b. in a military fashion.
   c. in small communities of self-directing workers.
   d. in communities of fellow believers housed in monasteries.
6. The most notable success in early socialist experiments was
   a. the New Lanark mill of W. Owen.
   b. the phalanstery of Charles Fourier.
   c. the anarchy promoted by Pierre Proudhon.
   d. the communal society proposed by the French revolutionaries.
7. The most important parliamentary act in nineteenth-century British history was the
   a. passage of the United Kingdom Act.
   b. passage of the Reform Act of 1832.
   c. decision to exile Napoleon to St. Helena.
   d. passage of the Factory Act of 1819.
8. The revolts of 1848 began in
   a. Belgium with an outbreak against Dutch rule.
   b. Paris with demonstrations against the July Monarchy.
   c. London with hunger marches in the slums.
   d. St. Petersburg with protests against the Crimean War.
9. Which country was least affected by the revolts of 1848?
   a. France
   b. Great Britain
   c. Italy
   d. Austria

IDENTIFICATION TERMS

de Saint-Simon, Henri

Fourier, Charles

Frankfurt Assembly (1848)

Franz Joseph of Austria

Gendarme of Europe

July Monarchy

Louis Napoleon (Napoleon III)

Manchester liberalism

Marx, Karl

Owen, Robert

Pius IX

Proudhon, Pierre

Reform Act of 1832

Romantic movement

Sardinia-Piedmont

Tories

Whigs

INFOTRAC COLLEGE EDITION

Enter the search term "Adam Smith" using Key Words.

Enter the search term "nationalism" using Key Words.

41

CONSOLIDATION OF NATIONAL STATES

The war of the peoples will be more terrible than those of kings.
WINSTON CHURCHILL

1851–1871	Louis Napoleon (Napoleon III): Second Empire (France)
1853–1856	Crimean War
1859–1870	Unification of Italy
1861	Freeing of serfs in Russia/Civil War in the United States
1862–1871	Unification of Germany
1867	*Ausgleich:* Dual monarchy established in Austria-Hungary
1870	Franco-Prussian War

AFTER THE DEFEATS of 1848, liberals and nationalists were in retreat during the next decade, and conservative statesmen were everywhere in control. But only twenty to thirty years later, many of the goals of the liberals had been reached, and nationalism was already one of the givens of policy making. The beginnings of modern political democracy were visible in several countries, notably Britain and the post–Civil War United States. The universal male franchise was introduced in several countries. Labor unions were legalized in many places, and in Russia the serfs were freed. The Western world was entering the next phase of the dual revolution—that is, the Second Industrial Revolution and the massive social changes that accompanied it. We will look first at individual countries.

RUSSIA

Since victory over Napoleon in 1814, the armed might of Russia had lain like a sleeping bear on Europe's eastern perimeters. The revolts of 1848–1849 had brought its army into Hungary to assist the Habsburg dynasty in its hour of crisis, and Nicholas I had rejoiced in his role of "Gendarme of Europe." Now the Romanovs' own hour of crisis approached, this time generated by foreign challenges.

Defeat in the Crimea

The first severe failure of the international alliances set up by the Vienna treaties was the **Crimean War** (1853–1856) between Russia on one side and England, France, and Turkey, on the other. An awkward war that no one wanted, it represented an accidental breakdown of the system established at Vienna a generation earlier. Russian expansionary ambitions led Czar Nicholas I to demand Turkish concessions in southeastern Europe. Once assured of British and French help, the Turks unexpectedly resisted. The conflict was mostly fought on the Crimean peninsula in the Black Sea (see Map 41.1).

Militarily, the war was a general debacle for all concerned. The Russian commanders and logistics were even less competent than those of the allies, so in time Russia had to sue for peace. The Peace of Paris of 1856 was a drastic diplomatic defeat for St. Petersburg, and for the next twenty years, Russia was essentially bottled up in the south,

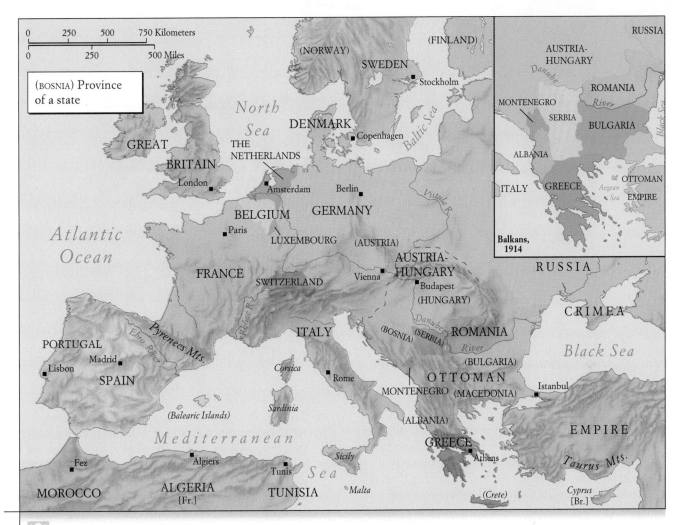

MAP 41.1   Europe after 1871.   The unification of the Germanies and of the Italian peninsula had been completed by 1871, but southeastern Europe was still in political flux. A disintegrating Turkey meant that Bosnia would soon fall under Austrian occupation, and a lost war against Russia would force the Ottomans to recognize the independence of Serbia, Montenegro, Romania, and Bulgaria in 1878. In 1912, a new war allowed the kingdom of Albania to emerge from the Ottoman empire, while Greece and Serbia were enlarged.

unable to gain the much desired naval access to the Mediterranean. The Russian Colossus, which had intimidated Europe since crushing Napoleon, was seen to have feet of clay. No longer could it be expected to play the role of reactionary watchman against revolutionary or even liberal sentiments. Now Russia's attention would be occupied by attempted solutions of its pressing internal problems. What were these, and how might they best be approached?

The Great Reforms

The military embarrassment in the Crimea hardened the determination of the new ruler, **Czar Alexander II** (ruled 1855–1881), to tackle Russia's number one social and economic problem: the question of the serfs. For the previous half century, educated Russians had been debating what could and should be done to bring the almost 50 percent of

the population who lived in legal bondage into freedom and productivity. Various czars since Catherine the Great had proposed various steps to better the serfs' condition, but in the end, little had been done. The serfs still lived in almost total illiteracy, ignorance, and superstition. Not only were they growing increasingly resentful of their noble landlords and masters, but they were an immense drag on the Russian economy. Living in stagnant poverty as they had for centuries, they had no money to consume anything except what they made or grew themselves. Nor could they contribute to the nation's capital for industrial investments.

In 1859, Alexander commanded a quick resolution of the serf problem, based on these principles:

- Freeing the serfs from the judicial and administrative control of their landlords and making them legally equal to other citizens with full personal liberty

⚜ **The Crimean War.** The war in the Crimea was the first to be photographed. Here, the English journalist Roger Fenton shows us an officer and men of the Fourth Dragoons in their encampment in 1855. At their side is one of the first military nurses, a colleague of Florence Nightingale. *(© The Granger Collection)*

🔊 Giving the serfs a substantial part of the estate land that they had previously worked for their master, and compensating the landlord with government bonds, redeemable by annual payments from the peasants

🔊 Anchoring the ex-serfs to the land by making them collectively responsible for paying the fixed tax of the village community (*mir*) and supplying a quota of conscripts for the army

Over the next two years, a special Court Commission worked out the complex details, and on February 19, 1861, the most massive emancipation order ever issued by any government abolished serfdom in Russia. About 55 million individuals—serfs and their dependents—were directly affected.

What was the result of the long-sought emancipation? It was only a very limited success. Many serfs were disappointed with their allotted portions of land, which were either small or of poor quality. And instead of outright possession of the land, they received only a tentative title subject to several restrictions imposed by the government. The serfs could not mortgage the land or sell it without permission from the village council, which was difficult to obtain. So, instead of creating a class of free, prosperous farmers as the authorities in St. Petersburg had hoped, the emancipation of the serfs actually made a good many worse off than before—much like the condition of many of the freed slaves in the U.S. South after the Civil War. Rural misery and ignorance were only very gradually and partially abated.

Besides emancipation, Alexander II presided over several other major reforms of Russian public life. These **Great Reforms,** as they are called, included the following:

🔊 *Local government.* The central government reorganized local and provincial authority changing its previously purely appointive nature. It allowed the election of a county commission, called the *zemstvo board.* Originally, the zemstvo boards had few real powers, but they acted as a catalyst of civic spirit and helped the local peasants become aware of what they could do to better their lives. From the zemstvo boards came many of the middle-class reformers and liberals who attempted to avert revolution before World War I by persuading the imperial government to make timely concessions to democracy.

🔊 *Judicial system.* The Russian court system was so antiquated and corrupt (bribing the judge was common) that it barely functioned. In 1864, Czar Alexander decreed a complete overhaul, and soon the courts were on the level of the western European countries. The class of lawyers and judges who emerged played a leading role in politics from then on.

🔊 *Army reform.* In 1873, the conscription, training, length of service, and many other aspects of the Russian army were completely revamped. The army became less a penal institution and more an educational and engineering facility, used by the government to do something about the very low level of rural education. The maximum service time was set at two years for most youth and less for the educated.

Seen in the longer perspective, however, what Alexander did not do was more important than what he did. Like several of his predecessors, he did not think the time ripe for Russia to have a constitution, an elected national legislature, or strong local government bodies. Russia remained what it had always been, an autocracy (government by a single person having unlimited power). The czar alone ultimately decided law and policy, and the people were viewed as simply passive recipients of the government's demands. This failure to change the basic governmental institutions was to be a crucial mistake. The continuing autocratic nature of Russian government blocked the way to peaceable political evolution and forced serious reformers to become revolutionaries.

Ironically, it was during the reign of the reforming Alexander II that the Russian revolutionary movement became for the first time a serious threat. In the 1870s, both socialism and anarchism found their first adherents in the urban **intelligentsia,** the intellectuals and activists drawn mostly from the thin ranks of the professional class. Every variety of revolutionary doctrine was to be found in the Russian underground by the 1890s, ranging from orthodox Marxism through peasant communes to nihilistic terrorism. As late as 1905, however, the government of the czar still seemed to be in undisputed control over the illiterate peasants and a very small and doctrinally divided group of socialist workers in the towns.

Escape by Balloon, Paris, 1870. In this dramatic photo, the head of the French government, Leon Gambetta, eludes the Prussian blockade of Paris by balloon. Despite Gambetta's efforts to continue resistance, the war was lost through the early mistakes of emperor Louis Napoleon. *(Corbis-Bettmann)*

France: The Empire of "Napoleon the Little"

The nephew of the great Napoleon won the presidential election in France that was held in the wake of the 1848 revolt. Riding on his uncle's name and claiming to be a sincere republican, Louis Napoleon—or "Napoleon the Little," as he was at once nicknamed by his enemies—was the first modern ruler who understood how to manipulate the democratic franchise to create a quasi-dictatorship. What he did in France during the 1850s showed the power of modern propaganda when controlled by an individual who knew how and when to appeal to his people.

Within a few months of his election, Napoleon sensed that there would be no effective opposition if he imitated his uncle and made himself emperor of the French, as **Napoleon III.** This *Second Empire* lasted twenty years, which divide into two distinct segments. Until the 1860s, it was an authoritarian regime led by one man's vision. After that, Napoleon gradually liberalized his rule and allowed political opposition. The main reason for the change was his increasingly unpopular foreign policy: a failed colonial adventure in Mexico in 1863–1864, his failure to stop an expanding Prussia, and his inability to protect the pope from the Italian secularists. These problems made trouble for Napoleon at home. He then had to encourage a previously tame legislature to share leadership responsibilities by allowing competitive elections.

Internally, Napoleon was more successful in changing the primarily agrarian France of 1851 into a mixed economy with the firm beginnings of industrial development in place by 1870. Paris was the only large industrial city and was regarded as a foreign place by much of the French public, in much the same way as midwesterners in the United States looked on New York City. But by 1870, capitalist industry was also taking root in many smaller cities, such as Lyon, Marseilles, Nancy, Brest, and Rouen. Britain and Germany were still far ahead of France in industrial development, but at least the French were beginning to make up the difference.

Napoleon and the Second Empire came to a disgraceful finish in the **Franco-Prussian War** of 1870 (discussed later), which was the emperor's last policy miscalculation. Foolishly taking the field, he was captured by the enemy, forced to abdicate, and died in quiet exile in England. At the end of the war, the first attempt at socialist revolution had taken place in Paris until the army crushed it with great bloodshed. This **Paris Commune of 1871** was very frightening to the majority of the French. From this time onward, the split between the conservative villages of the French provinces and the radical workers and intellectuals of "red" Paris that had originated in the French Revolution of 1789 was wide open. It would remain that way for much of the following century.

Following the war, the monarchists (who certainly at this juncture represented the majority of the French) failed to agree on a single candidate. This quarrel enabled those who favored a republic to gradually establish themselves in

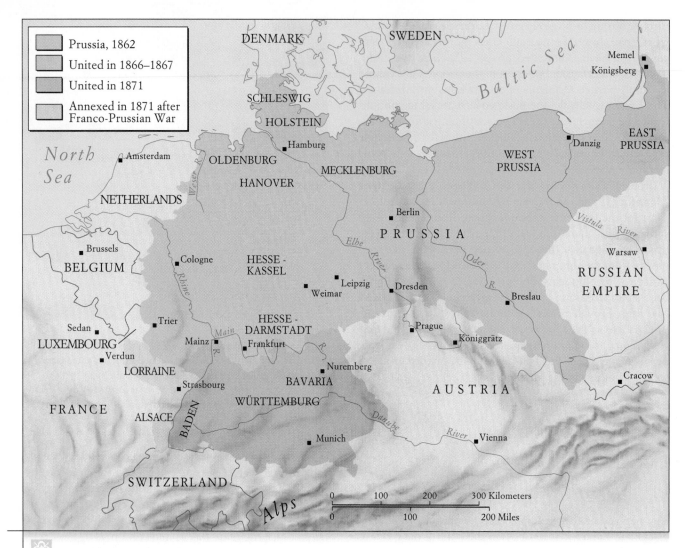

MAP 41.2   Unification of the German Empire.   After the battle of Königgrätz in 1866, the Austrians were put out of the running for primacy among German speakers. The surrender of French emperor Napoleon III at the head of his army at Sedan completed the task Bismarck had set himself.

power. By 1875, the **Third Republic** was more or less in place: it was a liberal state with a strong legislature (the National Assembly) and a very weak presidential executive. A confused mass of political parties ranged across the whole spectrum from extreme reactionaries to Marxists and anarchists. About the only political topic that most French agreed on during the later nineteenth century was the necessity of someday gaining revenge on Bismarck's Germany and reclaiming the "Lost Provinces" of Alsace and Lorraine (shown on Map 41.2).

THE UNIFICATION OF ITALY

One of the major changes in the political map of nineteenth-century Europe was the completion of the unification of Italy (see Map 41.3). This had been the goal of two genera-

tions of Italian statesmen and revolutionaries, going back to the Napoleonic wars. In the 1860s, unification was thrust through over the opposition of both Austria, which controlled much of northern Italy, and Pope Pius IX, who despised and dreaded a secular, liberal Italy. Austria's opposition could only be ended through warfare. The pope's opposition was never actually ended, but it was made harmless.

The father of Italian unification was the liberal-minded aristocrat Count **Camillo Cavour** (1810–1861), who became the prime minister of the kingdom of Sardinia in 1852. Based on the industrial city of Turin in northwestern Italy, Sardinia had long been the best hope of those who wanted a united, liberal Italy. It was better known as **Piedmont,** because the center of political gravity in the kingdom had long since moved from backward Sardinia to progressive and modern Turin at "the foot of the mountains." Cavour strongly supported economic progress, and during

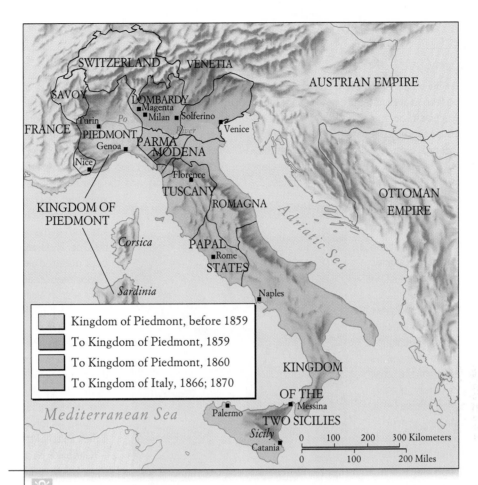

MAP 41.3 The Unification of Italy. The military and diplomatic triumphs of the 1860s produced an Italian kingdom that was composed of two quite different regions, North and South.

the 1850s, he built Piedmont into the leading economic force in all of Italy, as well as the major political power. Cavour was a moderate who believed in constitutional monarchy and firmly rejected radical social change.

Cavour fully realized that Austria would never willingly let go of its Italian provinces and that Piedmont alone was too weak to force it to do so (as had been demonstrated in 1848). Therefore, a foreign ally was needed, and that ally could only be France. Carefully, he drew Napoleon III into a so-called defensive alliance and then provoked a war in 1859. Faced with the French-Piedmont alliance, the Austrians were outmatched and forfeited the large Lombard province to Cavour.

As Cavour had reckoned, after the defeat of Austria, much of the rest of Italy threw in its lot with Piedmont. The newly christened Kingdom of Italy, based in Turin, now embraced about half of the peninsula. The rest was divided among the pope, the reactionary Bourbon king of Naples and Sicily, who wished to remain independent, and Austria.

The romantic and popular revolutionary **Giuseppe Garibaldi** now entered the scene, leading a volunteer army

("The Thousand Red Shirts") through southern Italy, routing the royal government of Naples and joining Sicily and southern Italy to the Italian kingdom in 1861 (see the Exercise of Authority box). A few months later Cavour died, with the job of unification-by-conquest almost done.

Two pieces of the picture still remained to be fitted in: the Austrian province of Venetia and the Papal States centered on Rome. Venetia was gained in 1866, as a prize for joining with Prussia in another brief victorious war against Austria. The Papal States, however, were guarded by France, where the Catholic population was insisting that Napoleon III preserve papal liberties. When the Franco-Prussian War broke out in 1870, the French garrison was withdrawn. The Piedmontese quickly annexed the Papal States and made Rome the capital of the all-embracing Italian kingdom. The pope was reduced to the status of quasi-prisoner within the Vatican City, a tiny enclave in the center of Rome. The relationship between the kingdom of Italy and the papacy remained frigid until the twentieth century. Not until the dictator Benito Mussolini came on the scene were formal relations finally established (1929). Papal

GIUSEPPE GARIBALDI
(1807–1882)

The creation of new national states inevitably involved bloodshed as well as negotiation. Every bit of territory within the European continent had long since been occupied by ethnic groups who by the nineteenth century had made their claims to national existence legitimate, though they still might lack sovereign statehood. The Italian and the German peoples entered unified political existence at almost simultaneous dates, in part owing to the extraordinary abilities of individuals. These men found varying ways to create and exercise personal authority. In Italy, Giuseppe Garibaldi's romantic charisma fascinated a generation of his countrymen.

Born in Nice in 1807, Garibaldi grew up in the full flush of the national feeling unleashed by the French Revolution and its extension through Napoleon's troops. He was a subject of the small kingdom of Sardinia-Piedmont, but as a dedicated republican, he took part in an abortive plot against the king and had to flee for his life to South America in 1835. There he participated in several attempts to install a republic in Brazil and to secure independence for Uruguay. He also became an enthusiast for the ideas of his fellow Italian Giuseppe Mazzini, perhaps the most admirable of the nineteenth-century revolutionaries in his steadfast conviction that the brotherhood of man could only rise from the smoking ruins of monarchic government.

In 1848, Garibaldi hastened back to his native land to join the fight against Austria. After its defeat, he reluctantly put aside his republican convictions and became an ally of Count Cavour's

Garibaldi. (© *The Granger Collection*)

diplomacy aimed at making the king of Sardinia, Victor Emmanuel II, the eventual king of united Italy. In 1859, Garibaldi again joined with Cavour in Sardinia (or Piedmont, as the kingdom was increasingly known) against the Austrians by embarking on the crowning adventure of an adventurous life: the conquest of Sicily and southern Italy for the forces of unity. At this time, Sicily and the southern third of the peninsula were governed very poorly by one of the most unpopular monarchs of Europe, Francis II of the house of Bourbon. With his One Thousand volunteers (who had been outfitted and trained in the north), Garibaldi succeeded in routing the royalists first in Sicily (at the battle of Calatafimi in June 1860) and then on the mainland (at the Volturno River). All of Italy except the Papal States around Rome and the city itself were now under the control of either Piedmont or Garibaldi. Finally, the Franco-Prussian War of 1870 allowed Victor Emmanuel to move his forces into Rome and make it the capital of the united Italy.

Garibaldi became a delegate to the new Italian parliament, but his true place in history was accorded to him by the Italian people, who regarded him as the chief hero of their long campaign to throw out foreign rulers and native oppressors. By the time of his death, he had become almost an object of worship among the common people of his country.

FOR REFLECTION

Whom do you think more important for success in leading a nation, the Cavours or the Garibaldis? Is there always room for both?

---

resentment and condemnation contributed to the early difficulties of the Italian state and discredited it to some extent in the eyes of devout Catholics in Italy and elsewhere.

In the generations that followed, the new Italy was a very mixed success story. Lacking all important industrial material resources except manpower, Italy was the weakest of the great powers. This country was in most ways really two, quite distinct countries: the industrializing, urban, liberal north and the agrarian, rural, feudal south.

The south (from Rome down) and Sicily were controlled by reactionary aristocrats, mainly absentee landowners whose impoverished peasants still lived in serfdom in everything but name. The Catholic Church was all-powerful and itself an ally of the aristocracy. The population outside the towns was almost entirely illiterate, superstitious, and quite unaware of anything outside their native region. The south had no modern industry or transport, and no prospects of any.

The north (from Florence up) was controlled by educated wealthy landowners and a large commercial middle class, who lived and worked in good-sized cities such as Turin, Milan, and Venice. These towns, which had ties to transalpine Europe, were rapidly industrializing, producing a proletariat who would soon be one of Europe's most fertile fields for socialist ideas. The average income in Milan was three or four times what it was in Palermo, Catania, or Naples. The northerners viewed the Sicilians and the south in general with contempt and despair, refusing to regard them as equal fellow citizens of the new state.

From the start, national politics and national economic policies were controlled by the Piedmontese and other northerners. The south was ignored or given a few crumbs in the budget to ensure that the party in office could control southern votes. The "national culture," as well as government money, was tilted heavily in favor of the north and would remain that way into the mid–twentieth century. Almost all of the millions of Italian emigrants to North and South America came from the overpopulated, backward south.

The Unification of the Germans

During the same years that the Italians were uniting into one state came the unification of Germany (see Map 41.2). As the new Italy was an extension of the kingdom of Sardinia, so the new Germany was an extension of the kingdom of Prussia. Like Italy, Germany was the product of both diplomacy and war. But here the similarities mostly ended.

The creation of the German Empire (*Deutsches Reich*), as it was called, was the most important single development in the later nineteenth century in Europe. Far more than Italy, Germany was an economic and military powerhouse, and it became the most important military force in the world by the 1880s. Germany would surpass Britain as the foremost industrial power as early as 1890 and would be rivaled only by the United States in the early twentieth century.

The fashion by which Germany was united would have a dominant influence on the later history of the country. It followed the conservative, even reactionary realization of the vision of two men: the Prussian king William I (ruled 1861–1888) and, more important, his chancellor and trusted friend **Otto von Bismarck** (1815–1898). Bismarck was the outstanding European statesman of the entire nineteenth century, and his shadow hung over the German nation until 1945. For good or evil, modern Germany was largely the product of Bismarck's mind and hand.

A Junker aristocrat, Bismarck deeply distrusted liberalism, while remaining a nationalist to the core. Like almost all nineteenth-century patriots, he wished to see the German people united rather than remain fragmented among the sixteen kingdoms and city-states left by the 1815 Treaty of Vienna. Above all, he wanted to complete what many years of Prussian policies had attempted with only modest success: to unify all Germans under the political leadership of Berlin. A chief reason for the failure thus far was the determined opposition of the other major Germanic state: Austria. Austria insisted on a seat in any pan-German political arrangement, and its size and prestige in the early

Bismarck and the Young Kaiser, 1888. The tension between the ambitious young William II and his chancellor Bismarck comes through even in this formal photo. William found it impossible to continue his predecessor's warm relations with the old man who had piloted Prussia and Germany since 1862. (*Bildarchiv Preussischer Kulturbesitz, Berlin*)

nineteenth century assured it a leading seat if such an arrangement ever came about.

The Prussians resisted Austria's pretensions, in part because they considered the Austrian empire not really a German territory at all. Within Austria's borders were more non-Germans than Germans, as we have seen. In 1848, this tension between **kleindeutsch** ("little German," Germans only) and **grossdeutsch** ("big German," or Germans predominantly) did much to wreck the hopes of the constitutionalists at Frankfurt and allow the reestablishment of absolutist monarchy in most of the Germanic lands.

Bismarck was a decided kleindeutsch adherent, and his policy aimed at removing the Austrians from German affairs as soon as possible. To this end, he cleverly manipulated the Vienna government into a situation where, no matter what Austria did, it came out looking opposed to German unity. This was notably the case in an otherwise insignificant war against Denmark in 1863–1864. Bismarck then provoked Austria into declaring war on Prussia, so that Austria appeared to be the aggressor in the eyes of the other Germans, who tried to remain neutral. The **Austro-Prussian War** of 1866 was over in one bloody battle, won unexpectedly by the Prussians using their new railway system and repeating rifles. Instead of seeking territory or money damages, Bismarck insisted only that Austria withdraw from German political affairs, leaving the field to Prussia.

The capstone of Bismarck's policy for unity was to provoke a third war, this one against the traditional enemy west of the Rhine. The Franco-Prussian War of 1870–1871 was

The Krupp Werke. One reason for the dramatic rise of Gemany's economic and military power after unification was the massive investment in metallurgical engineering. The buckets each hold about forty tons of molten steel, destined to be made into *panzer* (armor) for a new German cruiser in 1906. (*AKG London*)

the result of clever deception by the Prussian chancellor to maneuver the French (under Napoleon III) into becoming the formal aggressor. As Bismarck had reckoned, the other German states could no longer remain neutral in this situation. Fevered nationalist opinion forced the governments to join the Prussians, as fellow Germans, against the ancient enemy.

Soon the captured Napoleon III had to abdicate, and France sued for peace. Bismarck now put forward the Prussian king as emperor of Germany as a wave of national triumph swept up almost all German speakers. The Germans, after all, were the most numerous nation in Europe and had been artificially divided for many centuries. Only the Austro-Germans and the neutral Swiss stayed outside the new empire, which counted 70 million inhabitants and extended from Alsace (annexed from France) almost to Warsaw and from the North Sea to the Alps.

The new empire was a decidedly conservative state. Bismarck drew up a constitution that replicated that of Prussia. In the *Reichstag,* the national legislature, it was the Prussian delegation that counted, and votes in Prussia were based on property: one-third of the legislators were elected by the top 5 percent of property holders. The government ministers were responsible not to the Reichstag but to the king. Behind everything was the looming, stern figure of Bismarck, by now a national monument. His power would be almost unchallenged for the next nineteen years.

THE MULTINATIONAL EMPIRE OF AUSTRIA-HUNGARY

In the center of the European map stood the huge, backward Austrian empire. The fourth largest state in population, and third largest in territory, Austria under the guidance of its longtime foreign minister Metternich had played a major role in international affairs for a full generation after 1815. After the national-liberal revolts of 1848 had been crushed, a decade of absolutist rule had ensued under the young Kaiser Franz Joseph.

During this decade, considerable internal progress had been made, both economic and cultural, but these successes were nullified by setbacks in foreign policy and by the refusal of the defeated Hungarian nationalists to participate in central government. Since the Hungarians were the second largest group in the empire and had a long tradition of self-government, their boycott crippled internal politics.

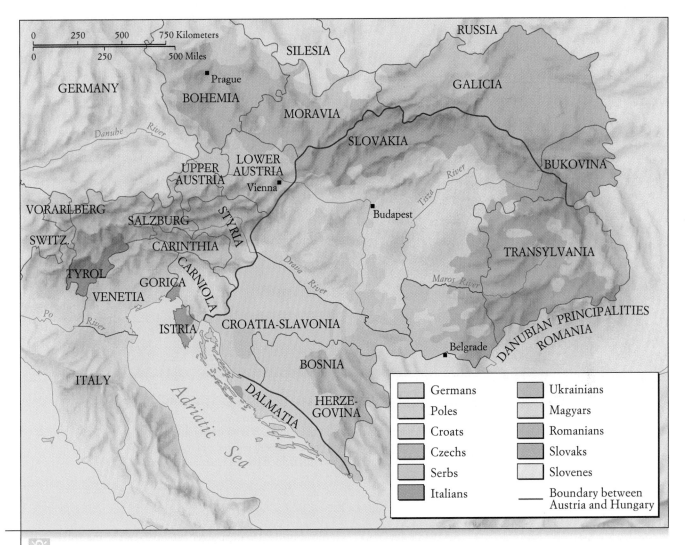

MAP 41.4 Ethnic Groups in the Dual Monarchy. The Austro-Germans and the Hungarian Magyars shared leadership of the empire of Austria-Hungary, but both were in a minority in their respective halves. The Ausgleich (Compromise) of 1867 was designed to keep the empire together while assuring their continued political domination.

After the defeats in Italy in 1859 and by Prussia in 1866, the kaiser had to come to terms with them. He did so in the **Ausgleich of 1867,** a compromise that divided Austria into roughly equal halves, Austria and Hungary. Each was independent of the other in everything except foreign policy, defense, and some financial matters. Each had its own constitution on generally liberal principles. The *Dual Monarchy,* as it came to be called, was a unique political arrangement held together by the person of the ruler (emperor in Austria, king in Hungary), the army, the Catholic Church, and a supranational bureaucracy and nobility. The Hungarians were temporarily placated.

The minority peoples within the empire—Czechs, Slovaks, Croats, Serbs, Italians, and others—were less satisfied (see Map 41.4). Those living in Hungary were now under the domination of the highly nationalistic Hungarians (Magyars), which they strongly resented. Those in Austria

were subordinate to the Austro-Germans, and for a time, the internal affairs of this half of the Dual Monarchy were more harmonious. But by the 1890s, the "national" question was heating up here as well. The fairly liberal, constitutional government was paralyzed by the obstructionist minorities in Parliament. To get anything done, the emperor had to rule by decree. Austria-Hungary became the prime European example of the negative aspects of nationalism.

THE UNITED STATES IN THE INDUSTRIAL AGE

At its independence from Britain, the United States was still an agrarian society, with its 4 million inhabitants concentrated along the eastern coast. Skilled tradesmen and master

The Strike Committee of the Matchgirls' Union. In 1888 one of the most famous labor battles of the century was fought between a major employer of the girls who made matches and the newly formed union led by Annie Besant. Besant, shown here in the middle, was an uncompromising reformer and campaigner against the very poor working conditions still common in the unskilled industries, especially for women. The strike was won, and this helped pave the path to better jobs for many females. *(Mary Evans Picture Library)*

craftsmen were in short supply, and 85 percent of the labor force were farmers and their auxiliary helpers and servants. Even in the urbanized areas of New England and the Middle Atlantic region, as late as 1800 there was practically no large-scale commercial production.

Industrial Progress

By the Civil War, seventy years later, this situation had changed markedly. Thanks to steady waves of immigrants from Europe and slaves from Africa, the United States had more inhabitants than Great Britain—about 30 million. Half a dozen cities had populations of more than 100,000, and farm labor now made up less than half of the total. The dependence on British engineering and machinery that had characterized the first generation after independence (and made the United States the best customer outside Europe for British exporters) was now entirely gone. American manufacturers and industrial techniques were rapidly proving they could compete throughout the world.

New England was the original center of American industry. Factories making consumer goods such as textiles and shoes, harness and wagons, and metal tools and kitchenware located there. They took advantage of both the abundant waterpower provided by the many rivers and the large pool of labor in the overcrowded and poverty-stricken rural areas. New England's expanding population had long since exceeded the supply of reasonably arable farmland. The new immigrants who came by the tens of thousands in the 1830s and 1840s often found they had only two choices: to take the plunge and try the unsettled frontier life in the west or to go to work in a mill or factory. Most chose the latter, believing its rewards were safer and more predictable.

Mill towns such as Lowell, Massachusetts, and Bridgeport, Connecticut, became common. They were similar in many ways to those in England but less dreary and unsanitary because of cheaper land and a different building style. Compared to the early industrial towns in Europe where workers for the most part faced exploitation and limited horizons, American towns offered a degree of social mobility. Although the myths of Horatio Alger ascents from rags to riches were indeed just myths, Americans probably did have far more opportunities to improve their condition than were available to the working class in Europe. The belief that a relatively high degree of economic equality and opportunity was and must remain open to Americans permanently shaped American political and social ideals.

The Nature of U.S. Industrialization

Two characteristics of U.S. industrialization are notable. The first was the advantage of not being the pioneer, a characteristic the United States shared with all other industrializing nations outside Great Britain. Americans were able to use British know-how and capital, and they avoided some of the technical and financial blind alleys that the English had experienced in their initial stages. By midcentury, the U.S. entrepreneurs in such vital areas as land and sea transport, iron making, and mining were catching up to or surpassing their teachers. The U.S. gross industrial product was already as large as that of the rest of Europe outside Britain.

The second characteristic was the "rugged individualist" nature of capitalism in nineteenth-century America. Men such as the railroad barons Cornelius Vanderbilt and Edward H. Harriman, the banking wizards John Hay Whitney and John Pierpont Morgan, and the iron makers Andrew Carnegie and Henry Clay Frick came into their own only after the Civil War, when American industry and finance exploded forward. But the tradition of enjoying total freedom from governmental and public opinion in one's method of business and use of money was already deeply ingrained and would not be modified until the twentieth century. This tradition stands in contrast to the experiences of both England and the Continent, where either government or a degree of social conscience exercised some controls over the way the early industrialists made and spent their money.

THE MODERN NATION-STATE

We have seen that in the quarter-century between 1850 and 1875, great political changes occurred in several major European states: Russia, France, Italy, Germany, and Austria-Hungary (review Map 41.1). These changes were accompanied by sweeping changes in the economy and the structure of society. Toward the period's end, the Second Industrial Revolution—powered by petroleum and electricity—was in full swing, bringing technological advances that had a direct impact on the everyday lives of everyday people.

What emerged in Europe and the United States during these years was in fact the modern nation-state, in which an ethnic group (the nation) exercises control over a territory (the state) through mass participation in government. Its political-governmental outlines had been initiated in the French Revolution but were not perfected until the industrial-technical breakthroughs of the late nineteenth century.

A host of familiar concepts first came into daily life during this period:

- mass political parties electing legislatures and executives who were more or less responsible to their voters;
- mass school systems turning out disciplined, trained minds to take over the technical tasks of a much more complex society and economy;
- labor unions representing the rapidly increasing numbers of workers negotiating with the representatives of impersonal corporations.

Protest and Repression. This engraving illustrates what many middle-class British and European people feared would be the inevitable result of labor organization. In 1887 a contingent of socialist workers attempted to hold a protest parade against current government policies, and at St. Martin's Lane in London were violently broken up by the "bobbies." Britain was among the last of the Western countries to allow unions and the right of strikers to demonstrate. (*Mary Evans Picture Library*)

All of these developments were characterized by a large group, a mass or class, coming into a predominant position, while the individual receded into the background.

THE NEW IMPERIALISM

The last half of the nineteenth century also witnessed an extraordinary surge in Western activity in the non-Western world. While the "scramble for Africa" was the most spectacular example (see Chapter 33), much of Asia and the Pacific islands were also the objects of a huge landgrab by the United States and Japan as well as the European powers.

What was behind this sudden burst of imperial expansion? One factor was the conviction in the European capitals that a state must either expand its power and territory or watch them shrink. There could be no standing still in the race for international respect. Another factor was the coming of the oceangoing steamship in the 1860s. With its ability to carry much larger cargoes over much longer distances on a cost-efficient basis, it changed the rules of international maritime trade. Now it became imperative for trading nations to obtain secure refueling harbors. That meant assured military control over a far-flung network of colonial ports.

Third, many statesmen assumed that new colonies would soak up the excess production of industrial consumer goods that was already looming in Europe and the United States. This economic consideration was generally accepted as a rationale for the industrialized nations to secure new markets in what we now term the developing countries.

Lastly, and by no means least, many well-intentioned folk at all levels of American and European society felt that it was, in Rudyard Kipling's phrase, the "**white man's burden**" to "civilize" the Asians and Africans, whether they desired that happy state or not. In other words, what was happening to the non-Western world was not a power play by rapacious foreign exploiters but an act of duty toward fellow humans who—perhaps without acknowledging it—needed the West's magnanimous aid. The combination of all these factors in varying degrees justified to both government and public the surge of Western military and economic power into the Asiatic and African lands that we examined in Part Four.

SUMMARY

The 1860s and 1870s produced major changes in almost all of the political and territorial maps of continental Europe. The modern nation-state with its mass-participatory institutions was coming into existence, although its pace varied from place to place. In Russia, attempts at basic reform fell short because of the Court's and nobility's reluctance to allow the people a full share in governing themselves. Instead, the reforms resulted in the growth of a revolutionary movement that would blossom in the early twentieth century. In France, the empire of Napoleon III brought progress internally but failed in foreign policy and was destroyed by the lost war with Prussia. Italy was finally unified in the 1860s, in part voluntarily and in part through conquest by the kingdom of Sardinia-Piedmont. What emerged, however, was two Italies, south and north, that had little in common.

The German chancellor Bismarck was the most successful of the statesmen who attempted to realize national destiny. Unified by war and nationalist fervor, Germans entered into a Prussia-dominated empire after 1871 and immediately became the most potent military force on the Continent. One of the countries the new empire surpassed was Austria-Hungary, a former rival now split by conflicting nationalisms.

In the United States, steady industrial growth on a regional level in New England was greatly expanded on a national scale after the Civil War. By the end of the century, the American economy rivaled Germany's for leadership of the industrial world. In the last half of the century, the West engaged in a new imperialism that was particularly focused on Asia and Africa.

TEST YOUR KNOWLEDGE

1. The biggest single governmental problem in mid-nineteenth-century Russia was
   a. how to defend the enormous borders against simultaneous attacks.
   b. how to make the czar's government more efficient.
   c. how to bring the serfs into the national economy.
   d. how to bring the military into the modern technical age.

2. The Paris Commune was
   a. an attempt to impose a socialist regime under Karl Marx on France.
   b. an imaginative attempt to introduce democracy through popular vote.
   c. an uprising against the imperial government that had lost a war.
   d. a kind of new religion prompted by anti-Christian radicals.

3. Cavour's role in unifying Italy was that of
   a. the diplomat-statesman.
   b. the rabble-rousing tribune of the people.
   c. the military commander.
   d. the right-hand man of the pope.

4. Garibaldi's contribution to Italy's unity is best described as that of
   a. the militant romantic.
   b. the calculating politician.
   c. the religious prophet.
   d. the financial wizard.

5. The crucial question for Bismarck as Prussia's chancellor in the 1860s was
   a. how to strengthen the army.
   b. how to crush the socialists' opposition.
   c. how to unite the German people politically.
   d. how to strengthen the constitutional rights of the citizens.

6. The Franco-Prussian War represented first and foremost
   a. a major shift in the European balance of power.
   b. a victory of a land power over a naval one.
   c. a lesson to would-be autocrats such as Napoleon III that the citizens' will cannot be ignored in modern politics.
   d. the rising powers of the socialists in dictating policy to government.

7. The most serious problem facing late-nineteenth-century Austria was
   a. the constant rebellions of the peasantry.
   b. the friction among the various nationalities.
   c. the pressure against its borders from the rising power of Germany.
   d. the lack of policy continuity at the top—that is, on the throne.

8. The United States became one of the top industrial powers
   a. after the Civil War.
   b. through profiting from the free labor of black slaves.
   c. as soon as New England had been colonized.
   d. by the expansion over the Mississippi River.

9. The "new imperialism" differed from the older variety by being
   a. more oriented toward the Pacific rimlands.
   b. more closely supervised by government officials.
   c. more driven by industrial market considerations.
   d. more individualistic in its leadership.

IDENTIFICATION TERMS

Czar Alexander II

Ausgleich of 1867

Austro-Prussian War

Bismarck, Otto von

Cavour, Camillo

Crimean War

Franco-Prussian War

Garibaldi, Giuseppe

Great Reforms

grossdeutsch

intelligentsia

kleindeutsch

Napoleon III

Paris Commune of 1871

Piedmont

Third Republic of France

white man's burden

INFOTRAC COLLEGE EDITION

Enter the search term "Crimean War" using Key Words.

Enter the search terms "Habsburg" or "Hapsburg" using Key Words.

42

ADVANCED INDUSTRIAL SOCIETY

*H*ence all society would appear to arrange itself into four different classes: (1) those that will work, (2) those that cannot work, (3) those that will not work, and (4) those that need not work.

HENRY MAYHEW

1848	*Communist Manifesto*
c. 1850–c.1910	Massive emigration from Europe
c. 1870s	Second Industrial Revolution begins
1870s–1914	Urbanization increases/Labor unions and mass democratic politics emerge/Marxist socialism strengthens

THROUGHOUT THE NINETEENTH CENTURY, the West (that is, western Europe and the United States) was clearly the dominant factor in world political and military developments. And this colonial subordination of much of the rest of the globe to Europe was a reflection above all of the West's large and increasing lead in technology and economic organization.

In the half century between 1860 and World War I, Europe itself went through a peaceful change of massive dimensions. As in the eighteenth century, a dual revolution was propelled by a shift in the sources of energy, which then was reflected in social organization and national politics. This Second Industrial Revolution was driven by petroleum and electricity. These two energy sources transformed urban life and made the city clearly the dominant social organism. Urban areas produced new businesses, new organizations of workers, new professions, and new lifestyles.

In these decades, socialism became for the first time a major force in several countries. As enunciated by Marx, it posed a severe threat from below to the combined aristocratic/bourgeois rule that had become normal in European politics and economies. Also, while the non-Western world was being incorporated into the European financial and commercial system, Europeans themselves were emigrating in massive numbers to selected areas of the globe, primarily for economic reasons. The Americas and particularly the United States were the favored destinations.

THE SECOND INDUSTRIAL REVOLUTION

As in the late eighteenth century, population growth and rising demand for consumer goods necessitated the search for new energy sources. Europe's overall population exclusive of Russia rose from 265 million to 401 million in the second half of the nineteenth century (see Map 42.1). Despite the stabilization of the average western European family at 2.5 children at the end of the century, the previous huge increase, combined with a rise in real income, created a large market for consumer goods and services of all types.

A definite rise in material standards of living was visible throughout Europe west of Russia. With fewer children's hands now necessary for labor, those who were born profited from better public health and nutrition to live longer, healthier lives. They could and did consume more. Goods

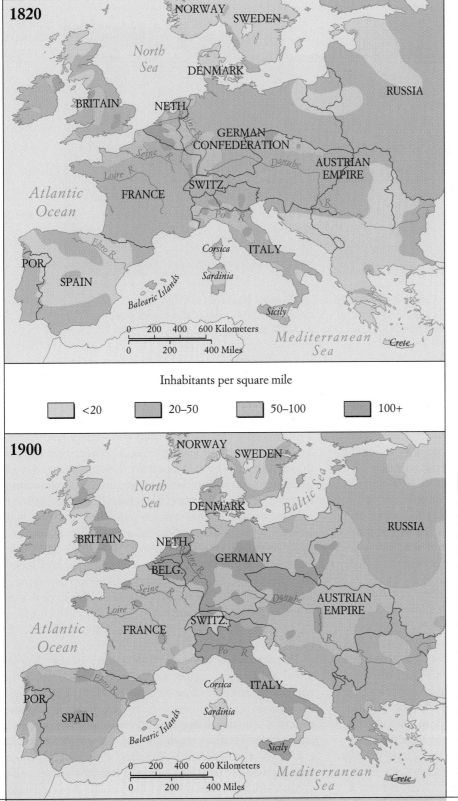

1820

NORWAY
SWEDEN
North
Sea
DENMARK
RUSSIA
BRITAIN
NETH.
GERMAN
CONFEDERATION
AUSTRIAN
EMPIRE
FRANCE
SWITZ.
Atlantic
Ocean
Po R.
Corsica
ITALY
Sardinia
POR.
SPAIN
Balearic Islands
Sicily
Mediterranean
Sea
Crete

0 200 400 600 Kilometers
0 200 400 Miles

Inhabitants per square mile

| | <20 | | 20–50 | | 50–100 | | 100+ |

1900

NORWAY
SWEDEN
North
Sea
Baltic Sea
DENMARK
RUSSIA
BRITAIN
NETH.
GERMANY
BELG.
FRANCE
SWITZ.
AUSTRIAN
EMPIRE
Atlantic
Ocean
Po R.
Corsica
ITALY
Sardinia
POR.
SPAIN
Balearic Islands
Sicily
Mediterranean
Sea
Crete

0 200 400 600 Kilometers
0 200 400 Miles

MAP 42.1 European Population Growth in the Nineteenth Century. The Italian peninsula and parts of central and eastern Europe saw the most dramatic increases in population density during the eighty-year period 1820–1900. In some rural areas in these lands, the lack of industry and the poor soil productivity had created an overpopulation crisis that was only ameliorated by emigration. Government was caught up in conflict with itself; emigration was discouraged and made difficult by national policy (particularly in Russia), while local authorities promoted it. In the latter third of the century, it was a commonplace for most of the younger male residents of whole villages and counties to emigrate to the New World. Some intended to return—and did so—but the majority stayed in the new homelands.

A Paris Street Scene. This view of the Montparnasse tram station was taken in 1900. The regularity of the building façades was one of the results of the massive rebuilding of this former slum undertaken by the government of Louis Napoleon in the 1860s. (© *The Granger Collection*)

that were almost unknown in European workers' houses in the early 1800s now became common: mechanically produced footwear and clothes, nursing bottles for babies, gas or electric lighting, and books and newspapers.

Adding to this internal market was the rapidly expanding overseas market, both in the European colonies and in some of the independent nations of America and Asia. The surge of imperial ventures that began in the 1850s brought major increases in the availability of raw materials as well as the number of potential consumers in the Asian and African marketplaces. The volume of world trade shot upward in the later nineteenth century, and the West controlled that trade entirely. Britain, Germany, and the United States were the main beneficiaries.

New Energy Sources

The big lead in industrial production that Great Britain had established in the early nineteenth century gradually narrowed after 1850. Belgium and northern France were the centers of the Continent's initial industries, followed by parts of Germany and Italy. After the unification of those two countries, their industrial growth accelerated sharply. As an important example, Germany's steel and iron production exceeded Britain's by 1893 and was almost double British production by 1914.

Whole new industries sprang up, seemingly overnight. Chemicals, oil refining, steamship building, turbines and machinery, and, toward the end of the 1890s, the automobile industry are outstanding examples. But perhaps the most important of all the new developments was the taming and application of electricity to both industrial and domestic uses.

Electricity had been recognized as a potentially useful natural phenomenon since the eighteenth century (the days of Ben Franklin), but no practical use could be made of it then. In the 1870s, this changed dramatically as a result of the work of German, American, and French researchers. The development of generators and transformers allowed direct current to be sent wherever desired cheaply and efficiently, then transformed into easily used, safe, alternating current. The first big power plant was constructed in 1881, and very soon electric power was being used to light streets, power trams, and bring artificial light into hundreds of thousands of city homes and factories. Soon after, electrical machinery was being used in thousands of industrial applications. Electric railways and subway systems were introduced in every major European city. Probably no other series of inventions contributed so much to easing the physical labor and improving the material life of ordinary people.

Petroleum was the second new energy source. The internal combustion engine, which drew its power from the controlled explosion of gasoline injected into cylinders, was invented in 1876. Although it was clearly an impressive means of applying energy, its full potential was not apparent until the German engineers Daimler and Benz put the engine on a carriage and connected the cylinder pistons with the wheels. Benz's work in the late 1880s is generally credited with the emergence of the gasoline-powered automobile as a practical, reliable mode of transport, though literally dozens of other German, French, American, and British experimenters also contributed in major fashion to its development.

Petroleum and its by-product, natural gas, were to have many other uses, including lighting, heating, and driving stationary engines and pumps. From petroleum also came a whole range of important new chemicals. Then as now, Europe west of Russia had very little oil and was dependent on imports from other places. American capital (Rockefeller's Standard Oil) and American exploration and drilling techniques soon led the world in the race for oil production.

The Second Industrial Revolution depended very much on scientific research. The Germans with their well-equipped university and industrial laboratories quickly took over the lead in this area and held it without serious competition for many years. Their carefully organized and well-funded research enabled the Germans to dominate European industry after 1870. The British, the former leaders, were very slow to realize that the rules of industrial competition had changed. They put little money into research, from either government or private hands. By 1890, Britain's technological expertise and innovation was falling steadily behind Germany's, and this growing gap had much to do with the rising competition between the two countries in political and diplomatic affairs.

New Forms of Business Organization

New forms of business organization accompanied the new energy applications. In the first century of the industrial age (1760–1860), the standard form of industry had been the private partnership or proprietorship. It was limited deliberately to a small handful of owner-managers, some of whom might work alongside their employees in the office or even on the shop floor. When more capital was needed for expansion, it was borrowed on a short-term basis for specific needs. The public was *not* invited in, and the banks were not partners but only facilitators in arranging funds.

In the Second Industrial Age (c. 1860–1920), the **corporation** rather than the partnership became the standard. And often the corporation was permanently financed by banks, which thus became part owners of the company. *Joint stock companies,* whose shares were traded on public stock exchanges in every European capital, were formed to raise huge amounts of capital from the investing public. The shareholders were technically the owners of the company, but, in fact, they had little or nothing to say about management policy. This separation of ownership and management was one of the most striking changes in business and commerce of all sorts in the later nineteenth century, and it continues to the present.

SOCIAL RESULTS OF THE SECOND INDUSTRIAL REVOLUTION

The Second Industrial Revolution accelerated several trends that had begun during the First. Four were particularly important:

1. *Urbanization.* The outstanding feature in Western demography throughout the nineteenth century was the rapid growth of urban areas. Britain was the first European country to urbanize. In 1851, the census revealed that more than half of the English people lived in towns and cities. (At this time, for comparison, only 22 percent of Americans were urban dwellers.) By 1900, Britain alone had more cities with populations of more than 100,000 than there had been on all of the Continent in 1800. Industrial jobs were a major reason for the migration to the cities, but they were by no means the only reason, as we saw in Chapter 39. Better education, leisure activities, and marital prospects were also strong incentives.

2. *Organization of labor.* After the failure of the 1848 revolutions, the workers on the Continent rarely attempted to gain better conditions by street riots or mass demonstrations. Instead, they took to organizing labor unions, which would fight for improvements in a legal way and attempt to gain government support against abusive employers. In so doing, the Continental workers were following the lead of the British, who had attempted to win reforms in their conditions of life and labor through the **Chartist movement** of the 1840s. Although its short-term goals were frustrated, the movement initiated a long-term change both in and outside Parliament toward greater democracy and fairer distribution of the country's wealth.

   In the 1870s, Great Britain became the first major country to fully legalize labor unions, giving them the right to strike, picket, and boycott. In the 1880s, France took the same course, and in 1890 Germany did also. By the turn of the century, all western European nations except Spain and Portugal had conceded the rights of labor to use all nonviolent means available in the struggle for a better life.

3. *Social reforms.* The unions did give the laboring classes a new and fairly effective way to express their discontents and sometimes win redress for them. By 1914, few workers had to endure the sort of systematically inhumane working conditions that were common during the First Industrial Age. Child labor laws and industrial safety regulations were now common and enforced by both national and local authorities. A few countries had some provisions for worker employment security and pensions (Bismarck's Germany led in these respects). Even worker health and accident insurance was frequently provided by the government, if not the employer.

   The early unions were sometimes socialist in orientation, sometimes not. By the 1890s, however, the Marxist revolutionary socialists were close to taking over the labor movement in several key countries. (The United States was a notable exception; Marxism never was popular there.) This frightened many employers and their partners in government. The last decade prior to World War I saw many bitter disputes between management and labor all over Europe. Labor violence was common.

✿ **Suffragettes.** One of the many late-nineteenth-century demonstrations for women's voting rights, this one in the United States. In most cases, the Western countries did not grant female suffrage until after World War I. (© *The Granger Collection*)

4. *Mass democratic politics.* A very important effect of industrial life was the coming of mass politics and parties. In the last third of the century, almost all European governments allowed all their male citizens to vote, regardless of property qualifications: Germany in 1871, France in 1875, Britain in 1884, and Spain in 1890. Only Russia, Hungary, and Italy stood firm against universal male suffrage as late as 1905. By the outbreak of World War I in 1914, all of Europe had male universal suffrage. This advance strongly stimulated the formation of large, tightly organized political parties. Prior to that time, the people who had the vote were property holders, relatively well educated, and generally aware of the issues of national politics. They did not need an organization to get out the vote, for they knew very well what was at stake in elections and made voting a major part of their public lives.

Now, the much-enlarged number of voters had to be informed of the issues and then organized into groups that would vote. The vehicle for doing this was a mass political party, equipped with newspapers, local organs and offices, speakers, and propaganda material. Most of the new voters were men of the working classes, and the new parties concentrated their efforts on them.

SOCIALISM AFTER 1848: MARXISM

The failure of the 1848 revolts inspired much analysis. National antagonisms and the passivity of the countryfolk were important, but the chief reason, all contemporary ob-

servers agreed, was the split between the liberal leaders—professionals and intellectuals—and the urban workers. This split allowed the conservatives to gain a breathing space after their initial panic and then to mount a political and military counterattack that was successful almost everywhere (see Chapter 40).

Why did the split between the middle-class liberals and the workers occur? The liberals generally did not want social reforms. They only wanted to substitute themselves for the conservatives in the seats of political power. The workers, on the other hand, were economically desperate and wished to gain for themselves the type of thoroughgoing change in the alignments of power that the French peasants had won in the wake of the 1789 revolution. When it became clear to the liberals that the workers wanted to go much further down the revolutionary road, they withdrew to the sidelines or actually joined with the conservatives as happened in Vienna, Paris, and Berlin. In the end, the protection of property meant more than political or social ideals.

Marxist Theory

One close observer of this development was **Karl Marx** (1818–1883). Marx, a German Jew whose family had been assimilated into Prussian Protestantism, grew up in the Rhineland town of Trier. Soon after his graduation from the University of Berlin in 1842, he became deeply involved in radical politics. Pursued by the Prussian police, he had to leave his native city and flee to France as a political refugee. There, he came to know his lifelong colleague, **Friedrich**

COMMUNIST MANIFESTO

The most well-known of the nineteenth century's various revolutionary challenges was the manifesto produced by Karl Marx and Friedrich Engels in 1848 as a platform for the tiny Communist League they had recently founded in London. Most later Marxist doctrine appeared in it in capsule form. The following excerpts concern mainly the theory of the formation of classes and the struggle between them in history.

The history of all hitherto existing society is the history of class struggle. Freeman and slave, patrician and plebian, lord and serf, guildmaster and journeyman, in a word, oppressor and oppressed, stood in constant opposition to one another, carried on an uninterrupted, now hidden, now open fight, that each time ended either in a revolutionary reconstitution of society at large, or in the common ruin of the contending classes. . . .

The modern bourgeois society . . . has not done away with class antagonisms. It has but established new forms of struggle in place of the old ones.

Our epoch, the epoch of the bourgeoisie, possesses, however, this distinctive feature: it has simplified the class antagonisms. Society as a whole is more and more splitting up into two hostile camps, into two great classes directly facing one another: Bourgeoisie and Proletariat. . . .

[T]he bourgeoisie has at last, since the establishment of modern industry and of the world market, conquered for itself, in the modern representative State, exclusive political sway. The executive of the modern State is but a committee for managing the common affairs of the whole bourgeoisie. . . .

In proportion as the bourgeoisie, i.e., capital developed, in the same proportion as the proletariat, the modern working class, developed; a class of laborers, who live only so long as they find work, and who find work only so long as their labor increases capital. . . .

Owing to the extensive use of machinery and to division of labor, the work of the proletarians has lost all individual character, and consequently, all charm for the workman. He becomes an appendage of the machine. . . . In proportion, therefore, as the repulsiveness of the work increases, the wage decreases.

All previous historical movements were movements of minorities. The proletarian movement is the self-conscious, independent movement of the immense majority, in the interest of the immense majority. The proletariat, the lowest stratum of our present society, cannot stir, cannot raise itself without the whole super-incumbent strata of official society being sprung into the air.

What the bourgeoisie produces above all, are its own grave-diggers. Its fall and the victory of the proletariat are equally inevitable.

The Communists disdain to conceal their views and aims. They openly declare that their ends can be attained only by the forcible overthrow of all existing social conditions. Let the ruling classes tremble at a communistic revolution. The proletarians have nothing to lose but their chains. They have a world to win.

Working men of all countries, Unite!

FOR REFLECTION

Do you agree that class struggles have largely defined history, especially in modern times? Do you think a just society will be reachable through violent revolution? *Must* be through violent revolution?

SOURCE: Excerpted from Karl Marx and Friedrich Engels, The Communist Manifesto (New York: Signet Classic, 1998).

Engels, the wealthy, radical son of a German industrialist. The two men formed a close working relationship that was ideal for Marx, who devoted his entire adult life to research and writing and organizing revolutionary socialist parties. (See the Tradition and Innovation box.)

In 1848, coincidentally, just prior to the revolt in France, Marx and Engels published perhaps the most famous pamphlet in all European history: the *Communist Manifesto.*

Marx predicted the coming of a new social order, which he called *communism,* as an inevitable reaction against the abuses of bourgeois capitalism. When this order would come, he did not predict, but he clearly expected to see communist society arise within his lifetime. It was equally clear that Marx and Engels expected communism would be born in a violent revolution by the industrial workers, the proletariat who had been reduced to abject misery and had little or no hope of escaping it as long as capital ruled. (See the Exercise of Authority box.)

The proletarian revolution was inevitable, according to Marx, and the only questions were the precise timing and how it might be helped along by those who wished to be on the side of progress and justice. Marx issued an invitation to all righteous persons to join with the ignorant and miserable proletariat in hastening the day of triumph. Once the revolution of the downtrodden was successful in gaining political power, a "dictatorship of the proletariat" (not further defined) was to be created, which would preside over the gradual transformation of society.

What was the ultimate goal of Marxist revolution? According to Marx, it was a communist society, in which private control/ownership of the means of production would be abolished and men and women would be essentially equal and free to develop their full human potential. For the first time in history, said Marx, the old boast of the Greeks that "Man is the measure of all things" would be fulfilled. A society would be created in which "the free

KARL MARX
(1818–1883)

The critical thing is not to understand the world, but to change it!

With this maxim as his polestar, the philosopher Karl Marx became the most notorious, most quoted, and most influential social reformer of the nineteenth and twentieth centuries. The recent demise of that distortion of his ideas called Soviet communism has put his name and reputation under a heavy cloud from which they may never recover. But for 150 years, Marx and Marxism provided much of the world's dissatisfied citizenry with what they perceived to be their best hope of better times.

Marx was born into a well-to-do Jewish family in Trier, Germany, which at that time was part of the kingdom of Prussia. He studied at the universities of Bonn and Berlin, where his major interest was philosophy, but his interests soon expanded to include economics and sociology, two sciences that were still in their infancies. By the mid-1840s, he was slowly shaping his radical critique of contemporary European society by drawing on all three disciplines: German philosophy, English economics, and French social thought.

Prevented by his Jewish background from realizing his original plan of teaching in a university, Marx returned to Trier after graduating from the University of Berlin. In 1842, he opened a small newspaper, the *Rhenish Gazette*, which was dedicated to promoting social and political reform. He soon got into trouble with the conservative authorities and had to flee to escape arrest. He lived briefly in Paris, where he came to know his lifelong supporter Friedrich Engels, son of a wealthy German manufacturer. Engels and Marx collaborated on the *Communist Manifesto*, published just weeks before the 1848 revolutions.

Soon Marx aroused the suspicions of the French authorities and had to move on. An attempt to enter German politics as a revolutionary leader failed, and again Marx had to flee his native country, this time to London where Engels was ready to help. Marx spent the rest of his life in English exile, living in genteel poverty with his German wife and several children.

The world around Marx was in the throes of the first wave of industrialism, and it was not an attractive place for most working people. Air and water pollution were common in the factory towns and in the working-class sections of the cities. Public health was neglected, medical help was restricted to the well-to-do, and welfare facilities of any type were almost nonexistent. Women and children worked at exhausting jobs for very low pay, and workers were frequently fired without warning to make room for someone else who agreed to work for less. Neither law nor custom protected the workers' rights against their employer. And among the employers, cut-throat competition was the rule. Government intervention to assure a "level playing field" in the marketplace was unknown. When governmental power was occasionally employed, it was always in favor of the status quo, which meant against the workers.

Marx observed this scene closely and was convinced that the situation must soon erupt in proletarian revolution. The explosion would come first in the most advanced industrial countries, which meant at this time Britain, parts of Germany and France,

development of each is the condition for the free development of all."

At the time, no government took notice of the *Communist Manifesto*. None of the important 1848 revolutionary groups had heard of it or its authors. But in time this changed. During the 1850s and 1860s, Marx and Engels gradually emerged as two of the leading socialist thinkers and speakers. From his London base (England had the most liberal political association and censorship laws in Europe), Marx worked on his great analysis of mid-nineteenth-century industrial society, *Capital* (1867–1873). This work was the basis of Marx's boast that his socialism was scientific, unlike the utopian (that is, impractical) socialism of earlier days.

Marx was a child of his times. The 1840s were the "dismal decade," years of the crudest exploitation of the workers by greedy or frightened employers. They were frightened because many were being driven to the wall by the relentless competition of the free market. As these small business owners desperately looked for ways to lower production costs, they usually tried to save by reducing wages. Since what Marx called a "reserve army" of starving unemployed was always ready to work at almost any wage, the most elementary job security was totally absent. The result was often an extremely low pay scale for the semiskilled and unskilled workers who made up most of the early industrial labor force. Marx was not alone in believing that this condition would persist until it was changed by militant force.

Marxist Organizations

In 1864, Marx played a central role in creating the **First International**—properly, the International Working Men's Association—in London. This organization had a short life span, falling apart because of internal dissension in 1876. Nevertheless, it served as a central interchange among the budding socialist parties of Europe and gave Marx a good platform for spreading his own brand of revolutionary thought.

When the Paris Commune arose in the wake of the lost war with Prussia in 1871, Marx mistakenly thought that the

and possibly the United States. While Engels provided financial assistance, Marx dedicated many years to working out a theory of history and social development that would make sense of the chaos and allow a rational hope of a better world in the future. Eventually, he produced *Das Kapital*, or *Capital*, the bible of scientific socialism, which was published in the original German in 1867 and translated into most European languages by the later nineteenth century. Almost all the work was done in the Reading Room of the British Museum, which Marx visited with clocklike regularity for decades.

In 1864, Marx organized the International Workingmen's Association. This so-called First International lasted only a few years before it collapsed in internal arguments about how the revolution of the proletariat should best be accomplished. Marx was always a headstrong character and was most unwilling to allow others to have their say. Like many prophets, he came to think that any who disagreed with him were ignorant or malicious. Engels was one of the few intimates who remained faithful to the master to the end.

In 1883, Marx died in the same poverty in which he had lived in the London suburb of Hampstead. At his death, the proletarian revolution seemed further away than ever, but the movement was slowly growing. It would make giant strides in several countries in the 1890s, and in far-off Russia, a country that Marx held in contempt for its backwardness, a certain Vladimir Ilich Ulyanov, better known as Lenin, was studying *Capital* with an eye to the Russian future.

FOR REFLECTION

Does this picture of Marx's life coincide with your general view of a committed revolutionary personality?

Karl and Jenny Marx. Marx spent most of his life in English exile with his long-suffering German wife, Jenny. *(Stock Montage, Inc.)*

dawn of social revolution had come and enthusiastically greeted the very radical oratory of the *Communards.* The Commune was speedily crushed, but socialist parties came into being everywhere after 1871 and grew steadily over the next decades. By the end of the century, they were in most countries the primary voice of the industrial working class. Their common denominator was a demand for radical rearrangement of the existing socioeconomic order. Some of these parties were anti-Marxist in doctrine, either preferring some form of anarchism (see the next section) or wishing to operate mainly through labor unions (a tendency that Marx anathematized as mere reformism). But most were Marxist and subscribed to the principles laid out in *Capital* by the master.

The most important socialist parties were in Germany, Austria, Belgium, and France. In southern Europe, they were outnumbered by anarchists and syndicalists (see the next section). In Britain and the United States, no socialist party had a wide following, and in Russia, the Marxists were still a tiny exile group at the end of the century.

RIVALS OF MARXISM

In Mediterranean Europe and Russia, the theory of politics called **anarchism** captured many minds. *Anarchism* is the rejection of the state and the powers that the modern state exercises over its citizenry. Its followers believe that all government is necessarily prone to corruption. Only such authority as is necessary to avoid conflict over property or civil rights of the citizens should be surrendered by the citizens to their government. Even then, the least possible authority should be granted and only on a small-scale, localized basis. Anarchists simply do not trust any government. They believe that sooner or later every government will succumb to the temptation to restrict its citizens' freedoms without just cause.

As a theory, anarchism goes back to the ancient Greeks. But the modern founders of anarchism are the Frenchman Pierre Proudhon, whom we have already encountered (see Chapter 40) and the Russian **Michael Bakunin** (1827–1876). Bakunin developed the *propaganda of the deed,* the idea that a dramatic, violent act was the most effective way to gather converts for anarchism. The deeds his followers performed were acts of political terror: they carried out bombings and assassinations in the hopes of shaking the structures of government from the top down. In the two decades between 1885 and 1905, the high point, about 300 notable lives were sacrificed to this belief, including several reigning kings and queens, prime ministers, presidents (including the U.S. president William McKinley in 1901), and assorted generals.

Was the propaganda of the deed successful? It succeeded nowhere. Both governments and popular opinion reacted strongly against the terrorists. Eventually, anarchism itself became discredited because of its association with political murders. After World War I, little was heard of anarchism until the 1960s, when it was briefly revived in the streets by protesting French and German university students.

Syndicalism is a form of political action by the working classes. It is founded on the belief that only the laboring classes and peasants should govern, because only they contribute a substantial asset to society through their work. Instead of the false verbal sparring and make-believe of the political parties, the laborers must create a large-scale association of persons employed in the same type of work. This association, called a *syndicate,* would represent the economic and social interests of the members and confer with other syndicates to find common political means for progress in economics and justice in society. Like anarchism, and unlike communism, syndicalism did not wish to abolish private property but to limit its political power and distribute it more evenly.

Syndicalism was stronger than socialism in Spain and Portugal and was a strong rival to it among the peasantry in Italy and France. Many working people in these countries condemned the unbounded greed that they saw in liberalism as practiced by the bourgeoisie. Syndical government offered the badly paid and insecure working classes and small peasants a theoretical way out without going to the socialist extreme of class warfare and the abolition of private property. It never succeeded in establishing control of a national government.

Reform and Revisionism

In Great Britain, the labor force was never much attracted to either socialism or its rivals as a solution to the dual problems of concentrated wealth and concentrated poverty. Instead, British workers in the later nineteenth century focused on gaining higher pay and better working conditions through a moderate reformism that centered on the right to strike and organize unions. In 1906, the reformist but non-Marxist **Labour Party** was formed on a platform of more equable distribution of wealth. The new party gradually attracted the vote of most union members and much of the lower middle class. It was able to replace the Liberal Party as the main opponent of the Conservatives after World War I.

In the 1880s, Chancellor Bismarck attempted to crush the appeal of socialism in Germany by an attack on two fronts. First, he outlawed the Marxist socialist party, which had been organized in 1875, claiming that it was a revolutionary group with the destruction of the state as its ultimate aim. Then he tried to show that socialism was unnecessary because the German state itself would look out adequately for the workers' welfare. During the 1880s, a series of new laws instituting unemployment insurance, accident and health protection, and worker pensions made Bismarck's Germany the most progressive state in the world in terms of social policy.

The blunt attack on the Marxists did not succeed. After a few years, there were more German socialists than ever, and in 1890, the antisocialist law was repealed. The German Social Democratic Party (SD) steadily gained votes, attracting not only workers but also the lower middle classes and civil servants. With several newspapers, a tight network of local offices, and an extensive member/financial base in the German labor unions, the German Social Democratic Party set the pace for socialists throughout Europe.

In 1899, a leading Social Democratic theorist, Eduard Bernstein, published a book in which he claimed that the SDs would soon become strong enough to take over the state in peaceful, constitutional fashion. Socialism would then be introduced through the workings of a parliament and government controlled by the Marxists. Thus, the idea of violent revolution in the streets was outmoded. According to Bernstein, Marx (who had died sixteen years earlier) could not foresee that capitalism would be so altered by democracy that the workers would be able to counter it through the ballot rather than on the barricades. The triumph of social justice could and should be obtained without bloodshed.

This idea was heatedly denounced by many in the **Second International,** the Europe-wide association of socialists founded in 1889. But the theory attracted the party leadership in the more industrially advanced countries, especially in Germany and France. By the coming of World War I, **revisionism** (the adaptation of Marxist socialism that aimed to introduce basic reform through parliamentary acts rather than through revolution) was a strong rival to orthodox Marxism as the true path to the workers' paradise.

EMIGRATION OVERSEAS

The largest human migration in world history took place from Europe to overseas destinations during the second half of the nineteenth century. What caused this move? In general, the triggers were economic, but the emigrations began with the political upheaval of 1848, when tens of thousands of Germans and Austrians looked to America for the freedoms they feared they would never have in their homeland.

HOME WORK: BERLIN 1898

One of the plagues of working life in the big European cities was the spread of home work into the tenements of the poor. Particularly the so-called needle trades depended on massive numbers of male and female production workers laboring in their own apartments for up to sixteen hours per day. Paid by the piece, the cutting and sewing was done in miserably overcrowded and unsanitary conditions. Often enough the family's one or two rooms had to serve as nursery, kitchen, sitting room, and bedroom as well as workplace. Children as young as nine were typically part of the "labor force." For the employer, the use of the workers' apartments meant saving the costs of not only the factory building and machinery but also the costs of worker pensions, sick pay, holidays, and so on, which he might otherwise have to bear. The following is excerpted from an 1898 exposé of conditions in Berlin:

> [T]he mother of a multitudinous family said, compared to her one-windowed room where her children slept, cried, played, and worked, she would far rather be in the factory where she had worked for awhile. As against the disorder and noise of her own household, the quiet and regularized factory environment was like a vacation, and she often could scarcely bring herself to return to her home after the workday. But the infant child was constantly sick, and she had to give up her factory job. Now she sewed blouses all day long, and for longer worktime she earned actually less. Besides this, at home the needs of the children were constantly thrust into her eyes, while the necessity of steady work to support them demanded her full attention, and so she was always neglecting one task in order to do another. Her life had become an exhausting chase, so that "I think each morning that I simply can't get up and start another day."

Another Berliner widow and mother of three told the census-taker in a few words her painful situation: "Because work and illness made it impossible to raise my children properly at home, I took them to an orphanage. But my mother's feelings couldn't be overcome, and after three months I brought them all home again. I hope that they can somehow raise and supervise themselves: I cannot."

Source: Annette Kuhn and Jorn Rusen, eds., Frauen in der Geschichte (Dusseldorf: Pädigogischer Verlag Schwann, 1982), vol. 2, pp. 229ff., citing two German authors of inquests in 1898 and 1904.

From about 2.5 million in the 1850s, total net emigration from Europe rose each decade until it peaked in the years just before World War I. By then, about 12 million people had left Europe in a ten-year period, a number about equal to the entire population of Scandinavia at that time. The war shut this stream down almost completely, and it never again reached those dimensions. In all, some 60 million Europeans emigrated during the nineteenth century and did not return. (About one of three emigrants to the United States eventually returned to the home country for reasons ranging from homesickness to deportation.)

Destinations

Where were all these people headed? The river of migrants flowed mainly to the New World, but Australia, New Zealand, and (for Russians exclusively) Siberia were also important destinations. The French colony of Algeria and the British colony of South Africa also attracted large groups of emigrants. (See Figure 42.1.)

In terms of proportionate impact on a given nation, Argentina was the most dramatic example of immigration in the world. About 3 percent of the total Argentine population arrived from Europe (mostly Spain and Italy) every year in the early twentieth century—three times the rate that the United States gained from the same source. But in absolute terms, the United States was easily the most popular single destination for emigrating Europeans. It received about 45 percent of the grand total of immigrants worldwide during the nineteenth century.

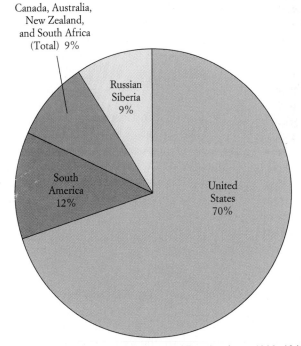

FIGURE 42.1 European Emigrants' Destinations, 1800–1960. The United States was easily the most preferred destination, with South America (mainly Argentina and Brazil) a distant second. What countries did the emigrants leave? Great Britain and Ireland supplied about 33 percent of the total; Italy, about 30 percent; and the rest of Europe, the remainder. The ethnic balance shifted steadily from northern and western Europe to southern and eastern as the nineteenth century matured. At the peak of European emigration in the decade just before World War I, an average of about 1.2 million emigrated annually.

The Dining Hall at Ellis Island. This 1906 photo captures the human faces who poured through the huge New York immigrant facility. By this time, the dominant nationalities were Italian and eastern European. New York City's population was over one-third foreign-born during this era. (© *The Granger Collection*)

Why did they leave? First and foremost, they were seeking better economic conditions. The rise and fall of emigration rates corresponded closely to European business cycles. In hard times, more left for the "land of golden opportunities." But a large proportion left because they were dissatisfied with domestic political and social conditions and had little faith that the future held any more promise than the present.

Types of Emigrants

Who were the emigrants? Most were not the very poor or ignorant. Instead, they were people who had been able to save a little or had relatives who were better off and helped them get a start. Many were small farmers who had too little land to ever get much farther up the ladder and feared for their sons' future when that little would be divided again by inheritance. Some were skilled craftsmen, who believed guild-type restrictions would prevent them from becoming independent entrepreneurs. Some were educated people who saw no chance of fully using their education in a class-bound society. In the later phases of the movement, many were indeed the poor and ignorant. They were as-

sisted by relatives who had emigrated earlier and had managed to establish themselves in their new land. Unmarried young men were the largest single contingent of emigrants, followed by young girls, usually the sisters and/or fiancées of males already in the new country.

The ethnic origins of the emigrants varied by chronology of departure. The majority of those who left for the New World in the middle of the nineteenth century were from Britain, Ireland, and Germany. In the later decades, they tended to be from eastern and southern European countries. By World War I, the Austro-Hungarians, Russians, Poles, and, above all, the Italians supplied the great bulk of the emigrants. A disproportionate number were Jews from the Russian empire (including Poland) who were fleeing racial persecution.

By the later nineteenth century, in the industrial economies of northern and western Europe, the working classes could find reasonably secure factory and white-collar jobs. Hence, they were less likely to emigrate than the unemployed and underemployed peasants and laborers of eastern and southern Europe. As a rule, the more literate and better prepared went to North America, Australia, or South Africa. South America received mainly those with lesser prospects.

Lower East Side of New York. This magnificent "slice of life" shows Mulberry Street, one of the chief street markets in slum New York, in about 1900. Much of the population of such neighborhoods spent little of the day inside their cramped apartments, if they could help it. *(Corbis)*

SUMMARY

A Second Industrial Revolution was fueled by the electrical and petroleum industries and the myriad uses to which these new sources of energy were applied in the last third of the nineteenth century. The corporation replaced the partnership, and joint stock companies became the usual means of raising capital in this same period.

In this second phase of industrialization, mass political parties became commonplace throughout western Europe. They sometimes represented newly organized labor and were almost always based on the rapidly expanding urban centers. By 1900, most industrial countries had introduced the universal male franchise. These developments con- tributed to the steady gains of socialism, particularly the Marxist variety after about 1870. Karl Marx's theories posited inevitable class warfare and a revolution of the pro- letariat against its capitalist oppressors. At the end of the century, this view was increasingly challenged by revision- ism and/or other rivals in the search for a more just distri- bution of national wealth.

The later nineteenth century also saw the most numer- ous emigration in recorded history, as up to 60 million Eu- ropeans opted to leave their homelands permanently and travel to the New World or other areas for better economic or political prospects.

TEST YOUR KNOWLEDGE

1. The Second Industrial Revolution was generated by
   a. the worker revolts of 1848.
   b. capitalist exploitation of the workers to the maximum ex- tent possible.
   c. industrial research and electrical energy.
   d. mining and iron making.

2. The countries that were in the forefront of the Second Indus- trial Revolution were
   a. Britain and the United States.
   b. the United States and Germany.
   c. Japan and the United States.
   d. Germany and Britain.

3. The most important of the new forms of business emerging in the late nineteenth century was the
   a. partnership.
   b. proprietorship.
   c. nonprofit company.
   d. corporation.
4. Labor unions first gained the legal right to organize and to strike in
   a. Germany.
   b. the United States.
   c. Britain.
   d. Holland.
5. Which of the following pairs is logically incorrect?
   a. Karl Marx and scientific socialism
   b. Eduard Bernstein and revisionist socialism
   c. Michael Bakunin and syndicalism
   d. Pierre Proudhon and anarchism
6. The bulk of the European emigrants of the nineteenth century were
   a. landless laborers seeking a new start in North and South America.
   b. dissatisfied small farmers, businessmen, artisans, and skilled laborers.
   c. Jews and others fleeing political persecution.
   d. relatively successful shop owners, artisans, and white-collar workers.
7. In the early twentieth century, the country supplying the largest number of emigrants to the United States was
   a. Germany.
   b. Ireland.
   c. Russia.
   d. Italy.
8. Which of the following was *not* a new phenomenon in the late nineteenth century?
   a. The corporation as the dominant form of business organization
   b. The spread of anarchist philosophy
   c. Emigration to the United States from Europe
   d. Revision of the Marxist plan of violent revolution

IDENTIFICATION TERMS

anarchism	*Communist Manifesto*	First International	revisionism (Marxism)
Bakunin, Michael	corporation	Labour Party	Second International
Chartist movement	Engels, Friedrich	Marx, Karl	syndicalism

INFOTRAC COLLEGE EDITION

Enter the search term "Marxism" using Key Words.
Enter the search term "socialism history" using Key Words.

Enter the search term "anarchism" using Key Words.

MODERN SCIENCE AND ITS IMPLICATIONS

Discovery consists of seeing what everyone has seen and thinking what no one has thought.

ALBERT SZENT-GYORGI

THE PHYSICAL SCIENCES
Biology
Physics
Astronomy

THE SOCIAL SCIENCES
Psychology
Anthropology and Sociology

THE MALAISE IN TWENTIETH-CENTURY SOCIETY

RELIGIOUS THOUGHT AND PRACTICE
Churches under Attack
The Christian Revival

IN THE WEST, the eighty years between 1860 and 1940 proved to be one of the most dazzling periods of innovation and change in intellectual history. In the last years of the nineteenth century, it was still possible for sophisticated persons to hold to a Newtonian view of the universe: the physical world was a composition of law-abiding matter, finite in its dimensions and predictable in its actions. Fifty years later, most of the natural sciences and especially physics, biology, and astronomy had been radically changed by some new factual data and many new interpretations of old data. The social, or "soft," sciences such as psychology, sociology, and economics had undergone a similar transformation, although here the novel ideas encountered more resistance because they could not be easily demonstrated as factually correct.

Religion, too, experienced striking changes. Long in retreat before an aggressive secularism, some Western Christians had come to believe that their religion was evolving like other human thought and that the Bible was properly subject to interpretations that would differ sharply in various ages and circumstances. But some "fundamentalist" denominations moved instead toward an uncompromising insistence on literal interpretation of the Bible as the sole source of God's unchanging truth.

THE PHYSICAL SCIENCES

In the second half of the nineteenth century, the mental frame of reference implied or dictated by rationalism and science became much more commonplace than ever before. By century's end, educated individuals throughout most of the Western world accepted the proposition that empirical science was the main source of accurate and valuable information. Religious revelation, authority, and/or tradition could not compete as legitimate rivals.

In the first half of the twentieth century, the preponderance of science over competing world-views became stronger still. Theology and philosophy, which previously had some persuasive claim to presenting a comprehensive explanation of human life, became the narrowly defined and exotic preserves of a handful of clerics and academics. In the universities, which became for the first time the recognized intellectual centers of the world, the physical

MR. BERGH TO THE RESCUE.

THE DEFRAUDED GORILLA. "That *Man* wants to claim my Pedigree. He says he is one of my Descendants."

Mr. BERGH. "Now, Mr. DARWIN, how could you insult him so?"

The Gorilla's Reproach. Thomas Nast was a well-known political cartoonist of the day, and this cartoon was one of his favorites. (*Corbis*)

sciences became increasingly specialized while attracting more and more students. Meanwhile, armies of scientific researchers garnered the lion's share of academic budgets and prestige. Though fewer and fewer were able to understand the intricacies of the new research, the general educated public still maintained its belief in the method of science as the most efficacious way of solving human problems. This viewpoint was weakened but survived even the cataclysms of the two world wars.

Biology

The shift from theology to science and hence from spiritual to material causation had begun with the Scientific Revolution of earlier days (see Chapter 35), but certain nineteenth-century ideas hastened its pace greatly. Darwinian biology was perhaps the most important.

In 1859, the Englishman **Charles Darwin** published ***The Origin of Species,*** a book that did for biology what Adam Smith's *Wealth of Nations* had done for economics. The controversy the book set off roiled European and American society for over a generation and generated acrid public

and private debate. In the end, the Darwinian view generally won out over its detractors.

What did Darwin say? Basically, he argued that through a process of **natural selection,** the individual species of plants and animals (inferentially including humans) evolved slowly from unknown ancestors. The organisms that possessed some marginal advantage in the constant struggle for survival would live long enough to create descendants that also bore those assets in their genes. For example, a flower seed with sufficient "feathers" to float a long distance through the air would more likely find suitable ground to germinate than those with few or none. Slowly over time, that seed type would come to replace others in a given area and survive where others died off.

This is a mechanical explanation of nature's variety and of the evolution of species. It is similar to stating that an automobile moves along a highway because its wheels are propelled by a drive shaft and axles, which are themselves driven by a motor. All true, of course, but it leaves out any mention of a person sitting in the driver's seat and turning the ignition key. Darwin carried Newton's mechanistic explanation of the cosmos into the domain of living things. In so doing, he eliminated the role of an intelligent Creator, or God, who had ordered nature toward a definite purpose and goal: glorifying himself and instructing humans. God was superfluous in Darwinian science and, being superfluous, should be ignored.

Darwin carried this theme forward with his 1871 ***The Descent of Man,*** which specifically included humans in the evolutionary process. It treated the morals and ethics they developed as the product of mechanical, naturalistic processes, not of an all-knowing and directing God. If it is the ability of our thumbs to close upon our fingers that chiefly distinguishes humans from apes, as some biologists believe, then what some call the human conscience may also be just a product of evolutionary experience, aimed at physical survival rather than justice and obedience to the will of a Creator-Judge.

Contrary to general impressions, Darwin did not explain why natural selection occurs or the factors that caused some variance from the norm (a mutation) that resulted in the survival of one species and the expiration of others. That task was left to an Austrian monk named Gregor Mendel, who worked out the principles of modern genetics in many years of unrecognized labor with the common pea in his monastery garden. And it should be added that Darwin's work was matched, simultaneously, by the independent research of Alfred Russell Wallace, another English amateur, who never sought or received public notice until after Darwin's work had taken over the stage. (For a sample of Darwin's writings, see the Science and Technology box).

CHARLES DARWIN REFLECTS ON *THE ORIGIN OF SPECIES*

Toward the end of his life, Charles Darwin wrote an autobiographical sketch for his children in which he outlined his feelings about his epoch-making work. The following excerpts are taken from his reflections on the modification of animal and bird species he had observed during his 1836 voyage on the *Beagle* to the Galápagos. The reference to success in adapting plants and animals to man's uses is to the ongoing breeding of improved livestock and crops. The reference to "Malthus on Population" is to the pamphlet that this author had given the world in 1798, claiming that the food supply would always lag behind the number of mouths to feed adequately.

It was evident that such facts as these [that is, certain species' changes] as well as many others could be explained on the supposition that species gradually become modified; and the subject haunted me. But it was equally evident that neither the action of the surrounding conditions, nor the will of the organisms (especially in the case of plants), could account for the innumerable cases in which organisms of every kind are beautifully adapted to their habits of life—for instance a woodpecker or tree-frog to climb trees, or a seed for dispersal by hooks or plumes. I had always been much struck by such adaptations, and until these could be explained it seemed to me almost useless to endeavour to prove by indirect evidence that species have been modified.

I soon perceived that Selection was the key-stone of man's success in making useful races of animals and plants. But how selection could be applied to organisms living in a state of nature remained for some time a mystery to me. In October 1838, that is fifteen months after I had begun my systematic inquiry, I happened to read for amusement "Malthus on Population," and being well prepared to appreciate the struggle for existence which everywhere goes on from long continued observation of the habits of animals and plants, it at once struck me that under these circumstances favourable variations would tend to be preserved and unfavourable ones to be destroyed. The result of this would be formation of new species.

After many hesitations and delays, Darwin finally decided to publish the book he had been incubating since 1837:

In September 1858 I set to work by the strong advice of Lyell and Hooker* to prepare a volume on the transmutation of species, but was often interrupted by ill health. . . . It was published under the title of the "Origin of Species" in November 1859. Though considerably added to and corrected in the later editions it has remained substantially the same book.

It has sometimes been said that the success of the *Origin* proved "that the subject was in the air," or "that men's minds were prepared for it." I do not think that this is strictly true, for I occasionally sounded not a few naturalists, and never happened across a single one who seemed to doubt about the permanence of species. Even Lyell and Hooker, though they would listen with interest to

Charles Darwin. Darwin's gravity assisted him to overcome the many critics and doubters who found his application of the theory of evolution to man offensive. *(Corbis)*

me, never seemed to agree. I tried once or twice to explain to able men what I meant by natural selection, but signally failed. What I believe strictly true is that innumerable well-observed facts were stored in the minds of naturalists ready to take their proper places, as soon as any theory which would receive them was sufficiently explained.

FOR REFLECTION

Do you agree that scientific discoveries are awaiting a theory that will sufficiently explain facts already "well observed"? What comes first, the theory that explains or the facts that back up the theory?

*Eminent British scientists and friends of Darwin.

SOURCE: Autobiographies: Charles Darwin; Thomas H. Huxley, ed. Gavin de Beer (Oxford: Oxford University Press, 1974), pp. 70–74, 84.

Physics

In physics the pathbreakers were **Ernst Mach** (1838–1916), **Wilhelm Roentgen** (1845–1923), **Max Planck** (1858–1947), and **Albert Einstein** (1879–1955). The fact that all four were educated in German universities is an indication of the emphasis on scientific research in the German educational system (see Chapter 41). This model was gradually extended throughout the Western world.

Mach's several publications in the 1880s and 1890s contributed importantly to the underlying concept of all twentieth-century physics: the impossibility of applying philosophical logic to physical matter. Mach believed that scientists could only determine what their intellect and equipment told them about matter, not what matter actually was or did. What a later German physicist would call the "Uncertainty Principle" had replaced the Newtonian world machine and substituted mere probability for law.

Roentgen discovered X rays, by which solid objects could be penetrated by a form of energy that made their interiors visible. His work, published at the end of the nineteenth century, immediately gave rise to experimentation with subatomic particles, especially in the laboratory of the Englishmen J. J. Thompson and **Ernest Rutherford** (1871–1937). Rutherford, who was a pioneer in the discovery of radioactivity and the splitting of the atom, is one of

The Young Einstein. This photo was taken about 1902, when Einstein was twenty-three and yet an unknown dabbler in theoretical physics. *(Topham Picture Library/Image Works)*

X-Ray Examination. The drawing shows the discoverer of the X ray, Wilhelm Roentgen, giving a young patient an examination with one of the earliest machines. Roentgen was awarded the Nobel Prize in 1901 for his hugely beneficial invention, which allowed surgeons to work with unprecedented success on the body's interior organs. *(Mary Evans Picture Library)*

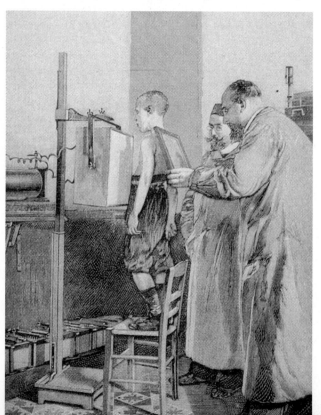

the great names of modern science. His work, in turn, was materially helped by the simultaneous research conducted by the French radiologist **Marie Curie** (1867–1934), whose laboratory work with radium proved that mass and energy were not separate but could be converted into one another under certain conditions.

Planck headed a major research lab for many years and revolutionized the study of energy with his *quantum theory,* by which energy is discharged in a not fully predictable series of emissions from its sources, rather than as a smooth and uniform stream. Quantum theory explained otherwise contradictory data about the motion of objects and subatomic matter such as electrons and protons.

Then, in 1905, the young Swiss German Einstein published the most famous paper on physics since Newton, the first of his theories on relativity. Einstein insisted that space and time formed a continuous whole and that measurement of both space and time depended as much on the observer as on the subjects of the measurement themselves. He saw time as a "fourth dimension" of space rather than as an independent concept. Eleven years later, Einstein published his ***General Theory of Relativity,*** which announced the birth of twentieth-century physics (and the death of the Newtonian model).

How does twentieth-century physics differ from the Newtonian conception? Several fundamental ideas are prominent:

- *Uncertainty.* In dealing with some forms of energy and with subatomic particles, modern science does not assume that cause-and-effect relations are reliable. Strong probability replaces certainty as the best obtainable result. No Newtonian laws apply except in the most crude fashions.
- *Relativity.* The observer's status affects the supposedly independent object observed. Some would say that the very fact of observation changes the nature of the object or process observed, so that no neutral observation is possible.
- *Interchangeability of matter and energy.* Under specified conditions, the Newtonian distinction between matter and energy falls away, and one becomes the other.

These mind-bending novelties have been recognized and acted on by only a small handful of specialists, mainly in the universities. They have removed modern physics from the comprehension of most ordinary people, even well-educated ones. The assumption, so common in the nineteenth century, that physical science would be the key to a fully comprehensible universe, in which matter and energy would be the reliable servants of intellect, was dashed by the physical scientists themselves. Their ever-more exotic research and its unsettling results widened the previously narrow gap between professional scientists and educated laypeople.

This intellectual divorce between the mass of people and the holders of specialized scientific knowledge has become a subject of concern that continues to the present day. The nonspecialists in positions of responsibility are often placed in an intolerable situation when dealing with economic policy, for example. Statesmen and politicians rarely comprehend the scientific background of the internal development policies they are implementing or their possible dangers. For another example, the naïveté of the early proponents of nuclear power plants, who had no understanding of the menace posed by a nuclear meltdown, became a major embarrassment, or worse. The lawmaking and political authorities were forced to rely on scientific advisers who had every professional interest in seeing the plants built. This dilemma of contemporary government is not going to be easily solved.

Thomas Edison in His Laboratory. The rapid advance of the physical sciences in the nineteenth century was almost immediately translated into technology. One of the outstanding examples of both scientist and technician was the American Thomas Edison, whose inventions such as the incandescent lightbulb were put to profitable use as they issued from his laboratory in New Jersey. *(Corbis)*

Astronomy

In astronomy the major changes in the scientific paradigm are more recent. The last fifty years have seen fantastic advances and an ongoing debate. The advances were mainly technological: huge new telescopes and radio devices, space vehicles that venture far into the cosmos to report on distant planets, and spectroscopes that analyze light emitted eons ago from the stars. As a result of this new technology, we know much more about the nature of the universe than before. Space probes have revealed that planets such as Mars and Saturn are physically quite different than previously thought, while the moon has become almost familiar territory. The universe is now thought to be much larger than once believed—indeed, perhaps infinite—and to contain millions or billions of stars.

Strictly speaking, the debate is not astronomical in character but rather metaphysical ("beyond physics"). It revolves around how this huge universe was created and how it will develop. The widely supported **"big bang" theory** holds that the universe originated several billion years ago with a cosmic explosion of a great fireball, which is still flinging fragments of matter—stars—farther out into space. Some think that the expansion will end with a general cooling and dying off of all life-supporting planets. Others believe that gravity will gradually slow the expansion and bring all the scattered fragments together again, only to have another big bang and repeat the process.

A third group—creationists—rejects both of these naturalistic explanations and holds to the Christian tradition that an Intelligent Being created the cosmos and all within it in accord with a preconceived plan. In the same way, a number of respected scientists accept the overwhelming evidence for the slow physical evolution of humans but insist that the separate, instantaneous creation of an immortal soul within *Homo sapiens* by a God is a perfectly possible hypothesis.

THE SOCIAL SCIENCES

The social sciences have human beings, collectively or individually, as their subject matter. They include psychology, sociology, anthropology, economics, and political science. These disciplines were strongly affected by the waves of new ideas and data produced by the physical sciences in the later nineteenth century. Just as the sciences of the seventeenth-century innovators slowly percolated into the consciousness of historians and political philosophers to produce the Enlightenment, so did the innovations and technological breakthroughs of the nineteenth-century physicists and biologists affect the world-views of the sociologists and psychologists who followed. The effect was probably most spectacular and controversial in psychology.

Psychology

Psychology has been radically altered by the widely held modern conviction that its major purpose should be to heal sick minds, rather than merely understand how the mind works. In the twentieth century, psychiatry—the healing process—has come to be an important branch of medicine. No one individual has been more crucial to this transformation than **Sigmund Freud** (1856–1939), a doctor from Vienna, Austria, who gradually developed a theory of psychiatric treatment called psychoanalysis.

The Consultation Room in Freud's Apartment. This is the famous couch on which Freud's patients reclined while the psychiatrist listened to their "free associations" and took notes. (*AP/Wide World Photos*)

Freud believed that not the conscious but the unconscious mind is the controlling factor of the deepest mental life. In effect, he was rejecting the principle of rationality—that is, that men and women are capable and desirous of reasoned acts—on which all previous psychological theory had been built. Psychoanalysis attempts to help the patient to recognize and do something about the distorted impressions of reality that produce social or individual disabilities. It is based on Freud's convictions that the sexual drive is the motor of the unconscious, that childhood events are almost always the source of mental and emotional problems in adult life, and that the eternal struggle between the libido, or pleasure principle, and the superego, which might be translated as conscience, will never be entirely resolved within the human mind.

Freud has had several competitors in explaining the mind's workings and how the sick might be cured. The Swiss **Carl Jung** (1875–1961) was one of Freud's early collaborators, but he broke with the master (as did many others) and founded his own psychological school. It emphasized religious symbolism and archetypal ideas shared by all humans in their unconscious as the bedrock of mental activity.

Ivan Pavlov (1849–1936) is considered the founder of behaviorism, a widely supported theory that insists that the rewards and punishments given to various types of behavior are the controlling factors of individual psychology. Pavlov's work with dogs in his native Russia before World War I made him famous. His work was supplemented by the Americans William James (1842–1910) and B. F. Skinner (1904–1990) in the early and middle decades of the past century.

In recent years, the former sharp division of psychologists into pro- and anti-Freud camps has softened. While much of Freud's theoretical work is now rejected or discredited from universal application, a good deal more has been accepted as conventional wisdom. When we use terms such as *inferiority complex, Freudian slip,* and *Oedipus complex* in everyday speech, we are paying verbal tribute to the Austrian explorer of the mystery of inner space. (For more about Freud, see the Tradition and Innovation box.)

Anthropology and Sociology

Both anthropology and sociology treat humans as a species rather than as individuals. These two new sciences flourished greatly in the twentieth century. Anthropology as a scientific discipline is an indirect product of Darwinian biology, though some work was done earlier. It is divided into two basic varieties: physical, dealing with humans as an animal species, and cultural, dealing with humans as the constructors of systems of values. Especially since World War II, great advances have been achieved in extending our knowledge of the human species far back into prehistoric time. Combining with archaeology and the new subscience of sociobiology, these paleoanthropologists have learned much about the physical and cultural aspects of earlier human life. They have posited several theories and ideas of the nature of humans that sharply contradict the previous, traditional concepts and that have strongly influenced current anthropological research.

Sociology also came of age in the late nineteenth century. Unlike most fields of science that are the product of many disparate contributors, it can trace its basic theory to a small handful of brilliant individuals. First in time was **Auguste Comte** (1798–1857), a Frenchman whose philosophical treatise, *The Positive Philosophy,* insisted that laws of social behavior existed and were just as readily knowable as the laws of physical behavior. In this view, humans advance through three stages of ability to perceive knowledge, culminating in the scientific stage just now being entered. Truth could and must be obtained by the application of positivism, by which Comte meant that only empirical, measurable data were reliable and that a philosophy that attempts to identify spiritual, nonmaterialistic forces or values was falsely conceived and impossible.

Comte's view of sociology as the culmination of all the sciences inspired many imitators. In the last years of the nineteenth century, the French sociologist Emile Durkheim (1858–1917) and the German Max Weber (1864–1920) were equally important as formative influences. In his special way, Karl Marx was perhaps the greatest of the nineteenth-century figures who studied the "science of society."

Several Americans were also in the forefront of sociology's development, especially in the early twentieth century when American universities took up the discipline with enthusiasm. The underlying premise of sociology seemed to be particularly appealing to American habits of mind: if one knew enough of the laws of social behavior, one could alter that behavior in positive and planned ways. This mode of thought fit well with the preeminently American view of society as an instrument that might be tuned by conscious human interventions. But in many minds, this optimism was eventually countered by profound misgivings about the course of human society.

One offshoot of the Darwinian discoveries in biology was a reexamination of human ethics. More especially, can a code of ethics originate through a particular set of environmental influences? If so, can one type of behavior be promoted over another in some rational manner? Do ethics themselves evolve, or are they permanently instilled by a Superior Being, as fundamentalist Christians believe?

Herbert Spencer (1820–1903) was the most noted of the upholders of social Darwinism, a philosophy that held that ethics are indeed evolutionary in nature and that free competition is the main engine of social progress. As among the plants and animals, the fittest will survive, as a ruthless nature demands. Though Spencer did not intend such a result, his philosophy of unbridled social competition made it all too easy for the powerful to justify their own position as the proper, even the inevitable reward for their superiority. As for the poor or the unfortunate, their misery was the

SIGMUND FREUD
(1856–1939)

The founder of modern psychotherapy, Sigmund Freud is one of the three Germans of Jewish descent who radically changed the physical and social sciences of the Western world in a relatively brief epoch. (The others were Albert Einstein and Karl Marx.) In some ways, Freud's contribution was perhaps even more penetrating than the others, as the popularized versions of his theories have long since become part of the everyday mental equipment of even minimally educated persons. His innovative work has proved extraordinarily controversial, even a century later.

Freud was born in Bohemia (now the Czech Republic), a province of the Habsburg empire. He entered medical studies at the University of Vienna in 1885 and lived in that city for almost his entire life. He became more and more interested in the interlinking of the mind and the body, especially as this was evidenced by hysteria, or the breakdown of certain bodily functions under extreme stress. His attempt to show that the underlying cause of hysteria (almost always found in females) was some type of sexual fear or trauma offended the prevalent ethical sensitivities and made him persona non grata among his medical cohorts. A few years later, his insistence on the sexuality of small children as well as the sexual meanings of dreams cemented this rejection by the Viennese public.

But Freud was not put off by the disdain of his colleagues. Between 1900 and 1910, he published several major studies in psychology and psychotherapeutic practice that won him international recognition. In this period, he developed his ideas on the possibility of reaching and healing unconscious sources of mental anguish by means of free association: encouraging the patient to "talk out" the mental link between outwardly unrelated topics or feelings. This came to be called *psychoanalysis*. The healer's role was to listen encouragingly rather than to intervene actively. In essence, the patient would in time come to recognize his or her ills and heal himor herself.

By the mid-1920s, most of the original work in Freud's psychotherapeutic theories had been completed. He remained at the head of the International Psychoanalytical Association and continued his private practice in Vienna, where he had married and raised a family. Most of his later writings are concerned with cultural topics rather than medical ones, including his very famous books *Civilization and Its Discontents* and *Moses and Monotheism*.

The antagonism Freud aroused through his insistence on the sexual nature of much human activity was only increased by his equal insistence on the primacy of the unconscious in directing human action. Freud's assertions that humans are only sporadically rational and sporadically aware of why they thought or did certain things fell at the time on stony ground, particularly in his native country. Many thought it no great loss when the "degenerate Jewish manipulator" Freud had to leave Vienna for London in the wake of the Nazi takeover in 1938. Already suffering from a painful cancer of the jaw, he died shortly after arriving there.

Sigmund Freud was a pioneer of the huge, dark spaces of the human psyche. Much of what he insisted on has now been revised or even rejected by the majority of psychiatrists, but it is perhaps no exaggeration to give him the title "Columbus of the Soul."

FOR REFLECTION

How much of Freud's insistence on sexuality as the prime motivator of unconscious activity do you agree with? What other motivators strike you as important inputs into the unconscious?

Sigmund Freud. (© *The Granger Collection*)

equally inevitable result of their natural inferiority. Social Darwinism was a temporarily fashionable pseudophilosophy at the end of the nineteenth century, and its adherents by no means entirely disappeared in the twentieth.

THE MALAISE IN TWENTIETH-CENTURY SOCIETY

With all the triumphs scored in understanding the physical universe, and the growing acceptance of science as the most certain path to useful knowledge, many people at the nineteenth century's end still felt uneasy about the road ahead. This malaise (apprehensive feeling) became much more tangible and widespread after World War I. What had happened to bring about this state of affairs?

In unintended ways, psychology has contributed as much to the insecurity and uncertainty that cloud modern lives in the West as the revolution in physics has. Both sciences often leave the observer with the feeling that things are not as they outwardly seem. In psychology, the brute instinct is as important as the reason. In physics, matter can suddenly turn into its opposite, nonmatter, and the course and nature of such transformations cannot be predicted accurately. Traditional knowledge is no longer applicable or insufficient, and traditional authority has shown itself incompetent to give clear answers to new questions. Freud himself claimed, with a note of ambivalent pride, that his work had finished the destruction of the medieval view of humans begun by the cosmology of Copernicus and continued by the biology of Darwin. While Copernicus had reduced humankind to being residents of a minor planet in a cosmos of many similar planets, Darwin had torn down the precious wall distinguishing beasts and man. Now Freud had shown that these human beings did not and could not fully control their own acts or perceptions.

One of the prominent features of the social sciences in the twentieth century was the spread of **cultural relativism.** The nineteenth century's assurance that whatever was the standard in Europe should become the standard of the world's behavior was largely demolished. The recent generations raised in Western culture are much less convinced that there is but one proper way to raise small children, inculcate respect for the aged, assign gender roles, and so forth, than was the case a century ago. An appreciation of the variety of ways to solve a generic task, such as instructing the young in what they will need to prosper, has become more common among Western people. It is interesting that this is happening at exactly the time when the rest of the world is voluntarily imitating the West in many respects. This cultural relativism is another face of the general abandonment of traditional ethnocentrism that is an earmark of late twentieth-century thought, in the West, especially, but throughout "the global village."

RELIGIOUS THOUGHT AND PRACTICE

During the nineteenth century, the Christian Church came under siege throughout Europe. Both Catholic and Protestant believers found themselves portrayed by numerous opponents as relics from a forgotten medieval age who were against progress, rationalism, and anything modern.

Churches under Attack

Attacks came from several quarters. Intellectuals, in particular, rejected the traditional arguments of religion and the clergy's claim to represent a higher order of authority than mere human beings. Liberals rejected the stubborn conservatism of the clergy and the peasants who were the church's most faithful followers. Marxists laughed at the gullibility of the pious believer ("pie in the sky when you die"), while agitating against the churches, which they regarded as slavish tools of the bourgeois class, like other institutions of the modern state.

These varied attacks had very substantial effect. By the 1890s, the European working class had almost entirely ceased to attend church. In France only a minority of the Catholic peasantry went to hear the priest on occasions other than their wedding day. Like the English and the Germans, the French urban workers were practically strangers to organized religion. In Italy and Spain, where the papal religion was still an established church, anticlericalism was common in all classes, even though most peasants still supported the church as an essential part of their life.

Positivist science was a strong weapon in the attackers' arsenal. The intellectual battle over Darwin's biology was won by the Darwinians by century's end, though the topic was still acrimoniously debated in some sectors. The long struggle over lay versus religious control of public education was settled everywhere in the West by the coming of state-supported schools in which the religious denominations were excluded or restricted. Religious belief was removed from the qualifications of officeholders, civil servants, and voters. Everywhere but Russia, by the 1870s, Jews and atheists were made fully equal with Christians in law, if not always in practice. Among the larger part of the educated and influential classes, secularism was taken for granted as the wave of the future in European (and American) civic culture.

The Christian Revival

Meanwhile, the churches everywhere were struggling to renew themselves and regain at least some of the lost ground. In parts of the United States, the fundamentalist Protestant creeds became strong rivals of the Lutherans, Anglicans, and other, less aggressively evangelical churches. The somewhat similar British Nonconformists (those Protestants who did not "conform" to the Anglican credo, such as Methodists, Presbyterians, Quakers, and Unitarians) showed formidable tenacity in their missionary work and the foundation of hundreds of schools.

In Germany, Chancellor Bismarck made a major error in attempting to consolidate support for his government by attacking the Catholic Church. This "Kulturkampf" ended in the 1880s with a rout of the Bismarck forces. The church emerged stronger than ever and founded a political party, which was the second largest in the German parliament by 1910. The necessity of meeting the Darwinian challenge and the positivist critics of the Bible made it obligatory for both Catholic and Protestant to reexamine the basis of literal belief in the Creation. Soon, a school of Christian Bible exegesis on scientific foundations contributed to a revival of intellectually credible research.

In 1891, the unfortunate tradition of papal rejection of all that was new was broken by Leo XIII's major encyclical (papal letter): ***Rerum novarum*** ("About new things"). In this, the pope strongly supported the ideals of social justice for the working classes and the poor, while continuing to denounce atheistic socialism. For the next fifty years, *Rerum novarum* provided a guideline for loyal Catholics who wished to create a more liberal, less exploitative economic order. They frequently found themselves opposed by the clergy and their coreligionists in positions of power throughout the Western world.

World War I dealt a heavy blow to all organized religions. Many members of the clergy in all denominations were caught up in the patriotic hysteria of the early weeks of the war and outdid themselves in blessing the troops and the battleships, declaring, "Gott mit uns!" (God's on our side). The ghastly reality of the trenches quickly put an end to such claims. Radical discontent at the endless bloodletting sharpened the critiques. The clergy were denounced as willing pawns of the various governments that controlled their incomes and status. After the 1917 Russian Revolution, Marxist propaganda skillfully intensified these negative feelings both inside and outside Russia.

A small minority reacted differently. They saw the war and the following period of upheaval as the inevitable results of a godless, mechanistic progressivism that had little of value to offer humans' spiritual nature. In the 1920s and 1930s, both Protestant and Catholic communities in the Western world experienced a perceptible, though limited, revival of Christian belief.

A few intellectuals, too, were ready to risk the contempt of their fellows by taking an overtly religious point of view in the interwar era. Among them were Paul Claudel and Etienne Gilson in France, Karl Jaspers and Reinhard Niebuhr in Germany, T. S. Eliot in Britain, and Dorothy Day in the United States. They were indeed a tiny minority, but that did not deter them from hoping and working for a Christian renaissance out of the blood and terror of the war.

SUMMARY

Advances in the physical sciences multiplied and fed off one another in the second half of the nineteenth century, leading to an explosive ferment in the opening half of the twentieth. Darwinian biology led the parade of theory and data that together profoundly altered the existing concepts of the physical universe and its creatures, including human beings. The Newtonian cosmology was overthrown by a New Physics pioneered by German researchers. Somewhat later, theoretical astronomy also entered a revolutionary era, which had its own impact on age-old habits of belief.

In the social sciences, the disputed revelations of Freud were equally disturbing to traditionalists. For those who followed the master, human consciousness was overshadowed by irrational forces beyond its awareness, and the soul was reduced to a biochemical entity, if it existed at all. What was left of traditional morality was ascribed to a psyche entangled in its own irrational fears and follies. Less controversially, sociology and anthropology emerged as accepted academic disciplines and provided new ways of contemplating humans as a community.

Throughout the nineteenth century, the Christian religion had been assaulted by self-doubt and persuasive scientific adversaries. Tardily, both Protestant and Catholic organs took up the challenge. Reaction against positivist science and changes in official church attitudes had assisted a slight recovery by the turn of the century. This limited revival was increased in the 1920s and 1930s by the revulsion against World War I.

TEST YOUR KNOWLEDGE

1. Darwinian biology was ultimately based on
   a. Christian theology.
   b. a mechanical view of the cosmos.
   c. a belief in random change in species.
   d. a belief in a kind of deism much like Newton's.
2. The Uncertainty Principle refers to modern
   a. psychology.
   b. physics.
   c. history.
   d. economics.
3. The most clear-cut similarity among later nineteenth-century physicists is
   a. their belief in Christianity.
   b. their training in German methodology.
   c. their reliance on individual research.
   d. their unhappy domestic lives.
4. Which of the following was *not* embraced by Freudian psychology?
   a. The superego is engaged in struggle against the libido.
   b. The sex drive lies at the bottom of much unconscious activity.
   c. Humans are basically seeking rational answers to their difficulties.
   d. Conscious actions are often reflections of unconscious motives.

5. Freud's theories of psychology
   a. encouraged the belief in rational planning as an answer to misery.
   b. were supported most ardently in his home city of Vienna.
   c. were thought to be insulting by many of his colleagues.
   d. were based on the study of behavior of animals.
6. Which of the following pairs is *least* logically paired?
   a. Mach and Einstein
   b. Freud and Jung
   c. Marie Curie and Ernest Rutherford
   d. Auguste Comte and Wilhelm Roentgen
7. Which pair fits *most* logically together in terms of their interests?
   a. Durkheim and Weber
   b. Niebuhr and Mach
   c. Jung and Einstein
   d. Darwin and Rutherford
8. As a general rule, twentieth-century Christian belief in the Western world
   a. became nearly extinct after World War II.
   b. developed an entirely new view of Christ.
   c. became much stronger as a result of World War I.
   d. recovered some support among intellectuals.

IDENTIFICATION TERMS

"big bang" theory	*The Descent of Man*	Jung, Carl	Planck, Max
Comte, Auguste	Einstein, Albert	Mach, Ernst	*Rerum novarum*
cultural relativism	Freud, Sigmund	natural selection	Roentgen, Wilhelm
Curie, Marie	*General Theory of Relativity*	*The Origin of Species*	Rutherford, Ernest
Darwin, Charles		Pavlov, Ivan	Spencer, Herbert

INFOTRAC COLLEGE EDITION

Enter the search term "Charles Darwin" using Key Words.
Enter the search term "Sigmund Freud" using Key Words.

Enter the search term "Social Darwinism" using Key Words.

44

WORLD WAR I AND ITS DISPUTED SETTLEMENT

The lights are going out all over Europe.
We shall not see them lit again in our lifetime.
LORD GREY, BRITISH FOREIGN MINISTER

MANY PEOPLE WOULD SAY that the nineteenth century and its convictions of inevitable Progress lasted until 1914, when "the lights went out all over Europe," as one British statesman put it. And the twentieth century began not in 1900 but in 1918, when by far the bloodiest and most bitter war fought until then finally ended.

World War I was a European fratricide and the deathblow to the belief that progress and prosperity were almost automatic. By 1918, much of the youth and the political ideals of the Western world lay in ruins on the battlefields and at home. Disillusionment was rampant, and the stage was set for revolution in several countries. From a war that had no true victors in Europe, the United States and Japan emerged as major powers, while the Western imperial image suffered damage that was never repaired in Asia and Africa.

PREWAR DIPLOMACY

After defeating France in the short Franco-Prussian War of 1870–1871, the German chancellor Bismarck knew that the French would be yearning for revenge. Weakening France to the maximum accordingly made good strategic sense. Thus, Germany seized the two border provinces of Alsace and Lorraine, a move that deprived an industrializing France of its main sources of iron and coal.

The Triple Alliance

Bismarck also wished to keep France isolated, knowing that France alone could not hope to defeat the newly united and powerful Germany. Toward that end, he promoted alliances with Austria-Hungary and Russia. These states were engaged in a strong rivalry over the fate of the weakened Ottoman Empire, and Bismarck intended to bind them together with Germany as the "swing" partner, so that neither would join France.

For more than twenty years, Bismarck's system worked well. A satiated Germany had what it wanted, and peace was preserved because France was indeed too weak to move alone and could not find allies. (Britain in this epoch was practicing "splendid isolation" from continental affairs and in any case had no quarrel with Germany and no friendship toward France.)

When newly unified Italy began to want to play a role in international affairs, Bismarck was able to persuade the Italians that their desires for colonial expansion would have a better hearing in Berlin than in Paris. Italy eventually joined Germany and Austria in the **Triple Alliance** of 1882, which said, in essence, that if any one of the three were attacked, the other two would hasten to its aid.

In 1890, however, the linchpin of the system was removed when the old chancellor was dismissed by the young Kaiser William II (ruled 1888–1918). William was not a man to remain willingly in the shadow of another. He was determined to conduct his own foreign policy, and he did so immediately by going out of his way to alienate Russia, imposing a new import tariff on Russian grain and allowing a previous treaty of friendship to lapse. As a result, the Russians suddenly showed some interest in negotiating with the French, who had been patiently waiting for just such an opportunity. In 1893–1894, France and Russia signed a defensive military alliance. The pact did not mention a specific antagonist, but it was clearly aimed at Germany.

The Anglo-French Entente and the Anglo-Russian Agreement

The cordial relations between Britain and Prussia-Germany, which had prevailed throughout the nineteenth century, gave way to an unprecedented hostility in the early 1900s for several reasons:

- Germany's industrial and commercial imperialists were demanding that Kaiser William carve out a big slice of the few remaining potential colonial regions before the French and British swallowed them all.
- The Boer War in South Africa (1899–1902) aroused considerable anti-British feeling among the Germans. These sentiments were quickly reciprocated by the British public, fed by the sensationalist penny press in London.
- Germany's announcement in 1907 that it intended to build a world-class navy was taken as a deliberate provocation that must be answered by British countermeasures.
- The belligerent "sword rattling" in which the impetuous and insecure kaiser indulged during the decade before 1914 contributed significantly to the developing tensions. Under William II, the German government often gave the impression that it was more interested in throwing its very considerable weight about than in solving diplomatic crises peaceably.

By 1904, the British had decided that post-Bismarck Germany was a greater menace to their interests than France, the traditional continental enemy. In that year, Britain and France signed the **Anglo-French *Entente*** (understanding). Without being explicit, it was understood that Britain would come to the aid of France in a defensive war. Again, no other power was named in the pact, but its meaning was quite clear.

The final step in the division of Europe into conflicting blocs was the creation of a link between Britain and Russia, which had been on opposite sides of everything since the Napoleonic wars had ended. Here, the French served as middlemen, and in 1907, Britain and Russia signed the **Anglo-Russian Agreement,** which was much like the Anglo-French Entente. Now Germany, Austria, and Italy on the one side faced Britain, France, and Russia on the other. The stage had been set. The action was sure to follow.

Causes of the War

What caused World War I? Like most wars, World War I had two types of causes: (1) the proximate cause, or the event that actually triggered hostilities, and (2) the more decisive remote causes, or the trail of gunpowder that led to the explosion.

The proximate cause was the assassination of Archduke Franz Ferdinand, the heir to the Austrian throne, on June 28, 1914, in the town of Sarajevo in Bosnia, at that time an Austrian possession. Bosnia had been transferred from Turkish to Austrian rule by international agreement in 1878, following one of several Serbian uprisings. The transfer from one alien overlord to another had not placated the Bosnian Serbs, who wished to join with the independent Serbian kingdom adjoining Bosnia (see Map 44.1). The archduke was murdered by a conspiracy of Serbian nationalist youths who were convinced that the assassination would somehow induce Austria to abandon its Serb-populated possessions. They were, of course, wrong.

The war also had several remote causes:

- *Nationalism.* Extreme nationalist sentiment had been rising steadily, particularly among the various small peoples who inhabited the areas of southeastern Europe held for centuries by the Turks. Some of these peoples were the clients of the Austrians, some were the clients of the Russians, and some had no patron. All were determined to seize as much territory as possible for their own nations when the capsizing Ottoman Empire finally sank.
- *International imperialism.* Austria, Russia, Britain, France, Germany, and Italy all shared in the frenzy of the new imperialism of the late nineteenth century. At the time, many believed that those who were not expanding their territories and populations would be the certain losers in the sharpening industrial competition among the developed nations. This doctrine of inevitable expansion and conflict among the capitalists was a cornerstone of Marxist propaganda.
- *Weariness of peace.* A long generation of peace (1871–1914) had allowed Europeans to forget how quickly war can fan the embers of discontent into revolution and anarchy. In addition, some influential persons in public life were convinced that war ennobled

MAP 44.1 The Balkan States, 1914. The intermixing of several ethnic and religious groups in southeastern Europe is a result of many centuries of immigration, conquest, and foreign overlordship. On the eve of World War I, Serbia, Bulgaria, Romania, and Greece were maneuvering for national advantage in the event that the long-awaited collapse of the Ottoman empire occurred.

the human spirit and that Europe had "suffered" through too many years of peace since 1815. They actually longed for the challenges of war as the ultimate test that would separate the wheat from the chaff among the nations.

After a month's ominous silence, the Austrian government presented the government of independent Serbia (from which the assassins had obtained their weapons and possibly their inspiration) with a forty-eight-hour ultimatum. Acceptance of the conditions would mean in effect the surrender of Serbian independence, while refusal meant war. The Serbs chose war.

MILITARY ACTION, 1914–1918

Within a week in early August, all but one of the members of the two blocs formed over the past two decades were also

at war. The exception was Italy, which bargained with both sides for the next several months. Austria-Hungary was joined at once by Germany, Turkey, and Bulgaria (in 1915). Joining Serbia were Russia, France, Britain, Italy (in 1915), and Romania (in 1916). The United States and Greece entered the fray in 1917 on the Entente or Allied side, as it was generally called.

In its military aspect, World War I was almost entirely a European phenomenon, although members of the Allies came from all continents by the time it was over. The battlefronts were (1) the *Western front* in France and Belgium, which was the decisive one (see Map 44.2); (2) the *Eastern or Russian front,* which reached from the Baltic Sea to the Aegean but was always secondary (see Map 44.3); and (3) the *Alpine front,* which involved only Italy and Austria-Hungary and had no major influence on the course of the conflict.

As so often, the military experts were mistaken, and the generals unprepared. This was particularly true on the

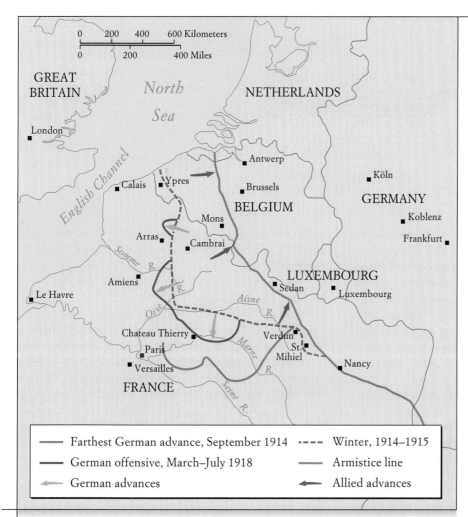

Apprehension of Gavrilo Princip in Sarajevo. What happened to the archduke's assassin? He was seized immediately by the Sarajevo police and rushed into prison before he could be lynched. He died in an Austrian prison from tuberculosis in 1918. (*The Bettmann Archive/Corbis*)

MAP 44.2 The Western Front in World War I. Neither the Germans nor the Allies were able to move more than a few miles forward after the initial German attack was contained in the fall of 1914. Artillery, minefields, and machine guns stopped any assault on the opposing trenches with massive losses.

Legend:

— Farthest German advance, September 1914

--- Winter, 1914–1915

— German offensive, March–July 1918

— Armistice line

← German advances

← Allied advances

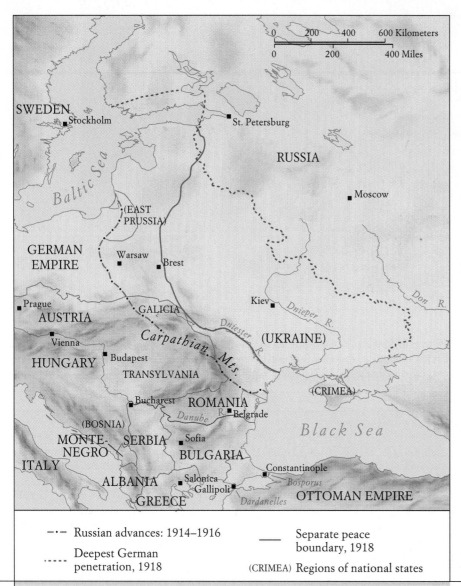

Western front. The experts had thought that thanks to rail-roads, motor vehicles, telephones, and radio communications, as well as the use of much heavier cannons and much larger armies than had been seen before, whichever side got the upper hand in the early days would have a decisive advantage. The offense would also have a big advantage over the defense, thought the experts. The war would be won within a few weeks by the superior attacker, just as in a chess game between experts in which one player gains the advantage in the opening moves.

Just the opposite happened: the defense proved superior to the offense. Instead of large numbers of motorized troops scoring breakthroughs against the enemy, the war turned out to be endless slogging through muddy trenches and hopeless, cruelly wasteful infantry attacks against machine guns while artillery knocked every living thing to perdition for miles around. Instead of lasting a few weeks, the war lasted four and a quarter ghastly years, with a loss of life far in excess of any other conflict ever yet experienced. (See the box for an account of a soldier's life in the trenches.)

The Bloody Stalemate

Originally, the **Central Powers** (as the German-Austrian allies were called) planned to hold off the Russians with minimal forces while rapidly smashing through neutral Belgium into France and forcing it to surrender. The plan very nearly worked. In late August 1914, the Germans got to within a few miles of Paris, only to be permanently stalled along the river Marne by heroic French resistance. Aided now by a British army that grew rapidly, the French were able to contain one tremendous German attack after another for four years.

From the English Channel to Switzerland, the battle lines did not move more than a few miles, as millions of

Erich Maria Remarque, All Quiet on the Western Front

In even the most horrifying nightmare, no one who enthusiastically marched or cheered on those who were marching into World War I could have foreseen the dehumanizing brutality that the four years 1914–1918 would bring. The German writer Erich Maria Remarque was conscripted into the imperial army soon after the outbreak of the war. In his 1927 novel, *All Quiet on the Western Front,* which became an international best-seller, he recounted what he had observed through the ghastly, violent experiences of young German soldiers like himself:

> We wake in the middle of the night. The earth booms. Heavy fire is falling on us. We crouch into corners. . . . Slowly the grey light trickles into the outpost, and pales the flashes of the shells. Morning has come. The explosion of mines mingles with the gunfire; that is the most dementing convulsion of all. The whole area where they go off becomes one grave. . . .
>
> The dull thud of gas shells mingles with the crashes of the high explosives. A bell sounds between the explosions, gongs and metal clappers warning everyone: Gas! . . . These first few minutes with the [gas] masks decide between life and death: is it tightly woven? I remember the awful sights in the hospitals: the gas patients who in day-long suffocation cough their burnt lungs up in clots.
>
> We lie under the network of arching shells and live in a suspense. Over us Chance hovers. If a shot comes, we can duck, that is all; we neither know nor can determine where it will fall.
>
> It is this Chance which makes us indifferent. A few months ago I was sitting in a dugout playing *skat;* after a while, I stood up and went to visit some friends in another dugout. On my return nothing more was to be seen of the first one: it had been blown to pieces with a direct hit. I went back to the second and arrived just in time to lend a hand digging it out. In the interval it had been buried.
>
> The brown earth, the torn, blasted earth, with a greasy shine under the sun's rays; the earth is the background of this restless gloomy world of automatons . . . into our pierced and shattered souls bores the torturing image of the brown earth with the greasy sun and the convulsed and dead soldiers, who lie there . . . who cry and clutch at our legs as we spring away over them. We have lost all feeling for one another. We can hardly control ourselves when our hunted glance lights on the form of some other man. We are insensible, dead men who through some trick, some dreadful magic, are still able to run and to kill.

Battle of Verdun. The fortress city of Verdun, near the German frontier, was utterly destroyed in a sixteen-month-long attack costing both sides over a half-million casualties. (*Archives Larousse, Paris, France/Bridgeman Art Library*)

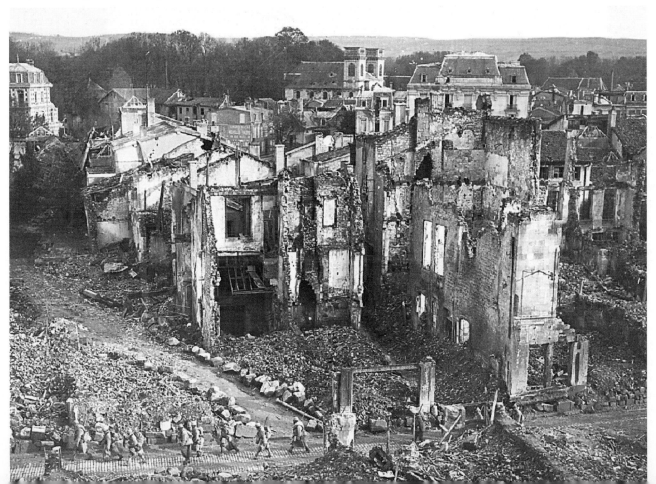

men on both sides met their death. The defense of the French fortress city of Verdun in 1916–1917 was the bloodiest slaughter of all. The defenders lost more than 600,000 killed and wounded and the attackers even more.

U.S. Entry and Russian Exit

The entry of the United States into the war in April 1917 was vitally important to the Allies. The American decision was triggered by the resumption of unrestricted submarine war by the German High Command. Strong protests after U.S. ships and American lives had been lost to torpedoes had brought a lull in attacks for almost two years, during which the United States maintained its formal neutral stance. In fact, President Woodrow Wilson and most of his advisers had been sympathetic to the Allied cause from the beginning. Yet the public's opinion was sharply divided. Many Americans were recent immigrants from the lands of the Central Powers and had emotional ties to them. Wilson found it politically inadvisable to try to intervene in the war until there was some persuasive reason for doing so. In early 1917, several ships carrying American passengers were sunk, giving the pro-Allied party in Washington a dramatic and plausible excuse for intervention.

The American entry into the conflict counterbalanced the collapse of the Russian war effort following the revolutions of 1917 (see Chapter 46) and the terrible losses suffered by the Allies in the Somme River offensive in the summer of 1916. The American war industry and military met the demands placed on them by the exhausted British and French surprisingly rapidly. Men and war supplies from U.S. ports during the winter and spring of 1918 allowed the desperate French to hold on against the final German offensive.

Collapse of the Central Powers

In the fall of 1918, the Central Powers suddenly collapsed. The Austrians asked for peace without conditions in mid-October, by which time the Bulgarians and Turks had already withdrawn. The High Command now advised the kaiser to accept the armistice conditions that President Wilson had presented some weeks earlier, which had been based on the **Fourteen Points** he had enunciated in a speech in January 1918. In summary, the Fourteen Points looked for a "peace without victors," self-determination for the repressed nationalities, disarmament, freedom of the seas to all, and an international body to keep the peace permanently.

On November 9, 1918, the kaiser handed power to a just-created provisional government. Mainly members of the Social Democratic Party, this government immediately asked for an end to hostilities. On November 11, the long bloodbath came to an end. Everywhere, German troops were still standing on foreign soil, and Germany itself had experienced none of the destruction wrought by war on Allied lands. Those facts were to be very important in future days. They allowed the impression that Germany had been defeated not by foreign troops or war exhaustion but by the betrayal of some scheming politicians.

THE HOME FRONT DURING THE WAR

After the outburst of manic enthusiasm that overtook all the belligerent populations in the first weeks of war (and the total failure of the Marxist socialists' hopes for an international general strike), both governments and people came to realize that a long, hard struggle lay ahead. Several steps had to be taken if the demands of this first "**total war**" were to be met. By 1916, all combatants had acted to ensure that civilians would fully support the battlefronts. Among the most important measures they took were the following:

- *Full mobilization of the civilian population.* Unlike all previous wars, World War I did not allow the unarmed masses to remain neutral. Led by Germany but soon imitated by France and the others, the governments insisted that everyone had a role to play in attaining victory. The governments made wholesale use of every type of propaganda available: print media, exhibitions, parades, veterans' speaking tours, and so on. Starting in 1915, they indulged in hate propaganda. Much of it was deliberate lies. All of it was meant to transform the civil population into a productive machine to fight the enemy. Food was rationed, and so were fuel and clothing. All active males aged seventeen to sixty were considered "soldiers in the war for production" and could be ordered about almost like the troops in battle. Even women were pressed into various kinds of unprecedented service as described later.

- *Government control of the economy.* Much more than in any previous war, the governments took command of the entire production system. Labor was allocated by bureaucratic command, and so were raw materials, currency, and imports of all types. New taxes were levied to prevent any excess profit from war contracts. Wage rates, rents, and consumer prices were also controlled by government order. All or almost all of these measures were novelties being tried for the first time.

- *Female labor.* Since millions of men were no longer available to the civil economy after 1914, women were induced to fill their places by various means, including high pay, patriotic appeals, and even coercion. Dozens of occupations that were previously "off-limits" to women were now opened to them, including jobs involving heavy physical labor or considerable authority. Women worked as police, tram drivers, truck drivers, bank tellers, carters, and munitions factory labor and held a host of civil service jobs previously reserved for men.

In this way, a new world of work opportunity opened for women. After some initial resistance by the labor unions,

Aerial Dogfight on the Western Front. Both sides quickly recognized the potential of the airplane for reconnaissance and artillery spotting. Spectacular dogfights between opposing planes were a daily occurrence. *(AKG London)*

women were generally accepted as replacements for men and given more or less equal pay. In particular, their ability to do repetitive industrial jobs exceeded male expectations and earned them new respect as productive employees. In every belligerent country, women made up at least 30 percent of the total civilian labor force by war's end—a far higher percentage than in peacetime.

Social Behavior

As in most wars, the insecurity of life and the desire to accommodate the young men going off to fight resulted in a slackening of traditional standards for both sexes, especially for women. Public demonstrations of affection between the sexes became acceptable even among the respectable classes. Women insisted on access to some form of mechanical birth control as extramarital and premarital sex became more common. Standards of conduct and dress for girls and women became more relaxed. Factory work inspired shorter and less voluminous dresses—it was even possible to show a bit of leg without automatically being considered "fast" by one's peers. Alcohol consumption by both sexes rose sharply despite attempts to discourage it by all governments (which were concerned about worker absenteeism in the war plants).

Female Workers, World War I. The draining off of males to battlefields after 1914 opened the way for millions of women to enter jobs previously unknown to them. In this 1917 photo, female paper mill workers show they can handle heavy labor. *(UPI/Bettmann Newsphotos/Corbis)*

Unlike previous wars, so many men were involved and the casualty rates suffered by most belligerents were so high that the slackening of moral restraint during the war had a profound and permanent effect on postwar society. Marriageable men were in short supply for years afterward, and the imbalance between men and women aged twenty to thirty-five influenced what was considered acceptable sexual conduct. After the war, it proved impossible to put young men and women back into the tight customary constraints of prewar society.

In addition, the many millions of conscripts in the armies had been torn out of their accustomed and expected "slots" in life. For better or worse, many, especially rural youth, never returned to their prewar lifestyles. "How're you gonna keep them down on the farm after they've seen Paree?" went the popular song in the United States. That was a relevant question, and not just for Americans.

Psychic Consequences

Perhaps the most significant of all the consequences of World War I was its effect on the collective European psyche. Three effects in particular stand out in retrospect:

1. *Political disillusionment.* Even while the war was being fought, many were disillusioned of its purpose and the prospects for meaningful victory, and their mood spread despite intensive propaganda campaigns by all the belligerent nations. After 1916, the war became a war of brutal attrition. Basically, both sides were trying to hold on until the other gave up. As the casualty lists lengthened without any decisive victories for either side, the survivors in the trenches and their loved ones back home came to doubt as never before in the wisdom of their political and military leaders. Men were dying by the millions, but what was being fought for remained very unclear. When the war ended, disillusionment with the peace was widespread even among the victorious Allies. Some thought it too mild, others too harsh. Despite Wilson's promises, the losers universally regarded the peace as one of vengeance.

2. *Skepticism toward authority.* The feelings of betrayal and disappointment were especially common among the veterans back from the battlefields. They regarded most military and political leaders as heartless blunderers who had no concern for ordinary people. All authority figures were suspect now: the clergy who had blessed each side's cannons, the diplomats who had not been able to prevent the war, and the teachers and professors who had led the foolish cheering at the outbreak of war. None of the old guides for right and wrong could be trusted.

3. *An end to the religion of science and progress.* Before 1914, most educated Europeans assumed that the next

generation would be able to solve most of the problems that still haunted their own. They believed material and spiritual progress were inevitable. The war ended that naïve optimism for soldiers and civilians alike. They had seen the mutual slaughter end with no clear achievement for the victors and with chaos for the losers. As the spiritual and economic costs to all sides became apparent, many people began to doubt whether there had even been any victors. The faith of the European bourgeoisie in liberalism, parliamentary government, and the triumph of science looked absurd in 1919, as the smoke of battle cleared and the cemeteries filled. Not progress, but revolution and a kind of vicious nihilism (belief in nothing) were on the day's menu.

The dismay was not universal, however. Some believed that a triumphant new day had dawned after the carnage. In the fine arts, a whole series of new ideas, new perspectives, and challenging new theories emerged during or soon after the war. (We will look at them in Chapter 50.) On the political side, many eastern and central European nationalists were gratified at the outcome of the war, for the peace negotiations fulfilled many of their dreams of regional dominance and sovereignty. The feminists were pleased as women gained the vote in almost every country, largely as a result of the promises made by desperate politicians during the war emergency. And the Marxist socialists or communists were filled with surging hopes of a Europe-wide proletarian revolution, brought on by the sufferings of the common people during the conflict and the general rejection of the prewar political order. These hopes were ignited by the success of the revolution in November 1917 and the installation of a Marxist socialist regime in Moscow (see Chapter 46, as well as the Family and Gender Relations box in this chapter).

The Peace Treaties, 1919–1920

The German surrender was based on acceptance of an armistice offered by the Allies in November 1918. A permanent peace arrangement was worked out in Paris during the first months of 1919. The last of five separate treaties with the losing nations (Austria, Hungary, Bulgaria, and Turkey, as well as Germany) was signed in August 1920.

The popular leader of the victorious Allies was clearly the American president Woodrow Wilson. Much of the European public saw him as a knight in shining armor because of his earlier proclamation of "a peace without victors" and his support of "**open diplomacy.**" But Wilson's popularity did not carry into the closed-door negotiations in Paris. He was soon blocked by the other Allied leaders, who were convinced that the president's slogans and plans were totally unrealistic. Georges Clemenceau, the French premier, and Vittorio Orlando, the Italian premier, were opposed to a peace without victors, which to them meant political sui-

cide or worse. David Lloyd George, the British prime minister, was originally a bit more sympathetic to the American, but he, too, turned against Wilson when the president attempted to make his Fourteen Points the basis of the peace. Each of the European leaders had good reasons for rejecting one or more of the points as being inapplicable or foolish, and they combined against the American on their mutual behalf. The points were eventually applied in a highly selective manner or ignored altogether.

The negotiations were conducted in secret (despite Wilson's earlier promises) and involved only the victors. Germany, Austria, Hungary, Bulgaria, and Turkey were each given a piece of paper to sign without further parlays. They were told that if they did not, the war would be resumed. Unwillingly, each signed during 1919–1920. Especially for the Germans, this peace was a bitter pill that would not be forgotten.

Conflicting Principles and Their Compromise

What came out of the Paris negotiations?

Territorially Germany lost 10 percent of its land and its population to the new states of Poland and Czechoslovakia. Alsace-Lorraine, the "Lost Provinces" of 1870, went back to France (see Map 44.4).

Austria's empire was completely dismantled, a process that had become inevitable during the closing days of the war when each of the major components had declared its independence from Vienna and the last Habsburg ruler had abdicated. The new **Successor states,** as they were called, were Austria, Hungary, Czechoslovakia, Poland, and Yugoslavia. In addition, the former Romania was greatly enlarged.

Bulgaria lost some land to Romania, Yugoslavia, and Greece.

Turkey's empire was also completely dissolved, and its Middle Eastern lands were partitioned among the Allies: Jordan, Palestine, Iraq, Syria, Arabia, and Lebanon became French or British protectorates. The Turkish core area of Anatolia came under a military dictatorship led by the ex-officer Mustapha Kemal.

Ethnically Some of Wilson's plans for self-determination became a reality, but others were ignored. The old multinational empires had collapsed and were replaced by states in which one ethnic group had at least a majority. But each of the eastern European Successor states included a large number of minority groups. Some were as much as 30 percent of the total. Czechoslovakia and Yugoslavia were the most vulnerable in this respect. The Germans living within Czechoslovakia made up close to a third of the population, and the Magyars, Germans, Albanians, and others in Yugoslavia were a strong counterweight to the dominant Slavs.

Everywhere, the attempts of the peacemakers to draw up ethnically correct borders were frustrated by strategic,

NICKY AND SUNNY

Over the centuries, the European royal families have had considerably more than their share of unusual characters. But neither Czar Nicholas II of the Romanovs nor his czarina, Alexandra, could be considered eccentric. Both were exceptionally handsome specimens, the czar standing over six feet tall and his wife, the former Princess Alix of Hesse, even more regal in appearance than her husband. With the exception of the hemophilia in Alix's family, neither had a physical or mental handicap of any substance that would present obstacles to a successful reign.

Alix was twenty-two when she was wed in 1894 to the twenty-six-year-old czar, who had just succeeded his dead father on the throne. In accord with the usual terms of a Russian noble wedding, she gave up her Lutheran faith and became a member of the Orthodox Church, taking the name Alexandra Feodorovna Romanov.

Nicholas II admired his father greatly and was determined to rule in a similar, ultraconservative fashion. Unfortunately for him, he did not possess his father's personality. Where Alexander III had been blindly self-righteous, Nicholas was hesitant. Where Alexander had ignored criticism, Nicholas was confused by it. Nicholas regretted the necessity of using his quite efficient secret police (*Okhrana*) against the revolutionaries; Alexander never regretted anything.

Alexandra soon convinced herself that she was the divinely ordained counterbalance to Nicholas's indecision and softness.

For several years after coming to Russia, she remained in the background, content to supervise the rearing of the five handsome children (four girls and a boy) she bore the czar in the years around 1900. But in 1908, a fateful meeting between Alexandra and the corrupt "holy beggar" Rasputin led to changes that eventually rocked the Russian government's very foundations. In a crisis, Rasputin was able, probably through hypnotism, to arrest the hemophilia threatening the life of the young heir-apparent Alexander. From that moment on, the czarina came increasingly under Rasputin's influence; by 1912, "our friend," as Alexandra called him, came to have real power in the appointment of officials and even in domestic policies.

Rasputin's wholly selfish motives served to reinforce Alexandra's natural inclinations in government. In letter after letter to her traveling husband, the czarina encouraged Nicholas to resist all concessions to constitutional government, liberal ideals, and anything smacking of democracy. She despised parliaments and all their works. She is said to have believed that the last truly great Russian leader was Ivan the Terrible; since his time, the rulers of Russia had made entirely too many concessions to the mob and to the rotten intellectuals.

When World War I broke out, Nicholas's government was in serious disarray, caught between the mock constitutionalism adopted after the aborted revolution of 1905 and the basic inclinations of the royal couple and their friends. In 1915, Nicholas left St. Petersburg and assumed direct command of the poorly

---

economic, geographic, or political considerations. The resulting ethnic map between Germany and the new Soviet Russia and between the Baltic and the Aegean Seas looked like a crazy quilt. Protections were formally extended to the minorities by the special treaties that all Successor states were required to sign upon entry into the League of Nations, a new international organization to maintain peace and promote amity among nations (discussed later in this chapter). Chauvinist governments soon were ignoring these protections almost without reprimand, for there was no mechanism to enforce them. National and religious minorities were often made the objects of systematic prejudice throughout the interwar era.

Politically   Germany was tagged with full responsibility for starting the war (**Paragraph 231 of the Versailles Treaty**), which no German could accept as true. This allowed the European Allies (Wilson would not) to claim reparations for wartime damages from the losers. The amount of damages was to be calculated (solely by the victors) at some future date. It eventually was announced as $33 billion (perhaps eight times that in year 2000 value).

The **reparations question** was to be one of the chief bones of contention in international affairs for the next fifteen years. (See the box for excerpts from the Versailles Treaty.)

The defeated states and some of the Successor states became republics, having lost their various royal/imperial rulers during the final days of the conflict. The last Habsburg emperor, Charles II, lived out his days in exile. The Hohenzollern kaiser was gone from Berlin (he died in Dutch exile), and the last Romanov czar died as a hostage of the Bolsheviks in 1918. The Turkish sultan was also gone, deposed by the Kemal government, which chose isolated Ankara rather than cosmopolitan Istanbul as its capital.

The new states of Czechoslovakia, Poland, and the three tiny Baltic states were parliamentary republics. Constitutional monarchies (Yugoslavia, Romania, Bulgaria, Albania) were continued in the Balkans. In all of these entities, democracy was given lip service and often little more.

Diplomatically   The Paris treaties created an organ new in world history, a **League of Nations** with universal membership that was to act as a permanent board of mediation when international conflicts arose. The league was Wilson's

trained and equipped armies. Alexandra, who had come to rely more and more on Rasputin's advice, was left in charge at the palace. The many letters exchanged between the couple (the Nicky/Sunny correspondence) show their deep mutual affection but also demonstrate how weak Nicholas was in contrast to his forceful—and hopelessly wrongheaded—wife. Even the murder of Rasputin by some patriots in December 1916 did not help matters; the rift between the palace and the hastily reconvoked parliament was by now too deep, and the Romanovs' unpopularity too widespread among the people. The March Revolution of 1917 was inevitable (see Chapter 46).

Under the Provisional Government, the royal family was placed under a loose form of house arrest in one of their homes. When the Bolsheviks took command in November 1917, they were moved to what appeared to be a safe haven in a provincial town. But the entire family was massacred by Lenin's personal order in July 1918, when it seemed that anti-Bolsheviks might free them and use them as a unifying force against the Leninists. Nicky and Sunny went bravely to their graves, according to eyewitness reports that have only become available to us in the last few years. All five of the dead children have now been definitively identified through DNA comparisons, though reports of a surviving daughter (Anastasia) circulated for more than half a century.

FOR REFLECTION

Do you think, under the traditional Russian system of absolute power in the hands of the czar, that Alexandra's guidance/interference in government was illegitimate? Or was she filling a vacuum left by Nicholas's dislike for the task?

The Romanov Family in 1905. The czarevich (crown prince) is in his mother Alexandra's arms. (© *The Granger Collection*)

brainchild, and to obtain it, he had been willing to accept all the injuries that had been inflicted on his other ideas by the European statesmen.

As it happened, despite his best efforts, Wilson was not able to sell his fellow Americans on the idea of the league. Partly because of concern about involving the United States indefinitely in Europe's tangled affairs, the U.S. Senate rejected the Paris treaties in 1919. The United States eventually made separate treaties with each of the defeated states, duplicating the Paris treaties with the exception of the League of Nations paragraph.

EVALUATION OF THE TREATIES

Criticism of the peace signed in Paris began as soon as the ink dried. And it came not only from the losing nations but from a good portion of the victors as well. Some of the victors' complaints came from fear that the losers had been left too well off. Many people in France feared that Germany could and would rise once more despite its partial dismem-

berment and the extraordinary costs of reparations. But some of these concerns arose from the conviction that the peace had been guided by vengeance and that all the high-flown principles of the Allied governments had been ignored in the dealings in Paris. After all, the peace negotiated in Paris was *not* a peace without victors, nor did it guarantee self-determination, nor did it end imperialism or carry through many of the other ideals that the wartime Allies had proclaimed.

The most scathing critique came from the young British economist **John Maynard Keynes,** who believed that the Allies had attempted to impose a "Carthaginian peace" (total destruction) on Germany that could not succeed. Keynes had enormous contempt for Wilson, and his opinions soon became fashionable among influential people in both Britain and the United States. Both groups regarded the French and Italians as greedy and stupid in their short-sighted fixation on temporary advantage.

The failure of the Versailles Treaty in the Senate was a major turning point in postwar diplomacy. With no commitment to the League of Nations, America could and did turn its attention to Europe only when and how it chose for

MAP 44.4 Europe after World War I. The war and the peace treaties carved seven entirely new states out of Russia and the Austro-Hungarian empire: Finland, Latvia, Estonia, Lithuania, Poland, Czechoslovakia, and Yugoslavia. Austria and Hungary were separated, and Romania, Italy, and Greece were enlarged.

twenty years. And without the assurance of U.S. support through the league, France was left to face a resurgent Germany by itself in the early postwar era. As a result, the French position became more hard-line than ever and drove France and Britain farther apart at the very time when close coordination was most necessary.

Perhaps the worst aspect of the peace was that it tried to ignore certain political realities. Russia, now under the Bol-

sheviks, was not even invited to send a representative to Paris and so was confirmed as a pariah nation and allowed no access to negotiations that would surely affect its status and future in world affairs. The losing nations, above all Germany, were presented with a fait accompli that was intensely disagreeable to them and that they believed was totally unjust. Neither Germany nor Russia, two of the strongest states in the world, was allowed to join the League

THE VERSAILLES TREATY, 1919

The Versailles Treaty has been argued over since it was signed, portrayed by supporters as a strict but just limitation on the powers of an aggressive Germany to make war, and by its critics as a vindictive act of revenge. Beyond clipping off 10 percent of German prewar territory and population, the treaty's numerous articles went into great detail on topics as widely separate as German citizens' rights in the former African colonies and the supplying of the Allied forces of occupation that were to be stationed temporarily in western Germany.

Some of the more pertinent articles for the status of postwar Germany are cited here:

Article 119. Germany renounces in favor of the Principal Allied and Associated Powers all her rights and titles over her overseas possessions. [These possessions were mainly in Africa, on the China coast and in the southern Pacific islands.]

Article 160. By a date which must not be later than March 31, 1920 the German Army must not comprise more than seven divisions of infantry and three divisions of cavalry.

After that date, the total number of effectives . . . must not exceed one hundred thousand men. . . .*

The Army shall be devoted exclusively to the maintenance of order within the territory and to the control of the frontiers.

The total effective strength of officers, including staffs, must not exceed four thousand. . . .

The German General Staff and all similar organizations shall be dissolved and shall not be reconstituted in any form. . . .

Article 180. All fortified works, fortresses and field works situated in German territory to the west of a line drawn fifty miles to the east of the Rhine shall be disarmed and disassembled. . . .

Article 198. The armed forces of Germany must not include any military or naval air forces. . . .

Article 231. The Allied and Associated Governments affirm and Germany accepts the responsibility of Germany and her allies for causing all the loss and damage to which the Allied and Associated Governments and their nationals have been subjected as a consequence of the war imposed upon them by the aggression of Germany and her allies.

Article 233. The amount of the above damage for which compensation is to be made by Germany shall be determined by an Inter-Allied Commission, to be called the Reparation Commission.[†]

*The 100,000-man limit was quickly gotten around, as part of the more or less open defiance of the Versailles armed force restrictions that took place after 1921. See Chapter 45.

[†]The total reparations figure due from Germany was $33 billion in gold, as presented by the Commission in 1921. Of this, about one-third was eventually paid, mainly in goods. See Chapter 45.

Source: Treaty of Peace with Germany

---

of Nations for several years. Germany was commanded to disarm almost entirely, yet no machinery was in place to enforce that demand, and none was ever created.

The league was supposed to be not only the enforcer of the Paris treaties but also the keeper of the peace for the indefinite future. Yet the weak Secretariat had no armed force at its disposal, and the league members never had any intention of creating one. The league's effectiveness was going to depend on the goodwill of the member governments, and some of those governments were filled with anything but goodwill toward their neighbors.

The 1919 treaties were certainly not as harsh as they have sometimes been painted, but they were certainly a long way from the hopes of the Wilsonians and much of the world's population, who were trying to recover from the "war to end wars." As it turned out, the treaties lasted less than twenty years. What Europe had found in 1919 was not peace, but a short armistice between two terribly destructive wars.

SUMMARY

The system erected by Bismarck to keep France isolated and helpless broke down after the impetuous William II took over the direction of foreign policy in Berlin. Within a decade, the blocs that would contest World War I had been formed. When a Serbian nationalist youth assassinated the heir to the Austrian throne in 1914, a general war broke out that, contrary to expectations, lasted for more than four years.

The battlefields where huge slaughters took place were matched in importance by the home fronts, where governments intervened in unprecedented ways to spur the civilian war effort. Women in particular were affected, as the desperate need for labor impelled politicians in all countries to forget prewar restrictions on female activity.

The war aims of all the combatants were poorly understood and never honestly expressed. As the casualty lists soared, a sense of disillusionment and anger toward established authority spread. Even the so-called victors experienced feelings of revulsion at the disparity between the huge sacrifices demanded and the minimal results gained. This revulsion was strengthened as it became apparent that the "peace without victors" was not to be. The social and psychic consequences of the war were enormous and permanent.

The Paris treaties were despised by the losers and satisfied few of the victors with their compromises between the optimistic visions of President Wilson and the hard realities of international and national politics. The former empires of eastern Europe were dismantled and a group of Successor states established in accord with political and strategic advantage rather than ethnic justice.

TEST YOUR KNOWLEDGE

1. The Bismarckian system of alliances for Germany was meant to
   a. restrain Russia and Austria and to isolate France.
   b. allow Austria to expand to the south and east.
   c. encourage peace with France indefinitely.
   d. force Russia to submit to German eastern expansion.
2. The Triple Alliance of 1882, which was renewed through 1914, was composed of
   a. Italy, France, and Britain.
   b. Austria, Russia, and Germany.
   c. Germany, Austria, and Italy.
   d. France, Britain, and Russia.
3. Which of the following was *not* a remote cause of World War I?
   a. Aggressive imperialism practiced by several nations
   b. An inclination toward the "supreme test" of war among some leaders
   c. The belligerent nationalism of the Balkan states
   d. Racial antipathies between colonies and their home countries
4. A chief novelty brought by World War I was
   a. the use of naval blockades.
   b. the desire of the belligerents to gain postwar economic advantages.
   c. the use of conscripts rather than all-volunteer armies.
   d. the massive intervention of government into the war economy in all nations.
5. Which of the following did *not* accompany the wartime use of females in the economy?
   a. Widening of the gap between the wages paid to male and female labor
   b. A demonstration of the women's ability to do many physical tasks

   c. Less male restrictiveness toward female public activities
   d. Less distinction between "male" and "female" jobs
6. In the spring of 1917, two unrelated events changed the course of the war; they were
   a. the failure of the submarine campaign and the entry of Italy into the war.
   b. the success of the socialist revolution in Russia and the first use of conscripts by France.
   c. the toppling of the czarist government in Russia and the entry of the United States into the war.
   d. the collapse of the French government and the entry of Britain into the war.
7. Subsequently, the most serious complaint against the Paris treaties was that
   a. they failed to punish the losers severely enough to keep them down.
   b. they failed to recognize basic international political realities.
   c. they did not give enough national self-determination.
   d. they ignored ethnic boundaries entirely when redrawing the map.
8. Czarina Alexandra was all but one of the following:
   a. A firm-willed and energetic woman
   b. An opponent of parliamentary government
   c. A politically reactionary character
   d. A reluctant and timid player in Russian governmental affairs

IDENTIFICATION TERMS

Anglo-French *Entente*	Keynes, John Maynard	Paragraph 231 of the Versailles Treaty	Successor states
Anglo-Russian Agreement	League of Nations		total war
Central Powers	open diplomacy	reparations question	Triple Alliance
Fourteen Points			

INFOTRAC COLLEGE EDITION

Enter the search term "World War, 1914–1918" using the Subject Guide.

Enter the search term "Versailles Treaty" using Key Words.

Enter the search term "Nicholas II" using Key Words.

1800–1920
INDUSTRY AND WESTERN HEGEMONY

	Law and Government	Economy
Europeans	After French Revolution, law is based on secular viewpoint rather than religious authority. Government becomes steadily more sophisticated, bureaucracy is universal in advanced societies. Colonial imperialism revives in midcentury and is extended to Asia and Africa by armed force and economic activity.	Industrialization develops throughout this period, with deep regional variations of pace and impacts. By 1920, northern and western Europe are far more industrial than the east and south. Capitalist structures and processes are challenged by newly organized Marxist groups in most countries. Mechanized, factory-based mode of production replaces handwork after Second Industrial Revolution.
West Asians and Africans	Both Muslim and African regions subordinated increasingly to Western imperialism. Islamic states in Middle East reduced to satellites or taken over entirely by Europeans. The Ottomans are helpless to defend their interests, and the empire crumbles. The African interior is penetrated after 1840 by various imperialist missions and by private individuals; the "scramble" for Africa is completed by 1890s.	Economy of West Asia heavily damaged by rise of Atlantic maritime trade and by the continuing decline of Muslim empires. Machine industry is still unknown at end of period, and a huge technological gap has opened between West and Muslim worlds. Africa less affected, partly because of lower levels of international trade and contacts and the lower intensity of European interest in Africa after abolition of transatlantic slaving.
South and East Asians	Tokugawa shogunate and Manzhou dynasty continue in Japan and China throughout most of the period. Both encounter Western penetration and aggression after 1840 but respond in sharply different fashions; the Meiji Restoration in Japan is very successful, but Manzhou China collapses into anarchy. The Mughals in India also fail to deal with West successfully and are eliminated as governors by both Hindus and Europeans. Southeastern Asia and Pacific islands are mainly appropriated by British and French colonists in second half of century.	China begins to feel overpopulation problem in early the part of period, while Japan continues to prosper and urbanize. The urban population and particularly the merchants in both countries gain prestige and some power in government, while the peasantry sinks. After Meiji Restoration (1867), Japan rapidly industrializes and soon is the leading economic power in Asia. China attempts economic reforms but cannot overcome mandarin traditionalism. India enters urban age and selective industrial development as the major British colony.
Americans	After 1825, both North and South Americans are independent peoples pursuing different goals in government and law. North Americans continue their heritage of constitutional and representative government within the republican form; South Americans also adopt republican form but are unable to translate it into effective constitutional democracy. Criollos continue to rule as before over the mestizo majority. The United States pioneers universal enfranchisement of whites and basic democratic forms, while the slavery question has to be decided finally by a bloody civil war.	After unspectacular but steady growth to 1860, North America's industrial economy, propelled by large-scale immigration, explodes after the Civil War. By 1920, the United States is the most potent industrial nation in the world. Latin America receives relatively little immigration and little capital investment until the early twentieth century; industry is minimal, and the overwhelmingly agrarian society is still controlled by a relative handful of wealthy families.

PEOPLES: EUROPEANS, WEST ASIANS, SOUTH AND EAST ASIANS, AMERICANS

Religion and Philosophy	Arts and Culture	Science and Technology
The Enlightenment and French and American Revolutions attack official churches and the link between state and church. Secularist philosophies become widely accepted, and after Darwin, traditional Christianity is seen as antiscientific by many educated persons. A philosophy of progress based on the advance of science becomes popular.	Major achievements in all plastic and pictorial arts. Neoclassicism followed by Romanticism and Realism as leading schools of art and literature. Late nineteenth and early twentieth centuries are especially significant for innovations. Beginnings of mass culture facilitated by rapidly changing technologies.	Physical and biological sciences' spectacular advances are rivaled toward end of this period by innovations in the social sciences. Technological breakthroughs multiply, utilizing new energy sources. Positivism is the ruling philosophy, challenged at end of nineteenth century by destructions of Newtonian physics and antirationalist trends in the arts.
This is the nadir of Muslim religious and cultural vitality. Secularism rejected by traditionalists, who dominate society. Toward end of period some signs of revival via Arab nationalism. Both North and sub-Saharan Africa dominated by Western cultural influences, and Christian missionaries exert significant influence on the non-Muslim areas.	Art forms in both Muslim and animist regions stultify or become imitative of previous work. Still some fine artisanry is produced in Persia, the Ottoman Empire, and the few parts of Africa where the machine products of West have not yet penetrated. Reduced wealth and a sense of impotence contribute to the decline of creativity.	This period is the nadir of Asian science and technology as compared with the West and with North America. Occasional attempts to remedy this lack through modern education are blocked by religious fundamentalism and by the anti-Western feelings of Muslim populace.
Muslims and Hindus peaceably contest for allegiance of northern Indians under Mughal rule, while both religions see the rise of strong minority sects. In China and Japan, Buddhism in several forms blends with Confucian and Dao beliefs (China) and Shintoism (Japan). Neo-Confucian philosophy in China also influences Japanese. Christian missionary efforts in all three countries bring relatively minor returns.	In China and Japan, the later eighteenth century is a high point in both pictorial and literary arts. Luxury items of bronze, porcelain, silk, and jade enjoy enormous prestige in West. Mughal arts are extraordinarily cosmopolitan and reach a high degree of excellence as political powers wane.	Until 1867, Japan continues to lag behind the West but then rapidly closes the gap in science and technology. China resists Western ways and does not develop the scientific outlook or sufficient Western contacts to make much difference. The traditional Muslim and Hindu views of life hinder India's progress in this respect, although a few upper-caste individuals respond to British examples and Westernize.
Secularism triumphs in the founding legal codes of both Americas, although Catholicism is the religion of state in all but name in most of Latin America. In the United States, separation of church and state is taken farther and becomes generally accepted. United States and Canada share in the general debate over the place of religion versus science that Darwin has begun. In Latin America, anticlericalism of most of the criollo intellectuals is carried to an extreme, confronting a clerical establishment that remains feudal.	Both Americas are still essentially dependents of European art forms and fashions throughout most of the period. Only in folk art or in the figure of an occasional eccentric can a native genius be discerned. Signs of rebellion against this are multiplying at the end of the nineteenth century, and the early twentieth century sees a definite change toward cultural autonomy, especially in the United States.	In North America in the later part of the period, the physical sciences and their accompanying technology make major advances, although still lagging the most developed parts of Europe. By 1920, the gaps have been closed in almost all fields. In Latin America, the gaps widen except for the tiny minority of educated and well-off people. A key difference in the two continents can be found in the educational systems and the place of the sciences within them.

EQUILIBRIUM REESTABLISHED: THE TWENTIETH-CENTURY WORLD
1920–PRESENT

Part Six examines the last eight decades of intensifying interaction between the East and West. These years have seen the unilateral military and political authority of the West modified and weakened throughout the non-Western world, while at the same time Western cultural forms have expanded into heretofore-untouched regions. New constellations of power, both military and economic, have arisen, sometimes to fall again, as in the case of communist Russia. East Asia has become a major nexus of development, and South and Southeast Asia have emerged from the shadow of colonial status with vigor and confidence. For Africa and Latin America, the story has not been so positive; both remain on the periphery of power and in an essentially dependent relationship with the West.

In the wake of the disastrous World War I, the central and eastern European nations generally gravitated into various forms of authoritarian government and bade sour farewell to the classical liberal ideals and presumptions about human nature. Fascism in superficially varied forms won popular support and governmental power in several countries.

Britain, France, Scandinavia, and the United States resisted this trend during the interwar period. But after 1930, it was not the liberal democracies, which seemed helpless and exhausted, that seized the imagination and captured the sympathies of many of the world's less fortunate peoples. They turned instead to the novel socioeconomic experiment mounted by the Bolsheviks after seizing power in a war-prostrate Russia. Under Josef Stalin's brutal aegis, traditional Russia was transformed by the Five-Year Plans and the Stalinist aberration of Marxism.

Catalyzed by the lust for revenge and the expansionary dreams of Adolf Hitler and his fellow Nazi visionaries, World War II broke out in 1939. The unnatural anti-Nazi partnership of Britain, the United States, and Stalinist Russia fell apart, however, immediately after the common enemy was overwhelmed. The Cold War began and lasted for a long and frequently terrifying generation of crises. For a time, the world seemed on the verge of becoming divided into the permanent fiefs of the two atomic superpowers, the United States and the Soviet Union. But western Europe, which had seemed finished in the ruins of 1945, got back onto its economic feet with American aid and by the mid-1950s was showing an astonishing vitality.

In eastern Europe, the allegedly revolutionary message of communism was revealed to be no more than the ideologically enlarged shadow thrown by a crude Great Power, rather than a new dispensation for humankind. This impression was was then demonstrated by the abject collapse of the spiritually bankrupt communist regimes at the beginning of the 1990s.

In the non-Western world, the reestablishment of national autonomy went through several stages. In the interwar era the formation of a critically important native intelligentsia was completed. The two world wars revealed the weaknesses of Western governments and generated much support for national self-determination throughout the world. Either by armed force or by moral suasion, the once-subject colonies became newly sovereign nations and took their place proudly in a United Nations organization that had originally been planned as a great power club. A kind of cultural and political equilibrium among the members of an increasingly polycentric world was in the process of being painfully and tentatively reasserted. Using the intellectual and moral resources opened to them by Western ideas and ideals, the other three-quarters of humanity were determined to make themselves heard and listened to as this violent century came to its end.

Chapter 45 opens this part by reviewing the attempt to make World War I comprehensible to its survivors. Chapter 46 is the story of the first generation of Soviet Russian government, from Lenin's coup to the enthronement of Stalin. Chapter 47 puts the totalitarian idea and particularly the Nazi dictatorship under the spotlight. Chapter 48 examines the momentous events in East Asia during the century between 1840 and 1949.

World War II is the subject of Chapter 49, which also looks at the strains that quickly broke down the victorious alliance against the Axis. Chapter 50 departs from our usual political-chronological standpoint to review some outstanding aspects of modern culture. The Cold War between the United States and the Soviet Union is the focus of Chapter 51. This is followed in Chapter 52 by an examination of the decolonizing phenomenon after the war and the staggering problems of the developing countries since the 1950s.

Chapter 53 reviews the history of the countries on the Pacific's western shores and of South Asia since the end of World War II. Africa is the subject of Chapter 54, which looks at the immense difficulties confronting the sub-Saharan states since the euphoria of independence. In Chapter 55, the same problem-oriented survey is made, this time of the Latin American countries throughout the twentieth century. In Chapter 56, the focal point is the Islamic community, particularly the Middle East. The collapse of the Marxist regimes in Europe is analyzed in Chapter 57. Our final chapter, 58, looks at some aspects of contemporary society, both East and West, and summarizes the immediate challenges awaiting in the new millennium.

45

A FRAGILE BALANCE: EUROPE IN THE TWENTIES

I do not worship the masses, that new divinity created by democracy and socialism. . . . History proves that it is always minorities . . . that produce profound changes in human society.

BENITO MUSSOLINI

1919	Weimar Republic established in Germany
1922	Mussolini in power in Italy
1923	France occupies Ruhr/Inflation in Germany
1925	Locarno Pact/Fascist dictatorship begins in Italy
1926	General strike in Britain
1927–1930	Economic and political stability

WORLD WAR I had profound and disturbing effects on Europe. The 1919 peace treaties were resented intensely by the losers and did not satisfy the winners. Most of the eastern half of the continent was in continuous upheaval for several years. Russia gave birth to the world's first socialist society in 1917 and then attempted to export its Bolshevik philosophy by legal and illegal channels. Defeated Germany underwent the world's worst inflation, ruining millions. In Italy, fascism came to power early in the postwar era. International rivalries and rampant nationalism made another conflict appear inevitable. But by the late 1920s, western and central Europe seemed more stable, and the threat of renewed war was more distant. For a few years, it seemed that Europe might weather the crisis that 1914 had set off.

POLITICAL AND ECONOMIC BACKDROP TO THE INTERWAR ERA

The United States and, to a lesser degree, Europe saw the democratization of politics. Political parties had ceased to be defined strictly by class. Some parties broadened sufficiently to include the working class *and* members of the middle class, aristocrats *and* intellectuals. (This process really accelerated in Europe only after World War II.) Property alone no longer dictated political affiliation. The nineteenth-century division into liberal and conservative made less and less sense as cultural experience, secularization, social philosophy, and other intangibles helped shape the political inclinations of a given individual. Any parties that continued to represent a single interest group at either end of the social scale were destined to give way to those that attracted a diverse mix. The only important exception was the Marxists, who claimed a proprietary interest in both progress and the proletariat.

Keynesian Economics

In national economics, the two major innovations of the first half of the twentieth century were (1) the recognition that governments could and probably should intervene to smooth out the roller coaster of the business cycle and (2) the spread and Russianization of Marxist communism.

John Maynard Keynes (1883–1946), the British economist whom we encountered in connection with his harsh critique of the Treaty of Versailles (see Chapter 44), proved to be the most influential economic theorist of the century. He insisted that government had the power and the duty to lessen the violent ups and downs of the business cycle by pumping new money into the credit system in hard times (such as the 1930s). By doing so, the millions of private investors, business owners, and speculators whose collective decisions determined the course of the economy would get the credit they needed to engage in new enterprise. Eventually, the increased tax revenues generated by this stimulus would recompense the government for its expenditures and enable it to prevent inflation from accelerating too rapidly. A growth economy with some inflation was both attainable and more desirable than the nineteenth-century "boom and bust" cycles that had caused much misery.

Keynes's thought did not find many adherents among government leaders before World War II. President Franklin D. Roosevelt instituted some halfhearted measures on Keynesian lines during the Great Depression of the 1930s, but they had relatively little effect. Only after 1945 were Keynes's ideas tried in earnest. Since that time, it has become standard procedure for Western governments to counter the economic cycle by "pump priming" in times of unemployment and deflation. Essentially, this means pouring new government expenditures into the economy at a time when the government's income (taxes) is declining. Since increasing taxes during a recession is politically very difficult, a government that follows Keynes's ideas must either borrow from its own citizens (by issuing bonds or treasury notes) or use its powers to inflate by running the money printing presses a bit faster.

The debate as to whether Keynes's ideas actually work continues. Certainly, governments have often abused Keynesian pump priming for the sake of political advantage. And it probably has contributed to long-term inflation, which hits the lower classes hardest. Since the 1970s, free-market theory and practice have experienced a significant revival—not the untrammeled market that the nineteenth-century liberals expounded, but rather a kind of partnership of business and government in the global markets that technology has opened. Examples include the economic policies of President Ronald Reagan in the United States and Prime Minister Margaret Thatcher in Britain. Most recently, several Southeast Asian nations and the postcommunist governments of eastern Europe have embraced this modified free-market idea. Such theory rejects the Keynesian view in part and accepts the inevitability of some ups and downs in the national economy, while encouraging the "survival of the fittest" in the global markets.

Marxist Successes and the Soviet Chimera

The other major phenomenon of international economics after World War I was the flourishing of the Marxist gospel among both workers and intellectuals in much of the world. That the inexperienced and supposedly incompetent "Reds" of revolutionary Russia (see Chapter 46) could turn the new Union of Soviet Socialist Republics (USSR) into an industrial great power by the 1930s seemed to demonstrate the correctness of Karl Marx's analysis of the world's ailments. What had been done in backward, isolated Russia, many reasoned, must and would be done in the rest of the world.

In the early 1920s, new communist parties, inspired and guided by the Russian pioneers, sprang up in every important country and many colonies. From the sitting rooms where intellectuals worried that they might be left behind "on the ashheap of history" to the docks and mines where painfully idealistic communist workers labored, the Marxist belief spread into all social groups and classes. Even some of the "bourgeois exploiters" saw the light and abandoned their own narrow class interests to join the forces of progress and equity.

During the Great Depression of the 1930s (discussed in Chapter 47), the Marxists made substantial progress not only among the miserable unemployed but also among the many intellectuals and artists who concluded that capitalism had definitively failed, that its day was done, and that the page had to be turned. The Marxist sympathizers delighted in contrasting the millions of out-of-work, embittered men and women in the Western democracies with the picture (often entirely false) painted by Soviet propaganda of happy workers going off to their tasks of "building Socialism in one country" (the Soviet Union) with confidence and dignity.

Germany in the Postwar Era

The new republican government in Berlin came under fire from its first day. It was mainly supported by the Social Democratic Party, which had adopted revisionism in the prewar years. It had the thankless task of attempting to fill the vacuum left by the military and civil collapse at the end of the war. Very soon the government was forced to accept the hated Versailles Treaty, an act that damned it in the eyes of the nationalists and conservatives forever.

Simultaneously, the new government was threatened by Russian-inspired attempts to spread the Bolshevik revolution among the German working classes. In early 1919, the German communists attempted to replicate what their Russian colleagues had done in November 1917. This coup d'état was put down by the German army, which had remained a powerful force under its conservative generals. The generals chose to go along with the despised Social Democrats rather than risk a communist takeover. This tacit partnership lasted throughout the 1920s. Several other attempted revolts inspired by the Communist Party were put down without serious trouble in the early 1920s.

The Effects of Inflation. Money to burn? This German housewife uses worthless currency to light a fire in her cooking stove. In the early 1920s, the value of the German mark had fallen incredibly. *(UPI/Bettmann Newsphotos/Corbis)*

many's total gross national product for five years! This was supposed to be paid in either gold or goods in annual installments over the next several years.

Paying such sums would have utterly bankrupted a wounded Germany, and the government attempted to reason with the French. But the Paris government would not negotiate. In 1921 and 1922, the Germans actually made most of the required payments, but in 1923, they asked for a two-year moratorium (suspension of payment). The French responded by sending troops to occupy Germany's industrial heartland, the **Ruhr** area along the lower Rhine. The occupying force was instructed to seize everything that was produced, mainly iron and coal. Berlin then encouraged the Ruhr workers to engage in massive nonviolent resistance through strikes that effectively shut down all production.

Inflation and Middle-Class Ruin

The Ruhr occupation and shutdown set off the final spiral of the inflation that had afflicted the German Reichsmark since 1919. The inflation ruined many people in Germany's large middle class, which had been the backbone of its productive society for many years. At the height of the inflation, money was literally not worth the paper it was printed on—one U.S. dollar purchased 800 *million* Reichsmarks in late 1923. A few speculators and persons with access to foreign currencies made fortunes overnight, but most people suffered. People who lived on fixed incomes, as did much of the middle class, were wiped out. Many were reduced to begging, stealing, and selling family heirlooms to avoid starving. They would not forget.

The inflation was ended by a government loan in U.S. dollars to the German national bank, which reassured people that the paper currency had something of value behind it once more. At the same time, in 1924, the U.S.-sponsored **Dawes Plan** induced the French to leave the Ruhr, forgo some of the reparations payments, and spread them over a considerably longer time period, if the Germans would resume payments. This agreement held up for a few years (1924–1929), but the psychic and financial damage to the strongest elements of German society could not be made good. They had seen the thrifty turned into beggars while clever thieves became wealthy. They hated the society and government that had permitted such things. From now on, many of them were looking for someone who could impose order on a world that had betrayed their legitimate expectations.

In July 1919, the government adopted a new fundamental law, called the Weimar Constitution after the town where it was framed. The constitution was a high-minded, liberal, democratic document. But the government it established was already so tarnished in the eyes of many that neither the constitution nor the state it created was considered truly German and legitimate. As long as economic conditions were tolerable and the menace of a communist coup remained, the **Weimar Republic** was not in too much danger from the conservatives. But once these conditions no longer prevailed, the danger was imminent.

Reparations

The most painful part of the Paris peace to Germany was the insistence of the French (less so the Italians and British) that Germany bore the full financial responsibility for war damages and therefore must pay reparations. After much delay, the Allies finally presented the full bill in 1921: $33 billion (in 1920 dollars)—approximately the value of Ger-

ITALIAN FASCISM

The peculiar contribution of the first half of the twentieth century to political doctrines was *totalitarianism,* the attempt by a dictatorial government to achieve total control

THEORY OF FASCISM

Benito Mussolini tried for years to avoid spelling out exactly what the aims of his fascist movement were and what the good Fascist Party member should believe. He did this in part because he rejected the restrictions such a definition would place on his freedom of intellectual movement and in part because explaining what fascism stood for was very difficult (though saying what it was against was relatively easy).

In 1932, however, after seven years of dictatorial powers, Mussolini decided that the time had come. An article entitled "The Political and Social Doctrine of Fascism," signed by Il Duce, appeared that year in the Italian national encyclopedia. The following are excerpts from this article, which is as close as Mussolini ever came to attempting a rationale of his movement:

> Fascism was not the nursling of a doctrine worked out beforehand with detailed elaboration; it was born of the need for action and it was itself from the beginning practical rather than theoretical; it was not merely another political party but, even in the first two years, in opposition to all political parties . . . a living movement.
>
> Fascism, the more it considers and observes the future and the development of humanity quite apart from political considerations of the moment, believes neither in the possibility nor the utility of perpetual peace. It thus repudiates the doctrine of Pacifism—born of a renunciation of the struggle and an act of cowardice in the face of sacrifice. War alone brings up to its highest tension all human energy and puts the stamp of nobility upon the peoples who have the courage to meet it. All other trials are substitutes which never really put men into the position where they have to make the great decision—the alternative of life or death. . . .
>
> Such a conception of life makes Fascism the complete opposite of that doctrine, the base of so-called scientific or Marxian Socialism, the materialist conception of history. . . . Fascism now and always believes in holiness and in heroism, that is to say, in actions influenced by no economic motives, direct or indirect. . . .
>
> After Socialism, Fascism combats as well the whole complex system of democratic ideology, and repudiates it, whether in its theoretical premises or in its practical applications. Fascism denies that the majority, by the simple fact that it is a majority, can direct human society; it denies that numbers alone can govern by means of periodic consultations [that is, elections], and it affirms the immutable, beneficial, and fruitful inequality of mankind.

Source: Mussolini and Italian Fascism, ed. S. W. Halperin (Princeton, NJ: Van Nostrand, 1964), citing the Encyclopedia Italiano (1931), vol. 14.

---

over a society's life and ideas. The first example of totalitarian government was **fascism** in Italy. (See the "Theory of Fascism" box for more.)

After the war ended, Italian workers and peasants became extremely discontented with their liberal parliamentary government. At the Paris peace talks, Italy gained much less than it had hoped. The economy was in critical condition because of the sudden end of wartime industrial contracts and the failure to plan for peace. Immigration to the United States, the traditional haven for unemployed Italians, ended when the United States enacted restrictive laws in the early 1920s. The Bolshevik success in Russia was well publicized by the socialists, who soon split into moderates and communists (as did every other European socialist party).

An ex-socialist named **Benito Mussolini** now came forward as a mercenary strikebreaker and bullyboy in the employ of frightened industrialists and landowners. His party took its name from the ancient Roman symbol of law and order, the fasces (a bundle of rods with an ax and protuding blade) carried by the bodyguard of the consul. At first very small, the Fascist Party grew by leaps and bounds in 1921–1922 with the secret support of the antisocialist government itself.

In October 1922, Mussolini pulled off a bloodless coup by inducing the weak King Victor Emmanuel III to appoint him as premier. This was grandiosely termed Mussolini's "**March on Rome.**" For two years, he ruled by more or less legal and constitutional methods. The fascists were only a small minority in parliament, but their opponents were badly divided. Then, in 1924, Mussolini rigged elections that returned fascists to a large majority of parliamentary seats. He proceeded to form a one-party state; by the end of 1926 he had forced the other parties to "voluntarily" disband or had driven them underground (like the communists). Those who protested or attempted resistance were harassed and imprisoned by a brutal secret police. (See the Exercise of Authority box for more on Mussolini.)

Fascist Economic and Social Policies

Fascist economics was a mixture of socialism-without-Marx and laissez-faire. Private property was never disturbed, but the state played a much larger role than heretofore in directing both industry and commerce. Labor was pressed into becoming an arm of the government. For a few years, this system worked reasonably well and avoided or dampened the class struggles that were plaguing much of democratically governed Europe during the 1920s and 1930s.

Until the mid-1930s, Mussolini was genuinely popular. So long as he did not involve Italy in war, a large majority of Italians were fascinated by his undeniable charisma and believed in his efforts to make Italy a major power for the first time. He promised action on behalf of the common people, and to some extent he delivered (*autostrade*—highways—pregnancy leaves, vacation pay, agricultural credit for the peasants, and the like). But his price was always total control of the nation's politics.

BENITO MUSSOLINI
(1883–1945)

The totalitarian state was first attempted in Italy. Its aura of singleminded unity and violence was carefully promoted by ceaseless sloganeering and use of every type of modern propaganda. Coercion of all who resisted was portrayed as the citizen's duty.

The Fascist Party of Italy was the creation of an ex-socialist named Benito Mussolini, the son of a blacksmith, who had obtained an education and become a journalist for socialist newspapers. In 1912, he had become the editor of the major Socialist Party newspaper; from that platform, he called for revolution and regularly denounced all wars in standard Marxist terms as an invention of the capitalists to keep the international proletariat divided and helpless. When World War I broke out, however, Mussolini renounced his pacifism and campaigned for intervention on the side of the Allies; for that, he was kicked out of the Socialists and proceeded to found a nationalist paper. When Italy entered the war in May 1915, he at once volunteered for front-line duty and in 1917 was wounded in action. He returned to his newspaper, *Il Popolo d'Italia,* and spent the rest of the war demanding that Italy find its overdue respect and national glory in combat.

The end of the war found an exhausted Italy deprived of much of what had been promised it by Britain and France in case of victory, by President Woodrow Wilson's insistence on a peace that allowed national self-determination. Mussolini rode the wave of chauvinist reaction and proclaimed himself the patriot who would lead the Italian nation to its just rewards. Appealing cleverly to the whole political spectrum, from the peasants and workers in desperate economic straits, to the ultraconservative landlords of the south, the fascist leader appeared to many Italians as the Man of Destiny.

By mid-1922, the fascist black-shirted "squads" were found in every Italian town, composed of disillusioned veterans, unemployed workers, and the flotsam and jetsam of unstable men seeking to find their place in a radically disrupted postwar era. Strengthened by a stream of undercover subsidies from the right-wing parties, the fascists moved into the vacuum in Italian politics left by the bankruptcy of the wartime government's policies.

The 1920s saw the first application of systematic violence, organized and directed from above, against political opponents in a European state. This violence, aimed at obtaining complete conformity of the populace to the wishes of a semimythic Leader (Il Duce), was promoted by innumerable slogans and distortions of the truth:

"Mussolini is always right."

"Believe! Obey! Fight!"

"Better to live one day as a lion than a hundred years like a sheep!"

"A minute on the battlefield is worth a lifetime of peace!"

"Nothing has ever been won in history without bloodshed."

Mussolini was able to enlist much of the intelligentsia and labor into his campaign for national glory during the 1920s, only to see many of them fall away from his ranks during the next decade as they came—belatedly—to see that the Leader's promises far exceeded his ability to deliver. Thanks to this scepticism, Mussolini was not able to attain total control of his people, but his example was to have a chillingly efficient imitator across the Alps, in Hitler's Nazi Germany. (See Chapter 47.)

Benito Mussolini. Il Duce greets the crowd from his office balcony on the occasion of the fifteenth anniversary of the Fascist Party, 1935. *(Corbis)*

FOR REFLECTION

Do appeals such as those described here still find resonance in contemporary politics? Can you give some examples?

EASTERN EUROPE

In the Successor states, parliamentary democracy and constitutional government were facing rocky roads after the war. By the mid-1930s, almost all of the eastern European states were run by authoritarian dictatorships. Czechoslovakia was the only one that retained its democratic and constitutional nature throughout the 1920s and 1930s. Not coincidentally, it was also by far the most industrially developed, with a vibrant, well-organized working class.

Poland, which had been newly re-created from slices of Germany and Russia, had no democratic tradition and huge economic problems. Its difficulties were compounded by the fact that one-third of its population were not Poles and did not want to be within Polish borders. By 1926, Marshal **Jozef Pilsudski,** a World War I military hero, had brushed aside the quarreling and ineffectual parliament and established a conservative dictatorship.

Hungary had lost more than half of its prewar territory and population, making economic progress impossible even during the relatively prosperous years of the later 1920s. Magyar nationalism was the sole shared rallying point for the socialist left and the chauvinist right. Manipulating the parties and acting as a sort of conservative father figure throughout the interwar era was Miklos Horthy, a former Austro-Hungarian officer who took the title of regent (for the former Habsburg emperor).

In Romania, the prewar monarchy carried over and provided a façade behind which the two chief parties maneuvered for control. Both were corrupt, and neither represented the interests of the vast majority: the impoverished and illiterate Romanian peasantry. Parliamentary government was a series of cynical deals between the parties or between them and the king.

In Yugoslavia, Bulgaria, and Albania, similar constitutional monarchies were in place. Here parties representing all segments of the population were present, but the small urban bourgeoisie exercised parliamentary control in its own interest and against the peasant majority. This manipulation was facilitated by the several divisions of the populace along ethnic and religious lines and by the maneuvers of a clique of "patriots" at the royal palace.

In all the eastern European states, fear of Bolshevism was intense among the governing classes even though the industrial workers were so few and the peasants so conservative as to make the Bolshevik appeal very limited. In most of these countries, the native Communist Party was soon outlawed. Its small, mostly urban memberships were driven underground.

The most pressing problem of the eastern European states was alike from Poland to Albania: their economies were still based on an underdeveloped, subsistence agriculture. Between 60 and 85 percent of the people either were outside the cash economy or derived an erratic and unreliable livelihood from low-paying grain or pastoral agriculture. So long as the world commercial picture was bright and they could export their primary products (grain, hides, lumber), the eastern Europeans could get along. But when the Great Depression of the 1930s began, this picture quickly changed.

Chauvinist nationalism was the universal blight of the eastern Europeans. Every state east of Germany had a large number of minority citizens, most of whom were living unwillingly under alien rule. Many of them (such as the Magyars in Czechoslovakia and Romania, the Germans in the same states and in Poland, and the Austrians in northern Italy) were vulnerable to **irredentism,** the movement to split away from one's present country in order to unite with a neighboring, ethnically similar state. The fact that Wilson's promise of self-determination was only partially fulfilled at Paris aggravated the condition of those who found themselves left outside their national borders. This situation would cause intense political problems throughout the interwar era in eastern Europe.

THE WESTERN DEMOCRACIES

The two major political and social democracies, Britain and France, had several advantages in the 1920s. At least formally, they had been the victors in a war that no European state really had won. Their economies and labor forces had been hard hit by the war, but not so badly as Germany's, and they had not suffered the destructive inflation of the losing powers. They had much deeper democratic roots than the other states, and their governments were committed to constitutional processes.

Britain

But this does not mean that Britain and France did not have serious problems. For Great Britain, the most serious were economic: (1) unemployment and (2) reduced availability of capital. The British labor force suffered severe and chronic unemployment throughout the entire interwar period for many reasons. During the war, the United States had replaced Britain as the financial center of the world. The British empire could no longer be relied on to absorb the products of English mines and factories. Wartime losses had dramatically reduced the earnings of the world's largest merchant marine, and British goods and services were now rivaled or overshadowed by several competitors (notably the United States and Japan) in world markets.

Reduced profits and trade opportunities were reflected in the long decline of capital invested by the British in Britain and around the world. Where once the English led all nations by a large margin in profitable investments such as tramway lines in Argentina, railroads in India, and fishing canneries in Japan, they now often lacked the capital to invest. Furthermore, Britain, which had once been the world leader in technology, had slipped behind the United

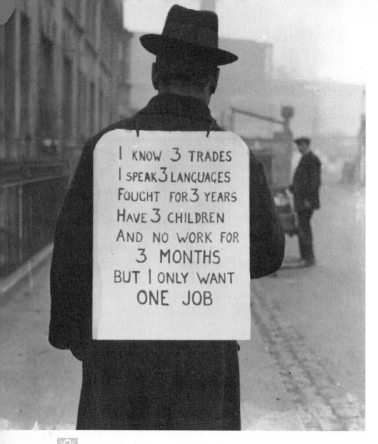

States and Germany in the late nineteenth century and was falling even farther behind now.

These conditions of unemployment and reduced capital explain the long depression that gripped Britain early and permanently during the interwar period, when millions were "on the dole" (welfare). One result was the sudden rise of the **Labour Party,** a non-Marxist socialist group, to second place in British politics. The new party displaced the Liberals and was even able to elect a Labour government in 1924 over its Conservative opponent. Labour carried great hopes, but it had no more success than the Conservatives and Liberals in curing the nation's ills. A union-organized general strike in 1926—the first in a democratically governed country—was also a failure. The unemployment rate stayed around 10 percent. No one had a quick answer to what was ailing Britain.

France

In France, on the contrary, economic problems were not apparent in the 1920s. France had a well-balanced national economy, and German reparations and the return of the rich provinces of Alsace and Lorraine after 1918 helped it. But like the other belligerents, France had been seriously weakened by the loss of 1.5 million of its most productive citizens in the war. And German reparations could only slowly make up for the $23 billion in estimated material damage to French property. France's most serious dilemma was more of psychic and/or social nature: the fear

Unemployment in Britain. Why were the British unable to solve their continuing unemployment problem, which became evident in the early 1920s as the economy contracted after the war? The wartime transfer of overseas markets and financial power to the United States was a major factor, as was the obsolescence of much English industry. *(Woodfin Camp & Associates, Inc.)*

General Strike in Britain. The May 1926 general strike in Great Britain was called by the trade unions to underline their protest at the continued high unemployment rate. One reason it failed to produce results was the flexibility displayed by the many nonstrikers in meeting the challenge, such as that of these office workers shown riding to work in a truck. *(© The Granger Collection)*

of a powerful, vengeance-minded Germany on its eastern border, and the deeply felt conviction that no cause, not even national survival, was sufficient to justify another such bloodletting.

The United States

In the United States, after the passion aroused by the fight over the League of Nations had subsided, a series of conservative Republican administrations (those of Warren Harding, Calvin Coolidge, and Herbert Hoover) had been content to preside over a laissez-faire and prospering domestic economy. Foreign policy questions were overshadowed by the general embitterment over the Europeans' "ingratitude" for U.S. contributions to the victory and the Allies' irritating laxity in repaying their war loans. The extensive social reform crusades of the early twentieth-century Progressives were put aside, and, in Coolidge's words, the business of America once again became business.

Fundamental domestic changes were taking place in this decade, although most were unnoticed at the time. (See the Tradition and Innovation box for more on the Roaring Twenties.) The Second Industrial Revolution was now complete. Corporations and the stock market they generated completely dominated both commerce and industry. The consumer economy became much larger thanks to new techniques such as assembly-line production, retail chain stores, and enormously expanded advertising. Suburban living became popular, and the blurring of traditional class divisions, which had always been an American characteristic, picked up speed. The well-dressed clerk could not be distinguished from the store manager in appearances and tastes. The blue-collar factory hand and the company's stockholders ate the same corn flakes for breakfast and sat in the same grandstand at the baseball game. And the automobile, led by Henry Ford's low-priced and mass-produced creations, swept the country.

The nation as a whole profited greatly from U.S. involvement in World War I, while the population had suffered very little damage compared to the European nations. By the early 1920s, the United States had replaced Britain as the Western Hemisphere's source of technology, trade, and finance and had become the prime creditor nation in world trade. Only a few pessimists were worried by the indiscriminate speculative activity on the New York Stock Exchange.

INTERNATIONAL RELATIONS ON THE EVE OF THE DEPRESSION

The late 1920s saw considerable hope that the lessons of world war had been learned and that war itself would soon become obsolete. After the failure of the Ruhr occupation and the ensuing economic chaos, the French spirit of vengeance against Germany gave way to a more cooperative stance. In 1925, the two countries signed the **Locarno Pact,** which was to be the high-water mark of interwar diplomacy for peace. Locarno allowed Germany to join the League of Nations in return for its promise to accept its frontier with France and Belgium as permanent. Soon afterward, the Soviet Union was also allowed to join the league. In the same spirit, a series of conferences and agreements were held toward the goal of limiting armaments worldwide.

By this time, the U.S. president was the internationally sophisticated Herbert Hoover, a different individual than his immediate predecessors Harding and Coolidge, neither of whom had ever set foot in Europe. With Washington's tacit blessings, the flow of investment money from the

Lindbergh Prepares for Takeoff. Colonel Lindbergh became an instant—if reluctant—hero with the first solo flight across the Atlantic in 1927. He is shown here just prior to takeoff in his all-metal monoplane, the *Spirit of St. Louis.* (Hulton-Deutsch Collection/Woodfin Camp)

THE ROARING TWENTIES

A large part of the reason for looking at World War I as a significant break between epochs of modern history is to be found in changes in popular culture. In literature, entertainment, apparel, communication media, social customs—in short, in most all facets of interpersonal and intergroup relations—the world of the late 1920s was very considerably changed from that of 1914. A few examples follow (and others will be dealt with in Chapter 50).

In transport and communication, the airline industry was transformed in a space of fifteen years from the manufacture of a few dozen fragile "kites" for daredevil backyard pilots to the production of hundreds of craft large enough to carry first mail, then passengers thousands of miles on a regular schedule. Telephony was limited to the large businesses and commercial users in a handful of Western countries prior to the war; residential service was quite unusual outside the larger cities. By 1925 in the United States (which led the world in this area, as in many other technical advances), the business without a phone was a rarity, and the telephone lines were rapidly taking the place of the telegraph everywhere.

It was more in the tone and content of literature than in its forms in which the changes announced themselves. The more profound analysis of motivation, the much franker treatment of gender relations, the use of novel technique, and many other breaks with tradition marked both the European and the American books of the twenties. Disillusionment was a frequent note except in the numerous ranks of the communists and their fellow travelers, who affected to see a new world coming.

Entertainment media became both more varied and more commercialized. The advent of the radio was in part responsible, as was the great popularity of the cheap phonograph record for musical reproduction. Professional sports experienced a steady upsurge in their spectator figures. The reduction of the work week allowed an increase in time for hobbies and vacation trips, though this trend, too, was markedly more apparent in the United States than in Europe. Most important was the coming of the movie theater, a topic looked at in detail in a later chapter.

Attention has been drawn in the previous chapter to the loosening of the restrictions on female attendance in public places and events during the wartime years. This relaxation continued in the 1920s, evincing itself not only in allowances for women to enter almost any establishment without the previously mandatory escorting male, but also in permissible language, forms of address, dress, and many types of social manners. In concrete terms, the young lady of, say, 1928 in Berlin, London, or Paris might appear unescorted in a hotel bar, greet and be greeted by some of the male patrons affectionately, order and drink a martini cocktail while smoking a cigarette, and then proceed on her way in her stylish outfit of knee-length silk and high heels, without anyone imploring the manager to cease allowing his premises to be abused by "loose women."

FOR REFLECTION

Women are supposedly the guardians of public morality. Is this true in your experience? Or is it another example of male delusion about the other sex?

United States to Europe, particularly Germany, was ever increasing as the profits (on paper) from speculating on the bubbling stock market made many Americans feel rich.

After 1928, Europe appeared to be en route to full recovery from the economic effects of the war. The Dawes Plan had helped reestablish German prosperity, and the Germans could thus manage their reduced reparations payments to France and Britain. These countries could then begin to repay the large loans they had received from the United States during the war.

For four years, this circular flow of money worked well for all concerned. The booming German economy received a great deal of private U.S. investment funds. The eastern European agricultural products were bought in large quantities by the western European industrial nations. Except in Britain, unemployment was under control.

Even the West's hostility and fear toward Bolshevism cooled, as the Russians ceased to trumpet their confident calls for world revolution and started to behave like reasonable, if somewhat unorthodox, business partners in world trade. It was indicative that by the later 1920s, Soviet diplomats had given up the workers' caps and boots they had donned ten years earlier and returned to formal dress of top hat and tails.

The fear that European workers would gravitate en masse toward Bolshevik Russia had proved to be exaggerated. Much communist energy was wasted in fighting the socialists who had refused to join the Communist (Third) International, founded and headquartered in Moscow. Even conservative politicians began to look upon the communists, whether in Russia or at home, as a less urgent danger than they had originally appeared. In 1929, European international relations seemed to be in a healing mode. The wounds of war were closing, and good economic times allowed old enemies to think of one another as potential partners. Hope was in the air.

SUMMARY

In the immediate postwar years, the political situation was extremely unstable in central and eastern Europe, with Russian Bolshevism seeking to expand westward and a series of new states without constitutional stability groping for survival. The Weimar Republic of Germany began its history encumbered with the guilt of signing the Versailles Treaty and presiding over a spectacular inflation, two handicaps that it could never overcome in the eyes of many citizens. In Italy, a demagogue named Mussolini bluffed his way to governmental power in 1922 and then proceeded to turn his country into a quasi-totalitarian state.

In the Western democracies, the search for economic recovery seemed to be successful in France, but less so in a subtly weakened Britain. The United States immediately withdrew from its European wartime activity and devoted itself to domestic affairs under conservative Republican administrations. It enjoyed general prosperity partly as a result of taking the role Britain had vacated in world financial and commercial affairs.

By the end of the decade, international conferences had secured partial successes in disarmament, border guarantees, and pledges of peace. The spread of Bolshevism seemed to have been checked, and the Russians became less threatening. As the decade entered its last year, most signs were hopeful for amity and continued economic progress.

TEST YOUR KNOWLEDGE

1. The postwar German state was the product of
   a. a communist coup following the military defeat in the war.
   b. the Allied Powers' intervention and postwar occupation.
   c. a liberal constitution written by the Social Democrats and their allies.
   d. a generals' dictatorship imposed to prevent an attempted communist takeover.

2. The unofficial name of the government set up in Germany after World War I was the
   a. Nazi state.
   b. Weimar Republic.
   c. Fascist Republic.
   d. Bolshevik Republic.

3. The nation that suffered most dramatically from inflation after World War I was
   a. France.
   b. Russia.
   c. Germany.
   d. Britain.

4. The Dawes Plan was a
   a. proposal by U.S. financiers to assure Germany's recovery and payment of reparations.
   b. U.S. government plan to carry through the punishment of Germany.
   c. British-French scheme to assure German payment of reparations.
   d. U.S. government plan to try to get the country out of the Great Depression.

5. Mussolini made his political debut as
   a. a communist organizer in postwar Italy.
   b. a strikebreaker.
   c. a military officer.
   d. a liberal parliamentary delegate.

6. The only eastern European state that retained a democratic government during the 1930s was
   a. Romania.
   b. Hungary.
   c. Czechoslovakia.
   d. Poland.

7. The nation that had the most deep-rooted unemployment problem in postwar Europe was
   a. Great Britain.
   b. Germany.
   c. France.
   d. Italy.

8. The high point for hopes of a lasting European peace was
   a. the signing of the Locarno Pact in 1925.
   b. the removal of the French from the Ruhr in 1923.
   c. the entry of Germany into the League of Nations.
   d. the diplomatic recognition of the Soviet Union by France and Britain in 1921.

IDENTIFICATION TERMS

Dawes Plan

fascism

irredentism

Labour Party

Locarno Pact

March on Rome

Mussolini, Benito

Pilsudski, Jozef

Ruhr

Weimar Republic

 # INFOTRAC COLLEGE EDITION

Enter the search term "Weimar Republic" using Key Words.
Enter the search term "Mussolini" using Key Words.

Enter the search term "fascism" using the Subject Guide.

46

THE SOVIET EXPERIMENT TO WORLD WAR II

*I*t is true that liberty is precious—so
precious that it must be rationed.

VLADIMIR LENIN

ONE OF THE CHIEF by-products of World War I was a
radical experiment in social organization that was destined
to last in Russia for seventy-five years. In 1917, the Russian
Marxists took advantage of the disruptions and weaknesses
caused by the war to carry out revolution. The first socialist state, the Union of Soviet Socialist Republics (USSR),
was born under the watchful eye of a handful of ambitious,
visionary men around Vladimir Lenin. Their communist
government, which proudly called itself "the dictatorship
of the proletariat," was a frightening phenomenon to most
of the rest of the world. But everywhere some men and
women were inspired by its example and wished to imitate
it in their own countries during the interwar period.

THE MARCH REVOLUTION, 1917

What events led up to the establishment of this new government? By 1917, the imperial government of Russia had
been brought to the point of collapse by the demands of total war. Twelve years earlier, an aborted revolution had finally brought a constitution and the elements of modern
parliamentary government to the Russian people. But the
broadly democratic aims of the Revolution of 1905 had
been frustrated by a combination of force and guile, and
the czar maintained a tight grip on the policymaking machinery as the war began.

In the opening years of World War I, the Russians suffered huge casualties and lost extensive territory to the Germans and Austrians. Their generals were the least competent
of all the belligerents. The czar's officials were unable or unwilling to enlist popular support for the conflict.

As the wartime defeats and mistakes piled up, the maintenance of obedience became impossible. By spring 1917,
the food supply for the cities was becoming tenuous, and
bread riots were breaking out. Finally, the demoralized garrison troops refused to obey orders from their superiors.
With no prior planning, no bloodshed, and no organization, the **March Revolution** came about simply by the unpopular and confused Czar Nicholas II abdicating his
throne. A committee of the *Duma* (the parliament), which
had been ignored and almost powerless until now, took
over the government of Russia. The Duma committee,
which called itself the **Provisional Government,** intended
to create a new, democratic constitution and hold free elections as soon as possible.

But the new government was a weak foundation on which to attempt to build a democratic society. It had no mandate from the people but had simply appointed itself. Leadership soon passed into the hands of Alexander Kerensky, a moderate, non-Marxist socialist who had little understanding of the depths of the people's antiwar mood. The peasants—about 80 percent of the population—were desperately tired of this war, which they had never understood and which they hated because it was devouring their sons. If peace were not soon achieved, they would refuse to grow and ship food to the cities, and Russian government of any kind must collapse. But Kerensky thought that Russia dare not make a separate, losing peace despite the ominous tide of discontent. He believed that only a victorious peace would allow the newborn Russian democracy to survive, and he was therefore determined to keep Russia in the war.

THE BOLSHEVIKS

The people's war weariness opened the way for the uncompromising Marxists, or **Bolsheviks,** led by the brilliant tactician **Vladimir Lenin** (1870–1924). Before the spring of 1917, Lenin had been a refugee from his native land, living in Swiss and German exile for twenty years, plotting incessantly for the triumph of the socialist revolution. He was the leader of a movement that had perhaps 100,000 members and sympathizers in the entire Russian imperial population of about 160 million.

Under Lenin's aegis, the Bolsheviks had changed Marx a great deal to make his ideas fit the Russian realities of the early twentieth century. Lenin insisted on a full-time, professional leadership supervising a conspiratorial, clandestine party. Unlike Marx, he believed that such a party could hasten the coming of the revolution and that the peasantry could be led into revolutionary action. Lenin thought that in a country such as Russia, where the urban proletariat was at most about 5 percent of the population in 1910, only a movement that galvanized peasant discontent stood a chance of success. Lenin was clear that the vague dictatorship of the proletariat that Marx had talked about would quickly become a dictatorship of the Bolsheviks. Within that party, the small group around Lenin, called the Central Committee, would rule in fact.

The Bolshevik leader returned to Russia immediately after the March Revolution, when the new government allowed total freedom to all political groups. Through the summer of 1917, Lenin and the Provisional Government under Kerensky dueled for power. The chosen arena was

Lenin in His Tomb. Embalmed at his death in 1924, the founder of the USSR rests in an elaborate mausoleum on Red Square in the heart of Moscow. Given an annual "touch-up," the body can remain in good condition for centuries, but it may soon be relocated to the Ulyanov family plot in a St. Petersburg cemetery. (*AKG London*)

LENIN'S SPEECH TO THE SOVIET

Immediately after the Bolshevik revolution of 1917 in Russia, Vladimir Lenin outlined his party's priorities and longer-range goals in a speech to the Petrograd (St. Petersburg) Soviet, which was now under the control of the Bolsheviks and their sympathizers. The uncompromising directness is typical of Lenin's speaking style. He was at this time entirely confident that the workers in the rest of the combatant nations would join Russia in revolt against their capitalist governments and that peace would come because the workers would refuse to fight their proletarian brothers any longer.

Comrades! The workmen's and peasants' revolution, the need of which the Bolsheviks have emphasized many times, has come to pass.

What is the significance of this revolution? Its significance is, in the first place, that we shall have a soviet government, without the participation of bourgeoisie of any type. The oppressed masses will of themselves form a government. The old state machinery will be smashed into bits, and in its place will rise a new machinery of government created by the soviet's organizations. From now on there is a new page in the history of Russia, and the present, third Russian revolution [that is, counting the abortive 1905 uprising] shall in its final result lead to the victory of socialism.

One of our immediate tasks is to put an end to the war at once. But in order to end the war, which is closely bound up with the present capitalistic system, it is necessary to overthrow capitalism itself. In this work we shall have the aid of the world labor movement, which has already begun to develop in Italy, England, and Germany.

A just and immediate offer of peace by us to the international democracy will find a warm response everywhere among the international proletariat masses. In the interior of Russia a large part of the peasantry has said: Enough playing with the capitalists! We will go with the workers!

We shall secure the confidence of the peasants by one decree, which will wipe out the private property of the landowners. The peasants will understand that their only salvation is in union with the workers.

We will establish a real control by labor in production. We have now learned to work together in a friendly manner, as is evident from this revolution. We have the force of mass organization which has conquered all, and which will lead the proletariat to world revolution.

We should now occupy ourselves in Russia in building up a proletarian socialist state.

Long live the world-wide socialist revolution!

FOR REFLECTION

Why could Lenin think at this juncture that other nations' proletariats would join with the Russians in revolution against their capitalist governments? Why would the "peasants understand that their only salvation is in union with the workers"?

---

the *soviets* (councils) of workers and soldiers, formed all over Russia in the weeks following the March Revolution. Chairing the supremely important St. Petersburg soviet was **Leon Trotsky** (1879–1940), Lenin's dynamic second-in-command, who was able to lead the body into the Bolshevik camp.

In the short term, the fate of the country necessarily would be determined by which group could secure the allegiance of the armed forces. The imperial army had been disintegrating since the spring, with mass desertions commonplace. The peasant soldiers hated the war, and a wide cleft had opened between them and their middle- and upper-class officers. Into this rift Bolshevik pacifist and revolutionary propaganda was pouring and finding a ready audience.

Kerensky decided to accede to the demands of his hard-pressed allies in the West and gamble everything on an ill-prepared summer offensive. This was soon turned into a rout by the Germans' counterattack. By September, the enemy was at the gates of St. Petersburg, and the army was visibly collapsing. The cities were on the point of mass starvation, and the peasants were taking the law into their own hands and dividing up the estates of their helpless landlords, much as their French counterparts had done a century and a quarter earlier.

THE OCTOBER REVOLUTION

By mid-October, Lenin had convinced a hesitant Central Committee that the time for revolutionary action was at hand. He insisted that the brilliantly simple Bolshevik slogans of "All power to the Soviets" and "Land, bread, peace" would carry the day despite the tiny number of Bolsheviks.

On the evening of October 26, Old Style (November 6 by the modern calendar), the Bolsheviks used their sympathizers among the workers and soldiers in St. Petersburg to seize government headquarters and take control of the city. The **Great October Revolution** of Soviet folklore was in fact a coup d'état that cost only a few hundred lives to topple a government that, as Lenin had insisted, had practically no support left. In the next few weeks, Moscow and other major industrial towns followed St. Petersburg by installing Bolshevik authorities after varying amounts of armed struggle in the streets. (See the Exercise of Authority box for Lenin's speech to the Soviet after the revolution.)

What about the 80 percent of the population outside the cities? For several months, the countryside remained almost untouched by these urban events, with one exception: in the villages, the peasants took advantage of the breakdown of government to seize the land they had long craved from the hands of the nobles and the church. For the peasants, the redistribution of land from absentee landlords to themselves was the beginning and the end of revolution. Of Marxist theory about collectivization of agriculture, they knew and wanted to know nothing at all.

Lenin moved swiftly to establish the Bolshevik dictatorship, using both armed force and the massive confusion that had overtaken all levels of Russian government after October. By December, large economic enterprises of all types were being confiscated. The first version of the dreaded political police, the **Cheka,** had been formed and was being employed against various enemies. The remnants of the imperial army were being bolshevized and turned into a weapon for use against internal opponents.

CIVIL WAR

Against heavy opposition from his own associates, Lenin insisted that Russia must make immediate peace with the Germans and Austrians. His rationale proved to be correct:

a civil war against the many enemies of Bolshevism was bound to come soon, and the party could not afford to be still fighting a foreign foe when it did. In March 1918, the harsh **Treaty of Brest-Litovsk** was signed with the Central Powers. The collapse of the Central Powers eight months later made this treaty a dead letter. By that time, the Bolshevik "Reds" were engaged in a massive and very bloody civil war, which was to last two and a half years and cause about as many Russian deaths as had occurred in World War I.

The Reds won this conflict for several reasons. They were far better organized and coordinated by a unitary leadership than were their opponent "Whites." Despite his total lack of military experience, Lenin's colleague Trotsky proved to be an inspiring and effective commander in chief of the Red Army, which he created in record time. The Reds had a big advantage in that they controlled most of the interior of European Russia, including the major cities of St. Petersburg and Moscow and the rail networks that served them (see Map 46.1). The opposition armies, separated by vast distances from one another, were often at cross-purposes. Moreover,

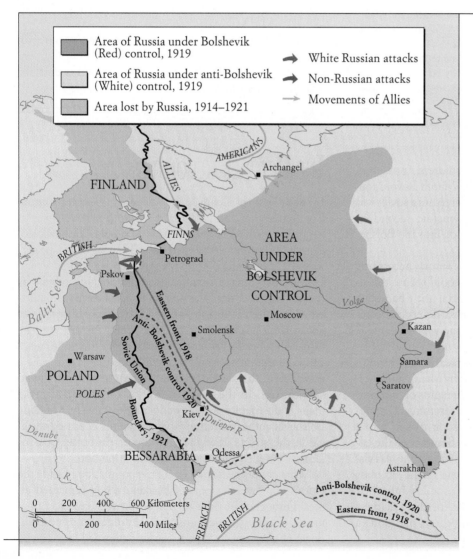

MAP 46.1   Russian Civil War, 1918–1921.   This map of the civil war shows the advantage of holding the interior lines of transport and communication, as well as the two leading cities (Moscow and St. Petersburg). The White armies and their foreign helpers were widely separated geographically and never had unified command or even coordination. By the summer of 1920, the Reds had defeated the Whites and were in control of most of the country.

the Whites were decisively defeated in the propaganda battles, in which the Reds played up the White generals' multiple links with both the old regime and the landlords. Personal rivalries also damaged the White leadership.

The intervention of several foreign powers in the civil war also became a Red asset, though it was intended to assist the Whites. In early 1918, fearing that the Bolsheviks would take Russia out of the war and that matériel meant for the old imperial army would fall into enemy hands, the French and British sent small forces into Russia. Inevitably, these forces clashed with the Reds, and the foreigners (including a small U.S. detachment in the far north) began actively assisting the Whites. Overall, the foreign intervention provided very little practical help for the Whites but gave the Leninists an effective propaganda weapon for rallying support among the Russian people.

Economic Revival and Internal Struggles

By the summer of 1921, the Bolsheviks were close enough to victory that they abolished their coercive "War Communism." War Communism was the label for rule at the point of a gun that Lenin had employed since 1918 through the Red Army and the Cheka. It had sustained the Bolshevik rule, but only at great costs. Along with terrible famine and the disruptions of civil war, it had reduced the Russian gross national product to about 20 percent of what it had been in 1913!

In place of War Communism, Lenin now prescribed the **New Economic Policy (NEP),** which encouraged small-scale capitalist business and profit seekers, while retaining "the commanding heights" of the national economy firmly in state hands. By this time, state hands meant Bolshevik hands. The Communist Party of the Soviet Union (CPSU), headed by Lenin and his colleagues, was in sole control of both economic and political affairs. By 1922, all other parties had been banned, and Russia was fast becoming a totalitarian state.

After being wounded in an attempted assassination, Lenin suffered a series of strokes starting in 1922. Power in everyday affairs was transferred to an inside group of the Central Committee, called the *Politburo* (Political Bureau). This group included Lenin's closest colleagues. Trotsky was the best known and seemed to hold the dominant position within the party's inmost circle. But when Lenin died in January 1924 without naming anyone to succeed him, a power struggle was already under way.

Stalin as a Young Bolshevik. These police file photos were taken in 1912 or 1913 and show the thirty-four-year-old Stalin after one of his several arrests as a suspected revolutionary. (*Woodfin Camp & Associates, Inc.*)

LEON TROTSKY
(1879–1940)

Lev Davidovitch Bronstein, better known by far as Leon Trotsky, was born to a prosperous Jewish farmer in southern Ukraine in 1879. Like many other Russian revolutionary figures, Trotsky's career as a radical challenger of the status quo began very early, while he was in high school in Odessa. In 1898, he underwent the traditional coming-of-age ceremony for eastern European reformers: arrest by the political police.

Exiled to Siberia in 1900, Trotsky escaped two years later and fled abroad, where he met Vladimir Lenin and other leaders of the budding Russian Marxist movement. Even in that highly intellectual and aggressive company, young Trotsky stood out by force of character and self-assurance. Opposed to Lenin's version of Marxism, Trotsky later adopted an independent standpoint of his own, refusing to submit to the discipline Lenin demanded of all his followers but not condemning Bolshevism outright. During the short-lived Revolution of 1905, Trotsky had momentary power as chairman of the Petersburg Soviet of Workers. He again was exiled and again escaped to Europe in 1907.

Still opposed in principle to Bolshevism during the early years of the war, Trotsky changed his mind after the March 1917 revolution. He now fell under Lenin's powerful personality and joined him as his right-hand man. Trotsky was second only to Lenin in preparing the October Revolution that brought them to power. After a brief stint as commissar for foreign affairs, Trotsky then took over as commissar for war in 1918. His brilliance as a strategist and his ruthlessness were major reasons for the Reds' victory in the civil war that wrecked Russia between 1918 and 1921.

In the struggle for succession to Lenin, which began as early as 1922, Trotsky seemed to most to be the inevitable choice. But Stalin and others were determined this would

Leon Trotsky. *(Bettmann Archive/Corbis)*

not happen and proved to be both less scrupulous and more in tune with party members' thinking than Trotsky. One step after another forced the civil war hero out of the Central Committee, then out of the commissariat for war, then out of the party, and finally, in 1929, into foreign exile. In 1940, after several moves, Trotsky was murdered on Stalin's orders in his final refuge in Mexico.

A tiny, unprepossessing figure with thick glasses, Trotsky was possessed of almost incredible energy and single-mindedness. He was totally uncompromising and totally convinced of his own correctness in things political. Like his hero Lenin, he never allowed what the Bolsheviks called "bourgeois sentiment" to interfere with his dedication to a communist triumph. Again like Lenin, his force of personality attracted a clique of followers who were entirely devoted to him. But he lacked the organizational skills of his master and was never interested in the day-to-day administrative detail.

Trotsky became a hero to some because of his unremitting and devastating criticism of Stalin's dictatorship, at a time—the 1930s—when few other reformers were willing to see just how repressive Stalin's regime had become. Trotsky believed, as Mao Zedong would later, that bureaucracy was the great danger to revolutions, and he condemned it among communists as well as capitalists. He was a steadfast adherent of "permanent revolution" and the opponent of Stalin's "socialism in one country." He believed that if the communist revolution did not spread, it would inevitably degenerate under a dictator such as Stalin. Trotsky's attempt to found an anti-Stalin Fourth International did not get very far, but his charisma and his vivid writings about the Russian Revolution of 1917 have guaranteed him a place in the pantheon of twentieth-century revolutionaries.

One of Trotsky's rivals was **Josef Stalin** (1879–1953), a tested party worker since early youth. He was esteemed by Lenin for his administrative abilities and hard work. At the end of his life, however, Lenin had turned against Stalin because of his "rudeness" and his contempt for others' opinions.

Lenin was too late in reaching this conclusion: Stalin, as the party general secretary (administrator), had already ce-

mented his position. Brilliantly manipulating others, Stalin was able to defeat first Trotsky and then other contestants for Lenin's position in the mid- and late 1920s. By 1927, he was the leader of the majority faction in the Politburo and thus of the Communist Party. By 1932, Stalin was becoming dictator of the Soviet Union's entire public life. By 1937, he was the undisputed master of 180 million people. (See the box for more on Trotsky.)

Under the NEP, both the agrarian and the industrial economy had made a stunning recovery from the lows of the early postwar era by late 1928. The peasants on their newly acquired private farms were apparently content. Industrial production exceeded that of 1913. To foreign businessmen interested in Russian contracts, it appeared that Bolshevism's revolutionary bark was much worse than its bite. One could, after all, do good business with the Soviets. But only a few months later, the entire picture changed.

THE FIVE-YEAR PLANS

At Stalin's command, the **First Five-Year Plan** of 1929–1933 was adopted. It would transform the Soviet Union in several ways. The "Second Revolution" had started.

Russia was still an overwhelmingly rural, agrarian society, backward in every way compared with western Europe or the United States. Throughout the 1920s, some party members had been discontented with the "two steps forward, one step back" concessions of the NEP. In their view, the good proletarian workers in the cities were still at the mercy of the "reactionary" peasants who fed them. Very little additional investment had been made in industry, the key to a socialist society.

In the fall of 1928, many of the more prosperous peasants decided to hold back their grain until they could get better prices in the state-controlled markets. Stalin used this "betrayal" as a reason to start the drive for agricultural collectivization and rapid industrialization. It would go on at a breathtaking pace until World War II brought it to a temporary halt.

Stalin's Five-Year Plan was intended to kill three major birds with one enormous stone. The age-old resistance of private landholders to any kind of government supervision would be broken by massive pressure to collectivize. Then, a huge increase in investment would be allocated to heavy industry and infrastructure (such as transportation and communication systems) to modernize the backward society. Third, the organization and efforts required to achieve the first two goals would enable the total integration of the citizenry into the CPSU-controlled political process.

Agrarian Collectivization

In 1929, Stalin began his **collectivization campaign** as a way to "win the class war in the villages"—that is, the alleged struggle between the poor peasants and those who were better off. The richer peasants (*kulaks*) were to be dispossessed by force. The poorer peasants were to be forced onto newly founded collective farms under party supervision.

As many as 10 million peasants are estimated to have died in the collectivization drive between 1929 and 1933, most of them in an artificially caused famine. Determined to break the peasants' persistent resistance, Stalin authorized the use of the Red Army as well as armed party militants against the villages. Millions were driven off their land and out of their houses and condemned to wander as starving beggars. Their former land, machinery, and animals were turned over to the new *collectives*. These enormous farms, which were run like factories with wage labor by party bosses, proved to be very inefficient, in part because the peasants heartily disliked their new situation and felt little responsibility and even less incentive to produce. Throughout the Soviet Union's history, agriculture remained a major weakness of the economy.

The collectivization struggle left deep scars, and its costs were still being paid a generation later. Stalin rammed it through because he believed it was essential if the Soviet Union were to survive. The ignorant, conservative peasants must be brought under direct government control, and their numbers reduced by forcing them into a new industrial labor force. Both these goals were eventually reached, but at a price that no rational economist could justify.

Industrial Progress

Stalin's second goal was rapid industrialization. Here again, the costs were very high, but their justification was easier. Soviet gains in industry between 1929 and 1940 were truly impressive. In percentage terms, the growth achieved in several branches of heavy industry and infrastructure was greater than any country in history has ever achieved in an equivalent period—about 400 percent even by conservative estimates. Whole industrial cities rose up from the Siberian or Central Asian plains, built partly by forced labor and partly by idealists who believed in Stalin and in communism's vision of a new life. Throughout the economy, "fulfilling the Plan" became all-important. Untouched by free-market realities and constraints, the Soviet managers plunged ahead in a wild race to raise total production.

The new industry turned out capital goods, not consumer items. Consumer goods such as clothes and baby carriages became more and more difficult to obtain, and their prices rose ever higher throughout the 1930s. When a suit of clothes could be found, it cost the equivalent of four months' wages for a skilled worker. Items such as refrigerators, automobiles, and washing machines were out of the question. Even basic food had to be rationed for a while because of the drop in production caused by collectivization. It is testimony to the extraordinary capacity of the Russian people to suffer in silence that so much was accomplished at such high costs with so little reward for those doing it.

The uprootings and hardships caused by the industrialization drive in the 1930s were nearly as severe as those caused by collectivization in the countryside. And much of the work on the new mines, canals, logging operations, and other projects was performed by Stalin's slave laborers. By conservative estimates, fully 10 percent of the 1930s Soviet gross national product was produced by prisoners of the NKVD (one of the several successive names for the Soviet political police).

JOSEF STALIN, HUSBAND AND FATHER

One of the stranger occurrences of twentieth-century history was the appearance of a Soviet Russian citizen at the New Delhi, India, embassy of the United States in 1966, asking for political asylum. The Russian's name was Svetlana Alliluyeva Stalin; she was the only surviving child of the Soviet dictator, Josef Stalin. At age forty, she had decided she had had enough of life in the country her father had formed.

Svetlana Stalin was born in 1926 to the second wife of Stalin, Nadezhda Alliluyeva, as her second child. Nadezhda (Nadja) had been only seventeen when she married, while Stalin was a thirty-nine-year-old widower. He had married a fellow worker in the underground revolutionary movement in 1905, with whom he had one son, Jakov, before her untimely death in 1907. As a harried and secretive Bolshevik revolutionary and political exile in Siberia, Stalin had had little time or opportunity to found a second family. But in the aftermath of the successful coup d'état of November 1917, he had courted and married the young Nadezhda, starting a new family in the Kremlin apartments.

Svetlana had been raised in the citadel of the Marxist revolution. As she wrote in her first memoir of her Soviet life, her father's ability to control the fate of millions was nothing to her compared to the fact of whether he did or did not take her on his lap for a brief moment between his endless conferences. Stalin may have been a distant and harsh-mannered father to her and her two brothers, but she makes it clear that for her early childhood years he fulfilled her modest demands.

The marriage of Josef and Nadezhda was too heavily burdened to survive, however. The increasing paranoia of the Soviet dictator intruded ever more into his family life. In 1932, Nadezhda committed suicide; the motives and the details remain a secret, even in post-Soviet Russia. The impact on Svetlana, now age six, was overwhelming; she had been closer to her warm-hearted and ever-present mother than to her father,

and she never recovered from her loss. Gradually alienated from her father, she married and divorced twice before she was thirty and led a tormented internal life—by her own words—even as a member of the Soviet elite.

During World War II, both Svetlana's half-brother Jakov and her brother Vasili were active in the Soviet forces. Jakov died in a German POW camp after his father had refused a proferred exchange of prisoners that would have freed him in return for some high-ranking German officers. Vasili survived the war as a combat aviator but met an early death from alcoholism, in part induced by Stalin's icy rejection of him as an incompetent.

In the United States, Svetlana published her memoir of her early life to worldwide success: *Twenty Letters to a Friend* (1967) was an instant best-seller. Becoming an American citizen, she married a Virginia architect in 1970 and added a new daughter to the two grown children from her Russian marriages. (Both of those had opted to remain in the USSR when their mother defected.)

The American marriage also failed, however, and in 1984 Svetlana temporarily returned to the Soviet Union, longing to see her older children and trying to find a foothold in that rapidly changing political environment. In 1986, she opted to return to the United States and then went to live her remaining years in Great Britain. Her erratic and painful course shows that after more than sixty years, she still lived in "Stalin's Shadow," as she has titled a second book of family recollections published not long ago. Like millions of other Soviet citizens who felt the dictator's iron fist, though never within his family orbit, she could only strive to put a permanently scarred life back together.

FOR REFLECTION

Does the revelation of a personal, "human" side of a dictator induce you to make allowances for his public evils and brutalities? Should it?

THE STALINIST DICTATORSHIP

The third goal of the Five-Year Plans was, in effect, a revolution by Stalin and a changed Communist Party against the Soviet peoples. In 1928, Stalin was chief of a CPSU that was still an elite organization. It was relatively small (about 6 percent of the adult population) and difficult to join. The party was tightly disciplined and composed of intellectuals, white-collar personnel, and some workers. It included very few peasants and very few women above the lowest ranks. Many members still knew little of Stalin and were totally unaware of the secret high-level struggles for control in the Politburo.

Stalin emerged as the Boss (*vozhd*) on his fiftieth birthday in 1929, when a tremendous fuss was made over his role

as Lenin's successor. From this time on, no one else in the Soviet hierarchy was allowed to rival Stalin in press coverage or authority. From the early 1930s, every party member lived in Stalin's shadow. He proved a master of Mafia-style politics, never forgetting who had helped and who had hurt him in his climb. Absolutely vindictive toward political rivals and enemies (they were the same to him), his character has long fascinated many Russian and foreign analysts. (See the Family and Gender Relations box.)

Stalin cultivated an image of mystery. Unlike his fellow dictators, he had no gift for speech making, and he never indulged in the dramatics that other dictators constantly employed in their public appearances. After 1935, he was rarely seen in public and then only under totally controlled circumstances.

Although he was a Georgian by birth, Stalin became a strong Russian nationalist and soon transformed what had been a truly supranational movement under Lenin into a Russian one. He took the international communist organization, called the **Comintern** and based in Moscow, and turned it into an organ of Russian foreign policy. No foreign communists dared to challenge the policies dictated by Stalin's stooges on the governing board of the Comintern, even when, as sometimes happened, those policies were directly opposed to the interests of the Communist Party in the foreigners' own country. In the communist world, Moscow alone called the tune.

The Purges: A Terrorized Society

Although Stalin had crushed his high-level opponents by 1933, he still had some opposition in the party. In 1935, he apparently decided that he must crush those opponents, too. He proceeded to do so over the next few years in a fashion that shocked and mystified the world.

Between 1936 and late 1938, Moscow was the scene of a series of **show trials,** where leading party members were accused of absurd charges of treason and sabotage. Virtually all of Lenin's surviving comrades had disappeared from public sight by 1939, and Stalin was alone as master. Hundreds of thousands of ordinary citizens were arrested at the same time for alleged "crimes against the state" and sentenced to prison or to the Siberian labor camps, where most eventually died.

Lenin and Stalin: A Faked Photograph. This photo of the two leaders, purportedly taken shortly before Lenin's death and used extensively by the Stalinist propaganda machine to show the closeness of their relationship, is known to have been "doctored." Stalin's figure was placed into the photo later. Lenin came to distrust Stalin in his last days but took only ineffective measures warning the party against him. *(Topham Picture Library/Image Works)*

Victory in the Five-Year Plan. Soviet propaganda for the "Workers Paradise" created by Stalin's dictatorship particularly liked to show the alleged enthusiasm of the peasantry for their new tasks. This was often the opposite of the truth. *(Sovfoto)*

The Soviet Drive for Literacy. An undeniable benefit of the Soviet Union to its people was the effective campaign for adult literacy introduced in the 1920s. By the end of the Second Five-Year Plan in 1937, most men and women had some ability to read and write. *(Sovfoto/Eastphoto)*

To this day, historians do not agree on an explanation of why the purge happened. What is known is that between 1935 and the end of Stalin's life in 1953, perhaps *10 million* Soviet citizens were at one time or another banished to prison camps without trial and almost always without proof of violation of current Soviet law. Everyone had a close relative or friend who had been spirited away, usually in the night, by the dreaded secret police. These "administrative measures," based on anonymous denunciations, were conducted completely outside the usual court system, and often the prisoners were never told their crimes, even after serving many years. Some survived, but very many did not. It was commonplace for the camp overseers to extend the original sentences, adding five more years for such "offenses" as trading a bit of bread for a pair of socks.

Stalin never offered an explanation, then or later. One thing is certain: if Stalin instituted the **Great Purge** to terrorize the party and Soviet society into complete obedience, he succeeded. Until his death, no one in the party, military, or general society dared oppose him openly.

How did Stalin's dictatorship compare with Adolf Hitler's—that other terrifying Western dictatorship of the twentieth century? One major difference should be noted: Stalin posed as the champion of the underdog everywhere, while Hitler was the champion only of the Germans. We will see in Chapter 47 that Hitler's narrowly racist ideology had no vision of the beneficial transformation of human society, whereas Stalin's international communism did. Stalin and his assistants were able to fashion that vision so that a significant portion of the world, from China to Cuba, came to believe it—for a time.

LIFE UNDER THE DICTATORSHIP

Stalin and his associates believed that a "new Soviet man" would emerge after a few years of Soviet rule. In this, they were sadly mistaken. The Soviet people continued to be old-style human beings with all their faults. But a new type of society did emerge in the Soviet Union, and it had both good and bad points.

Possibilities Expanded

On the good side, the forced-draft industrialization and modernization under the Five-Year Plans allowed a very large number of human beings to improve their professional prospects dramatically. Mass education enabled many people to hold jobs and assume responsibilities that they could not have handled or would never have been offered in the old society. Many illiterate peasants saw their sons and daughters obtain degrees in advanced technology, while the new Soviet schools turned out engineers by the millions. For example, Nikita Khrushchev, Stalin's successor as head of the Communist Party, worked as a coal miner in his early years.

Millions of Russian and Soviet women were emancipated from a life that offered them no real opportunities to use their minds or develop their talents. Despite much propaganda to the contrary, the Soviet leaders did not really believe in equality for women, and the highest positions remained overwhelmingly male until the Soviet Union's collapse. But the leaders *did* believe in additional skilled labor, male or female. By the end of the 1930s, most Soviet women worked outside the home. Living standards were very low, and the woman's additional income was crucial for many Soviet families. Still, the door to a more varied, more challenging life had been opened and would not be closed again.

A basic "safety net" was established for all citizens. Outside the camps, no one starved, and no one was allowed to die like an animal because of lack of human care. According to the Soviet constitution, every citizen had a right (and a duty!) to a job. Medical care was free, all workers received pensions, and education was open and free to all politically reliable persons. There were truly no ceilings to talent, provided that one either was a sincere communist or paid the necessary lip service to the system.

Liberties Suppressed

On the bad side were all the drawbacks we have already mentioned as inherent in the Stalinist dictatorship: lack of any political freedom, terror and lawlessness, and low standards of living. There were other disadvantages, too: religious persecution, cultural censorship, constant indoctrination with a simplistic and distorted Marxism, and constant interference with private lives. For a certain time, during the 1920s and early 1930s, many well-meaning people in and outside the Soviet Union were able to rationalize the bad aspects of Soviet life by balancing them against the good. They accepted the Stalinist statement "You can't make an omelet without breaking eggs." They believed that within a few years, Soviet society would be the envy of the capitalists in the West. Then, the glories of developed socialism would be wonderful to behold, and the evils of the transition period would be soon forgotten.

But the terror of the purges of the mid-1930s disillusioned many, and the continued iron dictatorship after World War II discouraged many more. Even the youths, who had been the most enthusiastic members of the party and the hardest workers, were disappointed that the enormous sacrifices made during World War II seemed to go unappreciated by the Leader. The CPSU lost its spirit and its moral authority as the voice of revolutionary ideals. In the postwar years, it came to resemble just another huge bureaucracy, providing a ladder upward for the opportunists and the manipulators. The only real talent necessary for a successful party career became to pretend to worship Stalin.

MATERIAL AND SOCIAL WELFARE IN THE INTERWAR SOVIET UNION

Material life under Stalin was very hard. Starting from a low level, Russians' living standards became far worse than those of any other European people. The new industrial cities were plagued by a continuing, unsolvable housing crisis. On average, people were living worse in 1950 than they had in 1930. The typical Moscow apartment housed four adults *per room,* and often they were members of unrelated families sharing a kitchen and a one-floor-down toilet. There was a total lack of privacy in urban apartments, with devastating effects on family living conditions. Until the mid-1950s, certain basic foods were still rationed—long after the defeated Germans had overcome such shortages.

Social problems were sometimes met head-on by government action, sometimes ignored. The divorce and abortion rates shot up in the 1920s in line with the communist-supported emancipation of Russian women. In the mid-1930s, Stalin reintroduced tight restrictions on abortion and divorce and rewarded women who bore many children with cash and medals ("Heroine of Socialist Labor"). The underlying reason for this change in policy was the shortage of labor in Soviet industry and agriculture, both of which were extraordinarily inefficient in their use of labor and suffered from endemic low productivity.

Soviet medical care was supposedly free to all but was very spotty in quality, and party membership was a definite advantage. Clinics were established for the first time throughout the countryside, but the problems of bad nutrition, superstition about prenatal and postnatal care, and the large Muslim population's distrust of all Western-style medicine were great handicaps to lowering the epidemic death rate or infant mortality.

Alcoholism remained what it had always been in Russia: a serious obstacle to labor efficiency and a drain on resources. Repeated government campaigns for sobriety had only limited effects on the peasants and urban workers. Home brew was common despite heavy penalties on its production.

Some common crimes were effectively reduced, at least for a time. (The Soviet government was always reluctant to provide accurate statistics on social problems, especially crime.) Prostitution became rare for a while, partly because the original Bolshevik attitude toward sex was quite liberal: men and women were equals and should be able to arrange their sexual activities as they saw fit without interference. Financial offenses, such as embezzlement and fraud, were almost eliminated because opportunities to commit them were originally almost nonexistent This was to change radically in later days. Theft, on the other hand, became very common, as all classes of people frequently had to resort to it to survive during the civil war; later, the attitude became that stealing from a government-owned shop or enterprise was not really a crime, as all property belonged to "the people," hence to no one. Violence against persons increased in the early Soviet period, when civil war, starving wanderers, and "class struggle" were commonplace and provided some cover for personal criminal acts. So far as could be seen from statistics, violent crimes then reverted to their original, prerevolutionary patterns.

SUMMARY

The Bolshevik revolution of 1917 was one of the milestones of modern history. For a long time, millions of idealists considered it the definitive dawn of a new age. No other modern social or economic movement has convinced so many different people that it was the solution to society's various ills.

Lenin's installation of a dictatorship by the Communist Party immediately after the revolution broke the ground for the Stalinist rule of later date. After a hidden power struggle, Leon Trotsky, the presumed successor to Lenin, was overcome by Josef Stalin, who had mastered the art of closed-group infighting better than any of his competitors. In a few more years, he had made himself the master of his country in unprecedented fashion.

In 1928, the introduction of the First Five-Year Plan was a Second Revolution. Agrarian life was transformed by collectivization of the peasants, and the USSR became a major industrial power. Midway through the 1930s, the Great Purge of both party and people began, with millions of innocent victims. Stalinist policies helped the material welfare of some large segments of the Soviet populace. These measures improved education, professional opportunities, and medical care and generally allowed the population to live a more modern lifestyle. But the Soviet peoples paid very high prices for these advantages. They gave up all political and economic liberties and suffered through a generation of great hardships under the dictatorial rule of the party and its omnipotent head.

TEST YOUR KNOWLEDGE

1. In the early 1920s, Lenin's closest associate and apparent successor as leader of the Soviet Party and state was
    a. Stalin.
    b. Trotsky.
    c. Khrushchev.
    d. Romanov.
2. By 1921 in Russia,
    a. a large part of the population was in arms against communism.
    b. the majority of Russians had become communists.
    c. a civil war had greatly worsened the damage sustained during World War I.
    d. the economy had almost recovered from wartime damages.
3. During the Five-Year Plans, the peasants were
    a. finally liberated from dependence on the government.
    b. ignored by the authorities, who were concentrating on industry.
    c. deprived of most of their private property.
    d. given a major boost in productivity by government action.
4. The Five-Year Plan called for
    a. subordination of the Communist Party to the government.
    b. rapid, forced industrialization.

    c. distribution of the farmlands to the peasants.
    d. war on the Western democracies.
5. The Great Purges started
    a. after an assassination attempt on Stalin himself.
    b. after evidence of a foreign spy ring within the party.
    c. because of a rebellion of party leaders against the Five-Year Plans.
    d. because of Stalin's suspicions about his associates' loyalty.
6. One of the chief rewards for the workers in the new Soviet Union of the 1930s was
    a. improved and expanded housing.
    b. mass educational facilities.
    c. a decisive voice in public affairs.
    d. security of life and property against the state.
7. Which of the following were *not* members of the new communist elite in the Soviet Union?
    a. Artists and writers
    b. Party officials
    c. Medical specialists
    d. Technical managers

IDENTIFICATION TERMS

Bolsheviks
Brest-Litovsk Treaty
Cheka
collectivization campaign

Comintern
First Five-Year Plan
Great Purge
Great October Revolution

Lenin, Vladimir
March Revolution
New Economic Policy
 (NEP)

Provisional Government
show trials
Stalin, Josef
Trotsky, Leon

INFOTRAC COLLEGE EDITION

Enter the search term "Russia Revolution" using Key Words.
Enter the search term "Bolshevik" using Key Words.

Enter the search term "Joseph Stalin" using the Subject Guide.

47

Totalitarianism: The Nazi State

One does not establish a dictatorship in order to make a revolution; one makes a revolution in order to establish a dictatorship.

George Orwell, *1984*

1920	Hitler takes charge of NSDAP
1923	Munich putsch fails
1924	*Mein Kampf*
1930–1932	Great Depression in Germany
1933	Hitler becomes chancellor/Enabling Law
1935	Nuremberg Laws on race
1936–1939	Nazi preparation for war
1938	"Kristallnacht"/Harassment of Jews intensifies

IN THE TWENTIETH CENTURY, a new form of state organization came into the world—the savage form called totalitarianism. It was an unprecedented denial of the traditional freedom of the individual citizen, in order to glorify and strengthen the powers of the state. Was totalitarianism the result of some peculiar, temporary combination of circumstances in the political-economic spectrum of the 1920s and 1930s? Or was what occurred in those years the result of the inevitable stresses generated by the modern nation-state, and therefore the possible harbinger of worse things still to come? The experts still argue about these questions.

Totalitarian states were always ruled by a dictator, but not all dictatorships were necessarily totalitarian. The interwar years (1919–1939) saw the rise of several dictatorships in various parts of the world. Most of these regimes were not totalitarian in character. In this chapter, we concentrate on the most aggressive and dangerous of the European totalitarian states: that erected by Adolf Hitler, the leader of Nazi Germany from 1933 until his death at the end of World War II.

Totalitarian Government

The word *totalitarian* comes from the attempt—more or less successful—to impose total control over the public life of a society. Totalitarianism is a twentieth-century phenomenon. Before then, such an attempt had not been made, in part because it was not technically possible but largely because other institutions such as the churches strongly resisted the very idea.

The atmosphere of unquestioning obedience to governmental authority that was a necessary prelude to totalitarianism was a product of World War I. The full mobilization of the civilian population behind the war effort was new in history. No one could escape. The wartime governments took full control of the economy, instituting rationing, allocations to industry, wage ceilings, and price controls. Citizens were expected to sacrifice their accustomed personal freedoms for victory. The majority readily accepted the government's crude censorship and propaganda. Those who refused were vulnerable to both legal and social retributions.

As we saw in Chapter 45, Benito Mussolini in Italy was the first political figure to see what might be accomplished by blending the techniques of wartime government with a mass appeal to national sentiment and the resentments of the masses. In his *fascisti,* he brought together traditional underdogs of society and gave them a chance to feel like top dogs. The fascists claimed to be the vanguard of an epoch of national glory, made possible by a radical change in the very nature of social organization and led by a man of genius: **Il Duce** (the Leader).

Five Characteristics

What did the totalitarian state and society mean in practice?

1. The traditional boundaries between public and private affairs of citizens were redefined or obliterated. What had been considered private was now declared public and thus a matter for governmental concern and control. Even family relationships and aesthetic values fell into this category.
2. The state itself became an extension of the Leader's will. Government policy was the implementation of what "the people" truly wanted, as interpreted by the Leader.
3. The bond between people and Leader was made concrete and visible by the party, a single, mass organization created to form a link between the two. The "people" were understood to include only those belonging to the majority ethnic group (Italians, Germans, or whoever). The others, "aliens," had no inherent rights at all and could be so treated.
4. Since the Leader and the people were joined by a mystic bond allowing the Leader to be the sole authentic interpreter of the collective will, there was no need for political competition or discussion. Parliaments and traditional parties could all be eliminated. They were merely selfish interests seeking to confuse the people and negate their true welfare, which lay in the Leader's hands.
5. The collective was all; the individual, nothing. Individual conscience, affections, and interests were to be rigorously subordinated to the needs and demands of the people and the Leader, as expressed through the party.

Antirationalism

Totalitarian governments often deliberately turned away from reason and cultivated a kind of *antirationalism* as a philosophy. Instincts were raised above logic—"thinking with the blood," as the Nazis put it. Such antirationalism was an outgrowth of the late nineteenth century, when a cult of violence appeared among some intellectual fringe groups in Europe. World War I then showed how far civilized humans could descend toward their animal origins. Instead of being revolted by the war, the totalitarian theorists often seized on those experiences as representing authentic human nature: violent, instinctual, collective.

Struggle was the key concept for the totalitarian states. The struggle of the people and their Leader was never completed. Victory was always conditional and partial, since another enemy was always lurking somewhere. The enemies were both domestic and foreign ("international Bolshevism," "Jewish conspiracies," "encircling capitalists"), and it was necessary to be constantly on guard against their tricks and destructive ploys.

Action was also essential, though it often lacked any clear goal. Mussolini once said, "Act forcefully . . . the reason for doing so will appear." In other words, don't worry about why something is done; the act of doing it will produce its own rationale in time. Inevitably, this approach often led to contradictory and illogical policies. But reasonable action was not high on the list of priorities.

Fear of communism, frustrated nationalism, and the accumulated resentments of the underdogs made a potent combination, and Mussolini rode that combination into power in the early 1920s. Once he had power, he quickly found ways to increase his popularity by initiating a self-proclaimed crusade for social justice, economic expansion, and imperial glory. Throughout the later 1920s and 1930s, Mussolini was attempting to erect a totalitarian state, but he was to be only partly successful. The master builders were elsewhere.

THE NAZI STATE: HITLER AND THE THOUSAND-YEAR REICH

The "honor" of creating the most ruthless totalitarian state was divided between the communist dictatorship of Josef Stalin in Russia (see Chapter 46) and the Nazi dictatorship of Adolf Hitler in Germany. We have seen that Stalin attained tremendous power by cynically manipulating an idealistic movement aimed at bringing first Russia and then the world into a new era of equality and freedom. The German dictator had no such visions, however.

Hitler's Early Career

Adolf Hitler was born an Austrian citizen in 1889. He was the only child of a strict father and a loving mother who spoiled him in every way her limited resources allowed. When he was seventeen, he went off to Vienna in hopes of an art career. Rejected as having no talent, he survived for the next few years on the fringes of urban society, living hand to mouth on money from home. He fully absorbed the anti-Semitism prevalent in Vienna at this time, and his constant reading convinced him of the falsity of typical "bourgeois" values and politics. But he despised Marxism, which was the most common hope and refuge of social outsiders like himself. When World War I broke out, Hitler was a young malcontent of twenty-five, still searching for some philosophy that would make sense of a world that had rejected him.

Enlisting immediately, Hitler distinguished himself for bravery under fire, receiving the Iron Cross. The wartime experience gave him his first idea of his life's purpose. With millions of other demobilized men, he spent the first months of the postwar era in a state of shock and despair, seeing the socialist government that had replaced the kaiser and accepted the Versailles Treaty as the betrayers of the nation. As time passed, he became determined to join those who were aiming to overturn the government.

In 1920, Hitler took over a tiny group of would-be re-formers and renamed them the National Socialist German Workers Party (NSDAP), or "Nazis" for short. Devoting his fanatical energy to the party, he rapidly attracted new members in the Munich area, where he had been living since before the war. In 1923, Hitler, supported by a few discontented army officers, attempted a *putsch* (coup d'é-tat) in Munich, but it failed miserably. Arrested for treason, he used the trial to gain national notoriety. He was sentenced to five years in prison by a sympathetic judge and used the year he actually served to write his autobiography and call to arms: *Mein Kampf* (My Struggle).

The Nazi Program

In wild and ranting prose, *Mein Kampf* laid out what Hitler saw as Germany's present problems and their solutions. It insisted on all of the following:

- *Anti-Semitism.* Jews were declared born enemies of all proper German values and traitors to the nation.
- *Rejection of the Versailles Treaty and German war guilt.* Hitler called the treaty the most unfair in world history, dictated by a (temporarily) strong France against a helpless, tricked Germany.
- *Confiscation of illicit war profits.* This measure was aimed mainly at Jews but also at non-Jewish German industrialists. This point reflected the Nazis' claim to be socialists (though anti-Marxist).
- *Protection of the middle classes from ruinous competition.* The Nazis made a special show of paying attention to the growing concerns of the shopkeepers and white-collar workers who feared that they were being forced downward on the economic ladder by big business.
- *Land redistribution for the peasants.* With this pseudoso-cialist measure, Hitler claimed to be protecting the peasants who were being squeezed out by large landholders.

The basic tenor of *Mein Kampf* and of Nazi speeches and literature in the 1920s was consistent: hatred for the existing situation in Germany and the determination to change it radically. The "Marxist-Zionist" government that had accepted the Versailles Treaty had given a "stab in the back" to the brave German army in 1918. Germany must be reborn and once again gain its rightful place! Whatever means were necessary to do this were justified, as only the strong would survive in a jungle world of competing nations.

After the failure of the Munich putsch, Hitler swore that he would come to power by constitutional, legal means. No one could later say that he had acted against the will of his people. From the moment that he was released from jail, he devoted himself tirelessly to organizing, speech making, and electioneering from one end of the country to the other.

Hitler was an extremely gifted rabble-rouser who quickly learned how to appeal to various groups in language that they could not forget. His targets were always the same: Jews, the signers of the Versailles Treaty, the communists, and the clique of businessmen and bureaucrats who supposedly pulled the strings behind the scenes. (For more about Hitler and his appeal, see the Religion and Philosophy box.)

Between 1925 and 1929, which were prosperous years for Weimar Germany, the Nazis made little headway among the masses of industrial workers, who remained loyal to either the Social Democrats or the large, legal German Communist Party. But the Nazis did pick up voters among the members of the middle classes who had been ruined in the great inflation and among the numerous white-collar workers who saw their relative status slipping in postwar Germany. As late as the elections of 1928, the Nazis received only 2.6 percent of the vote and 12 seats in the Reichstag. In comparison, the Communists had 77 seats, and the Social Democrats had 156. The rest of the Reichstag's 500 seats were held by moderate or conservative parties that regarded Hitler as a loose cannon who might possibly be useful against the socialists but could not be taken seriously as a politician.

The Great Depression's Effects

The collapse of the German (and world) economy in 1930–1931 set the stage for Nazi political success. In late 1929, the New York Stock Exchange went into a tailspin that soon had effects on every aspect of finance in the Western world. Germany was particularly affected because for years German industrialists and municipalities had been relying on American investment and loans. Suddenly, this credit was cut off as loans were called in on short notice. Instead of new investment, international finance and trade shrank steadily as each nation attempted to protect itself from external competition by raising tariffs and limiting imports.

The results for Germany were horrendous: the number of unemployed rose from 2.25 million in early 1930 to more than 6 million two years later (about 25 percent of the total labor force). And this figure does not count involuntary part-time workers or the many women who withdrew from the labor market permanently. In no other country, not even the United States, was the industrial economy so hard hit.

The governing coalition of Social Democrats and moderate conservatives fell apart under this strain. In the fre-

ADOLF HITLER
(1889—1945)

Despite many tries, no one has been able to explain satisfactorily why Adolf Hitler's political and social doctrines were so attractive to most German people. During the 1930s, few Germans were disturbed by his anti-Semitic and antiforeigner slogans, his manic nationalism, or his crude and violent ideas for renovating the German nation.

True, the plight of the Germans after World War I and the struggle for survival during the first years of the Great Depression contributed to their acceptance of Hitler's views. The orderly and progressive world of Kaiser William II had crumbled before their eyes. Germany was forced to yield to a partial Allied occupation and to give up most of its much-honored army and its equipment. Most irritating of all, Germany was forced to accept a peace treaty that branded it as the sole culprit for causing the ruinous war and was required to pay many billions of dollars as compensation to the victors.

The punishment was far greater than most had anticipated, and the common people suffered the consequences. Inflation, unemployment, and political turmoil spread. The fear of communism was acute among the middle classes, while the laborers and intellectuals struggled to make their voices heard. The old system was thoroughly discredited, and Germans looked for a new architect of morals. In 1923, a candidate appeared who had not yet found his proper voice. His name was Adolf Hitler.

Hitler had served during the war and like millions of other front-line soldiers emerged from that experience with contempt for the politicians and the traditional leaders of his people. He was looking for revenge against the "dark forces," which he sensed had thus far prevented him and those like him from assuming their rightful place in society and prevented Germany as a nation from reaching its rightful, dominant place in the world.

In 1920 Hitler found his chance at the head of a tiny party of malcontents. Rapidly expanding its membership through his mesmerizing ability to capture a crowd, Hitler entered into a half-baked scheme to take over the government in 1923, when the terrible postwar inflation and popular turmoil were at their height. The attempted coup failed with fourteen deaths. Hitler was tried for treason, turned the courtroom into a rostrum for his passionate attacks on the Jews and socialists, and was jailed for a year.

From 1924 on, the Nazi movement slowly gained strength. Hitler became an ever-more skilled manipulator of political propaganda and gathered around him a very mixed band of dreamers, brutes, ambitious climbers, and opportunists. Some of them firmly believed in the Führer and his self-proclaimed mission to save Germany and bring a New Order to Europe. Others hitched their wagons to his star without necessarily believing the wild rantings in *Mein Kampf*. Few took his promises to exterminate Jews and communists as anything more than a rabble-rouser's empty words.

Hitler's personality was a collection of contradictions. He despised organized religion and proclaimed himself untrammeled by common morality, yet he lived a life of ascetic restraint. A strict vegetarian and teetotaler, he frowned on the more boisterous and indulgent lifestyle of some of his followers (such as the fat hedonist Göring). He was fascinated by the power of the intellect and will yet held intellectuals in contempt. He would work thirty-six hours at a stretch yet went into nervous collapse and secluded himself from his officials in several political crises. He was a notorious charmer of susceptible women yet abstained from all sexual relations and was probably impotent.

He was perhaps the most murderous power holder of the twentieth century, committing endless atrocities against Germans and other human beings, yet he had a deep reverence for the arts and considerable artistic talent. Perhaps it is in his artistic personality that a hint of the truth lies: when his paintings were exhibited after the war, critics were impressed by his talent for rendering structural accuracy but noted his inability to sketch the human form.

FOR REFLECTION

Why do you think Hitler seized on the Jews as the German people's most dangerous enemy? Is it unusual for a political leader to hold sharply contradictory views of moral standards for himself versus for the mass of people?

---

quent elections necessitated by the collapse of the coalition, the middle-of-the-road parties steadily lost seats to the extremes on right and left: the Nazis and the Communists. In an election for the Reichstag in mid-1930, the Nazis won a total of 107 seats, second only to the weakening SDs.

As the economy continued downhill, Hitler promised immediate, decisive action to aid the unemployed and the farmers. In another national election in early 1932, the Nazis won 14.5 million votes of a total of about 35 million. The Nazis were now the largest single party but still lacked a majority. Their attacks on the government and the other parties intensified both verbally and, increasingly, in the streets.

The *Machtergreifung*

Finally, in a move aimed at moderating Hitler by putting him into a position where he had to take responsibility rather than just criticize, the conservative advisers of the old president, Paul von Hindenburg, appointed him chan-

SIEG oder BOLSCHEWISMUS

Nazis or Bolsheviks? This effective appeal to the German populace to choose between the Nazis or bolshevism was part of the campaign to discredit any moderate solutions to the Depression and its attendant misery. (© *The Granger Collection*)

cellor on January 30, 1933. Within eight weeks, Hitler had transformed the government into a Nazi dictatorship. And technically, he had accomplished this *Machtergreifung,* or seizure of power, by constitutional procedures, as he had promised.

How did this transformation occur? It involved two complementary processes: the capture of legal authority for the Nazis and the elimination of competing political groups. First, the Nazis whipped up hysteria over an alleged communist revolutionary plot. Under the constitution's emergency provision, Hitler as chancellor introduced the equivalent of martial law and used it to round up tens of thousands of his opponents in the next weeks. After the election that Hitler called for March (in which the Nazis still failed to gain a simple majority), all Communist and some Social Democratic delegates to the Reichstag were arrested as traitors. Finally, in late March, the Nazi-dominated rump parliament enacted the so-called *Enabling Act,* giving Hitler's government the power to rule by decree

until the emergency had passed. It did not pass for the next twelve years, until Hitler was dead in the ruins of Berlin.

The German Communist Party was immediately outlawed, and the Social Democrats were banned a few weeks later. One by one, the centrist and moderate parties disappeared, either by dissolving themselves or by being abolished by Nazi decree. In mid-1933, the Nazis were the only legal political organization left in Germany. In its various subgroups for women, youths, professional associations, farmers, and others, all patriotic Germans could find their place.

Hitler completed the process of consolidating power with a purge within the party itself. This was the infamous *"Night of the Long Knives"* in June 1934, when the paramilitary **Sturmabteilung** (Storm Troopers, or SA), who had been very important to the Nazi movement as bully-boys, were cut down to size. Using another of his suborgan-

Our Last Hope, Hitler. This poster depicting economic depression on a mass scale was part of Hitler's unsuccessful 1932 presidential campaign as the National Socialist Party candidate. (© *The Granger Collection*)

Unsere letzte Hoffnung: HITLER

✦ **An All-German Party Parade.** A major reason for the Nazi success was the masterly touch of drama accompanying the party's functions. The impression of overwhelming force was fostered by slogans and banners that proclaimed the party's strength in every part of the homeland. *(UPI/Bettmann/Corbis)*

izations, the new ***Schutzstaffel*, or SS,** Hitler murdered several hundred of the Storm Troop leaders. By doing so, he both rid himself of potentially serious rivals and placated the German army generals, who rightly saw in the brown-shirted Storm Troop a menace to their own position as the nation's military leaders.

THE NAZI DOMESTIC REGIME

When the Nazis took power, the NSDAP had an active membership of about 1 million and probably twice that many supporters who could be counted on to show up for major party affairs or contribute some money. By 1934, about 15 percent of the total population had joined the Nazi Party. The numbers rose steadily thereafter. By the middle of the war, about one-fifth of adult Germans belonged, though many joined under severe pressure and contributed nothing except mandatory dues.

Rank-and-file party members were drawn from all elements of the population, but the leaders were normally young men from the working and lower-middle classes. Like the Russian communists, the Nazis were a party of young men who were in a hurry and had no patience with negotiation or gradual reform. Unlike the communists, they

✦ **Nuremberg Nazi Rally, 1938.** The massive display of strength and unity so dear to the Nazis was nowhere better on view than at the regular rallies held in the Bavarian town of Nuremberg. In this photo, Hitler takes the salute from his labor union chief before congratulating the 50,000 participants on completing the West Wall along the French border. *(Hulton-Deutsch Collection/Woodfin Camp)*

saw themselves not so much as implementing a revolution but as restoring proud Germanic traditions that had been allowed to decay.

The party was represented in all parts of Germany, which was organized into *Gaue,* or districts under the command of a *Gauleiter* (a district party boss). As under the Bismarckian and Weimar governments, Prussia was the most important region in Germany. The brilliant and unscrupulous propagandist Joseph Goebbels (1897–1945) was Hitler's deputy here. Another member of Hitler's small circle of intimates was **Hermann Göring** (1893–1946), the rotund, wisecracking, and entirely cynical pilot-hero of World War I who was generally seen as the number two man in the hierarchy.

Hitler's policies were designed to make Germany into a totalitarian state, and they did so very rapidly. His right arm in this was **Heinrich Himmler** (1900–1945), the head of the SS and of the *Gestapo,* or political police. Himmler was Hitler's most loyal colleague, and he was charged with overseeing the internal security of the Nazi regime. Himmler's SS operated the concentration camps that had opened as early as 1934 within Germany. And later in the conquered territories, a branch of the SS conducted the Holocaust of the Jews, setting up the slave labor camps and installing a reign of terror against all possible resistance. (See the Exercise of Authority box for more on Himmler's ideas.)

Dehumanizing of the Jews. The Nazis viewed Jewish-Christian sexual relations as pollution of German blood. The woman's sign reads, "I am the biggest pig in the place and get involved only with Jews." The Jewish man's placard says "As a Jewish fellow, I take only German girls to my room." The public humiliation of such couples began immediately after the Nazis came to power in 1933. (© Keystone/The Image Works)

The "Jewish Question"

The most horrible of the Nazi policies was the genocide against the Jews. For the first time in modern history, a systematic, cold-blooded war of extermination was practiced against a noncombatant people, solely on the basis of race. The war against the Jews went through four distinct phases between 1933 and 1945:

1. From March 1933 to 1935, German Jews were publicly humiliated and excluded from government jobs.
2. In September 1935, the **Nuremberg Laws** prohibiting social contacts between Jews and "Aryans" (defined as persons with no Jewish blood for two generations on both sides of their family) made Jews into noncitizens. The government began to harass Jews constantly and push them into urban ghettos for easier surveillance.
3. In November 1938, new policies made it almost impossible for Jews to engage in public life and business and forbade emigration unless they surrendered all their property in Germany and went as paupers. By this time, many thousands of "antistate" Jews had been consigned to the camps.
4. At the **Wannsee conference** in Berlin in 1942, the **Final Solution** for the "Jewish problem" was approved by Hitler. The Jews were rounded up from the ghettos throughout Germany and occupied Europe and sent to the death camps in Poland. The Holocaust had begun and would not end until Germany's defeat in 1945. By then, some 6 million Jews from all over central and eastern Europe had been murdered, starved to death, or otherwise fallen victim to Himmler's henchmen. Of the more than 2 million Jews living in Germany itself in 1933, only a few tens of thousands had survived at the close of the war, overlooked or hidden by sympathetic neighbors.

Nazi Economic Policy

Economic policy in the Nazi state was a peculiar mixture of a fake "socialism" and an accommodation of the big businesses and cartels that had dominated Germany for a generation. As in Mussolini's Italy, the government's economic policies generated some measure of social reform. Workers and farmers were idealized in propaganda as the true Aryan Germans. But private property remained untouched, and the capitalist process was subjected to only sporadic and selective interference by the government. The labor unions, like every other type of public association, were fully subordinated to the party and became arms of the Nazi octopus. Strikes were illegal, and the Marxist idea of class conflict was officially declared nonexistent among Germans.

HEINRICH HIMMLER'S SPEECH TO THE SS

Heinrich Himmler was perhaps the most detested—and feared—man in the world, until he died at his own hand in the Nazi collapse in 1945. A totally insignificant-looking individual with rimless eyeglasses through which he peered nearsightedly, Himmler was the willing slave of the Führer. In return for his doglike devotion, he was entrusted with the leadership of the SS, the *Schutzstaffel,* or bodyguard of Hitler, which he built up into an elite branch of the German military.

Himmler was given the responsibility of implementing the "Final Solution" of the Jewish Question. The following selection is a partial transcript of a speech that Himmler gave to an SS conclave in Poland on October 4, 1943. Note the peculiar combination of secrecy and an attempt to excite pride in what the concentration camp guards were being asked to do.

I also want to make reference before you here, in complete frankness, to a really grave matter. Among ourselves, this once, it shall be uttered quite frankly; but in public we will never speak of it. Just as we did not hesitate on June 30, 1934,* to do our duty as ordered, to stand up against the wall comrades who had violated their duty, and shoot them, so we have never talked about this, and never will. . . . Each of us shuddered, and yet each one knew that he would do it again if it were ordered and if it were necessary.

I am referring to the evacuation of the Jews, the annihilation of the Jewish people. This is one of the things that can be easily said: "The Jewish people is going to be annihilated" says every Party member. "Sure, it's in our program, elimination of the Jews, annihilation—we'll take care of it." And then they all come trudging in, 80 million worthy Germans, and each one of them has his one "decent Jew." Sure, the others are swine, but *this* one is an A-1 Jew.

Of all those who talk this way, not one has seen it happen, not one has been through it. Most of you know what it means to see a hundred corpses side by side, or five hundred, or a thousand. To

have stuck this out and—excepting cases of human weakness—to have kept our integrity, that is what has made us hard. In our history, this is an unwritten and never-to-be-written page of glory, for we know how difficult we would have made it for ourselves if today—amid the bombing raids, the hardships and deprivations of war—we still had the Jews in every city as secret saboteurs, agitators, and demagogues. If the Jews were still situated in the body of the German people, we probably would have reached the 1916–1917 stage by now.

The wealth they had we have taken from them. We have taken none of it for ourselves . . . whoever takes so much as a Mark of it for himself is a dead man. A number of SS men—not very many—have transgressed, and they will die without mercy. We had the moral right, we had the duty toward our people, to kill this people who wished to kill us. But we do not have the right to enrich ourselves with so much as a fur coat, a watch, a Mark, or even a cigarette or anything else. Having exterminated a germ, we do not want in the end to be infected by the germ, and die of it. I will not stand by and let even a small rotten spot develop, or take hold. Wherever it may form, we together will cauterize it. All in all, however, we can say that we have carried out this heaviest of all our tasks in a spirit of love for our people. Our inward being, our soul, has not suffered injury from it.

FOR REFLECTION

Why does Himmler insist on the absolute honesty of the SS in dealing with Jews' property? What do you think he refers to when in the last sentence he talks of "our inward being, our soul"?

*The Night of the Long Knives, when the SA was eliminated.

Source: "The Holocaust Reader," in Readings in World Civilizations, ed. Lucy Dawidowicz (Metuchen, NJ: Behrman House, 1976). Copyright 1976, Behrman House, Inc.

Hitler had come to power partly on the strength of his promises to end the unemployment problem. From 1933 to 1936, he instituted measures that were effective at providing jobs. The huge road construction and public works programs he began in 1934 absorbed a large portion of the pool of unemployed. With rearmament, the military was greatly enlarged, and munitions factories and their suppliers received government orders. Raw materials were rapidly stockpiled. Synthetics for the vital raw materials that Germany lacked (petroleum, rubber, tin, and many other exotic minerals) were invented in government-supported laboratories and produced in new factories.

Already by 1936, Hitler was putting Germany on a war footing. Labor was allocated according to government priorities. Government ministries decided what would be imported and exported. In the western border region, a huge

"West Wall" was being erected. This system of fortifications would mirror the fortified French Maginot Line across the frontier. The *autobahns* (expressways) were crisscrossing the country, creating a system that could move men and material quickly in case of war.

By 1937, the number of unemployed was down to 400,000 (from 6 million), and a labor shortage was developing. Unmarried women and youths were put into more or less compulsory organizations to relieve the shortfall. In every German village and town, Nazi Youth organizations gave boys and girls age seven to twenty-one a place to get together with their peers for both work and fun while imbibing the Nazi viewpoints. The nation was prosperous, the Great Depression became a dim memory, and many millions of Germans were proud of their government and their **Führer.**

Hitler Youth. At the annual mass rally of Nazi organizations in Nuremberg the uniformed Hitler Youth were always given a prominent place to salute the Führer's carefully staged arrival. Membership was all but mandatory; those who didn't join were singled out for social ostracism. *(Hulton-Deutsch Collection/Corbis)*

MAP 47.1 Europe in 1939 at Eve of World War II.   Most of Europe was under dictatorial rule of various types by the end of the 1930s. The impact of the Great Depression pushed some of the former parliamentary democracies into the dictatorship column during the middle of the 1930s. Only Britain, France, and the Scandinavians kept alive the reality of democratic politics.

SUMMARY

Totalitarian government is a twentieth-century phenomenon that found several homes in Europe after World War I. One experiment with it occurred in Soviet Russia, and another in fascist Italy. But the German Nazi state was the most notable and aggressive example.

The defeat in 1918, the runaway inflation of the early 1920s, and the weak and unpopular socialist government combined to exert a devastating effect on German national morale. Millions of voters lost faith in liberal democracy and the parliamentary process. So long as the economic situation remained favorable, this political weakness was manageable. But the onset of the world depression brought on a crisis from which the gifted demagogue Adolf Hitler and his Nazi Party emerged triumphant in 1933. The Nazis could soon boast that the Führer made good his promises to his people. He had obtained government power legally, and an intimidated legislature gave him dictatorial authority soon after.

By the mid-1930s, rearmament and a vigorous social investment policy had restored German prosperity. The large majority of Germans were quite content with Hitler's guidance. His ranting anti-Semitism and brutal harassment of all opposition elements did not overly disturb the majority, who had found prosperity, security and sense of national purpose that had been badly lacking.

TEST YOUR KNOWLEDGE

1. The necessary prelude to the development of the totalitarian state was
   a. World War I.
   b. the French Revolution.
   c. the precepts of *Mein Kampf.*
   d. the Bolshevik Party charter.
2. Which of the following is *not* associated with modern totalitarian government?
   a. Continuous striving toward changing goals
   b. Distinctions between private behavior and affairs of public policy
   c. Subordination of the individual to the state
   d. Leadership exercised by a single semisacred individual
3. Hitler's major political ideas were formed
   a. during his early manhood in Vienna.
   b. as a reaction to the Great Depression.
   c. during his boyhood in rural Austria.
   d. after he formed the Nazi Party in the postwar era.
4. Which of the following did *not* help Hitler in his bid for political power?
   a. His sympathy for Marxist theory and practice
   b. The rivalry between the Social Democrats and the Communists

   c. The ineptitude of the democratic leaders in meeting the economic crisis
   d. Massive economic hardship
5. The German chancellorship came to Hitler in 1933 through
   a. legal appointment.
   b. a conspiracy.
   c. an overwhelming electoral victory.
   d. armed force.
6. The internal purge of the Nazi movement was called
   a. the Day of Judgment.
   b. the Night of the Long Knives.
   c. the Second Coming.
   d. The Führer's Triumph
7. The Nuremberg Laws
   a. outlawed the German Communist Party.
   b. laid out the details of the Nazi dictatorship in Germany.
   c. detailed who was Jewish and what that meant.
   d. were the formal rejection of the reparations bill from World War I.
8. Which was *not* true of Hitler's government during the 1930s?
   a. Its policy was increasingly anti-Semitic.
   b. It was successful in eliminating mass unemployment.
   c. It allowed only one party to represent the German people.
   d. Its economic policy abolished private ownership.

IDENTIFICATION TERMS

Der Führer	Hitler, Adolf	*Mein Kampf*	*Schutzstaffel*/SS
Final Solution	*Il Duce*	Munich *putsch*	*Sturmabteilung*/SA
Göring, Hermann	*Machtergreifung*	Nuremberg Laws	Wannsee conference
Himmler, Heinrich			

INFOTRAC COLLEGE EDITION

Enter the search term "Hitler" using Key Words.
Enter the search terms "Nazi" or "Nazism" using Key Words.

Enter the search term "totalitarianism" using the Subject Guide.

48

EAST ASIA IN A CENTURY OF CHANGE

The art of government is the organization of idolatry.

GEORGE BERNARD SHAW

THE EXPLOSIVE DEVELOPMENT of Western technology and military prowess in the nineteenth century had an impact on East Asia somewhat earlier than elsewhere. By the 1850s, China, Japan, and Southeast Asia had all felt the iron hand of the West in their commercial and political relations with the rest of the world.

How did these widely variant nations meet this unexpected challenge to their identities, generated by a Western culture to which neither of them had paid much attention previously? China and Japan could hardly have chosen more different ways of dealing with the new situation. Nor could the outcomes have been more different. By the opening of the twentieth century, China suffered a collapsing government attempting to preside over a society torn by unbridgeable gaps. In contrast, Japan had undergone one of the most remarkable self-willed transformations known to history. An aggressive imperialism brought Japan into conflict with a struggling China in the 1930s and later with the West. Meanwhile, Southeast Asia had gradually become a group of white-ruled colonies where European values and education were loosely and superficially imposed on the traditional cultures.

CHINA

The Qing (Manzhou) dynasty had originated outside China in Manchuria and had come to China as conquerors, ruling from 1644 onward. This last dynasty of imperial China was notably successful in its early generations (see Chapter 30) but by the mid–nineteenth century had weakened considerably. Problems such as overpopulation and resultant famine developed in parts of China, while the almost entirely agrarian/handicraft domestic economy stagnated.

The Manzhou Decline

China's modern history begins with the **Opium Wars** (1840–1842). In the eighteenth century, the British East India Company had developed a lucrative trade in Indian opium with south China. The drug had at long last given Westerners an exchange commodity for the luxury goods they imported from China and paid for with precious gold and silver. Previously little known in China, opium became

A NOVEL CURE FOR THE OPIUM PLAGUE

By no means were all Chinese officials blind to what was happening to their country in the nineteenth century or without ideas as to how to meet the crisis ensuing from the lost Opium Wars and the Taiping Rebellion. Yi Tsan sent this memorandum to the imperial throne in the 1860s:

The situation China faces today is unprecedented, and what has worked in the past, to our sorrow, no longer works today. In today's world all the nations have been suddenly thrown together, and the normal approach to making China wealthy and strong has become woefully inadequate. . . .

The Westerners' most effective weapon in butchering our financial well-being has been and still is opium, the poison of which permeates into every corner of the nation. We exchange precious silver for harmful drugs, and the total amount of silver that has flowed out of the country during the past fifty years is so large that we have cease to count. The more we ban the opium traffic, the more the people violate the ban. Meanwhile, the Westerners, sitting there comfortably and radiating a self-satisfied smile, collect their profit. They will not be satisfied until every Chinese looks like a skeleton and every Chinese penny goes into their pockets. . . .

However, as long as we cannot prevent people from taking opium, we might as well let people manufacture opium of their own, so at least we can reduce the amount of silver that flows from the country. Yet the government strictly enforces the law that bans the cultivation of native poppies. . . . The official policy seems to be that anyone who wishes to smoke opium must buy it from foreigners. In the name of eradicating the opium poison, our government and its officials, although unwittingly, have brought the greatest harm to our own country on behalf of opium traders from abroad. . . . It is true that under the treaties we cannot prevent foreigners from shipping opium to China; it is also true, nevertheless, that the treaties do not prohibit us from growing our own. As native opium will completely displace foreign opium in the domestic market in thirty or forty years, we can then do whatever we please about the opium problem without involving either the treaties or the foreigners. Then we can either impose heavy taxation on opium consumption or introduce strict rules governing opium traffic. In either case, opium will gradually disappear from the market and the number of opium smokers will slowly decrease until, eventually, there are neither opium nor opium smokers. All this, of course, requires patience.

FOR REFLECTION

How effective do you believe Yi's cure for the opium epidemic would be? Do you think that the suggested "heavy taxation" and "strict rules" would work to ensure the gradual disappearance of the drug once it was legalized?

SOURCE: Modern China, ed. and trans. Dun J. Li (New York: Scribner's, 1978), pp. 68–69.

---

a major public health problem in the coastal cities, and its illegal trade disrupted the empire's finances. After some ineffective protests to the East India officials and the British government, in the 1830s the Chinese finally decided to take strong measures to prevent the drug's importation. This led to a naval war, which was predictably one-sided, given the huge differences between British and Chinese weaponry and naval tactics.

In 1842, the Beijing government signed the first of the **"unequal treaties"** between a weakening China and the Western powers. China, in effect, lost control of some of its territory and its trade patterns to a foreign power. The treaties opened up the previously closed Chinese coastal towns to British merchants and consuls. (This was the beginning of the British colony of Hong Kong.) The resident British were subject to British law, not Chinese law. Though not specifically mentioned in the treaty, the opium trade would continue.

The treaty with Britain was followed by others with France and, later, with Russia and Germany. All of the treaties were similar. All were extorted from a Chinese government that was still attempting to deal with the West as its ancestors in the sixteenth and seventeenth centuries had

dealt with foreigners—as a superior dealing with inferiors. This was by now so far from reality that it became a bad joke among the Europeans. With the exception of some missionaries intent on bringing Christ to the Buddhist or Daoist masses, most Europeans in China in the nineteenth and twentieth centuries were there as imperialist fortune seekers. The Chinese resented them intensely, humiliated by their new inability to protect themselves from the "foreign devils." (See one official's scheme to meet an aspect of China's crisis in the Exercise of Authority box.)

The Taiping Rebellion The losses to the European powers, bad as they were, were overshadowed in the 1850s through early 1870s by the Taiping and Nien Rebellions. Of the two, the **Taiping** episode was the more widespread and more disastrous. For more than twenty years during which the Chinese suffered perhaps 20 million deaths, rebel generals led a motley band of poverty-stricken peasants and urban workers against the Qing emperors. The Taipings' success in the early years of the revolt brought them wide support from many educated Chinese who were sickened by the government's inability to resist the foreigners. The upheaval was encouraged by several factors:

ᴗ Discontent with the corruption and incompetence of the government officials

ᴗ The rapidly worsening problems of overpopulation in much of south China

ᴗ The strong appeal of the Taipings' economic reform proposals

ᴗ The total ineffectiveness of the Qing armed forces

For a few years, the Taipings set up a countergovernment in central China that controlled about half the total area of the country. Their leader, the visionary Hung Hsiu-chuan, had been exposed to Christian missions and believed himself to be Jesus' younger brother. Hung originally enjoyed sympathy from the West, in part because he seemed to want to imitate Western ways. Some thought he was the would-be founder of a Christian China.

But the Taipings also opposed opium smoking and further giveaways of Chinese rights to foreigners. The Western powers thus opted to support the Qing because they knew the government would give them little trouble in the future. At that point, the rebels began to quarrel among themselves; by 1864, they were breaking up. The government soon defeated them and executed Hung.

For a time, the Nien presented almost as fierce a threat to the Beijing emperor. They controlled large areas of the southwest and northwest of the empire and threatened to link up with the Taipings. Total collapse seemed imminent.

Failure of the Late Manzhou Restoration The government was unexpectedly saved by a group of provincial officials and landlords. They organized regional armies to take the place of the failed central forces. Their effort is known as the "late Manzhou restoration" of the 1870s.

The new governors were reformers, and their policy of **Self-Strengthening** aimed at giving China the means to hold its own against the foreign barbarians once more. They addressed the peasant's myriad problems by instituting land reform measures and encouraging new crops with more nutritive value. Long-neglected public works programs, such as flood control projects on the Yellow (Huang) and Yangtze Rivers, were taken in hand with good effect.

Self-Strengthening attempted to introduce Western methods and technologies, while retaining traditional Confucian values in the Chinese educated class. The examination system was tightened to eliminate favoritism, but candidates were still tested on the Confucian classics. Military and business affairs received much more attention than heretofore but continued to play a supporting role, rather than being allowed center stage in Chinese life.

How well did this attempt to blend West and East succeed? Unhappily for China, it did not work out well in the longer run. New leaders who could both quote the classics and design a steam-driven factory did not appear as hoped. And traditionalist, ultraconservative attitudes remained too strong to be overcome among the scholar-officials. The **Empress Dowager Cixi** (1835–1908), who managed to hold on to power for almost fifty years (1861–1907), was not opposed to reform in principle, but she was also not in favor of it. The only thing that mattered to her was retaining her own position. An expert in political infighting, she was a kind of evil genius of China's government, pulling the strings for many years in the name of her son and her nephew, both powerless child-emperors. (For more about this wily ruler, see the Family and Gender Relations box.)

Mainly because of her foot dragging, the Chinese military forces were in poor shape in the first Sino-Japanese war, fought with Japan in 1894–1895 over Korea. Japan was rapidly pulling this traditional buffer between Japan and China into its orbit in the 1890s. The Chinese were decisively defeated in the war. Japan later annexed Korea and thus announced that it was replacing China as the most powerful Asian nation (a shift that remained in effect until Japan's defeat in World War II).

Chinese Disintegration after 1895

The defeat in 1895 was an even ruder shock to the Chinese leaders than the string of humiliations by the Westerners had been. For many centuries the mandarins had looked upon Japan and the Japanese as pitiable imitators of infinitely superior China. Now modern weapons and armies had been shown to be superior to refined culture and Confucian integrity, even in non-Western hands.

In the wake of the defeat, China again had to submit to a wave of foreign imperialist pressure. Russian, German, and British, as well as Japanese, trade extortions were forced on the Beijing officials, backed by governmental threats. Christian missionaries were granted unprecedented freedoms to attempt the conversion of the mostly unreceptive natives. Coastal enclaves became special spheres of interest for one power or another. The Chinese government conceded that its ancient tributary of Vietnam was now the property of the French colonialists. Control of Korea had been surrendered to Japan (over the heads of the Koreans). Manchuria was all but given to the Russians in the north.

The **Boxer Rebellion** (1900) was an attempted answer to this wave of foreign exploitation. The Boxers were a fanatical, quasi-religious society who believed that they had nothing to fear from bullets. Rebelling at first against Beijing, they changed their course when the sly old empress joined with them in starting a crusade to cleanse China of the foreign devils. But the Boxers had no effective leadership or weaponry. After a few months, an international military force shipped off to China from various European capitals crushed the rebellion and further humiliated the tottering dynasty by demanding cash indemnities. The failure of the Boxers convinced even the most conservative leaders that the old, Confucian-based government could no longer be maintained. China had to change or disappear as a state, and a series of radical reform proposals now came forth from various quarters.

EMPRESS CIXI
(1835–1908)

The last effective ruler of the empire of China, the empress Cixi was an extraordinary woman who defied every cliché about Asian women. Born in 1835 to a provincial gentry family, she was married to the weak Qing emperor Hsien Feng as a child and bore him his only surviving child. When Hsien died in 1861, Cixi took full advantage of her position to have her young son named emperor while she exercised ruling powers in his name. This period, which lasted for twelve years, was the first time Cixi ruled a nation that traditionally despised women who attempted a public role. Two other periods were to follow.

All accounts agree that the empress was a person of more than usual intelligence, but her real strength was her ability to anticipate what others wanted and make sure that they were dependent on her goodwill to get it. She was a master of everyday psychology. She supervised a court and a government that had become so filled with intrigue that every action—indeed, almost every word—could carry multiple meanings.

The Qing dynasty had come to China as conquerors and insisted for a time on maintaining the signs that they, and not the "men of Han," as the Chinese called themselves, were in charge. But since the Opium Wars (1840–1842), the central government was under severe attack and had shown little imagination in trying to meet the challenge. Foreigners ranging from Christian missionaries to soldiers of fortune had overrun the port cities, turning the Chinese into second-class citizens in their own country. Native rebels, above all the Taipings, had almost overturned Chinese imperial government in the 1860s and 1870s. Much of the blame in the officials' eyes rested squarely on the woman at the head of the imperial court. But blaming her was one thing; removing her was another.

When her young son died in 1875, Cixi managed to have her infant nephew placed on the throne with herself, of course, as

Empress Cixi. Dressed in formal court costume, the empress is shown at the height of her powers around the turn of the twentieth century. *(Topham/Image Works)*

regent for the ensuing fifteen years. She outmaneuvered the boy's father, Prince Kung, and eliminated him from the court completely. Even after the nephew came of age and assumed power for himself, most decisions remained in the hands of the empress. When he attempted to put through some badly needed governmental reforms, she removed him and reassumed power herself in 1898. It was she who manipulated the Boxers into becoming her tool for defying the foreign powers that were carving up China.

A determined and intelligent ruler such as Cixi might have been able to bring the tottering Qing dynasty through its crisis, if she had not been so intent on simply preserving her own position. To do so, she was not above arranging the murder of those who opposed her at court, offering massive bribes, or using government monies for her private ends. The most sensational case was her use of the navy budget to rebuild the Beijing Summer Palace. China's most famous and most awe-inspiring ship was actually a life-size replica made of white marble and resting permanently in a reflecting pool at the palace!

Although not opposed to all reform, Cixi resisted many measures that were needed to modernize the decrepit bureaucracy and military. She played one group of provincial lords off another with great expertise, so that no single faction could challenge her directly. Even as an old woman of seventy-four, she was not ready to step aside and appointed a distant relative, the infant Pu Yi, as last emperor of China in 1908. A few weeks later, she was dead, and the empire itself was on its deathbed.

FOR REFLECTION

Do you think the traditional Chinese distaste for female rule accentuated or restrained Cixi's ambitions? What, if any, restraints did the Chinese system offer to prevent a ruler such as Cixi from injuring the country?

The New China Movement By the end of the nineteenth century, a small but growing handful of young Chinese had been given a Western-style education, generally through the influence of missionaries who had "adopted" them. The most important of these was the intellectual Kang Yu-wei (1858–1927), who argued against the common notion that Confucian philosophy represented an unchanging and unchangeable model of government and society. Kang taught that Confucius himself was a reformer and that reform was a basic ingredient of his philosophy. Kang believed that history was evolutionary, not static, and that history was moving forward in China, as in the rest of the world, toward democratic government.

Collectively, Kang's ideas were called the **New China Movement,** and they spread widely among educated people in the 1890s. By 1898, the stage was set for an attempt at revolution from above, similar to that carried out by Peter the Great in eighteenth-century Russia. But this attempt was not successful, and its supporters in Beijing were forced to flee for their lives. For a few more years, under the manipulations of the empress, the status quo prevailed. It was clear that if China were to be changed, it would have to be done from below by the exasperated and desperate people.

The Chinese Republic An important step toward a new China was the abolition of the Confucian examinations for government office in 1905. This move opened the way for aspiring officials with modern ideas, many of whom had been educated in the West or in rapidly westernizing Japan. The Western-educated liberal **Sun Yat-sen** (1866–1925) was the intellectual leader of an antigovernment reform movement that quickly swept the whole country. Sun was trained as a medical doctor in Honolulu and Hong Kong, and on returning to his country, he gradually became convinced that a revolution from below was the only answer to China's many ills. He took up the cause of reform ("Three Principles") among the overtaxed and impoverished peasantry, believing that China could regain political harmony only after a measure of social justice had been established.

The long-awaited revolution against the feeble and incompetent government came in 1911. After Cixi's death three years earlier, the dynasty was so weak that few would defend it when it was challenged. Originally, Sun was called to head the new parliamentary government, but to avoid civil war, the head of the Army, General Yuan Shikai, soon replaced him. The Republic of China was formally declared in 1912. The last child emperor was forced to abdicate and lived long enough to see the installation of Mao's communist government many years later.

For a few years, General Yuan was master of China and intended to become the next emperor. But his failure to stop the Japanese incursions on the coast during World War I made him unpopular, and he died in disgrace in 1916. For the next decade China was in anarchy, ruled by warlords (local strong men, often ex-bandits) with private

Boxer Rebel Awaits Beheading, 1901. Surrounded by European troops, Chinese hangmen prepare to behead a captured Boxer. *(Hulton Deutsch/Woodfin Camp)*

armies. More important was the fast growth of fanatical nationalism among the urban classes, particularly the educated youth. Sun was the theoretical leader of this movement, but he was a poor organizer, and the national party he founded, the **Kuomintang,** or KMT, split into many factions during the 1920s.

The whole nationalist-reformist phase of China's development in the early twentieth century is called the **May Fourth Movement** because of an incident in 1919 when thousands of Beijing students and youth protested the Versailles Treaty's gift of a part of China to Japan. The movement had no single leader, and its various subgroups went off in many directions. Eventually, the reform ideas it propagated would provide some of the momentum for the communist takeover after World War II. **Mao Zedong** himself was one of the outraged students who swore that China would no longer be the pawn of foreigners and capitalists who exploited Chinese backwardness.

Chiang Kai-shek's Regime

Sun Yat-sen's most able and aggressive lieutenant was **Chiang Kai-shek,** who headed the KMT's military branch. After the founder's death in 1925, Chiang moved quickly to take over leadership, while maintaining the liaison with the tiny Chinese Communist Party (CCP) that Sun had established in the early 1920s to assist in modernizing the state. In 1926, Chiang felt himself strong enough to go after the warlords who had made themselves into petty kings in the north and northeast and bring them under effective central control. This Northern Expedition was a success, and several

Chiang Kai-shek and Madame Chiang. The newsweekly *Time* selected Chiang and his spouse as "Man and Wife of the Year, 1937." Madame Chiang handled much of the diplomacy of China with the Western powers in this epoch. (© *1938 Time, Inc. Reprinted by permission*)

provinces were recovered. Strengthened by this and by the increasing support of Chinese financial circles, Chiang decided to finish off the communists who had displayed disturbing support in Shanghai and a few other coastal cities. In 1927, he conducted a sweeping blood purge of all suspected communists, killing tens of thousands before it was over. The CCP appeared to have suffered an irremediable defeat. Chiang was clearly in control and established himself as the president of a national KMT government in Beijing a few months later.

The Kuomintang government under Chiang (1928–1975) was a barely disguised dictatorship, led by a man who believed in force as the ultimate political argument. He had married a westernized Chinese plutocrat who successfully acted as his intermediary when dealing with Western governments throughout his long career. Chiang believed the obstacles to making China into a sovereign, respected state were first the Japanese and then the communists. As time passed, however, that order began to reverse. Under new leaders, the CCP had staged a quick recovery from the events of 1927 and, within a few years, had established a strong base among the peasants in south China.

Knowing that he did not as yet have the strength to challenge the superior weaponry and training of the Japanese,

Chiang threw his 700,000-man army against the communists. He drove them from their rural strongholds into the famous **Long March of 1934,** an epic of guerrilla war. Under their rising star Mao Zedong, an original force of perhaps 100,000 poorly armed peasants wandered more than 6,000 miles through western China. A year later, the 10,000 or so survivors of starvation and combat barricaded themselves in Shensi in the far northwest near the Mongolian border. Here, during the remainder of the 1930s, they preached the Marxist gospel to the desperately poor peasants around them.

In this, they were following Mao's new precept: the Chinese peasants are a true revolutionary force, and no revolution will succeed without them. Mao pursued peasant support in clever and concrete ways. He never spoke of collectivization but only of justice, lower interest rates, and fair distribution of land. The members of the CCP became village teachers—the first ever in this province—and made sure that the communist army did not behave like earlier Chinese armies and "liberate" what they needed and wanted from the helpless farmers. Soon the locals were sufficiently impressed with Mao's forces that they began to join them.

The Sino-Japanese War and the Maoist Challenge

Americans sometimes forget that for four years prior to Pearl Harbor the Japanese and Chinese were engaged in a bloody war. This conflict had actually begun with the Japanese aggression in Manchuria in 1931, but it had been sporadic until a minor incident in the summer of 1937 gave the Japanese commanders the pretext they had long sought. After a few months of unequal fighting, the two major cities of Beijing and Nanjing had fallen, and much of coastal China was under Japanese control.

Instead of submitting and becoming a Japanese puppet as expected, Chiang elected to move his government many hundreds of miles west and attempt to hold out until he could find allies. The move inland meant, however, that Chiang was isolated from his main areas of support. Furthermore, the KMT army and officials appeared to the local people around the new command city of Chongqing (Chunking) as a swarm of devouring locusts. Famine was endemic in this poverty-stricken region, and official corruption in the army and civil government was widespread. Morale deteriorated steadily under these conditions, especially since Chiang refused actively to fight the Japanese invader. After the attack on Pearl Harbor, he had decided that Tokyo would eventually be defeated by the Americans and that the communists under Mao were China's real enemy. Protected in his mountainous refuge, he wanted to husband his forces. When the war ended in 1945, Chiang was the commander of a large but poorly equipped and demoralized garrison army that had no combat experience and was living parasitically on its own people.

Mao in Yunan, 1930s. This undoubtedly staged photo wishes to show Mao's convivial side. During the desperate struggle against the forces of Chiang Kai-shek, there was usually little time for peasant interviews with the communist leadership. *(EastFoto)*

The Maoists, on the other hand, made steady progress in winning over the anti-Japanese elements among the people, especially the peasants. They claimed to be nationalists and patriots as well as reformers, and they fought the invader at every opportunity from their bases in the northwest. Mao set up a local government system that was far more just and more respectful of the peasants than the KMT had been. He introduced democratic practices that won the communists the support of many of the intellectuals and the workers. Mao's armed force grew by large numbers during the war years to a total of almost a million men in organized units, plus many thousands of guerrilla fighters behind the Japanese lines. The CCP set up mass organizations with branches in every village for women, youth, educators, and others.

Communist Victory At the Pacific war's end, Chiang's army was about three times the size of Mao's, and he was confident of victory. The civil war broke out soon after the Japanese surrender. The United States at first backed Chiang with supplies and money but could not counter the effects of years of corrupt KMT rule, inaction, and failure on Chiang's part to appreciate what China's peasant masses wanted. While the KMT armies deserted, the communist forces enjoyed wide and growing support. The superior fighting spirit and military tactics of the Maoists turned the tide decisively in 1948, when Beijing and the big port cities fell into their hands.

By October 1949, all of China was under Mao's control, and Chiang with several hundred thousand KMT men were refugees on the Chinese offshore island of Taiwan. Here, they set up a regime that called itself the Republic of China and was recognized as the legitimate government of China by the anticommunist world for some time to come. But "Red" China (properly the People's Republic of China, or PRC), with the world's largest population, was now presumably a devoted ally of the Soviet Union under the ruthless communist Mao and was aiming at world revolution side by side with the Soviets.

JAPAN

In the mid–nineteenth century, Japan's two centuries of seclusion under the Tokugawa shoguns ended, and the country began to be transformed.

The Emergence of Modern Japan

The trigger for Japan's modernization was the forceful "opening of Japan" by the American commodore Matthew

Perry in 1853 and 1854 (see Chapter 31). In the name of international commerce, Perry extorted a treaty from the shogun that allowed U.S. ships to dock and do business in Japanese ports. This treaty was soon followed by similar agreements with the European trading nations. With the country divided over whether to allow the "pale-faced barbarians" into the ports, a brief conflict broke out among the daimyo lords for the shogun's power, and a few resident foreigners were molested. In 1863, a retaliatory attack by Western naval forces revealed how far Japan had fallen behind in the arts of war.

Japan seemed on the brink of being reduced to the same helplessness as China, but at this point, a decisive difference emerged. Some of the daimyo and samurai faced the causes and consequences of Japanese impotence squarely: they decided to imitate the West as rapidly as possible. These men engineered the revolt against the shogunate in 1867 that is termed the **Meiji Restoration** because, in a formal sense, the emperor was restored to the center of political-governmental life and the shogunate was abolished. In control, however, was not the emperor but the powerful daimyo who had seen that the semifeudal shogunate was obsolete and now replaced it with a new style of government.

Starting in 1871, one major reform after another came out of the imperial capital in Tokyo (formerly Edo). All were modeled on the West. Unlike their neighbors across the China Sea, the Japanese leaders were willing and able to add up the pluses and minuses of accepting Western ideas and come to definite, consensual decisions about them. Then they systematically carried out reforms, even at the expense of cherished tradition.

Meiji Reforms

The major reforms of the Meiji Restoration included the following:

- *Military.* The daimyo-samurai feudal forces were removed in favor of a conscript army with a modern organization, modern weaponry, and professional discipline.
- *Financial.* A new national tax system and a new national bank and currency were established; credit facilities and corporations on the Western model were introduced.
- *Agrarian.* Land was redistributed, quasi-feudal dues abolished, and ownership was established clearly and securely by survey.
- *Constitutional.* In 1889, a group of notables framed an entirely new constitution. It gave the parliamentary vote to a small electorate and allowed the emperor considerable but not supreme power over the government elected by the parliament.

By no means did all Japanese support these reforms. The samurai majority were so discontented by their total loss of status (even their precious swords were taken from them in

1876) that they several times attempted to rebel, only to be crushed by the new army. The new tax system, which required money payments to the government rather than service to the daimyo, reduced many peasants from landowners to tenants and was very unpopular. But after twenty years, the reform element in Tokyo was unshakably entrenched.

Students were sent abroad by the hundreds annually to study Western science and Western government. For a time, everything Western was highly fashionable in Japan, from pocket watches to Darwinian biology. As elsewhere, the most potent of all the Western influences was the modern sense of nationalism, which struck Japanese youth just as strongly as it had Chinese. New political parties sprang up and vigorously contested the seats in the lower house of the Diet (parliament). The constitution of 1889 was modeled after the German constitution authored by Bismarck and reserved decisive powers to the wealthy voters and the imperial ministers. The emperor was sovereign, not the people. He was also commander in chief of the armed forces, and the ministers answered solely to him, not to the

Japan's First Railway. In 1872 the Tokyo-Yokohama rail line was opened, only a few years after the Meiji reform era began. Built under the direction of Western engineers, the line fascinated the Japanese, who portrayed it in traditional woodcut style. (© *Asian Art & Archaeology, Inc./Corbis*)

SUMO WRESTLERS

When Commander Matthew Perry "opened" Japan to the West by quasi-invasion in 1853, one of the treats given him by his reluctant hosts was a sumo exhibition. Perry related his rather negative impression in his journals:

> After we were seated . . . some twenty five or thirty huge men, naked with the exception of a narrow girdle around the loins, were paraded before us. Never have I seen grouped together so many brawny men, giving a better idea of an equal number of stall-fed bulls than human beings. These men were professional wrestlers. . . .
>
> On passing behind screens they were covered with robes which they retained until brought into the ring. This was a circular space of about twelve feet in diameter, carefully prepared and the earth broken up and smoothed, and every hard substance removed. On a signal being given, two whose names were called stepped into the ring and began to eye one another with threatening looks, rather dramatic to be sure, stamping the soft earth with their naked feet, stooping down and grasping handfuls of the earth with which they rubbed themselves . . . whether this was to imitate the action of the bull, who paws the earth when preparing for an attack, or for what purpose, I am ignorant, but it seemed to be very foolish.
>
> At last they placed themselves opposite to one another crouched upon their hams, each warily watching the eye and movements of his antagonist. Quick as lightning they sprang upon one another, and writhing their arms about the upper parts of the body of their opponent commenced a contest which was neither wrestling nor boxing. Each occasionally was whirled about by some extraordinary effort and thrown violently upon the ground. . . .
>
> One of the contestants invariably exhibited the greatest rage, constantly howling and screeching at the top of his lungs, making a noise similar to that of dogs in combat. This was evidently to show that he was the attacking party. . . . It was noticed by all the officers that the one who made the noise was in every instance overcome.

Source: Asia and Africa. Introductory Studies of Non-Western Societies, ed. P. Conover (Columbus, OH: Merrill, 1973), citing Perry, The Japan Expedition 1852–1854 (Washington, DC: Smithsonian Institution, 1968).

---

parliament. Only about 5 percent of the male population had the franchise for parliamentary elections.

At the same time, the Meiji leaders made sure that the ancient regime and the traditional values of the people were held in high esteem. The reformers strongly supported the Shinto faith, which revered the emperor as the quasi-divine leader of his country,. The constitution (which remained in force until 1945) explicitly stated that "the empire of Japan shall be governed by a line of emperors unbroken forever." The Meiji reformers made no attempt to throw out what they thought of as truly Japanese. Rather, the reform consciously—and successfully—aimed at making Japanese of all classes into good patriot-citizens.

Industrial development received much attention from the outset. Government funds were directed to railroad construction, shipyards, mines, and munitions under the supervision of foreign technicians. Later in the 1890s, many of these costly enterprises were sold at bargain rates to combinations of individual investors. Thus began the peculiar Japanese form of government-assisted large corporations called *zaibatsu,* which came to dominate the nation's economy. New banks were founded to provide credit for entrepreneurs, and the internal transport of people and goods was greatly eased by the construction of a dense network of railways. Mountainous terrain and the island geography had physically isolated much of Japan's population until the early twentieth century, but the railroads changed that.

Agriculture became more productive as taxes were paid in fixed amounts of money rather than produce, and peasants were able for the first time to buy, mortgage, and sell land freely. Silk was the big money crop, rising from 2.3 million pounds in 1870 to 93 million in 1929. Japan's mechanization of silk production practically blew the Chinese out of the world market they had previously dominated. Rice production—the key Japanese commodity—also rose sharply, more than doubling in tonnage produced in one generation's time.

Foreign Successes The foreign policy of Meiji Japan was aggressive and grew more so as time went on. The challenge to "big brother" China in 1895 was a great success. Another success was the gradual elimination of the unequal treaties signed with the Western powers in the 1850s and 1860s. Like China, the Japanese authorities had at first agreed to a series of treaties that allowed Westerners to enjoy extraterritoriality. Persistent negotiations reversed this situation by the end of the century, and Japan became the first Asian power in modern times to treat with Europeans as equals.

But the big breakthrough for Japanese foreign prestige was the Russo-Japanese War of 1904–1905. This war, the first between an Asian and a European nation that ended in victory for the Asians, announced to the world that Japan had arrived as a major power. The formal annexation of occupied Korea was a major result of the war, and the Japanese nationalists felt cheated that they had not obtained still more from the beaten Russians. They would have their chance a few years later, when the Bolshevik revolution and civil war made Russia temporarily helpless. After nominally participating on the Allied side in World War I, Japan attempted to seize eastern Siberia from the Soviets. Pressured mainly by

Tanks Patrolling Nanjing, 1937. The "rape of Nanjing" was the opening of the second Sino-Japanese war, 1937–1945. Here, Japanese armor patrols among the ruins of China's second city. *(Bettmann/Corbis)*

the United States, the Japanese agreed to evacuate in 1922 but kept their eyes firmly on the huge border province of Manchuria as a possible field for imperial expansion.

Between the World Wars

The foundation of civil government in Japan was aided substantially by the fact that economic prosperity for the upper and middle classes continued without setback for the entire reign of the first Meiji emperor (1868–1912). World War I then gave the entire economy a boost but also created severe inflation that caused serious rioting among the working class in 1918. The 1920s and 1930s saw a strengthening of the army in politics, a factor that Japan had not previously experienced. The career officers often resented their diminished position in Japanese life compared to what the samurai had once had. Considering themselves the most devoted and reliable exponents of all that was good in Japanese culture, they came to hold the civilian politicians in contempt.

In the early and most difficult years of the Great Depression, the officers' ambitions were particularly attracted to resource-rich Manchuria. In 1931, they in effect rebelled against the Tokyo civil government and seized the province from the very weak hands of China. From this point onward, Japan's army was engaged in an undeclared war against China and also against its own government in Tokyo. The Chinese war became an open struggle only after 1937, but the war against the civil government was already won in 1932. From that year, the military was in effective command of Japan's domestic and foreign policies. Any civilians who opposed the aggressive and self-confident generals and admirals were soon silenced.

In 1936, Japan, whose military shared the usual contempt for Marxism among army men, joined the Hitler-sponsored Anti-Comintern Pact. By 1937, Japan was formally at war with Chiang Kai-shek's government and had close to a million men in China. The alliance with Hitler (and Mussolini) was supposedly strengthened by the signing of the 1940 Tripartite (three-sided) Pact, but the Japanese resented not being informed of Hitler's decision to go to war against the West in 1939. When Germany decided to attack Russia in 1941, the Japanese were again not informed, and they decided to remain neutral despite the provisions of the pact and German anger. The Japanese had, in fact, little to do with their supposed ally throughout World War II. The war in the Pacific was indeed almost entirely distinct from the European conflict in timing, motivation, and contestants.

The Japanese attacked Pearl Harbor in December 1941 because the Tokyo military command was convinced that war was inevitable if the United States would not go along with Japan's plans for expansion in Asia. Since the U.S. government showed no signs of changing its expressed resistance after long negotiations, the Tokyo general staff wished to strike first and hoped that greater willpower would overcome greater resources (see Chapter 49).

For about eight months, it seemed that the Japanese might be correct. Then, with the great naval battles of the mid-Pacific in the summer of 1942, the tides of war changed. From that point on, it was apparent to most observers (including many of Japan's leaders) that the best Japan could hope for was a negotiated peace that would leave it the dominant power in the western Pacific. Those hopes steadily diminished and were finally dashed with the explosions over Hiroshima and Nagasaki in August 1945.

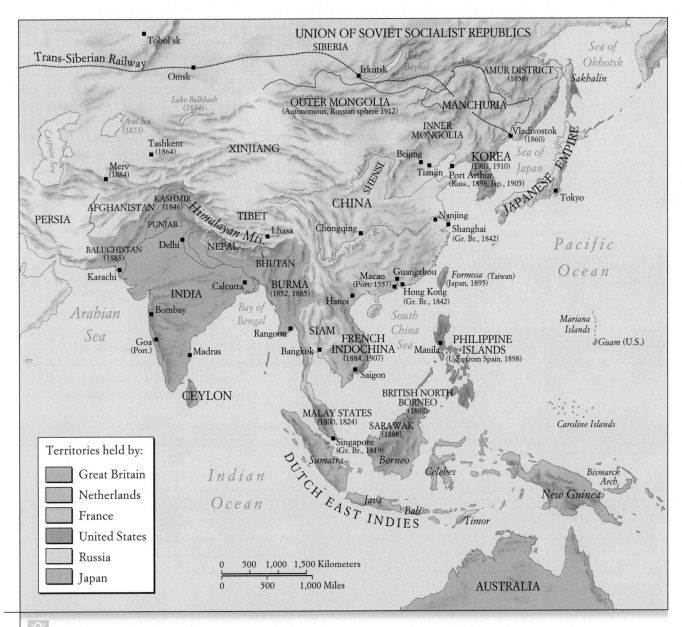

MAP 48.1 East Asian Colonial Territories, 1840–1940. Shown here are the accessions of colonial domains by the West in East Asia during the era of new imperialism. Only Thailand (Siam) escaped.

SOUTHEAST ASIA

Although China and Japan managed to maintain their formal independence from the Europeans, the Asians in the southeast of the continent and in the Pacific Islands were not so fortunate. In the nineteenth century, all those who had not already become part of a European empire fell under one or another of the great powers, except Thailand, which played off various rivals and thereby retained independence (see Map 48.1 and Chapter 31).

In the middle of the century, the kingdom of Burma, which had been independent for many centuries, fell under British rule through war and was united to British India. At the same time, the British colonial fiefs in Malaya and especially Singapore, the port at its tip, began to experience a great economic upsurge. The tin mines and rubber plantations that sprang forth in interior Malaya attracted much British capital and Chinese labor. By the end of the century, Singapore was a large city serving shipping from around the industrial world as well as East Asia. The political leadership was entirely British, but the Chinese dominated trade and commerce, and their business acumen enabled them to maintain equality with the Europeans in all except political matters.

The French presence centered on Indochina, or Vietnam, Laos, and Cambodia, as they are now called. The French had seized Indochina by stages, starting in the 1850s. They were aided by the same invulnerable naïveté that impeded an effective Chinese response to European aggression: the mandarins simply could not believe that their "superior" culture was endangered. In 1859, France used a pretext to seize Saigon and, a few years later, Cambodia. Following a brief war with China in 1885, the French then took over all of Vietnam and Laos.

In time, tens of thousands of French came to Indochina to make their careers and/or fortunes as officials, teachers, rubber plantation owners, and adventurers of all sorts. Like the British in Malaya, the French introduced some beneficial changes into the economy and society, making southern Vietnam, for example, into an enormously fertile rice bowl that exported its product throughout East Asia. Schools were opened in the villages, the practical slavery of women was ended, child marriages were forbidden, and new cash crops (rubber and coffee) were introduced. But as happened everywhere else in Asia, these improvements in social and economic possibilities mainly benefited a relatively very small minority of alien middlemen (mainly Chinese) and native landlords. And they were outweighed in nationalist eyes by the humiliations suffered at the hands of the European conquerors and overlords.

In the major maritime colonies of Dutch Indonesia and the Spanish Philippine Islands, the Europeans had a much longer presence, dating to the seventeenth century. The Indonesian islands had been placed under a very limited (in the geographic sense) Dutch rule in the 1600s when bold Hollanders had driven out their Portuguese rivals for the rich spice export trade. Since then little had changed until the mid–nineteenth century. At that juncture, the nature of colonial controls had tightened, and their impact expanded with the introduction of the "culture system" of coerced cropping of specific commodities. Dutch overlords gradually conquered and replaced native leaders, and a small group controlled large estates that produced coffee and sugar at high profits. Despite efforts to assist them after 1870, the Indonesian peasants suffered as massive population growth turned many of them into landless semiserfs for Dutch and Chinese landlords.

Alone among the Asian lands taken over by European rule, the Philippines became a nation in which the majority was Christian. This fact heightened the Filipinos' resentment when Spain continued to deny them political and social rights. The southern half of the Philippine archipelago was never brought under European rule, and here the Muslim faith was paramount among an aggregation of sultanates. A rebellion against the stagnant and faltering Spanish rule broke out in the northern islands in the late 1890s. It was still going on when the Americans became embroiled in war with Spain and captured the islands (1899–1900).

Since the United States was originally no more inclined to give the Filipinos independence than the Spaniards had been, the rebellion turned against the Americans and persisted for two more years before it was finally extinguished. What had been promoted as a "liberation" became an occupation. Even though American policy became steadily more benevolent and advantageous to the Filipinos and independence was promised in the 1930s, the Philippines had to wait another decade before attaining sovereignty immediately after World War II.

SUMMARY

China and Japan met the overwhelming challenge of Western intervention in vastly different ways. The Chinese mandarins, unwilling to leave the false security that Confucian philosophy and many centuries of assured superiority gave them, went down a blind alley of hopeless resistance and denial until they were pushed aside by rebellion and revolution at the beginning of the twentieth century. In contrast, the Japanese upper classes soon recognized the advantages to be gained by selectively adopting Western ways and used them to their own, highly nationalistic ends during the Meiji Restoration of the late nineteenth century.

China's halfhearted and confused experiment with a democratic republic came to an end in World War II, when the corrupt Chiang Kai-shek regime was unable to rally nationalist support against either the Japanese or Mao's communists. After two years of civil war, Mao took Chinese fate in his confident hands.

Japan's civil government was much more stable and successful than China's until the 1930s, when a restive and ambitious military establishment pushed it aside and put the country on a wartime footing with an invasion of China. Then, in 1941, they entered World War II with the attack on Pearl Harbor.

Elsewhere, almost all of Southeast Asia was a European colony, and by the early twentieth century, this region was experiencing a buildup of frustrated nationalism among both intellectuals and ordinary folk. This became even truer after the Asians witnessed the humiliation of Russia by Japan in 1905 and the mutual slaughter of Europeans in World War I. In retrospect, the late nineteenth and early twentieth centuries were the high point of European domination of Asia. After World War II, the tide would turn toward a closer balance in East–West relations.

TEST YOUR KNOWLEDGE

1. The beginning of China's clear inability to withstand foreign pressure is found in
   a. the outcome of the Opium Wars.
   b. the repression of the Boxer Rebellion.
   c. the defeat at the hands of the Japanese in 1895.
   d. the concessions in Manchuria to the Russians in 1901.
2. The bloodiest rebellion in China's history is called
   a. the Boxer Rebellion.
   b. the Nakamura Rising.
   c. the Taiping Rebellion.
   d. the Long March.
3. The "late Manzhou restoration" was
   a. a successful attempt by the bureaucracy to renew itself.
   b. a cultural movement in the late nineteenth century that replaced Western forms with Chinese models of literature and art.
   c. the regeneration of the government by local gentry leaders after the Taiping and Nien Rebellions were put down.
   d. the substitution of a new young emperor for the old empress by the army.
4. The Meiji Restoration in Japan saw
   a. the return of the emperor to supreme governing power.
   b. a turning away from the West to a renewed isolation.
   c. the reinstallation of the samurai and daimyo to power.
   d. the adoption of Western techniques and ideas by Japan's rulers.
5. The single most important foreign policy success of post-1853 Japan was
   a. winning the war against China in 1895.
   b. forcing the Boxer rebels to surrender in China in 1901.
   c. winning the war against Russia in 1904–1905.
   d. signing the Anglo-Japanese Treaty of 1902.
6. Which of the following places was not made into a European colony?
   a. Thailand
   b. Indonesia
   c. Malaya
   d. Burma
7. The most important Asian group in the foreign trade of Southeast Asia was the
   a. Japanese.
   b. Chinese.
   c. Vietnamese.
   d. Indians.

IDENTIFICATION TERMS

Boxer Rebellion

Chiang Kai-shek

Empress Dowager Cixi

Kuomintang (KMT)

Long March of 1934

Mao Zedong

May Fourth Movement

Meiji Restoration

New China Movement

Opium Wars

Self-Strengthening

Sun Yat-sen

Taipings

unequal treaties

INFOTRAC COLLEGE EDITION

Enter the search term "China history" using Key Words.
Enter the search term "Mao Zedong" using the Subject Guide.

Enter the search term "Japan history" using Key Words.

49

WORLD WAR II

I have been actuated by love and loyalty to my people in all my thoughts, acts, and life. They gave me the strength to make the most difficult decisions which have ever confronted mortal man.

ADOLF HITLER

THE RISE AND FALL OF COLLECTIVE SECURITY
The Spanish Civil War

HITLER'S MARCH TO WAR, 1935–1939
The Reoccupation of the Rhineland
Anschluss in Austria
Munich, 1938
The Nazi-Soviet Nonaggression Pact

WORLD WAR II
The European Theater
The Pacific Theater

THE ONSET OF THE COLD WAR
Wartime Alliance and Continuing Mistrust
The Original Issues

1931	Japanese Seizure of Manchuria
1935	Ethiopian War
1936–1939	Spanish Civil War
1938	*Anschluss* of Austria/Munich Conference
1939–1945	War in Europe
1941–1945	War in Pacific
1945	Yalta and Potsdam Conferences among Allies
1945–1948	Eastern Europe comes under Soviet control/ Cold War begins

FOR THE FIRST FIFTEEN YEARS after the end of World War I, the peace held together. Despite the bitter complaints of the losers, especially the Germans, the Paris treaties were backed up by French diplomacy and the potential application of military force by France and Britain. For a brief period in the late 1920s, the Germans voluntarily adopted a policy of "fulfillment," adhering to the provisions of the treaties. But with the worldwide economic collapse and the coming of Adolf Hitler to power in the early 1930s, the treaties were unilaterally rejected and an atmosphere of international hostility resumed. The impotence of the League of Nations was quickly evident, and Hitler successfully bluffed his way forward until he felt himself in an invulnerable position to undertake a war of vengeance and conquest.

THE RISE AND FALL OF COLLECTIVE SECURITY

When the French saw the U.S. Senate reject Woodrow Wilson's League of Nations and realized that the British were having second thoughts about continuing their wartime alliance, they hurriedly took independent steps to protect France from potential German revenge. To this end, France signed a military alliance with Poland, Czechoslovakia, and Romania, three of Germany's eastern neighbors. This *Little Entente* stated that if Germany attacked any of the signatories, the others would give assistance. Also, France stayed on good terms with fascist Italy through the 1920s. And the French consistently argued that the League must take unified action against any potential aggressor nation; an attack on one was an attack against all.

Even before Hitler's seizure of power, however, the Paris-inspired policy of "collective security" against a resurgent Germany was under severe strain. For one thing, the aggressive stirring of international revolutionary hopes by the Bolsheviks meant that Soviet Russia was an outcast (see Chapter 46). For years, it was not invited to join the League of Nations and even after a reluctant invitation was extended, it was not considered a suitable ally by the capitalist democracies. For another, Japan, a member of the league, totally disregarded the league's disapproval of its invasion of Manchuria in 1931 and got away without penalty. The league could only express its moral condemnation.

The league's impotence was revealed even more clearly in 1935 in a case that was much closer to European affairs. Hoping to revive his sagging popularity with the Italian people, Benito Mussolini started a blatantly imperialistic war with Ethiopia. The Ethiopians appealed to the league and obtained a vote that clearly branded Italy as an aggressor nation. But neither Paris nor London would take decisive measures such as banning oil shipments to Italy, which had no oil of its own. In the end, the triumphant invaders were not even threatened in their occupation of Ethiopia. The League of Nations had been shown to have no teeth. Collective security had been struck a hard but not yet lethal blow.

The Spanish Civil War

All hope for collective security was finished off by the Spanish Civil War, which broke out in the summer of 1936. Spain in the 1930s was a sharply divided nation. Its liberals had recently forced out an ineffectual monarch and declared a republic. But the public remained divided among every variety of leftist group, moderate democrats, and fascists. Like most of the Spanish upper classes, many army commanders were afraid that Spain might soon come under a communist government if current trends were not checked. To prevent such a takeover, they entered into a military revolt, supported by the Catholic Church, much of the peasantry, and most of the middle classes.

Despite open support for the rebel forces from both Mussolini and Hitler, the Western democracies refused to take sides and declared an embargo on shipments of arms and matériel to both contestants. In the circumstances, this was the same as assisting the rebels led by General Francisco Franco against the legitimate Spanish government.

Josef Stalin early decided that the Spanish conflict was a golden opportunity. It might allow the Soviet Union to gain popularity among the many Western antifascists who as yet could not sympathize with communism. The Comintern orchestrated an international campaign to assist the outnumbered and outgunned Spanish Loyalists in the name of a **Popular Front** against fascism. For two years, the Soviets abandoned their previous vicious propaganda against the democratic socialists in all countries. In some instances, Popular Front tactics were quite successful. Much Soviet military aid was sent to Spain, and some tens of thousands of volunteers from all over the world (including the United States) came to fight with the Loyalists.

But Hitler's and Mussolini's arms and advisers were more numerous and more effective in the long run. In the spring of 1939, the Loyalists surrendered, and Franco established himself as the military dictator of his country for the next generation. Though friendly to the fascist dictators, he stubbornly defended his freedom of action and

never allowed himself to be their tool. Like Sweden, Switzerland, and Portugal, Spain sat out World War II as a neutral.

HITLER'S MARCH TO WAR, 1935–1939

Since 1922, the fascist Mussolini had made no effort to conceal his contempt for the Western democracies, but Germany, much more than Italy, represented the real danger to the Paris treaties. Even before gaining power, Hitler had sworn to overturn the Versailles Treaty, and he proceeded to take Germany out of the League of Nations almost immediately—in 1933.

Did Hitler intend a major war from the outset of his dictatorship? This question is still much debated. Historians generally agree that he realized that the program of German hegemony described in *Mein Kampf* could only be made reality through war, because it entailed a major expansion of German territory eastward into Slavic lands (Poland and Russia). But he seems to have had no concrete plans for war until about 1936, when he instructed the General Staff to prepare them.

In 1935, Hitler had formally renounced the provisions of the Versailles Treaty that limited German armaments. This move had symbolic rather than practical importance, as the treaty limitations had been ignored even during the Weimar era. A few months later, he started conscription for a much larger army and the creation of a large *Luftwaffe* (air force). Neither France nor Britain reacted beyond a few words of diplomatic dismay and disapproval.

The Reoccupation of the Rhineland

In 1936, Hitler sent a small force into the **Rhineland,** the area of Germany west of the Rhine on the French borders. Under both the Versailles and Locarno agreements, the Rhineland was supposed to be permanently demilitarized. To the French, stationing German troops there was a direct threat to their security. But in the moment of decision, France said that it did not want to act alone, and Britain said it would not support France in an offensive action. What the British and French did not know was that the German army was more frightened of the consequences of the Rhineland adventure than they were. The General Staff strongly opposed the action, advising Hitler not to try this ploy, because the army as yet was in no condition to resist Allied attacks. Hitler insisted on proceeding with his bluff and scored a great psychic and diplomatic triumph over his own generals as well as the French. From this point, the quite erroneous legend of Hitler the master strategist was born.

From 1936 on, Germany was rapidly rearming, while France and Britain were paralyzed by defeatism or pacifism among both the general public and the government officials. In Britain, where the English Channel still gave a false feeling of security, many members of the Conservative government leaned toward appeasement of der Führer and were ready to abandon France. Much of the party leadership was more fearful of a Bolshevik revolution than of a fascist or Nazi society. Some hoped that a Hitler-like figure would rise in Britain and put "order" back into the Depression-wracked country. The French, for their part, put all their hopes into the huge defensive network—the Maginot Line—built during the 1920s along their eastern borders—and into their allies in eastern Europe.

Also in 1936, Hitler and Mussolini reached a close understanding, the Rome–Berlin **Axis Pact,** which made them allies in case of war. This agreement eliminated any hopes the French might have had that Mussolini would side with France and against Germany.

Anschluss in Austria

In 1938, the pace of events picked up. Hitler, an Austrian by birth, had always intended to bring about the "natural union" of his birthplace with Germany. The **Anschluss** (joining) was explicitly forbidden by the Versailles Treaty, but by this time that was a dead letter. In Austria, the Nazis had strong support. Most Austrians were German by blood, and they regarded the enforced separation from the Reich as an act of vengeance by the Allies. An earlier attempt at a Nazi coup in 1934 had failed because of Mussolini's resistance. Now, in 1938, Mussolini was Hitler's ally, and the Anschluss could go forward. It was completed in March by a bloodless occupation of the small country on Germany's southern borders, and Nazi rule was thus extended to another seven million people.

Next to fall was the Successor state of Czechoslovakia, a country created by the Versailles Treaty that Hitler had always hated. Linked militarily with France, it contained within its borders 3.5 million Germans, the Sudetenlander minority who were strongly pro-Hitler. Under the direction of Berlin, the Sudeten Germans agitated against the democratic, pro-Western government in Prague. Concessions were made, but the Germans always demanded more. After the Anschluss in Austria, it appeared only a matter of time before the Germans acted. The attitude of the British government was the key. If Britain supported Czech armed resistance, the French promised to honor their Little Entente treaty obligation and move against Germany.

Munich, 1938

In September 1938, Hitler brought the British prime minister Neville Chamberlain and the French premier Edouard Daladier to a conference at Munich, where they were joined by Mussolini. After several days of threats and negotiations, Hitler succeeded in extracting the **Munich Agreements** from the democratic leaders. The Czechs were sacrificed entirely, although Hitler had to wait a few months before taking the final slice. Chamberlain returned to Britain waving a piece of paper that he claimed guaranteed "peace in our time." One year later, Britain and Germany were at war.

Almost before the ink was dry on the Munich Agreements, Hitler started pressuring Poland about its treatment of its German minority. These Germans lived in solid blocs on the borders with Germany and in the so-called Free City of Danzig (Gdansk) in the Polish Corridor to the sea between Germany and its province of East Prussia (see Map 49.1).

Prodded by British public opinion and the speeches of Winston Churchill in Parliament, Chamberlain now at last moved firmly. In March 1939, he signed a pact with Poland, guaranteeing British (and French) aid if Germany attacked. Hitler did not take this threat seriously, as he knew that the Allies could aid Poland only by attacking Germany in the West. But the French, having put their military in an entirely defensive orientation behind the Maginot Line, were not prepared to go on the offensive. Of more concern to Hitler was the attitude of the other nearby great power, the Soviet Union.

The Nazi-Soviet Nonaggression Pact

At this point, the only convincing threat to Hitler's war plans was the possibility of having to face the Soviet Union in the east and the Allies in the west simultaneously—the two-front war that had proved disastrous in 1914–1918. But even at this stage, neither Chamberlain nor Daladier nor their conservative advisers could bring themselves to ask the communist Stalin to enter an alliance. In fact, the Russians were equally suspicious of the West's motives as Paris and London were of Moscow. Stalin had not forgotten that the Soviet Union had been excluded from the postwar arrangements and treaties. Nor had he overlooked the fact that when the chips were down, Britain and France had sacrificed their ally Czechoslovakia rather than coordinate action with the Soviet Union, as Stalin had offered to do through Czech intermediaries.

Even so, it was a terrific shock to communists and to all antifascists everywhere to hear, on August 23, 1939, that Stalin and Hitler had signed a **Nonaggression Pact.** By its terms, the Soviet Union agreed to remain neutral in a war involving Germany. In return, Hitler agreed that the Russians could occupy the three small Baltic states (Estonia, Latvia, and Lithuania), eastern Poland, and a slice of Romania. These areas had once belonged to imperial Russia and were still claimed by the Soviets. Both sides affirmed their "friendship." Hitler no longer had to worry about what Russia might do if he attacked Poland and the Allies came to the Poles' aid as they had promised. The Nonaggression Pact made war certain.

For communists all over the world, the pact represented a 180-degree turn in the party line, and they were

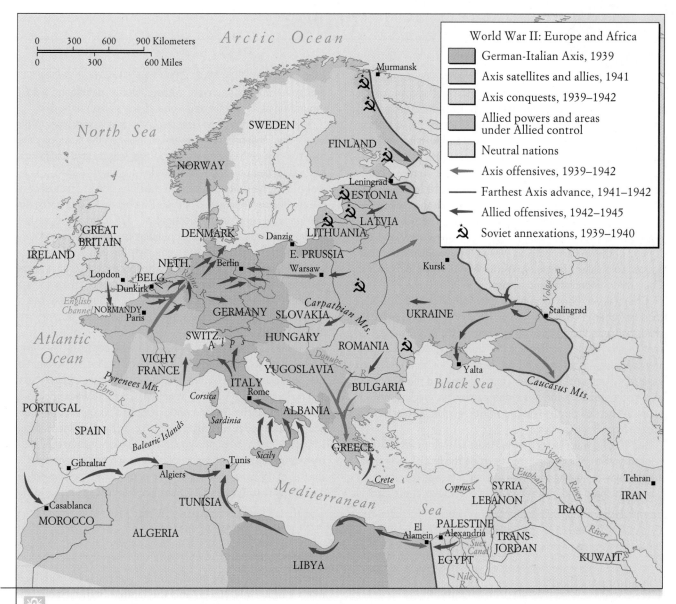

MAP 49.1 World War II in Europe. In contrast to World War I (1914–1918) World War II was decided militarily as much or more on the eastern fronts as in the west. Until the war's end, the largest part of Nazi forces was deployed in Russia and occupied eastern Europe. Civilian and military casualties far outstripped those of World War I, again mainly in the east, where slave labor was extensively recruited and the extermination camps were located.

entirely unprepared. Hitler was now the head of a friendly government. The Popular Front against fascism died overnight. Many members of the Communist Party outside the Soviet Union dropped out, unable to swallow this latest subordination of truth and others' national interests to the momentary advantage of the Soviets. But Stalin had gained some time. The Soviet Union did not enter World War II for almost two more years. Whether he used the time well to prepare for war is a topic of debate to the present day.

WORLD WAR II

World War II can be divided into three major chronological periods and two geographic areas, or theaters. Chronologically, the first phase of the conflict saw the German and later the Japanese victories and expansion from 1939 to late 1942. The second phase was the Allied counterattack from late 1942 through 1943, which checked and contained both enemies. The third phase was the steady Allied advance in 1944 and 1945, bringing final victory in August 1945.

WINSTON CHURCHILL
(1874–1965)

Each year the American newsmagazine *Time* selects a "Man of the Year" to appear on the cover of the last issue of the year. But a few years ago, *Time* decided that one individual should qualify as "Man of the Century." That person was the British statesman, author, artist, and warrior Winston Churchill. Yet some might ask which century Churchill best represents: the nineteenth, in whose traditions he immersed himself and fought for, or the twentieth, in which he found himself a natural hero, but somewhat out of step with the majority of his country's political and social viewpoints. The novelties introduced in British political life by mass democracy and the coming of the welfare state, as well as the worldwide backlash against colonialism following World War II, were difficult for Churchill to understand and accept.

Churchill was born to an American mother and a British aristocratic father in 1874. Born to privilege, Winston was a lonely child, unwanted and generally ignored by his parents. He was sent to the military academy at Sandhurst and served in India and the Sudan as an army officer. Resigning his commission to have more personal freedom, Churchill covered the Boer War as a correspondent for a London paper. He quickly made a name for himself through his journalistic exploits, especially his escape from Boer captivity.

In 1900, he was elected to the House of Commons as a Tory (Conservative). Four years later, he made the first of several political jumps by joining the rival Liberals and was rewarded by being appointed undersecretary for the colonies in the Liberal government of 1905–1908. Other high posts in succeeding Liberal governments followed, while Churchill developed a solid reputation as an incisive speaker and wily parliamentarian.

But in World War I, as First Sea Lord (that is, secretary of the navy), Churchill suffered a severe blow when the Gallipoli campaign, which he had strongly supported, was an abysmal failure. He was forced out of government for a time.

In 1924, he switched back to the Tory side as chancellor of the exchequer (minister of finance), a post he held until the Tories were defeated in the elections of 1929. During this period, he defended the idea of the continuing British empire and condemned Mohandas Gandhi's campaign for Indian self-government. He also led the opposition to organized labor and the general strike of 1926. These positions alienated large groups of voters for differing reasons, and after 1929 Churchill was out of government (but still in Parliament) for the entire decade preceding World War II.

During his "exile" in the 1930s, Churchill continued the writing career that had begun with journalism. But his passion for active politicking could not be satisfied with literary achievement, and he longed to get back into action. Churchill was appalled at the inability of the British upper classes to recognize the menace of Hitler and the fascist movements on the Continent. Again and again, he called on the government to strengthen the country's defenses and to take action against the Nazi aggression. In the fall of 1939, with a major war under way, the discredited government of Neville Chamberlain was forced out, and the

The European Theater

Geographically, the European theater (including North Africa) was the focus of Allied efforts until the German surrender in May 1945. Then, the emphasis shifted to the Pacific, but the anti-Japanese campaign was unexpectedly shortened by the atomic bombs and Japan's ensuing surrender. The United States, alone among the belligerents, played an important role on both fronts. The Pacific theater was fundamentally a conflict between Japan and the United States. The Soviet Union was drawn into the European war in mid-1941 but maintained neutrality with Germany's ally Japan until the final three weeks. (We will consider the Pacific war as an adjunct of the European theater, as indeed it was for all combatants except Japan and China.)

Phase 1: Axis Blitzkrieg   The German *blitzkrieg* ("lightning war") machine smashed into Poland on September 1, 1939 (see Map 49.1). Britain and France retaliated by declaring war on Germany two days later. Italy remained neutral for the time being (the Axis Pact did not demand immediate assistance to the other partner). So did Germany's other ally, Japan, and the United States, Spain, the Scandinavian countries, and the Balkan countries. The Soviet Union remained neutral as well, but it moved quickly to occupy the promised segments of eastern Europe in accord with the Nonaggression Pact.

Poland fell almost at once to the well-trained, well-armed Germans despite brave resistance. Soviet forces occupied the eastern half of the country. For several months, all was quiet. Then, in the spring of 1940, Hitler struck. France fell to the German tanks (now assisted by the Italians) within a few weeks. Denmark, the Netherlands, Belgium, and Norway were overwhelmed prior to France. By July, Britain stood alone against a Nazi regime that controlled Europe from the Russian border to the Pyrenees.

For the next several months, the Luftwaffe attempted to bomb England into submission, as many experts feared would be possible with the huge new planes and their large bomb loads. But the Battle of Britain, fought entirely in the air, ended with a clear victory for the defenders. The Channel was still under British control, and Hitler's plans for an

country turned to the man whose warning had proved so correct. Winston Churchill now stepped like some fierce, confident bulldog into the seat of power that he had been preparing for since boyhood. For millions of Britons, Churchill *was* the government, incarnating in his jowly face and stubborn chin the determination not to yield to the enemy's bombs or threats.

But almost immediately after final victory, his stubborn conservatism and unwillingness to cater to an electorate that had made enormous wartime sacrifices and now wanted the Labour Party's promised "welfare state." Six years later, with the public dissatisfied by Labour's inability to get the economy into high gear, another election returned the Tories and Churchill to power. He governed until his retirement in 1955.

The final ten years of Churchill's life were dedicated to writing his impressive *History of the English-Speaking Peoples,* to go on the shelf next to his magisterial *History of the Second World War* completed earlier. In 1953, he was awarded the Nobel Prize for literature.

Besides his political leadership, Churchill was known for his biting wit and mental quickness. Once the playwright and Labour supporter George Bernard Shaw sent him two tickets to a Shaw premiere. "Bring a friend, if you have one," wrote Shaw on the accompanying note. Churchill returned the tickets with regrets, saying that he could, however, use some for the second performance, "if there is one."

FOR REFLECTION

Do you think that Churchill deserves his honors as Man of the Century? Whom might you put up for that title instead?

Winston Churchill. Statesman, soldier, historian, journalist, and artist, Churchill was an extraordinary man in extraordinary times. *(The Bettmann Archive/Corbis)*

---

invasion, like those of Napoleon a century and a half earlier, had to be abandoned. Just before the fall of France, Churchill had replaced Chamberlain as head of the British government, and he personified the "British bulldog" who would never give up. His magnificent speeches and leadership rallied the British people, cemented the growing Anglo-American sympathies, and played a key role in the Allies' eventual victory. (See the Tradition and Innovation box for more on this leader.)

The high point of the war for the Nazis came in 1941, when attacks on Yugoslavia (April), Greece (May), and the Soviet Union (June) were all successful. The Germans gained huge new territories and turned all of eastern Europe into either a Nazi satellite (Romania, Bulgaria, Hungary) or an occupied land (the Ukraine, Poland, and western Russia). **Operation Barbarossa,** the code name for the attack on Russia, got off to a tremendous start, as Stalin's government was caught entirely by surprise despite repeated warnings from spies and Allied sources. In the first two days alone, some 2,000 Russian planes were destroyed on the ground, and a half million men were taken prisoner by the end of the first month. The Red Army, still recovering from the purge of its officers in 1937–1938, looked as though it had been all but knocked out of the war. At this critical point, Hitler overruled his generals and insisted on diverting many of his forces southward, toward the grain and oil of Ukraine and the Black Sea area, rather than heading straight for Moscow. As a consequence, the Germans were struck by the numbing cold of an early winter before they could take the capital, and Stalin was given precious time to rally and reinforce. For all practical purposes, the Germans had lost their chance for a quick, decisive victory on the Eastern front already in the fall of 1941.

Phase 2: Allied Counterattack   In December 1941, the attack on Pearl Harbor brought the United States into the war against Japan and its allies, Germany and Italy. In many ways, the U.S. entry into World War II and its later decisive role in it was similar to what had occurred in World War I. As the oppressive nature of the German occupation regime in Europe became known to the American public, opinion began running strongly in support of London and against

Ruins of Hamburg, 1945. The terrible destruction visited upon the German cities by Allied bombing is vividly displayed here. The port of Hamburg was destroyed in two days and nights in 1944 by a huge firestorm set off by incendiary bombs. (*Hulton Deutsch/Woodfin Camp*)

Berlin. Thus, the attack on Pearl Harbor only accelerated a process that was already under way toward the entry of the United States into the conflict.

Although the American peacetime military was very small and poorly equipped, U.S. industrial resources were immense and played the same important role that they had in 1917–1918. Neither Japan nor Germany had the wherewithal to hold out indefinitely against this power. In an economic sense, the outcome of the war was decided as early as December 1941.

But the Allies' eventual victory was far from clear at the time. The Germans had been checked in Russia but not defeated. Their Italian ally was not much help but did contribute to the takeover of North Africa and the Balkans, and the blockade of the British forces in Egypt. German submarines threatened Britain's supply lines from the United States for the next two years and were defeated (by the convoy system) only after heavy losses.

In the summer of 1942, the Russians were again pushed back hundreds of miles by superior German armor and aircraft. Stalin then ordered a "not one step backward" defense of the strategic city of **Stalingrad** on the Volga. Historians agree that the ensuing battle in the fall and winter of 1942 was the turning point of the war in Europe. The Nazis lost an entire army, which was surrounded and captured, and from this point on, they were defending more than attacking. At the same time, the Western Allies were at last counterattacking. In the summer of 1943, the Germans and Italians were driven from Africa, and the Allies landed in southern Italy. After a few months, the discredited Nazi puppet Mussolini fell, and Italy capitulated in September.

Phase 3: Allied Victory   In Europe, the tide had turned decisively in 1943. An Allied army landed in the south of France and started pushing northward. In the Balkans, the German occupiers were under heavy attack by partisans (guerrillas) supplied by the Allies. By late 1944, Greece, Yugoslavia, Bulgaria, and Albania had been cleared of Axis forces.

But the main theater of the war in Europe was on the Russian front, where the Germans had the bulk of their forces. Here, too, the Nazis were forced steadily back, and by the fall of 1944, they were again on German soil. Poland, Hungary, and Romania had all been freed of the occupiers. The Red Army became entrenched in those countries, while it pursued the retreating Germans.

The human losses on the Eastern front were immense. The Nazis had treated the occupied areas with great brutality, taking millions for slave labor in German factories and mines. Millions more starved to death. The large Jewish populations of Poland, Hungary, and Romania as well as the western Soviet Union were systematically exterminated in the gas chambers of Auschwitz, Belsen, Maidenek, and the other death camps set up by the SS.

Stalin's repeated calls for a **Second Front** in the West were finally answered by the June 1944 invasion across the English Channel by British, American, and Canadian forces (the invasion began on June 6, or **D day**). For the next several months, fighting raged in northern France and Belgium without a decision, but by the winter of 1944–1945, Allied troops were on Germany's western border. The next spring the fighting was carried deep into Germany from both east and west.

The Holocaust: The Extermination Camp at Auschwitz. After his initial success in the east, Hitler set in motion the machinery for the physical annihilation of Europe's Jews. Shown here is a group of Hungarian Jewish women and children who have just arrived at Auschwitz, a major extermination camp. The picture was taken shortly before their deaths. *(Yad Vashem/Film and Photo Archive)*

On May 1, 1945, a half-mad Hitler committed suicide in the smoking ruins of his Berlin bunker, as the Russians entered the city. Several of his closest associates chose the same death, but others fled and were hunted down for trial at Nuremberg as war criminals. Germany's formal surrender—unconditionally this time—took place on May 8. In accordance with previous agreements, the Russians occupied eastern Germany, including East Berlin. The British and Americans controlled the western part of the country.

The Pacific Theater

In the Pacific theater, naval battles in 1942 checked what had been a rapid Japanese advance (see Map 49.2). All of Southeast Asia and many Pacific islands had fallen to the flag of the Rising Sun, and the Japanese were threatening Australia and India by the middle of that year. But by the end of 1942, it was clear that the United States was recovering from Pearl Harbor. The **Battle of the Coral Sea** had nullified the Japanese threat to Australia, and British India proved ready to defend itself rather than passively submit, as Tokyo had hoped.

Even with the bulk of the U.S. war effort going toward Europe and the Russians remaining neutral, the Japanese did not have the raw materials or the manpower to keep up with the demands of prolonged conflict over so wide an area. (The Japanese high command knew this. They had counted heavily on the attack on Pearl Harbor to "knock out" American power in the Pacific or at least to make the United States amenable to a negotiated peace that would leave Japan in control of the western Pacific.)

In 1943–1944, the United States rolled the Japanese back, taking one Pacific island chain after another in bloody fighting. The Philippines were liberated from Tokyo's forces in late 1944 in a campaign led by the American commander Douglas MacArthur, the chief architect of the victory in the Pacific. The Japanese homelands were pummeled by constant bombing from these newly captured island bases.

Japanese Defeat and Surrender The end of the Pacific war came quickly after the Nazi capitulation. During 1944–1945, the Japanese occupation forces had been gradually forced from maritime Southeast Asia. Burma and Indochina had been cleared when the Japanese withdrew to return to their homeland. The long war between Japan and China was also now swinging in favor of the communist army under Mao Zedong (see Chapter 48).

The Americans were preparing for massive casualties in a planned invasion of the Japanese islands when they dropped atomic bombs on **Hiroshima** and Nagasaki in August 1945. Within a few days, the Japanese government indicated its readiness to surrender, and the formal act was completed on August 15, 1945. The sole condition was that Emperor Hirohito be allowed to remain on his throne.

Should the atomic bombs have been used? This issue has remained profoundly acrimonious. Critics say that the bombing of the two Japanese cities was admittedly aimed against civilians rather than military targets and cite the huge loss of civilian life (more than 70,000 of a population of about 200,000) in Hiroshima. This was entirely unnecessary, they say, because Japan would soon have surrendered

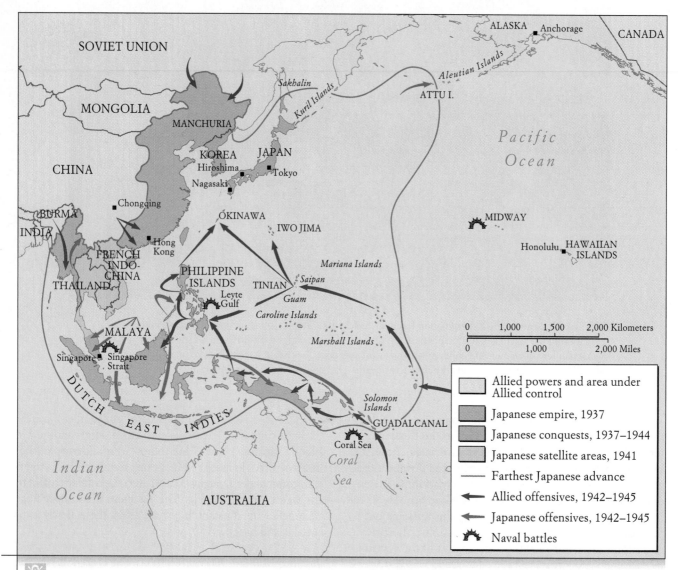

MAP 49.2 World War II in Asia and the Pacific. The failure of the Japanese to deal the United States Navy a lethal blow in the first months of the Pacific war meant that the war could not end in victory, as it would be only a matter of time until Washington could summon its far greater resources and drive the Japanese back. From 1943 onward, the best Tokyo realists could hope for was a negotiated peace that gave Japan some favored position in China.

to overwhelming Allied forces in any case. Another school of criticism thinks that the real reason for the bombing was that the U.S. government was looking ahead to the postwar era and wished to intimidate the Soviets.

On the other side, the defenders of President Harry S. Truman and the U.S. high command point out that the Japanese had shown fanatical determination to resist and would have stalwartly defended their home islands. Some estimates at the time allegedly thought more than a million U.S. casualties and countless more Japanese might have been expected before the fighting was over. To avoid such massive casualties, the atomic attack was entirely justified in their view.

In any case, the sight of the enormous mushroom cloud of an atomic explosion would hover like some ghastly phantom over the entire postwar era. The knowledge that humans now had the power to entirely destroy themselves was the most fearsome insight to come out of World War II.

The other balance sheets of the war were almost as terrible. More people died in World War II than in any other disaster in recorded history. The final count will never be known for certain, but it is thought that about 30 million people died as a direct result of hostilities around the world. The most devastating casualties were suffered by the Jews of Europe, followed by the Russians and the Germans. In material categories, much of central and eastern Europe was reduced to shambles by ground or air war, and many parts of Italy and France also suffered severe damage. Many Japanese and Chinese districts were in bad shape from bombings and (in China) years of ground war. Everywhere, the survivors stood on the edge of an abyss. Starvation, cold, epidemic disease, family disintegration, and psychic disorientation posed distinct threats to humane life in much of the world.

THE ONSET OF THE COLD WAR

During the conflict, the Allies had not been able to agree on their postwar aims. Between the Western Allies and the Soviets stood a wall of mistrust that had been veiled temporarily but had by no means been dismantled. As soon as the victory over the Axis powers was secured, the dimensions of this wall were again visible for all to see.

Wartime Alliance and Continuing Mistrust

The so-called Cold War between the Soviet Union and the West began as early as 1945. During the war against the Axis, three Allied summit conferences (Tehran in 1943, Yalta and Potsdam in 1945) had been held. The main concrete results of these meetings were to assure the Soviets of political-military dominion over eastern Europe after the war, to assign parts of conquered Germany to Allied armies of occupation, and to move Germany's eastern border a hundred miles to the west. Moving Germany's border would allow the Soviet border with Poland to be moved west a similar distance, fulfilling an old demand of the Soviets dating back to 1919.

The immediate trigger for inter-Allied suspicion was the Russians' clear disregard for their commitments in eastern Europe and Germany. At the **Yalta Conference** in February 1945, the participants had agreed that free elections would be held as soon as wartime conditions might permit, even though all of these nations fell under what was conceded to be a Soviet "sphere of interest." Already at the Potsdam Conference in July 1945, it was apparent that major problems were arising. From the Russian point of view, the assurance of freedom in any real sense for these nations was unjustified presumption on the West's part. Since 1918, the nations of eastern Europe had consistently been hostile to the Soviet Union and would undoubtedly continue to be so, given the chance. Therefore, the only freedom for them that the Soviets would agree to was the freedom to choose between various types of Soviet overlordship. The eastern Europeans could install their own native Communist Party dictatorship, or they could accept the Soviet one—in either case, backed up by the Red Army already on the scene.

Refugees Flee Yokohama. American bombing attacks on Japanese cities began in November 1944. Japan's crowded cities were soon devastated by these air raids. Many refugees took shelter in Yokohama until American bombers devastated the city on May 29, 1945. (© *Mainichi Shimbun, Tokyo*)

From the Western point of view (which increasingly meant the U.S. perspective), Stalin's government was violating the plain meaning of the promises it had made about eastern Europe and eastern Germany. Also, the tiny Communist Parties were being falsely portrayed as the voices of the majority of Poles, Hungarians, and the like by Soviet media, and governments composed of their members were being imposed on anticommunist majorities through rigged elections and political terror.

Both sides were correct in these accusations. The almost inevitable rivalry between the United States and the Soviet Union in the contest for postwar leadership was the basic reason for the Cold War. Which side was indeed the more culpable for the fifteen years of extreme tension that followed is not easily answered except by those who have a doctrinal commitment to Marxism or its capitalist opponents. The following assertions seem in order now.

Until Stalin's death in 1953, the Soviets were certainly trying to expand their direct and indirect controls over Europe. The large Communist Parties of France and Italy (which consistently obtained more than 25 percent of the vote in postwar elections) were regarded as Trojan horses by all other democratic leaders, and rightly so. These parties had shown themselves to be the slavish followers of Moscow's commands, and if they had obtained power, they would have attempted to turn those democracies into imitations of the Soviet Union.

The Big Three at Yalta, February 1945. This final summit meeting among the three Allied leaders—Churchill, Roosevelt, and Stalin—came a few months before the German surrender. It was devoted to arranging the Soviet Union's entry into the Pacific war against Japan and the fate of postwar eastern Europe. *(Imperial War Museum/Art Archive)*

World revolution was still seen as a desirable and attainable goal by some communists, possibly including Stalin. The progress of the Maoist rebellion against the Chinese government in the late 1940s certainly buoyed these hopes, while greatly alarming American opinion.

On the other hand, the U.S. military and some U.S. political leaders were almost paranoid in their fears of communism. They were prone to see Muscovite plots everywhere and to think all communists shared a monolithic commitment to Moscow's version of Marx, employing the same goals and methods. Like the most fanatical communists, they could not imagine a world where communists and capitalists might coexist. They viewed the exclusively U.S.-controlled atomic bomb as the ultimate "persuader" for a proper world order.

The Original Issues

During the immediate postwar years, several specific issues concerning Germany and eastern Europe brought the two superpowers—the United States and the Soviet Union—into a permanently hostile stance:

- *Reparations in Germany.* The Soviet Union claimed, more or less accurately, that the Allies soon reneged on their promises to give the Russians a certain amount of West German goods and materials, as reparations for war damage.
- *"Denazification" of German government and industry.* Again, the Russians were correct in accusing the West

of not pursuing the Nazi element very vigorously, as soon as the Cold War frictions began. By 1949, the Western powers had dropped denazification altogether, as an unwelcome diversion from the main issue of strengthening Germany as a barrier to the spread of communism.

- *The creation of a new currency for the Allied sectors of Germany in 1948.* Without consulting its increasingly difficult Russian occupation "partner," the West put through a new currency (the deutsche mark, which is still in use), which split the supposed unity of the occupation zones in economic and financial affairs.
- *The Berlin government and the Berlin blockade in 1948–1949.* The Russians showed no interest in maintaining the agreed-on Allied Control Council (where they could be always outvoted) and made East Berlin and East Germany practically a separate administration as early as 1946. In 1948, Stalin attempted to bluff the Western allies out of Berlin altogether by imposing a blockade on all ground access. The Allies defeated the **Berlin blockade** by airlifting food and vital supplies for six months, and Stalin eventually lifted it (see Chapter 51).
- *The country-by-country Soviet takeover of eastern Europe between 1945 and 1948.* From the moment the Red Army arrived, terror of every kind was freely applied against anticommunists. For a brief time after the war's end, the Communist Parties attempted service to democratic ideals by forming political coalitions with noncommunists who had not been compromised during the Nazi occupation. Under Moscow's guidance, these coalitions were turned into "fronts" in which the noncommunists were either powerless or stooges. Protests by Western observers were ignored or denounced. The communists then took the leading positions in all the provisional governments and used their powers to prepare for "free" elections. The elections were held at some point between 1945 and 1947 and returned a predictable overwhelming majority for the Communist Parties and their docile fellow travelers. Stalinist constitutions were adopted, the protecting Red Army was invited to remain for an indefinite period, and the satellite regime was complete.

Many other factors could be mentioned, but the general picture should already be clear: the wartime alliance was only a weak marriage of convenience against Hitler and was bound to collapse as soon as the mutual enemy was gone. After 1946 at the latest, neither side had any real interest in cooperating to establish world peace except on terms it could dictate. For an entire generation, the world and especially Europe would lie in the shadow thrown by the atomic mushroom, with the paralyzing knowledge that a struggle between the two superpowers meant the third, and final, world war. (For a more hopeful view of the postwar world, see the Exercise of Authority box on the United Nations.)

THE UNITED NATIONS CHARTER

In June 1945, the victorious Allies and many neutrals sent delegates to San Francisco, where for the previous two months the Big Five (the United States, Britain, the Soviet Union, China, and France) had been working out the details of a world organization dedicated to keeping the peace. The resultant charter created the United Nations Organization, later to be headquartered in New York. The United Nations membership roll has risen from the original 51 nations of 1945 to now include more than 180; practically every state in the world belongs and participates in the annual sessions of the General Assembly. Some also take a role in the Security Council, which is composed of the Big Five permanent members plus ten additional members serving two-year electoral terms.

The United Nations Charter reflects the ideals and hopes of the anti-Axis coalition; certainly, not all their hopes have been realized or even partly attained. But the preamble still constitutes one of the best statements of what the world *might* be one day:

> We the people of the United Nations, determined to save succeeding generations from the scourge of war . . . and to reaffirm faith in fundamental human rights, in the dignity and worth of the human person, in the equal rights of men and women and of nations large and small, and to establish conditions under which justice and respect for the obligations arising from treaties and other sources of international law can be maintained, and to promote social progress and better standards of life in larger freedom and for these ends to practice tolerance and live together in peace with one another as good neighbors, and to ensure . . . that armed force shall not be used, save in the common interest, have resolved to combine our efforts to accomplish these aims.

Some specific provisions of the charter's 111 articles have been put into operation in the ensuing fifty years; others, like the assumption that the Security Council would have the full support of the members, have proved naive:

Chapter 1: Purposes and Principles

Article 1

The Purposes of the United Nations are:

1. To maintain international peace and security, and to that end: to take effective collective measures for the prevention and removal of threats to peace, and for the suppression of acts of aggression . . . and to bring about by peaceful means, and in conformity with justice and international law, adjustment or settlement of international disputes or situations which might lead to a breach of peace;

2. To develop friendly relations among nations based on respect for the principle of equal rights and self-determination of peoples, and to take other appropriate measures to strengthen universal peace.

3. To achieve international cooperation in solving problems of an economic, social, cultural, or humanitarian character, and in promoting and encouraging respect for human rights and for fundamental freedoms for all without distinction as to race, sex, language, or religion.

Article 2

3. All members shall settle their international disputes by peaceful means in such a manner that international peace and security and justice are not endangered. . . .

5. All members shall give the United Nations every assistance in any action it takes . . . and shall refrain from giving assistance to any state against which the United Nations is taking preventive or enforcement action. . . .

Chapter 7: Enforcement Procedures

Article 42

[The United Nations] may take such action by air, sea, or land forces as may be necessary to maintain or restore international peace and security. Such action may include demonstrations, blockade, and other operations by air, sea, or land forces of Members of the United Nations.

Article 43

All Members of the United Nations in order to contribute to the maintenance of international peace and security, undertake to make available to the Security Council . . . armed forces, assistance, and facilities, including rights of passage, necessary for the purpose. . . .

Article 45

In order to enable the United Nations to take urgent military measures, Members shall hold immediately available national airforce contingents for combined international enforcement action. The strength and degree of readiness of these contingents and plans for their combined action shall be determined . . . by the Security Council with the assistance of a Military Staff Committee.

FOR REFLECTION

Do you believe that the United Nations is a workable idea for world peacekeeping duties? Does the UN Assembly have sufficient powers to fulfill the founders' plans for it? Should the United States fully support the United Nations or not?

SUMMARY

World War II came about through a series of aggressive steps taken by the fascist and Nazi dictatorships in the later 1930s against the defeatist and indecisive democratic states of western Europe. Hitler quickly recognized the weakness of his opponents and rode his support by most Germans to a position of seeming invincibility in foreign affairs. The remilitarization of the Rhineland was followed by the annexation of Austria and Czechoslovakia, and finally the assault against Poland in September 1939 that began the general war.

In the first three years of war, the battles were mainly decided in favor of the Axis powers led by Germany. But the Battle of Stalingrad and the defeat of the Axis in North Africa marked a definite military turning point in the fall of 1942. In a long-range sense, the entry of the United States into the war following the Japanese attack on Hawaii was the turning point, even though it took a full year for the Americans to make much difference on the fighting fronts.

By late 1944, the writing was clearly on the wall for both the Germans and the Japanese, and attention turned to the postwar settlement with the Soviet ally. Despite some attempts, this settlement had not been spelled out in detail during the war because of the continuing mistrust between East and West. As soon as the fighting had stopped (May 1945 in Europe, August 1945 in the Pacific), the papered-over cracks in the wartime alliance became plain and soon produced a Cold War atmosphere. The political fate of eastern Europe and the administration of defeated Germany were the two focal points of what proved to be a generation of conflict between the West, led by the United States, and the communist world, headed by Soviet Russia.

TEST YOUR KNOWLEDGE

1. Which of the following was *not* a German-instigated step toward World War II?
   a. The occupation of the Rhineland
   b. The invasion of Ethiopia
   c. The seizure of the Sudetenland
   d. The Nonaggression Pact of 1939
2. A chief reason for Britain's prolonged appeasement of Hitler was that
   a. the British government wanted a counterweight to France on the Continent.
   b. he was seen by some leaders as an anticommunist bulwark.
   c. the British government of the late 1930s was strongly pro-German.
   d. he was seen as a way to tame the eastern European troublemakers.
3. At the Munich Conference in 1938,
   a. Austria was sacrificed to a Nazi invasion.
   b. Czechoslovakia was abandoned by its Western allies.
   c. Soviet Russia was invited to join the League of Nations.
   d. Hitler and Mussolini decided on war.
4. World War II was started by the Nazi invasion of
   a. France.
   b. Austria.
   c. Poland.
   d. Czechoslovakia.
5. Which of these did *not* occur during the first phase of World War II?
   a. The German blitzkrieg against Denmark and Norway
   b. The D-day invasion of France
   c. The loss of the British and French colonies in South Asia
   d. The invasion of Russia and the conquest by Germany of the Balkans
6. Winston Churchill first became a public figure when he
   a. became the leader of the British government.
   b. was elected to Parliament.
   c. was a journalist in Africa.
   d. was a navy minister in World War I.
7. The turning point in favor of the Allies in World War II from a military point of view was
   a. the fall of 1942.
   b. the fall of 1944.
   c. the spring of 1940.
   d. the summer of 1941.
8. The focal point of the Yalta Conference among the Allied leaders in 1945 was
   a. the future of Japan.
   b. the postwar political arrangements in eastern Europe.
   c. the details of a peace treaty with Germany.
   d. the signing of a peace treaty with Italy.

IDENTIFICATION TERMS

Anschluss	D day	Operation Barbarossa	Second Front
Axis Pact	Hiroshima	Popular Front	Stalingrad
Berlin blockade	Munich Agreements	Rhineland	Yalta Conference
Coral Sea, Battle of	Nonaggression Pact		

INFOTRAC COLLEGE EDITION

Enter the search term "World War, 1939–1945" using the Subject Guide.

Enter the search term "Holocaust" using the Subject Guide.

Enter the search term "Winston Churchill" using the Subject Guide.

HIGH AND LOW CULTURES IN THE WEST

I *respect the idea of God too much to hold it responsible for a world as absurd as this one.*
GEORGES DUHAMEL

1880s–1890s	Post-Impressionist painting begins/Modernism in the arts
Early 1900s	Modernism in literature, music
1920s	Radio commercialized/Movies become major entertainment medium/Recorded music
1930s	Television invented/Cheap paperback books
1960s	FM radio/audiotape recordings/Business and research computing
1970s	First VCRs and video cameras
1980s	CD recordings/Large-screen TVs
1990s	The home computer age/The Internet

IN THE JUST-COMPLETED CENTURY, the arts and their audiences have undergone one more of those radical reorientations that we have termed revolutions when placed in a political or economic context. The twentieth century was unprecedentedly receptive to new cultural trends and new ways of communicating both ideas and feelings. Frenetic experimentation has been the hallmark of Western culture since World War I. Many forms have been borrowed from non-Western sources, and artists in several media have not hesitated to reject the historical traditions of their art. Popular media, with no traditions to restrict them, have sprung up like weeds, feeding on technological innovation.

In painting and literature, especially, an almost complete break with the modalities of earlier times was attempted and occasionally was successful. Such attempts often led to dead ends, however, and the older models were able to hold the allegiance of the audience majority. The century ended with a distinct gap between the "high" and the "low" cultures, which differ not only in the media employed but also in their content, their aims, and their audiences.

FRAGMENTATION AND ALIENATION

If we were to select a single keyword to describe twentieth-century Western culture, it might well be *fragmentation*. All authorities agree that never before have so many conflicting approaches to the common problems of human life and art been pursued. Value systems and aesthetic judgments collide head-on with depressing regularity. There often seems to be so little common ground that no lasting consensus can be achieved.

The sense of what is necessary and proper for the fulfillment of a satisfying human life, which the educated saw as a self-evident proposition in the eighteenth and nineteenth centuries, no longer seems to exist. Artists and writers insist that individual viewpoints, shaped by specific experience, are the only valid points of reference for creative work. The result is frequently an art from which unity of message, form, and technique has been eliminated. What remains often looks like chaos to the observer.

What has happened? Why and how has this fragmentation, or incoherence, occurred? Is it profoundly harmful to our society or merely another mode of cultural expression, as legitimate and creative as any that preceded it?

The creative arts in the past century have been dominated by alienated individuals who are in conflict with their human environment. *Alienation* means to become a stranger and find oneself at odds with the values of your fellows or unable to communicate with them. This is hardly a new phenomenon among artists. Since the beginning of modern times, artists have often felt like outsiders in society, as indeed many were. But in the past century this feeling has deepened and become more aggressively expressed. The early twentieth-century Dada movement repudiated all obligations to communicate intelligibly to the public. As its manifesto proudly stated, "Art is a private matter; the artist does it for himself; any work of art that can be understood is the product of a journalist." (See the box for more on Dadaism.)

The Dadaists were too extreme to be taken seriously by most, but many serious artists also believed that the artist's first duty was always to be true to him- or herself. In practice, this has meant that in painting, fiction, poetry, and to a lesser extent music and sculpture, innovative artists frequently abandoned the forms and even the contents of the classical past. Meterless verse, abstract figures in painting and sculpture, music composed of equal parts silence and dissonance, and stream-of-consciousness narrative were the essence of their art to many of the most noted recent practitioners.

How did the previous high culture audience react? Many found it all too confusing. Artists in all fields discovered that they had to choose between disproportionate sectors of the public when preparing their work. A dual-level audience had arisen: the elite who favored innovators though their art was "difficult" and the much larger group that included those who visited museums to admire the portraits of a Rembrandt, went to concert halls to hear the works of Bach and Beethoven, and read poetry that they felt they could understand at first sight. Between the two groups and the artists that each supports, there was and is little communication or shared ground.

Much modern art makes a great many people uncomfortable. The temptation to dismiss the creators as baffling egocentrics or outright frauds is strong. Sometimes, no doubt, this suspicion is justified. The fine arts in our times have become in some instances a commodity like any other, exhibiting the usual marketing techniques of clever agents

The Dada Artists and Their Mission

In the midst of World War I, a tiny group of artists—poets, painters, sculptors—living in neutral Switzerland announced the coming of a final stage in the liberation of art from representational restrictions. They adopted the name *Dada*, variously explained as a French word for "hobbyhorse," a nickname for one of their acquaintances, or just nonsense. For a few years, Dada and the Dadaists held a major spot in the international limelight, particularly in Paris and Berlin, the two major art capitals in the Western world. Their total rejection of traditional values in all the arts created a sensation.

One of the founders of Dada was Hugo Ball, a young poet. In a lecture in Zurich in the midst of war in 1917, he explained the inspiration of the new movement. It is easy to see how both the war and modern physics and psychology had had an impact on Ball's thinking:

I. The Age
Three things have shaken the art of our time to its depths, have given it a new face, and have prepared it for a mighty new upsurge: the disappearance of religion induced by critical philosophy, the dissolution of the atom in science, and the massive expansion of population in present-day Europe.

God is dead. . . . Religion, science, and morality—phenomena that originated in the states of dread known to the primitive peoples. An epoch disintegrates. A thousand year culture disintegrates. . . . Churches have become castles in the clouds. . . . Christianity was struck down. . . . The meaning of the world disappeared. . . .

II. Style
The artists of these times have turned inward. Their life is a struggle against madness. They are disrupted, fragmented, dissevered. . . . [The artists] are forerunners, prophets of a new era. Only they can understand the tonalities of their own language. They stand in opposition to society, as did heretics in the Middle Age. . . . They are forerunners of an entire epoch, a new total culture. They are hard to understand, and one achieves an understanding of them only if one changes the inner basis—if one is prepared to break with a thousand year tradition. You will not understand them if you believe in God, and not in Chaos.

[The artist] voluntarily abstains from representing natural objects—which seems to him to be the greatest of all distortions. . . . They become creators of new natural entities that have no counterpart in the known world. They create images which are no longer imitations of nature but an augmentation of nature, by new, hitherto unknown appearances and mysteries.

Source: Hugo Ball, Flight Out of Time: A Dada Diary, trans. Ann Rhines (New York: Viking, 1974), p. 219.

and sellers. But this is certainly not always the case. In the twentieth century, almost all the arts in the West experienced a tremendous burst of creativity, such as has not been seen since the Renaissance. Let's look at a few common characteristics of this explosion and then at a few of the individual art forms exemplifying them.

MODERNISM

Certain common features of recent Western art and culture can be summed up conveniently in the word **modernism.** It carries several implications, the foremost of which are as follows:

⁍ *Form is emphasized at the expense of content.* Since many modern artists were convinced that even a sympathetic and knowledgeable audience could not uniformly comprehend what they were saying, they minimized the message (content) and gave full attention to the medium (form). This obsession with form led to novels that shifted narrators and time frame without warning; poetry that seemed much more concerned with the printed format than with the sense of the words; and sculpture that was entirely "abstract"—that is, unrecognizable in life—and given such a title as *Figure 19.*

⁍ *A systematic and determined rejection of the classical models.* At no epoch of the past did artists so generally attempt to find new—perhaps shockingly new—ways to express themselves. Not only new techniques but also wholly new conceptions and philosophies of art were trotted out, following one another in rapid succession from the 1870s (painting), the 1890s (poetry), the 1900s (music and dance), to the 1910s (literature and sculpture).

⁍ *A conscious search for non-Western inspiration.* This was particularly true in the figurative arts—painting, sculpture, weaving, ceramics—in which East Asian and African and Polynesian forms had a great vogue.

Modern Painting

Painting has frequently been the pathbreaker in times of change in the high culture. What the eye can see is universal, making painted pictures capable of reaching the largest audiences in the most straightforward fashion. In the 1870s, the **Impressionists** began the long march away from realism and toward abstraction. The Impressionists (working mainly in Paris, which remained the painting capital until the 1950s) were concerned not with realism, which they wanted to leave to the newly invented camera, but with the nature of light and color. In the 1880s and 1890s, center stage went to the **post-Impressionists,** who focused on mass and line and were daring innovators in their use of color. Several of them (Paul Cézanne, Claude Monet) were the pioneers of twentieth-century forms and are revered as the creators of modern classics in painting.

At the end of the nineteenth century and the first decade of the twentieth, cubism and abstract art appeared, again first in Paris. The key descriptor of this new school is "nonrepresentational": the painter makes little or no attempt to represent external reality as the eye sees it. Piet Mondrian was perhaps the leading exponent of **abstractionism.** But the most influential figurative artist of the entire century was **Pablo Picasso,** a Spaniard who chose to live and work in France most of his very long and highly innovative life. (For more about Picasso and his work, see the Tradition and Innovation box.)

During the first decades of the twentieth century, expressionism and other, smaller schools emphasized the primacy of the emotions through line, color, and composition. After World War II, the Americans led by Jackson Pollock, Hans Koenigsberger, and others took the lead by combining pure abstraction and new ways of putting the paint on the canvas (sometimes by apparently random splattering). This **abstract expressionism** remained the chief form of avant-garde painting in the second half of the century, though it has a half dozen competitors including its diametrical opposite, a photographic neorealism. Many attempts to discover profundity in the commonplace and vulgar (pop art, op art) have also been made in the past fifty years—with limited success in the public.

Modern Literature

In literature the departure from tradition is as sharply defined and uncompromising as it has been in painting. Novelists, playwrights, and especially poets have turned their backs on the models of narrative and description enshrined by the past. They have experimented with every conceivable aspect of their craft: grammar and meter, characterization, narrative flow, point of view, and even the very language. Some poets and novelists employ what seems almost a private vocabulary, which, like the Red Queen's in *Alice in Wonderland,* means "what I want it to mean."

The inevitable upshot of this fevered experimentation has again been the loss of much of the traditional audience. Modernist poetry, for example, demands so much effort to follow the poet's vision that it is exhausting to most casual readers. Though a poem by Delmore Schwartz may be in every "serious" anthology of twentieth-century verse, it is seldom quoted by lovers of poetry. Instead, their lists of favorites are likely to include any of several poems by Robert Frost. With their familiar English and adherence to traditional rules of poetic construction, Frost's verse seems easily understood by a mass audience.

The same is true of novels and novelists. In both style and content, some modern writing is so intent on giving voice to the writer's subjective viewpoints that the essential communication of ideas and events gets lost or is never attempted. It is this *fascination with the self,* at the expense of

Jackson Pollock, 1951. The American painter, who was the founder and most noted exponent of abstract expressionism, charged his enormous canvases with raw energy. Splattering apparently random flecks from his brush onto the canvas, Pollock's work convinced most critics that it contained both form and content of genius. *(© Hans Namuth/Photo Researchers)*

the reader, that "turns off" a large part of the public from modernist fiction.

Two examples among hundreds may be found in the novels of the American Donald Barthelme (b. 1931) and the film scripts of the Frenchman Alain Resnais (b. 1922). Though praised highly by critics, their work is appreciated by only a select few who are willing to attempt the hard work of analysis they demand and who are not deterred by their deliberate obscurity. Time may indeed reveal that Barthelme and Resnais are great artists, but the large majority of the contemporary reading and filmgoing public seems content to remain happily ignorant of them and their work.

In some instances, the modernists have been rewarded by widespread recognition from the public as well as the critics. The artistry and originality of these authors are undeniable. **James Joyce** (1882–1941), **Samuel Beckett** (1906–1980), **Marcel Proust** (1871–1922), and **Virginia**

Woolf (1882–1941) had the creative power to overcome old forms and break new ground. Joyce was the author of two novels that were immediately recognized as marvelously original works. *Ulysses* (1917) and *Finnegan's Wake* (1934) employed the "stream of consciousness" technique to a degree and with an effect never seen before. Joyce succeeded in portraying the ordinary life of an individual as experienced by his unconscious mind, as though relating a dream. *Finnegan's Wake* was too abstruse for the public (much of its effect came from a huge series of very obscure puns), but *Ulysses* has become a modern classic.

Beckett's series of plays, written after World War II, were technically so inventive that they found an international audience despite their profound pessimism about humans and their fate. *Waiting for Godot* is his most famous work. Others include *Endgame* and *Krapp's Last Tape*. Beckett sees humans as unfortunate worms who sporadically delude themselves into believing that this life holds something besides disappointment and despair. It is a horrifyingly grim picture that this reclusive Irishman paints of humans and all their hopes.

Proust's portraits of upper-class Parisians in the beginning of the twentieth century were important not for what he said but for the way he said it. Proust was a neurotic who lived almost entirely in a cork-lined retreat in his wealthy home, exercising his memory and his imagination to attempt a total recall of the details of life. It is a testament to his success that his multivolume novel *Remembrance of Things Past* is universally accorded a place among the three or four most influential fictional works of the first part of that century.

Woolf's fiction, also written in the early decades of the twentieth century, has been highly influential in both matters of style and content. *To the Lighthouse* and *Mrs. Dalloway*, both published in the 1920s, are her most significant works of fiction. She also wrote a pathbreaking feminist tract, *A Room of One's Own*, which has found much resonance in the last twenty-five years.

Modern Philosophy

Philosophy has not been exempt from the profound changes in traditional thought that mark recent times in the West. Twentieth-century philosophical systems have been divided between those that seek a new basis for human freedom and those that deny freedom as a myth and insist on the essential meaninglessness of life. Much recent philosophy focuses on the role of language: how it is created and how it relates to material reality. Behind this interest is the conviction that the so-called spirit or soul has no existence other than a linguistic one; that is, because we talk about it, it exists.

The question of existence itself is the primary concern of **existentialism**, which has been perhaps the leading school of philosophy in this century. Existentialism, which originated in Europe, rejects the various higher meanings that

PABLO PICASSO
(1881–1973)

Rare indeed are the artists who can claim to be the originators of an entirely new technical conception of their art. Rarer still are those who can make that claim and also be the creators of the two most important paintings of an entire century. Pablo Picasso, a Spaniard who lived most of his life in France, is that exception. In his technical innovation, his tremendously original imagination, and his versatility, he had no peers in the twentieth century.

Picasso studied in Paris in the early 1900s after a brief training in Barcelona. At that time innovators from every European country and the Americas were eagerly flocking there to join the many established painters, sculptors, and authors. From the earliest days of his boyhood, Picasso had known what he wished to do with his life. His pursuit of artistic excellence was single-minded and uncompromising from that period on.

Picasso's painting career went through several more or less distinct phases. In his first years, his so-called Blue Period, he focused on the melancholy lives of the urban poor, using predominantly blue tones. Later, during his Rose Period, which began in 1905, he used a lighter palette of colors to convey more carefree scenes, many taken from life in the circus. In 1907, Picasso's *Les Demoiselles d'Avignon* became a sensation, first among his fellow artists and then among the artistic public at large. *Les Demoiselles* was the first major work of cubism and the signal for an entirely new conception of how the artist might present external reality on canvas. In showing the distorted figures of three young girls, the painting reflected in vivid colors the impressions of African sculptures that Picasso and the rest of artistic Europe had recently experienced. The rigid mathematical basis of cubism led directly to the abstractionist style, which Picasso himself never joined but which inspired a generation of painter-innovators after World War I.

In the 1930s as the war clouds gathered, Picasso refused for years to involve himself directly with political affairs. But in 1937 he surprised the world with a second landmark work, the passionate mural *Guernica*, in memory of the agony of that small and previously unnoticed city that had been heavily bombed by Franco's planes in the current Spanish Civil War. A condemnation of fascist brutality and war itself, the huge painting was the

Picasso. The twentieth century's most influential artist exhibits one of his post–World War II creations, in his home near Vence, on the French Riviera, 1960. *(Archive Photos/Popperfoto)*

religion or philosophers have attempted to find in human life. It demands that one accept the inherent pointlessness of life. At the same time, most existentialists, led by **Jean-Paul Sartre** (1905–1980), insist that humans are free to supply their own meaning, and in fact they *must* do so. Existentialism blossomed after World War II, when the anguish created by this second bloody conflict within a single generation seemed to spell the end of European and, perhaps, Western culture. Seen in historical perspective, existentialism may be understood as a reaction against the rather naïve optimism and faith in science as the great

"fixer" of human problems that marked the late nineteenth century.

Like the arts and literature, twentieth-century philosophy was strongly affected by the uncertainty and cultural relativism that may be traced to Darwinian and Freudian theory, on the one side, and post-Newtonian physics, on the other (see Chapter 43). In the present day, most adherents of one philosophical school would not dare accuse their opponents in another school of heresy or attempt to silence them. No one, it seems, has that type of self-assurance any longer in this culture of probabilities and relative ethics.

twentieth century's most remarkable work of artistic propaganda. It now is located in the Museum of Modern Art in New York City.

Picasso settled after World War II in southern France with his third wife and devoted himself mainly to sculpture and ceramics. Among his best-known work in this period was the long series on the life of the character from Spanish literature, Don Quixote, and his faithful Sancho Panza. Picasso was through and through a Spanish artist but refused to return to his beloved Catalonia (the area around Barcelona) until the tyrant Franco was dead. That meant never, for Franco outlived the artist.

Picasso's genius lay in his ability to see through the conventional forms and beyond them. So strong was his influence that much of what the world calls modern painting is identified by the signature "Picasso." He was a master of line, and much of his postwar work was in graphics rather than paint. With a few strokes of the crayon or pen, he could bring a scene to the viewer complete in every essential. In the ten years after World War II, he lent his name and reputation to the communists. Like many others, his commitment to truth as he saw it led him to an almost childlike faith in the good intentions of those who pretended to agree with him.

FOR REFLECTION

Do you think artists have an obligation to voice their protest or support of political activity, as leaders or molders of opinion? Or should they segregate their artistic lives entirely from their activities as citizens, if any?

Les Demoiselles d'Avignon. The breakthrough to cubist and geometric representation in painting is usually attributed to this painting by Pablo Picasso, completed in 1907. *(Picasso, Pablo, Les Demoiselles d'Avignon. Paris C [June–July 1907]. Oil on canvas, 8' × 7'8" (243.9 × 233.7 cm). The Museum of Modern Art, New York. Acquired through the Lillie P. Bliss Bequest. Photograph © The Museum of Modern Art, New York. © 2000 Estate of Pablo Picasso/Artists Rights Society [ARS], New York)*

This relativism is the other side of the coin of tolerance and sensitivity to others' values that the twentieth century so espoused—or at least paid lip service to.

POPULAR ARTS AND CULTURE

Popular, or low, culture has undergone an explosion in both variety and accessibility. The mass media (television, movies, paperbacks, radio, popular magazines, newspapers, tape and disc recordings) has never had such a large audience as in the late twentieth century. This audience transcends the political boundaries that previously fragmented and restricted it. New technology has been largely responsible for this explosion. Easily the most important at the moment are the vast reach of the Internet and the personal computer. But there have been important predecessors. At the very outset of the twentieth century, two inventions were quickly converted to commercial entertainment: the motion picture and the radio. Both were products of the two decades just before World War I and were developed by Europeans and Americans working in-

Sartre and Simone de Beauvoir. These two intellectuals established an extraordinary partnership in both their professional and personal lives in the postwar era. *(© Gisele Freund/Photo Researchers, Inc.)*

dependently (Thomas Edison, Guglielmo Marconi, the Lumiere brothers, Lee De Forest). After the war, both came into their own as channels of mass communication.

Movies

The movies (the more elegant term *cinema* was never accepted in the United States) were first shown in arcades and outdoors. The first narrative film was *The Great Train Robbery* (1903). New York City was the initial home of the motion picture makers, and the American industry was to be the pacesetter of the world cinema for most of the century. By 1920, stars such as **Charlie Chaplin,** Buster Keaton, and Mary Pickford were well established (Chaplin's worldwide commercial success is outlined in the Tradition and Innovation box). The studio system, whereby the film creators were financed and thus controlled by distant investors, was already in operation. This uneasy marriage of artistic creativity and hardheaded money making was to be the keynote of the international cinema and particularly of Hollywood, which replaced New York as the center of moviemaking in the United States during World War I. By 1927, the first talking movie was produced (Al Jolson in *The Jazz Singer*), and films were on the way to becoming the number one entertainment medium of the world—a position they retained until the advent of television after World War II.

Radio

Like the movies, radio emerged rapidly from the laboratory to become a commercial enterprise of major importance.

The brilliant Italian experimenter Guglielmo Marconi was successful in transmitting signals through the air ("wireless") over long distances in 1901. Two years later, the invention of the vacuum tube enabled voice and music to be carried. The demands of military communications during World War I sped up radio transmission technology and improved receivers. The first commercial radio broadcasts began in the early 1920s. Within a few years, networks of broadcasting stations had been formed by the same combination of creative scientists and entrepreneurs as in the film industry.

In Europe and other parts of the world, the government normally controlled radio broadcasting. These governments saw in radio the same possibilities for influencing the citizenry that were inherent in the postal service and the telephone network. In the United States, however, radio was from the start a commercial venture, and the ever-present advertisements were a standard part of the radio-listening experience.

Radio and movies provided not only entrepreneurs but also politicians and cultural leaders with undreamed-of means of reaching a national audience. Many people in positions of power quickly recognized this potential. The use of both media for propaganda as well as commercial and educational purposes was one of the key breakthroughs in the manipulation of democratic societies. The Soviet and Nazi leaders both made adept use of film and radio in the 1930s and 1940s.

But it was probably in the extension of knowledge of what was happening in the world—the "news"—that the radio set and the movie screen made their greatest contributions to twentieth-century culture. The radio told and the movie newsreel showed your grandparents' generation what was going on outside their own cultural circles in a way that neither books nor newspapers could rival. Not only politics but also manners, fashion, humor, language, and education were intensely affected. In the interwar period, about two of every five adults went to a movie at least once a week in Britain and the United States. Never before had such a large percentage of the population participated in a single form of recreational activity except eating, drinking, and possibly sex.

Music

Music for the masses came into its own in the twentieth century. The technology of Edison's phonograph and its lineal descendants the tape player, compact disc player, and laser were joined to forms of popular music that expressed a great deal more than the simple urge to sing and dance. Since the 1950s, various forms of rock and roll have captured the allegiance of much of the world's youth. The West's "youth revolt" of the late 1960s was a thoroughly international phenomenon, and its anthems were drawn equally from folk music and rock.

CHARLIE CHAPLIN
(1889–1977)

No one better personifies the huge impact that the motion picture industry had on the world public than Charlie Chaplin. Chaplin was an enormously talented actor, director, scripter, and producer of movies that thrilled audiences from Capetown to San Francisco. He was probably the best-known single name in the world from 1920 to 1960, eclipsing any statesman or general.

Born into poverty in 1889, Chaplin began his career alongside his performer parents in London music halls as an acrobatic clown. He came to the United States in 1913 as one of the dozens of European vaudeville performers who hoped to make their fame and fortune in this country through the booming movie industry. Since sound films had not yet been invented, it did not matter what language the actors used, only how effectively they could get the plotline across to an audience through strictly visual means. Facial expression and body movement were an actor's capital.

In 1914, Chaplin joined the Keystone Kops and their artistic director, Mack Sennett. This most famous of the early Hollywood comedy troupes specialized in crazy chase scenes and offered Chaplin a great opportunity to show off his own ideas as a comedian. Thus was born the most famous film figure of the century: the "Little Tramp" swinging his rolled umbrella in baggy pants and flapping coat. His ridiculous flat-footed walk identified him at once as one of the world's eternal underdogs. Yet there was nothing pathetic about this underdog. Often beaten about by the rich and the powerful, the Tramp had a wonderful touch for knowing when and how to strike back. He combined the broadest slapstick with a pathos that touched everyone's heart. And always the laughter rolled out from the audience like an irresistible wave.

By 1918, Chaplin had dropped his early ten-minute "loops" and started to make feature-length films under his own direction. Joining with such giants as Mary Pickford and Douglas Fairbanks, he formed his own production company (United Artists), assuring that he would have complete control of every aspect of filmmaking and distributing. Throughout the 1920s and 1930s,

Chaplin scored unparalleled success: *The Gold Rush, The Circus, City Lights, Modern Times,* and his first "talkie," *The Great Dictator* (1940). All rank among the best film comedies ever produced.

A hardheaded businessman in real life, Chaplin became very wealthy. He clearly was never as comfortable in his talking roles as he had been doing silent pantomime. After about 1936, he made only a small handful of films until his death in 1977. With the single exception of his hilarious parody of Hitler in *The Great Dictator,* none were as commercially or artistically successful as his "silents."

Chaplin's appeal was truly universal. His pictures were distributed from one end of the world to the other, and they are still shown regularly in the art theater circuit in the United States and in the mass markets of much of the rest of the world. Chaplin's genius lay in his ability to establish an immediate bond with his audience as someone like themselves but faster in wit and luckier in outcomes. For those purposes, the Little Tramp character was perfect: always vulnerable but never defenseless, the Tramp was the ultimate survivor.

In the Cold War hysteria of the 1950s, when Senator Joseph McCarthy was conducting witch-hunts for communists, Chaplin's refusal to become an American citizen (largely for tax reasons) and his naïve support of leftist causes made him an easy target for "Red-hunting" demagogues. Embittered, he went to live in Switzerland in 1952, staying there in semiretirement until a triumphant return to the United States twenty years later to receive a special award from the Academy of Motion Picture Arts and Sciences. He was survived by his fourth wife Oona O'Neill Chaplin (daughter of the playwright Eugene O'Neill) and his several children, including the actress Geraldine Chaplin.

FOR REFLECTION

Have you ever seen a Chaplin comedy? Would you agree that he was a comic genius? What allowed him to communicate to so many, varied audiences?

Charlie Chaplin in His Favorite Role: The Little Tramp. Always vulnerable but never defenseless, the Tramp was the ultimate survivor. (© *The Granger Collection)*

But rock itself was just the latest addition to a parade of musical types that drew from both European and African American sources in the early twentieth century. The European sources included the artificial folk songs of the Broadway stage and the vaudeville halls. More important was the black contribution—jazz. Jazz was the name given to that mix of gospel song, African rhythms, and erotic blues shouting that was popularized by black musicians in New Orleans and later in Memphis and Chicago. Once introduced into the mainstream white culture via traveling nightclub bands and early radio, jazz was cleaned up and tamed for middle-class consumption via phonographs.

The processing of folk songs and jazz into commercial products began with the "crooners" of the 1920s. It continued through the swing bands of the 1930s and 1940s, the beboppers and rock and roll of the 1950s, and the folk revival of the 1960s. Keeping close pace with the rise of stars such as Elvis Presley, the Beatles, the Rolling Stones, and the Supremes was the stream of mechanical innovations that made popular music an ever-present accompaniment to most of the rituals of life for Western people under age thirty. The high-fidelity stereo system, Walkman portable tape player, FM broadcasting technology, and automobile sound system all are part of this stream. Nowhere is the

The Ecko Scophony Model 202. Television was actually available with reasonably good transmission quality in the mid-1930s, but the price of receivers and the very limited broadcasts discouraged potential purchasers. Shown here is a British company's 1936 model, priced at 100 guineas, or about the equivalent of $80,000 in 2000 buying power. (*Topham Picture Library/Image Works*)

close and formative relation between technology and mass culture so clear as in the production, distribution, and consumption of popular music.

Television

The powerful impressions left by radio and movies on the popular mind were equalled or even overshadowed, however, by those delivered by a post–World War II development—television. Invented by Americans and Britons in the early 1930s, TV came into commercial use only after the war. Already by 1950, television had replaced radio as the prime entertainer in the American home, and a few years later, it was threatening to drive the neighborhood movie theaters out of business. Left behind by the Americans at first, Europeans closed the television gap in the 1960s. As with other forms of mass media, the European governments monopolized the broadcasting studios until private commercial stations were permitted in the 1970s and 1980s.

More even than films, television shows have the immediacy and emotional power of a picture, especially when that picture is edited (that is, manipulated to give a particular effect) by a knowing hand. Television's takeover of news reporting on all levels—local, national, international—is striking evidence of how deeply the flickering images of the small screen have penetrated into the world's life and thought. Most recently, even war in Iraq and Afghanistan has been captured by its cameras and fitted into its schedules. Newspapers, which were the chief news medium in the nineteenth century and the first half of the twentieth, are rapidly being converted into bulletin boards for local retail advertisers and human interest storybooks. A newspaper cannot compete with television for quick, colorful reporting of what is happening around us or around the globe.

MASS CULTURE AND ITS CRITICS

Between the high culture of the patrons of art museums, contributors to the Metropolitan Opera, and subscribers to the *New York Review of Books* and the low culture of the Elvis Presley cultists, readers of comic books, and fans of the National Football League exists a transition ground whose importance and nature are the subject of much debate. In a famous essay dating from the early 1960s, the critic Dwight MacDonald dubbed this large group of in-betweeners **Masscult.** MacDonald believed that Masscult was a disastrous phenomenon, representing the surrender of the higher to the lower echelon. He thought that the Masscult participants were rapidly losing the ability to tell the real from the phony and could not distinguish the art and music that came from an authentic artist from that generated by some advertising agency's robots. Better to have honest ignorance, he said, than the tasteless ba-

Andy Warhol. One of the icon figures of popular art forms in the 1960s and 1970s was the painter/photographer/filmmaker Andy Warhol. Warhol, here posing as one of the original "flower children," was the best-known leader of a peculiar band of "subterranean" artists who considered themselves rebels against mainstream culture but who were adept at profiting from it. *(© William Kennedy/FPG)*

nality of a half-educated flock of pretenders. Authentic culture—the culture that historically has created the models and set the standards of the world civilizations—has always been an elitist phenomenon and always will be. Insofar as it becomes amassed, it declines in value.

Others are not so sure. They argue that Masscult has come about because of the unparalleled access to education that the Western nations, at least, have enjoyed since World War II; the cultural variety that the communications explosion of the late twentieth century produced; and the openness to experiment and toleration of artistic novelty. In their view, Masscult is a praiseworthy reflection of the lower classes' efforts to rise up the ladder of cultural taste. These observers do not deny that Masscult's judgments and preferences are frequently misguided or manipulated. They merely ask when the masses of people ever before had a chance, such as they now enjoy, to educate themselves and refine their taste. In short, they ask MacDonald to give the Masscult time to mature and develop better taste and surer judgments. Then, the process will be reversed with the low

culture being uplifted, rather than the high culture being made banal.

Whichever side of this argument one takes, it is beyond dispute that twentieth-century technology has provided the large majority of the Western world's populations with access to cultural opportunities in an unprecedented fashion. Radio broadcasts, films, television, and cheap paperbacks have been followed by videocassettes and recorders, computer imagery, portable telephones, and a seeming unending parade of home entertainment devices that quickly filter down in the market's hierarchy from luxury items to common expectations. In the latest epoch, access to the cybernetic reality of the Internet and the instantaneous communication possibilities of E-mail and wireless telephony have further foreshortened the distance once separating all of us from one another. We are all now children of the electronic age, and the "technological imperative" that was once conceived of as operating only in the science labs has now transformed the consumer market: If it can be done, it will be done! And sold!

SUMMARY

The first half of the twentieth century saw an expansion of cultural opportunities for the masses that has no parallel. New means of communication across distance have joined with new leisure and widespread prosperity in the Western world to allow tremendously widened access to ideas, arts, and news. Commercial entertainment has become one of the chief industries of the modern age and reaches into every level of society with its wares of film, music, sports, and television shows.

Whether this trend is truly uplifting the formerly ignorant masses into the lofty realm of high culture is a topic of debate. Some think that the worthwhile has given way to the despicable. The high-culture purists have seen their position eroded by the modernist movement in the early part of the century, which permitted artists to forget their former obligation to communicate in easily comprehended ways. By doing so, much literature and pictorial art of a high-culture type were removed from the experience of ordinary people. They turned instead to the models of culture being supplied increasingly through commercially driven entertainment media. Such low-culture channels have always existed but could be ignored by the tastemakers until the twentieth century, when they have penetrated into so many levels of society as to become what some critics call Masscult, the legitimation of banality.

TEST YOUR KNOWLEDGE

1. Modernism in twentieth-century arts implies, among other things, that
   a. the message of the artwork to its audience should be uniformly understood.
   b. content is more important than form.
   c. the artist cannot be held responsible for differing perceptions of his or her work.
   d. the artist has the duty to attempt something novel in his or her art.

2. Abstract painting seeks to project
   a. a photographic vision of external objects.
   b. a blueprint for understanding reality.
   c. an internal mood or feeling divorced from external imagery.
   d. a portrait of the artist.

3. The art movement of the early twentieth century that attacked all accepted standards and forms was
   a. abstractionism.
   b. cubism.
   c. Dadaism.
   d. expressionism.

4. "Stream of consciousness" in prose was most memorably employed by
   a. James Joyce.
   b. Samuel Beckett.
   c. Jean-Paul Sartre.
   d. Sigmund Freud.

5. A characteristic of twentieth-century Western art forms was
   a. a reverence for the great classical masters.
   b. a timidity in attempting to devise new forms.
   c. an interest in non-Western ideas and forms.
   d. an obsession with propagandizing the audience.

6. The convinced existentialist believes that
   a. life is hardly worth living as it is devoid of all values.
   b. values are created for others by a handful of strong individuals.
   c. each age creates its own moral values.
   d. each individual must create his or her own values.

7. Popular music in the mid– and late twentieth century
   a. has been dominated by non-Westerners.
   b. has been much affected by technology.
   c. is less important to general culture than it has been in the past.
   d. is more limited to certain ethnic groups than before.

8. Which of the following would *not* be considered a good example of Masscult?
   a. A radio comedy broadcast
   b. A monument to Beethoven
   c. A *People* magazine feature on a new art gallery
   d. A television program on interior decorating

IDENTIFICATION TERMS

abstract expressionism

abstractionism

Beckett, Samuel

Chaplin, Charlie

existentialism

Impressionists

Joyce, James

Masscult

modernism

Picasso, Pablo

post-Impressionists

Proust, Marcel

Sartre, Jean-Paul

Woolf, Virginia

INFOTRAC COLLEGE EDITION

Enter the search term "modernism" using the Subject Guide.

Enter the search term "existentialism" using the Subject Guide.

51

SUPERPOWER RIVALRY AND THE EUROPEAN RECOVERY

We are eyeball to eyeball . . . and I think the other fellow just blinked.
U.S. SECRETARY OF STATE DEAN RUSK, OCTOBER 1962

1947	Marshall Plan and Truman Doctrine
1948–1949	Blockade of Berlin/NATO and Warsaw Pact
1950s	Western European economic recovery/Stalinization of eastern Europe
1950–1953	Korean War
1957	Treaty of Rome establishes European Economic Community (EEC)
1961	Berlin Wall
1962	Cuban Missile Crisis
1970s	Détente in Cold War
1979	Soviet invasion of Afghanistan

AS WORLD WAR II ended, the two great victorious powers were becoming increasingly suspicious of each other's intentions. Leadership in the Western world was passing to the United States from Britain and France for the indefinite future. In the East, Stalin's Union of Soviet Socialist Republics (USSR) was the engine of a drive to make the world over according to Marx. The two superpowers would have to find a way to settle their differences peaceably or plunge the world into atomic conflict that would leave both in smoking ruins. For the two decades after 1945, the question of atomic war overshadowed everything else in world affairs and dictated the terms of all international settlements.

The Cold War became the stage on which the other vast drama of postwar diplomacy was played: the ending, forcible or peaceable, of the colonial system in the non-Western world. The links between the two struggles were many. In those same decades (1945–1965), Europe staged a remarkable recovery from both the material and the spiritual damages of war. Although many had almost written off Europe as a loss, the nations in the noncommunist two-thirds of Europe were exceeding prewar levels of production as early as 1950. In the next thirty years, they succeeded in progressing far down the road to economic unity, and the ancient hopes of political unification looked increasingly attainable.

CONFLICT IN THE POSTWAR GENERATION

The hostility between the United States and the Soviet Union had both proximate and remote causes. We briefly reviewed the proximate causes in Chapter 49: the Soviets' insistence on "friendly" regimes along the western borders of their country and the arguments over the treatment of postwar Germany and the defeated Nazis. But these disputes were only specific reflections of the broader, more remote causes: the friction between two militarily powerful states, each of which had a tradition of strong nationalism and was convinced its politics and social organization were based on an exclusive truth. The Russian communists (who were at all times the directing force within the Soviet Union) believed that in Stalin's version of Marxism they had found the ultimate answers to the problem of making humans happy on Earth. The Americans thought their forebears had produced, and they had maintained, a political and economic system that reflected the justified aspirations of all right-thinking people everywhere. The war against fascism had briefly brought these two nations into the same political bed. Now that it was won, their latent ideological antagonism must inevitably make itself apparent. (See the box on "The Iron Curtain.")

The Division of Europe

Both superpowers realized that control of Germany meant control of most of Europe. The focus of conflict soon shifted from the elections and governments of the eastern European countries (which were clearly within the Russian zone of dominion) to defeated Germany. Germany was divided into originally three, then four occupation zones: Russian, American, British, and French. Already in 1946, arguments over industrial reparations from Germany had broken out. The Russians confiscated everything movable in their zone, shipping it back to the badly wounded USSR, while the Americans, British, and French soon decided that stripping Germany of its industrial capacity would only bring on political and social chaos and possibly a communist revolution.

To counter the menace of Soviet expansion and to speed up the still very slow recovery, in the summer of 1947, the **Marshall Plan** for reconstruction of the European economy was put forth by U.S. secretary of state General George Marshall. It proved to be one of the most successful foreign policy initiatives ever undertaken and was largely responsible for the beginning of the European recovery.

The **Truman Doctrine** was also announced in 1947. Named for the then-president, it committed the United States to defend governments throughout the world when they were threatened by communist-inspired subversion. This policy was a historic departure from the traditional U.S. position of refusing the "entangling alliances" warned against long ago by George Washington. The acceptance of the policy by the U.S. Congress and the public indicated that a decisive change in attitude had taken place since Woodrow Wilson's League of Nations was rejected in 1919. The United States was now prepared, however reluctantly, to shoulder the burdens of what was soon termed "free world" leadership.

The Soviet blockade of Berlin in 1948 (see Chapter 49) was decisive in showing there was no hope of reviving the wartime alliance and that Stalin was committed to expanding communism into the European heartland. The key to containment of this threat was a West-oriented Germany. Conjured from the three Western zones in September 1949, West Germany (*Bundesrepublik Deutschland*) was larger and more powerful than its Russian-created counterpart, the *Deutsche Demokratische Republik,* or East Germany, which came into existence a few weeks later.

THE IRON CURTAIN

In the spring of 1946, Winston Churchill, just retired by the voters from his job as British wartime prime minister, visited the United States as guest of President Harry Truman. In Westminster, Missouri, he gave a speech that caught the attention of the whole world and gave the phrase "Iron Curtain" to the language. His purposes were to alert the U.S. government and public to what was happening in Soviet-controlled eastern Europe and to assure a united stand against it.

> A shadow has fallen upon the scenes so lately lighted by the Allied victory. Nobody knows what Soviet Russia and its Communist international organization intends to do in the immediate future, or what are the limits, if any, to their expansionist and proselytizing tendencies. . . . From Stettin in the Baltic to Trieste in the Adriatic,* an iron curtain has descended across the Continent. Behind that line lie all the capitals of the ancient states of Central and eastern Europe. Warsaw, Berlin, Prague, Vienna, Budapest, Belgrade, Bucharest and Sofia, all these famous cities and the populations around them lie in what I must call the Soviet sphere, and all are subject in one form or another, not only to Soviet influence but to a very high and, in many cases, increasing measure of control from Moscow. . . . The Communist parties, which were very small in all these Eastern States of Europe, have been raised to pre-eminence and power far beyond their numbers and are seeking everywhere to obtain totalitarian control. . . .
>
> I do not believe that Soviet Russia desires war. What they desire are the fruits of war and the indefinite expansion of their power and doctrines. . . . Our difficulties and dangers will not be removed by closing our eyes to them. They will not be removed by mere waiting to see what happens; nor will they be removed by a policy of appeasement. What is needed is a settlement, and the longer this is delayed, the more difficult it will be and the greater our dangers will become.

*A line drawn between these two cities would enclose to its east the areas of Europe recently taken by the Red Army and made into Soviet satellites.

The Nuremberg Trial, 1946. Shortly after the German surrender, the Allies put several leading Nazis on trial for "crimes against humanity." The months-long trial was presided over by judges from Russia, the United States, Britain, and France. It resulted in the convictions of all but three of the defendants, who were sentenced to varying terms in prison or to death. Hermann Göring, the number two Nazi (far left, first row, back to camera), cheated the hangman by taking cyanide. *(Hulton Deutsch/Woodfin Camp)*

The North Atlantic Treaty Organization (**NATO**) was similarly an outgrowth of the East–West struggle. Created in April 1949, it was Washington's solution to the need for an international military organ dedicated to stopping the spread of communism. It originally counted twelve western European and North American members—later increased to fifteen—who pledged to come to the aid of one another if attacked. The Soviet answer quickly came with the **Warsaw Pact,** which made the communist governments of eastern Europe military allies. The pact merely formalized what

The Berlin Airlift. After Stalin blocked all surface routes into West Berlin, the Allies responded by starting an airlift of supplies from their occupation zones in western Germany into the isolated city. Beginning in June 1948, it continued for eleven months until the Soviets allowed overland access again, tacitly admitting defeat. *(The Bettman Archive/Corbis)*

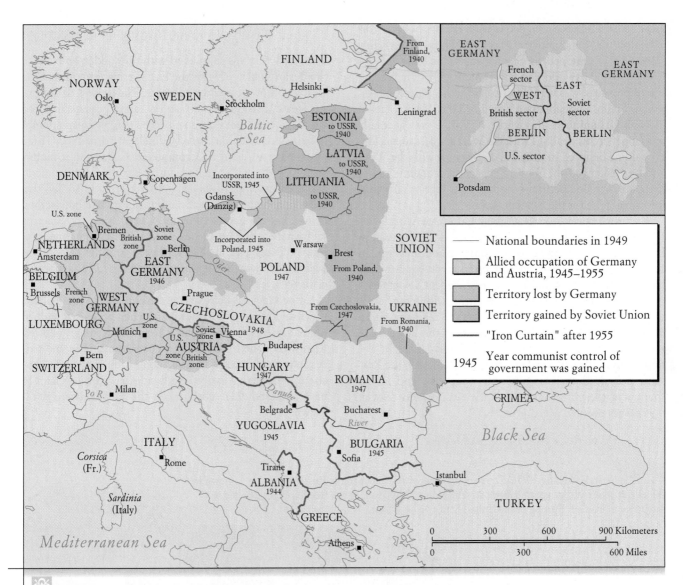

MAP 51.1   Cold War Europe, 1945–1990. The Soviet Union immediately reclaimed those territories in eastern Europe granted it by the Nonaggression Pact of 1939 and added half of East Prussia. Yugoslavia was thrust from the Soviet bloc in 1948, and Austria was unexpectedly granted a neutral status by agreement among the occupying nations in 1955. Germany remained divided until the autumn of 1990.

had been true since the series of Marxist takeovers in 1945–1948.

Not only Germany but now all Europe was thus divided into two enemy blocs, along with a handful of militarily in-significant neutrals (Austria, Finland, Spain, Sweden, and Switzerland). (See Map 51.1.) The situation whereby the Continent was more or less at the military mercy of two non-European powers, Russia and the United States, was a definite novelty in history. In the late 1940s and through the 1950s, it appeared that whatever the Europeans might be able to do about their own prosperity, they would remain the junior partners of outside powers in military affairs and diplomacy.

Grudging Coexistence

In 1950, the **Korean War** broke out when South Korea, a U.S. satellite, was invaded by North Korea, a Soviet satel-lite. Within a year, the conflict had become an international war with the United States providing the leadership in the South, and the Chinese (*not* the Soviets) coming to the aid of their hard-pressed North Korean allies. The fighting ended in deadlock, and a truce was finally signed in 1953 (which still exists).

Josef Stalin also died in that year, and with him died the most aggressive phase of the Cold War. His successors, however fanatical their communist belief, were never so given to paranoia as Stalin had been in his later years. After a behind-the-scenes power struggle, **Nikita Khrushchev** (1894–1971) emerged as Stalin's successor, chief of the Communist Party and the government. Khrushchev, the son of peasants, was very different from the secretive, mysterious Stalin. Though just as convinced that Marxism must inevitably triumph in the whole world, he was generally more open in his dealings with the West and less menacing. He said he believed in peaceful coexistence with the West, and he challenged the West to engage in economic rather than military competition—a challenge that would turn into a bad joke for the Russians later.

Khrushchev was not about to give up what World War II had brought to the Soviet Union or to release the eastern Europeans from their bonds to communism, however. In 1956, when the Hungarians rose up in revolt against their highly unpopular satellite government, he sent Soviet tanks to restore order and keep Hungary firmly within the Soviet orbit. The failure of the NATO powers to take any action made it clear that the West had accepted the Soviet-style regimes in eastern Europe, however much it might denounce their illegality and repression. Since 1949, the Russians possessed their own atomic weaponry, and in the shadow of the mushroom cloud, the *pax Sovietica* (Soviet peace) was deemed acceptable.

From Cuban Missiles to the Invasion of Afghanistan

The Cold War was sharpened with the sudden erection of the **Berlin Wall** in 1961 by the East Germans to prevent the steady outflow of political refugees. The success of this unparalleled division of a city and a nation perhaps inspired Khrushchev to make an unexpected gamble in an attempt to help his Cuban Marxist ally, Fidel Castro, in 1962. Three years earlier, Castro had conquered Cuba with a motley army of insurgents, kicked out the corrupt government, and then declared his allegiance to Marxism. An abortive U.S.-sponsored invasion at the Bay of Pigs had been a total failure. Fearing another attempt, Castro asked the Russians for military help. Khrushchev decided to install intermediate-range rockets with nuclear warheads, and the project was well under way when it was discovered by U.S. aerial surveillance over Cuba.

After a few days of extreme tension, the Soviets backed down and removed their weapons when presented with an ultimatum by President John F. Kennedy. Kennedy allowed Khrushchev some room for maneuver by making some concessions on U.S. bases in Asia, along with a promise not to attempt another invasion. Both sides could thus claim to have achieved their goals when the missiles were withdrawn.

Budapest, November 1956. The fierceness of the resistance to the Russian invasion is shown in this scene of one of Budapests's major streets. Many of the Hungarian "freedom fighters" fled to sanctuary in western Europe or the United States. *(Hulton Deutsch Collection/Corbis)*

CUBAN MISSILES IN 1962

In the fall of 1962, the stunning discovery that the Soviets had secretly deployed nuclear-tipped intermediate-range missiles in Castro's Cuba ignited the most dangerous incident in the generation-long Cold War. Aerial photography of the island during September and October gradually confirmed that Russian engineers were building missile launch sites and bringing in a large number of missiles by ship. If fired, the missiles already transported could destroy much of the eastern United States.

Faced with the cruelest dilemma of any postwar presidency, John F. Kennedy had to frame a response that was absolutely firm yet restrained and not provocative. A nuclear war might well have been the price of miscalculation. After the Soviets were quietly put on notice that Washington was aware of what was going on, and they had not responded, Kennedy decided it was necessary to "go public" with the news. For some days, the White House continued the agonizing search for the most unambiguous wording, designed to put maximum pressure on the Soviet leader Nikita Khrushchev while giving him an opportunity to retreat without losing face. On October 22, Kennedy made a televised address to a nervous nation and world:

Good evening, my fellow citizens.

This government, as promised, has maintained the closest surveillance of the Soviet military build-up on the island of Cuba. Within the past week, unmistakable evidence has established the fact that a series of offensive missile sites are now in preparation on that imprisoned island. . . .

This secret, swift, and extraordinary build-up of communist missiles—in an area well known to have a special and historical relationship with the United States and the nations of the Western hemisphere—in violation of Soviet assurances, and in defiance of American and hemispheric policy—this sudden, clandestine decision to station strategic weapons for the first time outside Soviet soil is a deliberately provocative and unjustified change in the status quo which cannot be accepted by this country if our courage and our commitments are ever to be trusted again by either friend or foe.

. . . All ships of any kind bound for Cuba from whatever nation or port will, if found to contain cargoes of offensive weapons, be turned back.

. . . It shall be the policy of this nation to regard any nuclear missile launched from Cuba against any nation in the Western hemisphere as an attack by the Soviet Union on the United States, requiring a full retaliatory response upon the Soviet Union.

. . . I call upon Chairman Khrushchev to halt and eliminate this clandestine, reckless, and provocative threat to world peace, and to stable relations between the two nations. . . .

After a few horribly tense days, the Russians agreed to dismantle and withdraw their missiles in return for a face-saving pledge on Kennedy's part that the United States would not attempt another invasion of Castro's island. The crisis was over.

Source: Elie Abel, The Cuban Missile Crisis (Philadelphia: Lippincott, 1966).

The world fright over the **Cuban Missile Crisis** stimulated the nuclear powers to make more serious efforts to reduce the level of hostility (see the box). In 1963, they signed the **Nuclear Test Ban,** limiting the testing of atomic weapons in the atmosphere. Under the new leadership of Willy Brandt, the West German government after years of resistance moved to recognize the postwar borders to its east and thus to establish better relations with its communist neighbors and with the Soviet Union. This German *Ostpolitik* (Eastern policy) was a key point in reducing tensions in Europe.

By the mid-1960s, then, the Cold War was less confrontational. The ideology of communist revolution had become a very minor part of the Soviets' baggage in international affairs; it had been replaced by the predictable, selfish interest of a great power with imperialist motives. The Soviet Union was becoming a conservative state—a stable factor in world politics—despite its revolutionary slogans. The best evidence of this shift was the failure of the Soviets to provide military support for the communist side in the Vietnam conflict during the later 1960s (see Chapter 53).

The progress of **détente** (relaxation) between the Soviet Union and the West was marred but not derailed by the Soviet invasion of Czechoslovakia in 1968, when that nation attempted to oust its Stalinist overlords through a peaceful revolution. The United States was again not inclined to involve NATO in this "internal matter," and communist rule was reimposed without bloodshed. Coming in a year when many Western nations experienced explosive internal frictions between government and citizens, the Czechs' misfortunes were soon forgotten in the West.

The NATO alliance itself was not so close-knit by this time. Under war hero General **Charles de Gaulle,** France had no sympathy for what it considered the American obsession about the Soviets. The bombastic Khrushchev had been replaced in 1964 by a tight group of *apparatchiks* headed by Leonid Brezhnev (1906–1982) who showed little commitment to any type of revolution or foreign policy gambles.

De Gaulle and many others thought western Europe was no longer seriously threatened by violent communist intervention, and France withdrew its military from NATO command in 1962. (See the Exercise of Authority box for more about de Gaulle.)

The decline of NATO reflected the shift from foreign to domestic policy issues that preoccupied European leaders

CHARLES DE GAULLE
(1890–1969)

The first president of the Fifth Republic of France, Charles de Gaulle was easily the most important French statesman of the twentieth century. Born to a devout Catholic family in 1890, de Gaulle went into the officer corps and fought in World War I with distinction before his capture in 1916. While in a German prison camp, he realized that the military was the best field to demonstrate his strongest personal feelings: dedication to the glory of France.

De Gaulle was much impressed by the potential of tank warfare, which had been only lightly and inconclusively used in World War I. In 1934, he published *The Army of the Future*, a call to the General Staff to prepare for a coming war in which mobile units spearheaded by massive tank forces would make the trench warfare of 1914–1918 outmoded. He also called for far more attention to the air force. But the French Army establishment regarded these ideas as radical, and for a time de Gaulle's career was blocked.

France fell to German armor attacks in 1940, but de Gaulle refused to accept the surrender and fled to Britain. For the next four years, he devoted himself to organizing and leading the Free French, a military and civilian movement of all who wished to continue the fight against the Nazi occupiers. By 1944, several of the overseas colonies were governed by the Free French, and its military units landed with the other Allies on D day (June 6, 1944). Paris was liberated from German occupation by a French division.

Immensely popular at the end of the war, de Gaulle was elected provisional president in 1945, but when it became clear that the politicians

Charles de Gaulle and Konrad Adenauer. *(The Bettmann Archive/Corbis)*

in the 1960s. Generated originally by student discontent with the outmoded educational and cultural institutions carried over from the prewar era, protests of every type (the "youth revolt") soon erupted against the policies and politics of governments and other forms of traditional authority. These protests—often violent—reached a peak in 1968, when European disaffection with NATO support of the U.S. war in Vietnam and with the continuing arms race between the East and West reached tidal wave proportions. Not only was the defense against a fading Marxism becoming superfluous, but to European minds, there were far more urgent and profitable areas for their governments to pursue.

EUROPE'S ECONOMIC RECOVERY

Cast into the shadows by the disasters of the first half, Europe had reemerged by the last quarter of the twentieth century as the most important locale of technical, financial, and commercial power in the world. The word *renaissance* is not too strong to use in describing the developments in western Europe since 1945. In that year, the Continent was an economic ruin for the most part, and two external powers were contesting for supremacy over what was left intact.

By 1965, the western European countries had surpassed every measure of prewar prosperity and were rapidly regaining independence of action in politics.

Factors Promoting Prosperity

What had happened to encourage this rebirth? Five factors in particular can be identified:

- *Marshall Plan aid* was remarkably successful in restarting the stalled economies of both the former enemies and the allies. For five years (1947–1951), Austria, West Germany, France, Britain, Italy, and others benefited from this fund of U.S. dollars available for loan. The conditions imposed by supervisory agencies assured a new spirit of collaboration not only between governments but also between government and employers for the benefit of the general public.

- *Social reforms* were enacted immediately after the war to provide benefits for ordinary citizens that they had long sought. Pensions for all, universal medical insurance, family allowances, paid vacations, paid schooling, and other changes all gave the working classes a new sense of being part of the process. Now they felt they had a stake in the success of their country.

were not so enthusiastic about his authoritarian style, he resigned in a huff after only a couple of months. For the next twelve years he lived in retirement waiting confidently for the people's call.

In 1958, in the wake of the French defeat in Indochina, the gathering rebellion in Algeria, and constant instability in government, the call finally came. A new, de Gaulle–inspired constitution created the Fifth Republic. De Gaulle then assumed the much-strengthened presidency and gave France ten years of stability and prosperity. He crushed an attempted army revolt on the way to settling the bloody war in Algeria. Insisting on French equality with the United States, he gradually withdrew his forces from NATO and evolved a remarkable partnership with another stubborn old man, Chancellor Konrad Adenauer of West Germany. The two former enemies had become convinced of the need for a permanent Franco-German alliance if Europe were to find peace. The alliance was created within the framework of the European Community, now the European Union.

In a sense, de Gaulle's success in giving France stability led directly to his ultimate defeat. The wave of discontent began with the famous Parisian student strike of 1968. Tens of thousands of new working-class students had flocked into the few French universities during the prosperous 1960s, to find themselves frustrated in an unbendingly conservative academic system. They turned to radical protest in the streets, and although the action was put down by police and army, the public reacted vehemently against the amount of force employed. De Gaulle's government now looked to many to be bankrupt of any constructive ideas. In the following year, when an opportunity came to display displeasure by rejecting a constitutional amendment, it was taken by the same middle-class voters who had so strongly embraced de Gaulle ten years earlier. Reading the results as a rejection of himself, de Gaulle resigned the presidency in 1969 and again retired to his native Normandy, where he died at age eighty.

Even his most vehement enemies were obliged to acknowledge his role in modern French history, when he had almost single-handedly created the image of a country that may have been temporarily overwhelmed by a brutal enemy but was far from giving up the struggle. De Gaulle's sense of mission, of being the almost divinely appointed savior of his people, carried over into an obstinacy that made him difficult to work with. But that same obstinacy overcame massive wartime obstacles for the embattled general and gave him the moral authority as president to lead the disunited and cynical French into a better civic life. He was France's great modern lawgiver, as Napoleon had been a century earlier.

FOR REFLECTION

De Gaulle's authoritarian nature was partly inspired by his Catholic upbringing and his military background. Is authoritarianism always a debit factor for a governing figure? Why might twentieth-century France have been particularly susceptible to electing such a person to supreme power?

- ❧ *Effective national planning* provided intelligent direction for the economy without eliminating individual enterprise and its profit reward. The "mixed economy"—with some industries and financial institutions directly controlled by the government, some totally private, and many in between—came to be the rule from Scandinavia to Portugal.
- ❧ *A large, willing labor pool* in most countries allowed employers and entrepreneurs to expand at will when they saw opportunities. The unions, which had generally opposed employers as a matter of principle in the prewar era, now cooperated because socially conscious politicians protected and expanded their rights to a point where they now had an important voice in management.
- ❧ *Free trade was made general.* The tariff, quota, and license barriers of the 1930s were gradually junked among the NATO countries; the various national currencies were made easily convertible and transferable; and international investment—much from the United States—was simplified and directly encouraged.

For these reasons, the growth of the western European economies was little short of sensational after the immediate postwar years. West Germany led the way in these "economic miracles" of the 1950s, but France, Italy, and the Benelux nations (Belgium, Luxembourg, and the Netherlands) were close behind. Only Britain did not do very well because of an overly tradition-bound mentality and the breakup of the Commonwealth trading bloc that had long given British industry a false sense of security from competition.

The *average* rate of growth in western European gross national product during 1948–1972 was approximately 4.5 percent per annum—an unbelievable achievement over a full quarter-century. Some nations did much better. And no recessions or business crises occurred.

The United States promoted much of this economic development by pouring in new capital first through the Marshall Plan and then much more through private investment by U.S. companies. By the 1960s, many Europeans were becoming concerned that their economies were being tied too closely to the United States or that Europe had become a kind of voluntary satellite to the Colossus across the Atlantic.

In retrospect, it is clear that the early 1960s represented the apex of American economic influence and political power in Europe. Subsequently, the intervention in Vietnam combined with the erosion of the dollar's value to weaken U.S. moral and financial prestige. President Richard M. Nixon's reluctant decision to allow the dollar to

Volkswagen Assembly Line, 1954. This plant, a frequent target of Allied bombers a few years earlier, led the way into mass production of cheap automotive transport for millions of European consumers. *(AP/Wide World Photos)*

find its own level in the international gold market (1971) immediately demonstrated that the U.S. currency had become overvalued, and the Swiss franc and the German mark began to rise steadily against it. The financial event dramatized the more general economic changes that had been taking place under the surface, bringing Europe collectively back into a status of balance with the United States (and far overshadowing the Soviet Union).

European Unity

As the economies of the various western European states recovered and then boomed in the 1950s, the old dream of supranational union quickly took on new life. For a couple of generations, some Europeans had looked to the day when the nations would give way to some kind of federation (with or without a powerful central organ). Now at the end of a gruesome war that had been caused in part, at least, by German and French enmity, these visionaries saw their best opportunity ever. With the strong backing of the United States, itself a successful federation, they would turn Europe into a new and peaceable political organism.

The main actors in this movement were the leaders of the Christian Democratic parties in Italy, France, Belgium, and West Germany. These middle-of-the-road Catholic parties had become the leading political forces in their countries immediately after the war. Their leaders in the early 1950s were gifted men, such as Alcide de Gasperi in Italy, Konrad Adenauer in West Germany, and Robert Schuman in France. They shared a consensus on future politics for the Continent. They believed that inter-European wars were an absolute disaster and must be avoided through political controls over each nation by some type of international group. Being realists, they thought that the best way to form this political association was to create economic ties among the potential members, which would grow so strong and all-embracing that an individual government could not logically consider waging war against its partners. First would come the economic bonds, then the social, and eventually the political ones.

In chronological order, the most important steps in this process of unifying western Europe (communist Europe was for obvious reasons a hostile bystander until the 1990s) were the following:

- 1947: The founding of the *Organization for European Economic Cooperation (OEEC)*. The OEEC was the supervisory arm of the Marshall Plan aid to Europe.

- 1951: The founding of the *European Coal and Steel Community*. France, West Germany, the Benelux nations, and Italy agreed to subordinate their individual needs in coal and steel to a supranational council. The system worked splendidly, and the six countries formed the nucleus of the Common Market of Europe.
- 1957: The **Treaty of Rome,** the founding charter of the **European Economic Community (EEC).** The EEC was the fundamental organ for European unity in the past forty years, and the current European Union evolved from it. The EEC is responsible for the *Common Market,* which now embraces most of Europe's countries in a single, nondiscriminatory trading system. The EEC was meant to become the vehicle by which Europe would be drawn into social as well as economic integration. It has largely achieved these aims for its original twelve members, which have now expanded to fifteen.
- 1992: The **Maastricht Treaty.** This treaty gave extensive powers to the European Parliament (created in 1957 by the Treaty of Rome) and facilitated economic and financial intercourse among the member states.

The name of the organization (headquartered in Brussels) that supervises these affairs is now simply the *European Union (EU).* By 1998, labor, money, credit, raw materials and manufactures, communications, and personal travel flowed across the national boundaries of fifteen European states with few, if any, restrictions. In 2002, a single, unified currency, the *euro,* went into effect. All European states, except traditionally neutral Switzerland, have joined or are candidates to join the EU. Several of the former communist states have applied for membership. Even without those states and the former Soviet Union, the EU now contains the largest, richest single market in the world—almost 400 million consumers.

The Communist Bloc, 1947–1980

Eastern Europe (that is, Poland, Hungary, the Czech and Slovak Republics, Romania, former Yugoslavia, Bulgaria, and Albania), where the communists took over after World War II, developed very differently. Here, the orthodox Marxist program was put into effect, following the lead of the Soviet Union. For several years, the development of heavy industry and transportation was the number one priority. Labor and capital were placed into heavy industry at the expense of agriculture and all consumer goods.

This Stalinist phase lasted from the late 1940s to the mid-1950s. As in the Soviet Union, it resulted in a huge increase in industrial capacities and the partial industrialization of these previously backward, peasant economies. Urban areas in particular grew by leaps and bounds as the abundant excess labor of the rural areas was siphoned off by the demand for workers in the new industry. As in Soviet Central Asia a generation earlier, whole new towns sprouted out of the fields, built around the new steel plant or the new chemical complex. Agriculture was collectivized and then relegated to permanent stepchild status in the budget.

After Stalin's death in 1953, somewhat more attention was paid to the consumer's needs, although the standard of living in communist Europe lagged far behind that in western Europe at all times. Khrushchev, Stalin's successor, summed up the period between 1955 and 1970 when he called it "goulash communism," communism that would put some meat in the pot. By the early 1960s, it was possible for people with professions or skills and perhaps with good Communist Party connections to live fairly comfortably and to hope for a better future still for their children. Salaries and wages were very low by Western standards, but medical care and education at all levels were free, and rents and food prices were low. In this way, the communist governments more or less satisfied a large proportion of their subjects economically, especially those who had been on the lower end of the social ladder in precommunist days.

In the 1970s, however, in one communist-ruled country after another, the economic advance halted and went into reverse as far as most consumers were concerned. The Marxist "command economy," which was always struggling with major defects, now showed increasing signs of breaking down altogether. Workers' discontents radically increased, and the governments' attempts to placate them with concessions backfired. As periodicals and television reception from the West were legalized and Western tourism increased, eastern Europeans had a better opportunity to see how miserably they fared in contrast to their Western counterparts.

The "technology gap" was growing more rapidly than ever before to the huge disadvantage of the communists not only in international economics but also at home. The average man in Warsaw, Budapest, or Moscow recognized how far behind his society was and how hopeless its chances of catching up were. And the average working woman was rapidly tiring of the dubious benefits that communism had given her: a double task inside and outside the home, lower pay than males and "glass ceilings" in her work, declining health care, and other handicaps in both public and private life. In the face of this rising wave of discontent, the rigid old men who were in charge of the Communist Party and government in all of the eastern European communist lands were paralyzed. They simply did not know what to do, short of abandoning the system to which they had devoted their lives and that had treated *them,* at least, quite well. As the 1970s became the 1980s, all of the European communist countries drifted and stagnated at the top, while the steam was building up below. And, of course, the safety valve of protest—democratic politics and free elections—did not exist. We take up subsequent developments in Chapter 57.

SUMMARY

The field of ruins that was Europe in 1945 gave birth to new economic and political life in a surprisingly short time. With U.S. aid, but mainly by their own determination and energy, the western Europeans came back strongly and created a stable, prosperous economy by the 1960s. Progress in economic unity gave strong encouragement to hopes of eventual sociopolitical integration of the European heartland.

During the same two postwar decades, the Cold War waxed and waned in accord with U.S. and Soviet initiatives and gambles such as the Berlin Blockade. So long as Joseph Stalin lived, it seemed impossible to find an accommodation that would take the world out from under the atomic mushroom cloud. His successor, Nikita Khrushchev, proved more flexible despite erecting the Berlin Wall in 1961 and the missile adventure in Cuba in 1962. Peaceful coexistence became the slogan of the day, leading to a considerable relaxation in East–West relations by the mid-1960s.

Internally, the eastern European communist states went through a Stalinist phase of heavy industrial development that transformed these peasant economies into modern, urban-based ones. But the industrial development was not matched by an increase in living standards, and the previous gap between East and West in this respect grew steadily larger in the 1970s. By the early 1980s, the slowdown in the chase for prosperity was noticeable everywhere in the Soviet bloc, and discontent was rising.

TEST YOUR KNOWLEDGE

1. The economic "miracle" of West Germany during the 1950s was founded on
   a. a mixed state and private economy.
   b. free-market capitalism with few restrictions.
   c. the decision to create a model welfare state.
   d. extensive imports from Britain and the United States.
2. The most dangerous phase of the Cold War's early period (1946–1950) was
   a. the Russian attempt to blockade access to West Berlin.
   b. the Russian decision to assist North Korea's invasion of South Korea.
   c. the arguments over proper operation of the military government in Berlin.
   d. the Western Allies' attempt to get a democratic government in Poland.
3. Khrushchev emerged as successor to Stalin in the Soviet Union
   a. from the public election held in 1954.
   b. after much backstage maneuvering.
   c. on a platform of anti-Stalinism and more democracy in the Communist Party of the Soviet Union.
   d. because of his wide popular appeal to Russians.
4. What is the correct chronology of these events?
   a. Berlin Wall erection, Berlin blockade, Cuban Missile Crisis, Korean War
   b. Berlin blockade, Korean War, Berlin Wall erection, Cuban Missile Crisis
   c. Korean War, Berlin blockade, Berlin Wall erection, Cuban Missile Crisis
   d. Korean War, Cuban Missile Crisis, Berlin blockade, Berlin Wall erection

5. The Common Market in Europe was originated by
   a. the Treaty of Versailles in 1919.
   b. the wartime Alliance of the United States, Britain, and the Soviet Union.
   c. the NATO treaty in 1949.
   d. the Treaty of Rome in 1957.
6. Which statement about communist Europe's economic progress is most correct?
   a. Much industrial progress from 1945 to 1955, then tapering off to stagnation in the 1970s
   b. Poor results until Stalin's death, then rapid improvement until the 1970s
   c. Gradual change from agrarian to industrial economy during the 1950s and 1960s with a switch to consumer products successfully undertaken in the 1970s and 1980s
   d. A continuous disaster of poor planning and lack of expertise
7. Early postwar leadership in western Europe was generally held by
   a. socialist parties that severed ties with the communists.
   b. coalitions of communists and socialists.
   c. moderate conservatives in the Christian Democratic parties.
   d. strong conservatives rejecting all aspects of socialism.
8. General Charles de Gaulle was
   a. the United States' most dedicated ally in NATO.
   b. the founder of the Free French movement in World War II.
   c. the leader of a coup against the civil government in the 1960s.
   d. the supreme commander of French forces during the early months of World War II.

IDENTIFICATION TERMS

Berlin Wall	European Economic	Maastricht Treaty	*Ostpolitik*
Cuban Missile Crisis	Community (EEC)	Marshall Plan	Treaty of Rome
de Gaulle, Charles	Khrushchev, Nikita	NATO	Truman Doctrine
détente	Korean War	Nuclear Test Ban	Warsaw Pact

INFOTRAC COLLEGE EDITION

Enter the search term "Cold War" using the Subject Guide.
Enter the search terms "Soviet Union relations with the United States" using the Subject Guide.

Enter the search term "Single European Market" using the Subject Guide.

52

DECOLONIZATION AND THE THIRD WORLD

The moment the slave resolves that he will no longer be a slave, his fetters fall. Freedom and slavery are mental states.

MOHANDAS GANDHI

THE FIFTY YEARS after World War II saw the end of the colonial empires built up since 1500 by the European powers. In the Western colonies, the end came soon after the war. In 1945, many hundreds of millions of Asians, Africans, Polynesians, and others were governed by Europeans from distant capitals. By the end of the 1970s, practically none were. These unexpected developments gave birth to the so-called Third World as a counterforce to the superpower blocs of the Cold War years.

In the late 1980s, the last of the colonial powers, the Soviet Union, confessed its inability to coerce continued obedience from its eastern European and Asian satellites and released them from imposed communist rule. A short time later, the collapse of the Soviet Union itself allowed the emergence of several new independent states from its ruins (see Chapter 57).

Decolonization or the "retreat from empire," as it has been frequently called, was a major turning point in world history. Europe (and North America and Japan) continues to exercise great power over the non-Europeans, but today this influence is more subtle. It is basically economic rather than political and military in nature. It is now inconceivable that a Western country would attempt to install an openly colonial regime in any non-Western land, if only for fear of the penalties it would suffer from its own neighbors. Since the collapse of the Soviet system in the early 1990s, the same can be said of the Russians. Colonialism as an overt political relationship is "history."

DECOLONIZATION'S CAUSES

What brought about this unexpectedly rapid end to a story that dated back to the sixteenth-century Western expansion? The movement toward decolonization had several major causes. In certain instances, such as India, Vietnam, and the Philippines, the rise to independent, sovereign status was the culmination of a generation or more of struggle—sometimes with gun in hand. In other cases, such as Zaire (now the Republic of Congo), Libya, and Iraq, independence came as a more or less sudden "gift" from the home country, often to a population that was quite unprepared for the event. Whatever the individual circumstances, all the independence-seeking colonies profited from some general developments that had occurred during the immediate postwar years:

- *Rising nationalism in Asia and Africa.* National pride and a burning resentment of Western dominion were in all cases the driving forces of decolonization. European rule had sown the seed of its own dissolution in the colonies by creating a small but vitally important native intelligentsia. The products of European-founded schools, these individuals had sometimes obtained higher education in the mother country. There they had learned not only academic subjects but also to reject the inferior status they suffered at home. They also absorbed Western nationalism and Western techniques of political organization (both legal and illegal). (The value of imitating Western models was quickly learned; see the box on "Vietnam's Declaration of Independence.") In a few cases, such as the Vietnamese **Ho Chi Minh** (1890–1969) in France, they encountered and adopted Marxism as a path to successful revolution. The Asian militants' efforts to build a popular following were aided by the repeated humiliations Japan inflicted on European/American armies and navies early in World War II, which revealed that the colonial powers were not invincible.

- *Loss of European moral authority.* In the nineteenth and early twentieth centuries, most Europeans looked upon their colonies with the sense that in ruling them they were doing the right thing—that is, meeting their duties as carriers of the "white man's burden." By the 1950s, the conviction that they were destined to rule others had been much weakened by the experiences of the two world wars and by the postwar spirit of egalitarian democracy. The Europeans' self-assurance was gone. They no longer possessed the morale that is necessary to govern others effectively.

- *Temporary prostration of Europe.* After the war until about 1960, Europe's six overseas colonial powers (Belgium, Britain, France, Italy, the Netherlands, and Portugal) were absorbed with repairing the damage caused by the war and/or reforming the low-tech economies, social antagonisms, and obsolete educational systems they had carried over from the 1930s. The public had no interest in supervising "difficult" colonials or pouring badly needed capital and labor into colonial projects that, like many previous ones, might never work out.

- *Opposition to the continuation of colonies in both Allied war aims and U.S. policy.* The stated aims of the United Nations, founded at the end of World War II by the Western powers, were clearly anticolonial. And the United States, which played such a major role in postwar Europe, had always felt uneasy about holding

Ho Chi Minh with His Generals. The Vietnamese leader of the long war against France and then the United States plots his next moves. "Uncle" Ho was an outstanding representative of the large group of Third World nationalists determined to lead their peoples into independence by any means possible after World War II. (© *Black Star*)

colonies, even its own. (It acknowledged Philippine independence as early as 1946.)

In light of these facts, the Western countries' more or less voluntary release of their colonies between 1946 and 1962 becomes more understandable. By the latter date, only the Soviet Union was still an important colonial country, holding eastern Europeans as unwilling satellites and suppliers.

DISMANTLING OF WESTERN COLONIES

How did decolonization proceed? Britain led the way by making good on the Labour Party's wartime promise to release India from the British Commonwealth. For many years, British Conservative governments had steadfastly opposed the peaceable but unrelenting movement for independence led by the Hindu Congress Party and its founder, **Mohandas Gandhi** (1869–1948). Gandhi's magnificent ability to reveal the moral inconsistencies in the British po-

VIETNAM'S DECLARATION OF INDEPENDENCE, 1946

Ho Chi Minh remained in Vietnam throughout World War II, organizing and leading the Viet Minh guerrillas against the Japanese occupiers. Ho and his people expected to be treated as allies by the French after the war, but instead they were told they must return to colonial status. In September 1945, the Viet Minh leadership made this reply, which draws cleverly on the history of both France and the United States to justify itself. Note that Ho by no means had the "entire Vietnamese people" behind him at this juncture and was hoping to bluff the French and embarrass the Americans with this Vietnamese Declaration of Independence. That independence was in fact achieved only after thirty years of near-continuous fighting.

"All men are created equal. They are endowed by their Creator with certain inalienable rights; among these are Life, Liberty, and the pursuit of Happiness." This immortal statement was made in the Declaration of Independence of the United States of America in 1776. In a broader sense, this means: all the peoples of the earth are equal from birth, all the peoples have a right to live, to be happy, and to be free.

The Declaration of the French Revolution made in 1791 on the Rights of Man and Citizen also states: "All men are born free and with equal rights, and must always remain free and have equal rights."

Those are undeniable truths.

Nevertheless, for more than eighty years, the French imperialists, abusing the standard of Liberty, Equality, and Fraternity, have violated our Fatherland and oppressed our fellow citizens. They have acted contrary to the ideals of humanity and justice. . . .

They have built more prisons than schools. They have mercilessly slain our patriots; they have drowned our uprisings in rivers of blood. . . .

In the field of economics, they have fleeced us to the backbone, impoverished our people, and devastated our land. . . .

In the Autumn of 1940 when the Japanese Fascists violated Indochina's territory to establish new bases in their fight against the Allies, the French imperialists went down on bended knee and handed over our country to them. Thus, from that date our people were subjected to the double yoke of the French and the Japanese. Their sufferings and miseries increased. . . .

After the Japanese had surrendered to the Allies, our whole people rose to regain our national sovereignty and to found the Democratic Republic of Vietnam.

The truth is that we have wrested our independence from the Japanese, and not from the French. The French had fled, the Japanese have capitulated. Our people have broken the chains which for nearly a century have fettered them and have won independence for the Fatherland.

For these reasons, we, members of the Provisional Government, representing the entire Vietnamese people, declare that from now on we break off all relations of a colonial character with France; we repeal all the international obligations that France has so far subscribed to on behalf of Vietnam, and we abolish all the special rights that the French have unlawfully acquired in our Fatherland.

Source: Selected Works of Ho Chi Minh, vol. 3 (Hanoi: 1960–1962).

---

sition made him an unbeatable opponent, however, and the Labour Party had been gradually won over to his point of view. (For more on Gandhi and his nonviolent methods, see the Exercise of Authority box.)

In 1945, Labour won the first postwar election, and negotiations with Gandhi and his associate **Jawaharlal Nehru** were begun. It soon became clear that the Hindu leaders could not speak for the large Muslim minority, which demanded separate statehood. The British government, immersed in the severe postwar problems at home, tried in vain to resolve this dilemma. In 1947, independence was granted to India on a ready-or-not basis.

The immediate result was a very bloody civil war, fought by Hindus and Muslims over the corpse, so to speak, of Gandhi, who had been assassinated by a fanatic. From this war came two new states, India and Pakistan (and eventually Bangladesh, the former East Pakistan), which remain hostile to this day and engage in frequent border disputes and mutual misunderstandings. It was a shaky beginning to the decolonization movement.

Elsewhere, however, the British generally managed things more adroitly. Burma and Sri Lanka (Ceylon) gained their independence peaceably by mutual agreement in the late 1940s. **Ghana** (Gold Coast) became the first colony in sub-Saharan Africa to be granted self-government. It was then recognized as a sovereign member of the voluntary association called the *British Commonwealth* in 1957. Almost the entire list of British colonies, from Malaysia to Belize (British Honduras) in Central America, quickly followed. By the mid-1960s, even such minor holdings as the islands of the south Pacific (Fiji, the Solomon Islands) and the Bahamas were granted either self-government under the Crown or full independence.

In France, the attitude of the public and government toward retaining the colonial empire underwent a sharp shift around 1960. This reversal was generated by the unhappy results (for France) of its colonial wars in Vietnam (1945–1954) and Algeria (1958–1961). Both of these proved lost causes that led to many thousands of French casualties and much discontent at home. In 1958, the war hero General Charles de Gaulle became president of France and almost immediately began to change course on the colonial question. Within four years, most of the former possessions had been granted independence and membership in a French version of the British Commonwealth. The members of this community remain closely linked with

MOHANDAS GANDHI
(1869–1948)

The worldwide reputation of Mohandas Karam-chand Gandhi, the Hindu national and spiritual leader, resulted from his deeds as a nonviolent revolutionary. His acts of defiance against what he considered an unjust and coercive colonial government were uniquely successful. He is rightly seen as the father of Indian independence and the model for peaceable defiance of injustice by authority. Gandhi was above all else an upholder of human dignity. Believing that all life was precious and should not be wasted, he steadfastly opposed the use of violence, in any cause. His followers titled him the Mahatma, or "great soul." Even the British colonial government came to recognize and respect his moral elevation and dedication to his people.

Gandhi was born to a merchant family of middling caste in Porbandar, India, in 1869. When he was thirteen, he was married in traditional fashion to a distant relative. Five years later, he went to England to study law. He returned to India to practice, but after two years, he decided to try his luck in the British colony of South Africa. There he soon became a leader of the large group of Hindu immigrants and defended their rights against systematic racial discrimination. During this period, Gandhi became a man of extraordinary spiritual strength. He gave up Western dress and customs, dressed in the worker's traditional loincloth and homespun shirt, and began a life of complete celibacy.

In 1915, he returned to India and at once became active in the budding Indian national independence movement. But he supported Britain in World War I, counting on London to grant Indians much more self-government after the conflict was over. When this did not happen, Gandhi began his campaigns of civil disobedience against the injustices of colonialism and the subordination of Indians to the British colonial authorities. His most famous act of protest was the Salt March of 1930, which brought him to world attention. Gandhi led hundreds of thousands in a long walk across India to the sea as a protest against a British tax on salt (the one commodity that poverty-stricken Hindus had to buy for money).

After this, Gandhi was in and out of British jails or in London as spokesman for the idea of Indian independence. The

Mohandas Gandhi. *(AP/Wide World Photos).*

bald little man in a loincloth could not be ignored, however much the interwar governments wished he would go away. In World War II, Gandhi refused to support Britain until the government made a definite promise of independence. For this he was jailed again, but he was freed in 1944 to take part in the negotiations over India's postwar status that culminated with the division of India into its Hindu and Muslim portions and the independence of both from European rule.

Because he refused to countenance Hindu repression against the minority Muslims, some fanatics considered Gandhi a traitor to the Hindu cause. In early 1948, one of them shot and killed him while he was praying. The entire subcontinent, Muslim and Hindu alike, went into mourning.

Gandhi's example of nonviolent civil disobedience has been followed throughout the world since his death. In the United States, Martin Luther King, Jr., attributed much of his success in organizing American blacks to lessons learned from Gandhi. But not all of Gandhi's lessons and examples were popular or heeded by his own people. His hope that Indians could return to a preindustrial lifestyle, weaving their own clothes and growing their own foods, seemed to many otherwise sympathetic people to be impossible. His protégé and successor to the presidency of the Hindu National Congress Party, Jawaharlal Nehru, strongly disagreed with his mentor on these topics. After Gandhi's death, the Congress Party became a normal, faction-filled political organization rather than the Mahatma's personal instrument to mold Indian national consciousness. But Gandhi is still revered among ordinary Indians, and he would unquestionably rank at the head of any list of modern Hindus.

FOR REFLECTION

Do you think Gandhi's hope for a return to preindustrial lifestyle in India was realistic? What advantages might an independent India have enjoyed from such a return? Was the split between Hindu and Muslim that created separate states of India and Pakistan inevitable? Desirable?

Flight from Terror. Millions of Muslim refugees fled the outbreaks of ethnic violence that marked the 1947 division of British India into two sovereign states. Hindus living in the new Pakistan suffered similar fates. (*Associated Press*)

France in economics and culture but go their individual ways in international affairs. With some bitter exceptions, the French were successful, as were the British, in retaining a position of privilege and influence in their former colonies. Despite rabid nationalism among the former subjects, the ties generated by common languages and education often survived the political scission.

The Belgians, Dutch, and Portuguese, on the other hand, were all forced from their Asian and African possessions by a combination of uprisings and international pressure exerted in the United Nations. These small European countries had relatively more prestige and wealth invested in their colonies and gave them up only reluctantly. The Belgians lost the huge African Congo by threatened rebellion in 1961. The Dutch let go of their Indonesian empire only after prolonged and vain fighting against the nationalists in the late 1940s. The Portuguese gave up their outposts in Africa also under severe pressure from a guerrilla war beginning in the early 1970s.

PROBLEMS OF THE THIRD WORLD

What have the former colonies achieved in the generation or more since attaining their independence? Have they been able to fulfill the hopes of the nationalist intellectuals and the dedicated dreamers who were so instrumental in their creation?

Until the mid–twentieth century, the writing of history in the United States or any other Western country was very largely concerned with the acts of a relatively small minority: the inhabitants of Europe and North America. But the largest part of the world's population has long been located elsewhere. The majority live in what was formerly called the "Third World" (that is, of neither the American nor the Soviet side of the Cold War) of less developed and scarcely developed countries such as Togo, Afghanistan, and Bolivia. In these countries, the per capita cash income is perhaps one-twentieth of the West's, and this material poverty is reflected by a basically different set of cultural values and customs.

In fact, three-fourths of the nearly 6 billion people inhabiting the world in 2000 lived in the less developed countries. This predominance in numbers has not yet been translated into cultural and economic predominance—and perhaps never will be. But with the global village beckoning in the twenty-first century, we in the West had better prepare to encounter and assist these people if we intend to live in peace. Many observers believe the gap that currently exists between the developed and less developed countries cannot be sustained much longer without severe repercussions.

What is a Third World society? The rapid economic and social development of some non-Western nations in recent years makes it imperative to distinguish among countries that used to be lumped together under that term. Thus, the following description applies to only the least developed nations of the world, some of which are in the Americas, but mostly located in Asia and Africa. Economically speaking, it is a society in which poverty is the rule, and some form of agriculture still makes up a high proportion (over

50 percent) of the gross national product. Unskilled labor is predominant in both town and country; the industrial and larger commercial enterprises are commonly controlled by or dependent on foreign capital. Industry is most often engaged in unsophisticated processing of raw material, often for an export market.

Politically speaking, it is a society in which a small elite, often derived from the bureaucracy of the colonial era, controls access to power and wealth. One political party controls public life, often with dictatorial power. Large landholders are dominant in the countryside, overshadowing or intimidating the far more numerous peasants and landless laborers. Nationalism is frequently carried to the point of mindless chauvinism, and disdain for the colonial past is a patriotic duty that masks many postcolonial failures.

Socially speaking, it is a society in which the overpopulation problem is severe and is getting worse each year. Males still exercise control over females within the family and have far more rights and prestige outside it. Education is highly desired and prestigious but often is ill designed for the present tasks. The clan or the extended family is far more important than in developed countries. Upward mobility is still quite possible but is becoming rarer and an unhealthy imbalance between burgeoning town and stagnant country life is steadily more apparent.

Internationally speaking, it is a society that is in most ways still dependent on the more developed countries—sometimes as much so as when it was formally a colony.

Since independence, it has been treated by both the West and the former Soviet bloc basically as a pawn in their foreign policy designs, and its weak bargaining powers have almost surely been further reduced by the ending of the Cold War.

Since the collapse of the Soviet bloc and the discrediting of Marxist economics (see Chapter 57), the tension between the rival ideologies of communism and capitalism can no longer be turned to third-party advantage in the competition for political and economic power. Additionally, the leaders of the Western world have given the highest priority for international aid programs to the Russians and eastern Europeans, to avoid chaos as those peoples attempt to make the transition to a free market. Consequently, less aid has been available for the less developed countries.

In some nations, the standard of living has actually declined since they attained independence. Africa is a particularly tragic case. The famine and banditry afflicting much of the **Sahel** (Sudan, Somalia, Ethiopia) in recent years are manifestations of this decline. So are the dictatorships that are the rule in African governments. Where dictators are absent, it is often only because tribal enmities (Somalia, Rwanda), religious warfare (Sudan), or a combination of these (Ethiopia, Republic of Congo) have prevented a single individual or party from seizing power. Almost everywhere, the root causes of these evils are a population that is too large for the available resources, the misuse of poorly

Queen Elizabeth Greets a Ghanian Chieftain. Her state visit to independent Ghana in 1961 was a triumph of British diplomacy in keeping friendly contact with the emerging states of former British Africa. (*John Bulucer/Camera Press London*)

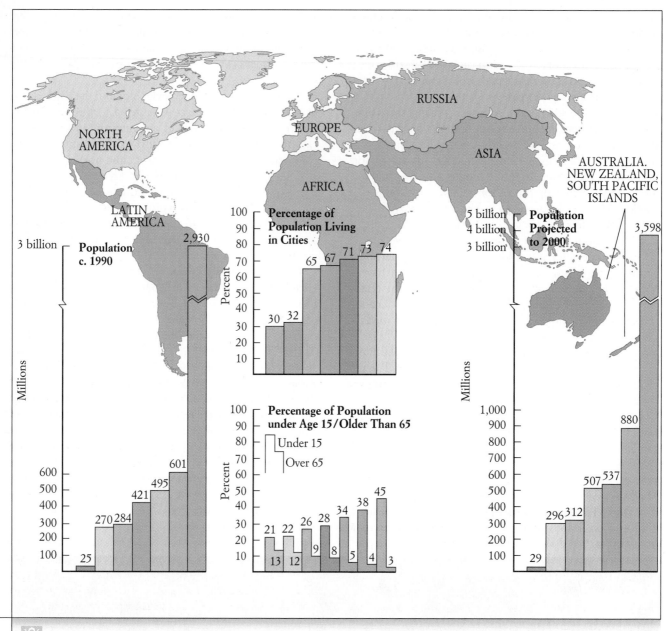

MAP 52.1 **Global Population Growth.**

understood imported technology, and a terrifying maldistribution of wealth.

The Population of the Earth

A book appeared in the 1970s with the arresting title *The Population Bomb.* Written by a respected biologist, Paul Ehrlich, at an American university, it warned that a time was rapidly approaching when the Earth would face mas-

sive, prolonged famine. The rate of population growth in the less developed countries threatened to overwhelm the Earth's capacity to grow food (see Map 52.1).

Professor Ehrlich's prognosis of early famine proved erroneous. The Green Revolution plus a series of good crop years around the globe actually increased the ratio of available food to mouths. But many believe Ehrlich's basic argument is still valid: inevitably, starvation will come. They point to the examples of the African Sahel, Bangladesh since independence, and many of the Andean populations in South America to assert that the number of consumers is exceeding the available resources. It is just a matter of time, they argue, until the well fed will be using lethal weapons to hold off the starving hordes.

Other observers, however, argue that Ehrlich and similar doomsayers are not taking the so-called **demographic transition** into account. This transition occurs when parents stop viewing many children as a familial and economic necessity and instead produce a smaller number of better cared-for children. Historically, this has occurred when a society becomes industrialized and urbanized. Children then become less economically necessary to the family, and a lower mortality rate means that most will live to maturity. Hence, parents no longer need to have many children to ensure that some will survive to care for them in their old age.

Since the three continents (Africa, Asia, and South America) where the large majority of the nonindustrial peoples live are rapidly developing urban and industrialized societies, it was hoped that the birthrates would drop substantially within a generation. This has not happened. In Latin America, parts of Asia, and much of Africa, birthrates have remained at levels double or triple Western rates. The "gap" between the present-day medical and technological capacities to preserve and prolong life and the cultural demands to have children early and frequently so that some will survive into adulthood has not closed as swiftly as was hoped. Efforts to lower the birthrate by artificial means (condoms, the Pill) have worked in some places but failed in others. The most impressive results have been obtained in communist China through massive government intervention in private life as well as constant propaganda for one-child families. Neither of these measures would be acceptable in most countries.

Yet, some means of controlling the hugely increasing demands of the world's population on every type of natural resource (including privacy, quietude, or undisturbed contemplation) must be found soon, presumably. The human inhabitants of Spaceship Earth are increasing in geometric fashion. The Earth's first half-billion inhabitants took perhaps 50,000 years to appear, and the second half-billion appeared over 500 years (1300–1800). But the last half-billion of the 1990 total of 5.5 billion people came aboard in a period of ten to twelve years! The large majority of this last half-billion live in the less developed countries, where the rate of natural increase—births over deaths without counting migration—is two to four times that of the industrial world.

Misapplied Technology

The developed countries' postwar attempts to assist the former colonies and the Latin American states sometimes compounded the difficulties those nations were already experiencing. In nations with a superabundance of labor, where the economy could not supply more than a few months' paid labor for many citizens, the World Bank and other international agencies frequently promoted industrial projects that actually *lessened* job opportunities. Instead of encouraging the continued use of shovels and baskets or similarly technologically primitive but economically productive means of moving earth, for example, the agencies shipped in bulldozers and large dumptrucks to construct a new dam or mine. In agriculture, a local government's request for modern heavy equipment for plowing or the newest mechanical milking machines for its dairies would be granted, even when the predictable net result for the local labor market would be devastating. The cowherd and other laborers thus thrust out of work only contributed to the problems of the poverty-stricken villages or the overcrowded city slums. This preference for short-term "show" rather than long-term improvement characterized many of the Third World's domestic and internationally funded postwar projects.

Ill-conceived technology also frequently had unfortunate ecological consequences. The Aswan Dam project in Egypt is a good example. Built with Soviet aid in the 1950s, the huge dam and the lake it created radically altered the ecology of the lower Nile. Although the lake (despite tremendous loss from evaporation) supplied tens of thousands of acres with water for irrigation, downstream from the dam the changes were entirely for the worse. A variety of snail that previously had not lived in the lower Nile waters began to flourish there, causing a massive outbreak of epidemic disease. The schools of Mediterranean fish that had previously been fed from the flooding Nile delta disappeared; with them went the food supply of many Egyptians and the livelihood of many more who had netted the fish and sold them. The new upstream lands now under irrigation from Lake Nasser could not make up the deficit for the hungry Egyptian peasants because almost all of these lands were devoted to cotton or other industrial crops for export.

All told, the efforts of the Third World nations to achieve industrial and/or agrarian development in the thirty years following World War II were unsuccessful in raising living standards for the masses of people. Some groups did prosper, and some regions did much better than others, notably the western rim of the Pacific Ocean. But in much of Africa and Latin America, the few rich got richer, the many poor stayed poor, and those in between did not multiply as hoped. The maldistribution of wealth is best displayed by some comparative figures. In the industrialized Western nations, the personal income of the uppermost 10 percent of society is about five times the income of the bottom 10 percent. In the comparatively well-off Mexico, the disparity in income has grown over the past decades, until by the 1990s the upper 10 percent were receiving *twenty-seven times* as much as the bottom 10 percent.

SUMMARY

Decolonization came in the first quarter-century after World War II, as the colonial powers realized that economic exhaustion and anticolonial sentiment made it impossible to retain their former possessions in Asia and Africa. Beginning with the difficult and bloody severance of India and Pakistan from the British empire, the colonial structures were dismantled or toppled by armed revolts between 1947 and 1974. While the British gave their remaining subjects uncontested self-government and then sovereignty in the 1960s, the French were at first less pliant. First in Vietnam and then in North Africa, they engaged in extended warfare that eventually resulted in defeat and withdrawal. Only then under de Gaulle did they achieve a workable postcolonial relationship. The French mistakes were imitated by the Dutch, Belgians, and Portuguese, all of whom had to be driven out of their colonies by nationalist rebellions during the 1940s through the 1970s. In the Soviet instance, the attempt to retain satellites persisted into the 1980s.

The Third World that emerged from the postcolonial settlements was a hodgepodge of different states and societies. But to some degree all suffered from generic handicaps in dealing with the "First World" West and the "Second World" communist states. Maldistribution of national wealth, misapplication of technological assets, and the overwhelming growth of population were three of the worst.

TEST YOUR KNOWLEDGE

1. Which was *not* a strong motivation for the rapid decolonization after World War II?
   a. U.S. opposition to continued colonial holdings
   b. The war-caused weakness of most colonial powers' economies
   c. The weakening of Europeans' confidence in their ability to rule others well
   d. The communists' accusations of Western imperialism
2. Which of the following African countries fought a long war against a colonial power and eventually won its independence?
   a. Nigeria
   b. Egypt
   c. Algeria
   d. South Africa
3. The decolonization process went ahead with the least violence in
   a. Southeast Asia.
   b. French North Africa.
   c. British Africa
   d. Portuguese Africa.
4. The last surviving major colonial power was
   a. Portugal.
   b. the Soviet Union.
   c. the United States.
   d. France.
5. What proportion of the world's population currently lives in the less developed countries?
   a. One-half
   b. Two-thirds
   c. Three-fourths
   d. Four-fifths

6. One of the prominent identifying factors for a Third World society is a
   a. prospering rural and agrarian economy.
   b. steady drain of population into the cities.
   c. reluctance to accept foreign aid.
   d. equal status for young males and females.
7. Which of the following was *not* a factor in lessening the West's attention to the problems of the Third World in recent years?
   a. The collapse of the communist hopes of revolution
   b. The diversion of foreign aid to the former communist lands of Europe
   c. The inability of Third World nations to collaborate effectively in international negotiations
   d. The slowing rate of population growth in most ex-colonial countries
8. The "demographic transition" means
   a. a change from a youthful to an elderly population.
   b. a change from an excess of males to an excess of females in a given population.
   c. the evolution of a bigger, stronger average size in human bodies.
   d. the change from high birthrates to lower ones as a population modernizes.

IDENTIFICATION TERMS

demographic transition   Ghana   Nehru, Jawaharlal   Sahel
Gandhi, Mohandas   Ho Chi Minh

 # INFOTRAC COLLEGE EDITION

Enter the search term "decolonization" using Key Words.
Enter the search term "Gandhi" using Key Words.

Enter the search term "developing countries" using the Subject Guide.

THE NEW ASIA

A *revolution is not a dinner party.*
MAO ZEDONG

THE TWO LEADING Asian powers had both suffered greatly during the war and were temporarily restricted in their international roles while recovering. China and Japan continued to take sharply differing paths to establishing modern societies. China chose the path of revolution and became the world's largest Marxist state. Japan adapted Western ideas and technology to fit its own culture and became for a time the world's exemplary economic success.

While World War I had brought relatively minor change to these areas, World War II proved to be the wellspring of major transformations. Many areas in eastern and southern Asia had been in colonial status and were intent on gaining full independence as soon as the war was concluded. The U.S.-held Philippines were the first to do so, followed by India and the European possessions in Southeast Asia and the Pacific islands. By the end of the twentieth century, several newly independent states had attained international significance by taking full advantage of a rapidly changing global economy.

MAO'S CHINA, 1949–1976

The People's Republic of China (PRC) was proclaimed by a triumphant Mao Zedong in the fall of 1949. It entered into a formal alliance with the Soviet Union a few months later. Government and all social institutions were reorganized on Soviet communist lines, and for the first ten years, the Soviets were both its helpers and its mentors.

The conquest of the world's largest population had essentially been the work of one man—Chairman (of the Chinese Communist Party's Central Committee) Mao, with the help of some brilliant assistants, especially Zhou Enlai. Although Mao had profited from some Soviet arms and economic support and guidance since the 1930s, in its fundamentals Chinese communism was his creation. No one else, not even Stalin, had played much of a role beside him in Chinese eyes. This was to be a critical factor in the years to come.

Mao was convinced that in an agrarian society like China's (about 90 percent of the population were peasants), the correct path to socialism could only lie through a revolutionary peasantry. Thus, at all times during his rule, keeping the peasants with him was his chief concern.

What the urbanites thought and did was of secondary importance. Mao's long and fruitful contacts with the rural folk also seem to have made him increasingly distrustful of intellectuals—a very untraditional attitude for a Chinese leader and one that would have horrendous effects in the 1960s Cultural Revolution.

In its first three years (1949–1952), the regime instituted the basic policies it would employ to assure political and social control indefinitely. In the countryside, land was expropriated from the landlords, and many—perhaps millions—of them were killed or imprisoned. The land was first redistributed to the peasants and then in 1955–1957 collectivized as the Soviets had done in their Five-Year Plan. Although millions more were killed or allowed to starve in the great famines of 1960–1962, the peasants did not resist as fiercely as in the Soviet Union. Why not? In part, it was because of the ancient Chinese tradition of regarding the central government as the legitimate source of authority and in part because so many desperately poor peasants supported the new arrangements ardently.

The new social organ called the *commune* was made the basis of rural production and of government, with disastrous effects for both the agricultural and the industrial economies. The communes were so large (about 25,000 persons) and their responsibilities were so unclear that they could not function. Even in good years, food production barely matched the rapidly increasing population as a result of poor planning and low incentives. When bad

harvests came after 1960, mass famine was inevitable. To keep the industrial plant working at all, grain was confiscated from the communes mercilessly, and the peasants starved just as they had in Russia earlier, under war communism and during the Five Year Plans. Eventually, the communes were abolished, and smaller units created that resembled the traditional villages except that land and work were collectivized.

The Chinese pursued industrial expansion in the same fashion as the Soviets had earlier, emphasizing heavy industry at the expense of consumer goods. A Stalinist Five-Year Plan instituted in 1953 produced substantial results in metals, coal, and other basic goods for industry. But Mao had become impatient with Soviet models and plans. In 1958, he personally introduced the **Great Leap Forward.** This attempt at overnight mass industrialization was an enormously costly failure (the infamous "backyard steelmaking," for example). It accelerated the growing gap between the Chinese and their Russian mentors, especially between Mao and Nikita Khrushchev.

The Russians criticized Mao for foolishly attempting the impossible and also for allowing himself to be made into the sort of Great Father in China that Stalin had been in Russia. In 1956, Khrushchev had just finished revealing Stalin's true nature to a shocked communist world, and he had no intention of allowing Mao to step up onto the vacant pedestal. On his side, a confident Mao made it clear that while he was no great admirer of Stalin or any other foreigner,

The Little Red Book of Chairman Mao. Chinese Red Guards mass in Beijing to celebrate the appearance of the Chairman. For many millions during the Great Proletarian Cultural Revolution, the *Thoughts of Mao* as printed in the famous little red book were a command and an inspiration. *(Sovfoto/Eastphoto)*

MOTHERS AND DAUGHTERS-IN-LAW IN CHINA

Two American women were able to stay as observers of women in post-Mao China during the 1980s, and they later collaborated in authoring a book on what they saw. The following excerpts are adapted from the chapter on "Family Relations."

Nowhere is the contrast between pre-Liberation and contemporary China more obvious than in the circumstances under which a young bride enters her new home. In pre-liberation China [when wives always moved into the husband's family] . . . for a young woman, having no protection, vulnerable to abuse from her mother-in-law, the only hope of finding allies . . . was to bear children. In post-1949 China the increased possibility of free choice and companionate marriage, particularly in the cities, made the husband a potential ally. And while a bride still had to forge relations with her husband's family, she was no longer expected to break off ties with her birth family.

These dramatic changes obscured more subtle continuities . . . a woman was marrying not just a husband, but an entire family as well. As in the past, she was the potentially disruptive family member, and was therefore often considered the cause of any domestic conflict.

In pre-liberation China, the paramount concern of a young bride was what her husband's family would be like, and how cruel or abusive her mother-in-law would be. So central was this last question to her future life that it was reflected in one of the most common ways of referring to marriage; not "to wed a husband" but "to find a mother-in-law."

In the early 1980s, a young wife had far more legal protection and social independence, and a mother-in-law less power. This was partly because political campaigns targeted for criticism mothers-in-law who abused their sons' wives . . . Sometimes a mother-in-law was even expected to shoulder the burden of household chores while her son and daughter-in-law worked. Conversely, the lack of welfare facilities for the elderly in rural areas often made them dependent on their married children. . . .

Thus the age-old conflict between mothers- and daughters-in-law, far from being resolved, assumed new dimensions. . . . In contrast to the 1950s, almost no stories exposed the abusive or unreasonable behavior of a mother-in-law and suggested that she reform. Instead the literature focused on the disrespectful, if not downright evil, behavior of daughters-in-law [and] aimed to persuade women to do what the traditional family system had formerly forced them to do—respect their mothers-in-law, take care of the elderly, and preserve domestic harmony.

FOR REFLECTION

How did the changed relationship between mother and daughter-in-law reflect the communists' insistence on eliminating Confucian ethics? What would you imagine the usual relationship between father and son-in-law might be under the Marxists, and why might it differ sharply from the female in-laws' relations?

SOURCE: E. Honig and G. Herschatter, *Personal Voices: Chinese Women in the 80s* (Stanford, CA: Stanford University Press, 1988).

---

he believed that true revolutions demanded a nearly supernatural Leader, with whom the ignorant masses might identify—something that Khrushchev never pretended to be or was capable of being.

Furthermore, Mao told the Russians that they had been diverted from the authentic revolutionary path by their fears of losing what they had in a war with capitalism and, moreover, that he intended to take their place as spokesman of the oppressed masses. By 1960 the barely concealed **Sino-Soviet conflict** was splitting the communist ranks. The rift became fully public at the time of the Cuban Missile Crisis, when the Maoists derided the Soviets' fear of U.S. "paper tigers," while Moscow denounced Beijing's readiness to plunge the world into atomic war.

Mao had long been convinced that the Soviet revolution had been suffocated by bureaucratization, and he was determined that China would not share this fate. In 1965, he suddenly called for the **Great Proletarian Cultural Revolution.** This extraordinary upheaval was meant to—and did—turn Chinese society on its head for a number of years. Like Stalin's "second revolution" of 1929, Mao's plan went far beyond political rearrangement. He wished to create a truly new relationship among party, people, and the

exercise of revolutionary power. The attack was aimed primarily at the intellectuals, particularly those in the CCP's cadres of officials. (See the Family and Gender Relations box for an example of how other relations changed.)

To achieve his main end, Mao was prepared to undertake what seemed an impossible task: to rid the Chinese people of their reverence for tradition. He called on the youthful **Red Guards**—mainly students—to make war on the older generation and its "empty formalisms." Mao himself was a profoundly skeptical spirit who distrusted all systems, even those he had created. He wished to introduce the permanent, self-perpetuating revolution, which he thought the Russians had given up in return for peace and a pseudo-Marxist society.

For the next three or four years, China experienced barely controlled, officially inspired anarchy. Professors were publicly humiliated, learned doctors were made to scrub the floors in their hospitals, scholars were abused for having foreign language books in their libraries, and Communist Party secretaries were accused of sabotage. Factional fighting in the party was allowed and encouraged, sometimes in the streets. The economy, only now recovering from the Great Leap Forward's mistakes, again suffered severe damage. Managers and skilled personnel were sent as outcasts to the villages to "learn the revolution's lessons" as barnyard sweepers or potato diggers. For a time, the only qualification for getting a responsible post was to have memorized the *Thought of Chairman Mao,* immortalized in the "**little red book**" that tens of millions of Chinese waved daily like an amulet against unknown evils. In 1969, the anarchy had become so bad that Mao had to call off the Red Guards and put the army in charge of everyday affairs. (For a sampling of the *Thought of Chairman Mao,* see the box.)

The tensions between China and the Soviet Union had erupted in the **Amur River War** as troops stationed on both sides of the frontier sporadically fired on each other. The military chiefs told Mao they could not guarantee what might happen if Russia attacked while the unrest continued. Still, until Mao's death in 1976, the spirit of the Cultural Revolution lived on, especially among the millions of radical, barely literate youth who thought the demolition of the Communist Party's apparatus and the government's disarray presented a once-in-a-lifetime chance for them to get ahead.

Within weeks of Mao's death, the inevitable reaction set in. The Cultural Revolution was first partially and then entirely condemned as a mistake. A collective leadership of party officials moved cautiously but steadily to put Mao's contributions into perspective. In 1980, his portraits, formerly everywhere, were silently removed from all public places. The era of the godlike chairman and his omnipresent little red book was definitely over.

The Goddess of Democracy. Chinese university students modeled this plaster creation after the Statue of Liberty and used it as their rallying point in Tienanmen Square before the massacre of May 1989. Mao's huge portrait looks on disapprovingly. *(Jeff Widener/AP Photo)*

Chinese Youth Defies Tanks. The never-identified youth stood alone to stop the tanks heading to Tienanmen Square in May 1989. After a brief hesitation, the vehicles rolled around him and continued to another destination. *(Jeff Widener/AP Photo)*

RECENT CHINA

Under Deng Xiaoping (1904–1997), an elderly but vigorous pragmatist, the Chinese Communist Party groped its way forward into the vacuum left by Mao's demise. A new spirit and new policies were strongly encouraged by various legal changes and official propaganda. To become rich, or at least well-to-do, was no longer a sin against the state and one's fellow citizens. In Deng's words, China would remain *socialist in spirit,* regardless of the semicapitalist economic system it seemed to be adopting. Deng, who had long been associated with the moderate wing of the party, was particularly interested in establishing better relations with foreign capitalists who might help China to recover from Mao's mistakes.

Spurred by President Richard M. Nixon's surprise visit to Beijing in 1972, the China–U.S. relationship had grown somewhat warmer since the ending of the U.S. presence in Vietnam. The Soviet invasion of Afghanistan (1979) increased Chinese interest in coming to a better understanding with the other superpower. Hence, in the 1980s, with U.S. encouragement, considerable progress was made in opening the country to foreigners and democratizing the secretive Communist Party and its iron controls over the political life of the populace. But in 1989, the rapid spread of a critical, questioning atmosphere among the university students eventually frightened the leaders, and they cracked down in the infamous **massacre in Tienanmen Square** in the heart of Beijing. Hundreds, perhaps thousands, of young people died fleeing the guns of their own army.

Since that time, China's government has been walking a fine line between diplomatic isolation and a partial acceptance of Western demands for relaxation of its repressive political measures. Recent indications are that the increasing worker/peasant discontent with their economic lot under Marxism will be considerably more persuasive to the policymakers in Beijing than foreign opinion. Whether Marxist or capitalist, China is now recognized as one of the four most potent international powers. With its aspiring and hard-working population of more than 1.2 billion, China will be a major factor in the global economy as well as in Asia in the future.

POSTWAR JAPAN TO 1952

The defeat and occupation of the Japanese islands by a foreign force (for the first time in history) was a tremendous shock. But it soon proved to be a constructive shock, unleashing a great deal of new energy and innovative thinking. Despite heavy war damage and loss of life, both military and civilian, Japan's economy rebounded with unexpected speed and then proceeded to shoot far ahead of anything it had achieved before.

The government of occupied Japan was an American-supervised affair under General Douglas MacArthur. Unlike the situation in occupied Germany after its defeat, a native civilian government was allowed to function, but it was limited to carrying out the directives of MacArthur's staff. All of MacArthur's many reform decrees in politics and social matters were accepted almost without criticism by the Japanese. Spiritually and materially exhausted by war and defeat, they were in a mood of self-questioning, very unusual for this proudly nationalist and confident nation. They seemed ready to accept a new basis for their social and political organization, and their willingness to change made the American occupation a great success.

In the first two years of his regime, MacArthur's office initiated radical changes in the traditional Japanese system, culminating in an entirely new constitution that established a government similar to the British government. The parliament (Diet) was declared the most important branch of government, with sovereignty residing in the Japanese people. The emperor remains but only as a symbol. Japan "forever renounces war as a sovereign right of the nation," maintaining only a small Self-Defense Force.

The war in Korea (1950–1953) was key in elevating the United States from conqueror to protector. The active support given to the North Korean communist army by Mao's China after 1951 made the U.S. armed forces in South Korea and elsewhere in the western Pacific an indispensable guardian for disarmed Japan. Japanese of all persuasions generally recognized the need for U.S. military protection, even though some were disturbed by the U.S.-instigated transformations in their social relations and political culture.

INDEPENDENT JAPAN

In 1952, the occupation ended and Japan again became a sovereign state. It signed a treaty of alliance with the United States that extended the U.S. nuclear umbrella over Japan in any future war. In return, the United States was guaranteed the right to have naval and military bases on Japanese soil for the indefinite future. Although minimally opposed at the time, this treaty caused tensions later, when the Socialist and Communist Parties denounced the treaty as a tool of U.S. imperialism. By then, however, it was clear that Japanese politics tended toward the conservative and that an anti-U.S. position had little appeal. A homogeneous people who value tradition and group approval, the Japanese have never shown much interest in social experimentation or political radicalism.

For the first few years, the Liberal Party was the leading force in independent postwar politics. The Liberals merged with their closest rivals in 1955 and became the Liberal Democratic Party (LDP). For almost forty years, the LDP formed every Japanese government. Despite the name, it was a conservative party, dominated by the big business interests that have always worked closely with government in Japan. The LDP finally went down to defeat in 1993, when it was the culprit in a series of political corruption scandals that rocked the country and the business establishment. Always more an aggregation of financial and economic interests than a political unit, the LDP split into factions and lost out to a coalition of opponents. In most recent days, the LDP's factions have become almost separate parties, fighting one another in the Diet and allowing Socialists and other groups to contest the national leadership effectively. Japan has become a fully democratic state, with governments that reflect both the strengths and weaknesses of that condition.

Economic Progress

The economic success of postwar Japan was admired throughout the world and was even considered as a possible model by the older industrialized states of the West. What explains this success? A combination of external and internal factors contributed to Japan's prosperity from the 1950s through the 1980s.

Externally, Japan benefited from several developments. When the United States assumed the burden of its defense, the budgetary expenditures that would have gone into nonproductive weaponry, housing, and pensions for the military were saved and could be invested in the civilian economy. The Korean War stimulated Japanese industry in many different ways. Also, Japan is entirely dependent on imported oil, and oil was very cheap during the initial postwar decades. International credit institutions such as the World Bank and the International Monetary Fund were eager to lend for investment and the acquisition of technology. Japan soon showed itself to be a willing student and a highly reliable credit risk.

Internally, Japan had the world's highest personal savings rate, and the banks reinvested the savings in new industry. The Japanese labor force was disciplined and skilled and had been well educated in one of the world's most effective primary and secondary school systems. The Japanese population rose throughout the postwar era, providing a large labor pool as well as a growing internal market. Under strong government urging, labor continued to work with employers rather than take an adversarial position. Unions were rewarded with extensive powers in the workplace.

Most of all, in the opinion of many, Japan's postwar surge was due to the consistent support of business by the government, which made large sums available for ongoing research and development and aggressively promoted business interests in its diplomacy. The *zaibatsu* combines, which originally had been broken up by the Americans, were allowed to reconstitute themselves in a slightly different fashion and with even more political and financial clout. New industrial giants such as Sony and Honda were the product of bold entrepreneurs. Industry and government directed a major effort toward expanding foreign trade, and Japanese trade with almost every noncommunist country rose without interruption during the postwar decades. Japanese goods, including electronic products, automobiles, watches, and cameras, conquered the consumer markets of the globe. The "Made in Japan" label, which had been synonymous with cheap imitations in the prewar era, became a symbol of advanced design and the world's best quality.

All these factors combined to give Japan the highest rate of growth in gross national product (about 10 percent per annum) in the world during the quarter-century between 1950 and 1975. Since then, the rate of growth has slowed due to several factors: other Asian countries began to compete effectively in the global markets; unsound credit extension saddling banks with enormous loan defaults; and widespread corruption in government–business relations weakened Japan's capacities and self-confidence. In the 1990s, the country slipped into a recession that is not yet overcome.

Japanese Society

Both rural and urban populations benefited from the postwar surge in material progress. After many generations of Buddhist simplicity and restraint, the Japanese have recently become a nation of consumers in the Western sense. Automobiles, television sets, cameras, and all the other manifestations of personal luxury we have become accustomed to are at least equally evident in Japan's cities. The standard of living is about as high as that in the United States. But many flaws in the picture of prosperity have recently come to light. Much of the surge in the postwar economy, especially in the 1980s, was generated by wild speculation in real estate, enabled by easy bank credit. This "bubble" broke with the first tremor in Japan's export balances, leaving huge numbers of aborted projects and paper losses in its wake. The government has shown itself unable to solve the tangles involved. Housing, for example, remains an acute problem because of the massive influx from the countryside and the shortage of available land where people wish to live. A well-paid manager working in Tokyo may have a two-hour, nerve-grinding commute because finding an affordable apartment any closer is impossible.

More disturbing than the economic stagnation to many is the visible erosion of respect for elements of the nation's Buddhist heritage that has taken place during the last two decades. Some blame this on the Americanization begun in the occupation years and promoted since then by American entertainment media. Others see the lost war itself as the fundamental reason why less respect is shown for the older generation and for all authority. In any case, urban youths in particular are increasingly unwilling to continue the age-old deference to the elderly. Embracing the consumer mentality, they resent having to provide support for a generation of older people who can no longer work and take care of themselves. Increasingly these tasks are pushed off onto governmental agencies, as in the West. This unprecedented "war of the generations," as some alarmists have termed it, is exacerbated by the housing shortage and outlandish rents in the cities, which force young people to remain in the parental home much longer than they desire.

How have Japanese women fared in this era? They find themselves in a multifaceted struggle to gain economic equality with their husbands and brothers. The constitution gave them legal and political equity but deliberately failed to alter a system that firmly separated male and female. In very recent years, Japanese working women have gained some access to jobs that were formerly male preserves, but they still lag behind women in other industrial societies. The "glass ceiling" in Japan may be the most prevalent and impenetrable in the world.

The formerly predominant agricultural sector has been much diminished in the last half-century: now less than 10 percent of the population lives on farms, and many of Japan's villages have become the more or less unwilling locales for second-home colonies of the city dwellers rather than their former self-contained societies. Even more telling of the reduced prestige of the farmer is the recent government decision to allow importation of foreign rice and the implied abandonment of the centuries-old "rice economy" and its commitment to the peasant as the mainstay of Japan's prosperity.

As for leisure and play, the ancient habit of allowing men to go places and engage in activities that were quite out of bounds to women has not been seriously challenged to the present day. Company-sponsored visits to geisha bars and nightclubs are still a routine part of white-collar professional life, as is ritualized drunkenness. The wife, on the other hand, usually has undisputed control over the household budget and the handling of the younger children and is at least the equal of her husband in family decision making. Most Japanese women are quite content with this state of affairs, and divorce rates are relatively low, though climbing. (See the Family and Gender Relations box in this chapter for further information.)

SOUTH AND SOUTHEAST ASIA SINCE INDEPENDENCE

The Indian subcontinent emerged from the colonial era divided between antagonistic Hindu and Muslim segments. It eventually yielded the major separate states of India, which is predominantly Hindu, and Pakistan and Bangladesh, which are mostly Muslim.

India

Today India's social and economic problems are severe, but its adherence to constitutional and political means to devise solutions is an inspiration to democrats throughout the world. Shortly after India gained its independence, Mahatma Gandhi's assassination left the Hindu masses in confusion and sorrow but did not interfere with the erection of the new India. As leader of the majority Congress Party, Gandhi's close associate and designated heir **Jawaharlal**

UNSOLD GOODS AND GIANT GARBAGE

Traditional Japanese politeness has never excluded blunt expressions, especially for those who for one reason or another are vulnerable to social re-proof. A Western resident of Tokyo in the 1980s gives us a more current view of femininity, followed by a few examples of contemporary insults by either sex.

One way to chart the meaning of femininity in Japan is to listen to how the landscape itself is described. A "male hill" is the steeper side of the hill, while the more gently sloping grade is termed the "female hill." . . . Another way of using nature to summarize the character of the sexes is the proverb "Men are pine trees, women are wisteria vines," which means men are the strong base to which women cling.

The positive traits associated with women are bundled up and tied together in the word *onna-rashisa*. Dictionaries define it in terms of being kind, gentle, polite, submissive, and graceful. Sometimes "weak" is included, spurring feminist scholars to protest.

On the other hand the Japanese have several insults based on the linking of women with certain character faults. "Rotten as a woman" is an insult hurled at Japanese men by accusers of both sexes. . . . Both men and women are offended when someone denounces them as "womanish." . . . Women are also the standard for inferiority; one way to show contempt for a man is to call him "less than a woman." Females being inferior to males has been considered so unremarkable that no parallel expression exists.

Although few Japanese stay single for life, there is a large and devilishly clever arsenal of Japanese words for ridiculing people—specifically women—who remain unwed past the so-called marriageable age. The older unmarried woman is "unsold goods." She has become a "widow without going," a play on the popular term for marrying, "to go as a daughter-in-law." . . . One anxiety shared by many women who stay single for life is the fate of their remains after death. According to Japanese custom, women are laid to rest in the family grave of their husband. A woman deemed "unsold merchandise" may have trouble entering the family grave beside her parents if, for example, her older brother's wife opposes. . . .

People in Japan always sort their garbage into three categories for easier disposal: combustible trash like eggshells, fire-resistant rubbish like beer cans, and last but not least, "giant garbage," *sodai gomi*, the big, coarse, hard-to-handle junk like broken refrigerators. Or like retired husbands, in the cruel slang of the 1980s.

Women call their own husbands "giant garbage" to complain that they mope aimlessly about the house, good for nothing, always getting in the way. Until they retired from demanding salaried jobs, these *sodai gomi* spent so little time at home that they never developed their own household niche. While wives devote all their energy to the home, husbands define themselves in terms of their job, as is revealed by another wifely insult for retirees who have been stripped of the company name that provided their identity. They are "unlabeled canned goods."

FOR REFLECTION

Do these two examples conform to your understanding of Japanese women's domestic arrangements with their men?

SOURCE: Kittredge Cherry, Womansword (New York: Kodansha International, 1987).

Nehru (1889–1964) sprang into the breach. Unlike Gandhi, Nehru believed that Western-style industrialization was absolutely necessary to avoid social chaos in India, and he set the country firmly on that path during his fifteen years at the government's head. He also believed that India could best live with neighboring Muslim Pakistan by showing it a strong hand. In practice, this policy meant that India and Pakistan were on a quasi-war footing for the next three decades, largely over the ownership of the rich border province of **Kashmir,** where Muslims predominated but India ruled.

Nehru led India toward a moderate democratic socialism that owed little to Marx and much to the British Labour Party. A mix of state ownership and free enterprise was worked out that has been relatively successful. For many tens of millions of Indians, living standards have risen in the past half-century. But for perhaps 60 percent of the total of 750 million, there has been discouragingly little change from the poverty of preindependence days. The most acute challenge to Indian prosperity, as in so many other developing nations, remains the high rate of population growth. Various governmental campaigns for fewer births have not been very successful in the traditionalist villages where most Indians live.

After Nehru's death, in 1966 his daughter **Indira Gandhi** (no relation to the Mahatma) became the first female prime minister of an Asian state and continued his vision of a modern, industrial India. Her increasingly dictatorial style created conflicts with many Congress Party leaders, however, and she was turned out of office in the 1975 general election, only to return in 1980. These peaceable electoral transitions were evidence of the maturity that India—the world's largest democracy—had achieved in its government only a generation after colonial subordination. It was an impressive and heartening performance.

The picture of stability and political consensus has been rudely marred in recent years by increased ethnic and religious friction. The Kashmir problem has become acute with repeated exchanges of gunfire. In the northwest, the Sikh minority is demanding autonomy for their Punjabi

Indira Gandhi. The first Asian female prime minister proved herself an adept politician. However, the intense maneuvering required to unite the many factions of the Congress Party became too much for her patience, and her increasingly authoritarian stance defeated her party in national elections in 1975. She returned to power a few years later and was assassinated in 1984 by Sikh fanatics. *(Bettmann/Corbis)*

province. Its denial by the government of Indira Gandhi was the trigger for her assassination in 1984. In the far south, Tamils and Sinhalese are fighting one another in a long drawn-out, nasty, but little-publicized guerrilla war. Outraged by what he thought was the government's favoritism, a Tamil fanatic killed Indira Gandhi's son and successor, Rajiv Gandhi, in 1991. And in the last several years, recurrent riots between militant Hindus and the Muslim minority have sharpened interfaith mistrust.

Given these deep-seated animosities, it is all the more remarkable that Indian democratic government has held together almost without lapse. The Congress Party, which represents about 80 percent of the Hindu population, has thus far resisted the strong temptation to make itself into a monolithic party in the African style and force the minorities to conform to its will. Within this party, would-be strongmen (or -women) have been checked before becoming dangerous. The large, well-equipped army has not meddled in politics, nor have any civilian adventurers attempted to gain power by using the military.

Pakistan and Bangladesh

When the British withdrew from the subcontinent in 1947, the large Muslim minority demanded separate and sovereign status in a state of their own. The widespread distribution of the Muslim population made it impossible to

Indian Village. This scene could be replicated in thousands of villages across the subcontinent. It has not changed in any essential way in 2,000 years or more. The cattle are given equal consideration as humans for food and shelter in accord with Hindu belief. *(The Image Works)*

create this state as a single unit so West and East Pakistan came into existence. All Muslims not already within their borders were encouraged to migrate to them. Together the two Pakistans included about one-fourth of the former British colony's population but considerably less than one-fourth of its human and material resources. These new states suffered from severe handicaps: their economies were undeveloped, and they had no infrastructure and very few potential leaders. Under the leadership of the devout Mohammed Ali Jinnah, the two Pakistans were committed from the outset to the supremacy of Islam in public life. This religious emphasis contributed to Pakistan's alienation from, and suspicions of, Nehru's determinedly secular India.

The geographically widely separated states soon discovered that they had nothing in common except Islam, and that was simply not enough to hold them together. With India's assistance, East Pakistan became the independent nation of Bangladesh in 1971. As measured by gross national product per capita, the overpopulated and flood-prone Bangladesh is about the poorest country in the world. Pakistan is not much farther up the ladder despite a generation of rival Chinese and American foreign-aid programs. Even before the 2001 Afghani conflict, the burden of caring for 3 to 4 million Afghani refugees from the lengthy civil war in that country has added to Pakistan's difficulties during most of its existence. What complications will arise for Pakistan from the overthrow of the fundamentalist Islamic government of the Taliban in neighboring Afghanistan remains, at this writing, impossible to guess. In the circumstances, it is remarkable that Pakistan has managed to retain a semblance of democracy, even occasionally holding free elections, though military dictatorships such as the present one of President Musharraf have more often held sway.

Southeast Asia since World War II

Stark contrasts are found in the postwar history of mainland and offshore Southeast Asia. During the middle decades of this century, some areas of the region may have experienced more violence than any other place on Earth while others developed quite peaceably. Since the expulsion of the Japanese invaders in World War II, insurgents of one stripe or another have challenged the governments of Southeast Asia in several guerrilla campaigns (see Map 53.1). In former French Indochina (that is, Cambodia, Laos, and Vietnam), these insurgencies produced communist governments after long struggles. In Malaya (Malaysia) and the Philippines, leftist guerrillas challenged unsuccessfully in the later 1940s, while in the Dutch East Indies (Indonesia), the campaign for national independence was triumphant. Both Thailand and Burma (Myanmar) withstood significant minority rebellions, but these uprisings were more tribal than revolutionary in nature.

The War in Vietnam   The lengthy war in Vietnam began as a nationalist rebellion against the French colonial overlord in the immediate postwar years. Under the Marxist-nationalist Ho Chi Minh, the Viet Minh guerrillas were at last able to drive the French army from the field and install a communist regime in the northern half of the country in 1954. At this point, the U.S. government under President Dwight D. Eisenhower took over the French role in the south, installed an American-funded puppet, and agreed to hold free elections for a national Vietnamese government. But the Americans became convinced that Ho would successfully manipulate any elections, and, as a result, none were ever held. In the ensuing Kennedy administration in the early 1960s, the decision was made to "save" the client government in Saigon from a communist takeover by countering increasing guerrilla activity in the south with U.S. ground and air power. Then President Lyndon B. Johnson, who had inherited a small-scale war, was determined to bring it to a successful conclusion and believed that he could do so without crippling the simultaneous War on Poverty in the United States or his effective support for civil rights for the U.S. black population.

He was wrong on both counts. By 1968, half a million U.S. troops were on the ground in Vietnam. The entire nation was debating the wisdom and the morality of engaging in this faraway, bloody, and apparently unending conflict that appeared on television screens nightly. The War on Poverty had been curtailed by both budgetary and political constraints. The campaign for civil rights had run into African American resentments, and there was a sharp decline of white liberal support for a president who continued to slog through the morass of Vietnam.

Johnson in effect resigned the presidency by deciding not to seek reelection in 1968, and his Republican successor Richard M. Nixon eventually opted to withdraw U.S. forces in the early 1970s under cover of a supposed "Vietnamization" of the conflict. A patched-together peace was signed with North Vietnam's government in 1973 after a year of negotiations, and the South Vietnamese took over their own defense. By 1975, the corrupt and demoralized Saigon authorities had fallen to their communist opponents, and North and South Vietnam were reunited on standard communist political and economic principles.

Until recently, the country was relegated to a diplomatic limbo by both West and East. The failure of the Soviets to assist their fellow communists in Vietnam fully brought to light the change in the Cold War and the conclusive nature of the break between the Soviet Union and China. In contrast to 1962, when Khrushchev was willing to gamble in Cuba, the Soviet government under Leonid Brezhnev preferred to forgo a foothold in South Asia and a propaganda advantage in the Third World rather than risk a war where Soviet security was not at stake. For its part, China was an active supplier of the guerrillas but carefully avoided placing its full resources behind the Vietnamese. After the

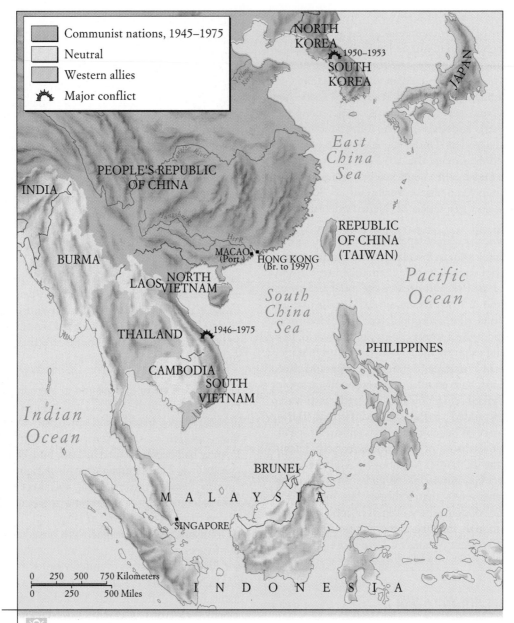

Communist nations, 1945–1975
Neutral
Western allies
Major conflict

MAP 53.1 Postwar Conflicts in East Asia. The Cold War was sporadically a "hot" one in East Asia. Communism made major gains in the thirty years after the conclusion of World War II but was checked in South Korea and the Philippines. In the 1990s, it suffered from the general decline in Marxism's prestige throughout the world.

communist reunification, frictions between the supposed allies reached the point where the Chinese briefly invaded Vietnam and withdrew only after giving a lesson to the recalcitrants in Hanoi. Relations between the two countries continue to be strained as Vietnam's commitment to Marxism weakens and the fear of a recurring Chinese dominance is reawakened (see Chapters 19 and 31). In most recent times, the still-communist regime in Hanoi has sought ties with all sources of potential aid for its lagging economy, and thus seems to be following the same path in its economic policies as its large neighbor to the north.

Important though the Vietnam conflict was in international affairs, its most striking consequences were probably within the United States itself. Many Americans now over age forty formed their views of government, the duty of citizens, and public affairs in general as a result of some type of personal involvement with the issues of the Vietnam War. The 1960s upheavals generated by war protest movements and resistance to what many saw as a wrong-headed and arrogant Washington were second only to the black civil rights movement as a milestone in the domestic affairs of the United States in the twentieth century.

Ginza Shopping District. Postwar Japan has undergone another of its rapid adaptations to Western influences, this time to the global marketplace introduced to the country by the American occupation regime. Here, the Ginza shopping district in downtown Tokyo reflects the new consumer economy of the 1970s. (© *Dallas and John Heaton/Corbis*)

Progress and the Promise of Future Prosperity   Other nations of Southeast Asia have been much more successful than the unfortunate Vietnam in escaping from poverty and technological backwardness. Although handicapped by rapid population growth and a still-heavy dependence on agriculture and exports of raw materials in a high-tech world, they are overcoming these obstacles to prosperity.

The **"four little tigers"** of the Pacific Rim—South Korea, Taiwan, Singapore, and Hong Kong—have followed the course plotted by the Japanese. Until very recently, they maintained superior growth rates in the drive to establish an electronically driven, information-based economy. They are being joined by Malaysia, and just behind these five are Thailand and Indonesia. Throughout the western Pacific, to foment rapid economic growth based on a modified free

market has become the first priority for government, whether Marxist or capitalist in formal ideology. From its backwater status in the early part of this century, industrialized East and Southeast Asia have become a vital part of a mutually dependent global interchange.

With relatively abundant resources, high literacy rates, stable village agriculture, and few border conflicts, much of Southeast Asia stands a good chance of making the difficult transition from a premodern to a modern economy and society within another generation. (The financial misalignments and speculative bubbles that burst in 1998 in several nations put a severe but probably short-lived ripple in this picture of progress.) The major long-term danger is still excessive population growth and the pressures it puts on the social fabric. But this threat is not as acute as elsewhere and

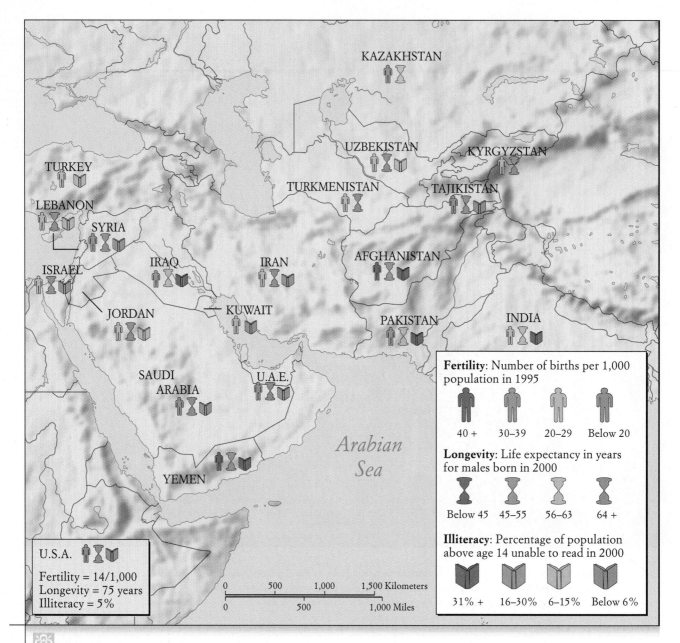

MAP 53.2 Poverty Index for West Asia. Three demographic factors are closely linked to opportunity, stability, and relative income in the developing countries: fertility in females, longevity in males, and illiteracy. High fertility is always linked to a shorter lifespan and to high rates of illiteracy. This map and Map 53.3 show the relative placement of individual countries based on the three social indicators on this poverty index.

is partly countered by steady growth in industrial development, which has drained off the rural excess in constructive fashion.

The most successful exemplars are Hong Kong and Singapore, two city-states with entrepreneurial business as their driving force. Both have found profitable niches in the evolving global interchange of goods and services. (How well Hong Kong can retain this special position after its reannexation to mainland China in 1997 is an open question.)

Next come South Korea, Taiwan, and Malaysia, where skilled and politically ruthless leaders encouraged the growth of modern economies. The authoritarian rule that was the norm between 1950 and 1980 is now being replaced by more open and truly democratic arrangements, as the prosperity created for the rich under the earlier generation filters down and widens choices and horizons. Indonesia, the Philippines, and Thailand come next on the ladder of prosperity, while the war-wounded and isolated Burma (Myanmar), Cambodia, and Vietnam bring up the rear (see Maps 53.2 and 53.3).

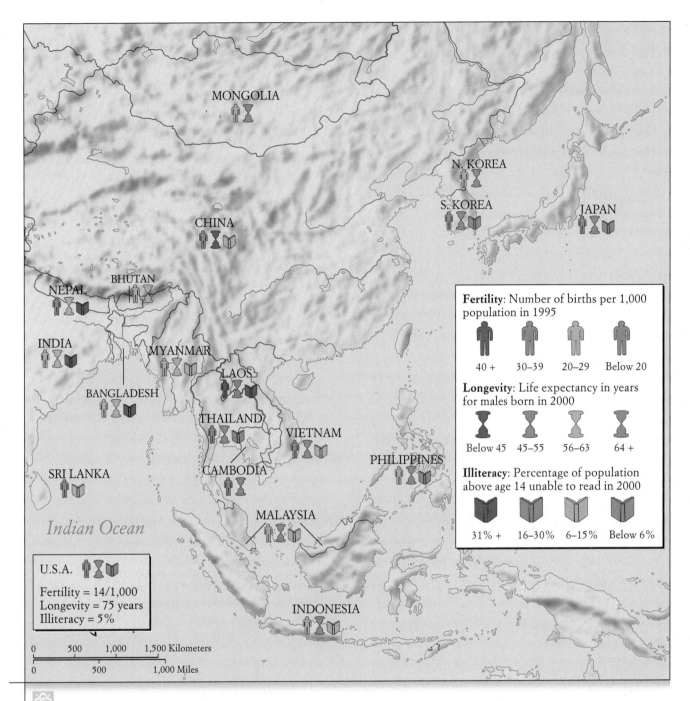

Fertility: Number of births per 1,000 population in 1995

40 +   30–39   20–29   Below 20

Longevity: Life expectancy in years for males born in 2000

Below 45   45–55   56–63   64 +

Illiteracy: Percentage of population above age 14 unable to read in 2000

31% +   16–30%   6–15%   Below 6%

U.S.A.

Fertility = 14/1,000
Longevity = 75 years
Illiteracy = 5%

0   500   1,000   1,500 Kilometers

0   500   1,000 Miles

MAP 53.3   Poverty Index for East Asia.

SUMMARY

In the second half of the twentieth century, East Asia saw two world powers arise, communist China and capitalist Japan. Going sharply divergent ways since they contested one another for predominance in World War II, both nations have come to play important roles in world affairs. In China, this role has been primarily military and political. In the case of Japan, it has been entirely economic and commercial until the present.

As founder of the Chinese Communist Party, Mao Zedong had tremendous influence after his victory in the civil war in the 1940s. His break with his Soviet mentors ten years later divided communism into hostile camps. It also allowed Mao to follow his own path into a communism that focused on the peasants and the necessity of continual revolution. After his death in 1976, his successors soon rejected this path, and the present leaders are experimenting with an unstable mix of socialism in politics and capitalism in the economy. The radical change in generations of leaders that lies just ahead puts a large question mark over the entire situation.

In Japan, the economy and society were modernized and westernized under the American occupation. The American-sponsored constitution allowed a new political culture to take shape that found a wide and positive response in a nation ready to accept change. A sustained partnership between government and business encouraged an unprecedented surge in productivity undisturbed by social or political discontents until very recently. Now one of the world's great economic powerhouses, Japan stands at the verge of decision on its international role in politics and diplomacy.

The Indian subcontinent emerged from the colonial era divided between antagonistic Hindu and Muslim segments. India has shown admirable maturity in retaining democratic politics despite the heavy pressures exerted by ethnic and religious frictions among its several peoples and inadequate, though substantial, economic development. Pakistan faces intimidating problems generated by retarded civic development and by the commitment to hostility with neighboring India.

In Southeast Asia, the picture has brightened in recent years after a third of a century of violence and wars. Worst of these was the Vietnam conflict, which also had serious repercussions on the United States internally. Several of the former colonies of Southeast Asia are making a successful transition to the high-tech global economy and have excellent prospects.

TEST YOUR KNOWLEDGE

1. China's attempt to make itself industrially independent of outside aid during the 1950s is called the
   a. Self-Strengthening movement.
   b. Red Guard challenge.
   c. China First movement.
   d. Great Leap Forward.
2. What major change in international affairs became fully apparent in the early 1960s?
   a. China and the United States joined forces against the Soviet Union.
   b. China and Japan became allies.
   c. China and the Soviet Union became allies for the first time.
   d. China and the Soviet Union became hostile toward one another.
3. Mao started the Great Proletarian Cultural Revolution because he
   a. believed that China was in danger of imminent attack.
   b. thought that it was the proper time to introduce political democracy.
   c. believed that all revolutions should be constantly renewed.
   d. wanted to forestall the Soviets' move toward coexistence.
4. Which of the following statements is *not* true of postwar Japan?
   a. It had the world's highest rate of personal savings.
   b. It had the world's highest sustained growth in gross national product.
   c. It had the world's most favorable balance of trade.
   d. It had the world's highest rate of personal consumption.
5. Japan's postwar political scene has been mainly controlled by the
   a. Socialist Party.
   b. Liberal Democratic Party.
   c. emperor through his political allies.
   d. labor unions.
6. In very recent years, Japanese working women have
   a. returned to their prewar habits of withdrawing into the home.
   b. been the world's leaders in asserting their political presence.
   c. made some gains in attaining equal pay and opportunity.
   d. finally broken through the "glass ceiling."
7. Since independence India has
   a. been a military dictatorship.
   b. maintained a large degree of democracy.
   c. been steadily at war with one or another of its neighbors.
   d. become a single-party, quasi-fascist society.
8. During the Vietnam War, the Soviet Union
   a. tried to aid the insurgents in every way possible.
   b. consistently tried to bring peace by acting as middleman.
   c. took a bystander's role rather than assisting the insurgents.
   d. healed the conflict with China to assist Ho Chi Minh.

IDENTIFICATION TERMS

Amur River War
"four little tigers"
Gandhi, Indira
Great Leap Forward

Great Proletarian Cultural
  Revolution
Kashmir

little red book
massacre in Tienanmen
  Square

Nehru, Jawaharlal
Red Guards
Sino-Soviet conflict

INFOTRAC COLLEGE EDITION

Enter the search term "Mao Zedong" using the Subject Guide.
Enter the search term "China history" using Key Words.

Enter the search term "Vietnamese conflict" using the Subject Guide.

AFRICA AFTER INDEPENDENCE

The African woman does not need to be liberated. She has been liberated for many thousands of years.

L. SENGHOR, PRESIDENT OF SENEGAL

1955–1965	Decolonization of most of Africa
1963	Organization of African Unity founded
1960s–1970s	Trend toward dictatorship and one-party states/Cold War interventions by United States, USSR, China
1970s–1980s	Overpopulation problem/Drought, civil wars, AIDS, runaway urbanization wrack the continent
1990s	More stable, open governments appear in several states/Apartheid dies in South Africa/Muslim fundamentalism gains in northern tier

AFRICA IS NOW the most problematic area of the world in the most basic terms of the prosperity and perhaps even survival of some of its peoples. In contrast to East and South Asia, the decolonization process and political independence have signally failed to bring the happy solutions that leaders and much of the general population had counted on forty years ago. The majority of the continent's fifty-odd independent nations have undergone major economic and social transitions, and the results so far are not encouraging. Millions have died needlessly from famine, civil wars, and political terror. Millions of others have been reduced to misery as refugees.

What is particularly disturbing to both African and non-African observers is that the cycle of economic deterioration and political repression shows no sign of having run its course. With the exception of South Africa, most indicators are still pointing downward for the continent. The hopes of a generation ago have been severely disappointed.

THE IMMEDIATE POSTINDEPENDENCE YEARS

The decolonization of Africa proceeded very rapidly (and unexpectedly peacefully, for the most part) between 1955 and 1965 (see Map 54.1). About thirty-five states derived from the former European colonies emerged in that decade. Since then, independence has been obtained through armed action in the Portuguese colonies in 1975, in the British settler colony of Rhodesia in 1980, and in Eritrea in 1993.

Aside from resurrecting some African names from the precolonial era (Mali, Ghana, and Zaire, among others), the new states showed remarkably little inclination to try to wipe out the two generations of European presence. The various kingdoms and empires that had been established as recently as the mid–nineteenth century by black and Muslim rulers were not reestablished, nor was a serious effort made to do so. Instead, the colonial borders were continued without change. Where they were challenged by secession, as in the Congo, Nigeria and Ethiopia, they were defended—not always successfully—by armed force. It soon became clear that, despite the severe obstacles to a truly national unity

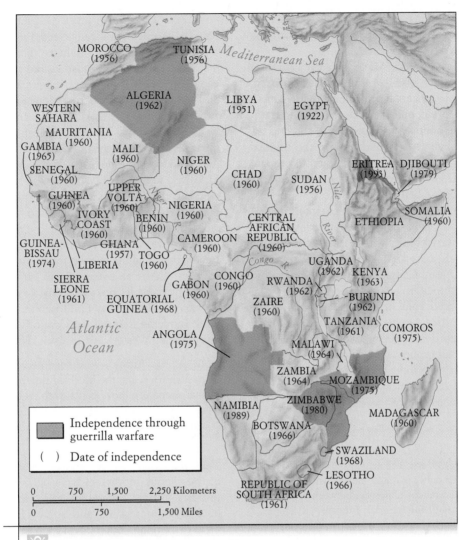

MAP 54.1 Africa Becomes Independent. Independence came with a rush for most African states in the years 1955–1965. Many of them were not prepared for it and lacked a cadre of trained officials to step into the shoes of departing Europeans.

which the colonial era borders imposed, the new leaderships were determined to keep them. If they acceded to a neighboring state's dismantling, they saw that they were inviting the same misfortune in their own.

It often is said that African independence movements were fueled by nationalism, but this term means something different in Africa than elsewhere. African nationalists were not attempting to bind together a culturally distinct people under a single government within a common territory, as the nineteenth-century European nationalists had tried to do. Instead, the African nationalists wanted modernization and equality with the whites. African nationalism is therefore at base not an ethnic phenomenon but a social and economic one.

The first years of independence saw a wave of optimism about Africa's prospects and specifically about the intentions and abilities of the native leaders to install democratic parliamentary republics. In several sub-Saharan states

(Tanzania, Kenya, Ghana, and Senegal are examples), men of cosmopolitan culture and political subtlety were placed at the helm. These men were thoroughly familiar with Western forms of government and values. Most had been residents of Europe and the United States. In other states (Zaire, Guinea, Angola, Sierra Leone), less known and less subtle leaders asserted themselves, sometimes through coups against the original elected governments.

The pro-democracy bent disappeared almost immediately, however. The presidents and prime ministers became dictators within five to ten years of independence. Original multiparty systems were replaced by an all-embracing (and completely artificial) "people's union" or "national assembly" single party a year or two later. Ghana, the first colony to gain independence, is a good example. The Western-educated **Kwame Nkrumah** (1909–1972) was a popularly elected president in 1957. In 1960, he pushed through a new constitution that made him effectively the sole authority, and he banned the opposing politicians and made Ghana a one-party state in 1964. He reigned over it as self-glorifying dictator until deposed by an army rebellion.

This sequence of events occurred so regularly as to form a pattern in every part of Africa—Muslim and sub-Saharan, West and East. Why? The answers must be tentative. First, like eastern Europe, preindependence Africa had no tradition of Western-style political institutions and customs associated with parliamentary give and take. In the colonial era, only the British and French had attempted to prepare their colonies for self-government along such lines, and the process had barely begun before World War II.

When the war ended, the combination of circumstances mentioned in Chapter 52 brought the colonies into a semblance of parliamentary politics with a rush. In most, the "Westminster model" based on British precedents was adopted under European inspiration. But this type of government, based on the interplay of a majority party and a loyal opposition whose voice must be permitted to be heard, was alien to Africa. On the contrary, Africa did have a strongly rooted tradition of personal leadership and loyalty to a lineage or kin group, which allowed no place for compromise if victory was in its grasp. Political party divisions in postindependence Africa were normally along such kin group lines, or what the West would call "tribalism."

Boys and Mercedes-Benz. The delight on the boys' faces as they admire the car is only a partial counterbalance to the reminder of the vast differences in lifestyles between the "Wabenzi" (the Benz tribe) and the other Africans. (© M. & E. Bernheim/Woodfin Camp & Associates)

In addition, foreign interests sometimes promoted the removal of a democratically elected regime and its replacement by a group, civil or military, that favored the foreigners. This pattern was most visible in nations that were caught up in the Cold War struggles among Russia, China, and the West for control of various parts of the continent. Ethiopia, Somalia, Angola, and Mozambique are examples.

The breakdown of democratic parliamentary government very frequently resulted in the establishment of a military dictatorship. The first in sub-Saharan Africa appeared in Ghana in 1966, but such dictatorships were soon endemic from Nigeria to Somalia and from Algeria to Angola. Some of the generals have come into power with a vision of what they wished to accomplish, but too many have simply wanted power and its accompanying opportunities to get rich. Worst of all have been those who combine the worst features of African tribalism and European terror: the repulsive Jean-Bedel Bokassa in the Central African Republic, Idi Amin in Uganda, and Joseph (Sese Seko) Mobutu in Zaire (now the Republic of Congo). The abrupt summary given by one Western Africanist is difficult to counter:

> In general, Africa is a misgoverned continent. During the past thirty years, the idealism that has characterized various nationalist movements, with their promises of popular self-determination, have given way in most states to cynical authoritarian regimes. (J. Ramsay, *Africa,* 4th ed. [Dushkin, 1991])

Yet some signs indicate that a better day is dawning. Some of the vicious repressors have been forced out. Popular protests against several of the one-party dictatorships have been increasing, and some of them (Republic of Congo, Benin, Ivory Coast) have succeeded in winning the right to establish legal opposition. Only the passage of time will reveal whether this is a trend throughout the continent or only a brief remission in the pattern of authoritarian government.

THE AFRICAN ECONOMY

Postindependence economies in Africa were naturally the outgrowths of colonial era policies. In the interwar years, all of the European powers had encouraged the rise of monoculture plantations, producing single crops such as cacao, rubber, coffee, and palm oil for export to the developed world. These plantations were owned and developed by Westerners, but the actual work was done by laborers who were sometimes forced to work on the plantations if they could not pay taxes in cash. In the colonies with sizable mineral resources, such as Congo, Rhodesia, Angola, and a few others, mines employing African labor were similarly owned by Westerners.

Domestic manufactures were relatively scarce, as they were discouraged by the home countries, which exported goods to the colonies. African enterprises tended to turn out substitutes for imports. For example, a factory might make soap that would otherwise be imported but not as-phalt for paving roads.

The final epoch of the colonial era had changed African economics in a number of ways. Migratory labor, for exam-ple, became more prominent all over the continent. Some went to a new area because of money wages or the demands of coerced labor in lieu of taxes. The cash economy intro-duced along the new railways and river steamships made it necessary for people who had never seen cash before to earn it, if they wished to buy the new goods introduced by the Europeans. The emphasis on export crops meant that gradually a great number of Africans who had previously produced all their own food from their gardens and gath-ering now had to purchase it, as they would any other commodity.

As a producer of raw materials, Africa was hit hard by the Great Depression of the 1930s. Prices on the world market dropped much faster for raw materials than for fin-ished manufactures or consumer goods, so African farmers and miners received less for their exports but had to pay relatively more for their imports. With World War II, the market for raw materials of all kinds revived, and the post-war period until independence was prosperous for African producers. This prosperity was a major reason why Africans and non-Africans alike were optimistic about prospects for the new states. Africa (especially tropical Africa) was thought to be hovering on the verge of an eco-nomic "takeoff."

Their optimism was disappointed, however. The takeoff turned out to be a slow crash for most of Africa in the years since independence. For quite some time, the building cri-sis was disguised by international loans and credits. The 1960s saw an influx of foreign aid—mainly through the United Nations and the **World Bank,** but partly from indi-vidual countries. Many African nations undertook huge de-velopment projects, only some of which made economic sense. "Bigger is better" seemed to be the password. Broad four-lane highways were built in capital cities that had only a few thousand cars, big new terminals in airports that had five flights on a busy day, and twenty-story government of-fice buildings that towered over the cardboard shacks of the poor while remaining half-empty.

Huge amounts of aid money were wasted or stolen by both locals and the foreign contractors, who scented easy pickings and paid the necessary bribes. To a large extent the bribery and waste were products of the Cold War, as the United States and the Soviet Union (and China in some in-stances) jockeyed for position in a dozen African countries. The United States kept the money flowing to the corrupt and murderous Mobutu regime in power in Zaire because he favored the West. The Soviets were only too pleased to support the Mengistu government in Ethiopia because this

African Market. The people in this marketplace in Burkina Faso are almost all female, which is usual in West Africa, where women dominate local trade networks. The color and bustle of the open-air market is an important facet of life in African towns. (© *Cynthia Johnson/Gamma Liaison*)

tyrannous and blood-stained clique called itself "Marxist-Leninist." Neither side protested or lifted a finger against the insane Idi Amin in Uganda because of vain hopes of in-ducing him to join them.

After the OPEC-generated oil shock of the 1970s, the African states found themselves slipping rapidly backward. Except for Nigeria and Angola, very few oil wells existed south of the Sahara, and the quadrupling of oil prices in 1973 hit the developing industries and the general citizenry hard. Inflation quickly got out of hand. The governments attempted to meet the crisis by redoubling their exports, thus encouraging still more monoculture of cash crops such as cotton and rubber. This in turn discouraged domestic food crops, such as rice and sweet potatoes. By the end of the decade, several formerly self-sufficient countries were importing part of their food. Nigeria, for example, chose to use a good chunk of its oil revenues to pay a subsidy to im-porters of food, thus keeping food prices low for con-sumers but putting local farmers out of business. When the oil bubble burst in the 1980s, Nigeria faced sharply re-duced revenues from petroleum and far fewer farms to feed its increased population.

✥ **African Contrasts.** In every African urban center, the contrasts between the newly arrived ex-villagers' poverty and the opulence of the better-connected population is intense. The attempt to discourage movement to the cities has not been successful anywhere. *(Sygma)*

The true dimensions of the problem only became visible in the 1980s. Several events coincided to bring this about: the diminishing domestic foodstocks; the very bad drought in Ethiopia, Somalia, and the Sudan; civil wars in the Sudan, Chad, Angola, Mozambique, and Ethiopia; and the sharp reduction in foreign aid flowing into Africa from international bodies and Cold War opponents. The injurious effects of all these were magnified by the continuing rapid increase in population, which was only partly offset by the equally rapid spread of AIDS in several countries.

In the twenty years from 1960 to 1980, in only about 20 percent of African nations did gross national product (GNP) grow at an annual rate of 2 percent or better, which is considered to be a moderate standard of progress. Nine countries actually had negative growth in this period. In the 1980s, however, the record was still worse. The small farmers and herdsmen who make up a majority in every country in tropical Africa have suffered most from the overpowering changes since independence. Farm output since independence has increased by 2 percent per year at best in most countries, while population growth has averaged more than 3 percent everywhere. One-quarter of sub-Saharan Africans live in what the World Bank calls "chronic food insecurity"—that is, they are hungry.

The abandonment of traditional diet and work patterns in the villages has driven many men to seek work in the ex-ploding cities. Increasingly, labor is flowing from the countryside to the towns, which almost never have adequate employment opportunities for it. Unable to find regularized employment, people are driven into the streets, as in India or Latin America, where they live by hawking bric-a-brac, cooked food, Coca-Cola, or plastic toys to passersby as poor as themselves. Previously, theft was almost unknown in African society, but it has now become common, as has street violence in the cities. Hunger and deprivation are the reasons.

THE POPULATION BOMB: ROUND 2

The economic and social problems enumerated here are to a very large degree the result of one overwhelmingly important fact: Africa is producing too many people for the means available to satisfy their rising expectations. Africa has the world's highest birthrates, averaging 3.3 percent per annum in 1990 (see Map 54.2). In some countries, the rate of national population increase has been more than 4 percent. (Most recent figures show some decline in African birthrates.) As yet, no African country has made a serious effort to control its surplus population. Several governments still maintain that there *is* no overpopulation problem, only a resource availability problem. But this position

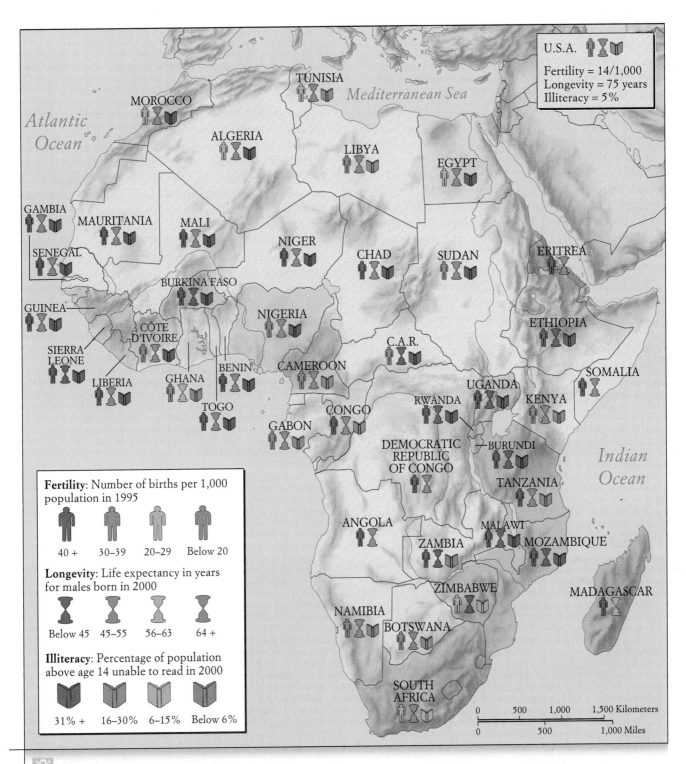

U.S.A.
Fertility = 14/1,000
Longevity = 75 years
Illiteracy = 5%

Fertility: Number of births per 1,000 population in 1995

40 +   30–39   20–29   Below 20

Longevity: Life expectancy in years for males born in 2000

Below 45   45–55   56–63   64 +

Illiteracy: Percentage of population above age 14 unable to read in 2000

31% +   16–30%   6–15%   Below 6%

MAP 54.2 Poverty Index for Africa.   Three demographic factors are closely linked to opportunity, stability, and relative income in the developing countries: fertility in females, longevity in males, and illiteracy. High fertility is always linked to a shorter lifespan and to high rates of illiteracy. The map above shows the relative placement of individual countries based on the three social indicators on this poverty index.

cannot be sustained in the face of any serious investigation of the facts of African ecology.

Only about 10 percent of African surface soil is suitable for any type of crop cultivation. Much of the farming is carried out on marginal land that is subject to repeated droughts, which come in long cycles. Africa has only 8 million hectares (each hectare = 2.47 acres) of irrigated land, versus Asia's 135 million. In exactly the same way as in the Amazon basin, one of Africa's most valuable products is being rapidly diminished: the tropical rain forest. Once the big trees (mahogany, above all) are cut down, the nutrient-poor land they have shaded is next to useless for agriculture and is poor even for pasturage. But the lumber has immediate export value, and that has been a sufficient inducement for governments desperate for revenues and private owners greedy for cash.

The concentration on export crops and timber has seriously disrupted the African ecological balance, and the explosive growth of population has increased the pressures. Nomadic herders in the Sahel, for example, have had to increase their flocks of camels, goats, and cattle, because in a drought cycle, such as was experienced in the 1970s and early 1980s, the animals could not prosper and grow sufficient meat for human consumption. But these increased numbers put even more stress on the vegetation they browse on, magnifying the effects of the drought. As a result, in this area the Sahara is rapidly expanding southward, as the natural vegetation is eliminated.

The popular image of Africa as a vast expanse of jungles and plains filled with lions and elephants is, of course, wildly distorted and always has been. But a great deal of big game is left in Africa in certain regions, and the tourist money that it attracts is a major contributor to some African nations (Kenya, Zimbabwe, and Tanzania lead the list). But as the population has grown in those countries, large regions where lions previously roamed have had to be opened to human habitation. The upshot, predictably, is a conflict between human and animal uses of the land, which, again predictably, the animals always lose. That, in turn, harms the tourist trade, reducing the money available to the governments to assist the excess population in the struggle to stay alive.

The current surge in African population numbers has produced several vicious circles of this sort. The "population bomb" that the ecologists in the 1970s feared would threaten the livability of the entire planet proved to be exaggerated—*except* in tropical Africa where, in some senses, it has exploded. (Recall from Chapter 52 the dire predictions of Paul Ehrlich and his associates. A prime reason that they have not come true thus far, at least, was the Green Revolution in agriculture. Through a combination of fertilizers and new hybrids, yields of corn, rice, and wheat were greatly increased in much of Asia and Latin America. But this outcome did not occur in Africa, where yields have remained low throughout the postindependence period and probably cannot be raised much.)

FOUR AFRICAN STATES

Four African nations—Kenya, Algeria, Senegal, and Zimbabwe—illustrate the troubled internal politics of African states since independence.

Karib Dam. One of the most publicized industrial projects of the postwar era in Africa was this huge hydroelectric generation site on the Zambezi River. Its electricity enabled the rapid development of the copper resources in Zambia and Zimbabwe. *(Michael Busselle/Corbis)*

JOMO KENYATTA
(1890–1978)

The history of twentieth-century Africa offers few examples of politicians who have successfully made the transition from colonial-era opposition to independent leaders of a nation. Felix Houphouet-Boigny of the Ivory Coast was one, Sekou Toure of Guinea another, and the Grand Old Man of Kenya, Jomo Kenyatta, a third.

Kenyatta, the son of a poor farmer, had the good fortune to be accepted at a Presbyterian mission school near his birthplace. He was a member of the majority Kikuyu tribe, which would assist his later rise in national affairs, even though Kenyatta was unusual in insisting on the subordination of tribal to national welfare in the campaign for independence. He accepted Christian baptism in 1914, many years after leaving the mission school, and served the British as a laborer during the campaigns against the Germans in East Africa. In the early interwar period, Kenyatta joined the Kikuyu associations that were permitted by the colonial overlords as a beginning of self-government. He became the general secretary of the Kikuyu Central Association in 1928 and the editor of its paper in the following year (the first newspaper published by Africans in East Africa).

At this time, politically minded Kikuyu were primarily concerned with inducing the government to restrain or reverse the large-scale land theft practiced by the whites in the fertile highlands of Kenya, and Kenyatta became a well-known figure in this campaign. He visited London to testify before one of the several investigatory commissions in 1929. In 1931, he was again sent to London by the association, and this time he remained for fifteen years. He married an English woman and had a son by her while studying at the London School of Economics under the famed anthropologist Bronislaw Malinowski. In 1938, Kenyatta published a paper originally prepared for Malinowski, *Facing Mount Kenya,* which created a major stir as a program for eventual African independence. At the end of World War II, Kenyatta, Kwame Nkrumah, and several other Africans in Britain founded the Pan-African Federation, the first association of African nationalities.

Returning to his native land, Kenyatta spent the postwar years organizing the Kenya African National Union (KANU) and serving as the influential head of an African teachers' college. In 1952, the Mau Mau guerrilla/terrorist campaign against the British settlers began in Kenya, the first of its kind on the continent against the colonial powers. Kenyatta, on no evidence of any kind, was hauled up to a biased court, tried, found guilty of treason, and sentenced to seven years in prison. Refusing compromise offers, he served out his full term, becoming a continent-wide symbol of Africa's irresistible surge toward independence. Under international pressure he was freed in 1961 and immediately returned to his work for KANU, looking toward participation in the government of a new Kenya.

By this time, the British authorities had accepted the inevitability of the independence of the former colonies despite the adamant resistance of many white settlers. New constitutions had been effected in the later 1950s that pointed toward autonomy and then independence for the black majority. In 1963, Kenya held national elections for self-government, which were easily won by KANU on a platform of black-white cooperation and moderation. In 1964, Jomo Kenyatta, a vigorous figure in his seventies, had the satisfaction of becoming the first president of a sovereign Kenyan republic, a post he held until his death fourteen years later.

Jomo Kenyatta. (© Jason Laure/Woodfin Camp & Associates)

Kenya

The Texas-sized East African country of Kenya was a British colony until 1963, when the London-trained anthropologist **Jomo Kenyatta** (c. 1890–1978) became the first president (see the box). Kenyatta had been accused of collaborating with the Mau Mau guerrillas who had begun attacking the British settlers as early as 1952 in an attempt to drive them out. The accusation was groundless, but Kenyatta spent years in jail nevertheless, which made his name known to every Kenyan and made him a folk hero to

CHANGING TIMES IN KENYA

The following spontaneous comment on what should be done to make a better life possible comes from a Kenyan village woman, speaking with an interviewer in the late 1970s. The married women of black Africa, and particularly those areas like Kenya that had seen most of the good land already taken up, often were left alone by their menfolk for months or even years at a time. The men saw the city as the only possible locale for entering the new money economy that had gradually supplanted the traditional barter/labor system of the villages. Sometimes they returned, sometimes not. In the meantime, the women were willy-nilly entering a new life:

What we need in this village is teachers to teach women handicrafts and sewing and agricultural skills. We have organized a women's group. I am one of the leaders. . . .

It is better to educate a girl than a boy, although one should educate both. Girls are better. They help a lot. See this house? My daughters built it for me. If you don't have any daughters, who will build for you? The boys will marry and take care of their wives—that's all. They don't care about mothers. . . .

My mother has eleven children; she is my father's only wife. She works in the fields and grows the food we eat. She works very hard, but with so many children it is difficult to get enough food or money. All my sisters and brothers go to school. One is already a teacher, and that is why I am trying to learn a profession. If I can get enough schooling I can serve the country and my own family. . . . My life is very different from my mother's. She just stayed in the family until she married. Life is much more difficult now because everybody is dependent on money. Long ago, money was unheard of. No one

needed money. But now you can't even get food without cash. Times are very difficult. . . .

If I were in a position of authority, I would really try to educate women. Right now, girls are left behind in education. It costs money, and parents think it is more important to educate boys. But I think that if people are intelligent, there is no difference. Girls and boys should be educated the same. I would make rules and teach women who are not educated and who have never been to school. They, too, must understand what today's problems are. If I have any spare time, I want to learn new things. I would like to learn how to manage my life, my future life, and have enough say in things so that my husband and I could understand one another and share life with our family. And I would change the laws so that men would understand women and their needs and not beat them as they do. . . .

Women feel very hurt because they think their men don't recognize them as human beings. They are unhappy because of this inequality. I am lucky . . . my husband is good. He never took another wife. We are still together. . . . My wish would be that men and women could live as two equal people.

FOR REFLECTION

What similarities and contrasts do you see between this and the Japanese woman's changing role described in Chapter 53? Do you think that a traditional society like Kenya's can modernize and still retain the subordination of women to men? Why or why not?

SOURCE: P. Huston, Third World Women Speak Out (New York: Praeger, 1979). Copyright © 1979 Praeger.

---

his Kikuyu tribe, the most numerous of several Kenyan ethnic groups. Kenyatta began auspiciously by assuring the 100,000 British that they were still welcome under African rule. Africanization of land and commerce was pursued and gave many Kikuyu, in particular, a rapid entry into modern and urban living.

By the early 1970s, however, Kenyatta had become the effective dictator of a one-party state. He had silenced the major opposition party by jailing its leaders, and within his own party, the Kenya African National Union (KANU), he had even resorted to assassinations. Tribal politics soon displaced the concept of national welfare, and the Kikuyu did not hesitate to oppress their fellow citizens for their own advantage.

Kenyatta's successor, Daniel arap Moi, has been in command of the country since 1978, and his rule has become steadily more repressive. Barely a shred of democratic government is left, while corruption at the top is rampant and the country's urgent problems are ignored. Possessing one of the most industrialized economies in Africa and some of the best agricultural land, Kenya has gone backward rather

than forward in the twenty-three years under Moi's dictatorship. An exploding rate of population growth in the past (as high as 4 percent per annum, the highest in Africa) has contributed to the country's downward spiral. (See the Tradition and Innovation box for more about Kenya.)

Algeria

Algeria until the 1990s had tried to walk the narrow line between democratic politics and a destabilized society. After a bloody rebellion, the Algerians attained their independence from France in 1962. One-party or military rule has been in effect ever since. The government has been a collective with a fair degree of democratic practice until recent years. The 1970s windfall from rising oil and gas prices—Algeria is a major producer of both—helped for a time to ease the shortcomings of an otherwise faltering economy. When the oil boom was over in the mid-1980s, hundreds of thousands had to leave Algeria for France to search for employment. Their remittances to the home country are crucial for the domestic economy, which has been completely

🔹 **Victims of Famine in Sudan, 1985.** These women and children are awaiting food rations in a makeshift camp set up by United Nations relief teams in the southern Sudan during the Sahel-wide famine of 1985. Many hundreds of thousands died. *(Chris Rainier/Corbis)*

unable to supply the rapidly growing population with sufficient jobs.

In the last fifteen years, the political group that had brought Algeria to independence has clearly lost its popularity and has had to allow opposition parties to appear. Most important among them are Islamic fundamentalists who draw support from their coreligionists outside the borders and wish to create a strict Islamic state. Their popularity is growing. Only the illegal decision of the government to cancel scheduled elections in 1992 saved it from a crushing defeat. Since then, some fundamentalists have not hesitated to pursue their goals through indiscriminate terror against the government. The authorities have responded with bloody repression and a veritable state of siege. More than 30,000 lives have been lost thus far. As a result, the country has been teetering on the edge of social dissolution for years while its overpowering economic problems remain untreated.

Senegal

Senegal, a West African coastal state about the size of Indiana, became independent in 1960 under the leadership of the renowned poet **Leopold Senghor.** Senghor was an outstanding example of the black intellectuals trained under the French in the early twentieth century who would become pioneers of *negritude* (assertions of a peculiarly African culture) and African nationalism. Islam arrived in Senegal in the twelfth century, and as in most of West Africa, the population is predominantly Muslim. Unlike much of independent West Africa, however, Senegal has clung to multiparty democracy. The quasi-religious, quasi-social associations called **Muslim Brotherhoods,** which

have up to three-quarters of a million members within this 8 million population, are the backbones of the various political parties.

President Senghor never had to resort to the political strong-arm tactics of most of Senegal's neighbors, and he retired from office in 1980 a revered figure. He was succeeded in a relatively open election by his protégé Abdou Diouf, who has been reelected twice and generally continues the moderate policies initiated by Senghor. After a period of one-party rule, Diouf has again permitted open parliamentary opposition. A small guerrilla force aiming at more radical measures has been controlled without major bloodshed.

Senegal is a good example of an African country that has chosen to remain close to its former colonial master, in this case, France. French is the official language of this multiethnic state, French firms and technicians are important throughout the gradually industrializing economy, and French troops (the remnant of the famed Foreign Legion) are stationed near the capital city of Dakar as a peacekeeping force. In return, Senegal has benefited from numerous special arrangements that favor members of the French-sponsored Economic Community of West Africa in their dealings with France and, through France, with the European Union.

Zimbabwe

Zimbabwe, which is about the size of Montana, emerged into independent existence in 1980, the fruit of a lengthy and sometimes bloody guerrilla war against the British settlers. The conflict began in 1966, when the settlers defied London's commands and set up their own independent government based on white minority rule, calling their creation Rhodesia. The whites, who constituted only 5 percent of the population, were eventually worn down and entered into negotiations with the guerrillas. In 1980, the state was renamed Zimbabwe, symbolizing the coming of black African rule by evoking the ancient city-state. **Robert Mugabe,** head of the Zimbabwe African National Union (ZANU) and a leader of the guerrilla war, was elected prime minister in the first national election in which blacks participated as equals. Until recently, he had taken a relatively moderate approach to the Africanization of white-owned businesses, land, and cultural institutions despite his party's formal commitment to what it terms African socialism. Economic progress in this quite rich country has been solidly impressive in the years since independence. The farmers who make up by far the largest single occupational group have increased production per acre significantly, aided by government credits and advice. Some industry has been established by blacks and the very small but economically important white minority. Social progress has also been substantial in health and education.

Mugabe has followed the same path as innumerable other African politicians in looking to establish an overarching unity among disparate ethnic groups by monopolizing political legitimacy. Since the beginning, he has actively persecuted his chief internal opponents. ZANU swallowed the major opposition party by coerced merger (1987) and has frequently harassed and threatened to ban the others. Adding to the tensions is the fact that the political map is based on ethnic lines dividing the dominant Shona tribe of Mugabe and the minorities. Resistance to Mugabe has been gradually increasing. He has been hurt internally by the evolution of South Africa away from *apartheid* (the term for segregation of the races in South Africa) and into black rule, because he had long been a leader of the antiapartheid forces internationally and has used that role to justify his often repressive domestic policies. In the last three years, Mugabe has tried to cement his position by encouraging and directing the illegal takeover of white-owned land by his followers. In the general election of 2002, Mugabe's win has been challenged by both his domestic rivals and international observers. As of this writing, the outcome remains unclear.

PROSPECTS AT THE START OF THE CENTURY

What will the twenty-first century hold in store for Africa? If one were to listen to the daily news bulletins as the sole source of information, it would be easy to predict a future of chaos, famine, and brutality. These have been a depressingly large part of Africa's fate in the recent past and are presumably what will happen for the indefinite future. This view can be supported by an infinitude of social data.

The continent has most of the world's poorest people. In 2000, the per capita GNP for Mali was $190. It was $155 for Madagascar, $235 for Tanzania, and $200 for Niger. In the same year, U.S. per capita GNP was $16,444. Life expectancies for males and females were forty-five and forty-eight, respectively, in Senegal, forty-two and forty-seven in Angola, forty-five and forty-nine in Mozambique, and thirty-eight and forty in Chad (perhaps the world's lowest). For the United States, they were seventy-four and seventy-eight.

Chad had one physician for every 53,000 residents in 1990. The infant mortality rate in sub-Saharan Africa averages about 125 per 1,000. In the United States, it is about 10 per 1,000. The adult literacy rate in many countries of Africa is below 50 percent overall and far lower among village dwellers. Higher education (postsecondary) is still a rarity, and the large majority of higher degrees are issued for the traditional specialties such as law, the humanities, foreign literature, and education. Relatively few students are interested in the applied sciences, engineering, or health specialties, which are precisely the disciplines most needed in their countries. These curricula lack prestige unless they can be studied at a foreign university, a dream open to few Africans.

One of the more gloomy and recalcitrant situations is the huge menace of the AIDS epidemic, which started in Africa and has hit that continent much harder than any other part of the world. According to reliable estimates, in parts of tropical Africa about 30 percent of the population is infected with the HIV virus, and already far more people have died from the disease in Africa than in the rest of the world combined. Until very recently, official countermeasures have been weak and ineffective. Strapped by scarce funding and an absence of basic public health facilities, the African governments are relying on the international health authorities to find a solution and bring it to Africa.

In a different arena, the internal and international conflicts afflicting Africa are frightening. Beside the strengthening challenges of the Islamic fundamentalists in the north, almost every country south of the Sahara has some ethnic group that is acutely unhappy with the state of affairs in the national capital. As of 2002, major rebellions were engaged in at least seven countries. Riots and street demonstrations against the current regimes were taking place in another half-dozen. Only in the Republic of South Africa, now completing the transition from generations of white-dominated apartheid to majority black rule, is there solid evidence of a new harmony. (See **Nelson Mandela**'s words in the Exercise of Authority box.) The **Organization for Pan-African Unity (OAU),** founded in the wake of the independence surge in the 1960s as both a sounding board and a peacekeeper for the continent, has proved ineffectual in the latter role. It has long since become a club of autocrats who never wish to reprimand one of their neighbors for fear that the example might then be applied to themselves.

Elementary School in West Africa. Often overcrowded, elementary schools are now found in most African villages, and universal education is an acknowledged responsibility of the government. The sexes are usually segregated, as in this math class for seven- and eight-year-olds. (© *Earl & Nazima Kowall/Corbis*)

In the economy, all of the African states are more or less deeply indebted to the World Bank and a series of private international banks from which they have borrowed large sums in the 1960s and 1970s. Since the prospect that these monies will ever be returned has disappeared, the lenders now insist on internal economic reform in the guise of so-called **Structural Adjustment Programs (SAPs).** The SAPs supposedly will restart stalled African economies and allow increased export earnings. But the SAP goals are contingent on painful governmental measures to reduce chronic inflation, reduce subsidies to exporters and importers, or take other steps equally unpopular with the voting public and/or the influential wealthy. As a result, the governments have very little incentive to implement them, once the loan is obtained. With all of these economic and political negatives, is it still possible to look at the first generation of independent Africa as a learning experience that may produce much of value for the continent's peoples? In several instances, a ray of light has entered the political and economic darkness that has engulfed Africa during the past twenty years. Here are a few examples:

- Several of the one-party autocracies established in the 1970s have been forced to surrender power or loosen their grip on it during the past few years. Malawi, Benin, the former Zaire, the Ivory Coast, and Mozambique, among others, have to some extent democra-

tized their politics, thanks to popular protest or armed rebellion.

- The end of the Cold War competition for allies has allowed a measure of sanity to creep back into relations between the First and Second Worlds and the African Third. Fantasts, tyrants, and kleptocracies (rule of thieves) are no longer supported on the ground that if "we" don't, "they" will.

- International lenders are no longer willing to put up money for construction of personal or national shrines in the form of steel plants with no markets, international airports with no traffic, and hydropower plants with no customers. New projects now must be rationally justified and be suited to the real needs of the country.

- After many unhappy experiences, African governments have toned down or stopped their previous emphasis on cash export crops and focused instead on family farming to meet the constantly growing domestic food demand.

- A change in attitude has been displayed by several African governments and political parties toward women and their roles in society. Women are receiving active support and being encouraged to make their voices heard not only in politics but in the working economy and in public affairs generally. (See the Tradition and Innovation box on Kenyan villagers.)

INAUGURAL ADDRESS BY NELSON MANDELA

The rise of Nelson Mandela to the presidency of the Republic of South Africa must be one of the more amazing events of recent African history. Imprisoned for twenty-five years as a subversive by the white South African government, Mandela remained the rallying point for all those who believed that the day of apartheid must finally pass.

Raised the son and heir of a thoroughly traditional African tribal chief, Mandela broke with his family and culture to gain a legal education in the city. As a thirty-six-year-old black lawyer, he entered the still subterranean world of African nativist politics and rapidly rose to prominence before his career was cut off by prison.

For his mainly black followers in the African National Congress, Mandela's convincing majority in the first universal balloting ever permitted in South Africa was a day of great elation and a satisfying end to an "extraordinary human disaster." But the white and Colored minorities were naturally nervous about what the future might hold. Would Mandela allow his more passionate black adherents to take revenge for their long exclusion from power and from human dignity? Would he remember the humiliations he had suffered both before and during his long imprisonment at the hands of the dominant Afrikaner whites? Or would he attempt to calm the waters stirred by a sometimes bloody electoral campaign and look into the future rather than at the past? His inaugural address of May 10, 1994, was eagerly awaited.

Today, all of us by our presence here . . . confer glory and hope to newborn liberty. Out of the experience of an extraordinary human disaster which lasted too long must be born a society of which all humanity will be proud.

Our daily deeds as South Africans must produce an actual South African reality that will reinforce humanity's belief in justice, strengthen its confidence in nobility of the human soul, and sustain all our hopes for a glorious life for all.

The time for the healing of the wounds has come. The moment to bridge the chasms that divide us has come. The time to build is upon us. . . .

We have triumphed in the effort to implant hope in the breasts of the millions of our people. We enter into a covenant that we shall build the society in which all South Africans, both black and white, will be able to walk tall, without any fear in their hearts, assured of their inalienable right to human dignity—a rainbow nation at peace with itself and the world. . . .

We dedicate this day to all the heroes and heroines in this country and the rest of the world who sacrificed in so many ways and surrendered their lives so that we could be free. Their dreams have become reality. Freedom is their reward.

We understand . . . that there is no easy road to freedom. We know it well that none of us acting alone can achieve success. We must therefore act together as a united people, for national reconciliation, for nation building, for the birth of a new world.

Let there be justice for all. Let there be peace for all. Let there be work, bread, water, and salt for all. Let each know that for each the body, the mind, and the soul have been freed to fulfill themselves. . . .

Let freedom reign! God bless Africa!

FOR REFLECTION

Accused of revolutionary activity, Mandela chose to appeal to a "higher law" in his own defense before a South African court. Do you think such a defense was justified?

Nelson Mandela. *(Reuters/Archive Photos)*

Africa's future as a part of human society is impossible to predict. This rich continent, with its immense variety in both natural phenomena and human activities, may continue to suffer from a welter of civil wars, tyrannical politics, and economic hardship internally and peripheral status internationally. But it could be that the first generation or two of freedom was a period of growing pains and that the twenty-first century will see a recovery from past internal mistakes, followed by a steady rise from neocolonialism to equality in the world community. "Out of Africa, always something new," said the Roman sage Pliny in 65 C.E., and his words remain true today.

SUMMARY

The second largest continent has seen some evil days since attaining freedom from colonial status in the 1960s and 1970s. The fond hopes of participatory democracy were largely gone to dust within a few years, as single-party or outright dictatorial regimes took power. Where guerrilla wars had been necessary to attain independence, the warriors imposed themselves in the guise of united fronts or similar vehicles of personal power. In other cases, free elections produced the rule of an ethnic or tribal group, whose leadership soon reacted to opposition by creating a dictatorship. In still others, the military reacted to civilian squabbles by brushing them aside. In all instances, the attempt to introduce the Westminster model of parliamentary government has had a rocky path. Corruption has been endemic and has been stimulated by foreign aid and trade arrangements.

In the economy, the new states continued the colonial era's emphasis on cultivating export crops and mining but added a new dependency on international credits for some ill-conceived "prestige" projects. When combined, these factors made Africa vulnerable to conditions no government could control: famine in the wake of droughts, low raw material prices on the world market, and rising food imports to feed an exploding population. In most African countries, the economy has at best been stalled and has often shown actual losses in GNP during the past decade. In very recent years, an encouraging shift has occurred toward economic realism and political toleration. Attacking the overpopulation problem is the continent's most pressing task. What the future holds in both politics and living conditions is impossible to know, but Africa will need both luck and assistance from the developed world to overcome its present handicaps.

TEST YOUR KNOWLEDGE

1. Which of the following statements about African nations is false?
   a. They have fewer educational facilities now than before independence.
   b. They all have primarily rural populations.
   c. They are all aware of their impoverished status in contrast to the West.
   d. They have almost all experienced a colonial past.

2. In terms of the Green Revolution, Africa
   a. benefited more than elsewhere in food supply.
   b. benefited less than elsewhere.
   c. grew no crops that could have benefited from the revolution.
   d. experienced practically no effect because of the nomadic lifestyle of many inhabitants.

3. In Africa, since independence, the most common population movement has been
   a. from the cities to the rural areas.
   b. from the inland cities to the coastal areas.
   c. from the nomadic life to the farm villages.
   d. from the farm villages to the cities.

4. From 1965 to very recently, the general trend of government in Africa has been toward
   a. one-party dictatorships.
   b. monarchies.
   c. socialist states.
   d. parliamentary democracies.

5. Which of the following countries experienced ethnic war after independence?
   a. Nigeria
   b. Algeria
   c. Egypt
   d. Ghana

6. Of the four countries analyzed, which currently has the most stable and most democratic politics?
   a. Senegal
   b. Algeria
   c. Zimbabwe
   d. Kenya

7. One of the following reasons does *not* apply to the causes for African economic missteps since independence:
   a. Misguided notions of establishing national prestige
   b. Desire for personal enrichment
   c. Desire to spread the benefits to maximal numbers of citizens
   d. Frequent use of bribery

8. Which of the following was *not* a consequence of post–World War II medical advances in the sub-Saharan regions?
   a. The extension of medical services to many rural areas
   b. Considerably longer life expectancy
   c. Decline in population gain rates
   d. Decline in infant mortality rates

9. The career of Jomo Kenyatta can best be summarized as
   a. from terrorist to democratic statesman.
   b. from patriot to terrorist.
   c. from imitator of Europeans to African patriot.
   d. from ignorant native to sophisticated Westerner.

IDENTIFICATION TERMS

Kenyatta, Jomo

Mandela, Nelson

Mugabe, Robert

Muslim Brotherhoods

Nkrumah, Kwame

Organization for Pan-
  African Unity (OAU)

Senghor, Leopold

Structural Adjustment
  Programs (SAPs)

World Bank

 # INFOTRAC COLLEGE EDITION

Enter the search term "Africa" using the Subject Guide.
Enter the search term "Kenya history" using Key Words.

Enter the search term "Nelson Mandela" using the Subject
Guide.

LATIN AMERICA IN THE TWENTIETH CENTURY

Those who make peaceful revolution impossible will make violent revolution inevitable.

JOHN F. KENNEDY

1900–1933	Repeated intervention in Caribbean affairs by the United States
1910–1920	Mexican Revolution
1930s	Cárdenas presidency in Mexico
1933	President Franklin Roosevelt begins Good Neighbor Policy
1940s–1955	Perón in Argentina
1948	Organization of American States founded
1959	Castro takes command in Cuba
1961	Bay of Pigs invasion of Cuba
1970s	Military governments in most of Latin America established
1980s–EARLY 1990s	U.S. intervention in Grenada, Nicaragua, Panama, Haiti
1990s	Reestablishment of constitutional governments in most of continent

IN THE TWENTIETH CENTURY, the histories of the twenty countries making up Latin America varied sharply in detail but were generally similar overall. In all cases, the politics and international relationships of the Latin countries were fundamentally influenced by the economic and social problems they faced—problems that were roughly alike from Mexico to Argentina. All of the countries also had to come to terms with the United States, the dominant power in the Americas with the ability—repeatedly demonstrated—to intervene in hemispheric affairs at will.

The worldwide depression of the 1930s was a turning point for the Latin Americans in an economic sense, as some of the larger countries attempted to recover from their loss of export markets by adoption of economic nationalism. Though not completely successful, they did manage a partial escape from the neocolonialism to which they had formerly acquiesced. Since the end of World War II, other attempts have been made to introduce more or less radical changes in both the political and economic structures, but with the exception of a faltering and controversial Marxism in Cuba, these efforts have not been sustained for more than a few years.

PERSISTENT DEPENDENCY

Because of its economic backwardness, Latin America remained dependent on the United States and Europe throughout the nineteenth and early twentieth centuries (many would say until the present). This did not mean merely that Latin America was dependent on outside areas for imports of goods and services it did not produce. In addition, Latin America became increasingly dependent on foreign capital for domestic investment of all types.

Latin America did not lack export markets. On the contrary, throughout the nineteenth century, demand in the Western world was rising for its raw materials: Bolivian tin, Brazilian coffee and rubber, Chilean copper and fertilizer, Mexico's silver and oil, and Argentina's meat and grain. But instead of providing a general stimulus to the Latin economies, the benefits derived from these exports were limited to a mere handful of wealthy families or to foreigners. The native families either used the profits for their own extraordinarily wasteful lifestyles or squandered them on poorly considered schemes. Little was invested in rational, farsighted ways by either government or the rich. No attempt was made to strengthen the social fabric by encouraging the poor and the unskilled to become educated and thus qualify themselves to participate in the political process. For that matter, there was no attempt at securing social justice of the most basic sort.

In very many cases, the real beneficiaries of the exploitation of Latin America's raw materials were the foreign investors who supplied the necessary capital to get production under way: American mining corporations, European coffee plantation owners, and British shipping firms. None of their profits went into the pockets of *any* of the natives, let alone the workers. And to assure the continuance of this arrangement, corruption in government was endemic.

The rising disparities between the rich handful and the poor majority created an atmosphere of social unrest in much of the continent. At times in the nineteenth century, the disenchanted and the desperate were able to find a popular leader (*caudillo*) who frightened the wealthy with his threats to install democratic reform. In every case, either the ruling group was able to bribe and co-opt the caudillo, or another army-led "revolution" forcibly removed him. In some cases, when the traditional ruling group did not remove the disturber swiftly enough, the United States acted instead. Beginning with the Mexican War of the 1840s, examples of U.S. intervention became more numerous in the twentieth century after the Spanish-American War of 1898 brought the North Americans more directly into the Latin world.

The obstacles facing the Latin American countries are similar in many respects, even though their political systems and societies are different, in some cases dramatically so. National economic policy throughout modern Latin America has aimed at escaping from the basic pattern of impoverishment: exporting cheap raw materials and importing expensive manufactured goods and technical expertise. A few countries made significant progress in the middle years of the century, usually in combination with a radicalization of internal politics. For example, in Argentina in the 1940s, the lower classes enthusiastically supported the dictator **Juan Perón** when he attacked both domestic class privileges and Argentina's import dependency on the United States. In the 1930s under President **Lázaro Cárdenas,** the Mexicans went further; they actually expropriated U.S. oil firms (with compensation) and withstood the wrath of the Giant to the North until a negotiated agreement was reached.

But in general, the economy of the southern continent (and of its Caribbean outliers) remained nearly as much under the control of external forces as it had been since colonial days. Until well into the twentieth century, the majority of the South American and all of the Central American states remained agrarian societies. They exported raw materials such as coffee, grain, beef, timber, petroleum, and copper ore. They imported the vital elements of industry and personal consumption such as machinery, steel, automobiles, transformers, and telephone wire. In such an equation, the raw material exporters are always at a disadvantage in the marketplace, because their products can almost always be found elsewhere or be replaced by new technologies.

New and Old Social Problems

By the mid–twentieth century, the Latin American countries were divided into two major groups: the more industrialized and urban societies, which included Argentina, Brazil, and Chile (the ABC countries) and, with reservations, Mexico; and the majority, which remained agrarian and rural. In the first group, the migration of much of the population into the handful of major towns accompanied industrialization, accentuating the accustomed isolation of the countryside from the highly centralized government. The peasants in their adobe villages or the laborers in the mine and ranch country saw the capital city as a distant seat of invisible (and parasitic) powers, rather than as the source of leadership in addressing national problems. In the cities, the industrial working class was growing rapidly and began to play a new role in national affairs in the 1930s and 1940s under the guidance of populist politicians.

In the nonindustrial majority of countries, the people at large remained isolated from the government as they had always been and continued their traditional political passivity. The illiterate mestizo, mulatto, and Indio peasants remained in a very backward condition, dominated in every sense by the (often absentee) landowners and with no hope of the social and economic mobility that the cities to some degree offered.

The social and political complexion of a given Latin American country depended largely on the number of its immigrants between about 1890 and 1930. In a select group consisting of the ABC countries plus Uruguay and Costa Rica, immigration from Spain and Italy in particular was large enough to establish and maintain a European culture in the cities and extinguish whatever Amerindian culture the countryside may have once possessed. At first glance, these countries seemed to have very favorable prospects for extensive and intensive development. With the exception of Brazil, they had little or no history of slavery and its accompanying social distinctions. Race was not a factor. Basic natural resources were generally adequate to abundant, and good farmland was in sufficient supply. In short, these countries seemed to have enough actual and potential wealth to meet their growing population's needs for a long time to come *if* no human-made obstructions to the exploitation and distribution of that wealth were imposed.

It was precisely such obstructions that led to much of the social tension in Latin America in the twentieth century. In the ABC countries (less so in Uruguay and Costa Rica), the Creole latifundists and their caudillo partners in government prevented the land from being subdivided for the immigrant latecomers in the nineteenth and twentieth centuries. Social discontent in the cities thus could not be relieved by settling the vast and underdeveloped countryside. Mineral wealth such as Chile's copper or Venezuela's oil remained in a few, mainly foreign, hands. Industry and commerce were almost as tightly controlled as the fertile lands were by the nonavailability of credit. In the absence of a vibrant economy that would act as the rising tide that lifts all ships, these nations attempted to find answers to their problems in political doctrine. After 1920 or so, the proffered solutions ranged from a demagogic nationalist populism to total dependency on foreign (meaning mostly U.S.) interests and investment.

Until recently, Latin America's most intractable social problems were in countries such as Colombia, Peru, and Bolivia, where a large Amerindian or mestizo population continued to rival the Iberian culture of the dominant *criollos* (Creoles). As late as the 1940s, the criollos normally responded to the perceived menace by attempting to exclude the natives completely from national affairs.

Now, the ancient chasms between the landowning class and their peon laborers and between criollos and mestizos have been further complicated by the widening gap between urbanites and rural dwellers. In the last thirty years or so, everywhere in Latin America the demographic picture has changed markedly. Propelled by high birthrates as well as migration, the cities are growing at an incredible rate. The *barrios* and *favelas,* the shantytowns that surround every city and often contain more people than the city proper, are the future of Latin society if current trends are not reversed. Overcrowding, unsanitary makeshift accommodations, and the absence of even elementary public services (schools, police, pure water, and the like) are taken for granted in these slums, where some shacks have harbored three generations already. In the meantime, the villages and small towns have become even less important in the affairs of the nation than before. Always a disproportionately urban-based economy, Latin America is becoming a series of huge heads weakly supported by anemic bodies.

Unemployment, both urban and rural, is endemic and constant. No reliable figures are kept because it is impossible to do so, but perhaps one-third of the adults in the cities have nothing that U.S. citizens would recognize as a steady job. Income distribution is as bad or worse now than it ever has been. Even by the standards of the developing world, Latin America has the most skewed distribution of cash income imaginable. A very small group of industrialists, latifundists, and import–export business owners are rewarded handsomely, while a very large number of unskilled urban and agricultural workers have next to nothing. In the middle, the number of professionals, white-collar employees, managers, and small business owners is increasing, but usually they are still too few, too unorganized, and insufficiently independent to play an important role in civic affairs.

ECONOMIC NATIONALISM

One result of acute social stratification and continuing economic dependency on foreigners has been the wavelike rise of radical reform movements with strongly nationalist overtones. Interestingly, the leaders of such protests have often been military men. The widespread foreign perception of Latin American military leaders as reactionaries who automatically uphold the status quo has become increasingly erroneous. Depending on the circumstances, they have frequently been at the forefront of economic nationalism.

The reform leaders of the past century were also often strongly influenced by the idea of a Mussolini-type corporate state, in which all sectors of the population would supposedly find adequate representation. The most popular of these broad-based movements appeared in Mexico under Cárdenas in the 1930s and in Argentina a decade later under the Peróns.

Mexico under Cárdenas

The spasmodic and multisourced revolution that took place in Mexico between 1910 and 1920 was, as has been mentioned, the only genuine social and political change in

Mexican Rebels Challenge the Government. In the extreme south of Mexico, where small cliques have controlled the state government of Chiapas for many years, an armed rebellion speaking for the rights of the peasantry broke out in 1995. After some hundreds of casualties, the federal government agreed to negotiations that are still continuing. (*© Salaber/Gamma Liaison*)

JUAN AND EVA PERÓN

In the entire history of Latin America, the husband-and-wife team of Juan and Eva Perón is unique. Colonel Juan Domingo Perón (1895–1974) was an Argentine army officer who became the country's virtual dictator in the middle decades of this century. Eva Duarte de Perón (1919–1952) was his wife and coruler until her early death from incurable cancer. To this day, they arouse feelings of love and hate among the Argentine people that have no parallel.

The Peróns rode to power on the wave of nationalism and class antagonism that afflicted many of Latin America's more developed countries in the early twentieth century. Perón was a career officer who joined with a handful of others to oust the visionless political authorities governing Argentina during World War II. Strongly nationalist and generally sympathetic to fascist ideas of reform, these men were viewed with suspicion by the U.S. government. Perón himself was pushed out by his fellow *junta* members in 1945, but massive popular protest organized by his wife got him out of prison and made him the leading candidate for the presidential election of 1946. The U.S. State Department's heavy-handed intervention against him practically assured his election by resentful Argentines.

Evita Perón came from a typically poverty-stricken working-class background. The illegitimate child of a village seamstress and an unknown father, she was raised among ignorance and misery. Guided by an iron determination to make something of herself, she left her mother and went off to the great city of Buenos Aires at age fifteen. The details of her life in the next several years vary depending on who is telling the story. Her enemies delighted in picturing her as a part-time actress who was not overly scrupulous in how and where she made her living. Her admirers picture her as a victim of an unjust and brutally oppressive society, who used her intelligence and beauty to lift herself up out of the mud she was born into. In 1943, this strikingly attractive, aspiring minor actress met the equally aspiring Juan Perón, who made her first his mistress and two years later his wife. A year after that, she became in effect his copresident.

Working together, husband and wife immediately began a program of social and economic reforms that seemed revolutionary to the upper classes who had been accustomed to ruling the country as a private club. Although their bark was frequently more severe than their bite, the program of Perónismo did assure the Argentine workers and peasants a considerably enlarged role in politics at the direct expense of the older ruling group. Evita Perón became the equivalent of minister of labor and social welfare, and from those positions, she built up a huge following among the poor and the ignored. These *descamisados,* or shirtless ones, were the backbone of the Perónist regime for the next ten years.

The Peróns capitalized on the long-smoldering resentment felt by many Argentines against the dependency on foreign nations that had been the fate of all of Latin America throughout the postindependence period. A strange coalition of labor, na-

the first half of the twentieth century. Out of it finally came a single-party government committed to social equalization and redistribution of both wealth and power. In this mestizo country where a small number of *haciendados* had held all power for generations, such goals were unprecedented—and unfulfillable. In the 1920s, the governing party (later termed the Partido Revolucionario Institucional, or PRI) despite much talk did little to advance social causes. But under the impact of the depression and the Marxist experiment in Russia, President Cárdenas (governed 1934–1940) tried to give substance to some of the revolution's slogans. He confiscated and redistributed much land to Amerindians and peasants in the poverty-stricken north, expropriated foreign mineral firms, and insisted on Mexican sovereignty in every sense. In so doing, he set the pattern of Mexico for the Mexicans, which most of his successors in office have followed.

His efforts to achieve security and a political voice for the lower classes, however, have generally not been followed, and the gap between the haves and the have-nots in Mexico remains vast. The PRI became an intricate web of established social powers ranging from labor leaders to intellectuals, all of whom expected—and got—a calculated payoff for their support. Despite undoubted abuses, particularly corruption at the top, the Mexican system has recently allowed an increasing pluralism in politics. The old allocation of political powers to solely a few recognized groups broke down, and scandal has ended the PRI's former death grip on high-level affairs. National elections in 2000 brought the leading opposition party to power, and new president Vincente Fox has promised major structural reform. Despite the difficult economic times Mexico has undergone in the last several years, there are many indications that the country is emerging from neocolonial status and headed into a more stable as well as more democratic epoch.

Argentina under Perón

In Argentina, Juan Perón and his military and industrialist backers in the 1940s were ardent nationalists, who dreamed of making Argentina the dominant power in Latin America—a status for which it seemed destined by its size, natural resources, and entirely European immigrant population.

tionalist intellectuals, industrialists, lower clergy, and much of the military supported the Perónist program in its early years. Each of these elements could gain something from the grab bag of Perónismo.

While Juan Perón concentrated on meeting the industrialists' hopes for greater profits and protection from foreign competitors, his wife used her enormous powers to assist the millions who lived at the bottom of the economic ladder. She led the efforts to establish a public health system and to assure some degree of schooling for every child. Her army of male and female admirers considered her a saint.

Evita's death in 1952 marked the beginning of the Perón decline. Without her charisma (which her husband had never shared), the cracks in the coalition rapidly surfaced. The higher military became increasingly uncomfortable with Perón's alliance with the Left and with labor. When Perón mounted a campaign against the Roman Catholic clergy, he was excommunicated in 1955. A few months later, he was chased out by a military coup similar to the one he had used to begin his own rise to power twelve years earlier.

For the next eighteen years, Perón lived in exile, while his country went through waves of political terror and economic decline at the hands of both the old civilian establishment and military juntas. Finally, confronted with the demands of the loyal Perónistas, an unwilling military was forced to allow the nearly eighty-year-old Perón to return and be elected president once again in 1973. But the fire was gone, and the old man died a year later without having had the time or, perhaps the will, to again disturb the course of his country's political life. While Juan Perón has become only another name to his younger country-

❀ **Juan and Evita Perón.** This 1951 photo shows the couple acceding to the "demand" of the Argentine people that they run for reelection. *(Bettmann/Corbis)*

men and women, Evita's controversial reputation continues almost undiminished among them. For generations of Argentines, she remains the person who defines "whose side are you on?"

FOR REFLECTION

What do you think of a woman who unabashedly uses her sexuality to secure power and prestige? Do you believe that ends justify means in politics?

Perón was one of a group of officers who threw out the elected government in 1943 and soon made himself into its leader. Perón's pro-German sympathies guaranteed that the United States would condemn him, which all but ensured his election in 1946 on a vehemently nationalist platform. His wife Eva (the "Evita" of song and story) was a product of the slums who knew her people intimately. She was always at his side in public, and her personal charisma and undoubtedly sincere concern for the Argentine working classes made her an idol whose popularity among the populace exceeded the colonel's. In terms of political impact, she was the most important woman in twentieth-century American politics, North or South. Her early death in 1952 was in a sense the beginning of the decline of the movement her husband headed. (See the Tradition and Innovation box for more on this incomparable pair.)

Perón (or Evita) understood something that eluded most Latin American reformers: to overcome the apathy of the rural dwellers and the tradition of leaving government in the hands of a few, it was necessary to appeal to people in a way that they could respond to, directly and with passion. Such an appeal must concentrate on their many eco-

nomic and social discontents. Perón played on this theme very effectively, organizing huge rallies of the lower classes and making inflammatory speeches against the foreign and domestic "exploiters" while simultaneously, though quietly, assuring the entrepreneurs and big business of government contracts and concessions of unprecedented size. It was a fine balancing act between encouraging the egalitarian desires of the ***descamisados*** (shirtless ones) and reassuring the rich that nothing unbearable was in store and that anyone else in Perón's place would probably be worse. Perón was helped by the fact that the early years of his rule (1946–1955) were a time of large profits for raw material producers, of whom Argentina took a place in the first rank. Like Africa in the immediate postindependence era, the Argentine economy prospered mightily, and the bigger pie allowed a bigger slice for all.

By 1954, however, Perón was confronted by a gradually strengthening democratic opposition. Attempting to keep his popularity among the workers, he allowed the radical-socialist wing of the Perónistas more prominence, which alienated his industrial and business support. In that year, he also made the mistake of taking on the Catholic

Church—which had originally been favorable toward Perónismo—by attacking its conservative higher clergy. In 1955, the military drove Perón into exile.

During the ensuing decades, the military or its puppets again ruled Argentina, giving way to civil rule only in 1982 after the self-incurred disaster of the brief Falkland Islands War with Britain. Only in the early 1990s did this potentially rich country stabilize politically and find its way—briefly—out of the social conflicts and mismanagement of the economy that mark its history. Like all of Latin America, its economic well-being and social harmony depend still largely on events and processes in which it is essentially a bystander, as the very recent national bankruptcy has again demonstrated.

The appeal of nationalism remains strong and will become stronger as the masses of Latins gradually are brought into contact with the world beyond their barrios by the international trade arrangements such as the **North American Free Trade Agreement (NAFTA)** that now links the United States with Canada and Mexico. The so-called Southern Tier free trading area currently being hammered out among Argentina, Brazil, and Chile seems to be next, and it will presumably be followed by a full-scale globalization of the Latin economies. Whether this setup will bring tangible benefit to the masses of the poor or only to those who are already on the upper steps of the financial ladder remains to be seen. In any case, those who clamor for political power in the name of "the people" will always find a ready audience in this sadly unbalanced society. What Mexican peons saw in Cárdenas and Argentinian descamisados in Perón was a leader who, whatever his faults, claimed to stand on *their* side of the social and economic barricades. And that was a rarity they appreciated.

The Shark and the Sardines

What about the powerful neighbor to the north? During the first two-thirds of the twentieth century, the Yanquis repeatedly played a heavy-handed and frankly conservative role in Latin American international affairs. One leader who had experienced firsthand what American influence could do in a small country (Guatemala) called it the relationship of the "shark with the sardines." That may be overstating the case slightly, but there is no doubt that in ways both open and covert, Washington was the court of final appeal in Latin foreign relations and, in some cases, not just foreign relations.

The United States first began to pay close attention to Latin America during the Spanish-American War (1898–1900), which was fought, in part, over the rights of the Cuban people to independence. In the ensuing thirty years, Washington intervened at will in Latin and Caribbean affairs. Incidents ranged from Theodore Roosevelt's creation of Panama as a suitable place to build his desired canal to

Mining in Brazil. The wholesale degradation of the natural environment practiced in almost all of the Latin American states since World War II is dramatically shown in this photo of an open-pit gold mine in the Amazon. Such sites rarely or never recover their pristine appearance; government regulation is minimal and often ignored by foreign investors. (© *Antonio Ribeiro/Liaison*)

the sending of armed forces against Mexico and Haiti and the use of the Marines to squelch the rebels of General Sandino—the original Sandinistas—in Nicaragua.

After World War I, U.S. capital and finance took the vacated place of the Europeans with a rush. The dependence of some of the Central American **"banana republics"** on the plantations of the United Fruit Company was merely the most notorious example of the economic imperialism that was practiced throughout Latin America. Cuba's huge sugarcane farms and mills were 80 percent owned by U.S. investors. The big oil strikes in Venezuela were brought in by U.S. firms using U.S. engineers. Mexico's original petroleum fields were dependencies of U.S. firms until nationalization, and 20 percent of the land surface of Mexico's border states was owned or leased by foreign investors in the 1920s, to name only a few examples.

But the story of Latin dependency on the United States has another side. Had it not been for Yankee investment and commerce, the countries to the south would have been even less developed economically and would have sunk deeper into their grossly obsolete system of production and consumption. Until World War II, it's largely true that the Caribbean and northern Latin America (with the exception of Cárdenas's Mexico) were U.S. colonies in everything but name. The bigger question remains: What would have been the Latins' fate in this period in the absence of the United States? Through their own efforts and expertise, they would never have achieved reasonable living standards for even a small segment of their peoples during the first half of the past century (and perhaps not in the second, either). If the U.S. capitalists had not been involved, would the Latin Americans have found more benevolent and selfless sources of help outside the Americas? It seems very doubtful.

In Franklin D. Roosevelt's presidency (1933–1945), the United States embarked on a **Good Neighbor Policy,** treating the Latins more as sovereign nations than as colonies. For many years, no troops were landed to assure a "stability" acceptable to the United States, but still no one had any doubt where true sovereignty lay in the Western Hemisphere. With World War II and the coming of the Cold War, Washington became more concerned about the political allegiance of the Latin states. In treaties signed immediately after the war, the United States pledged political and economic assistance to the other signatories. In 1948, the **Organization of American States (OAS)** was founded under American auspices and served several useful commercial, cultural, and legal purposes besides its primary one of assuring democratic and pro-Western governments in the hemisphere.

Fidel Castro in Havana. The Cuban revolutionary leader enjoys his triumph in making his first address to the Havana populace after chasing out the corrupt Batista regime in 1959. The display of guns was a frequent note in Castro appearances during his early years in power. *(Bettmann/Corbis)*

But the real catalyst for U.S. activity was the coming of Fidel Castro to revolutionary power in Cuba (with a program described in the Exercise of Authority box). Originally the organizer of a hopelessly outnumbered band of idealists, Castro surprisingly overturned the corrupt and unpopular Batista government at the beginning of 1959. After a year of increasing tension, he declared himself a Marxist and began systematically persecuting those who disagreed with that philosophy, while denouncing the United States as the oppressor of freedom-loving Latin Americans. After he nationalized the very extensive U.S. businesses in Cuba, a state of near-war existed between the two countries, culminating in the abortive Bay of Pigs invasion by U.S.-financed anti-Castroites in 1961. A year later, the placement of long-range missiles on the island by the Soviets brought the world to the brink of nuclear war (see Chapter 51).

Since then, relations between the Castro government and Washington have remained frigid. The Cuban revolution, despite some real achievements for the people of the island (literacy, public health, technical education, housing), has proved unable to guarantee a decent material life, especially since Castro's original Soviet and Chinese supporters have collapsed or withdrawn their aid. The revolu-

FIDEL CASTRO'S MANIFESTO

Fidel Castro attempted to begin a revolutionary movement in Cuba in 1956, three years before a second attempt was successful. The attack on the Moncada Barracks was a failure, and Castro was captured, but he was given an opportunity to broadcast his appeal to the Cuban people by the trial judges. His summation in his own defense is entitled *History Will Absolve Me*. The Cuban revolutionaries regard it as the fundamental statement of Castro's beliefs:

> When we speak of the people we do not mean the comfortable ones, the conservative elements of the nation, who welcome any regime of oppression, any dictatorship, any despotism, prostrating themselves before the master of the moment. . . . When we speak of struggle, the people means the vast unredeemed masses to whom all make promises and whom all deceive; we mean the people who yearn for a better, more dignified and more just nation. . . .
>
> Seven hundred thousand Cubans without work. . . .
>
> Five hundred thousand farm laborers, inhabiting miserable shacks, who work four months of the year and starve the rest. . . .
>
> Four hundred thousand industrial laborers and stevedores whose retirement funds have been embezzled, whose benefits are being taken away . . . whose salaries pass from the hands of the boss to the moneylender. . . .
>
> One hundred thousand small farmers who live and die working on land that is not theirs, looking at it in sadness as Moses looked at the Promised Land, to die without ever owning it. . . .
>
> Thirty thousand teachers and professors who are so devoted, dedicated and necessary to the better destiny of future generations and who are so badly treated and paid. . . .
>
> Twenty thousand small businessmen, weighted down by debt . . . and harangued by a plague of grafting and venal officials.
>
> Ten thousand young professionals . . . who come forth from school with their degrees, anxious to work and full of hope only to find themselves at a dead end with all doors closed. . . .
>
> These are the people, the ones who know misfortune and, therefore, are capable of fighting with limitless courage!
>
> To the people whose desperate roads through life have been paved with the bricks of betrayal and false promises, we were not going to say: "We will eventually give you what you need," but rather—"Here you have it, fight for it with all your might, so that liberty and happiness can be yours!"

FOR REFLECTION

How closely did Castro's action follow his words when he did manage to secure power in Cuba? Should it have been such an unpleasant surprise to the U.S. government of Dwight Eisenhower when Castro proceeded to nationalize all U.S. industrial properties? Do Castro's statements affect your own understanding of how he has been able to retain power in Cuba for over forty years?

SOURCE: Fidel Castro, *History Will Absolve Me* (London: Cape, 1968).

---

tion has also proved unsuitable for export to the rest of the continent, as Castro had once intended. No other Latin state ever "went communist," although a few Marxist-leaning governments have been elected (notably, those of Salvador Allende in Chile in 1971 and of the Sandinistas in Nicaragua in the 1980s). All of these have been overtly and covertly undermined by the United States, as have also the attempts by Marxist-led guerrillas or terrorists to seize power. The fiasco of Marxist theory and practice in eastern Europe (see Chapter 57) has all but eliminated this threat to capitalist and democratic governments in the continent. (See Map 55.1.)

The U.S. Role in Recent Latin Affairs

In the early days of the Kennedy administration (1961–1963), under the emblem of anti-Castro action, the United States entered into an **Alliance for Progress** with the Latin American states. More than $10 billion were set aside for economic development loans and credits, more than twice the money allocated to postwar Europe under the Marshall Plan. But as so often happens with government programs that are intended to make a quick impression on the electorate, much of the money went to make the rich richer or

wound up in the wrong pockets. The single most effective, externally funded program for Latin American development was the quiet work on improving crop yields, done mainly in Mexico during the 1950s and 1960s. This botanical laboratory project gave a tremendous boost to world food grain production, resulting in some places in the Green Revolution that we have mentioned earlier. Its success is a main reason why the threatened world famine has thus far been confined to regions of Africa and has not menaced Latin America and the entire developing world.

In recent years, U.S. involvement with the Caribbean nations has again become openly interventionary and reactionary, but generally within dimensions that the OAS as a whole has been willing to approve. Presidents Ronald Reagan (Grenada, Nicaragua), George Bush (Panama), and Bill Clinton (Haiti) have acted forcefully to protect what they conceived to be U.S. strategic, political, or economic interests in the area. But a return to the pre-1930 system of "gunboat diplomacy" by the United States is hardly possible, even if it were desirable. A major change in the levers of control occurred in 2000 when the Panama Canal became part of the sovereign territory of Panama. Other pending political questions include possible independence

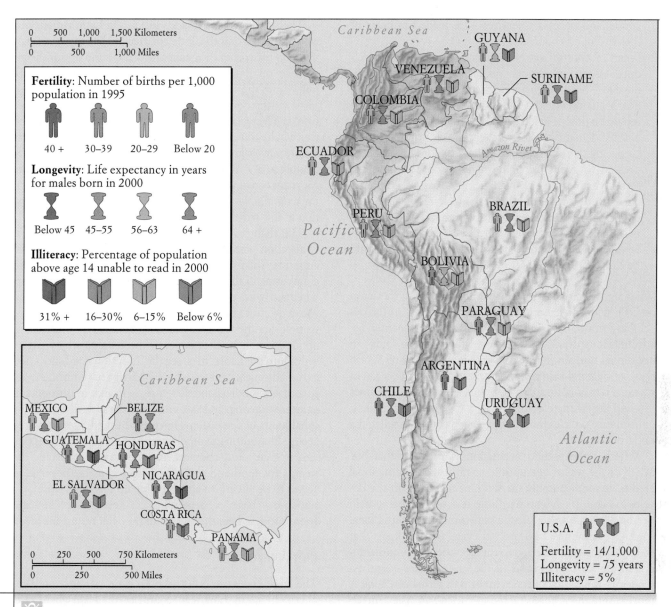

MAP 55.1 Poverty Index for Latin America. Three demographic factors are closely linked to opportunity, stability, and relative income in the developing countries: fertility in females, longevity in males, and illiteracy. High fertility is always linked to a shorter lifespan and to high rates of illiteracy. The map above shows the relative placement of individual countries based on the three social indicators on this poverty index.

for Puerto Rico (a U.S. territory for the past century) and the fate of Cuba after the inevitable demise of the seventy-five-year-old Castro.

CURRENT ISSUES AND PROBLEMS

In Latin America as elsewhere, economic and social issues are linked together. In Latin America as a whole, just as in Africa, probably the highest-priority social problem is controlling a rate (2.9 percent) of population growth that is too high for the resources available. Also as in Africa, a number

of governments would contest this assessment, saying that faulty or nonexistent access to resources, both domestic and foreign, generates most social frictions in their countries. There is, in fact, something to be said for this argument. In the eyes of many Latin Americans, the developed world, and especially the United States, has taken unfair and shortsighted advantage of the underdeveloped world during the past century and continues to do so in the following ways:

1. The terms of foreign trade—that is, the rate at which raw materials are exchanged for manufactures, consumer

goods, and necessary services—are loaded in favor of the developed countries.

2. Financial credits have been extended to the underdeveloped American nations on an unrealistically "businesslike" basis (high interest and short terms), which nearly guarantees that the loans cannot and will not be repaid on time, if at all. This condition then becomes the basis of demanding still harsher terms for the next loan.

3. Currently, the underdeveloped nations are being pressed to avoid using the main resources they possess—what nature has given them—to assure a more secure future for the developed minority. Environmental concerns are being used to justify interference in internal affairs such as how many trees are cut down, or where beef cattle should graze, or how many fish should be caught.

What are we to make of these complaints? First, there can be little doubt that Latin America, like the rest of the developing world, has been forced to accept consistently disadvantageous trade conditions, while getting only an occasional and undependable sop in the form of World Bank or bilateral loans and grants. Since World II, a ton of wheat, a bag of coffee, or a container of bananas purchases less and less of the electrical machinery, office equipment, or insurance policies that the developed countries sell to the underdeveloped.

Whether the second accusation is true is debatable. Much of the waste, corruption, or misuse of international credits was indisputably the work of recipients in the developing countries, who had little fear of ever being held personally responsible. At the same time, the international lending community has rarely if ever "pulled" loans that were clearly being diverted to the illicit benefit of individuals. In any case, the terms of the international loans extended to the Latin countries in the past have been notably more severe than those granted to Africa and Asia. The efforts to repay have handicapped Latin America's domestic investment and contributed to the fragile condition of the current Latin economies.

The third charge has a very complex background but demands a decisive answer because it will affect us all in a powerful fashion. The Latin Americans (and others) are saying in essence, "You, the developed societies, have now woken up to the dangers of pollution and abuse of the environment but want us, the less developed, to pay the price of implementing rational policies while you have enjoyed the short-term benefits of irrationality." It was all right, in other words, for nineteenth-century American timber companies to cut down every tree over a foot thick in Michigan, but it is not all right for twentieth-century Brazilian timber companies to cut down mature mahogany in the Amazon basin. Multiply this example by hundreds, and you will have the position adopted by the Latin Americans and most other leaders of the developing countries in response to the environmental concerns of the developed world.

The developed world adds salt to the Latin Americans' wounds by paying too little for that mahogany tree compared to the cost of the chain saw that cut the tree or the insurance on the boat that transports the tree to a U.S. mill—both the saw and the insurance, of course, were supplied by the developed world. And further salting comes from the fact that the fine piece of furniture made from the tree will be too expensive to grace an ordinary Latin American home owing to the high costs and profits of the U.S. manufacturer. What benefits NAFTA has brought to the Mexican consumer, as compared to the U.S. manufacturer, for example, is a hotly argued but still-unanswered question at this writing.

The flight to the cities we have already mentioned in connection with modern Africa is equally strong in Latin America. Towns such as Lima or Bogotá, which were still slumbering in the early twentieth century, have been overwhelmed with peasant migrants in the last thirty years. Mexico City, so far as anyone can tell, is now the largest metropolis in the world, with an estimated population of about 15 million. (For some of the reasons why villagers move into the Latin cities, see the Tradition and Innovation box.) The majority live in shabby barrios or unfinished, do-it-yourself subdivisions that spring up like mushrooms in an ever-widening circle around the older town. Many of the inhabitants of these slums have established a settled, even secure life, but many others are living on a tightrope, balancing petty and sporadic income against constant demands for food and fuel. Much of the urban population seems to be "living on air," hustling up unskilled work on a day-to-day basis or depending on networks of kin and friends to see them through until they can return the favor.

Rich and Poor

The chasm between rich and poor is deeper and more apparent in Latin American countries than anywhere else. Africa has relatively few very rich and not many people who are well-to-do. In most of Asia, wealth is fairly evenly distributed except in one or two cities in each country. But in South America, the extremes of very poor and very rich are growing, while the number of those in the middle is more or less stagnant. There are a great many very poor and a very small but growing number of rich—and the contrast between them is a powder keg in most Latin American countries.

So visible and disturbing is the polarization of Latin American society that the Catholic Church, long the main bastion of conservatism and reaction, has taken the lead in country after country as a voice for the poor. A peculiar combination of Marxist social theory and Catholic humanitarianism has come to life in several countries, notably Brazil, to speak for the common people against a social and economic system that has exploited them for many generations. Hundreds of priests, nuns, and higher officials of the church have been imprisoned or even murdered by military

MEXICAN VILLAGERS

In the early 1970s, an American anthropologist stayed for a number of months in an isolated highlands village in central Mexico. She witnessed the beginnings of the transition of Hueyapan from a quasi-medieval to a twentieth-century society, a phenomenon that was taking place simultaneously throughout Latin America in this epoch:

During the 1930s, '40s and '50s villagers with a little capital rented large fields from lowlanders. . . . Instead of being paid in money, peons were given corn seed and enough land to plant. In a good year, a man could harvest enough to carry him and a family of six or seven through the year. Although they left their wives and young children at home, men usually took along their older sons and daughters. . . . While the young boys joined the men in the fields, the women and girls worked as corn grinders and cooks. . . . At the end of their stay they received [as their wages] as many liters of unground corn to take back as they had managed to grind for their patrones.

Villagers would spend June, July and August in the lowlands, planting and caring for their vegetables. They would return to Hueyapan until December, at which time they would go down again for another month to harvest the crops.

[In recent years there have been important changes in this pattern, however.] As in the 1950s [corn-grinding] mills started to replace their labor, more and more women began to migrate to Mexico City and Cuernavaca to work as maids. Although a few men left the village to work in factories, the number was negligible compared with that of women. . . . [Also] most of the young people who leave to work in urban centers have settled permanently in the cities. Absorbed into the ever-growing ghettos of the poor, these Hueyapenos return to the village only occasionally to see their families. . . . On their visits, the new migrants take home money and many of the material objects associated with the city. In this way they are contributing to the process that is incorporating Hueyapan into the consumer-oriented economy of Mexico.

Even in this most Indian of all Latin societies, the disadvantage of being an Indian made itself apparent:

To be Indian in Hueyapan is to have a primarily negative identity. Indian-ness is more a measure of what the villagers are not or do not have vis-à-vis the hispanic [sic] elite than it is of what they have or are. . . . When I visited the homes of people in the village, from the wealthier to the more impoverished, I was often greeted with "Please excuse us, we are only poor little Indians here." . . . Nobody, they assumed, expected an Indian to have either the economic means or the good manners to treat an honored guest properly. . . .

Most villagers responded to their Indian-ness in one of three ways, all of them negative. Some people, mostly the old and illiterate, were fatalistic: such was their unfortunate lot and who could expect more of them ? Others believed that although Indians, they could at least try to hide their impoverished cultural condition, so that things would appear "less sad, less poor, less Indian." . . . A third response was to try to lose their Indian identity. . . . When villagers used the word "Indian" it was almost always to insult one another or to make a self-deprecating comment or joke.

FOR REFLECTION

What effects do you think will eventually result from the imbalance of the sexes in Hueyapan, so far as the viability of the village as an independent social unit is concerned? Do you believe the Mexican government has any responsibility to intervene in this transformation? Could it?

SOURCE: Adapted slightly from Judith Friedlander, Being Indian in Hueyapan (New York: St. Martin's, 1975).

---

and civilian reactionaries in the past fifteen years. Archbishop Oscar Romero of El Salvador was shot down while saying mass in his own cathedral for speaking out against the bloody excesses of the military in the civil war in El Salvador in the 1980s. The Romeros of two generations ago would have been blessing the army's guns.

Changing Styles in Government

Latin America since 1930 has thus tried several different styles of government, including socialism, corporatism, and nationalist populism in an effort to achieve greater social justice and economic prosperity. Most of these have quickly degenerated into dictatorship. All have proved either ineffective or corrupt or were unable to retain their momentum. Castro's Cuba remains the one experiment with scientific socialism, and even its defenders acknowledge that it has failed its people economically in the last ten years.

In the 1960s, it appeared quite possible that Latin American Marxists, inspired by Castro's success, would attempt to seize power in several countries. Economic nationalism was faltering, and little social reform had been effected. Terrorist activity became a menace to the upper classes in Argentina and Brazil, where urban guerrillas operated. The military establishment in country after country pushed aside the ineffectual politicians and governed directly on a platform of law and order. Encouraged by government policymakers, Western banks loaned huge sums to the Latin American nations. Foreign debt increased by more than twelve times in the 1970s, to a point where with the slightest economic reversal the Latin American nations could not pay even the interest on time.

The 1970s were the low point for constitutional government. At one point in that decade, only three of the twenty Latin American nations were still ruled by elected governments. Everywhere else, the military attempted to meet the increasing demands for social and economic reform by

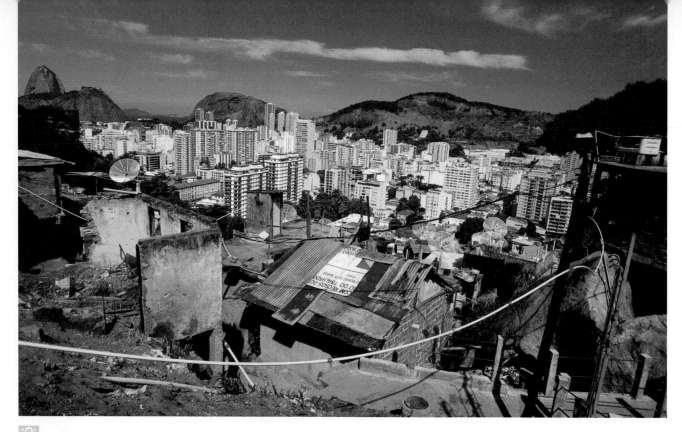

🏵 *Favela* **in Rio.** The distance from the slum to the golden beaches of Rio's Copacabana is not far in miles but a world away in terms of atmosphere and psychology. Sugar Loaf Mountain, rising behind the cityscape, is a beacon to the ambitious. (© *Jon Spaull/Panos Pictures*)

going outside the political process. Almost always these attempts failed or were discarded before they had a chance to take hold. (A wild inflation was the main enemy of the reform plans. At one time, the value of the Argentine peso against the U.S. dollar was dropping at the rate of 10 percent per *day*.)

In the 1980s, the pendulum swung back to civilian rule, and by the end of that decade, only a few countries were still ruled by men in uniform. Argentina and Brazil again led the way. The military in Buenos Aires stepped down in disgrace after foolishly provoking a war with Britain over the Falkland Islands, and a few years later, the Brazilian generals gave up power to the first duly elected government in a quarter-century.

Democratic, constitutional government is still a fragile flower most of the time in most of the continent. But it made some strong gains in the 1980s and 1990s. The ending of the Cold War has had a beneficial effect on U.S.–Latin American relations, as the United States no longer worries that some type of hostile, Soviet puppet regime will be installed in these near neighbors. But the emergence from neocolonialism is a painfully slow process that will continue well into the twenty-first century even in the most hopeful scenarios. Moreover, the relative backwardness of Latin America, as part of the developing world, will cause it to continue to be a breeding ground for social discontent. The continent's future will depend largely on whether and how that discontent is resolved.

SUMMARY

The twenty nations in Latin America have many overriding similarities, despite some differences. Everywhere, policymakers are concerned with the question of economic development—how to achieve it and how to manage it. Everywhere, the relationship between the United States and the Latin American nations is vital to the future stability and prosperity of the continent. Various types of economic nationalism, sometimes introduced by the military, have been the Latin American response to their status as poor relations of the more developed nations of the world. Cárdenas in Mexico and Perón in Argentina were perhaps the most noted examples in the past sixty years, but many others have appeared and will continue to do so. Forty years ago, Castro offered a Marxist response to neocolonial status in Cuba, but Marxism has had minimal appeal outside that country, despite initial efforts to spread it. Its future is very dim.

Social problems, especially the maldistribution of wealth and the pressures generated by a high birthrate, haunt the continent south of the Rio Grande. One of the most striking manifestations of these problems is the uncontrollable growth of the cities and their shantytown surroundings. Political solutions to Latin American problems have been at best sporadic and partial. But after the failure of the military regimes of the 1970s, there has been a vigorous recovery in parliamentary government. In the 1990s, some hopeful signs indicate that constitutional democracy will triumph permanently.

TEST YOUR KNOWLEDGE

1. After the Great Depression of the 1930s began, the larger Latin American states
   a. became totally dependent on imported goods.
   b. carried out long-delayed agrarian reforms to favor the peons.
   c. started on a program of economic nationalism.
   d. suffered economic collapse.
2. The most socially conscious Mexican president in this century was
   a. Lázaro Cárdenas.
   b. Porfirio Díaz.
   c. Benito Juarez.
   d. Pancho Villa.
3. The most widely recognized female in recent Latin American history was probably
   a. St. Theresa.
   b. Eva Perón
   c. Carmen Miranda.
   d. Violeta Chamorro.
4. Juan Perón was forced from power in 1955 by
   a. a mass uprising.
   b. a free election.
   c. U.S. intervention.
   d. a military plot.
5. Which of the following countries did *not* experience U.S. military intervention in the twentieth century?
   a. Nicaragua
   b. Colombia
   c. Panama
   d. Haiti
6. In the 1970s, the government and politics of most Latin American countries experienced
   a. a swing toward the Marxist left.
   b. intervention by military-based conservatives.
   c. a swing toward social welfare programs.
   d. a renewal of clerical influence.
7. In the later 1980s and 1990s, Latin America has experienced a strong movement toward
   a. democratically elected governments.
   b. military coups d'état.
   c. Marxist dictatorships.
   d. fascist governments.

IDENTIFICATION TERMS

Alliance for Progress

banana republics

Cárdenas, Lázaro

descamisados

Good Neighbor Policy

North American Free Trade Agreement (NAFTA)

Organization of American States (OAS)

Perón, Eva and Juan

INFOTRAC COLLEGE EDITION

Enter the search terms "Latin America economic aspects" using Key Words.

Enter the search terms "Latin America political aspects" using Key Words.

Enter the search terms "Latin America history" using Key Words.

THE REEMERGENCE OF THE MUSLIM WORLD

The people of [the Muslim world] sometimes make much more history than they consume locally.

SAKI (H. H. MUNRO)

1917	Balfour Declaration on Palestine
1920s	Ataturk leads Turkey/Saudi Arabia united by Ibn Saud
1946–1948	Mandate territories become independent states
1948	Israel founded and Israeli-Arab War begins
1956	Suez Canal nationalized by Egypt
1964	PLO founded to fight Israel
1973	OPEC oil boycott
1979	Iranian Revolution/Soviet intervention in Afghanistan
1980–1988	Iraq–Iran War
1985	Soviet withdrawal from Afghanistan
1991	Gulf War against Iraq
1993	Peace Agreement between Israel and PLO
1999–	Renewed Israeli/Palestinian confrontation
2001–	bin Laden terror network in West/War in Afghanistan

FOR THE FIRST TIME in centuries, the Muslim peoples are at the center of world events and are playing major roles in international affairs. The term *Muslim world* refers to far more than the Middle East or the Arab countries (see Map 56.1). Muslims now number about one-sixth of humanity, and Islam is the dominant religion in thirty-eight countries, reaching from Southeast Asia to the Atlantic coast of Africa. The 148 million Arabs are mostly Muslims, but a great many of the one billion Muslims are not Arabs. In this chapter, however, we will focus on the Arab Middle East because that is where the major events and processes defining the Muslim relationship with the world have taken place in the twentieth century.

The single most important factor in Middle Eastern history over the last seventy years has been geology. By far the largest known oilfields in the world are located under Saudi Arabia and the other Persian Gulf Muslim countries. Their development was the key to the massive change in relations between Muslims and non-Muslims in the later twentieth century, particularly since the oil boycott of 1973.

THE MUSLIM COUNTRIES UNTIL WORLD WAR I

As we saw in Chapter 32, the three Muslim empires of earlier times in Asia were either overthrown or much weakened by the nineteenth century. The Mughals in India, the Safavid Persians, and the Ottoman Turks had been overwhelmed by Western military and financial powers where they came into conflict with them. By the mid-1800s, the British had made most of India into an outright colony, and Persia was effectively divided between Russian and British spheres. The Ottomans had been repeatedly defeated by Russia in Europe and had been forced to watch as even the facade of their political overlordship in North Africa faded away. Only in the Near East did some substance of Turkish control remain.

But these political and military weaknesses were not the only indicators of decline. The Islamic world would have to overcome a series of psychological and technical barriers if it were to reassert its equality with the West. The fundamental tradition of Islam, wherever it attained power, was

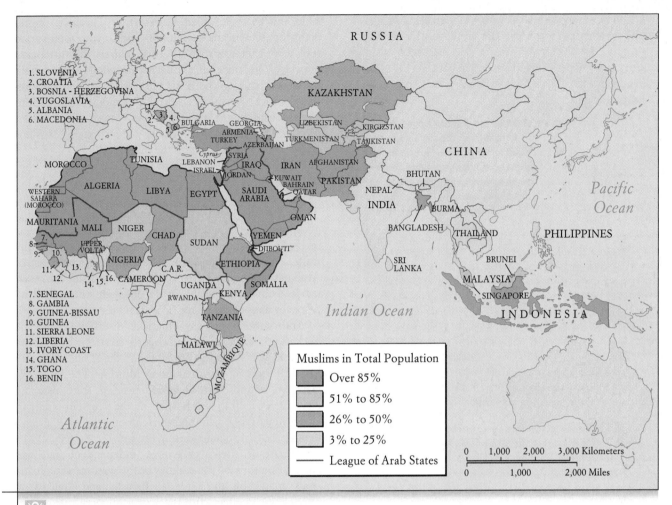

MAP 56.1   Modern Islam, 2000.   Although the Islamic heartland remains the Middle East and North Africa, Islam is growing steadily in black Africa and is the majority faith of over thirty countries around the globe.

to understand itself as a community of righteous believers who were actively spreading the sole authentic word of God and establishing his rule on Earth. For 1,000 years, since the time of the Prophet, this viewpoint had been the driving force behind the expansion of the religion around the globe.

From about the middle of the eighteenth century, however, this view could no longer be sustained, as the unbelievers took over former Muslim territories from the Balkans to the islands of Southeast Asia. The learned and the powerful men of Islam reacted in two differing ways. Some assumed that these reverses were temporary and would soon be made up. Others looked—for the first time—to the West for inspiration in technology and, above all, military science, to help them to counter and overcome Western superiority.

Unfortunately for Muslim ambitions, the first trend prevailed over the second. The ulema and the imams of the Ottoman domains could not accept the secularism of post–

French Revolution Europe, but they grudgingly recognized that Muslim practice would have to incorporate some Western elements if they were not to be utterly overwhelmed. Yet they still believed in the inherent superiority of the community of God (*Dar al-Islam*) over the unbelievers (*Dar al-Harb*). As a result, they only sporadically and inconsistently attempted to adopt some European science and technology without changing the very conservative cast of Islamic education and government, which frowned on innovation.

Those few who attempted to bring large-scale Western ideas into Islam were opposed by a vast body of traditions and prejudices. Even some of the Ottoman sultans who recognized that resisting the West without the assistance of Western science and education would be hopeless were unable to carry through their plans of reform against the twin obstacles of tradition and fatalistic apathy. By the mid–nineteenth century, Islam, as a religious community and as a political association, was in a nearly moribund

MUSLIMS AND UNBELIEVERS

As in most scriptures issuing from a prophet's message, the searcher can find in the Qur'an support for contradictory positions on many topics. This is especially so in the matter of the proper relationship between the Muslim and the unbeliever. A noted Western interpreter of Islam comments:

> There is in Islam a tradition of unquestioning obedience to authority. There is also a tradition of rebellion against authority perceived as unjust or illegitimate. Both traditions are firmly rooted in scripture and tradition: both were expanded and developed in theory and practice by subsequent generations of Muslims. In the same way, it is not difficult to find scriptural and juridical authority for both war and peace with the unbelievers. In the Qur'an the enemies of God are specified as the unbelievers, and they are doomed to hellfire (2:98; 41:19, 28). The believers are commanded to "strike terror into God's enemy and your enemy." But the struggle need not be to the death. "If the enemy incline toward peace, do you also incline toward peace and trust in God" (8:60–62). According to a striking passage, repeated several times in the Qur'an, "if God had wished, He would have made all humankind one community" (11:118; 16:93; 42:8). But, by God's choice, the world is divided into different nations and religions, and God determines who shall embrace the truth and who shall go astray. And in this, surely, there is a powerful argument for compassion and tolerance.

Source: B. Lewis, The Multiple Identities of the Middle East (New York: Shocken, 1998), p. 130.

state. Unwilling to adapt beyond a few superficial phenomena, the Muslim nations were seemingly destined to a future in which they were the permanent pawns of the European powers.

RESPONSES TO MUSLIM WEAKNESS

By the 1890s, this inability to resist external pressure had produced two quite different responses in the Muslim world. The first was the beginnings of what is now called *Islamic fundamentalism.* The second was *pan-Arabism* or *Arab nationalism,* which are related but not identical attempts to create a sense of unity among the Arab peoples of the Middle East and North Africa.

Islamic fundamentalism was and is marked by a thoroughgoing rejection of Western influences and Western ideas, including such notions as political democracy, religious toleration, the equality of citizens, and various other offshoots of the Age of Enlightenment and the American and French Revolutions. To a fundamentalist (the word is a recent appellation), the task of civil government is to bring about the reign of Allah and his faithful on Earth—nothing less and nothing more. Any obstacles that stand in the way of this process should be swept aside, by persuasion if pos-

sible, but by force (jihad) if necessary. There can be no compromise with the enemies of God or with their varied tools and facilitators such as secular schools, mixed-religion marriages, and nonconfessional parliaments. In the Mahdi's bitter resistance to the British in Sudan, and Shamil's resistance to the Russians in central Asia, modern Islamic fundamentalism found its first heroes. Many others would come forth in the twentieth century. (The box on "Muslims and Unbelievers" elucidates the question.)

Pan-Arabism is an outgrowth of Arab national consciousness that began to be articulated in the late nineteenth century, especially among Egyptians and Syrians. (Note that the word *Arab* or *Arabic* refers to an ethnic group, not a religious one. There are many Arab Christians in Egypt, Lebanon, and Syria, and they were among the leaders of Arab nationalism.) The long delay in the rise of Arab nationalism compared to Western varieties can be attributed to the inclusive nature of Islam, which had no place for national or ethnic divisions.

Arab nationalism was originally directed against the Turkish overlords, and it had become so strong by the time of World War I that the British found the Arabs willing allies in the fight against their fellow Muslims. The Arabs' reward was supposed to be an independent state, reaching from Egypt to Iraq and headed by the Hussein family of *sheikhs* in Arabia, who had been among the most prominent of the British allies during the war.

The Arabs' dream of a large, independent state was ended, however, by the realities of the wartime diplomatic deals made by the French, British, and Italians in 1916–1917. In effect, Turkish prewar imperial rule was replaced by European rule. Originally intended as outright colonies, the postwar Near Eastern Arab lands were converted into "**mandates**" in the care of the British and French until such time as the Arabs proved their ability to act as responsible sovereign powers.

What was the difference between a mandate and a colony? The distinction proved exceedingly fine. For all practical purposes, Syria and Lebanon were French colonies from 1919 to 1946, and Jordan, Palestine, and Iraq were British ones. When the Hussein-led nationalists protested and rebelled, they were put down with decisive military action. Egypt, where the British had had an occupation force since 1882, got a slightly better arrangement. There nationalism was strong enough to induce the British to grant the Egyptians pro-forma independence in 1922. British troops remained, however, and real independence was withheld until the 1950s because of British concerns about the Suez Canal and their "lifeline to India."

During the 1920s and 1930s, the small gains effected by individual Arab groups gave momentum to the Pan-Arab movement, which tried to get Arabs everywhere to submerge their differences and unite under one political center. The example of Saudi Arabia was held up as a possible model. Under the fundamentalist sheikh Ibn Saud, most of the Arabian peninsula was unified in the 1920s by conquest

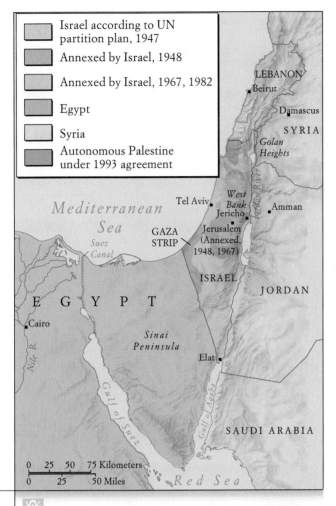

MAP 56.2 Israel and Its Arab Neighbors, 1947–1994.
The extraordinary complexity of the conflict between Jews and
Arabs stems in large part from the many years of peaceable
intermixing of populations, making it impossible to separate
them and to place them under separate governments without
coercion. As in the Balkan states, the very success and duration
of the past peace have made the current conflict more savage.

and voluntary association and turned into a poverty-ridden
and primitive but sovereign state. But the Pan-Arabists
could show few other gains by the time World War II broke
out. The colonial grip on individual regions was too strong,
and the disunity and jealousies that had plagued Arab politics for a long time showed no sign of abating.

THE TURKISH REPUBLIC

The exception to the continued subordination of the Muslim states or societies was the new Republic of Turkey. In
the aftermath of the defeat as Germany's ally in World War
I, the sultan's government had lost all credibility in Turkish

eyes. Backed by Great Britain, the Greek government attempted in 1919 to realize the "Great Idea" of restoring the
former Byzantine empire and making the interior of Turkey
(Anatolia) once more a Greek colony. A Greek army landed
on the Turkish coast and began to move inland.

At this critical point, a leader emerged who almost
single-handedly brought his people back from the edge of
legal annihilation. This was **Mustafa Kemal,** called **Ataturk**
(father of Turkey). Kemal had been a colonel in the Ottoman army. In 1919–1921, he organized the national resistance to the invaders and won a decisive victory against
the poorly led Greeks. Alone among the defeated in World
War I, Turkey was eventually able to secure a revision of the
original peace. The new treaty recognized the full sovereignty of the Turkish state within the borders it now has.
The former Arab provinces were abandoned to the Western
mandates.

But this was no longer Ottoman Turkey. Kemal was
elected the first president (with near dictatorial powers) of
the new parliamentary republic. Until his death in 1938,
Kemal retained the presidency as he drove Turkey and the
Turks to a systematic break with the past. Modernization
and Westernization were the twin pillars of Kemal's policies
as he focused on separating Turkish civil society from Islamic culture.

In every visible and invisible way Kemal could devise,
the citizens of modern Turkey were distinguished from
their Islamic ancestors. Western-style dress was introduced
and even made mandatory for government workers. The
veil was abolished. The revered Arabic script was replaced
by the Latin alphabet. Women were made legally equal and
could divorce their husbands. Polygamy was forbidden.
Western schooling was introduced and made compulsory
for both sexes. A new legal code was introduced, with no
preference for Muslims. The capital was moved from half-
Greek Istanbul to pure Turkish Ankara.

By the time of his death, Kemal had indeed kept his
promise to do for the Turks what Peter the Great had attempted to do for the Russians: to thrust them forward several generations and bring them into Europe. Despite
intense resistance from conservative Muslim circles, Kemal
had managed to turn his people into a superficially secular
society in less than twenty years. He had also given a
model emulated by like-minded reformers all over the non-
Western world.

PALESTINE

The thorniest of all problems in the Middle East after
World War I was the fate of the British mandate of Pales-
tine (Israel). During the war, the hard-pressed British had
made promises to both the Ottoman-ruled Arabs and the
Zionists, who claimed to represent most European Jews.
These promises conflicted with one another. In the **Balfour
Declaration** of 1917, the British had agreed to support a

THE ARAB VIEWPOINT ON JEWISH PALESTINE

The most intransigent international question in the entire post–World War II era has not been the fate of Berlin, or Korea, or Vietnam but rather the question of Palestine. This former Ottoman province was ceded to British "mandate" (that is, supervision) by the settlement of World War I. In the interwar era, the area had a solid majority of Arabs and a slowly increasing minority of Jews, many of whom were recent immigrants inspired by the vision of creating a Jewish state.

At the end of World War II, the United States and Britain created a commission to investigate the future of Palestine. The following excerpt from the Arab leaders' memorandum to the commission shows their fundamental opposition to the idea of a Jewish Palestine, or the state of Israel. The memorandum turned out to be a chillingly accurate prognosis:

1. The whole Arab people is unalterably opposed to the attempt to impose Jewish immigration and settlement upon it, and ultimately to establish a Jewish State in Palestine. . . . They cannot agree that it is right to subject an indigenous population against its will to alien immigrants, whose claim is based upon an historical connection which ceased many centuries ago. . . .

2. Zionism is essentially a political movement, aiming at the creation of a state: immigration, land-purchase and economic expansion are only aspects of a general political strategy. If Zionism succeeds in its aim, the Arabs will become a minority in their own country; a minority which can hope for no more than a minor share in the government, for the state is to be a Jewish state, and which will find itself not only deprived of that international status which the other Arab countries possess but cut off from living contact with the Arab world of which it is an integral part. . . .

8. In the Arab view, any solution of the problem . . .

i. must recognize the right of the indigenous inhabitants of Palestine to continue in occupation of the country and to preserve its traditional character.

ii. must recognize that questions like immigration which affect the whole nature and destiny of the country should be decided in accordance with democratic principles by the will of the population.

iii. must accept the principle that the only way by which the will of the population can be expressed is through the establishment of a responsible representative government.

iv. This representative government should be based upon the principle of absolute equality of all citizens irrespective of race and religion. . . .

vi. The settlement should recognize the fact that by geography and history Palestine is inescapably part of the Arab world; that the only alternative to its being part of the Arab world is accepting the implications of its position, that is, complete isolation, which would be disastrous from every point of view. . . .

The idea of partition and the establishment of a Jewish state in a part of Palestine is inadmissible for the same reasons of principle as the idea of establishing a Jewish state in the whole country. If it is unjust to the Arabs to impose a Jewish state on the whole of Palestine, it is equally unjust to impose it in any part of the country. . . . It would also be impossible to devise frontiers which did not leave a large Arab minority in the Jewish state. This minority would not willingly accept its subjection to the Zionists, and it would not allow itself to be transferred to the Arab state. . . . [A Zionist state] would inevitably be thrown into enmity with the surrounding Arab states and this enmity would disturb the stability of the whole Middle East.

Source: The Israel-Arab Reader, 2d ed., ed. Walter Laqueur (Harmondsworth: Penguin, 1970).

"Jewish national homeland," but this could be achieved only at the expense of the Arab majority. These Arabs had shared Palestine with the biblical Jews and had been the majority people there for many generations. To these Arabs, a "national homeland" sounded like a Jewish-controlled state in which they would be only a tolerated group, and they accordingly did not like the idea. (See the box for more on the Arab point of view.)

Jewish immigration to Palestine had begun in a minor way as early as the 1880s but had only taken on potentially important dimensions after the founding of the international Zionist movement by the journalist Theodor Herzl at the turn of the twentieth century. Under the well-meaning but muddled British colonial government, Arabs and Jews began to take up hostile positions in Palestinian politics during the 1920s. By the late 1930s, this hostility was taking the form of bloody riots, suppressed only with difficulty by the British police. Despite restrictions imposed from London, Jewish immigrants poured into Palestine from Hitler's Germany and eastern Europe, where vicious anti-Semitism had become commonplace. At the outbreak of World War II, perhaps 30 percent of Palestine's inhabitants were Jews.

At the end of the war, the British in Palestine as elsewhere were at the end of their strength and wished to turn over the troublesome Middle East mandates as soon as possible to the United Nations. The pitiful remnants of the Jews of Nazi Europe now defied British attempts to keep them from settling illegally in Palestine. Attempts to get Arabs and Jews to sit down at the negotiating table failed, and the frustrated British announced that they would unilaterally abandon Palestine on May 14, 1948. Faced with this ultimatum, the United Nations eventually (November 1947) came out with a proposal for dividing the mandate into a Jewish state and an Arab state—a compromise that, needless to say, satisfied neither side. By the time the United Nations proposal was put forth, fighting between irregular Arab and Jewish militias was already under way. Full-scale war followed on the British withdrawal.

The results of the 1948 war—the first of six armed conflicts in the past half-century between Israel and its Arab neighbors—were strongly favorable to the new Jewish state. Unexpectedly, it held its own and more against its several enemies. But the triumphant Israelis then expelled many hundreds of thousands of Palestinian Arabs from their ancestral lands, creating a reservoir of bitterness that guaranteed hostility for decades to come.

In 1964, after fifteen years of intra-Arab dissension about how best to deal with the Israeli presence, the **Palestine Liberation Organization (PLO)** was formed by Arab extremists. Its single goal was the destruction of the state of Israel, and it pursued that goal with terror and bloodshed for almost thirty years until 1993. In this effort the PLO was assisted by most of the Arab states, which saw Israel as a enemy that could not be tolerated in their midst. This enmity, like all other conflicts during the Cold War era, became caught up in the general hostility between the United States and the Soviet Union, with the former siding strongly with the Israelis and the latter with the Arabs.

The Palestinian *Intifada*. Beginning in 1989 under PLO leadership, the Palestinian Arabs in the Gaza Strip and the West Bank occupied territories challenged Israeli claims to these areas. Rock-throwing youth rioted in the streets in a persistent *intifada,* or uprising, which forced Israeli countermeasures and gave the Tel Aviv government a black eye in the world press. A second intifada began after the breakdown of the 1993 agreement, the Oslo Accord. *(© Esaias Beitel/ Gamma Liaison)*

Wedding Procession in a *Kibbutz*. A tractor is the limousine for the just-married couple in this Israeli *kibbutz.* Tens of thousands of young Jews emigrated to Israel during the 1950s and 1960s to take part in the spartan, communal life on the *kibbutzim,* agrarian setttlements on the former wastelands and deserts of the Jewish state. *(Ted Spiegel/Corbis)*

AYATOLLAH KHOMEINI
(1902–1989)

Early in 1979, the massive street demonstrations that had become a daily occurrence in Tehran succeeded in persuading the shah of Iran to leave the country for exile. His place was quickly taken by an unlikely figure: the Ayatollah Ruhollah Khomeini, a blazing-eyed, ramrod erect man in his seventies, garbed in the long kaftan of a strict Muslim believer. Khomeini had been forced into exile by the shah's police fifteen years earlier. Now the tables had turned, and it would be Khomeini, not the once all-powerful shah, who ruled Iran's forty million inhabitants until he died.

The *ayatollah* (the word means "theologian") was a member of Iran's leading sect: the Shiite Muslims, who make up only about 10 percent of the world's Muslim population but have long been the dominant religious group in Iran. Since the 1960s, conservative Shia had opposed the secularizing policies of Muhammad Reza Shah Pahlavi. They believed in a rigid in-

Ayatollah Khomeini. *(© T. Comiti/Gamma Liaison)*

terpretation of the Qur'an, whereby government should be the strong right arm of the religious establishment (the ulema). Not surprisingly, neither the shah nor his close advisers shared this view. Using all the apparatus of the modern state, including a barbaric secret police, they made the lives of the ayatollah and his followers miserable and assassinated many. Among the dead was Khomeini's elder son, who was murdered in Iraq.

With the resources of a modern army and police at his command, and with the full support of the U.S. government in his general policies, it seemed unthinkable that the shah's throne was in danger from a small group of unarmed religious fanatics. That was true until the mid-1970s when it became apparent that the government's initial social reforms—the White Revolution—were failing, thanks in part to massive corruption. Always a country of economic extremes, Iran became the model of a society in which a tiny elite became fantas-

THE RETURN OF ISLAM

Bernard Lewis, a leading expert on the Muslim world, recently wrote an essay entitled "The Return of Islam" that deals with the resurgence of Islamic activity in the past few years. He emphasizes that the West has always misunderstood the nature of Islam and has tried to equate it with Christianity in Europe with unfortunate results. Islam is much more than a religion as the West understands that term, and is certainly not limited to the private sphere as Christianity has been since the French Revolution. Islam does not recognize the separation of church and state, nor of religious belief and civil practice. Rather, for the good Muslim these concepts are a unity and always have been. They can no more be separated than can the human personality be parted from the body it inhabits.

Lewis goes on to say, "It was not nation or country that, as in the West, formed the historic basis of identity, but the religio-political community." For this reason, Arab nationalism has never been as successful as, say, French national-

ism was. Muslim Arabs felt a higher identity embracing them than the mere fact of being Syrian or Egyptian. "The Fatherland of a Muslim is wherever the Holy Law of Islam prevails." This feeling is not new. Even at the high point of secular nationalism in the Middle East, during the interwar years when the Turkey of Kemal Ataturk was blazing the path, there was a strong undercurrent of religiously based patriotic feeling that rejected secularism as severely as it did Western imperialism.

But only in recent decades have Muslim fundamentalists come into the spotlight in world affairs. In several countries—Afghanistan, Jordan, Libya, Sudan, and Yemen—they enjoy widespread and vociferous public support to the point of dominating public life and intimidating their civic rivals. In some others—Algeria, Egypt, Saudi Arabia, Syria, and Turkey—they are a minority but seem to be gaining ground against the secularists who still control the governments. In still others—Iran, Indonesia, Morocco—the balance is neatly held and can shift momentarily. But it is evident that fundamentalist Islam is a potentially major determinant of international affairs in the twenty-first century. In very retically wealthy, while the ever more numerous poor got the merest crumbs from their table. Surrounded by his elite friends, the shah compounded the bad impression by spending huge sums on personal and familial luxuries.

Khomeini had begun denouncing the shah's mistakes in the 1960s. Even in exile he was regarded as the spirit of the opposition in Tehran. He was adept at linking the devout villagers with the urban middle classes and reform-minded intellectuals who were coming to hate the shah's misrule. The police attempt to beat the increasing numbers of street demonstrators into flight only created martyrs for the movement. Thousands were arrested weekly; their places were instantly filled by new recruits. The peasant soldiers watched their parents and relatives being beaten, and the army became too unreliable to be used against the demonstrators. From his waiting place in Paris, Khomeini's messengers flew back and forth carrying instructions to the faithful. They boiled down to one demand: the shah and all he stood for must go.

When Khomeini took over, the world knew nothing of him or what he desired. That changed very soon, as he imposed strict Qur'anic standards on every aspect of Iran's constitutional and social affairs. He generally opposed all non-Muslim views but was especially contemptuous of the West and, above all, the Americans. Regarding the U.S. government as the foreign power most responsible for Iran's misery, he cut off all relations and began whipping up crowd hatred of the "Great Satan" in Washington. In November 1979, the demonstrators broke into the U.S. embassy and took fifty-two hostages in an attempt to force the Washington authorities to turn over the ailing shah to revolutionary justice in Tehran. The shah soon died of cancer, but the hostages were held for over a year until their release was negotiated.

By then, Khomeini (who never took an official post but directed all policy in Tehran) was looked upon in the West as a deranged tyrant. His rigid views and his conviction that he had supernatural approval made it next to impossible to approach him with realistic compromises. While the Cold War raged, the West was delighted to see him attack Iran's small Communist Party and to listen to his denunciation of "godless Marxism," but he was equally adamant against the democracies and all they stood for. His own country seemed on the verge of civil war when he died, but the transition of power went smoothly, with clerics of the ayatollah's type gradually giving way to more moderate politicians.

Khomeini's legacies to his people will long be the subject of acrid dispute. While many regarded him as a saint, his ideas were always opposed by a hard core of secularists, which has grown since his death and the reinstitution of a parliamentary government.

FOR REFLECTION

Do you believe that the ayatollah's attitude toward the U.S. government was justifiable? Is taking hostages from among officials of a foreign country an unheard-of action in modern times? Can you give examples?

cent days, the emergence of Al Qaida, the network of Muslim terrorists headed by the Arab Osama bin Laden and presumed responsible for the September 2001 attack on New York's skyscrapers, has put a different and much more immediately menacing face on the fundamentalist movement.

THE IRANIAN REVOLUTION

Three outstanding events or processes in the twentieth century have together defined many of the spiritual and material bases of the Muslim universe. The first was the establishment of the secular Republic of Turkey by Mustafa Kemal Ataturk. The second was the oil boycott of 1973–1974, organized and implemented by the Arab members of the **Organization of Petroleum Exporting Countries (OPEC).** The third was the Iranian Revolution of 1979, led by the Ayatollah Khomeini.

The modern state of Iran is the successor to the great Persian empires of ancient times. Its inhabitants, who are not Arabs, have been Muslims almost without exception since the Arab conquest in the 640s. In many epochs, the Iranians have been among Islam's most distinguished leaders. Nevertheless, they are separated from the majority of Muslims in one decisive way: they are Shiite Muslims and have been that sect's major stronghold for seven centuries.

Modern Iran came into being in the aftermath of World War I, when a military officer named Reza Shah Pahlavi (ruled 1925–1941) seized power from a discredited traditional dynasty and established an authoritarian regime modeled on his Turkish neighbor. His son, **Muhammad Reza Shah Pahlavi** (ruled 1941–1979) continued his Westernizing and secularizing policies. By the 1970s, considerable progress had been made in the cities, at least. The country had a substantial middle class, technically advanced industry (especially connected with petroleum engineering), an extensive Western educational system, and mechanized agriculture. Its immense oil deposits generated sufficient income to pay for large-scale government projects of every sort, and these proved very profitable for a select few contractors and their friends in the bureaucracy.

Ski Resort, Iran 1994. The Muslim women in their black chadors presumably are not going to ski. Ayatollah Khomeini's exhortation to recover the pious lifestyle was backed up by public humiliation of those women who defied it and continued to dress in the Western manner. *(David Turnley/Corbis)*

But the shah had neglected to see to the well-being of much of the urban and most of the rural population. Government corruption was universal, the army and police were all-powerful, and traditional religious values were held in more or less open contempt by the ruling clique. On top of that, many people viewed the shah and his advisers as slavish puppets of the West, who had neither understanding nor respect for the greatness of Islamic Persia.

The upshot was a massive swell of protest, inspired and led by the exiled **Ayatollah** (theologian) **Ruhollah Khomeini.** Under the banners of "Back to the Qur'an" and "Iran for the Iranians," Khomeini skillfully led his people into revolution and then returned in 1979 to take the helm of the government that succeeded the bewildered shah. For the next decade, the ayatollah implemented what he had promised Iran from afar: a thoroughly Islamic, uncompromisingly anti-Western, antisecular government. Resistance to this course was brushed aside by his authoritarian attitude that made no concessions. The atheistic Soviets were denounced almost as heartily as the Americans, whose long-standing support for the shah as a Cold War counter against the Soviets had

earned Khomeini's especial hatred. (For more about Khomeini, see the Religion and Philosophy box.)

In the ayatollah's Iran, Muslim fundamentalism found its most dramatic and forceful exponent so far. But it was by no means a necessarily attractive scenario for other, secular Muslim states, and within a year of the ayatollah's return, Iran was at war with a Muslim neighbor. In 1980, Iraq attempted to take advantage of the upheaval next door to seize some disputed oil-bearing territory from Iran. The eight-year conflict that followed was one of the bloodiest in recent history, claiming at least one million lives (mainly Iranian) and dealing both countries blows from which they have not yet recovered.

With its much smaller population, Iraq would have been defeated early in the war had it not been for the active financial support and armaments supplied by other states. Led by the Saudis, many Arab leaders thought that the ayatollah's brand of fundamentalism posed a serious threat to all of them and wished to see it contained or defeated. The rabid anti-Western positions embraced by Khomeini (notably, the holding of U.S. hostages in 1979–1980) also induced the Western states to support Iraq in various covert ways, actions that they would soon regret.

THE OIL WEAPON

What was the number one history-making event or series of events in the 1970s, as seen in retrospect? Most would now say that it was not the Cold War between the United States and the Soviet Union, or the American adventure in Vietnam, or the rapid steps being taken toward European unity. It was the worldwide economic crisis started by the OPEC oil boycott.

In 1973, the favoritism shown by the West and especially the United States toward Israel was answered during that year's brief Arab-Israeli conflict (sometimes known as the **Yom Kippur War** because it began on the Jewish holiday) by the Arabs' decision to withhold all oil shipments to the United States and its NATO allies. Since the Middle East had long been the dominant supplier of world petroleum markets, the impact was immediate and catastrophic. Prices of crude oil quadrupled within a few months. The economies of the Western nations and Japan were put under great strain. Even the United States, which came closest to oil self-sufficiency of all the affected nations, faced shortages.

A major recession, the worst since the 1930s, with unemployment rates zooming to 13 percent in western Europe, was one of the results. Soaring energy costs caused consumer prices for practically every necessity of life to spiral upward even as demand decreased. As mass unemployment was accompanied by double-digit inflation in the mid- and late 1970s, a new word came into the vocabulary—*stagflation.* This unlovely compound referred to the worst of all economic worlds, the combination of stagnation and inflation.

The postwar boom, which had lasted a quarter of a century, definitely ended, and most of the West remained in a painful business recession well into the 1980s. Some countries have never entirely recovered from the great oil shock. Their labor markets have been permanently altered by the disappearance of many blue-collar production jobs that depended on cheap energy. (The 1973 shock was later reinforced by events in Iran. In 1979–1980, international oil prices again quadrupled for several years because of fears of a supply pinch following the Iranian Revolution and the outbreak of the Iran–Iraq War.)

This windfall in Arab oil profits did not last more than a decade, and the OPEC nations were eventually forced to adjust their prices to a diminished world demand. But the brief havoc in oil supplies—which the West had always thought were shielded from producer-country influence—established a new respect for Arab political potency. What Western consumers knew after 1973 was that a handful of heretofore peripheral and insignificant Middle Eastern and North African kingdoms had risen on a tide of crude oil to become at least transitory major players in world politics. The surge in price made some of the major producers (notably, the largest of all, Saudi Arabia) immensely rich in dollars, and money here, as elsewhere, spelled both economic and political power. No longer could any industrial nation afford to ignore what OPEC was doing and planning. For the first time in at least two centuries, the Muslim East had attained importance through its own initiatives, rather than merely because of what one or another alien group was doing there.

The Gulf War

In 1990, the ambitious and bloodstained Iraqi dictator Saddam Hussein, victor in the just-concluded conflict with Iran, believed the time ripe for a settlement of accounts with his oil-rich neighbor at the head of the Persian Gulf, Kuwait. In an undisguised grab for additional oil revenues, Saddam invaded the tiny country and declared it annexed, thinking that he would present the world with an accomplished fact backed up by a large and well-armed army.

To his surprise, the West reacted violently and was very soon joined by most of the non-Western world, including the Soviet Union and most Arabs. These latter feared the effects of opening up the question of the territorial borders derived from the colonial era, and they also rejected Saddam's transparent bid to become the pan-Arab arbiter of the Middle East. Almost all of the United Nations presented Saddam with the most unified front that organization had seen since its inception. The Iraqi dictator refused to back down, however. It took a powerful air and ground attack led by the U.S. on his forces in 1991 to induce him to withdraw with heavy losses (the Gulf War). As of 2002, multiple military and economic sanctions against Saddam's government imposed by the United Nations have as yet failed to frustrate his capabilities of making war and topple him from power, and Saddam continues to defy his myriad enemies in and outside Iraq. The Middle East remains the world's most intransigent area for diplomatic or coercive peacemaking.

THE MUSLIM NATIONS TODAY

The relative importance of the Muslim nations in today's world can be viewed from sharply differing perspectives. Some observers, who focus on the continuing weakness of the domestic political infrastructure and the technological dependency of most Muslim societies on Western societies, tend to dismiss the twentieth-century resurgence as a temporary "blip" that will have no permanent effects on the overall picture of Western world domination.

Others, focusing on such disparate phenomena as the shocking capabilities and determination of the Al Qaida terrorists, the continuance of the Saddam Hussein regime

War and Famine in Afghanistan. Veiled Afghani women line up for a distribution of wheat in the city of Herat a few days after the anti-Taliban forces of the Northern Alliance took over the city in January 2002. Afghanistan has been wracked by more than twenty years of warfare, beginning with the Soviet army's invasion in 1979 and continuing to the U.S. campaign against the Al Qaida network of Osama bin Laden. *(AP Photo/Vahid Slemi)*

in Iraq and Mu'ammar Qaddafi in Libya, and the sophisticated financial initiatives of the Saudi Arabian government to protect its oil revenues, are of the contrary opinion. They believe that the Muslims have placed themselves firmly and permanently on the world stage. In this view, the West would be making a huge mistake to leave the Islamic peoples out of its calculations on any important international issue. It appears that the latter view is becoming generally accepted.

The Arabs

It is difficult to generalize accurately about the Arab nations. The various Middle East countries inhabited by Arabs are commonly known by their control over much of the world's oil and their enmity with Israel. But even these supposedly basic facts are subject to sharp variances both over time and between countries. The oil trade has become much less confrontational and less politicized, but the Arab–Israel hostility seems resistant to any solution. Even the extraordinary diplomatic efforts of U.S. president Bill Clinton in the early 1990s, like those of President Jimmy Carter before him, produced only a mirage of peace, rather than its actuality. In 1993, Clinton was able to induce the government of Israel and the Palestinian Liberation Organization (PLO) to sign a "path to peace" agreement. But in the past several years, this so-called Oslo Accord has been repeatedly tossed aside by hardliners on both sides, and the bloodshed resumed. At times it has appeared that the on-going conflict is needed by some of the Arab leadership to divert popular attention from their domestic economic problems, which have persisted despite both oil profit windfalls and international aid. At other times, the Jewish leadership has been deliberately provocative in its assertions of control over Palestinian people and places and its support of new Israeli settlements.

Egypt, with the largest population of the Arab world, is in an especially difficult position. With few resources beyond the fields of the Nile valley, it has become entirely dependent on U.S. and World Bank assistance and migration to rich Saudi Arabia to maintain an even minimal living standard for its people. Economic desperation, especially in contrast to the oil wealth of the Saudis, Iraqis, and others, has added fuel to other resentments, which have given rise to a militant Islamic fundamentalism in Egypt and other nations.

But the potential resolution of the Arab-Israeli conflict also poses the danger that without the common enemy, the Arab nations will be forced to recognize what most leaders already tacitly acknowledge: they lack any mutual policies and goals except for adherence in one degree or another to Islam. And that fact will almost certainly fuel the rising antipathies between the fundamentalists and the current ruling group of secularist and nationalist politicians. The clash between these two focuses on the struggle for the allegiance of the rural majority.

Will the villagers continue to support the urban politicians who have promised them a better life but have delivered on that promise only partially and sporadically since 1945? The secularists include such very different past and present personalities as **Gamal Abdel Nasser** and Anwar Sadat in Egypt, Saddam Hussein in Iraq, Ahmad Ben Bella in Algeria, King Hussein in Jordan, and Hafiz al-Assad in Syria. All of them wanted to lead their nations into a Westernized technology and economy, while giving perhaps only lip service to Western-style political and civil rights.

On the other side of the equation are the Islamic fundamentalists, led by such men as the former associates of Khomeini in Iran, the members of the terrorist network established under Osama bin Laden, the Afghani Taliban movement, and the leaders of the Muslim Brotherhoods, as well as many others whose names are as yet unknown to the world. They are quite willing to accept most of the modern world's material and technical achievements, but only if the power of selection remains securely in their own hands, and if it is understood that the society using these achievements must be fully in tune with the words of the Qur'an as interpreted by themselves. Between these two visions of proper government in the Arab world—and by extension, the Muslim world—there seems to be little common ground.

The Non-Arabic Nations

The Muslim countries of Africa and southern Asia have thus far shown little interest in coordinating their activity, foreign or domestic, with the Arabs. This attitude is partly due to the circumstances in which Islam was introduced and grew in these parts of the globe. As the offspring of converts who retained strong bonds to their previous culture, the African and Asian Muslims have not generally been as single-minded and exclusive as their Arab fellows in religious affairs.

Since attaining independence in 1949, Indonesia, the largest Muslim state and boasting the fourth largest population in the world, has felt its way forward by the technique of "guided democracy," originally under the charismatic leader of the anticolonial struggle, Sukarno and, until 1998, under the secularist General Suharto. (Guided democracy claims to be more authentic in representing the popular will than the Western parliamentary governments. It purports to reconcile clashing points of view by the benign guidance of a single leader.) Preoccupied with ethnic-religious conflicts and the problems created by a burgeoning population with quite limited resources (rich oil deposits are by far the most important), the government has shown no interest in forming associations even with nearby Muslim states. In this melting pot of religions, fundamentalism is growing but still relatively minor as a political force.

Pakistan and Bangladesh are the next largest Muslim states. Throughout its short history, Pakistan has been entirely occupied with its recurrently dangerous quarrel with India over Kashmir. Both countries now possess nuclear weapons; both have large populations of minorities who have little identification with the governing groups. In most recent times the chaos in neighboring Afghanistan has made Pakistan more important in Western eyes, balancing the former tilt towards India. Internally, a series of military takeovers—the latest of which is now in its third year— has prevented any real commitment to democratic politics, which is perhaps impossible given the huge political and economic problems created by events over which the government has comparatively little control.

On its side, Bangladesh has been struggling since its creation with abject poverty in an economy that ranks as one of the world's poorest. Lacking any notable human, mineral, or energy resources, both of these countries have remained on the periphery of both Muslim and world affairs and are heavily dependent on aid from foreign sources ranging from China (Pakistan) to the United States (both). Neither has shown any interest in making common policy with other Muslim countries (they could not get along even with one another in an earlier joint state). Both have been ruled by secularist generals or their civilian accomplices and puppets most of the time since their creation (see the Tradition and Innovation box for an interesting—but temporary—exception in the case of Pakistan's Benazir Bhutto). Fundamentalist Islam is as yet only weakly represented in both of these states but is gaining ground in Pakistan, where there are millions of refugees from wartorn Afghanistan.

As a summary labeling, the politics and governments of the Muslim states were still far from democratic in most instances. The monopolistic party with an authority figure at its head was the rule (as random examples, Hosni Mubarak in Egypt, Saddam Hussein in Iraq, and Mu'ammar Qaddafi in Libya). Ethnic minorities and/or religious "deviants" were treated roughly by the central authorities if they showed the slightest resistance. Civil wars, declared and undeclared, raged in several nations, both between competing sections of the Muslim populace and between Muslims and their religious and cultural rivals (Iraq, Sudan, Algeria). Whole regions containing groups unfriendly to the regime were systematically punished, sometimes by armed force, as in Turkey and Iraq.

The domestic economic condition varied from reasonably stable (the oil-blessed Middle East) to very shaky (most of North and West Africa). Indonesia and Malaysia were so badly shaken by recent fiscal and economic miseries as to bring down entrenched dictators, governments, and parties. Even rich Saudi Arabia proved not immune from the worldwide recession of 2001–2002. In most countries, "connections" with the bureaucracy were usually necessary for successful enterprise, corruption was rampant, and necessary government investments in infrastructure (roads, airports, sewer lines, and the like) were still conspicuous by their absence. All in all, the reentry of Islam into a prominent place in the modern world has not been easy, and the ride ahead promises to be perhaps even rougher, not only for the countries concerned but also for their non-Muslim neighbors.

WINDS OF CHANGE

In November 1988, the first national election in many years allowed Pakistanis to select a new parliament and prime minister. The voters responded by selecting the first woman ever to head a Muslim country: Benazir Bhutto, head of the Pakistan People's Party.

Bhutto had been involved deeply in politics since her twenties, when she returned from England to her native land. Her father, Ali Bhutto, was then the prime minister; he had been the People's Party leader since several years earlier, when he had won a much disputed election against the candidate of the Pakistani army. Only a few months after his daughter's return, in September 1977, Ali Bhutto was removed from office and placed under army arrest. Eighteen months later, he was put on trial for murder, found guilty by a military court, and executed despite worldwide protests.

Meanwhile, Benazir Bhutto was placed under house arrest, and she remained there for the better part of the period between 1977 and 1984. The military clique that ruled Pakistan in that epoch was clearly apprehensive of the political appeal "this impetuous girl" exerted on her father's followers. Bhutto had gained some experience in politics during her undergraduate years at Radcliffe College (the female undergraduate school at Harvard) and more at Oxford, where she was the first foreign woman to be

Benazir Bhutto. (© Teit Hornback/Gamma Liaison)

elected head of the debating club, the Oxford Union. Even while being held under arrest, she was able to take the reins of the People's Party. General Zia Khan, the president of the republic, repeatedly tried to persuade Bhutto to agree to be silent and take no part in public affairs in return for her freedom, but she was not so inclined despite occasional bouts of solitary confinement as punishment. In 1984, an exasperated Zia forced her into exile.

In 1986, a discouraged military stepped down from day-to-day political leadership and revoked the martial law it had imposed nine years earlier. Bhutto came home at once and was greeted by the largest crowd ever seen at a political function since Pakistani independence forty years earlier. Finally, national elections were permitted in 1988. Bhutto displayed a flair for populist campaigning clearly enjoying "pressing the flesh" of her constituents.

Her party won a solid plurality, which put her in the office of prime minister, a post she held for less than a year when her party was forced out on charges of corruption. Corruption there undoubtedly was, but the real issues were gender—there were still many who could not swallow the idea of a female leading a Muslim land—and traditional political rivalries. Bhutto's party lost the 1990 election to a coalition of religious and traditionalist parties. In the chaos of Pakistani politics, however, nothing seems to be of long duration, and in the elections in 1993, the People's Party came back again, and Bhutto with it. This time her government lasted over two years before it was again forced to resign by a parliament dominated by the People's Party's enemies. At this writing, the Pakistani military has again taken charge of the government, and Bhutto is once more on the sidelines, perhaps permanently.

Bhutto has countered her particular vulnerability as a female in a strongly patriarchal Islamic land with considerable finesse. Western reporters repeatedly attempted to "get a story" in the early days of her governmental career by asking her to comment on the differences between the liberated college student life she led in her twenties and the responsibilities of leadership of a devout Islamic country. But she eluded these questions by asserting that she is a "Muslim woman in a Muslim land" and that she has no intention of saying or doing anything that might offend the principles of her patriotic fellow citizens. Bhutto knows too well that one of the most potent weapons in the hands of her political enemies is the suspicion that this Western-educated, glamorous, and outspoken woman must at times have deviated from the strict standards of seclusion and behavior that the Qur'an and fundamentalist Islam impose on females. So far, at least, she has managed to stay one jump ahead of her detractors and remains active in Pakistani affairs despite the recurrent military suspension of civil government in that unhappy country.

FOR REFLECTION

Do you think that there is a place for women in the highest offices of a fundamentalist Islamic country, or should the conflicts necessarily engendered among the citizenry by such ideas rule out such ambitions?

SUMMARY

The Muslim world has returned to an important role in world politics and economics during the twentieth century after two or three centuries of insignificance. Making up about one-sixth of the globe's population, Muslims from West Africa to Southeast Asia have been able to reassert themselves into Western consciousness, especially since the oil boycott of the 1970s. The first real change was the creation of the secular Turkish republic after World War I. This state served as a model to many other Muslim thinkers and politicians and fostered the creation of nationalist associations throughout the Middle East and North Africa. The Arab-Israeli struggle over Palestine was a galvanizing force from the 1930s onward to the present. It was followed by the creation of the Arab-sponsored Organization of Petroleum Exporting Countries, the oil boycott, and the rise of an aggressive Islamic fundamentalism in the 1970s and 1980s. Fueled by a decade of extraordinary profits from oil, some Muslim countries have experienced a tremendous burst of modernization. Others, lacking oil, have remained at or near the bottom of the world prosperity scale.

After a long oblivion, Islamic religious purists are staging a strong comeback in several countries, notably since the revolution in Iran. Although all previous Pan-Arabic and Pan-Islamic appeals have foundered on sectarian and national rivalries, it is possible that the present surge of fundamentalism could erect and maintain such an alliance. The fundamentalists' uncompromising rejection of Western ideals such as religious toleration and political equality, combined with their appeal to an alienated underclass in poverty-stricken Muslim countries, makes them a potentially dangerous force not only for their secular rivals at home but also for international peace.

TEST YOUR KNOWLEDGE

1. After World War I, the chief exception to continued colonial rule among Muslim countries was
   a. Egypt.
   b. Turkey.
   c. Iraq.
   d. Lebanon.
2. The historical movement to unite all Arabs under single political leadership is
   a. Arabs First!
   b. Pan-Arabism.
   c. the Arab Awakening.
   d. Arab Unity.
3. Kemal Ataturk believed that
   a. Turks must remain Muslim to retain a national identity.
   b. Turks must expand beyond their old borders to solve their national woes.
   c. Turks had an obligation to liberate their Muslim comrades in Europe.
   d. Turks must adopt a Western lifestyle.
4. The state of Israel traces its creation to
   a. an Arab-Jewish pact in World War II.
   b. a United Nations decision to create two states from British Palestine in 1947.
   c. U.S. military intervention after World War II.
   d. a war against Egypt and Syria in 1963.
5. At the time of the Balfour Declaration on Palestine, that country's population
   a. was in its majority Muslim Arabs.
   b. was about half Arab and half Jew.
   c. was almost zero.
   d. was polled on its preferences for the postwar era.
6. The trigger for the Arab-sponsored oil boycott in 1973 was
   a. the U.S. air raid on Colonel Qaddafi in Libya.
   b. the Israeli raid on Yasir Arafat's headquarters in Tunisia.
   c. the support given by the West to Israel in the Yom Kippur War.
   d. the revenge of Saudi Arabia for the West's support of the shah in Iran.
7. The Iranian Revolution in 1979 was aimed against
   a. the shah of Iran and his Soviet backers.
   b. the shah and his U.S. backers.
   c. the communists who had seized power.
   d. the Sunni Muslims who had captured the shah.
8. The Muslim-majority state with the largest population is
   a. Pakistan.
   b. Indonesia.
   c. Algeria.
   d. Saudi Arabia.

IDENTIFICATION TERMS

Ataturk, Mustafa Kemal

Balfour Declaration

Khomeini, Ayatollah
  Ruhollah

Muhammad Reza Shah
  Pahlavi

mandates

Nasser, Colonel Gamal
  Abdel

Organization of Petroleum
  Exporting Countries
  (OPEC)

Palestine Liberation
  Organization (PLO)

Yom Kippur War

Zionists

INFOTRAC COLLEGE EDITION

Enter the search term "Ataturk" using Key Words.

Enter the search term "Palestine" using the Subject Guide.

Enter the search term "Iran" using the Subject Guide.

57

THE MARXIST COLLAPSE

M*en have always been mad, and those who think they can cure them are the maddest of all.*

VOLTAIRE

IN 1989, AN ASTOUNDED WORLD watched the spectacle of the impossible happening in eastern Europe: the rapid collapse of the Marxist communist system. A year later, the doubly impossible happened in the Soviet Union: the peaceable abolition of the Communist Party's control of government. One year after that, the Soviet Union itself was abolished, and its component ethnic regions became independent states.

Rarely, if ever, has such a totally unexpected and complete reversal of the existing state of international political affairs occurred in such a brief span. The Cold War—which had defined all other international arrangements for a long generation—was abruptly terminated. And an integrated system of political and military controls, governing an economic apparatus that had ruled from fifty to seventy-five years over 300 million people, was simply thrown into the ashcan and the table swept clean. The most memorable Revolution of the Proletariat, so vehemently proclaimed by the followers of Karl Marx, turned out to be the one that ended the reign of Marxism itself.

THE IMMEDIATE POSTWAR ERA

As we saw earlier, the Soviet government under Josef Stalin emerged triumphant from the "Great Patriotic War." The Red Army stood in the center of Europe, hailed by some, at least, as the liberator from the Nazi yoke. While the impatient Americans quickly demobilized their forces, Stalin proceeded to reap the fruits of his very costly victory over the Nazi enemy.

The Communization of Eastern Europe

Under the Allies' Yalta Agreement of 1945, the Russians were to carry through free, democratic national elections in the eastern European countries as soon as conditions permitted. The divisions among the Big Three (Britain, the Soviet Union, and the United States), which became evident at the war's end, made it impossible to specify more exactly when and how the elections should be held. The Yalta Agreement, was in fact a tacit acknowledgment by the West that Stalin and his Red Army would be in control east of the Elbe for at least the immediate postwar years. The best that

Washington and London could hope for was the election of governments that would be Soviet-friendly without being outright puppets.

But Stalin, whose suspicion of the West was intense, was not inclined to accommodate himself to any type of independent leadership among the eastern Europeans. As early as 1944, in Bulgaria, Yugoslavia, and Albania, communists had seized power through armed resistance movements that had fought the Nazi occupiers and their domestic collaborators. The governments so composed were not yet clearly satellites of Moscow, though communists played leading roles.

In Romania and Hungary, the Soviet-supervised intimidation of the numerous anticommunists took longer. Peasant anticommunist parties held on until 1947, when they were finally eliminated by arresting and executing their leaders. In Greece, however, a wartime agreement resulted in Stalin's abandoning the Greek communists when they attempted to seize power through an uprising. Stalin's failure to support the communists in the civil war (1944–1948) that ensued assured the eventual victory of the royalist side supported by the West.

Alone among the eastern European border states, Czechoslovakia had never had unpleasant experiences with Soviet Russia, and the Czechoslovak Communist Party had sizable popular support. So aided, the communist leaders pulled off a bloodless coup d'état in early 1948. They immediately installed a thoroughly Stalinist regime.

But the vital test case of whether the West would accept Stalin's long-term plans for eastern Europe was Poland. During the war, the Polish wartime government-in-exile had been promised the firm support of the Allies in recovering their country. Many Poles fought bravely in the British Royal Air Force (RAF) and distinguished themselves in the Allied Italian and French campaigns. In 1944, Stalin broke with the Polish exile government in London over the question of who was responsible for the massacre in the Katyn Forest (thousands of Polish army officers had been murdered in Soviet-occupied Poland in 1940) and then put together a group of Polish communists to act as his cat's-paw in liberated Poland. Despite Western protests, the pro-Soviet group, backed by the Red Army, gradually made political life impossible for their opponents. After a series of highly predictable elections under Soviet "supervision," Poland's decidedly anticommunist and anti-Russian population was forced in 1947 to accept a Soviet satellite regime. The Baltic countries of Estonia, Latvia, and Lithuania received even less consideration. The advancing Red Army simply treated them as recovered provinces of Soviet Russia.

Thus, throughout eastern Europe, a total of about 110 million people from the Baltic to the Adriatic Sea had been forced under Stalinist rule by Soviet puppets. If truly free elections had been held in most of the area, the Communist Party would have received perhaps 10 to 20 percent of the vote, but in the circumstances that fact was irrelevant.

The Stalinist Regime

The Soviet Union recovered rapidly from the horrendous damage caused by the Nazi invasion, thanks partly to stripping the Soviet Zone of Germany of all industrial goods and also to the forced "cooperation" of the eastern European satellites. For the first several years, the postwar economic policy was a continuation of already familiar Soviet goals and methods. The lion's share of investment went into either new construction or reconstruction of war-ravaged heavy industry and transportation. The first postwar Five-Year Plan reached its goals in considerably less time than planned. By 1950, the Soviet Union was an industrial superpower as well as a military one. It surpassed faltering Britain and still overshadowed recovering Germany, France, and Italy. New Soviet oilfields in central Asia, new metallurgical combines in the Urals, and new Siberian gas and precious metal deposits were coming on stream constantly.

But in basic consumer goods, the postwar era was even worse than the deprived 1930s. The housing shortage reached crisis proportions in the cities. To have a private bath and kitchen, one had to be either a high party official or an artistic/literary favorite of the day. Personal consumption was held down artificially by every means available to a totalitarian government: low wages, deliberate scarcity, diversion of investment to heavy industry, and constant propaganda stressing the necessity of sacrificing to "build a socialist tomorrow."

In the eastern European communist states, the backward agrarian economies of the prewar era were changed by the same methods employed in the Soviet Union in the 1930s: coercion of the peasantry, forced (and wildly inefficient) industrialization, and the absolute control of the national budget and all public affairs by the single party. The eastern European Communist Parties and their leaders were more or less exact replicas of the Soviet Communist Party and Stalin from the late 1940s until at least the late 1950s. The positive and negative results they obtained resembled those obtained in the Soviet Union fifteen to twenty years earlier, with one important exception: unlike Stalin, who transformed himself into a Russian nationalist when it suited him, the Soviet puppets in eastern Europe were never able during his lifetime to appeal to the deep-seated nationalism of their own peoples. On the contrary, they bore the burden of being in the general public's eye what they were in fact: minions of a foreign state.

In 1948, Stalin declared the Yugoslav leader Marshal Tito an enemy of communism and undertook a campaign against him that embraced everything but actual war. Tito's crime was that he had objected to the complete subordination of his party and his country to Soviet goals—a process that was well under way everywhere else in eastern Europe.

After a period of hesitation, the United States decided to assist Tito with economic aid. By so doing, Washington allowed the Yugoslav renegade to escape almost certain catastrophe for his country and himself. Tito, still a stalwart Marxist, responded by changing his foreign policies from unquestioning support of the Soviet Union to a prickly neutrality. By 1956, Yugoslavia was busily experimenting with its own brand of social engineering, a peculiar hybrid of capitalism and socialism that for a time seemed to work well enough to attract considerable interest among many African and Asian nations.

From Stalin to Brezhnev

Tito's heresy was the beginning of the slow breakup of international Marxism into two competing and even hostile camps. The phases of the breakup can best be marked by looking at the Soviet leadership and its policies after the death of Stalin (by a stroke, supposedly) in 1953.

Goulash Communism

Nikita Khrushchev (1894–1974), a longtime member of the Politburo, succeeded to the leadership first of the Communist Party and then of the Soviet state by gradual steps between 1953 and 1955. A son of peasants, Khrushchev was a very different sort of individual than Stalin. Having suffered in fear through the Stalinist purges himself, he was determined that the party, and not the secret police, would be the seat of final power. By 1957, the dreaded KGB had been put back into its cage, and Khrushchev, after a couple of close calls, had succeeded in breaking the Stalinist wing of the party that considered him to be the heedless and ignorant underminer of the system it believed indefinitely necessary.

Khrushchev's difficulties within the hierarchy of the CPSU sometimes revolved around his crude and volatile personality, but substantive frictions occurred over foreign and domestic policy as well. In foreign policy, Khrushchev allowed the tensions with the Maoist Chinese party to reach a complete break in 1959, splitting the vaunted unity of the world Marxist movement and introducing the unheard-of scandal of competing Marxist governments. In 1961, despite his proclamation of **peaceful coexistence,** he challenged the West and particularly the new U.S. president, John F. Kennedy, by allowing the Soviets' East German satellite to build the **Berlin Wall** in defiance of existing access agreements. Finally, Khrushchev took and lost the huge gamble of the Cuban Missile Crisis of 1962. To save Fidel Castro's vulnerable communist regime in Cuba, the Soviets tried to introduce atomic missiles within ninety miles of Florida (see Chapter 51) and were forced to give way by the United States.

But Khrushchev ultimately was brought down more by his domestic political innovations than by his foreign policy. Most important by far was his attack on Stalin at the Twentieth Congress of the Party in February 1956. At this highest party meeting, Khrushchev gave a long, supposedly **secret speech** in which he detailed some (though by no means all) of the sins of the dead idol, whom a generation of Russians had been trained to think of as a genius and incomparable savior. Khrushchev's denunciation, which immediately became known outside as well as inside Russia, marked a turning point in international Marxist affairs. Never again would Stalin occupy the same position in the communist pantheon and never again would a European communist leader be looked upon as a demigod.

Foreign reactions soon appeared. In the autumn of 1956, first the Poles and then the Hungarians attempted to act on Khrushchev's revelations about Stalin by shaking off Soviet political and military controls. Both were unsuccessful, but the Soviet party would never again have the same iron control over its satellites. Grudgingly, the CPSU had to admit that there were "many roads to socialism" and that each communist party should be allowed to find its own way there.

Secondarily, Khrushchev's "harebrained" attempts to change the structure of the CPSU and to install a mistaken agrarian policy contributed to his political demise. Party leaders came to see him more as a debit than an asset to Russian power and prestige, and in 1964 Khrushchev was unceremoniously ushered into premature retirement by his enemies within the Politburo. He lived out his final years in seclusion, but at least he was not executed by the new authorities—a welcome departure from the Stalinist model.

Khrushchev confidently expected the Soviet system to outproduce the capitalists in the near future and devoted much effort to improving the lot of the Soviet and eastern European consumers during his ten years in office. He coined the telling phrase "goulash communism" to explain what he wanted: a system that put meat in the pot for every table. Some progress was indeed made in this respect in the 1950s and 1960s when consumption of goods and services rose substantially. The very tight censorship over the arts and literature imposed by Stalin was also loosened temporarily. But the Khrushchev era was by no means a breakthrough into market economics or political democracy. It was an advance only in comparison to what went before.

Stagnation

Khrushchev was replaced by **Leonid Brezhnev** (1906–1982), an apparatchik who had climbed the party ladder by sailing close to the prevailing winds. Worried about the long-term effects of the denunciation of Stalin, Brezhnev and his associates presided over a degree of re-Stalinization of Russian life. He cracked down hard on writers who did not follow party guidelines and on the small but important number of dissidents who attempted to evade censorship by *samizdat* (self-publishing). At the same time, he endorsed Khrushchev's policy of increasing consumption. In the

1970s, the living standards of ordinary Russians finally reached upward to levels that had been current in western Europe in the Great Depression of the 1930s.

The hallmark of Brezhnev's foreign policy was a determination to retain what had been gained for world communism without taking excessive or unnecessary risks. The best example of this attitude was the so-called Brezhnev Doctrine applied in Czechoslovakia in 1968. Several months earlier, Alexander Dubcek, a reformer, had been voted into the leadership of the still-Stalinist Czech Communist Party and proceeded to attempt to give his country "socialism with a human face." The Soviet leadership watched this loosening of the reins with intense and increasing concern. The generals warned that Czechoslovakia must not be allowed to escape its satellite status.

In **August 1968** Brezhnev acted: Soviet and eastern European army units poured into Czechoslovakia in overwhelming numbers. The Czechs had no alternative but to surrender. Dubcek was forced out, and a faithful puppet installed in his place. Despite verbal denunciations, the Western countries accepted this resolution of the issue without lifting a hand. As in Hungary twelve years earlier, it was clear that the NATO nations were not prepared to risk a world war on behalf of the freedom of eastern Europeans. Anticommunists in the satellite nations realized that their freedom to act independently could only come about if (1) the Soviet Union gave them leave or (2) the Soviet Union itself radically changed its system of government. Neither prospect seemed likely within a lifetime in 1968.

Brezhnev remained in power (1964–1982) longer than any Soviet leader except Stalin, but his effect on the Soviet state was in no way comparable. Where Stalin had turned the Soviet Union on its head, Brezhnev was intensely conservative. His eighteen years as chief of the state and party were marked by a general loss of momentum in every aspect of Soviet life except the military. Opportunists and career seekers completely dominated the CPSU. Corruption in its top ranks (starting with Brezhnev's own son-in-law) was rampant and went unpunished. Using party connections to obtain personal privileges, such as rights to buy in special stores and permission for foreign travel, was taken for granted. Intellectuals and artists had once considered it an

MAP 57.1 Eastern Europe and Former Soviet Union. Although in eastern Europe only Yugoslavian borders were changed as an immediate result of the dissolution of the communist regimes, the borders of the Soviet Union were radically rearranged into four independent states and eleven members of a Commonwealth of Independent States (CIS). The Russian Republic is by far the most important of these, followed by Ukraine and Kazakhstan.

honor to join the party, but now its prestige had degenerated to the point that authentically creative people refused to join.

For a time, the increased emphasis on consumer goods in the 1970s masked what was happening to the **command economy**: the overall productivity of Soviet labor was declining while government investments were being misapplied. Pushed by his generals, Brezhnev went along with a huge increase in the military budget to match the U.S. atomic weaponry. Two forces thus converged to squeeze Soviet consumers from about 1975 onward: increased unproductive investment in military hardware and personnel, and declining civilian gross national product.

The *era of stagnation,* as it was later dubbed, made itself apparent in daily life in different ways. For many people, the most depressing was that Soviet living standards continued to lag far behind the West. Instead of catching up by 1980 as Khrushchev had once rashly predicted, the gap was increasing. After sixty-five years of communist promises, Soviet consumers still faced long lines outside shops selling inferior goods; unexplained shortages of meat, produce, and even bread in the cities; a housing shortage that never seemed to improve; and five-year waits to buy the very expensive but poor quality automobiles.

The Soviet Union was actually slipping backward, not just compared with the United States and western Europe but also relative to Japan, South Korea, and Taiwan. In fact, the Soviet Union was rapidly becoming a Third World country in every way except military technology and power. The entire postwar communications revolution had bypassed eastern Europe. Even a private telephone was a rarity for all but the higher party ranks and a few favored urbanites. Computers and their electronic spin-offs were few in number and obsolete compared with those in the West. The efficiency and productivity of communist industry and agriculture in both the Soviet Union and the satellites were far below world standards. They showed no signs of improvement as the ailing Brezhnev wheezed on into the 1980s. Had it not been for recently opened Siberian gas and oil resources, the U.S. Central Intelligence Agency estimated that Soviet domestic product would have actually *diminished* in the last years of Brezhnev's era.

The End of Communist Rule

The problems were not limited to the Soviet Union. By the 1980s, the gerontocracies (rule of the aged) of eastern Europe were also beginning to show signs of doom. Poland, the largest of the Soviet satellites, was the catalyst. The Polish leaders had failed to provide sufficient consumer goods for years and were almost ousted by a nationwide peaceable protest in 1980–1981. This **Solidarity** movement, which was led by shipyard electrician **Lech Walesa,** was then repressed by a communist general, who tried to rule by martial law for the next several years against massive popular resistance. Although Poland was the most dramatic example, by the mid-1980s, all of the eastern European states were experiencing a rising tide of popular rage at the inability of the Marxist leaders to provide a decent standard of living. Yet the leaders insisted on clinging to their obsolete and discredited ideology while attacking their critics as misinformed or subversive.

In 1985, **Mikhail Gorbachev** (b. 1931) rose to the leadership of the Soviet Union promising to reform both the sputtering economy and the CPSU itself. He pushed his program of *perestroika* (restructuring) and *glasnost* (openness) slowly, however, as it became apparent that both the party and much of the populace were fearful of a future in which the old rules might not hold anymore. Two full generations of Soviet citizens had accustomed themselves to "the system," and they had learned that reforms and reformers tended to disappear in disgrace, while the system went on.

Nevertheless, it became clear that economic restructuring and the regeneration of the tired party could not proceed without basic political reforms that allowed free criticism and initiative. In 1987–1988, Gorbachev took the plunge in this direction, spurred by heroic Soviet dissidents such as the physicist Andrei Sakharov, by his own convictions, and by the necessity of reducing the tremendously costly arms race with the United States. As long as that race went on, the money necessary for productive economic investment would not be available, and the communist world would fall further behind the West.

Gorbachev therefore initiated a rapid winding down of the Cold War, meeting several times with President Ronald Reagan of the United States to sign agreements on arms control and troop reductions in divided Europe. Gorbachev also made gestures of reconciliation to China, and in 1989, he withdrew Russian troops from Afghanistan. They had been engaged there in a highly unpopular war—the Soviet Vietnam—on behalf of Soviet puppet rulers since 1979, while the United States supported the opposing guerrilla forces. Afghanistan proved to be the last of the surrogate wars fought between the two rival systems all over the globe since 1946.

The most remarkable of Gorbachev's domestic initiatives was his drive to separate the Communist Party from the government of the Soviet Union. Between 1988 and 1991, the CPSU first secretary presided over a series of moves that transformed the Soviet state. He initiated a true multiparty democracy with a parliament and a radically revised constitution. The CPSU's seventy-year monopoly on political life was abolished. A Congress of People's Deputies and a Supreme Soviet (a standing parliament) were elected and took office in 1989. Immediately, bitter conflicts arose between the worried communist hard-liners in the parliament and its sizable noncommunist minority.

Gorbachev's cautious moves toward democracy had greatly upset the old guard CPSU activists and bureaucrats,

MIKHAIL GORBACHEV
(1931–)

No one realized it at the time, but the accession of Mikhail Gorbachev to supreme power in the Communist Party of the Soviet Union was the beginning of the end of the reign of the communists and, eventually, of the Soviet Union itself. This was hardly the intent of the party members who elected him in 1985 to the position of First Secretary of the CPSU. They expected him to grapple with the many serious problems that were afflicting the country after twenty years of weak leadership and to restore the communist state to a condition of parity with the United States. Above all, the party members were hoping that Gorbachev could break up the logjam in the Soviet economy that had prevented them and their fellow citizens from obtaining the consumer goods that the capitalist West had enjoyed for a generation. They were very tired of the stagnation that had overtaken the Soviet Union since the 1970s in every area except military hardware.

Gorbachev seemed a proper choice for this difficult job. At fifty-four, he was the youngest leader the party had seen in almost half a century. He was a well-educated lawyer with a reputation for practicality and great energy. His early speeches made it clear that he perceived the economy's failings and was determined to do something about them. Assisted by his charming wife Raisa, he was an instant hit ("Gorby! Gorby!") in his ventures abroad as spokesman for a "new USSR," a country that was quite ready to drop its previous threatening gestures and take its place in a rational and peaceable world. Within two years, he had collaborated with President Ronald Reagan to end the Cold War and begin real disarmament in Europe and around the world.

Gorbachev insisted that the communist government and especially its economic aspect needed perestroika (restructuring) to be competitive with the West and satisfy the needs of the citizenry. His attempts to begin this were fiercely opposed by many of the party leaders, who were more concerned about retaining their privileges under the old system than improving the economy. And his measures never went far enough to satisfy the liberal elements. They saw that as long as the so-called command economy existed in Russia, the hoped-for loosening of political and social controls could not be attained. They therefore pushed Gorbachev to reform the government and the organs of censorship, in step with a reformed economy.

Gorbachev responded, but only grudgingly and partially. He truly believed in the Communist Party's mission to bring about a more just and more rational society, not only in Russia but everywhere. He could not accept the view that communism's day had ended, and he originally wished to keep the party in control of the country's politics. He believed that if the CPSU were reformed along the lines he wished, it could legitimately claim that position.

At the same time, Gorbachev marched with the liberals toward a truly open and democratic political system. The party's monopoly on electoral candidates and on the whole political system was dismantled by 1989, when multiparty elections for a new Soviet parliament were held. For the first time in two

Boris Yeltsin Defies the Attempted Coup. In August 1991, Yeltsin, the president of the Russian Republic, mounted a tank drawn up before the Parliament Building to read out his refusal to surrender governmental powers to the hard-liners. At this time, Soviet leader Gorbachev was being held under arrest by the coup participants. (*AP/Wide World Photos*)

generations, Soviet citizens could express themselves without fear, travel abroad, and deal freely with foreign visitors. Dissidents were released from the jails. The once dreaded KGB and other police forces were openly criticized and their powers abolished. Rock music could be freely played, and Western books and newspapers were available to anyone who could afford them. Even the Soviet newspapers printed the news without censorship. All of this was collectively termed *glasnost,* or openness such as Soviets had never seen.

But Gorbachev's problems mounted faster than he could solve them. The non-Russian nationalities everywhere used their new freedom to protest against Russian domination. Soon, several of them declared themselves independent of Moscow and began fighting among themselves for supremacy in the regional scene. The stagnant economy did not respond as hoped to the partial free market introduced by Gorbachev's advisers. The attempt to change gradually was a fiasco. It satisfied no one and had resulted in shortages of all sorts by 1988. An already shaky production and distribution system broke down even further. Russians blamed Gorbachev for their mounting troubles, and non-Russians wanted "out" of a system that was abhorrent to them.

In late summer 1991, the final blows fell on perestroika and on Gorbachev himself. The hard-line element in the Communist Party attempted a poorly organized coup d'état against the government. It failed miserably, not because of Gorbachev but because of the resistance mounted by his chief rival, the demagogic ex-communist Boris Yeltsin. In December the belatedly disillusioned Gorbachev resigned his party and presidential posts and turned over power to Yeltsin. Assured of a good pension but otherwise ignored by a public that had no use for him, he withdrew to become the director of a think tank in Moscow, surrounded by the ghosts of what might have been.

Gorbachev at the Soviet Parliament, 1990. Having invited a much wider and more authentic electoral process to fill the seats in the new Parliament, party leader Gorbachev found himself in the unheard-of position of having to defend his policies before it. Resolute critics such as the great physicist Andrei Sakharov were not easily silenced or put off. *(Sovofoto/Eastfoto)*

FOR REFLECTION

Why didn't Gorbachev attempt a rapid and thorough reform of the economy? What do you think would have been the result if he had? Do you think Gorbachev would have been a better leader than Yeltsin during the '90s or than Vladimir Putin is currently?

but they had not gone nearly far or fast enough to satisfy the growing numbers of anticommunists and the supporters of thoroughgoing reform. A convinced believer in the possibilities of Marxism, the Soviet Union's last president also knew that thorough-going reforms were necessary. Gorbachev was a classic case of the moderate who is criticized by both extremes and cannot bring himself to join either one for survival. The result was his political death in the summer of 1991. An attempted coup by CPSU hard-liners was foiled by the reformers led by Boris Yeltsin, but it simultaneously revealed how naïve Gorbachev had been about his friends and his enemies. He was discredited and was soon pushed aside by Yeltsin. (For more about Gorbachev, see the Exercise of Authority box.)

The failed coup undermined not only Gorbachev's prestige but also the authority of the Communist Party. Yeltsin had already demonstratively resigned from it, and he was now joined by millions of others. Within a few months, the party was declared illegal in Russia (though this decree was later reversed by court action), and its ranks faded to a few hundreds of thousands of embittered and demoralized members. To use Leon Trotsky's cruel words to the anti-Bolsheviks in 1917, it had been "thrown on the ash-heap of history." Its enormous property and financial resources were either taken over by the government of Yeltsin or offered to private hands, in line with a vast "privatization" campaign that was introduced spasmodically, and with great difficulty, into the industrial and consumer economy as a whole. The dismantling of communism in the economic sphere, in fact, was going to prove as challenging as its introduction had been some three-quarters of a century earlier.

The Breakup of the Soviet Union

Gorbachev had failed to recognize the depth of discontent in the Soviet Union. Above all, the fires of nationalism were finding steady fuel from the possibility—for the first time in a century of czarist and communist rule—of expressing ethnic discontents openly. Indeed, glasnost proved to be a tremendous boost to the many peoples in this truly multiethnic union who wished to end their connection with Russia as well as with communism. Among them were Turkic and Mongol Asiatics who were second-class citizens in their own countries, Muslim fundamentalists who rejected Russia and communism with equal passion, and Ukrainian and Baltic nationals who had never accepted their coerced incorporation into the Soviet Union. (See Map 46.2 in Chapter 46.)

Once the reins were loosened, all of the western and southwestern borderlands of the Soviet Union were potential breakaways. Within two years of the initiation of glasnost, Armenians and Azeris were fighting one another over ancient disputes in the far Caucasus, Russian immigrants were being hunted down by wrathful Kazakhs in the new Kazakhstan, and the three Baltic republics of Latvia, Estonia, and Lithuania were demanding total independence. They were soon joined by Ukraine, Georgia, Moldova, and some of the Muslim provinces along the southern borders of Siberia. By mid-1991, the Soviet political structure of a federation dominated by the huge Russian Republic was in a state of collapse. The final straw came in August with the bungled coup, whose conspirators claimed their goal was to reestablish the union, though their first concern was to restore the rule of the Communist Party.

What eventually emerged from the events of 1991 was the **Commonwealth of Independent States (CIS),** whose very name reflects the difficulty of finding some common ground among its varied members once the lid of communist rule was blown off. Eleven of the fifteen Soviet republics opted to join the commonwealth, while four (the Baltic states and Georgia) refused. The CIS was always a very weak confederation—the smaller members would not agree to anything else—and was politically, economically, and territorially dominated by the Russian Republic. In recent years it has become all but meaningless, replaced by bilateral agreements between sovereign states of the former Soviet empire. Russia, now led by Yeltsin's successor, Vladimir Putin, is still a politically and economically fragile entity.

EASTERN EUROPE'S REVOLUTION OF 1989

In the fantastic fall of 1989, the communist governments of Czechoslovakia, East Germany, Bulgaria, and Romania were thrown out by peaceful protests or more violent means. Earlier, the Hungarian communists had saved themselves temporarily only by agreeing to radical changes, and the Polish Communist Party had in desperation agreed to share political power with Walesa's Solidarity. A bit later, in 1990, the Yugoslav and the Albanian Communist Parties were cast aside. Thus, Soviet-style communism was decisively rejected by all who had had the misfortune to live under it for a long generation in eastern Europe.

As in the Soviet Union, the primary cause of the eastern European **Revolution of 1989** was the failure of the system to deliver on its promises of economic progress. This failure reinforced the nationalist resistance to Russian dominion, which most eastern Europeans traditionally felt but which had been temporarily silenced in the postwar years. When Gorbachev showed that he believed in democratic ideas and was not inclined to keep eastern Europe under communist control by force as his Soviet predecessors had, the cork came flying out of the bottle of discontent. (See "The End of the Berlin Wall" box.) How did the eastern Europeans go about ridding their nations of communism? The means varied from the massive, peaceful protests mounted by the East Germans and Czechs (the "Velvet Revolution" in Prague), to the more gradual pressures brought by a wide spectrum of anti-Marxists in Bulgaria and Albania, to the lethal street fighting in Romania. In all countries, the Communist Party attempted to retain some support by renaming itself and participating as a legal party in the free elections held throughout postcommunist Europe in 1990 and 1991. As in Russia, the frictions and disappointments of the transition to a free-market economy and a democratic polity allowed some former party leaders a second chance. A number of "reform communists" were able to vindicate themselves in the eyes of their fellow citizens and retained or regained important posts in the Baltics, Hungary, Romania, and other states.

Generally speaking, the discredited old leaders were allowed to retire without being subjected to witch-hunts. There was no attempt to bring any but a handful of the most hated to trial. The most respected of the anticommunist leaders, including Walesa of Poland and **Vaclav Havel** of the Czech Republic, were inclined to put the past behind them as rapidly as possible and to forgive and forget those who had harassed and imprisoned them in the name of "the future."

PROBLEMS OF THE POSTCOMMUNIST ERA

The immediate economic problems of the new governments of eastern Europe and the former Soviet Union were immense. They had to cope with a backward, collectivized agriculture that required far too much of their available labor and produced too little. Markedly inadequate consumer distribution networks and services had been the rule for forty years. Communications and information technology were decades behind current Western practice. The interest payments on the foreign debt accumulated by communist governments seeking popularity in the 1970s were eating up an intolerable percentage of the gross national product. Above all, the industrial sector, packed with superfluous workers by a standard communist policy of maintaining full employment through artificial means, was

THE END OF THE BERLIN WALL

The ultimate symbol of the Cold War between East and West came to be the ten-foot-high concrete line of the Berlin Wall. Erected by the East German government with Soviet approval and assistance in August 1961, it ran along the boundary between East and West Berlin in an attempt to stem the increasing numbers of East Germans who sought asylum in the free and economically prospering West Germany. The "death zones" on the eastern side of the wall were just that: hundreds of people lost their lives attempting to sneak or burst their way across the barrier in the 1960s and 1970s. President John F. Kennedy's "Ich bin ein Berliner" speech at the wall in 1963 committed the Western alliance to the defense of the West Berliners and the eventual removal of the hated barrier to German unity.

The abrupt decision of the tottering East German government in November 1989 to allow free passage across the Berlin boundary signaled the end of the wall and of the Cold War. It heralded the demise of communism in eastern Europe and, a little later, the Soviet Union. On November 9, 1939, the demoralized East German border guards gave up their defense of a collapsing state. The American historian Robert Darnton gives his eyewitness account:

> The destruction of the Wall began in the early evening of Thursday, November 9th, soon after the first wave of East Berliners . . . burst upon the West. A young man with a knapsack on his back somehow hoisted himself upon the Wall . . . he sauntered along the top of it, swinging his arms casually at his sides, a perfect target for bullets that had felled many other Walljumpers . . . border guards took aim, and fired, but only with power waterhoses and without much conviction. The conqueror of the Wall continued his promenade, soaked to the skin, until at last the guards gave up. . . .
>
> A few minutes later hundreds of people . . . were on the Wall, embracing, dancing, exchanging flowers, drinking wine . . . and chipping away at the Wall itself.

Another view comes from an East Berlin woman:

> I was performing with my cabaret group in Cottbus, about three hours' drive away from Berlin, when someone said they'd heard on the radio that the Wall had been opened. We all dismissed that as rumor. But you didn't know what to believe, there were so many rumors going around. About an hour after the performance, we were driving back and heard it on the radio ourselves. When we arrived in Berlin, we immediately drove across into the West. . . . The city center, on Ku'damm, was one big party. After an hour we came back, and my friend dropped me off at my home.
>
> Bert, my husband, was away on a business trip and the kids were already asleep. Thirty minutes later, my friend called me back and said he couldn't sleep. I couldn't, either! so we decided to go back again. It was something like two or three in the morning. . . . I didn't come back till it was time for my kids to get up.
>
> The next weekend Bert and I and the kids went off on a trip to West Germany. People were passing out drinks along the autobahn. There were huge lines. I took a glass of something and thought: what kind of funny lemonade is this? It was champagne!
>
> That first week people were marvelous. There was an openness, a new spirit.

Source: Robert Darnton, Berlin Journal, 1989–1990 *(New York: Norton, 1991), p. 75.*

✿ **The Wall Comes Down.** A horde of willing volunteers turned up on November 9, 1989, and every succeeding day for a month to help smash down the hated wall that had divided Berlin and the Berliners for almost three decades. *(© Alexandra Hvakian/Woodfin Camp & Associates)*

performing miserably. Most large companies were actually bankrupt, a fact masked by government ownership and subsidies. The biggest plants were almost always antiquated in technology, pollution ridden, and inefficient. Their low-quality output could not be sold in hard-currency markets and had to be forced upon the domestic market or other communist countries.

The postcommunist democratic governments had to make the difficult choice between adopting free-market capitalism in one sudden sink-or-swim shift or attempting to achieve a mixed economy less traumatically through a gradual transition from state to private ownership. With the exception of Poland, which introduced basically free markets all at once, the governments opted for the gradual or

❀ **Vaclav Havel.** After an irresistible wave of public protests brought down the former regime, the playwright and political dissident Vaclav Havel was inaugurated as the first postcommunist president of the Czech Republic in 1990. Because no lives were lost during the uprising, the Czech revolt against the communist government is known as the "Velvet Revolution." *(AP/Wide World Photos)*

partial approach. Some, like the Russians and Romanians, have tried to introduce free or freer markets, only to have to back off when they ran into popular resistance.

At the time of this writing, the Poles appear to have been more successful, but all the countries have had at times severe difficulties in satisfying the justified demands of their citizenry for a better life. The first fruits of the postcommunist economic order were rapid inflation, endemic corruption, large-scale unemployment at bankrupt state-owned enterprises, and the highly visible division of the new free-market society into haves and have-nots. For many farmers, unskilled workers, and pensioners, the new situation could not be coped with and was a definite worsening of their material status. Although these evils have abated in the past decade, they and similar problems of transition from the command economy remain strong enough to influence many negative estimates.

Many citizens, especially the older generation, have been embittered at the surging crime rates, the appearance of a "mafia" of newly rich and corrupt *biznezmeni,* and other unsavory phenomena of a disoriented and dislocated society. The prolonged inability of the Yeltsin government in Russia to attain fiscal stability and organize its revenues had injurious repercussions throughout all of eastern Europe, frightening off much potential Western investment that was badly needed.

These economic facts have of course been reflected in the internal political sphere. Most of the eastern European

states (Romania was an exception) quickly installed complete personal freedom, honest elections, a free press, and effective justice and security. But these changes were not enough to ward off a certain disillusionment with the fruits of the 1989 revolutions. It should be remembered that the eastern Europeans are laboring under a special handicap. They have never had a prolonged period of political freedom and constitutional government. In most of their countries, the years of parliamentary democracy could be measured on the fingers of both hands (see Chapter 45). The postwar Marxist repression of the educated and the middle classes and its artificially imposed "class solidarity" have made the necessary consensus for parliamentary give-and-take even more difficult to achieve. Worst of all, the violent, negative nationalism that was the curse of the early twentieth century was lying just below the Marxist surface, as the spectacular and tragic disintegration of former Yugoslavia has demonstrated. The eruption in Kosovo between Serbs and Albanians and the bloody repression of the Chechnya rebellion in Russia were other severe blows to hopes for an easy transition from communist coercion to democratic harmony.

Clearly, the tasks of establishing effective, responsive, and just government in these multiethnic countries are enormous and will not be solved until well into the twenty-first century, if at all. In the international arena the outlook is currently more promising. Russia under the leadership of Vladimir Putin has shown itself committed to reasonable partnership with the West, even to the point of acceding to its former satellites joining the European Union (see Chapter 51) and accepting military and financial aid from the United States—an unthinkable change from Soviet practices. It now seems logical to expect Russia to accept the permanent sovereignty of the east European states. But whether Marxist or free, eastern Europe represents a continuing challenge to a world that seeks mutual and peaceable human development.

SUMMARY

The astonishingly rapid collapse of the Soviet political and economic dominion in the years 1989–1990 came as a surprise to even the most perspicacious observer. An accumulating discontent with the multiple failures of the communist system to provide freedom or a decent material life for its citizenry joined with the long-standing resentments of non-Russian nationalists under Soviet rule to bring down the Marxist-Leninist regimes like falling dominos. The collapse of the Soviet Union brought forth a series of claims to independence by the peoples along the western and southern borders of the traditional Russian state, claims that had to be recognized, however reluctantly. The former Soviet satellites in eastern Europe broke entirely free of their former masters in Moscow and underwent a sometimes painful and halting reintegration into the general European community. Both they and the new Russia found their way into the new millennium laden with difficulties in their economy and in political questions, particularly a rampant nationalism that had survived the communist era.

TEST YOUR KNOWLEDGE

1. Stalin's main objective in eastern Europe in the immediate postwar era was
   a. to hunt down and punish Nazis and their sympathizers.
   b. to secure military assistance against a possible Western attack.
   c. to generate a better supply of consumer goods.
   d. to repair war damage to the Soviet Union and assure communist control.
2. The Western Allies considered the most vital country in postwar eastern Europe to be
   a. Czechoslovakia.
   b. Poland.
   c. Hungary.
   d. Yugoslavia.
3. A major reason for Khrushchev's sudden expulsion from leadership of the CPSU in 1964 was
   a. his submission to the Maoists.
   b. his embarrassment over the attempt to place missiles in Cuba.
   c. his disregard of the building pressure for consumer goods.
   d. his efforts to emulate Stalin too closely.
4. The creator of the term *goulash communism* was
   a. Gorbachev.
   b. Khrushchev.
   c. Stalin.
   d. Yeltsin.
5. The Brezhnev Doctrine
   a. put the world on notice that the Soviet Union was preparing an invasion.

   b. asserted that the Soviet Union would always be the leader in world Marxism.
   c. said that eastern Europe must choose between communism and capitalism.
   d. said that an existing satellite state cannot be allowed to become independent.
6. As the head of the Communist Party in the late 1980s, Gorbachev's fundamental problem
   a. was his inability to see the need for change.
   b. came from foreign sources such as the Afghan war.
   c. was his indecision about the extent of necessary reforms.
   d. was his continuing belief in the probability of war against the United States.
7. After being deposed in 1989, the leaders of the various eastern European Communist Parties generally were
   a. hunted down and accused of crimes against their people.
   b. imprisoned without trial or shot.
   c. allowed to retain their posts.
   d. sent into retirement without being accused of crime.
8. In economics, the postcommunist governments of eastern Europe generally
   a. continued with the Marxist system without change.
   b. introduced a completely free market in a short time.
   c. sought to convert to a free market in gradual steps.
   d. retained the basic idea of a "command economy."

IDENTIFICATION TERMS

August 1968	Commonwealth of	Havel, Vaclav	secret speech
Berlin Wall	Independent States (CIS)	peaceful coexistence	Solidarity
Brezhnev, Leonid	*glasnost*	*perestroika*	Walesa, Lech
command economy	Gorbachev, Mikhail	Revolution of 1989	

 # INFOTRAC COLLEGE EDITION

Enter the search term "Soviet Union history" using Key Words.
Enter the search term "Europe Communism" using Key Words.

Enter the search term "perestroika" using the Subject Guide.

AT THE START OF A NEW MILLENNIUM: THE ROAD AHEAD

There is no solution to the problems of birth and death except to enjoy the interval.

GEORGE SANTAYANA

1945	United Nations founded
1948–1973	Economic boom in West
1950s–1960s	End of Colonial Era
1963	Nuclear Atmospheric Test Ban
1970	Widespread recognition of environmental crisis begins
1970s–1980s	Female economic equality drive
1986	Chernobyl nuclear plant meltdown
1991	Atmospheric pollution documented over Antarctica
1990s	Global warming recognized
SEPTEMBER 11, 2001	An Age of Terror opens?

A SHORT AND VIOLENT CENTURY BEHIND US

A recent book* by the well-known historian John Lukacs claims that the twentieth century really lasted only the seventy-five years between the outbreak of world war in 1914 and the collapse of communism in 1989. According to Professor Lukacs, these two landmarks loomed over the twentieth century, the first announcing its commencement, the second its end. Leninist communism was a child that was born of chaos in World War I, grew to menacing adulthood in World War II, and died of senility and intellectual poverty in the 1980s. In retrospect, an out-of-control nationalism, not communism, was the true menace to world civilization in the twentieth century, Lukacs insists. Recent events in Yugoslavia, Rwanda, Armenia, Chechnya, and other places seem to support his thesis.

TECHNOLOGY AND POLITICAL CULTURE

It is a shopworn cliché to say that our globe has shrunk incredibly in the last generation. Mass communications and instantaneous transfer of data and ideas from one corner of the Earth to the others have worked a transformation that contemporary human beings have not yet fully grasped. We do not yet understand the dimensions of the problems that have arisen, let alone their solutions.

A chief difficulty is that our technology has far outrun our ethics and our political culture. We can do things that have tremendous power for good or evil in the lives of human beings—our own and those in the future—but we don't know how to determine "good" or "evil" in a consensual fashion. In a world that has become immensely more interdependent, the old chimera of "I win, so you lose" is still being pursued by rivals of all types. This is as true in economic development and environmental protection as it is in international wars and ethnic conflicts. The

---

*John Lukacs, *The End of the Twentieth Century and the End of the Modern Age* (New York: Ticknor & Fields, 1993).

Identity and Loyalty. The transfer of identities and loyalties from a neighborhood or a family to a far more impersonal and distant locale can perhaps best be witnessed during a Superbowl game. These Bostonians are celebrating New England's victory in 2002. *(Darren McCollester/Getty Images)*

results are often chaotic and sometimes fatal for whole groups.

One of the noteworthy contradictions of the contemporary world is the fact that as advances in electronics are making physical distance almost irrelevant to communication, economic and social factors are splitting the human community into pieces that seem to have little to communicate to one another. The Northern Hemisphere abounds in personal luxuries and social resources of every type; the Southern Hemisphere has few and is unable to generate them. Several countries have already experienced a Third Industrial (or Postindustrial) Revolution, but it has not begun in many others, some of which, indeed, have remained largely untouched by the first two.

Contemporary society is a kaleidoscope of significant differences, often concealed beneath a thin veneer of similarities that are generated in the West and then adopted worldwide. Women apply much the same cosmetics, for exactly the same reasons, throughout the modern world; from Kenyan villages to New York apartments, children play with plastic toys mass-produced in Taiwanese factories. But these superficial uniformities of cultural behavior are deceptive. A better acquaintance or the arrival of a crisis lays bare the lasting differences. Many of them are direct reflections of the extreme variations in the economies of the most and least developed nations in the world of the twenty-first century.

THE ECONOMIC BASIS: CONTRASTS

Despite the best efforts of well-meaning individuals in powerful positions, the personal income gradient from the heights of developed countries to the lower slopes of the underdeveloped remains as steep as ever. In the 1990s, the enrichment of the already prosperous was steadily matched by the impoverishment of the already poor. According to the World Bank, in 1950 the average *per capita* income of the developed countries was ten times that of the underdeveloped. In 2000, it was over forty times! Cash income *per capita* in Ethiopia, the current poorest nation in the world, was about *1/300th* of that in the United States ($101 versus $32,778, according to the United Nations statistics). And there are a few countries, such as Sweden, Switzerland, and Denmark, in which the per capita income figure exceeds that of the United States.

Both the socialists and the supporters of the free market have advanced various schemes for improving the living standards of the poor, but in the most poverty-stricken economies these have failed. Africa, in particular, has sunk deeper into misery. The West, on the other hand, we can now see was on the threshold of the *longest sustained economic advance in modern history,* a quarter-century of burgeoning prosperity for both the owning and the laboring classes, which would result in important social, political, and cultural changes by the century's end. The failure of most of the less developed nations, particularly in Africa and Latin America, to provide anything like a comparable living standard for their citizens has created a dangerous gap between the two worlds of rich and poor, worlds that can also be characterized as the Northern versus the Southern Hemispheres. Neither the doctrinaire prescriptions of the Marxists nor the "unseen hand" of the free-marketeers have served to halt this sharpening division between haves and have-nots. And despite the hopes of some, the consequences of the increased "globalization" of world trading patterns shows many debatable or downright debilitating features for the have-nots.

Twentieth-Century Approaches to Social Reform

The collapse of the Soviet communist bloc in 1989–1991 was the unforeseen end of a system of economics and politics that had haunted the Western democracies for seventy years. In the interwar years and immediately after World War II, communism seemed likely to spread throughout the world either by revolution or by parliamentary procedure. In the underdeveloped lands, many millions saw it as the best hope at a decent material life for them and their children. In some countries such as China and Cuba, it did bring an initial surge of social and economic justice to the masses and earned their strong support for a generation. They were willing to pay for their better economic prospects by giving up the political and social freedoms they had only minimally and imperfectly enjoyed under the previous, capitalist system.

But this was not true of the Western countries, including eastern Europe. Here, when the people had a choice, they firmly rejected the political, economic, and intellectual sacrifices demanded by communism. The Western socialist parties severed all connections with Soviet communism during the 1950s and even distanced themselves from many of the long-treasured ideas of Karl Marx. Reformism rather than revolution and gradualism rather than radical change became the order of the day among the social democrats.

What had previously been considered a peculiarly American viewpoint—that the secret of social harmony was in making a bigger pie rather than rearranging the slices—came to prevail in all the Western nations. Furthermore, although never clearly admitted, this view came to be the new Soviet orthodoxy after Stalin's death. Revolution in the eyes of a Brezhnev or even Khrushchev was reserved for developing countries, where any other means of effecting change was out of the question. And such a revolution was only desirable where it served Soviet foreign policy. By the 1970s, it is fair to say that only Castro in Cuba and Mao in China gave more than lip service to Marx's original doctrines of social and economic egalitarianism. The Marxist dream of the proletariat achieving a universal earthly heaven was put on the shelf indefinitely.

Prosperity in the Developed Societies

So long as the economic boom in the West lasted, social changes *did* come as both a reflection and a cause of vast improvement in the workers' living and working conditions. Indeed, these improvements were what nullified the appeal of communism in Europe, as the Soviet system proved unable to generate anything like them.

Western workers (extending "Western" to mean Japan since about 1980) work about one-fourth fewer hours weekly to earn wages that purchase about two and a half times as much in real terms as in 1950. They have guarantees of job security, wage or salary increases, vacation and sick time, insurance against accidents and ill health, extended unemployment pay, family leave, and other benefits that would astound workers of the 1940s. Higher education is vastly more accessible, with state scholarships or stipends for student living expenses the rule in all countries. Material conditions have vastly improved also. In the United States, most salaried and about half of the wage-earning people own their homes. In Europe and Japan, where rentals are the urban standard, working-class families can afford more space, and private automobiles are now commonplace even among manual workers. Upward mobility out of the working classes into the technical or professional groups has been very extensive everywhere. In these very real senses, social progress in the West has been consistent and effective since 1945, though it has not been carried out in the name of an ideology or even a set of principles.

Losing Ground in the Developing Countries

The developing world shows a contrary pattern. The shift from manual to white-collar work, and from agriculture to technological pursuits, has been slow and halting, at best. Productivity has in some places and job types actually declined, as in much of sub-Saharan family farms. Social mobility has increased, but only a small proportion of persons with access to education and "connections" have moved upward. *Downward mobility* has probably been more common than upward in Africa and Latin America, where large groups of previously independent small landowners or tribal community members have been forced out of their traditional niches or impoverished by demographic and economic pressures. The near-total absence of organizations such as independent trade unions or farmers' associations leaves these people vulnerable to changes imposed by modern urban life with no one to help defend their interests. The Latin American peon and African mineworker can rarely improve their economic or social prospects except by migration to the city with its attendant dangers and frequent failure.

THE OTHER HALF OF HUMANITY

In 1964, a French wife and mother had to obtain the written permission of her husband to open a bank account in her own name. Ten years later, after a ferocious verbal battle, the French parliament legalized abortion on the request of the pregnant woman. These two facts are as useful as any to symbolize the changes in the status of women brought about by the struggle for **women's liberation** in the last several decades.

The Second Sex, as Simone de Beauvoir's influential book called women, has been steadily closing the vast gap that once stood between them and men in the social and economic arenas of the Western world. Most countries now have laws on the books (sometimes unenforced) that prohibit paying women less than men for the same work, discriminating on the basis of gender for promotions or entry into a profession, refusing credit to women, denying them contractual rights, denying women custody of minors, and so on. In 2000, women made up 56 percent of all U.S.university graduates, up from 20 percent in the 1950s. Forty-six percent of the students entering U.S. law schools are women, a number that has approximately quadrupled since 1980. By 2010, it is estimated that females will be more than one-third of the total number of lawyers.

These indications of rapid change are by no means limited to the economic and labor sectors. The formerly "normal" quality of marriage for young women has been radically questioned. About a quarter of American women between eighteen and forty-five were single (that is, divorced or unmarried) in 1960; over half were by 2000. More than half of all first marriages end in divorce. In the United States, one-third of all babies are born to unmarried women, up from about 8 percent forty years earlier. The proportion is higher still for first-borns. Unwed motherhood has become so common in some sectors of the population that it no longer requires comment or explanation. Two generations ago, it would have been grounds for social ostracism.

FAMILY AND THE INDIVIDUAL

The dramatic changes in family life over the past generation are evident in several ways. The two-parent, two-generation, male breadwinner and female housewife model, which has been the norm for Western urban families since the nineteenth century, has clearly become but one of several *alternative lifestyles.* With most mothers working at least part-time outside the home, children under six are com-

Economic Feminism, 1970s. The battle for women's rights shifted during the 1960s and 1970s from a political to an economic and social focus as millions of single and married women entered the Western workforce for the first time. Here, women in the United States march in a street demonstration for equal pay and benefits. *(Margot Granitsas/The Image Works)*

monly cared for by paid employees. The removal of the biological mother from primary responsibility for the young child's welfare during the most impressionable years will presumably have wide-ranging but as yet unknowable effects on the importance and permanence of the nuclear family relation.

The increasing *numbers of female-headed households and economically independent females* in all Western and some non-Western countries are putting women into a position of potential political power quite unparalleled in recent history. But to the dismay of the more aggressive feminists, so far this potential power has not been realized. Despite the occasional emergence of leaders such as Indira Gandhi and Golda Meir and a steady upward trend for females in legislative bodies worldwide, women have shown themselves generally unmoved by appeals to feminism as a political, as contradistinct from a socioeconomic, force. One cogent reason is that as divorce and abandonment by the male grow more common, so does common-law marriage in which enforcing legal responsibility for maintenance of spouse or children is difficult, if not impossible. Annually, many millions of women, from the villages of Africa to the ghettos of U.S. cities, find themselves thrown into permanent poverty by the breakup of their living arrangements with a man. Grappling with acute problems of survival, poor women have had little interest and/or energy to organize for longer-term political goals.

A third phenomenon in recent familial history is that the social identification that individuals in the past received from their family has largely become superfluous or is consciously rejected. It is the individual, not the family or the clan, who exercises choice, creates opportunity, accepts responsibility, earns renown, and generally makes his or her mark in the Western world (and increasingly, everywhere else). While this may be seen as a further large step toward democracy and fair play, it also has very definite negative aspects for both individual and society. The feeling of alienation from others that was mentioned in the chapter on modern cultures is highly stressful. It has been most apparent in those locales where the traditional family has become weakest: the urban, mobile, wealthy West where the individual is an atom among atoms rather than a link in a chain. The degree to which this has become true can be easily demonstrated by a simple question to the reader of these lines: Do you know where you are going to be buried? Probably, you have no idea where this traditionally most sacred rite will be carried out or who will do it—an unthinkable thing to confess until very recently in human history.

LOOMING PROBLEMS

The United Nations and National Sovereignty

One of the touchiest of all topics in the current political discourse has been the degree to which national sovereignty

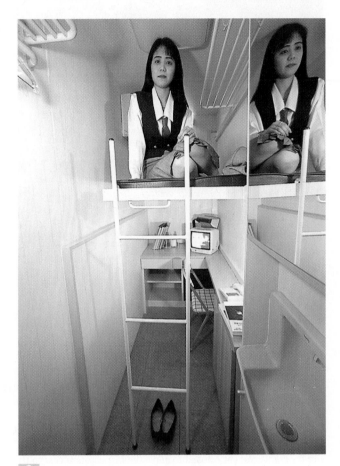

Isolation in a Tokyo Apartment. The extraordinary costs of housing in the Japanese capital are dramatized by this dormitory scene. The young woman will have to spend a large part of her leisure time in these surroundings; anything more spacious is beyond her means. *(Torin Boyd/Getty Images)*

must be surrendered to a supranational organization to preserve peace. The United Nations Organization (UN) was founded in 1945 by the victorious Allies to do what its predecessor, the League of Nations, was unable to do: guarantee international peace.

Unlike the league, the UN has a potentially very powerful executive organ in the Security Council. The council has wide authority, including the power to take air, sea, and land military action against aggression.

The UN General Assembly has no such powers and can only debate and recommend to the Security Council. All states of the world have an equal vote in the General Assembly, which in effect means that the developing countries have a very large voice in the UN's nonmilitary aspects, such as labor, cultural affairs, and public health through the International Labor Organization (ILO); the United Nations Educational, Scientific, and Cultural Organization (UNESCO); and the World Health Organization (WHO), respectively. These organs have played an important and

Security Council Meeting. In December 1999, the Security Council voted to send inspectors to Iraq to investigate that country's capacity for "weapons of terror." As it had for several years prior, the Iraqi government refused to allow the inspectors access to the suspected sites and defied the council's sanctions. *(© AFP/Corbis)*

positive role in world affairs for the last fifty years, even while the political and military performances of the UN were disappointing to many sympathetic observers.

The reason for their disappointment was that ultimate powers were retained by the sovereign states and not by the UN Secretariat (executive office). When a major state saw that its interests were being threatened by UN intervention of some type, it either exercised its veto in the Security Council or ensured by other means that there would be no effective interference. Throughout the Cold War era, the UN was able to intervene effectively only on the very few occasions when both blocs could agree that a given conflict was intolerably dangerous (namely, the Israeli-Arab contest) or when one side chose to boycott the proceedings (namely, the UN decision to defend South Korea in the 1950s). The smaller powers, on the other hand, were frequently forced to conform to Security Council resolutions aimed at controlling their political and military inclinations and initiatives. Thus, the UN's guardianship of the peace was applied on two levels: one for the powerful and another for the less so.

In the most recent times, the relative collaboration between the United States and Russia in international affairs has given the UN an unprecedented freedom of action in maintaining peace and redressing injustice that might lead

to war. The successful coalition against Iraq in the Gulf War of 1991 was an outstanding example of what can be done. Others were the universal condemnation of the terrorist acts of the Al Qaida group in 2001 and the support for the antiterrorist campaign in Afghanistan that followed. Perhaps this type of vigorous action will become more common now that there is truly only one superpower, and Cold War maneuvering has ended. But it is equally possible that the anti-Iraq and antiterrorist coalitions were an exceptional response to a clear-cut case of aggression. Instead, the frustrations and failure that marked the attempted intervention to establish peace in the Yugoslav and Somali civil wars of the 1990s may be the rule.

Control of Nuclear Weapons

Another pressing problem awaiting solution is the proliferation of nuclear weaponry. So long as only the United States, the Soviet Union, Britain, and France had atomic weapons, the "deadly secret" of creating them could be contained. But in the late 1960s, the Chinese under Mao went ahead with their own research effort, and by the mid-1970s, they had cracked the atomic code. The Israelis and South Africans were next, followed closely by the Indians and Pakistanis. The mushroom cloud is spreading over wider territories and can be set off by more and more hands. Much recent diplomatic history, such as the strong support of the Yeltsin and Putin governments in Russia by the United States, is closely linked with the fear that Cold War weapons stocks might be accessed or stolen by terrorists. The same fears are generated by contemplation of what could be done by release of epidemic disease germs. It is certain that such attempts have already been made. Many think that it is just a matter of time before some terrorist band or desperate government will attempt atomic—or biological—blackmail.

The entire question of terror employed for political or military ends came into sudden focus with the September 2001 attacks on New York City by fanatical Muslims belonging to the Al Qaida network. It was a day of mass death from enemy action, the first time that this country had ever suffered such an event on its own soil. Whether it will be followed by others cannot at this time be known. What is certain is that the easy assumption by most of us that malicious violence on a massive scale, for political purposes,

was something that happened elsewhere to other people has been shattered, perhaps forever. September 11 was "the day that changed everything."

Environmental Deterioration

We have all heard so much about the threats to the continued survival of the human race that we may be tempted to throw up our hands and trust to good luck or hope that another habitable planet is found before this one becomes unlivable. Nevertheless, certain environmental dangers are both real and can be addressed effectively, if only we have the will to do so. The most urgent near-term problems facing us in the new millennium seem to be the following:

> *Excessive and unbalanced consumption of nonrenewable energy.* Each year, the average U.S. citizen consumes roughly thirty-five times as much energy (fossil fuel, water, electric) as a person in India and about three times as much as an individual in Italy or France. The tremen-

September 11, 2001. Smoke rises from the site of the World Trade Center towers in downtown New York City moments after the collapse of the 110-story buildings. Hijacked airplanes were used as the instruments of destruction by terrorists thought to be members of the Al Qaida international network of Islamic extremists. *(AP Photo/Suzanne Plunkett)*

dous difference between the developed North and the underdeveloped South in global affairs is nowhere more apparent than in energy consumption. The less developed countries, with about 60 percent of world population, consume only 12 percent of the energy produced in the world; the rest is consumed by the developed countries. And if per capita use remains the same in 2030 as it is today, the world will need to produce 50 percent more energy just to keep pace with population growth.

Food production in Africa. Owing to sharply rising populations and the systematic use of marginal land for agriculture, African food supplies have been actually declining in large areas of the continent. Several countries, including Somalia, Sudan, Chad, and Tanzania, are now permanently dependent on imported food and have become beggars in the world economy.

Reduction of the tropical forest belt. It has only recently been recognized that the tropical forests, as the purifiers of the polluted atmosphere and the stabilizers of world climate, are absolutely vital to the whole world. Some of the rain forest countries around the equator (Malaysia, Brazil, Indonesia) are attempting to check the generation-long decimation of this vital resource, but their efforts are belated and are pushed only half-heartedly by governments that are often in league with the timber companies and need the foreign exchange that timber brings. Beyond that, tremendous domestic political pressure is generated by the land-hunger of rapidly growing populations.

Pollution and radioactive wastes. Many developing countries are almost entirely ignorant of or disregard the most elementary pollution control measures. Their industries and mines—frequently controlled by owners in the developed countries—poison the Earth, air, and water on a large scale. The meltdown at the Chernobyl nuclear plant in Ukraine fifteen years ago was the most spectacular example of the dangers posed by inadequate or nonexistent policing and protection. Many others might be cited. These potential catastrophes have no respect whatever for national borders, and the long-term, slow effects of pollution may be worse than the occasional explosive event such as Chernobyl.

This list is by no means comprehensive and deals only with what the author of this book believes to be the problems with the most immediate international repercussions. During the life spans of students reading these lines, the developed world (the United States foremost) will either master the most urgent of these problems or substantially change the hitherto known environment of human beings from a life *with* nature to a life *against* or *outside* nature. Whether this latter style of life is possible and at the same time "humane" is an open question.

CHOICES

We earthlings live on a small planet, which is only a minor part of a nine-planet solar system, which is itself one of hundreds, perhaps, within a still-expanding cosmos. We will soon either succeed (temporarily) or fail (permanently) in our attempt to keep the Earth livable for creatures like ourselves. It is now quite possible for humans to damage their habitat so drastically that it will no longer be a fit place for the species. What will be done in these regards in the next decades is largely up to people like yourselves, the educated men and women of a powerful country.

At bottom, there are only two rational approaches to the solution of basic environmental problems: *conservation,* which is the attempt to retain (conserve) existing systems, and *technology,* which is the attempt to discover superior replacements. The conservationists argue that the Earth's natural systems are the results of eons of slow evolution; that of all earthly beings, humans alone rebel against those systems rather than live with them; and that this rebellion, though it may be successful in the short run, spells ruin in the longer. The technicians argue that evolution is only one path to an acceptable, sustainable system and that humans can and must try to find other paths when the natural one proves inadequate or has been blocked. The choices that must be made between these differing approaches will largely determine the quality and character of your lives.

Indeed, choices of every kind lie before you, as they have before all of your predecessors. Like them, you will often not be sure of what must be or should be done. Like them, you will have to seek guidance from many sources: religion, science, parents, and the study of history. The answers from history especially will often be unclear or cryptic; they may have sections missing or lend themselves to more than one interpretation. But it is the historical answer that will usually be most applicable and most comprehensive: this is what humans, in all their variety, have done successfully to meet and overcome problems somewhat like those you currently encounter. And like all your predecessors on this Earth, you will have to hope that you have understood correctly and have taken a constructive, viable path as you join the long parade of men and women, moving forward into the infinite future.

IDENTIFICATION TERM

women's liberation

 # INFOTRAC COLLEGE EDITION

Enter the search terms "wealth redistribution" or "wealth distribution" using Key Words.

Enter the search term "feminism" using the Subject Guide.

Enter the search term "social problems" using the Subject Guide.

1920–Present
Equilibrium Reestablished

	Law and Government	Economy
Westerners	Rise of mass democracy in politics creates new-style party government where money, but no longer birth, plays important role. Law increasingly reflects popular attitudes, as interpreted by party heads. Property rights under attack while civil rights advance. Totalitarian governments appear in many nations after WW I and ensuing Great Depression of 1930s. After WW II, long economic boom allows democratic recovery and stability in West outside Soviet bloc. Soviet communism expands for a generation, then goes bankrupt.	There are two distinct economic periods. 1920–1945 sees the decline and near collapse of free market in West and widespread impoverishment of middle classes and agriculturalists. 1945–present has seen a long boom, interrupted for several years by the oil crisis of 1970s. Japan emerges as leading financial power in 1980s. The European Community becomes economic reality, whereas Soviet bloc stagnates and then collapses. The global economy is rapidly forming under Western dominance.
Africans	Law and government continue on colonial lines until after WW II. Decolonization brings unstable mixture of African traditional law and political structures with European models. Western forms are often at odds with precolonial content. Post-independence problems encourage authoritarian, single-party governments. Tribalism and corruption are major problems.	Increasing emphasis on export crops and mining converts some areas to food-deficit regions. There is very little manufacturing, even after end of colonial regimes. Increasing international aid in attempt to overcome declining agricultural productivity and dependency on imports of all types. Due to large increases in population, most national economies are in crisis by 1990s.
Muslim	Minority attempts to introduce modern Western law, education, and politics are made throughout Muslim world after WW I with minimal success, except for Turkey. After WW II a strong backlash favoring strict fundamentalist Islam develops, led most recently by Iran. Governments of Islamic countries range from a limited Western constitutionalism to undisguised theocracy. Nationalism is a powerful force, particularly among Arabs.	Middle East oil is the one major export, generating dependence on international customers. Much effort was exerted to avoid this by using oil funds for varied domestic investments. Arab states and Indonesia are relatively successful in doing so, but oil production still remains the key to their prosperity. Poor Muslim countries are very unstable and still are not integrated into world economy constructively.

PEOPLES: WESTERNERS (EUROPEANS, NORTH AMERICANS, JAPANESE, BRITISH DOMINIONS), AFRICANS, MUSLIMS, EAST AND SOUTH ASIANS, LATIN AMERICANS

Religion and Philosophy	Arts and Culture	Sciences and Technology
The "post–Christian era." Secularism is elevated to a formal doctrine in most countries, assisted by the rise in influence of Marxism through 1960s. Failure of Marxism in 1980s underlines the crisis of sterility in Western philosophical ideas. Concurrent sharp rise in Western interest in Eastern religion and philosophies.	Art and its audience become fragmented. No recognized models or authority. Much influence from non-Western sources. Abstraction in pictorial arts matched by rejection of traditional models in all other arts among the avant-garde. Literature and philosophy are either "serious" or popular; there is no middle ground. Mass cultural forms (TV, movies, music, magazines) are often dictated by commercial considerations.	Science becomes the defining reference for knowledge and truth. Social sciences (economics, psychology, etc.) rise to prominence. Technology makes enormous strides, removing physical labor as obstacle to almost any task and enabling "information revolution" through computers and electronic apparatus.
Christian missions make inroads into traditional animism in central and southern regions. Islam dominates the north, west, and eastern coasts. Most Africans blend one or the other formal doctrines with local animisms. Education for the masses begins after 1950, and increases after decolonization completed.	Sub-Saharan pictorial and plastic arts become widely recognized for first time, partly due to increased archaeological finds. Modern African artists blend Western training with native motifs and media. Independence brings much greater opportunities for artists, domestically and internationally. Literature continues to be in Western languages, hence limited in audience at home, where oral folklore is still the main way of transmitting cultural values.	Physical and social scientists are still relatively few and depend on foreign sources for training, financing, and direction. Higher educational facilities remain oriented toward nonscientific programs and degrees, emulating nineteenth-century colonial culture. Technology imported from West and Japan sometimes has devastating impact on local cultures and economies.
The secularism of some intellectuals and political reformers is sharply opposed by the traditionalists. Only after WW II do the religious fundamentalists learn how to propagandize effectively with a nationalist appeal. Islam in their view is combined with strong rejection of the West's public and private values.	Much increased literacy results in revival or first appearance of literature in several Muslim states. Oil wealth of 1970s provides major governmental patronage of the arts in Arab states. Nationalism is reflected in art forms and revived interest in folk art.	As in the rest of the non-Western world, physical and life sciences were dependent on Western training and goal setting. This rapidly changed to autonomous science in much of Muslim world since approximately 1970. Emphasis on science and technology in higher education apparently accepted by fundamentalist Muslims as modern necessity.

1920–Present
Equilibrium Reestablished

	Law and Government	Economy
South and East Asians	Former British possessions have generally retained Western outlook on law and government. French and Dutch territories less committed to these ideals. In several, Marxist socialism provided a format for combining nationalism with radical reform. Governments currently range from liberal democratic constitutionalism to oppressive dictatorships. China's mutated Marxism is in a category of its own, combining political censorship with economic and social freedoms.	South and East Asia give a mixed picture of economic progress. In Bangladesh, Sri Lanka, and Burma, the traditional agrarian and poverty-stricken economy has barely changed or has gotten worse due to rapid population increases. South Korea, Taiwan, and Malaysia have undergone stunning change in moving toward modern industry and services in the past thirty years. Japan's modified and highly successful free market example has proved influential, but huge China is the X quantity in Asia's economic picture.
Latin Americans	The fundamental laws continue to be European (Napoleonic codes), and the governmental structures resemble those of the West. The enormous social gap between rich and poor often frustrates the intent of the constitution, however, and makes a segregated legal procedure inevitable. Government often represents only the uppermost minority, though this is slowly changing in most of the continent.	A fully Westernized urban lifestyle is supported for a minority by relatively modern industrial economies. In most of the continent, however, the agrarian and deprived mestizo/mulatto population has made little progress in a century. As in Africa, a very rapid population increase prevents substantial or permanent gains from international investments and loans. Most of Latin America continues to be a dependent of the Western nations.

PEOPLES: WESTERNERS (EUROPEANS, NORTH AMERICANS, JAPANESE, BRITISH DOMINIONS), AFRICANS, MUSLIMS, EAST AND SOUTH ASIANS, LATIN AMERICANS

Religion and Philosophy	Arts and Culture	Sciences and Technology
Asians have retained their religious and cultural independence from the West, even during the colonial era. Buddhism in its several versions is still the most popular of the mass cults, while Islam and Daoism are major competitors in the southeast and China. India remains Hindu, while secular views gain everywhere among the educated. The superficial cultural phenomena have become increasingly Westernized.	Cultural autonomy in Asia is expressed in the arts now as always. A recognizably non-Western approach is manifested through several regional variations in the fine arts as well as in folklore and artisanry. Literature and philosophy have been deeply affected by Western influences in the last generation, but remain distinct. Higher education now resembles that in the West, with the same emphases in the advanced countries.	The formerly huge gap between the physical and life sciences in South and East Asia and in the West has almost been closed. Technology still lags, largely as a result of shortages of investment funds rather than lack of knowledge or willingness.
Catholicism has split into a reform-minded and a traditionalist party within the clergy as it gradually loses its automatic acceptance among the masses touched by modern secularism. The formal link between state and church is nearly gone. Education is still an unmet need in the mestizo and Indian countries, and literacy rates are still low.	Particularly in fiction, Latin American authors have won world acclaim, and the fine arts with some exceptions have also prospered in this century. Formal culture is still restricted to the wealthy and the urban middle class, however. Between them and the rural majority, the cultural chasm still lies open.	Retarded, labor-rich economy has slight connection with technology. The sciences and technology are still heavily dependent on Western and particularly American models and direction. Higher education has been very slow in reorienting itself toward a modern curriculum in these fields, while the mainly foreign-owned companies are not research oriented.

GLOSSARY

A

Abbasid dynasty The caliphs resident in Baghdad from the 700s until 1252 C.E.

Abbot/abbess The male/female head of a monastery/nunnery.

Abstractionism A twentieth-century school of painting that rejects traditional representation of external nature and objects.

Act of Supremacy of 1534 A law enacted by the English Parliament making the monarch the head of the Church of England.

Actium, Battle of The decisive 31 B.C.E. battle in the struggle between Octavian Caesar and Mark Anthony, in which Octavian's victory paved the way for the Principate.

Age of the Barracks Emperors The period of the Roman Empire in the third century C.E. when the throne was repeatedly usurped by military men.

Agincourt The great victory of the English over the French in 1415, during the Hundred Years' War.

Agricultural revolution The substitution of farming for hunting-gathering as the primary source of food by a given people.

Ain Jalut A decisive thirteenth-century battle in which the Egyptians turned back the Mongols and prevented them from invading North Africa.

Ajanta Caves Caves in central India that are the site of marvelous early frescoes inspired by Buddhism.

Allah Arabic title of the one God.

Alliance for Progress The proposal by U.S. president John F. Kennedy in 1961 for large-scale economic assistance to Latin America.

Alliance of 1778 A diplomatic treaty under which France aided the American revolutionaries in their war against Britain.

Anabaptists Radical Protestant reformers who were condemned by both Lutherans and Catholics.

Anarchism A political theory that sees all large-scale government as inherently evil and embraces small self-governing communities.

Anasazi Pre-Columbian inhabitants of the southwestern United States and creators of pueblo cliff dwellings.

Ancien régime "The old government"; the pre-Revolutionary style of government and society in eighteenth-century France.

Anghor Wat A great Buddhist temple in central Cambodia, dating to the twelfth-century C.E. Khmer empire.

Anglo-French entente The diplomatic agreement of 1904 that ended British-French enmity and was meant as a warning to Germany.

Anglo-Russian agreement The equivalent to the Anglo-French entente between Britain and Russia; signed in 1907.

Angola-to-Brazil trade A major portion of the trans-Atlantic slave trade.

Animism A religious belief imputing spirits to natural forces and objects.

Anschluss The German term for the 1938 takeover of Austria by Nazi Germany.

Anthropology The study of humankind as a particular species.

Antigonid kingdom One of the Hellenistic successor kingdoms to Alexander the Great's empire.

Apartheid The Afrikaans term for segregation of the races in South Africa.

Appeasement The policy of trying to avoid war by giving Hitler what he demanded in the 1930s; supported by many in France and Britain.

Archaeology The study of cultures through the examination of artifacts.

Aristocracy A social governing class based on birth.

Ark of the Covenant The wooden container of the two tablets given to Moses by Yahweh on Mount Sinai (the Ten Commandments); the Jews' most sacred shrine, signifying the contract between God and the Chosen.

Aryans A nomadic pastoral people from central Asia who invaded the Indus valley in about 1500 B.C.E.

Ashikaga clan A noble Japanese family that controlled political power as shoguns from the 1330s to the late 1500s.

Assur The chief god of the Assyrian people.

Ataturk, Mustafa Kemal The "father of the Turks"; a World War I officer who led Turkey into the modern age and replaced the sultanate in the 1920s.

Audiencia The colonial council that supervised military and civil government in Latin America.

August 1991 coup The attempt by hard-line communists to oust Mikhail Gorbachev and reinstate the Communist Party's monopoly on power in the Soviet Union.

Ausgleich of 1867 The compromise between the Austro-Germans and Magyars that created the "Dual Monarchy" of Austria-Hungary.

Austro-Prussian War The conflict for mastery of the German national drive for political unification, won by the Bismarck-led Prussian kingdom in 1866.

Avesta The holy book of the Zoroastrian religion.

Axis Pact The treaty establishing a military alliance between the governments of Hitler and Mussolini; signed in 1936.

Axum The center of the ancient Ethiopian kingdom.

Ayllu Quechua name for the clan organization of the Peruvian Indians.

Aztec Latest of a series of Indian masters of central Mexico prior to the arrival of the Spanish; developers of the great city of Tenochtitlán (Mexico City).

B

Babylon Most important of the later Mesopotamian urban centers.

Babylonian Captivity The transportation of many Jews to exile in Babylon as hostages for the good behavior of the remainder; occurred in the sixth century B.C.E.

Babylonian Captivity of the papacy See **Great Schism.**

Bakufu The military-style government of the Japanese shogun.

Balfour Declaration The 1917 public statement that Britain was committed to the formation of a "Jewish homeland" in Palestine after World War I.

Banana republics A dismissive term referring to small Latin American states.

Bantu A language spoken by many peoples of central and eastern Africa; by extension, the collective name of the speakers.

Barbarian Greek for "incomprehensible speaker"; uncivilized.

Battle of the Nations October 1813 at Leipzig in eastern Germany. Decisive defeat of the army of Napoleon by combined forces of Prussia, Austria, and Russia.

Bedouin The nomadic inhabitants of interior Arabia and original converts to Islam.

Benedictine Rule The rules of conduct given to his monastic followers by the sixth-century Christian saint Benedict.

Berbers Pre-Arab settlers of northern Africa and the Sahara.

Berlin blockade The 1948–1949 attempt to squeeze the Western allies out of occupied Berlin by the USSR; it failed because of the successful Berlin Airlift of food and supplies.

Berlin Wall The ten-foot-high concrete wall and "death zone" erected by the communist East Germans in 1961 to prevent further illegal emigration to the West.

Bhagavad-gita The best-known part of the *Mahabharata,* detailing the proper relations between the castes and the triumph of the spirit over material creation.

Big bang theory The theory that the cosmos was created by an enormous explosion of gases billions of years ago.

Bill of Rights of 1689 A law enacted by Parliament that established certain limits of royal powers and the specific rights of English citizens.

Black Death An epidemic of bubonic plague that ravaged most of Europe in the mid–fourteenth century.

Boer War/Boers The armed conflict in 1899–1902 between the Boers (the Dutch colonists who had been the initial European settlers of South Africa) and their British overlords; won by the British after a hard fight.

Bolsheviks The minority of Russian Marxists led by Lenin who seized dictatorial power in the October revolution of 1917.

Boule The 500-member council that served as a legislature in ancient Athens.

Bourgeoisie The urban upper middle class; usually commercial or professional.

Boxer Rebellion A desperate revolt by superstitious peasants against the European "foreign devils" who were carving up China in the new imperialism of the 1890s; quickly suppressed.

Brahman The title of the impersonal spirit responsible for all creation in Hindu theology.

Brahmin The caste of priests, originally limited to the Aryans and later allowed to the Indians with whom they intermarried.

Bread and circuses The social policy initiated by Augustus Caesar aimed at gaining the support of the Roman proletariat by freely supplying them with essential food and entertainments.

Brest-Litovsk Treaty of 1918 The separate peace between the Central Powers and Lenin's government in Russia.

Bronze Age The period when bronze tools and weapons replaced stone among a given people; generally about 3000–1000 B.C.E.

Burning of the books China's Legalist first emperor attempted to eliminate Confucian ethic by destroying the Confucian writings and prohibiting its teaching.

Bushido The code of honor among the samurai.

Byzantine empire The continuation of the Roman imperium in its eastern provinces until its fall to the Muslim Turks in 1453.

C

Cahokia sites The locales of North American Indian ceremonial sites in the valley of the Mississippi, established sometime prior to the fifteenth century.

Caliph Arabic for "successor" (to Muhammad); leader of Islam.

Carthage Rival in the Mediterranean basin to Rome in the last centuries B.C.E. before ultimate defeat.

Caste A socioeconomic group that is entered by birth and rarely exitable.

Caudillo A chieftain (that is, a local or regional strongman) in Latin America.

Censors Officials with great powers of surveillance during the Roman republic.

Chaeronea The battle in 338 B.C.E. when Philip of Macedon decisively defeated the Greeks and brought them under Macedonian rule.

Chartists A British working-class movement of the 1840s that attempted to obtain labor and political reform.

Chavin Early Peruvian Indian culture.

Cheka An abbreviation for the first version of the Soviet secret police.

Chichén Itzá Site in the Yucatán of Mayan urban development in the tenth to thirteenth centuries.

Civil Code of 1804 Napoleonic law code reforming and centralizing French legal theory and procedures.

Civil constitution of the clergy 1791 law in revolutionary France attempting to force French Catholics to support the new government and bring clergy into conformity with it.

Civilization A complex, developed culture.

Command economy The name given to communist economic planning in the Soviet version after 1929.

Committee of Public Safety The executive body of the Reign of Terror during the French Revolution.

Commonwealth of Independent States (CIS) The loose confederation of eleven of the fifteen former Soviet republics that was formed after the breakup of the Soviet Union in 1991.

Conciliar movement The attempt to substitute councils of church leaders for papal authority in late medieval Christianity.

Conquistadores Title given to sixteenth-century Spanish explorers/colonizers in the Americas.

Consuls Chief executives of the Roman republic; chosen annually.

Coral Sea, Battle of the Naval engagement in the southwest Pacific during World War II, resulting in the removal of a Japanese invasion threat to Australia.

Corpus Juris "Body of the law"; the Roman law code, produced under the emperor Justinian in the mid-500s C.E.

Counter-Reformation Series of measures that the Catholic Church took in the 1540s to counterattack against the Protestants, including a thorough examination of doctrines and practices and an emphasis on instruction of the young and of all Christians.

Creationism A cosmology based on Christian tradition that holds that the universe was created by an intelligent Supreme Being.

Crecy Battle in the Hundred Years' War won by the English in 1346.

Crimean War Conflict fought in the Crimea between Russia and Britain, France, and Turkey from 1853 to 1856; ended by the Peace of Paris with a severe loss in Russian prestige.

Criollo Creole; term used to refer to whites born in Latin America.

Cultural relativism A belief common in the late twentieth-century West that there are no absolute values to measure contrasting cultures.

Culture The human-created physical and/or mental environment of a group.

Cuneiform Mesopotamian wedge-shaped writing begun by the Sumerians.

Cynicism A Hellenistic philosophy stressing poverty and simplicity.

 D

Dada A brief but influential European art movement in the early twentieth century that repudiated all obligations to communicate intelligibly to the general public.

Daimyo Japanese nobles who controlled feudal domains under the shogun.

Dao de Jing (*Book of Changes*) Daoism's major scripture; attributed to Lao Zi.

Daoism (Taoism) A nature-oriented philosophy/religion of China.

Dawes Plan A plan for a dollar loan and refinancing of post–World War I reparation payments that enabled recovery of the German economy.

D day June 6, 1944; the invasion of France from the English Channel by combined British and American forces.

Declaration of the Rights of Man and Citizen The epoch-making manifesto issued by the French Third Estate delegates at Versailles in 1789.

Deductive reasoning Arriving at truth by applying a general law or proposition to a specific case.

Delian League An empire of satellite *polei* under Athens in the fifth century B.C.E.

Deme The basic political subdivision of the Athenian *polis*.

Demesne The arable land on a manor that belonged directly to the lord.

Democracy A system of government in which the majority of voters decides issues and policy.

Demographic transition The passage of a large group of people from traditional high birthrates to lower ones, induced by changing economic conditions and better survival chances of the children.

Dependency In the context of national development, the necessity to reckon with other states' powers and pressures in the domestic economy and foreign trade.

Descamisados "Shirtless ones"; the poor working classes in modern Argentina.

Descent of Man The 1871 publication by Charles Darwin that applied selective evolution theory to mankind.

Détente Relaxation; the term used for the toning down of diplomatic tensions between nations, specifically, the Cold War between the United States and the Soviet Union.

Dharma A code of morals and conduct prescribed for one's caste in Hinduism.

Dhimmis "People of the Book": Christians, Jews, and Zoroastrians living under Muslim rule and receiving privileged treatment over other non-Muslims.

Diaspora The scattering of the Jews from ancient Palestine.

Diffusion theory The spread of ideas and technology through human contacts.

Directory The five-member executive organ that governed France from 1795 to 1799 after the overthrow of the Jacobins.

Divine right theory The idea that the legitimate holder of the Crown was designated by divine will to govern; personified by King Louis XIV of France in the seventeenth century.

Diwan A council of Islamic government ministers in Istanbul during the Ottoman empire.

Domesday Book A complete census of landholdings in England ordained by William the Conqueror.

Dorians Legendary barbaric invaders of Mycenaean Greece in c. 1200 B.C.E.

Dream of the Red Chamber The best known of the eighteenth-century Chinese novels.

Duce, il "The Leader"; title of Mussolini, the Italian dictator.

 E

East India Company A commercial company founded with government backing to trade with the East and Southeast Asians. The Dutch, English, and French governments sponsored such companies starting in the early seventeenth century.

Economic nationalism A movement to assert national sovereignty in economic affairs, particularly by establishing freedom from the importation of foreign goods and technology on unfavorable terms.

Edo Name of Tokyo prior to the eighteenth century.

Eightfold Path The Buddha's teachings on attaining perfection.

Ekklesia The general assembly of citizens in ancient Athens.

Emir A provincial official with military duties in Muslim government.

Empirical data Facts derived from observation of the external world.

Empirical method Using empirical data to establish scientific truth.

Empiricist A school of Hellenistic Greek medical researchers.

Enclosure movement An eighteenth-century innovation in British agriculture by which formerly communal lands were enclosed by private landlords for their own benefit.

Encomienda The right to organize unpaid native labor by the earliest Spanish colonists in Latin America; revoked in 1565.

Encyclopédie, The The first encyclopedia; produced in mid-eighteenth-century France by the philosophe Diderot.

Enlightenment The intellectual reform movement in eighteenth-century Europe that challenged traditional ideas and policies in many areas of theory and practice.

Epicureanism A Hellenistic philosophy advocating the pursuit of pleasure (mental) and avoidance of pain as the supreme good.

Equal field system Agricultural reform favoring the peasants under the Tang dynasty in China.

Equity Fairness to contending parties.

Era of Stagnation The era of Brezhnev's government in the Soviet Union (1964–1982), when the Soviet society and economy faced increasing troubles.

Era of Warring States The period of Chinese history between c. 500 and 220 B.C.E.; characterized by the breakdown of the central government and feudal war.

Essay Concerning Human Understanding An important philosophical essay by John Locke that underpinned Enlightenment optimism.

Estates General The parliament of France; composed of delegates from three social orders: clergy, nobility, and commoners.

Ethnic, Ethnicity The racial, cultural, or linguistic affiliation of an individual or group of human beings.

Etruscans The pre-Roman rulers of most of northern and central Italy and cultural models for early Roman civilization.

European Economic Community An association of western European nations founded in 1957; now called the European Union, it embraces fifteen countries with several more in candidate status.

Excommunication The act of being barred from the Roman Catholic community by decree of a bishop or the pope.

Existentialism Twentieth-century philosophy that was popular after World War II in Europe; insists on the necessity to inject life with meaning by individual decisions.

Exodus The Hebrews' flight from the wrath of the Egyptian pharaoh in c. 1250 B.C.E.

Extended family Parents and children plus several other kin group members such as in-laws, cousins, uncles and aunts.

F

Factory Acts Laws passed by Parliament in 1819 and 1833 that began the regulation of hours and working conditions in Britain.

Factory system Massing of labor and material under one roof with a single proprietorship and management of production.

Fallow Land left uncultivated for a period to recover fertility.

Fascism A political movement in the twentieth century that embraced totalitarian government policies to achieve a unity of people and leader; first experienced in Mussolini's Italy.

Fathers of the Church Leading theologians and explainers of Christian doctrine in the fourth and early fifth centuries.

Fertile Crescent A belt of civilized settlements reaching from lower Mesopotamia across Syria, Lebanon, and Israel and into Egypt.

Feudal system A mode of government based originally on mutual military obligations between lord and vassal; later often extended to civil affairs of all types; generally supported by landowning privileges.

Final Solution Name given by the Nazis to the wartime massacres of European Jews.

First Consul Title adopted by Napoleon after his coup d'état in 1799.

First Emperor (Shi Huangdi) The founder of the short-lived Qin dynasty (221–205 B.C.E.) and creator of China as an imperial state.

First Five-Year Plan Introduced in 1929 at Stalin's command to collectivize agriculture and industrialize the economy of the Soviet Union.

First Industrial Revolution The initial introduction of machine-powered production; began in late eighteenth-century Britain.

First International Title of original association of socialists, in 1860s Europe.

Five Pillars of Islam Popular term for the basic tenets of Muslim faith.

Floating world A term for ordinary human affairs popularized by the novels and stories of eighteenth-century Japan.

Forbidden City The center of Ming and Qing government in Beijing; entry was forbidden to ordinary citizens.

Four Little Tigers Singapore, Taiwan, South Korea, and Hong Kong in the 1960s–1980s economic upsurge.

Four Noble Truths The Buddha's doctrine on human fate.

Fourteen Points The outline for a just peace proposed by Woodrow Wilson in 1918.

Franco-Prussian War The 1870–1871 conflict between these two powers resulting in German unification.

Frankfurt Assembly A German parliament held in 1848 that was unsuccessful in working out a liberal constitution for a united German state.

Führer, der "The Leader" in Nazi Germany—specifically, Hitler.

Fujiwara clan Daimyo noble clan controlling the shogunate in ninth- to twelfth-century Japan.

G

Gendarme of Europe Name given by liberals to the Russian imperial government under Czar Nicholas I (1825–1855).

General theory of relativity Einstein's theory that introduced the modern era of physics in 1916.

Gentiles All non-Jews.

Geocentric "Earth centered"; theory of the cosmos that erroneously held the Earth to be its center.

Ghana The earliest of the extensive empires in the western Sudan; also a modern African state.

Ghetto Italian name for the quarter restricted to Jews.

Gilgamesh One of the earliest epics in world literature, originating in prehistoric Mesopotamia.

Glasnost The Russian term for "openness"; along with *perestroika*, employed to describe the reforms instituted by Gorbachev in the late 1980s.

Glorious Revolution of 1688 The English revolt against the unpopular Catholic king James II and the subsequent introduction of certain civil rights restricting monarchic powers.

Golden Horde The Russia-based segment of the Mongol world empire.

Golden mean Greek concept of avoiding the extremes; "truth lies in the middle."

Good Neighbor Policy President Franklin D. Roosevelt's attempt to reform previous U.S. policy and honor Latin American sovereignty.

Gothic style An artistic style, found notably in architecture, that came into general European usage during the thirteenth century.

Gracchi brothers Roman noble brothers who unsuccessfully attempted reform as consuls in the late republican era.

Grand vizier Title of the Turkish prime minister during the Ottoman era.

Great Elector Frederick William of Prussia (1640–1688); one of the princes who elected the Holy Roman Emperor.

Great Leap Forward Mao Zedong's misguided attempt in 1958–1960 to provide China with an instantaneous industrial base rivaling that of more advanced nations.

Great Proletarian Cultural Revolution The period from 1966 to 1976 when Mao inspired Chinese youth to rebel against all authority except his own; caused great damage to the Chinese economy and culture.

Great Purge The arrest and banishment of millions of Soviet Communist Party members and ordinary citizens at Stalin's orders in the mid-1930s for fictitious "crimes against the State and Party."

Great Reforms (Russia) Decrees affecting several areas of life issued by Czar Alexander II between 1859 and 1874.

Great Schism A division in the Roman Catholic Church between 1378 and 1417 when two (and for a brief period, three) popes competed for the allegiance of European Christians; a consequence of the Babylonian Captivity of the papacy in Avignon, southern France.

Great Trek The march of the Boers into the interior of South Africa where they founded the Orange Free State in 1836.

Great Zimbabwe The leading civilization of early southern Africa.

Grossdeutsch* versus *Kleindeutsch The controversy over the scope and type of the unified German state in the nineteenth century; *Kleindeutsch* would exclude multinational Austria, and *Grossdeutsch* would include it.

Guild A medieval urban organization that controlled the production and sale prices of many goods and services.

Gupta dynasty The rulers of most of India in the 300–400s C.E.; the last native dynasty to unify the country.

Habsburg dynasty The family that controlled the Holy Roman Empire after the thirteenth century; based in Vienna, they ruled Austria until 1918.

Hacienda A Spanish-owned plantation in Latin America that used native or slave labor to produce export crops.

Hagia Sophia Greek name ("Holy Wisdom") of the cathedral in Constantinople, later made into a mosque by Ottoman Turkish conquerors.

Haiku A type of Japanese poetry always three lines in length. The lines always have five, seven, and five syllables.

Hajj The pilgrimage to the sacred places of Islam.

Han dynasty The dynasty that ruled China from c. 200 B.C.E. to 221 C.E.

Hangzhou Capital city of Song dynasty China and probably the largest town in the contemporary world.

Hanoverians The dynasty of British monarchs after 1714; from the German duchy of Hanover.

Harem Turkish name for the part of a dwelling reserved for women.

Hegira "Flight"; Muhammed's forced flight from Mecca in 622 C.E.; marks the first year of the Muslim calendar.

Heliocentrism Opposite of *geocentrism*; recognizes sun as center of solar system.

Hellenistic A blend of Greek and Asiatic cultures; extant in the Mediterranean basin and Middle East between 300 B.C.E. and c. 200 C.E.

Helots Messenian semislaves of Spartan overlords.

Heresies Wrong belief in religious doctrines.

Hetairai High-class female entertainer-prostitutes in ancient Greece.

Hinayana Buddhism A stricter, monastic form of Buddhism, claiming closer link with the Buddha's teaching; often called Theravada. Headquartered in Sri Lanka and strong in Southeast Asia.

Historiography The writing of history so as to interpret it.

History Human actions in past time, as recorded and remembered.

Hittites An Indo-European people who were prominent in the Near East around 1200 B.C.E.

Hohenzollerns The dynasty that ruled Prussia-Germany until 1918.

Hominid A humanlike creature.

Homo sapiens "Thinking man"; modern human beings.

Horus The falcon-headed god whose earthly, visible form was the reigning pharaoh in ancient Egypt.

Hubris An unjustified confidence in one's abilities or powers leading to a tragic end.

Huguenots French Calvinists, many of whom were forced to emigrate in the seventeenth century.

Humanism The intellectual movement that sees humans as the sole valid arbiter of their values and purpose.

Hungarian Revolution The Hungarians' attempt to free themselves from Soviet control in October 1956; crushed by the Soviets.

Hyksos A people who invaded the Nile delta in Egypt and ruled it during the Second Intermediate Period (c. 1650–1570 B.C.E.).

Ideographs Written signs conveying entire ideas and not related to the spoken language; used by the Chinese from earliest times.

Iliad The first of the two epics supposedly written by Homer in eighth-century Greece.

Imperator Roman title of a temporary dictator given powers by the Senate; later, emperor.

Impressionists Members of a Paris-centered school of nineteenth-century painting focusing on light and color.

Inca Title of the emperor of the Quechuan speaking peoples of Peru prior to arrival of the Spanish.

Indochina, Union of Official term for the French colonies in Indochina until their dissolution in the 1950s.

Inductive reasoning Arriving at truth by reasoning from specific cases to a general law or proposition.

Infamia Roman term for immoral but not illegal acts.

Inquisition Roman Catholic agency that was responsible for censorship of doctrines and books; mainly active in Iberian lands in the fifteenth through seventeenth centuries.

Institutes of the Christian Religion John Calvin's major work that established the theology and doctrine of the Calvinist churches; first published in 1536.

Intelligentsia Russian term for a social group that actively influences the beliefs and actions of others, seeking reforms; generally connected with the professions and media.

Investiture Controversy A dispute between the Holy Roman Emperor and the pope in the eleventh and early twelfth centuries about which authority should appoint German bishops.

Iranian Revolution The fundamentalist and anti-Western movement led by the Ayatollah Khomeini that seized power from the shah of Iran through massive demonstrations in 1979.

Irredentism The attempt by members of a nation living outside the national state to link themselves to it politically and/or territorially.

Isis A chief Egyptian goddess, represented by the Nile River.

Jacobins Radical revolutionaries during the French Revolution; organized in clubs headquartered in Paris.

Jacquerie A French peasant rebellion against noble landlords during the fourteenth century.

Janissaries From Turkish *yeni cheri,* meaning "new troops"; an elite troop in the Ottoman army; consisted of Christian boys from the Balkans.

Jesuits Members of the Society of Jesus, a Catholic religious order founded in 1547 to combat Protestantism.

Jewish War A rebellion of Jewish Zealots against Rome in 66–70 C.E.

Jihad Holy war on behalf of the Muslim faith.

Judea One of the two Jewish kingdoms emerging after the death of Solomon when his kingdom was split in two; the other was Samaria.

July Monarchy The reign of King Louis Philippe in France (1830–1848); so called because he came to power in July 1830.

Junkers The landowning nobility of Prussia.

Jus gentium "Law of peoples"; Roman law governing relations between Romans and others.

Justification by faith Doctrine held by Martin Luther whereby Christian faith alone, and not good works, could be the path to heavenly bliss.

K

Ka The immortal soul in the religion of ancient Egypt.

Ka'aba The original shrine of pagan Arabic religion in Mecca containing the Black Stone; now one of the holiest places of Islam.

Kabuki A type of popular Japanese drama depicting heroic and romantic themes and stories.

Kadi An Islamic judge.

Kamakura shogunate Government by members of a noble Japanese family from the late twelfth to the mid–fourteenth century in the name of the emperor, who was their puppet.

Kami Shinto spirits in nature.

Kampuchea Native name of Cambodia, a state of Southeast Asia bordered by Thailand and Vietnam.

Karma The balance of good and evil done in a given incarnation in Hindu belief.

Karnak The site of a great temple complex along the Nile River in Egypt.

Kashmir A province in northwestern India that Pakistan also claims.

Kellogg-Briand Pact A formal disavowal of war by sixty nations in 1928.

KGB An abbreviation for the Soviet secret police; used after *Cheka* and *NKVD* had been discarded.

Khmers The inhabitants of Cambodia; founders of a large empire in ancient Southeast Asia.

Kiev, Principality of The first Russian state; flourished from C. 800 to 1240 when it fell to Mongols.

King of Kings The title of the Persian emperor.

Kleindeutsch "Small German"; adjective describing a form of German unification that excluded the multinational Austria; opposite of *grossdeutsch.*

Knights Type of feudal noble who held title and landed domain only for his lifetime; generally based originally on military service to his overlord.

Korean War 1950–1953 war between United Nations, led by the United States, and North Korea; precipitated by the invasion of South Korea.

Kuomintang (KMT) The political movement headed by Chiang Kai-shek during the 1930s and 1940s in China.

Kush Kingdom in northeast Africa that had close relations with Egypt for several centuries in the pre-Christian epoch.

Kyoto Ancient capital of the Japanese empire and seat of the emperor.

L

Labour Party Political party founded in 1906 by British labor unions and others for representation of the working classes.

Late Manzhou Restoration An attempt by Chinese reformers in the 1870s to restore the power of the central government after the suppression of the Taiping rebellion.

League of Nations An international organization founded after World War I to maintain peace and promote amity among nations; the United States did not join.

Left The reforming or revolutionary wing of the political spectrum; associated originally with the ideals of the radical French Revolution.

Legalism A Chinese philosophy of government emphasizing strong authority.

Legislative Assembly The second law-making body created during the French Revolution; dominated by the Jacobins, it gave way to the radical Convention.

Legitimacy A term adopted by the victors at the Congress of Vienna in 1815 to explain the reimposition of former monarchs and regimes after the Napoleonic wars.

Levée en masse General conscription for the army; first occurred in 1793 during the French Revolution.

Leviathan A book by Thomas Hobbes that supported the necessity of the state and, by inference, royal absolutism.

Liberum veto Latin for "free veto"; used by Polish nobles to nullify majority will in the Polish parliaments of the eighteenth century.

Lineage A technical term for family or clan association.

"Little Red Book" Contained the thoughts of Chairman Mao Zedong on various topics; used as a talisman during the Cultural Revolution by young Chinese.

Locarno Pact An agreement between France and Germany in 1925.

Lollards Name of unknown origin given to the English religious rebels of the 1380s and who later protested against the privileges of the clergy and were vigorously persecuted.

Long March The 6,000-mile fighting retreat of the Chinese communists under Mao Zedong to Shensi province in 1934–1935.

Lyric poetry Poetry that celebrates the poet's emotions.

M

Maastricht Treaty Signed in 1991 by members of the European Community; committed them to closer political-economic ties.

Macao Portuguese colony-island off China's coast; founded 1513.

Machtergreifung "Seizure of power"; Nazi term for Hitler's rise to dictatorial powers in Germany.

Maghrib or **Maghreb** Muslim northwest Africa.

Mahabharata A Hindu epic poem; a favorite in India.

Mahayana Buddhism A more liberal, looser form of Buddhism; originating soon after the Buddha's death, it deemphasized the monastic life and abstruse philosophy in favor of prayer to the eternal Buddha and the bodhisattvas who succeeded him.

Mahdi Rebellion A serious rebellion against European rule in the Sudan in the 1890s, led by a charismatic holy man ("mahdi") whose death and British attack ended it.

Majapahit The main town of a maritime empire in fourteenth-century Indonesia.

Mali The African Sudanese empire that was the successor to Ghana in the 1300s and 1400s.

Manchester liberalism The economic practice of exploiting the laboring poor in the name of the free market.

Manchuria Large province of northeastern China, seized in the nineteenth century by Russia and Japan before being retaken by the Maoist government.

Mandarins Chinese scholar-officials who had been trained in Confucian principles and possessed great class solidarity.

Mandate Britain and France governed several Asian and African peoples after World War I, supposedly as agents of the League of Nations.

Mandate of heaven A theory of rule originated by the Zhou dynasty in China, emphasizing the connection between imperial government's rectitude and its right to govern.

Manor An agricultural estate of varying size normally owned by a noble or the clergy and worked by free and unfree peasants/serfs.

Manu Legendary lawgiver in India.

Manus "Hand"; Latin term for the legal power of a person over another.

Manzhou Originally nomadic tribes living in Manchuria who eventually overcame Ming resistance and established the Qing dynasty in seventeenth-century China.

Marathon The battle in 490 B.C.E. in which the Greeks defeated the Persians, ending the first Persian War.

March on Rome A fascist demonstration in 1922 orchestrated by Mussolini as a preliminary step to dictatorship in Italy.

March Revolution of 1917 The abdication of Czar Nicholas II and the establishment of the Provisional Government in Russia.

Maritime Expeditions (China's) Early fifteenth-century explorations of the Indian and South Pacific Oceans ordered by the Chinese emperor.

Marshall Plan A program proposed by the U.S. secretary of state George Marshall and implemented from 1947 to 1951 to aid western Europe's recovery from World War II.

Masscult The banal culture that some think replaced the traditional elite culture in the twentieth-century West.

Matriarchy A society in which females are dominant socially and politically.

Matrilineal descent Attribution of name and inheritance to children via the maternal line.

May Fourth Movement A reform movement of young Chinese students and intellectuals in the post–World War I era; Mao Zedong was a member prior to his conversion to Marxism.

Maya The most advanced of the Amerindian peoples who lived in southern Mexico and Guatemala and created a high urban civilization in the pre-Columbian era.

Medes An early Indo-European people who, with the Persians, settled in Iran.

Meiji Restoration The overthrow of the Tokugawa shogunate and restoration of the emperor to nominal power in Japan in 1867.

Mein Kampf *My Struggle;* Hitler's credo, written while serving a prison term in 1924.

Mercantilism A theory of national economics popular in the seventeenth and eighteenth centuries; aimed at establishing a favorable trade balance through government control of exports and imports as well as domestic industry.

Meritocracy The rule of the meritorious (usually determined by examinations).

Messenian Wars Conflicts between the neighbors Sparta and Messenia that resulted in Messenia's conquest by Sparta in about 600 B.C.E.

Messiah A savior-king who would someday lead the Jews to glory.

Mestizo A person of mixed Amerindian and European blood.

Metaphor of the Cave Plato's explanation of the difficulties encountered by those who seek philosophical truth and the necessity of a hierarchy of leadership.

Mexican Revolution The armed struggle that occurred in Mexico between 1910 and 1920 to install a more socially progressive and populist government.

Middle Kingdom The period in Egyptian history from 2100 to 1600 B.C.E.; followed the First Intermediate Period.

Milan, Edict of A decree issued by the emperor Constantine in 313 C.E. that legalized Christianity and made it the favored religion in the Roman Empire.

Minoan An ancient civilization that was centered on Crete between C. 2000 and C. 1400 B.C.E.

Missi dominici Agents of Charlemagne in the provinces of his empire.

Modernism A philosophy of art of the late nineteenth and early twentieth centuries that rejected classical models and values and sought new expressions and aesthetics.

Mohenjo-Daro Site of one of the two chief towns of the ancient Indus valley civilization.

Moksha The final liberation from bodily existence and reincarnation in Hinduism.

Monarchy Rule by a single individual, who often claims divine inspiration and protection.

Mongols Name for collection of nomadic, savage warriors of Central Asia who conquered most of Eurasia in the thirteenth century.

Mongol yoke A Russian term for the Mongol occupation of Russia, 1240–1480.

Monotheism A religion having only one god.

Monroe Doctrine The announcement in 1823 by U.S. president James Monroe that no European interference in Latin America would be tolerated.

Mughal A corruption of "Mongol"; refers to the period of Muslim rule in India.

Mulatto A person of mixed African and European blood.

Munich Agreement The 1938 meetings between Hitler and the British and French prime ministers that allowed Germany to take much of Czechoslovakia; the agreement confirmed Hitler's belief that the democratic governments would not fight German aggression.

Munich putsch The failed attempt by Hitler to seize power by armed force in 1923.

Municipia The basic unit of Roman local government; similar to a present-day municipality.

Muslim Brotherhoods Associations of Islamic groups that have strong fundamentalist leanings and practice mutual aid among members.

Mystery religion One of various Hellenistic cults promising immortal salvation of the individual.

N

Nantes, Edict of A law granting toleration to French Calvinists that was issued in 1598 by King Henry IV to end the religious civil war.

Napoleonic settlement A collective name for the decrees and actions by Napoleon between 1800 and 1808 that legalized and systematized many elements of the French Revolution.

National Assembly The first law-making body during the French Revolution; created a moderate constitutional monarchy.

Natural selection The Darwinian doctrine in biology that change in species derives from mechanistic changes induced by the environment.

Navigation Acts Laws regulating commerce with the British colonies in North America in favor of Britain.

Nazism The German variant of fascism created by Hitler.

Neanderthal man A species of *Homo sapiens* flourishing between 100,000 and 30,000 years ago and that mysteriously died out; the name comes from the German valley where the first remains were found.

Negritude A literary term referring to the self-conscious awareness of African cultural values; popular in areas of Africa formerly under French control.

Neo-Confucianism An eleventh- and twelfth-century C.E. revival of Confucian thought with special emphasis on love and responsibility toward others.

Neolithic Age The period from c. 7000 B.C.E. to the development of metals by a given people.

New China movement An intellectual reform movement in the 1890s that attempted to change and modernize China by modernizing the government.

New Economic Policy (NEP) A policy introduced at the conclusion of the civil war that allowed for partial capitalism and private enterprise in the Soviet Union.

New imperialism The late nineteenth-century worldwide colonialism of European powers interested in strategic and market advantage.

New Kingdom or **Empire** The period from c. 1550 to 700 B.C.E. in Egyptian history; followed the Second Intermediate Period. The period from 1550 to c. 1200 B.C.E. was the Empire.

Nicaea, Council of A fourth-century conclave that defined essential doctrines of Christianity under the supervision of the emperor Constantine.

Niger River The great river draining most of the African bulge.

Ninety-five Theses The challenge to church authority publicized by Martin Luther, October 31, 1517.

Nineveh The main city and later capital of the Assyrian empire.

Nirvana The Buddhist equivalent of the Hindu *moksha;* the final liberation from suffering and reincarnation.

NKVD An abbreviation for the Soviet secret police; used after *Cheka* but before *KGB.*

Nonaggression Pact of 1939 The treaty between Hitler and Stalin in which each agreed to maintain neutrality in any forthcoming war involving the other party.

North American Free Trade Agreement (NAFTA) An agreement signed by the United States, Canada, and Mexico in 1993 that provides for much liberalized trade among these nations.

North Atlantic Treaty Organization (NATO) An organization founded in 1949 under U.S. aegis as a defense against threatened communist aggression in Europe.

Nuclear family Composed of parents and children only.

Nuclear test ban The voluntary cessation of aboveground testing of nuclear weapons by the United States and the Soviet Union; in existence from 1963 to the present.

Nuremberg Laws Laws defining racial identity that were aimed against Jews; adopted in 1935 by the German government.

O

October Revolution of 1917 The Bolshevik coup d'état in St. Petersburg that ousted the Provisional Government and established a communist state in Russia.

Odyssey Second of the two Homeric epic poems, detailing the adventures of the homeward-bound Ulysses coming from the siege of Troy; see also *Iliad.*

Oedipus Rex Part of a triad of tragedies written by the classical Greek playwright Sophocles concerning the life and death of Oedipus and his daughter, Antigone.

Oil boycott of 1973 The temporary withholding of oil exports by OPEC members to Western governments friendly to Israel; led to a massive rise in the price of oil and economic dislocation in many countries.

Old Kingdom The period of Egyptian history from 3100 to 2200 B.C.E.

Old Testament The first portion of the Judeo-Christian Bible; the holy books of the Jews.

Oligarchy Rule by a few.

Olmec The earliest Amerindian civilization in Mexico.

On the Origin of Species Charles Darwin's book that first enunciated the evolutionary theory in biology; published in 1859.

Operation Barbarossa Code name for German invasion of the Soviet Union in 1941.

Opium Wars Conflicts that occurred in 1840–1842 on the Chinese coast between the British and the Chinese over the importation of opium into China. The Chinese defeat began eighty years of subordination to foreigners.

Oracle bones Animal bones used as a primitive writing medium by early Chinese.

Orange Free State One of the two political organisms founded after the Boer Great Trek in southern Africa.

Organization for Pan African Unity (OAU) The present name of the association of sub-Saharan African nations founded in 1963 for mutual aid.

Organization of American States (OAS) An organization founded in 1948 under U.S. auspices to provide mutual defense and aid; now embraces all countries on the American continents except Cuba.

Organization of Petroleum Exporting Countries (OPEC) Founded in the 1960s by Arab governments and later expanded to include several Latin American and African members.

Osiris A chief Egyptian god, ruler of the underworld.

Ostpolitik German term for Chancellor Brandt's 1960s policy of pursuing normalized relations with West Germany's neighbors to the east.

Ostracism In ancient Greece, the expulsion of a citizen from a *polis* for a given period.

P

Paleolithic Age The period from the earliest appearance of *Homo sapiens* to c. 7000 B.C.E., though exact dates vary by area; the Old Stone Age.

Paleontology The study of prehistoric things.

Palestine Liberation Organization (PLO) An organization founded in the 1960s by Palestinians expelled from Israel; until 1994 it aimed at destruction of the state of Israel by any means. Superseded by the autonomous Palestinian Authority created in 1997.

Pan-Arabism A movement after World War I to assert supranational Arab unity, aimed eventually at securing a unified Arab state.

Pantheism A belief that God exists in all things, living and inanimate.

Paragraph 231 of the Versailles Treaty The "war guilt" paragraph, imputing sole responsibility for reparation of all damages to Germany.

Pariah An outcast; a person having no acknowledged status.

Paris Commune A leftist revolt against the national government after France was defeated by Prussia in 1871; crushed by the conservatives with much bloodshed.

Parthenon The classic Greek temple to Athena on the Acropolis in Athens center.

Patents Royal documents conferring nobility.

Patria potestas The power of the father over his family in ancient Rome.

Patriarchy A society in which males have social and political dominance.

Patricians (*patres*) The upper governing class in ancient Rome.

Pax Mongolica The Mongol peace; between c. 1250 and c. 1350 in most of Eurasia.

Pax Romana The "Roman peace"; the era of Roman control over the Mediterranean basin and much of Europe between c. 31 B.C.E. and 180 C.E. or later.

Peace of Augsburg Pact ending the German religious wars in 1555, dividing the country between Lutheran and Catholic hegemony.

Peaceful coexistence The declared policy of Soviet leader Nikita Khrushchev in dealing with the capitalist West after 1956.

Peloponnesian War The great civil war between Athens and Sparta and their respective allies in ancient Greece; fought between 429 and 404 B.C.E. and eventually won by Sparta.

Peon A peasant in semislave status on a hacienda.

Perestroika The Russian term for "restructuring," which, with *glasnost,* was used to describe the reforms instituted by Gorbachev in the late 1980s USSR.

Persepolis With Ecbatana, one of the twin capitals of the Persian empire in the 500s B.C.E.; destroyed by Alexander the Great.

Persian Wars The conflict between the Greeks and the Persian empire in the fifth century B.C.E., fought in two installments and ending with Greek victory.

Persians An early Indo-European tribe that, along with the Medes, settled in Iran.

Petrine succession The doctrine of the Roman Catholic Church by which the pope, the bishop of Rome, is the direct successor of St. Peter.

Pharaoh The title of the god-king of ancient Egypt.

Philosophes A French term used to refer to the writers and activist intellectuals during the Enlightenment.

Phonetic alphabet A system of writing that matches signs with the sounds of the oral language.

Piedmont "Foot of the mountains"; the north Italian kingdom that led the unification of Italy in the mid–nineteenth century.

Plastic arts Those that have three dimensions.

Platea The land battle that, along with the naval battle of Salamis, ended the second Persian War with a Greek victory over the Persians.

Plebeians (*plebs*) The common people of ancient Rome.

Pogrom Mob violence against local Jews.

Polis The political and social community of citizens in ancient Greece.

Polytheism A religion having many gods.

Popular Front The coordinated policy of all antifascist parties; inspired by the Soviets in the mid-1930s against Hitler.

Porte, The A name for the Ottoman government in Istanbul.

Post-Impressionist A term for late nineteenth-century painting that emphasizes color and line in a then-revolutionary fashion.

Praetorian Guard The imperial bodyguard in the Roman Empire and the only armed force in Italy.

Precedent What has previously been accepted in the application of law.

Prehistory The long period of human activity prior to the writing of history.

Pre-Socratics Greek philosophers prior to Socrates who focused on the nature of the material world.

Primogeniture A system of inheritance in which the estate passes to the eldest legitimate son.

Princeps "The First" or "the Leader" in Latin; title taken by Augustus Caesar.

Principate The reign of Augustus Caesar from 27 B.C.E. to 14 C.E.

Proconsuls Provincial governors and military commanders in ancient Rome.

Proletariat Poverty-stricken people without skills; also, a Marxist term for the propertyless working classes.

Provisional Government A self-appointed parliamentary group exercising power in republican Russia from March to October 1917.

Psychoanalysis A psychological technique that employs free associations in the attempt to determine the cause of mental illness.

Ptolemaic Kingdom of Egypt The state created by Ptolemy, one of Alexander the Great's generals, in the Hellenistic era.

Pueblo culture Name given to the southwest U.S. Indian culture beginning c. 1000 B.C.E.

Punic Wars The three conflicts between Rome and Carthage that ended with the destruction of the Carthaginian empire and the extension of Roman control throughout the western Mediterranean.

Purdah The segregation of females in Hindu society.

Purgatory In Catholic belief, the place where the soul is purged after death for past sins and thus becomes fit for Heaven.

Puritans The English Calvinists who were dissatisfied by the theology of the Church of England and wished to "purify" it.

Pyramid of Khufu (Cheops) The largest pyramid; stands outside Cairo.

 Q

Qing dynasty The last Chinese dynasty, which ruled from 1644 until 1911; established by Manzhou invaders after they defeated the Ming rulers.

Quadruple Alliance The diplomatic pact to maintain the peace established by the Big Four victors of the Napoleonic wars (Austria, Britain, Prussia, and Russia); lasted for a decade.

Quanta A concept in physics indicating the expenditure of energy.

Quechua The spoken language of the Incas of Peru.

Qur'an The holy scripture of Islam.

 R

Raison d'état The idea that the welfare of the state should be supreme in government policy.

Raja Turkish for "cattle"; used to refer to non-Muslims.

Red Guard The youthful militants who carried out the Cultural Revolution in China during the 1960s.

Red International See **Third International.**

Reform Bill of 1832 Brought about a reform of British parliamentary voting and representation that strengthened the middle class and the urbanites.

Reformation The early-sixteenth-century upheaval led by Martin Luther that modified or in some cases rejected altogether some Catholic doctrine practices; led to the establishment of Protestant churches.

Reign of Terror The period (1793–1794) of extreme Jacobin radicalism during the French Revolution.

Reparations Money and goods that Germany was to pay to the victorious Allies after World War I under the Versailles Treaty.

Republican government A form of governing that imitates the Roman *res publica* in its rejection of monarchy.

Rerum novarum An encyclical issued by Pope Leo XIII in 1890 that committed the Roman Catholic church to attempting to achieve social justice for the poor.

Restoration (English) The period of the 1660s–1680s when Charles II was called by Parliament to take his throne and was thus restored to power.

Revisionism The late-nineteenth-century adaptation of Marxist socialism that aimed to introduce basic reform through parliamentary acts rather than through revolution.

Revolution of 1989 The throwing out of the communist governments in eastern Europe by popular demand and/or armed uprising.

Rigveda The oldest of the four Vedas, or epics, brought into India by the Aryans.

Romanov dynasty Ruled Russia from 1613 until 1917.

Rome, Treaty of The pact signed by six western European nations in 1957 that is the founding document of the European Union.

Rubaiyat The verses attributed to the twelfth-century Persian poet Omar Khayyam.

S

Safavid The dynasty of Shi'ite Muslims that ruled Persia from the 1500s to the 1700s.

Sahel The arid belt extending across Africa south of the Sahara; also called the Sudan.

Sakoku Japan's self-imposed isolation from the outer world that lasted two centuries until 1854.

Salamis The naval battle that, with the battle of Platea, ended the second Persian War with a Greek victory.

Samaria One of the two kingdoms into which the Hebrew kingdom was split after Solomon's death; the other was Judea.

Samsara The recurrent reincarnation of the soul; a concept shared by Hinduism and Buddhism.

Samurai Japanese warrior-aristocrats of medieval and early modern times.

Sanhedrin The Jewish governing council under the overlordship of Rome.

Sanskrit The sacred language of India; came originally from the Aryans.

Sardinia-Piedmont. See **Piedmont.**

Sati (suttee) In India, the practice in which a widow committed suicide at the death of her husband.

Satrapy A province under a governor or *satrap* in the ancient Persian empire.

Savanna The semiarid grasslands where most African civilizations developed.

Schutzstaffel **(SS)** Hitler's bodyguard; later enlarged to be a subsidiary army and to provide the concentration camp guards.

Scientific method The method of observation and experiment by which the physical sciences proceed to new knowledge.

Second Front The reopening of a war front in the west against the Axis powers in World War II; eventually accomplished by the invasion of Normandy in June 1944.

Second Industrial Revolution The second phase of industrialization that occurred in the late 1800s after the introduction of electricity and the internal combustion engine.

Second International Association of socialist parties founded in 1889; after the Russian Revolution in 1917, the Second International split into democratic and communist segments.

Secret speech Premier Nikita Khrushchev of the USSR gave an account in February 1956 of the crimes of Joseph Stalin against his own people that was supposed to remain secret but was soon known internationally.

Secularism The rejection of supernatural religion as the arbiter of earthly action; emphasis on worldly affairs.

Seleucid kingdom of Persia The successor state to the empire of Alexander the Great in most of the Middle East.

Self-strengthening The late nineteenth-century attempt by Chinese officials to bring China into the modern world by instituting reforms; failed to achieve its goal.

Seljuks Turkish converts to Islam who seized the Baghdad government from the Abbasids in the eleventh century.

Semitic Adjective describing a person or language belonging to one of the most widespread of the western Asian groups; among many others, it embraces Hebrew and Arabic.

Serfdom Restriction of personal and economic freedoms associated with medieval European agricultural society.

Seven Years' War Fought between France and England, with their allies, around the world, 1756–1763; won by England, with major accessions of territory to the British empire.

Shang dynasty The first historical rulers of China; ruled from c. 1500 to c. 1100 B.C.E.

Sharija The sacred law of Islam; based on the Qur'an.

Shi'ite A minority sect of Islam; adherents believe that kinship with Muhammad is necessary to qualify for the caliphate.

Shiki Rights attached to parcels of land (*shoen*) in Japan.

Shinto Native Japanese animism.

Shiva A member of the high trinity of Hindu gods; lord of destruction but also of procreation; often pictured dancing.

Shoen Parcels of land in Japan with *shiki* (rights) attached to them; could take many forms and have various possessors.

Shogunate The government of medieval Japan in which the *shogun*, a military and civil regent, served as the actual leader, while the emperor was the symbolic head of the state and religion.

Show trials First used for the staged trials of alleged traitors to the Soviet system in 1936–1937; generically, a political trial in which the conviction of the accused is a foregone conclusion.

Sikhs Members of a cult founded in the sixteenth century C.E. seeking a middle way between Islam and Hindu belief; centered on the Punjab region in northern India.

Sino-Soviet conflict Differences in the interpretation of Marxism were accentuated by conflict over proper policy vis-à-vis the United States in the 1950s and 1960s in Moscow and Beijing.

Sino-Tibetan languages The family of languages spoken by the Chinese and Tibetan peoples.

Social Darwinism The adaptation of Darwinian biology to apply to human society in simplistic terms.

Social Democrats Noncommunist socialists who refused to join the Third International and founded independent parties.

Solidarity The umbrella organization founded by Lech Walesa and other anticommunist Poles in 1981 to recover Polish freedom; banned for eight years, but continued underground until it was acknowledged in 1989.

Song dynasty The dynasty that ruled China from c. 1127 until 1279, when the last ruler was overthrown by the Mongol invaders.

Songhai A West African state, centered on the bend of the Niger River, that reached its fullest extent in the sixteenth century before collapsing.

Spinning jenny A fundamental improvement over hand-spinning of cotton thread, developed by an English engineer in the 1780s.

Spirit of the Laws One of the basic tracts of the eighteenth-century Enlightenment, written by Baron Montesquieu and adopted by many reformers of government throughout Europe.

Springtime of the Peoples The spring and summer of 1848 when popular revolutions in Europe seemed to succeed.

Stalingrad The battle in 1942 that marked the turning point of World War II in Europe.

Stalinist economy Involved the transformation of a retarded agrarian economy to an industrialized one through massive reallocation of human and material resources directed by a central plan; imposed on the Soviet Union and then, in the first years after World War II, on eastern Europe.

Stamp Act A law enacted by the British Parliament in 1765 that imposed a fee on legal documents of all types and on all books and newspapers sold in the American colonies.

State The term for a territorial, sovereign entity of government.

Stoicism A Hellenistic philosophy that emphasized human brotherhood and natural law as guiding principles.

Structural Adjustment Programs (SAPs) Programs designed by the World Bank to achieve economic improvement in developing countries; frequently failures.

Stuprum A Roman legal term denoting acts that were both immoral and illegal; contrast with *infamia,* which was an immoral but not illegal action.

Sturmabteilung (SA) The street-fighting "bully boys" of the Nazi Party; suppressed after 1934 by Hitler's orders.

Successor states Usual term for the several eastern European states that emerged from the Paris treaties of 1919 as successors to the Russian, German, and Austro-Hungarian empires.

Sudan The arid belt extending across Africa south of the Sahara; also called the Sahel.

Sufi Arabic name for a branch of Islamic worship that emphasizes emotional union with God and mystical powers.

Sui dynasty Ruled China from c. 580 to c. 620 C.E.; ended the disintegration of central government that had existed for the previous 130 years.

Sui juris "Of his own law"; Roman term for an individual, especially a female, who was not restricted by the usual laws or customs.

Sultanate of Delhi The government and state erected by the conquering Afghani Muslims after 1500 in north India; immediate predecessor to the Mughal empire.

Sumerians The creators of Mesopotamian urban civilization.

Sunni The majority group in Islam; adherents believe that the caliphate should go to the most qualified individual and should not necessarily pass to the kin of Muhammad.

Supremacy, Act of A law enacted in 1534 by the English Parliament that made the monarch the head of the Church of England.

Suzerain The superior of a vassal to whom the vassal owed feudal duties.

Swahili A hybrid language based on Bantu and Arabic; used extensively in East Africa.

Syndicalism A doctrine of government that advocates a society organized on the basis of syndicates or unions.

T

Taipings Anti-Manzhou rebels in China in the 1860s.

Taj Mahal The beautiful tomb built by the seventeenth-century Mughal emperor Jahan for his wife.

Tale of Genji First known novel in Asian, if not world, history; authored by a female courtier about life in the Japanese medieval court.

Tang dynasty Ruled China from c. 620 to c. 900 C.E. and began the great age of Chinese artistic and technical advances.

Tel el Amarna The site of great temple complexes along the Nile River in Egypt.

Test Act Seventeenth-century English law barring non-Anglican Church members from government and university positions.

Tetrarchy "Rule of four"; a system of individual rule established by Diocletian at the end of the third century C.E; failed to achieve its goals

Theocracy The rule of gods or their priests.

Theravada Buddhism A stricter, monastic form of Buddhism entrenched in Southeast Asia; same as Hinayana Buddhism.

Thermidorean reaction The conservative reaction to the Reign of Terror during the French Revolution.

Third Estate The great majority of Frenchmen: those neither clerical nor noble.

Third International An association of Marxist parties in many nations; inspired by Russian communists and headquartered in Moscow until its dissolution in 1943.

Third Republic of France The government of France after the exile of Emperor Napoleon III; lasted from 1871 until 1940.

Third Rome theory A Russian myth that Moscow was ordained to succeed Rome and Constantinople as the center of true Christianity.

Third World A term in use after World War II to denote countries and peoples in underdeveloped, formerly colonial areas of Asia, Africa, and Latin America; the First World was the West under U.S. leadership, and the Second World was the communist states under Soviet leadership.

Tienanmen Square, massacre on The shooting down of thousands of Chinese who were peacefully demonstrating for relaxation of political censorship by the communist leaders; occurred in 1989 in Beijing.

Tilsit, Treaty of A treaty concluded in 1807 after the French had defeated the Russians; divided Europe/Asia into French and Russian spheres.

Time of Troubles A fifteen-year period at the beginning of the seventeenth century in Russia when the state was nearly destroyed by revolts and wars.

Titoism The policy of neutrality in foreign policy combined with continued dedication to socialism in domestic policy that was followed by the Yugoslav Marxist leader Tito after his expulsion from the Soviet camp in 1948.

Toltec An Amerindian civilization centered in the Valley of Mexico; succeeded by the Aztecs.

Torah The first five books of the Old Testament; the Jews' fundamental law code.

Tories A nickname for British nineteenth-century conservatives; opposite of Whigs.

Totalitarianism The attempt by a dictatorial government to achieve total control over a society's life and ideas.

Transvaal Second of the two independent states set up by the Boer Great Trek in the early nineteenth century in South Africa.

Trent, Council of The council of Catholic clergy that directed the Counter-Reformation against Protestantism; met from 1545 until 1563.

Tribunes The chief representatives of the plebeians during the Roman republic.

Triple Alliance A pact concluded in 1882 that united Germany, Austria-Hungary, and Italy against possible attackers; the members were called the Central Powers.

Triumvirate "Three-man rule"; the First Triumvirate was during the 50s B.C.E. and the Second in the 30s B.C.E. during the last decades of the Roman republic.

Truman Doctrine The commitment of the U.S. government in 1947 to defend any noncommunist state against attempted communist takeover; proposed by President Harry Truman.

Twelve Tables The first written Roman law code; established c. 450 B.C.E.

Ulema A council of learned men who interpret the *sharija;* also, a council of religious advisers to the caliph or sultan.

Umayyad dynasty The caliphs resident in Damascus from 661 to 750 C.E.

Uncertainty principle The modern theory in physics that denies absolute causal relationships of matter and, hence, predictability.

Unequal treaties Chinese name for the diplomatic and territorial arrangements foisted on the weak Qing dynasty by European powers in the nineteenth century; also, the commercial treaties forced on just-opened Japan by the same powers and the United States.

Upanishads The ancient Hindu holy epics dealing with morals and philosophy.

Utopia "Nowhere"; Greek term used to denote an ideal place or society.

Utopian socialism The dismissive label given by Marx to previous theories that aimed at establishing a more just and benevolent society.

Vassal In medieval Europe, a person, usually a noble, who owed feudal duties to a superior, called a *suzerain.*

Vedas The four oral epics of the Aryans.

Verdun, Treaty of A treaty concluded in 843 that divided Charlemagne's empire among his three grandsons; established what became the permanent dividing lines between the French and Germans.

Vernacular The native oral language of a given people.

Villa The country estate of a Roman patrician or other wealthy Roman.

Vizier An official of Muslim government, especially a high Turkish official equivalent to prime minister.

Wakf An Islamic philanthropic foundation established by the devout.

Wandering of peoples A term referring to the migrations of various Germanic and Asiatic tribes in the third and fourth centuries C.E. that brought them into conflict with Rome.

Wannsee Conference The 1942 meeting of Nazi leaders that determined the "final solution" for the Jews.

Wars of the Austrian Succession Two 1740s wars between Prussia and Austria that gave important advantages to Prussia and its king, Frederick the Great.

War of the Roses An English civil war between noble factions over the succession to the throne in the fifteenth century.

Warsaw Pact An organization of the Soviet satellite states in Europe; founded under Russian aegis in 1954 to serve as a counterweight to NATO.

Waterloo The final defeat of Napoleon in 1815 after his return from Elban exile.

Wealth of Nations, The The short title of the pathbreaking work on national economy by Adam Smith; published in 1776.

Wehrgeld Under early Germanic law, a fine paid to an injured party or his or her family or lord that was equivalent to the value of the injured individual.

Weimar Republic The popular name for Germany's democratic government between 1919 and 1933.

Westphalia, Treaty of The treaty that ended the Thirty Years' War in 1648; the first modern peace treaty in that it established strategic and territorial gains as more important than religious or dynastic ones.

Whigs A nickname for British nineteenth-century liberals; opposite of Tories.

"White man's burden" A phrase coined by Rudyard Kipling to refer to what he considered the necessity of bringing European civilization to non-Europeans.

World Bank A monetary institution founded after World War II by Western nations to assist in the recovery effort and to aid the Third World's economic development.

Yalta Conference Conference in 1945 where Franklin D. Roosevelt, Joseph Stalin, and Winston Churchill (the "Big Three") met to attempt to settle postwar questions, particularly those affecting the future of Europe.

Yamato state The earliest known government of Japan; divided into feudal subdivisions ruled by clans and headed by the Yamato family.

Yin/yang East Asian distinction between the male and female characters in terms of active versus passive, warm versus cold, and the like.

Yom Kippur War A name for the 1973 conflict between Israel and its Arab neighbors.

Yuan dynasty Official term for the Mongol rule in China, 1279–1368.

Zama, Battle of Decisive battle of the Second Punic War; Roman victory in 202 was followed by absorption of most of the Carthaginian empire in the Mediterranean.

Zambo Term for mulattos in Brazil.

Zhou dynasty The second historical Chinese dynasty; ruled from c. 1100 to c. 400 B.C.E.

Zionism A movement founded by Theodor Herzl in 1896 to establish a Jewish national homeland in Palestine.

Zulu wars A series of conflicts between the British and the native Africans in South Africa in the late nineteenth century.

ANSWERS TO TEST YOUR KNOWLEDGE

CHAPTER 26
1. c, 2. a, 3. c, 4. d, 5. a, 6. c, 7. a, 8. d, 9. d

CHAPTER 27
1. c, 2. b, 3. c, 4. b, 5. d, 6. a, 7. a, 8. b, 9. c

CHAPTER 28
1. a, 2. d, 3. a, 4. a, 5. d, 6. a, 7. d

CHAPTER 29
1. a, 2. b, 3. d, 4. b, 5. d, 6. a, 7. a, 8. a, 9. c

CHAPTER 30
1. b, 2. d, 3. b, 4. c, 5. b, 6. c, 7. d, 8. c

CHAPTER 31
1. d, 2. a, 3. c, 4. c, 5. b, 6. c, 7. c, 8. b, 9. b, 10. d

CHAPTER 32
1. d, 2. b, 3. d, 4. a, 5. a, 6. c, 7. b, 8. b

CHAPTER 33
1. d, 2. b, 3. a, 4. b, 5. a, 6. c, 7. b, 8. b

CHAPTER 34
1. b, 2. b, 3. b, 4. b, 5. d, 6. c, 7. a, 8. d, 9. c

CHAPTER 35
1. b, 2. a, 3. b, 4. b, 5. d, 6. b, 7. a, 8. a

CHAPTER 36
1. a, 2. b, 3. d, 4. d, 5. c, 6. a, 7. c

CHAPTER 37
1. a, 2. c, 3. d, 4. b, 5. d, 6. b, 7. d, 8. a, 9. b, 10. a

CHAPTER 38
1. d, 2. c, 3. c, 4. b, 5. b, 6. c, 7. a

CHAPTER 39
1. a, 2. d, 3. a, 4. a, 5. b, 6. b, 7. a, 8. b

CHAPTER 40
1. a, 2. d, 3. c, 4. b, 5. c, 6. a, 7. b, 8. b, 9. b

CHAPTER 41
1. c, 2. c, 3. a, 4. a, 5. c, 6. a, 7. b, 8. a, 9. c

CHAPTER 42
1. c, 2. b, 3. d, 4. c, 5. c, 6. b, 7. d, 8. c

CHAPTER 43
1. b, 2. b, 3. b, 4. c, 5. c, 6. d, 7. a, 8. d

CHAPTER 44
1. a, 2. c, 3. d, 4. d, 5. a, 6. c, 7. b, 8. d

CHAPTER 45
1. c, 2. b, 3. c, 4. a, 5. b, 6. c, 7. a, 8. a

CHAPTER 46
1. b, 2. c, 3. c, 4. b, 5. d, 6. b, 7. c

CHAPTER 47
1. a, 2. b, 3. a, 4. a, 5. a, 6. b, 7. c, 8. d

CHAPTER 48
1. a, 2. c, 3. c, 4. d, 5. c, 6. a, 7. b

CHAPTER 49
1. b, 2. b, 3. b, 4. c, 5. b, 6. c, 7. a, 8. b

CHAPTER 50
1. c, 2. c, 3. c, 4. a, 5. c, 6. d, 7. b, 8. b

CHAPTER 51
1. a, 2. a, 3. b, 4. b, 5. d, 6. a, 7. c, 8. b

CHAPTER 52
1. d, 2. c, 3. c, 4. b, 5. c, 6. b, 7. d, 8. d

CHAPTER 53
1. d, 2. d, 3. c, 4. d, 5. b, 6. c, 7. b, 8. c

CHAPTER 54
1. a, 2. b, 3. d, 4. a, 5. b, 6. a, 7. c, 8. c, 9. c

CHAPTER 55
1. c, 2. a, 3. b, 4. d, 5. b, 6. b, 7. a

CHAPTER 56
1. b, 2. b, 3. d, 4. b, 5. a, 6. c, 7. b, 8. b

CHAPTER 57
1. d, 2. b, 3. b, 4. b, 5. d, 6. c, 7. d, 8. c

BIBLIOGRAPHY

PART FOUR
CHAPTER 26

Boxer, C. R. *The Portuguese Seaborne Empire, 1415–1825,* 1969. The best account of the achievement of tiny Portugal.

Cipolla, C. M. *Guns, Sails, and Empires,* 1965. A fascinating account of technical progress and its effects on human relationships in an age of exploration.

Crosby, A. W. *The Columbian Exchange: Biological and Cultural Consequences of 1492,* 1972. The most important book on this subject in the last generation.

Curtin, P. *The African Slave Trade,* 1969, and J. L. Watson, ed., *Asian and African Systems of Slavery,* 1980, are among the most interesting and authoritative treatments.

Díaz de Castillo, B. *The Conquest of New Spain,* trans. and ed. J. Cohen, 1988. The best of the conquistador accounts.

Elliot, J. H. *The Old World and the New,* 1970, considers the mutual impacts of the discoveries.

Fernandez-Armesto, F. *Columbus,* 1991. The most recent biography, reflecting new information.

Innes, Hammond. *The Conquistadors,* 1969. A lively illustrated rendition that is also sympathetic.

Kirkpatrick, F. *The Spanish Conquistadores,* 1968, is a standard work on the opening of the Caribbean and Central America.

Lovejoy, P. *Transformation in Slavery: A History of Slavery in Africa,* 1983.

McNeill, W. *The Pursuit of Power: Technology, Armed Force and Society since 1000 A.D.,* 1992.

Parry, J. H. *The Age of Reconnaissance,* 1981. The classic account of the early voyages. Wonderfully clear prose.

———. *The Discovery of South America,* 1979. Tells how new discoveries affected the Europeans. Excellent illustrations.

———. *The Establishment of European Hegemony 1415–1715,* 1961, is a short treatment.

———. *The Spanish Seaborne Empire,* 1966. The standard account of Spain's push into the Americas.

Sale, K. *Conquest of Paradise,* 1990. Highly critical of the Spanish policies.

Tracy, J. D. *The Rise of Merchant Empires; Long Distance Trade in the Early Modern World 1350–1750,* 1990. An anthology treating various empires and locales.

Wolf, E. *Europe and the People without History,* 1982. Critical of the Westerners' arrogance in dealing with others.

Wright, S. *Stolen Continents,* 1995. The discovery of America, from the points of view of the Aztecs, Inca, and North American Indians.

CHAPTER 27

Bainton, R. *Here I Stand,* 1950. Remains perhaps the best biography of Martin Luther.

Bouwsma, W. *John Calvin,* 1988. A good recent biography of the most influential of the Protestant leaders.

Cameron, E. *The European Reformation,* 1991. An excellent overview.

Jensen, D. L. *Reformation Europe,* 1990. An excellent survey of the Reformation period.

Haigh, C. *Elizabeth I,* 1998 is probably the best biography of the Virgin Queen. See also J. Ridley, *Elizabeth I,* 1988.

Kelly, H. A. *The Matrimonial Trials of Henry VIII,* 1975. Another good work on English affairs of state and religion.

McNeill, J. *The History and Character of Calvinism,* 1954. The best survey of what Calvinism meant theologically and as a way of living.

O'Connell, M. *The Counter-Reformation, 1559–1610,* 1974. A fair-minded balancing of Protestant and Catholic claims as well as a history of the Catholic responses.

Ozment, S. *Protestants: The Birth of a Revolution,* 1992. Also useful for students. The same author's *The Age of Reform, 1250–1550,* 1980, is a very good survey of the conditions in Europe that led to agitation against the papal church.

Scarre, G. *Witchcraft and Magic in Sixteenth and Seventeenth Century Europe,* 1987.

Youings, J. *Sixteenth Century England,* 1984. Places the English Reformation in the context of English society and culture. See also the fine work of A. G. Dickens, *The English Reformation,* 1989.

CHAPTER 28

Avrich, P. *Russian Rebels 1600–1800,* 1972. Just what it sounds like, focusing on the Razin and Pugachev revolts.

Aylmer, G. E. *Rebellion or Revolution? England, 1640–1660,* 1986. Interestingly written.

Cipolla, C. *Miasma and Disease,* 1992. A very engaging account of how diseases were perceived and reacted against by seventeenth-century Europeans.

Dunn, R. *The Age of Religious Wars, 1559–1689,* 1979. Probably the best short account.

Goubert, P. *Louis XIV and Twenty Million Frenchmen,* 1966. A survey of French society during the seventeenth century.

Hill, C. *God's Englishman: Oliver Cromwell and the English Revolution,* 1970, and A. Fraser, *Cromwell: The Lord Protector,* 1974, are both reliable aids to understanding what England went through in the seventeenth century and what sort of people the Puritans were.

Jessop, T. F. *Thomas Hobbes,* 1960. A good, short biography.

Kamen, H. *The War of the Succession in Spain,* 1969. Very good on Europe's foreign affairs in the late seventeenth century. The same author's *Spain 1469–1716,* 1983, is insightful on the causes for the decline of Spanish power.

Laslett, P. *Locke's Two Treatises of Government,* 1970. Both texts in full, with incisive introductions to them.

Lee, S. J. *The Thirty Years War,* 1991. Also good is S. H. Steinberg, *The Thirty Years War and the Conflict for European Hegemony 1600–1660,* 1966.

Lewis, W. H. *The Splendid Century,* 1953. An entertaining and very readable account of French life in the seventeenth century.

Wolf, J. *Louis XIV,* 1968. The standard, highly readable biography of this king who set the mold for so many of his contemporaries.

CHAPTER 29

Artz, F. *From the Renaissance to Romanticism,* 1962. An excellent brief survey of the formal culture of the Europeans in the sixteenth and seventeenth centuries, East and West.

Blum, J. *Lord and Peasant in Russia from the Ninth to the Nineteenth Century,* 1961. The best available survey of Russian serfdom down to its abolition.

Carsten, F. W. *Origins of Prussia,* 1954. Discusses how the Great Elector created a state from a collection of territories.

Coles, P. *The Ottoman Impact on Europe, 1350–1699,* 1968. Tells how the Turks terrified much of Europe for centuries until they lost their military edge.

Evans, R. J. W. *The Making of the Habsburg Monarchy, 1550–1700,* 1982. A detailed summary of how this dynasty flourished and expanded its power.

Kann, R. A., and Z. David. *The Peoples of the Eastern Habsburg Lands, 1526–1918,* 1984. A unique overview of the history of the nationalities and regions comprising the Austrian empire's eastern half.

Massie, R. *Peter the Great,* 1980. A first-rate popular biography that later served as the basis for a TV series seen around the world. Long, but continually interesting.

McKay, D., and H. Scott. *The Rise of the Great Powers, 1648–1815,* 1983. A general account with much attention to the three great Eastern empires.

Stoye, J. *The Siege of Vienna,* 1964. Gives much insight into why the Turks never recovered from the failed siege of 1683.

Sumner, B. H. *Peter the Great and the Emergence of Russia,* 1962. Good though somewhat outdated in its estimate of the great ruler's impact on his people.

Wandruszka, A. *The House of Habsburg,* 1964. A sympathetic but still reliable survey of this dynasty in its long history.

CHAPTER 30

Cahill, J. *Chinese Painting,* 1977. On this topic, see also R. Thorpe, *Son of Heaven: Imperial Arts of China,* 1988, which is richly illustrated. For literature see Wu-chi Liu, *An Introduction to Chinese Literature,* 1966, and M. Sullivan, *The Arts of China,* 1999.

Gernet, J. *Daily Life in China on the Eve of the Mongol Invasion,* 1962.

Miyazaki, I. *China's Examination Hell: The Civil Service Examinations of Imperial China,* 1964. A memorable look into what Chinese education emphasized and why.

Naquin, S., and E. Rawski. *Chinese Society in the Eighteenth Century,* 1987. A perceptive overview of a great civilization before its decline.

Ricci, M. *The Journals,* 1953. An edition of the Jesuit's interesting account of life in China in the sixteenth century.

Schirokauer, C. *A Brief History of Chinese and Japanese Civilizations,* 1989. Very helpful and clearly written. E. O. Reischauer, J. Fairbank, and A. Craig, *East Asia: Tradition and Transformation,* 1973, is a good introduction to both China and Japan. For more detail, try the relevant volumes in the *Cambridge History of China,* 1978.

Spence, J. *The Search for Modern China,* 1990. Especially recommended for its general account of affairs in the later Ming period. Spence has written a series of major works on China in this period. His *Emperor of China: Self-portrait of Kang Hsi,* 1974, is a fine biography of the outstanding statesman of eighteenth-century China.

Wakeman, F., Jr. *The Great Enterprise,* 1985. A good analysis of the way the Manzhou emperors attained control of their huge new conquest.

Wang, Chi-chen, ed. *The Dream of the Red Chamber,* 1958. The best short English translation of the classic novel.

CHAPTER 31

Andaya, B. and I. *A History of Malaysia,* 1982.

Akutagawa, R. *Rashomon and Other Stories,* 1959. A twentieth-century storyteller re-creates medieval Japanese society, including the sketch that served as the basis for the famous movie.

Beasley, W. G. *A Modern History of Japan,* 1973.

Boxer, C. *The Christian Century in Japan 1549–1650,* 1951.

Chandler, D. *A History of Cambodia,* 1983.

Cooper, M., ed. *They Came to Japan,* 1981. A series of pieces about Japan and the Japanese by European visitors.

Dunn, C. J. *Everyday Life in Traditional Japan,* 1969. A vivid discussion of social habits and groups in Tokugawa Japan. Highly recommended for giving a "feel" of Japanese lifestyle.

Endo, S. *The Samurai,* 1984. An exciting novel of seventeenth-century Japan and the Franciscan priests who journeyed there to establish trading relations and win converts.

Hane, M. *Japan: An Historical Study,* 1972. A fine general history.

Henderson, H. *An Introduction to Haiku: An Anthology of Poems and Poets from Basho to Shiki,* 1977.

Hibbitt, H. *The Floating World in Japanese Fiction,* 1982. A revealing analysis of the world of Kabuki.

Keene, D. *An Anthology of Japanese Literature,* 1955, and *Japanese Literature: An Introduction to Western Readers,* 1953. Keene has written a series of very helpful introductions to Japan's literature, and these are especially good. More specialized is his *World within Walls: Japanese Literature of the Pre-Modern Era, 1600–1867,* 1973.

Kidder, J. E., Jr., *The Art of Japan,* 1985, is beautifully illustrated.

Mason, P. *Japanese Art,* 1993. A good review for the thoughtful student.

Morris, I., trans. *The Life of an Amorous Woman and Other Writings* by Ihara Saikaku, 1977.

Osborne, M. *Southeast Asia.* 1990. Brief, illustrated history by a reliable source, focused on modern times.

Reischauer, E. *Japan: The Story of a Nation,* 1990. A highly readable general history, as is the book by C. Schirokauer mentioned in the bibliography to Chapter 40.

SarDesai, D. *Southeast Asia; Past and Present,* 1989. A good survey, mainly looking at post-eighteenth-century affairs.

Tarling, N. *A Concise History of Southeast Asia,* 1966.

Varley, H. P. *Japanese Culture: A Short History,* 1981.

CHAPTER 32

Andric, I. *The Bridge on the Drina,* 1948, and other novels by this Nobel Prize winner tell more than any factual history of the Christian-Muslim interrelationship in the Balkans.

Basham, A. S. *A Cultural History of India,* 1975. Covers the entire Muslim period, before and during the Mughal epoch.

Bernier, F. *Travels in the Mogul Empire,* 1968. An account of a European's experiences in the mid–seventeenth century.

Hansen, W. *The Peacock Throne,* 1972. A fine general history of the Mughals, very readable.

Holt, P. M., A. K. S. Lambton, and B. Lewis. *The Cambridge History of Islam,* vols. 1 and 2, 1970.

Ikram, S. M. *Muslim Civilization in India,* 1964. A standard work on Mughal and other Muslim principalities.

Inalcik, H. *The Ottoman Empire: The Classical Age, 1300–1600,* 1973. A solid scholarly overview of the empire at its height.

Kinross, P. *The Ottoman Centuries,* 1977. Recommended for its many episodes and anecdotes that illustrate Turkish attitudes and origins.

Kissling, J. J., et al. *The Last Great Muslim Empires,* 1996. Looks at the three great empires of early modern epoch in a comparative view.

Lewis, B. *Istanbul and the Civilization of the Ottomans,* 1963. Written by a renowned interpreter of the Muslim Arabic world.

Lewis, R. *Everyday Life in Ottoman Turkey,* 1971. Revealing and entertaining.

Lippman, T. *Understanding Islam,* 1992. A good survey of what Westerners can learn from Islam and the Muslim society.

Merriman, R. *Suleiman the Magnificent, 1520–1566,* 1944. Remains the best biography of this world shaker.

Mujeeb, M. *The Indian Muslims,* 1967. Strong on Mughal culture.

Saunders, J. J. *The History of the Mongol Conquests,* 1971. A straightforward account of the tremendous explosion caused by Chinghis Khan. D. Morgan, *The Mongols,* 1986, is more oriented toward the Mongols as people, throwing much light on their culture and habits.

Shelov, J. M. *Akbar,* 1967. A first-rate biography of the greatest Mughal.

Southern, R. W. *Western Views of Islam,* 1962. Enlightening on why the Western world paid little attention to the Muslims after the decline of their military powers.

Thapar, R., and P. Spear. *A History of India,* vols. 1 and 2, 1970. A very well-written, socially oriented book.

CHAPTER 33

Blackburn, R. *The Making of New World Slavery,* 1997, is an overview of the trade in human beings after 1500.

Chaudhuri, K. N. *Trade and Civilization in the Indian Ocean: An Economic History from the Rise of Islam to 1750,* 1985. A specialized account of the history of East Africa, with much on the Arab slave trade.

Davidson, B. *African History,* 1968. Still useful though obsolete on the earliest times. Davidson has written extensively on all aspects and periods of African history.

Fage, J., and R. Oliver, eds. *The Cambridge History of Africa,* vols. 1–4, 1977–1985. One of the several multivolume histories that Cambridge University has sponsored on the non-Western world. The same pair have written *A Short History of Africa,* 1986, which is a standard introductory work. It is particularly good on modern times.

Henderson, L. W. *Angola: Five Centuries of Conflict,* 1979. Gives insight into the effects of Portuguese rule in southwest Africa. The same theme is explored in A. F. Ryder, *Benin and the Europeans, 1485–1897,* 1969.

Morehead, A. *The White Nile,* 1960, and *The Blue Nile,* 1962. Exciting narratives on the topic of European exploration in Africa.

Nicholls, C. S. *The Swahili Coast,* 1971. A standard text on East African city-states.

Pakenham, T. *The Scramble for Africa,* 1991.

Ritter, E. *Shaka Zulu,* 1983. See also J. D. Omer-Cooper, *The Zulu Aftermath,* 1969, for what happened after Shaka's defeat.

Robinson, R., and J. Gallagher. *Africa and the Victorians,* 1961. Set a new course in studies of imperial rule.

Shillington, K. *A History of Southern Africa,* 1989. Has many illustrations to accompany a well-written text.

CHAPTER 34

All of the following titles have bibliographies that will assist the inquiring student greatly.

Barman, R. J. *Brazil: The Forging of a Nation, 1798–1852,* 1988. Good overview of how Brazil came to be a sovereign nation.

Bazant, J. *A Concise History of Mexico,* 1978. The best single book in English on this topic for the student.

Burns, E. B. *Latin America: A Concise Interpretive History,* 1986. Just what the title announces; a well-known and authoritative work.

Halperin-Donghi, T. *The Aftermath of Revolution in Latin America,* 1973, and R. Graham and P. H. Smith, *New Approaches to Latin American History,* 1974. Two of the most rewarding studies of the early independence period.

Lynch, J. *The Spanish American Revolutions,* 1986. Perhaps the best short treatment of what happened in the Spanish colonies between 1808 and 1825.

Masur, G. *Simon Bolivar,* 1969. The best biography of the Liberator.

Roeder, R. *Juarez and His Mexico,* vols. 1 and 2, 1947. The standard study of the great Mexican patriot and his times.

Scobie, J. *Argentina: A City and a Nation,* 1971, and J. Mamalakis, *The Growth and Structure of the Chilean Economy from Independence to Allende,* 1976. Two good studies of individual nations that profited from European immigration in the nineteenth century but remained in a dependent relationship.

Tannenbaum, F. *Ten Keys to Latin America,* 1962. A survey of Latin history from the vantage point of ten characteristics of Latin society.

Whitaker, A. *The United States and the Independence of Latin America, 1800–1830,* 1941. Until now, the best survey of the relations between North America and the Latin Americans in this period.

Part Five
CHAPTER 35

Anderson, M. S. *Europe in the Eighteenth Century,* 1987. A general survey of political and cultural trends and a good place to start research on almost any eighteenth-century topic.

Andrade, E. *Sir Isaac Newton,* 1974. A short biography of the most famous of the early scientists.

Butterfield, H. *The Origins of Modern Science,* 1951. A classic readable account of how science came to be what we now understand it to be.

Chisick, H. *The Limits of Reform in the Enlightenment: Attitudes toward the Education of the Lower Classes in France,* 1981. A very interesting examination of its topic.

Cranston, M. *The Noble Savage: Jean-Jacques Rousseau,* 1991 is the best current biography of the reformer.

Darnton, R. *The Business of Enlightenment: A Publishing History of the Encyclopedie, 1775–1800,* 1979. Fun to read and tells a great deal about the philosophes. The same author's *The Great Cat Massacre and Other Episodes in French Cultural History,* 1984, is equally good.

Gay, P., has written several books on the Enlightenment and is one of the most readable authors who deal with cultural history.

Hampson, N. *A Cultural History of the Enlightenment,* 1968. A brief, fact-filled survey of how society was affected. On the same lines is F. Artz, *The Enlightenment in France,* 1968.

Hill, B. *Eighteenth Century Women: An Anthology,* 1984. A good survey of women's lives in various social classes.

Jacob, J. R. *The Scientific Revolution: Aspirations and Achievements, 1500–1700,* 1998.

Koestler, A. *The Sleepwalkers,* 1959. An enthralling study of how the great breakthroughs in early science were made.

Rosen, E. *Copernicus and the Scientific Revolution,* 1984. Shows how astronomy and physics were transformed and what the effects of that transformation were.

Spencer, S., ed. *French Women and the Age of Enlightenment,* 1984. A good insight into the salons and other contributions made by women. On this topic see L. Schiebinger, *The Mind Has No Sex! Women in the Origins of Modern Science,* 1989.

CHAPTER 36

Bailyn, B. *The Ideological Origins of the American Revolution,* 1967. A standard work.

Calhoon, R. M. *Loyalists in Revolutionary America,* 1973.

———. *Revolutionary America,* 1976, is a short introduction to the events of 1763–1787.

Higgonet, P. *Sister Republics: Origins of the American and French Revolutions,* 1988. A comparative study of much value.

Maier, P. *From Resistance to Revolution,* 1972, looks at the influence of the radical thinkers among the rebels against Britain. The same author's *The Old Revolutionaries,* 1980, portrays five of the leading American patriots.

Mill, J. S. *On Liberty.* A mid-nineteenth-century tract, which, though somewhat difficult, has never been superseded as the platform of the classic liberal in the political arena.

Morgan, E. S. *The Birth of the Republic, 1763–1789,* rev. ed., 1977. A good short overview. The same author has written *Inventing the People: The Rise of Popular Sovereignty in England and America,* 1988.

Palmer, R. R. *Age of the Democratic Revolution,* 1964, is a deservedly classic interpretation of the political and constitutional importance of the events in the former colonies.

Warren, C. *The Making of the Constitution,* 1947, is especially adapted to student needs.

Wood, G. *The Creation of the American Republic, 1776–1787,* 1972. Speaks to our point in this chapter that the war in America was not revolutionary in any but the international sense.

CHAPTER 37

Bergeron, L. *France under Napoleon,* 1981. Covers all aspects of French society under the emperor with a light but learned touch.

Cobb, R. *The People's Armies,* 1987. The tale of the first *levées en masse* creating the modern conscript army.

Connelly, O. *The French Revolution and the Napoleonic Era,* 1991. A constantly interesting account.

Dickens, C. *A Tale of Two Cities.* An exciting and more or less historical account of how British liberals reacted to the Terror of 1793.

Doyle, W. *Origins of the French Revolution,* 1981, and its earlier and differently angled companion piece by J. Lefebvre, *The Coming of the French Revolution,* 1947, are both invaluable.

———. *The Oxford History of the French Revolution,* 1989. Very strong on both the revolutionary and the imperial periods, divided into convenient segments.

Geyl, P. *Napoleon: For and Against,* 1949. A famous collection never surpassed for readability and stimulus.

Hampson, N. *Terror in the French Revolution,* 1981. A thorough and highly readable account of Robespierre and his associates.

Hufton, O. *The Poor in Eighteenth Century France,* 1974. The best exposé of the problem of poverty amid plenty; explains how the French situation differed radically from that of the Americans.

Jones, P. *The Peasantry in the French Revolution,* 1988. Tells how far the peasants supported the Jacobin ideas and ideals.

Jordan, D. *The King's Trial: Louis XVI vs. the French Revolution,* 1979. A compelling and very readable story of the unfortunate king who could not quite comprehend what was happening to him and to his country.

Levy, D. G., et al., eds. *Women in Revolutionary Paris, 1789–1795,* 1979. A collection of documents that show how active the poor women of Paris were in the years of rebellion.

Markham, F. *Napoleon,* 1963. One of the best biographies of the great leader. Another good one is V. Cronin, *Napoleon Bonaparte,* 1972. His military campaigns are well treated in D. Chandler, *The Campaigns of Napoleon,* 1966.

———. *Napoleon and the Awakening of Europe,* 1954. Focuses on the impact of the revolution on national feeling, both in and outside France.

Nicholson, H. *The Congress of Vienna,* 1946. A witty and thoughtful history of the nineteenth century's most famous political conclave.

Palmer, R. *Twelve Who Ruled,* 1941. Has not been surpassed as a study of the Jacobin leadership.

Robiquet, J. *Daily Life in France under Napoleon,* 1963. One of the Daily Life series.

CHAPTER 38

Cameron, R. *A Concise Economic History of the World,* 1989, is one of those books whose titles are exactly fulfilled in the text. Its treatment of early industrialization is clear and very useful.

Deane, P. *The First Industrial Revolution,* 1965, is also good, as is *The Industrial Revolution* by C. M. Cipolla, 1973, which looks at Europe generally but with focus on Britain.

Evans, E. G. *The Forging of the Modern State: Early Industrial Britain 1783–1870,* 1983, is a standard appreciation of the beginnings and development of industrial life.

Landes, D. *Unbound Prometheus: Technological Change and Industrial Development in Western Europe from 1750 to the Present,* 1969. Probably the best single treatment of the whole topic of industrialization; clearly written and easy to follow for students who have no background in economics.

Pollard, S. *Peaceful Conquest: The Industrialization of Europe 1760–1970,* 1981, is very useful in its earlier chapters to give an idea of how the British inventions migrated. A broader view is given in P. Stearns, *The Industrial Revolution in World History,* 1993.

Taylor, G. R. *The Transportation Revolution 1815–1860,* 1968, looks at the United States, but its conclusions are applicable anywhere in the West.

Taylor, P., ed. *The Industrial Revolution: Triumph or Disaster?* 1970, is a discussion of positive and negative aspects.

Tilly, L., and J. Scott. *Women, Work, and Family,* 1978, is a survey of the female workforce in early industrial society. It is an updating of I. Pinchbeck's pioneering *Women Workers and the Industrial Revolution,* 1930.

CHAPTER 39

Bridenthal, R., and C. Koontz. *Becoming Visible: Women in European History,* 1976 and several later editions. A selection of articles and very good bibliography on the changing role of women as mothers, wives, and workers. See also vol. 2 of B. Anderson and J. Zinsser, *A History of Their Own: Women in Europe from Prehistory to the Present,* 1988, which has a huge bibliography.

Heilbroner, R. *The Worldly Philosophers,* 1967. An introduction to economic liberalism as it appeared in the nineteenth century.

Mayhew, H. *London Labour and London Poor,* 1851 (many reprints). A classic journalistic account of the lives of the ordinary poor people in the early years of the Industrial Age. A fascinating series of vignettes of street life. Highly recommended.

McKeown, T. *The Modern Rise of Population,* 1976. Has a lot to say about the changes induced by better nutrition and sanitation after the late eighteenth century.

Moraze, C. *The Triumph of the Middle Classes,* 1966; E. Gauldie, *Cruel Habitations: A History of Working-Class Housing, 1790–1918,* 1974; and G. Himmelfarb, *The Idea of Poverty: England in the Early Industrial Age,* 1984. All are very readable accounts of certain aspects of industrial society in the nineteenth century.

Pilbeam, P. *The Middle Classes in Europe 1789–1914,* 1990 is an important study of the entrepreneurial and mercantile classes.

Pinchbeck, I. *Women Workers and the Industrial Revolution,* 1930. A pioneering study of females. See also P. Robertson, *The Experience of Women: Pattern and Change in Nineteenth Century Europe,* 1982, for a survey of female public and private life.

Shorter, E. *The Making of the Modern Family,* 1975. A controversial—some would say outrageous—essay.

Taylor, A. J., ed. *The Standard of Living in Britain in the Industrial Revolution,* 1975. A collection of important articles on the pros and cons of industrial life for the masses of workers.

Taylor, G. *The Transportation Revolution, 1815–1860,* 1968. Looks at the social effects of steam-driven transport.

CHAPTER 40

Briggs, A. *The Making of Modern England, 1784–1867,* 1967. An excellent study of why Britain was spared upheavals as violent as those on the Continent in the nineteenth century.

Bullen, R., and F. R. Bridge. *The Great Powers and the European State System, 1815–1914,* 1980. An excellent overview of international affairs in Europe after Vienna.

Deak, I. *The Lawful Revolution: Louis Kossuth and the Hungarians, 1848–49,* 1979. An enlightening treatment of the ethnic and national conflicts in the Austrian empire.

Droz, J. *Europe between Revolutions, 1815–1850,* 1967. A survey, as is A. Sked, ed., *Europe's Balance of Power 1815–1848,* 1979.

Heilbroner, R. *The Worldly Philosophers,* 1967. Has already been mentioned as a good introduction to the economic liberals.

Kissinger, H. *A World Restored,* 1957. A good defense of Metternich and his policies, written by President Nixon's secretary of state. Compare A. J. May, *The Age of Metternich, 1814–48,* 1963, which is not so sympathetic, and the concise biography by A. Palmer, *Metternich,* 1972.

Namier, L. *1848: Revolution of the Intellectuals,* 1964. Highly critical of the failure of the liberal leaders in the German-speaking lands.

Sperber, J. *The European Revolutions 1848–1851,* 1994, is a thorough and reliable account of what happened throughout Europe in these years.

Stearns, P. *Eighteen Forty-eight,* 1974. Especially good on the social background of the rebellions throughout Europe. This theme is also well treated in P. Robertson, *Revolutions of 1848: A Social History,* 1960.

Wright, G. *France in Modern Times,* 1960. A well-written and consistently interesting study. See also R. Magraw, *France 1815–1914.*

CHAPTER 41

Baumgart, W. *Imperialism,* 1982. A first-rate study of British and French expansion in the late nineteenth century. See also on this topic B. Davidson, *Modern Africa,* 1989; R. Robinson and J. Gallagher, *Africa and the Victorians,* 1961; M. Edwardes, *The West in Asia, 1850–1914,* 1967; and H. M. Wright, ed., *The "New Imperialism,"* 1976.

Clark, G. K. *The Making of Victorian England,* 1962. A good brief introduction.

Cochrane, T. C. *Business in American Life,* 1977. One of the dozens of good books on the rise of business and industry in mid-nineteenth-century America. On the Civil War's effect, see P. J. Parish, *The American Civil War,* 1975.

Crankshaw, E. *Bismarck,* 1981. A reliable biography of the founder of the modern German state; so are G. Kent, *Bismarck and His Times,* 1978, and B. Waller, *Bismarck,* 1997.

Emmons, T. *The Russian Landed Gentry and the Peasant Emancipation of 1861,* 1968. The standard treatment of the abolition of serfdom in Russia. See on Russian history generally D. Saunders, *Russia in the Age of Reaction and Reform 1801–1881,* 1992.

Macartney, C. A. *The Habsburg Empire, 1790–1918,* 1969. A very well-written, detailed history of the problems of the Austrian empire and the attempts to solve them, which ultimately failed. On this, see also the less detailed A. Sked, *The Decline and Fall of the Habsburg Empire, 1815–1918,* 1989, and A. J. May, *The Habsburg Monarchy, 1867–1914,* 1951, which covers the foreign and domestic affairs of the Austro-Hungarian state.

Seton-Watson, H. *The Russian Empire, 1801–1917,* 1967, is a liberal interpretation of the last century of the czars' government, while B. Lincoln, *The Great Reforms,* 1991, deals extensively with the shattering impact of the Crimean War on Russian government and society.

Smith, D. M. *Cavour,* 1985. The classic biography of the Italian statesman. For the context, see Smith's *Italy: A Modern History,* 1969.

Smith, W. H. C. *Napoleon III,* 1972. Covers the life and affairs of Napoleon III in a readable and comprehensive style. See also A. Plessis, *The Rise and Fall of the Second Empire, 1852–1871,* 1975.

Stavrianos, S. *The Balkans, 1815–1914,* 1968, and B. Jelavich, *History of the Balkans,* vols. 1 and 2, 1983, are excellent sources of information on southeastern Europe from the late eighteenth century to the present.

Williams, R. *Gaslight and Shadows,* 1957. A fascinating work on the Paris of Napoleon III.

Woodham-Smith, C. *The Reason Why,* 1953. A really good example of how entertaining history can be when written with skill and commitment. It is the story of the Crimean War, that low comedy of military errors.

CHAPTER 42

Berlanstein, L. R. *The Working People of Paris, 1871–1914,* 1985, and E. Weber, *Peasants into Frenchmen: The Modernization of Rural France, 1870–1914,* 1980, are complementary works of importance and authority.

Erickson, C. *Emigration from Europe, 1815–1914,* 1976. The best single-volume work on the topic.

Gillis, J. *Youth and History: Tradition and Change in European Age Relations, 1770 to the Present,* 1981. A fascinating survey, focusing on the nineteenth century.

Joll, J. *The Anarchists,* 1964. A survey of what these idealists wanted. See also B. Tuchman's relevant chapter in her work cited later under "Social History."

Kraut, A. M. *The Huddled Masses: Immigrants in American Society,* 1982. See also O. Handlin's several books on immigrants to America and their fate here. For immigrants to Latin American countries, see the bibliography for Chapter 58.

Landes, D. *The Unbound Prometheus,* 1969. Remains an excellent introduction to both the First and the Second Industrial Revolutions.

McLellan, D. *Karl Marx: His Life and Thought,* 1974. Probably the best single introduction, but there are many other volumes on the life and action of the greatest of the socialist theorists. F. Mehring, *Karl Marx: The Story of His Life,* 1976, is another good biography.

Milward, A., and S. B. Saul, *The Development of the Economies of Continental Europe, 1850–1914,* 1977. A good textbook on its subject, including all European nations.

Social History

Social history is explored from numerous points of view in several books.

Burnett, J. *History of the Cost of Living,* 1969. An eye-opener as to how much was spent by whom on what. J. Laver, *Manners and Morals in the Age of Optimism,* 1966, treats of the various classes' views of what was proper and improper. See also J. Gillis, *Youth and History,* 1981, cited earlier, as well as P. Stearns, *Old Age in European Society,* 1976, which looks mainly at France.

Maynes, M. J. *Schooling in Western Europe: A Social History,* 1985, is a standard treatment of the history of mass education.

Smith, B. *Changing Lives: Women in European History since 1700,* 1989

Tobias, J. *Urban Crime in Victorian England,* 1972. A pioneering effort to reconstruct the incidence and seriousness of crime in London. See also the same author's *Crime and Industrial Society in the Nineteenth Century,* 1967.

Tuchman, B. *The Proud Tower,* 1963. An extraordinarily readable selection of pieces on various topics in European social history before 1914.

Vicinus, M. *Suffer and Be Still: Women in the Victorian Age,* 1972. Goes far to supplement the Smith book cited above; see also R. Bridenthal and C. Koontz, *Becoming Visible: Women in European History,* 1976, and B. Anderson and J. Zinsser, *A History of Their Own: Women in Europe from Prehistory to the Present,* 1988.

Walkowitz, J. *Prostitution and Victorian Society,* 1980, provides a look behind the scenes of Victorian prudery.

Weber, A. *The Growth of Cities in the Nineteenth Century,* 1899. An old but still useful analysis of urban growth. Accompanying it to show the dominant position of the city by the mid–nineteenth century are J. P. McKay, *Tramways and Trolleys: The Rise of Urban Mass Transport in Europe,* 1976; D. Pinckney, *Napoleon III and the Rebuilding of Paris,* 1972; and G. Masur, *Imperial Berlin,* 1970.

CHAPTER 43

For general overviews of Western thought in this era, try J. H. Randall, *The Making of the Modern Mind,* 1976, and the Baumer and Chadwick volumes noted later. R. Paxton's *Europe in the Twentieth Century,* 1985, provides good background. The social dimensions of changing views are treated in P. Stearns and H. Chapman, *European Society in Upheaval,* 1991.

Baumer, F. L. *Modern European Thought: Continuity and Change in Ideas, 1600–1950,* 1977. An excellent introduction to the background as well as to the topics treated in this chapter.

Bowler, P. *Evolution: The History of an Idea,* 1989.

Chadwick, O. *The Secularization of the European Mind in the Nineteenth Century,* 1975. A very incisive study of the changes that put organized churches on the defensive by the later nineteenth century.

Gay, P. *Freud: A Life for Our Time,* 1988. Admiring biography by a well-known intellectual historian. See also S. Wollheim, *Sigmund Freud,* 1971.

Irvine, W. *Apes, Angels, and Victorians,* 1955. A highly literate study of the great debate over Darwinism in England.

Ruse, M. *The Darwinian Revolution,* 1979. A useful and readable introduction.

Stromberg, R. *European Intellectual History since 1789,* 1993. An excellent survey, clear and opinionated. More demanding on the reader but very stimulating is H. S. Hughes, *Consciousness and Society,* 1956.

CHAPTER 44

Each of the nations involved presented lengthy collections of diplomatic documents as well as passionate arguments as to why the outbreak of war was someone else's fault. Nearly ninety years later, the question of war guilt is still debated; this list mentions only a few of the available books.

Falls, C. *The Great War,* 1961. The best short account of the military aspect, but see also B. H. Liddell-Hart, *The Real War, 1914–1918,* 1964. For the generally neglected Eastern Front, N. Stone, *The Fall of the Empires,* 1968, is concise and very readable.

Fussell, P. *The Great War and Modern Memory,* 1975. A brilliant résumé of what the war meant to a generation of British survivors and how it shaped their lives thereafter in ways both conscious and unconscious.

Gilbert, M. *The First World War,* 1994.

Keynes, J. M. *The Economic Consequences of the Peace,* 1920. This attack on the Versailles Treaty was very influential in both Britain and the United States. Perhaps the most readable of the many accounts of the Versailles negotiations is H. Nicholson, *Peacemaking 1919,* 1938.

Marwick, A. *The Deluge,* 1970. A good social history of the effects of war in Britain. For other countries, see R. Wall and J. Winter, eds., *The Upheaval of War: Family, Work and Welfare in Europe, 1914–1918,* 1988. F. Chambers, *The War behind the War, 1914–1918,* though published in 1939, is still unsurpassed for a summation of the war on the home fronts. G. Braybon, *Women Workers in the First World War: The British Experience,* 1981, fulfills its title's promise. Finally, R. Albrecht-Carrie has put together an insightful anthology entitled *The Meaning of the First World War,* 1965, which deals with several aspects of the war's consequences in society.

Remak, J. *The Origins of World War I,* 1967, and L. Lafore, *The Long Fuse,* 1971, are standard sources for the remote causes of World War I and short enough to be easily digested.

Tuchman, B. *The Guns of August,* 1962. One of the most brilliant examples of history-as-story.

Winter, J. M. *The Experience of World War I,* 1989. Particularly strong in its pictorial record.

Wohl, R. *The Generation of 1914,* 1979. What World War I meant to the European youth who fought it. On the same topic, see V. Brittain, *Testament of Youth: An Autobiographical Study of the Years 1900–1925,* 1980. An unforgettable account of the actual fighting is given in A. Horne, *The Price of Glory: Verdun 1916,* 1979, which accurately portrays the horrors of the trenches on the Western Front. J. Romain, *Verdun,* 1939, presents a fictional version based on firsthand experience. E. Remarque's novel *All Quiet on the Western Front,* 1929, and J. Ellis's memoir *Eye Deep in Hell,* 1976, are two of hundreds of personal recollections of this conflict that stress how senseless it seemed to the common soldier.

Part Six
CHAPTER 45

Carsten, F. L. *The Rise of Fascism,* 1982. A good starting point that might be supplemented by E. Weber, *Varieties of Fascism,* 1964, which is strong on the social aspects of the movement in several countries.

On France and Britain, see N. Greene, *From Versailles to Vichy: The Third Republic, 1919–1940,* 1970; C. S. Maier, *Recasting Bourgeois Europe: Stabilization in France, Germany and Italy in the Decade after World War One,* 1975; A. J. Taylor, *English History, 1914–45,* 1965, a witty survey that hits all the bases in incomparable style; and C. Mowat, *Britain between the Wars,* 1955, which is still very useful for its detail on politics.

Gatzke, H. *Stresemann and the Rearming of Germany,* 1965. An analysis of the most disputed of the Versailles restrictions and how they were evaded.

Gay, P. *Weimar Culture,* 1970, and W. Laqueur, *Weimar,* 1972. Both are recommended highly for their literary qualities as well as the exciting subject matter.

Marks, S. *The Illusion of Peace: Europe's International Relations 1918–1933,* 1976. A thorough overview of diplomacy up until Hitler's ascent.

Seton-Watson, C. *Italy from Liberalism to Fascism,* 1967, and D. Mack Smith, *Mussolini's Roman Empire,* 1976, cover the background and the early years of Italian fascism. An equally good but different approach is E. Wiskemann, *Fascism in Italy: Its Development and Influence,* 1969. The outstanding biography of Mussolini is D. Mack Smith, *Mussolini,* 1982.

Seton-Watson, H. *Eastern Europe between the Wars,* 1946. Gives as good a summary of what went wrong in interwar eastern Europe's politics and why, as has been written in English. See also *The Columbia History of Eastern Europe in the Twentieth Century,* 1992. A host of histories of individual countries are available.

Sontag, R. *A Broken World, 1919–1939,* 1971. Perhaps the best of the diplomatic histories of Europe between the wars.

CHAPTER 46

A huge literature on the Soviet Union is available, much of which has been seriously marred by ax grinding and propaganda. In the last ten years, for the first time since 1917, Russian (and other) historians have had free access to many archives formerly out of bounds, and a flood of new and interesting interpretations of Soviet events and personages is appearing.

Conquest, R. *Harvest of Sorrow,* 1990. An account of the great famine of the early 1930s during the collectivization drive.

———. *V. I. Lenin,* 1972. A good though hostile biography meant for students; A. Ulam's *The Bolsheviks,* 1968, is more extensive on Lenin and treats his major associates as well.

Davies, R. W. *The Socialist Offensive: Collectivization of Soviet Agriculture, 1929–30,* 1980. Provides an examination of collectivization. A generally more favorable survey of the Stalin years is given in P. Nettl, *The Soviet Achievement,* 1965, which focuses on the industrial and social transformations of the Five-Year Plans.

Fitzpatrick, S. *The Russian Revolution 1917–1932,* 1991. One of the best short treatments.

Koestler, A. *Darkness at Noon,* 1956. The most famous novelistic interpretation of Stalin's purges. On this, see also R. Conquest, *The Great Terror: A Reassessment,* 1990, and the brilliant essay by a Marxist but anti-Stalinist Russian, R. Medvedev, *Let History Judge,* 1972, which looks into many other sins of Stalin as well. The most comprehensive account of the terror under Stalin as it was experienced by ordinary Russians is A. Solzhenitsyn, *The Gulag Archipelago,* vols. 1–3, 1964.

Lincoln, B. *Red Victory: A History of the Russian Civil War,* 1989.

Malia, M. *Soviet Tragedy,* 1994.

Massie, R. *Nicholas and Alexandra,* 1971, is a dramatic biography of the royal pair that is thoroughly historical in nature and very well written.

Reed, J. *Ten Days That Shook the World,* 1919. An eyewitness account by a young American who sympathized with Lenin's revolution. It captures the feelings of those who believed a new dawn had come.

Tucker, R. *Stalin as Revolutionary,* 1973, and its sequel, *Stalin in Power,* 1992, are psychological studies of the most powerful individual in world history. See also the very good biography by I. Deutscher, *Stalin: A Political Biography,* 1967, and that by R. McNeal, *Stalin, Man and Ruler,* 1988.

Wildman, E. *The End of the Russian Imperial Army,* 1980. Excellent on the reasons why the czar's army could not continue the struggle in 1917.

A sympathetic biography of Trotsky is found in I. Deutscher, *The Prophet Armed, The Prophet Disarmed,* and *The Prophet Outcast,* 1953, a classic biography in three volumes, dealing with events from his youth through his murder by Stalinist agents in 1940.

CHAPTER 47

A general analysis of fascist totalitarianism is given in S. G. Payne, *Fascism: Comparisons and Definition,* 1980. See also E. Weber, *Varieties of Fascism,* 1964, cited in Chapter 45.

Bullock, A. *Hitler: A Study in Tyranny,* 1964, and J. Fest, *Hitler,* 1974, are both highly readable and reliable biographies of the Nazi leader. J. Lukacs, *The Hitler of History,* 1997, is idiosyncratic and enlightening.

Craig, G. *Germany, 1866–1945,* 1978. A survey that goes far to illuminate what brought Hitler and his party to power, as well as giving the kernel of Nazi thought and action while he was in power.

Gordon, S. *Hitler, Germans, and the "Jewish Question,"* 1984, and L. Dawidowicz, *The War against the Jews, 1933–45,* 1975, both give insight into the madness—and its rationalization by the Nazi leadership. A new and massive study by S. Friedlander, *Nazi Germany and the Jews* is under way.

Koehl, R. *The Black Corps,* 1983, and H. Krausnick and M. Broszat, *Anatomy of the SS State,* 1964, are thoroughgoing examinations of the black-shirted elite corps that terrified Hitler's opponents in the concentration camps.

Koontz, C. *Women in the Fatherland: Women, the Family and Nazi Politics,* 1987.

Marks, S. *The Illusion of Peace,* 1976, and R. Sontag, *A Broken World, 1919–1939,* 1971, are good surveys of international relations in Europe in the 1920s and 1930s.

Peukert, D. J. *Inside Nazi Germany,* 1987. Read this analysis of who supported the Nazis, and why, along with the exciting journalistic account in W. Shirer, *Rise and Fall of the Third Reich,* 1964. W. S. Allen, *The Nazi Seizure of Power: The Experience of a Single German Town, 1930–35,* 1971, is a definitive treatment of its subject and very well written.

Spielvogel, J. *Hitler and Nazi Germany,* 1996. A brief overview.

Watt, D. C. *How War Came,* 1989. A systematic and reliable study of diplomacy just prior to World War II.

CHAPTER 48

A general overview of China and Japan in this period is given in C. Schirokauer, *Modern China and Japan: A Brief History,* 1982, and in E. O. Reischauer et al., *East Asia: Tradition and Transformation,* 1973. See also the histories of both nations cited in the bibliographies of Chapters 40 and 41.

China

Eastman, L. E. *Seeds of Destruction: Nationalist China in War and Revolution, 1937–49,* 1984. An excellent account of what happened to Chiang Kai-shek's government and army.

Fairbank, J. K. *China: A New History,* 1992. By the master of American Sinology in the twentieth century.

Fay, P. W. *The Opium War,* 1975, and A. Waley, *The Opium War through Chinese Eyes,* 1958, are important to understanding how the Europeans established themselves in China.

Latourette, K. *A History of Christian Missions in China,* 1929. Shows the anti-Christian background of the Boxer Rebellion. See also J. Fairbank, *The Missionary Enterprise in China and America,* 1974, for a focus on the U.S. presence and its effects.

Schiffrin, H. *Sun Yat-sen and the Origins of the Chinese Revolution,* 1968. Explains the desperation of the younger generation of reformers in the late nineteenth century.

Schwartz, B. I. *Chinese Communism and the Rise of Mao,* 1951. Covers the pre-1949 Communist Party of China and its leaders. Other aspects of the early twentieth-century revolutionary ferment are looked at in B. Schwartz, ed., *Reflections on the May Fourth Movement,* 1972.

Snow, E. *Red Star over China,* 1942. A sympathetic account by an American journalist of Mao's peasant republic in Shensi.

Spence, J. *The Gate of Heavenly Peace: The Chinese in Their Revolution, 1895–1945,* 1986. A fine account of how the modernizing movement was shaped by several representative men and women.

Spence, J. *God's Chinese Son: The Taiping Heavenly Kingdom of Hong Xiuquan,* 1996, details the Taiping rebellion.

Wakeman, F., Jr. *The Fall of Imperial China,* 1975. A standard treatment of the last decades of the empire.

Japan

Bernstein, G., ed. *Recreating Japanese Women 1600–1945,* 1991. An anthology with much useful information.

Butow, R. *Tojo and the Coming of the War,* 1961. Looks at inter-war militarism in Tokyo.

Craig, A. M., ed. *Japan: A Comparative View,* 1979. A controversial and thoroughly interesting book, strong on comparisons between Japan and others.

Dore, R., ed. *Aspects of Social Change in Modern Japan,* 1967, and J. Hunter, *The Emergence of Modern Japan: An Introductory History since 1853,* 1989, are good for political and social overviews. Economic topics are well covered in G. C. Allen, *A Short Economic History of Japan, 1867–1937,* 1972.

Iriye, A. *After Imperialism: The Search for a New Order in East Asia,* 1978. One of the best surveys of Japanese foreign policy in the opening half of the century.

———. *Pacific Estrangement: Japanese and American Expansion 1897–1911,* 1972 looks at the Japanese empire in the western Pacific.

Keene, D., ed. *Modern Japanese Literature: An Anthology,* 1960. Perhaps the best introduction to twentieth-century Japanese novels, stories, and general literature.

Kiyooka, E., trans. *The Autobiography of Fukuzawa Yukichi,* 1966. A good view into the transition between traditional and Westernizing Japan in the late nineteenth century. R. Ward, ed., *Political Development in Modern Japan,* is an anthology that surveys post–Meiji Restoration affairs.

Myers, R. H., and M. R. Peattie, eds. *The Japanese Colonial Empire, 1895–1945,* 1984. See also the two Iriye books listed earlier.

Southeast Asia

Histories that focus on individual countries are generally most useful for the period examined in this chapter, but M. Osborne's history and P. Sar-Desai's work are good introductions to the entire region; both are listed in the bibliographies for Chapters 31 and 53, respectively.

Karnow, S. *Vietnam: A History,* 1983. Stronger for the twentieth century, but a good overall picture of a complicated land.

Ramusack, B., and S. Sievers. *Women in Asia,* 1999, looks at both south and southeast Asia.

Steinberg, D. J. *The Philippines: A Singular and Plural Place,* 1994. One of the very few choices available in English.

Wyatt, D. *Thailand,* 1982, is a general history.

CHAPTER 49

The diplomatic and political background to World War II will be found in R. Sontag, *A Broken World, 1919–1939,* 1971, and E. Wiskemann, *Fascism in Italy: Its Development and Influence,* 1969, which have been cited in the bibliography for Chapter 45 dealing with the 1920s; and S. Marks, *The Illusion of Peace,* 1967, and D. C. Watt, *How War Came,* 1989, which have been cited in the bibliography for Chapter 47.

Carr, R. *The Civil War in Spain,* 1986. A standard history of this conflict, which still reverberates in Spanish life in the 1990s. See also H. Thomas, *The Spanish Civil War,* 1961.

Churchill, W. S. *The Second World War,* 6 vols., 1948–1954. The most elegantly written history by the man who led Britain throughout the conflict. Packed with fascinating detail and highly personal, eyewitness accounts of historic moments from the late 1930s onward to the war's end.

Dallin, A. *German Rule in Russia, 1941–1945,* 1957. Gives a thorough analysis of what Nazi rule of an enemy nation actually meant in terms of its horrors. For the Eastern Front, this should be supplemented by the most memorable "worm's eye" account to come out of the conflict: G. Alzey, *The Forgotten Soldier,* 1965, a young German recruit's memoir of his three years in Russia.

Costello, J. *Love, Sex and War. Changing Values 1939–1945.* A social history of the war's impact in Britain. On the general topic of the home front see also E. R. Beck, *Under the Bombs: The German Home Front 1942–1945,* 1963; T. R. Havens, *The Valley of Darkness: The Japanese People and World War Two,* 1978.

Feis, H. *Churchill–Roosevelt–Stalin: The War They Waged and the Peace They Sought,* 1957. A reliable history of the tense relations among the Big Three.

Keegan, J. *The Second World War,* 1990. A brilliant military history, rivaled by B. H. Liddell Hart, *History of the Second World War,* 2 vols., 1971. See also the huge crop of more sensational but still accurate works on specific incidents or areas such as J. Toland, *The Last Hundred Days,* 1976, which details the final days of the war, or L. Collins and D. La Pierre, *Is Paris Burning?* 1965, which tells how the French capital was saved from the fate ordained for it by Hitler.

Kogon, E. *The Theory and Practice of Hell,* 1958. On the Nazi concentration camps.

Michel, H. *The Shadow War: The European Resistance, 1939–1945,* 1972. The story of the undercover war against the Nazi and fascist occupiers.

Weinberg, G. *A World at Arms: A Global History of World War II,* 1994. This and the two following items are the best histories of the war available.

Wright, G. *The Ordeal of Total War,* 1967, and P. Calvocaressi and G. Wint, *Total War,* 1972, are good accounts of the worldwide conflicts and how they impacted both the home fronts (Wright) and the other belligerents (Calvocaressi and Wint).

CHAPTER 50

Chafe, W., and H. Sitkoff, eds. *A History of Our Time,* 1991.

Cole, B., and A. Gealt. *Art of the Western World,* 1989. A good summary of what modern Western art has been attempting, and its relative failure with the public.

Eberly, P. *Music in the Air,* 1982. A penetrating review of pop music.

Johnson, P. *Modern Times,* 2d ed., 1995. See also the bibliography for Chapter 51.

Maltby, R., ed. *Passing Parade: A History of Popular Culture in the 20th Century,* 1989. First-rate selection of items and articles, from the earliest spy stories to CDs.

May, L. *Screening Out the Past: The Birth of Mass Culture and the Motion Picture Industry,* 1980.

Wheen, F. *Television,* 1985. A good short history of the medium.

CHAPTER 51

On the Cold War's development from 1945 onward, there are a number of reliable histories, including several that take the position that both superpowers were responsible for the initiation of the Cold War and its long continuance.

Kolko, G. *The Politics of War,* 1969. Probably the best known of the "revisionist" accounts that lay the blame for the Cold War more on the United States than on the Soviet Union. W. LaFeber, *America, Russia and the Cold War,* 1985, is a similar attempt. On the other side, Dean Acheson, the secretary of state under President Truman, has written *Present at the Creation,* 1969, a strong defense of the policy he helped make. J. Gaddis, *The United States and the Origin of the Cold War, 1942–1947,* 1972, is a balanced account leaning toward making Stalin responsible, while J. Lukacs, *A History of the Cold War,* 1968, berates both sides sharply. W. Loth, *The Division of the World 1941–1955,* 1988 is well respected in its scholarship. A. Ulam, *The Rivals: America and Russia since World War II,* 1971, is perhaps the best summary of the whole picture to its publication.

Europe's recovery in the quarter century after 1945 is detailed in several worthwhile books:

Ardagh, J. *The New French Revolution,* 1969. Describes the big changes in France since the war and explains why de Gaulle was so popular for a time.

Barzini, L. *The Italians,* 1970. Fun to read and insightful.

Johnson, P. *Modern Times: The World from the Twenties to the Eighties,* 1983. A vigorously opinionated (conservative) and stimulating history of everything imaginable.

Laqueur, W. *Europe in Our Time,* 1992.

———. *Europe since Hitler,* 1991. A very good survey.

———. *The Germans,* 1985. Love and hate judiciously balanced.

Marwick, A. *British Society since 1945,* 1982.

Paxton, R. *Twentieth Century Europe,* 1992. As good as Laqueur but takes in a bigger time frame.

Postan, M. M. *An Economic History of Western Europe, 1945–1964,* 1967. Lively book that makes economics almost fun to read about.

Riddell, P. *The Thatcher Decade,* 1989. Surveys the "reign" of Britain's most successful postwar leader.

Sampson, A. *The Changing Anatomy of Britain,* 1982.

White, T. *Fire in the Ashes,* 1953. A perceptive American journalist visits western Europe just beginning its recovery.

CHAPTER 52

Fanon, F. *The Wretched of the Earth,* 1968. A searing attack on the Western neocolonialists, with emphasis on Africa, by a black psychiatrist from the Caribbean.

Lipton, M. *Why Poor People Stay Poor: Urban Bias in World Development,* 1977. Highly recommended to help understand why so little has been accomplished for the rural majority.

von Albertini, R. *Decolonization,* 1971.

Ward, B. *Rich Nations and Poor Nations,* 1964. Despite its age, a book that is still relevant to world economic divisions. Most often cited as the best overview in English, but not an easy read.

Africa

Achebe, C. *Things Fall Apart,* 1959, and *A Man of the People,* 1966. Two novels of precolonial and postindependence Nigeria by the best-known contemporary African novelist.

Berger, I., and E. White. *Women in Sub-Saharan Africa,* 1999.

Davidson, B. *Let Freedom Come,* 1978. A distinguished Africanist reviews trends and events in independent Africa.

Hargreaves, J. D. *Decolonization in Africa,* 1988.

Horne, A. *A Savage War of Peace: Algeria, 1954–1962,* 1971. The best account in any language.

Iliffe, J. *The African Poor,* 1987. Highly recommended to students wishing to know what the lives of most Africans are like.

Lloyd, P., ed. *The New Elites of Tropical Africa,* 1966. Looks at the "wa-benzi" types that emerged after independence.

Asia

Collins, L., and D. La Pierre. *Freedom at Midnight,* 1975. Vivid account of the coming of Indian independence.

Dahm, B. *Sukarno and the Struggle for Indonesian Independence,* 1969.

Fall, B. *A History of Vietnam,* 2 vols., 1964. A French journalist's enlightening account.

Goldschmidt, A., Jr. *A Concise History of the Middle East,* 1991. Up-to-date except for the most recent events.

Nehru, J. *An Autobiography,* 1972. By a self-anointed visionary and the most important Indian statesman since World War II.

Tinker, H. *South Asia: A Short History,* 1990. One of the few overviews available.

CHAPTER 53

For both modern China and Japan, see the works by Fairbank, Reischauer, Schirokauer, and Spence in the bibliography for Chapter 48. More specific topics are treated in the following works.

Japan

Bernstein, G. *Haruko's World: A Japanese Farm Woman and Her Community,* 1983.

Bestor, T. *Neighborhood Tokyo,* 1989. Deals with contemporary urban life.

Dore, R. *Shinohata: Portrait of a Japanese Village,* 1978, and *City Life in Japan,* 1982. Interesting accounts of the grassroots changes in postwar society.

Hendry, R. J. *Understanding Japanese Society,* 1987. One of the most useful attempts.

Heymann, T. *On an Average Day in Japan,* 1992. Interestingly written comparison of Japan and the United States in several social areas.

Kawai, K. *Japan's American Interlude,* 1960. Studies the effects of the American postwar occupation.

Reischauer, E. *The Japanese,* 1977. Very good general history.

Robins-Mowry, D. *The Hidden Sun: Women of Modern Japan,* 1983.

Smith, D. *Japan since 1945: The Rise of an Economic Superpower,* 1995.

Vogel, E. *Japan as Number One: Lessons for America,* 1977.

China

Cheng, N. *Life and Death in Shanghai,* 1986. A story of what the Cultural Revolution did to ordinary people.

Dietrich, C. *People's China: A Brief History,* 1986.

Fairbank, J. K. *The United States and China,* 1983. Tells the relationship's ups and downs up through the early 1980s.

Hinton, W. *Fanshen: A Documentary of Revolution in a Chinese Village,* 1960. A firsthand account of what happened after the communist takeover.

Karnow, S. *Mao and China: Inside the Cultural Revolution,* 1972. A very good journalist's inside story of the way the Mao-inspired upheaval was tearing China apart.

Meisner, M. *Mao's China, and After,* 1986. A good history written for students.

Morrison, D. *Massacre in Beijing,* 1989. A reaction to the Tiananmen Square events in June 1989.

Schell, O. *To Get Rich Is Glorious,* 1986. A study of Deng's leadership after Mao's death.

Sullivan, M. *Arts and Artists of Twentieth Century China,* 1996. The most recent history of the topic, both pre- and post-1949.

Whalley, S., Jr. *Mao Tse-tung: A Critical Biography,* 1977. Written immediately after the leader's death, as was D. Wilson, ed., *Mao Tse-tung in the Scales of History,* 1977.

Zhang, Xinxin, and Sang Ye. *Chinese Lives: An Oral History of Contemporary China,* 1987. A fascinating collection by a pair of experienced reporters.

India and Pakistan

Bhatia, K. *Indira Gandhi,* 1974. A good biography.

Freeman, J. M. *Untouchable: An Indian Life History,* 1979, and K. Bhatia, *The Ordeal of Nationhood: A Social Study of India since Independence,* 1971, are excellent social histories.

Naipaul, V. *India: A Wounded Civilization,* 1977. A consistently challenging, critical examination of the country of the distinguished novelist's father.

Tharoor, S. *India: From Midnight to the Millennium,* 1997. A history of the most recent quarter-century.

Tinker, H. E. *South Asia: A Short History,* 1990. Provides a good overview of both major states in South Asia.

Wiser, W. and C. *Behind Mud Walls, 1930–1960,* 1984. A gripping account of life as experienced by two Westerners in a typical Indian village over a generation's time.

Wolpert, S. *A New History of India,* 3d ed., 1988. The final part covers the most recent period, since independence.

Southeast Asia

THE VIETNAM WAR

Fitzgerald, F. *Fire in the Lake,* 1970. Analyzes why the Viet Cong were able to sustain their costly war effort despite overwhelming U.S. superiority in weapons.

Herring, G. *America's Longest War: The U.S. and Vietnam, 1950–75,* 1979. Told from the American side, but informed about the Vietnamese.

Kahin, G. M. T. *Intervention: How America Became Involved in Vietnam,* 1986. Gives a clear account of this complex situation.

Karnow, S. *Vietnam: A History,* 1983. An exceptionally vivid and fair-minded history that focuses on the U.S. role since the mid-

1950s. This book was the companion to the highly respected television documentary on the war broadcast by PBS.

Other Topics

Legge, J. *Sukarno,* 1972. A good biography of the founder and controversial leader of Indonesia in its early years of independence. See also M. Risklef, *A History of Modern Indonesia,* 1981.

Sar-Desai, D. R. *Southeast Asia: Past and Present,* 1989. Has good coverage of the twentieth century and particularly post-1945 events.

Steinberg, D. J. *The Philippines: A Singular and a Plural Place,* 1971.

Turnbull, C. M. *A History of Singapore, 1819–1975,* 1977. A comprehensive history of this city-state since the British entered the scene as colonial masters.

Vogel, E. *The Four Little Dragons: The Spread of Industrialization in East Asia,* 1991.

Wyatt, B. *Thailand,* 1992.

Woronoff, J. *Asia's Miracle Economies,* 1986. Looks intensively at the "Four Little Tigers."

CHAPTER 54

In addition to the general histories mentioned in the bibliography for Chapter 33, see also the following:

Berger, I., and E. White. *Women in Sub-Saharan Africa,* 1999. One of a series recently published on women in the developing world.

Burke, F. *Africa,* 1970. A brief and easily digested summary history. Maps and charts help make the story.

Davidson, B. *Let Freedom Come,* 1978, and *The African Genius,* 1969. A journalist turned historian, Davidson has written several studies of tropical Africa since the 1960s; these are among the more notable.

Dwyer, D. J. *The City in the Third World,* 1974. Treats Africa along with Asia and Latin America.

Fieldhouse, D. *Black Africa 1945–1980,* 1986.

Harden, B. *Africa: Dispatches from a Fragile Continent,* 1990.

Harrison, P. *The Greening of Africa: Breaking through in the Battle for Land and Food,* 1987. A perhaps all-too-optimistic survey of agrarian problems and their possible solutions.

Iliffe, J. *The African Poor: A History,* 1987. A marvelous work and a very unusual one.

July, R. *A History of the African People,* 5th ed., 1997.

Martin, P., and P. O'Meara, eds. *Africa,* 1995. A collection of worthwhile articles on the modern era.

Patterson, K. *History and Disease in Africa,* 1978. Written prior to AIDS.

Robertson, C., and I. Berger, eds. *Women and Class in Africa,* 1986. An anthology of twentieth-century topics.

Turnbull, C. M. *The Lonely African,* 1962. A case study of what happens when the traditional ideas and communities no longer suffice but have not been effectively replaced.

CHAPTER 55

Several general histories of all of the American continent south of the Rio Grande are available; all contain good bibliographies for further research. R. Graham, *Independence in Latin America,* 1994; E. Williamson, *The Penguin History of Latin America,* 1992; and B. Keen, *A History of Latin America,* 1996, are the most up-to-date.

Berryman, P. *Liberation Theology,* 1994.

Burns, E. B. *Latin America: A Concise Interpretive History,* 1990.

Fagg, J. E. *Latin America,* 1977. A standard history, though now somewhat out-of-date.

Gilbert, A., and J. Gugler. *Cities, Poverty and Urbanization in the Third World,* 1992.

Lernoux, P. *Cry of the People,* 1982. A sympathetic exposé of how the poor are maltreated; by an American journalist.

Skidmore, T. E., and P. H. Smith. *Modern Latin America,* 1992. Focuses on recent times.

Tanenbaum, F. *Ten Keys to Latin America,* 1956. Still relevant.

Winn, P. *Americas: The Changing Face of Latin America and the Caribbean,* 1992.

Individual Nations

ARGENTINA

Ferns, H. *Argentina,* 1969. A good survey to the date of publication. C. Scobie, *Argentina: A City and a Nation,* 1971, is worthwhile for its account of how the potentially richest country in the Southern Hemisphere failed its chances in the twentieth century. More current and less focused on Buenos Aires is D. Rock, *Argentina 1518–1987,* 1987. A good biography of Perón was written by J. A. Page in 1983.

BRAZIL

Burns, E. B. *A History of Brazil,* 1980, is good, as is the more personalized and sensational R. DaMatta, *Carnivals, Rogues, and Heroes,* 1991.

Degler, C. N. *Neither Black nor White: Slavery and Race Relations in Brazil and the United States,* 1971. A classic comparison of the two biggest slaveholding societies in the New World.

CHILE

Kinsbruner, J. *Chile: An Historical Interpretation,* 1973, and B. Loveman, *Chile,* 1988, are both good general histories, with the latter having an economic slant.

CUBA

Mesa-Lago, C. *The Economy of Socialist Cuba,* 1981. An introduction to what Castro sought to do, and sometimes did. Another point of view is given in L. Perez, *Cuba: Between Reform and Revolution,* 1988.

MEXICO

Meyer, M. C., and W. L. Sherman, *The Course of Mexican History,* 1991. Very detailed for serious researchers. For material on Cardenas, see J. Bazant, *A Concise History of Mexico,* 1978.

Riding, A. *Distant Neighbors,* 1989. An interesting account of how Mexican society "works," from an American point of view.

CHAPTER 56

Arab-Israeli Conflict

All of the following are generally fair-minded in their treatment of this extremely sensitive topic.

O'Brien, C. C. *Siege: The Saga of Israel and Zionism,* 1986.

Reich, B. *Israel: Land of Tradition and Conflict,* 1985.

Smith, C. *Palestine and the Arab-Israeli Conflict,* 1988.

Individual Countries

Goldschmidt, A., Jr. *Modern Egypt,* 1988. Treats the recent years better than any other source.

Keddie, N. *Roots of Revolution: An Interpretive History of Modern Iran,* 1981. Takes the story through Khomeini's coming.

Munson, H., Jr. *Islam and Revolution in the Middle East,* 1988. Looks at Iran and the Arab countries in the last three decades.

Pelletiere, S. C. *The Iran–Iraq War,* 1992.

International Affairs/Muslim Fundamentalism

Bill, J. A., and R. Springbork. *Politics in the Middle East,* 1990. A comprehensive study.

Donohue, J., and J. Esposito. *Islam in Transition,* 1982. An anthology of Muslim writers' views on social organization.

Gellner, E. *Muslim Society,* 1980. A sympathetic account of the rise and growth of Muslim fundamentalism. Another view is reflected in S. Sullivan and F. Milan, *Iranian Women since the Revolution,* 1991.

Odell, P. *Oil and World Power,* 1986.

Voll, J. O. *Islam: Continuity and Change in the Modern World,* 1982. The final chapters give a compact overview of recent Islamic history from Indonesia to North Africa.

CHAPTER 57

Eastern Europe

Ash, T. G. *The Magic Lantern: The Revolution of 1989 as Witnessed in Warsaw, Budapest, Berlin, and Prague,* 1990. See also the same author's *The Polish Revolution: Solidarity,* 1984. Both are written with flair and insight.

Banac, I., ed. *Eastern Europe in Revolution,* 1992. A collection of mainly good articles.

Brown, J. F. *Eastern Europe and Communist Rule,* 1988. A rich source of information on postwar affairs, unfortunately published just a year before everything changed.

Cohen, L. *Broken Bonds: The Disintegration of Yugoslavia,* 1993. A clear account of how and why that state fell apart after the communist lid was raised.

Glenny, M. *The Return of History,* 1991. A British journalist's account of why the eastern Europeans rebelled against communism. The same author's *The Fall of Yugoslavia,* 1992, gives the story of the civil war through late 1992.

Rothschild, J. *Return to Diversity: East Central Europe since 1989,* 1992. One of the best of the vast crop of political histories of eastern Europe under communism and after.

The Former Soviet Union

Brzezinski, Z. *The Grand Failure: The Birth and Death of Communism in the Twentieth Century,* 1988. An important explanation of why Gorbachev could not save the Soviet Union.

Gwertzman, B., and M. T. Kaufman. *The Decline and Fall of the Soviet Empire,* 1992. The same pair put together *The Collapse of Communism,* 1991, which is similarly composed of contemporary newspaper accounts from the *New York Times.*

Laqueur, W. *The Long Road to Freedom,* 1988. Why glasnost and perestroika came, and why they could not succeed as Gorbachev had desired.

Smith, G. *The Nationalities Question in the Soviet Union,* 1990. A good review of more than twenty nations and how they reacted to Gorbachev's program in the late 1980s.

Smith, H. *The New Russians,* 1990. Written just prior to the collapse of the Communist Party and the Soviet government, this very readable analysis by a *New York Times* Moscow correspondent is an updating of an earlier book, also on Russian society.

White, S. *Gorbachev and After,* 1991. Also see R. G. Kaiser, *Why Gorbachev Happened,* 1992.

CHAPTER 58

Banks, O. *Faces of Feminism,* 1982. A comparison of British and American feminist movements.

Brown, L., ed. *Reports by the Worldwatch Institute.* This publisher has issued annual reports on the state of the environment since the 1970s; they are accepted as the most reliable and insightful of their kind.

Cherlin, A. *Marriage, Divorce, Remarriage,* 1981.

Clark, A. *Profiles of the Future: An Inquiry into the Limits of the Possible,* 1984. By the renowned sci-fi author.

Critchfield, R. *The Golden Bowl Be Broken: Peasant Life in Four Cultures,* 1988. Very engagingly written account of ordinary life in the developing world.

Dudly, W. *Death and Dying,* 1992. One of the Opposing Viewpoints series published by Greenhaven Press particularly for students.

Greider, W. *One World, Ready or Not,* 1997. A peek at the global economy and its political-social offspring.

Guttmann, A. *From Ritual to Record: The Nature of Modern Sport,* 1978. An excellent analysis. See also S. Freeman and R. Boyes, *Sport behind the Iron Curtain,* 1980, for a view of how the communist lands employed sport as propaganda.

Iglitzin, L., and R. Ross, eds. *Women in the World: A Comparative Study,* 1976. An anthology concerning the freedoms or restrictions placed on women in the recent era.

Kennedy, P. *Preparing for the Twenty-first Century,* 1993. One of the leading historians of modern times gives his views on the prospects of the immediate future.

Kübler-Ross, E. *On Death and Dying,* 1974. One of the best-known works on the "ultimate health problem" and how it can be faced.

Lorraine, J. *Global Signposts to the 21st Century,* 1979. A very interesting discussion of what one man sees as the coming age's characteristics.

Lukacs, J. *The End of the Twentieth Century and the End of the Modern Age,* 1993. A stimulating, opinionated, sometimes-maddening discussion of the challenges facing the West after the demise of communism. A different focus rules in the various works of A. and H. Toffler, who have led in the creation of a new intellectual discipline—futurism. See, for example, their *Previews and Premises,* 1984, and *The Politics of the Third Wave,* 1995.

Moorcroft, S., ed. *Visions for the Twenty-first Century,* 1993. An anthology of short, very wide-ranging topical essays, written by experts or interested amateurs in their fields.

Schell, J. *The Fate of the Earth,* 1982, and P. Harrison, *Inside the Third World,* 1986, are very illuminating surveys that warn without sensationalizing the plight of the two-thirds of humanity who live in the underdeveloped countries. See also A. B. Mountjoy, ed., *Third World: Problems and Perspectives,* 1978. Particularly good for a statement of the non-Western viewpoint that time has validated is M. ul-Haq, *The Poverty Curtain: Choices for the Third World,* 1976.

Smith, B. G. *Changing Lives: Women in European History since 1700,* 1989.

Turner, B. L., et al., eds. *The Earth as Transformed by Human Action: Global and Regional Changes in the Biosphere in the Last 300 Years,* 1990.

Wager, W. W. *The Next Three Futures: Paradigms of Things to Come,* 1991. A well-known academic futurist provides scenarios of what is successively awaiting us in the twenty-first century.

World Commission on Environment and Development. *Our Common Future,* 1987.

INDEX

PHOTO CREDITS